Undaunted

How the Sixth Lubavitcher Rebbe, Rabbi Yosef Yitzchak Schneersohn, Saved Russian Jewry, Reimagined American Judaism, and Ignited a Global Jewish Renaissance

David Eliezrie

UNDAUNTED

HOW THE SIXTH LUBAVITCHER REBBE
RABBI YOSEF YITZCHAK SCHNEERSOHN
SAVED RUSSIAN JEWRY
REIMAGINED AMERICAN JUDAISM
AND IGNITED A GLOBAL JEWISH RENAISSANCE

The Toby Press

Undaunted
How the Sixth Lubavitcher Rebbe, Rabbi Yosef Yitzchak Schneersohn, Saved Russian Jewry, Reimagined American Judaism, and Ignited a Global Jewish Renaissance

First Edition, 2025

The Toby Press LLC
POB 8531, New Milford, CT 06776–8531, USA
& POB 4044, Jerusalem 9104001, Israel

www.korenpub.com

Cover photo courtesy of Baltimore Sun

The publication of this book was made possible through the generous support of *The Jewish Book Trust*.

ISBN 978-1-59264-726-2, *hardcover*

Printed and bound in Turkey

In Loving Memory of

Yakova Tzvia Cleff

יקבה צביה קלף

יקבה צביה בת יהושע לייבל

Beloved wife, mother, and grandmother – a true אשת חיל.
May her memory be for a blessing.

Isadore and Roberta Schoen

Contents

A Note to the Reader ix
Preface xv

Chapter One: Lubavitch 1
Chapter Two: Tomchei Temimim 27
Chapter Three: The Secret Covenant 63
Chapter Four: Armed Men at Midnight 105
Chapter Five: Exile to Riga 131
Chapter Six: The Royal Wedding 157
Photos 171
Chapter Seven: The Voyage 175
Chapter Eight: Poland – Starting Anew 205
Chapter Nine: The World is Shattered 239
Chapter Ten: America Iz Nisht Andersh 271
Chapter Eleven: A Global Vision 325
Afterword: A Maamar in Brooklyn 365
Special Acknowledgment 368

Appendix 1 369
Appendix 2 373
Endnotes 379
Index 525

A Note to the Reader

There are moments when divine providence shines through like a bright sun. That occurred a few years ago when "Isadore Schoen" overheard a discussion between me and Rabbi Mendel Kalmenson at JLI's National Jewish Retreat. We were discussing the need for a comprehensive biography of the sixth Lubavitcher Rebbe, Rabbi Yosef Yitzchak Schneersohn. I told Kalmenson that I had long dreamed of writing such a book, but that I had been held back by the need for research funding. Standing nearby was Izzy, and to our surprise, he said, "That's not a problem." The generosity of Izzy and his gracious wife Roberta have made this book a reality.

Others also lent a hand to the project. I am deeply grateful for the support of Shmuel and Sharone Goodman and the friendship of Patricia Vienna, who each helped immensely.

One of the treasures of the Chabad community is JEM, Jewish Educational Media, under the direction of Rabbi Elkanah Shmotkin. This great reservoir of historical information contains thousands of interviews about the Rebbes of Chabad. The pages of this book have been greatly enriched by those memories. Thank you to Rabbis Elkanah Shmotkin, Yechiel Kagan, and Zalman Ceitlin.

A huge thanks to Mussi Sharfstein. She helped craft the manuscript from its inception, challenging assumptions, skillfully editing, and time and again, to her astonishment, finding relatives in the story.

This book has been enhanced by the advice and insight of Rabbi Eliezer Zaklikowski; the vast knowledge of Rabbi Yossi Keller, author of *The History of the Lubavitcher Yeshivah in the United States*; and the research of Rabbis Aron Kastel, Yoel Shernofsky, and Nachum Zajac.

Along the way, many have helped with advice, insight, and inspiration. I offer my gratitude to Professors Glenn Dynner, David E. Fishman, Ilia Luria, Rafael Medoff, and Jonathan Sarna; Rabbi Dr. Aaron Rakeffet; JDC archivist Misha Mitsel; and Rabbi Dovid Kamenetsky. Special thanks to Rabbi Sholom DovBer Avtzon, author of the biography series on Chabad Rebbes. The Chabad community is blessed with many intellectually curious scholars and historians. Each in their own way have made important contributions to understanding the storied history of Chabad. Thank you to Rabbis Mendy Bronfman, Chaim Dalfin, Mordechai Dinerman, Zalman Hertzel, Yosef Kaminetzky, Elyashiv Kaploun, Uri Kaploun, Dovid Margolin, Peretz Mochkin, Boruch Oberlander, Yossi Paltiel, Ari Raskin, Eli Rubin, Michoel Seligson, and Nissan Rupo.

Many others offered ideas and support. Thanks to Rabbis Zalman Abraham, Yifrach Abramov, Lipa Brennan, Chaim Shaul Brook, Chaim Cunin, Yossi Cunin, Sholom Deitsch, Mordy Einbinder, Mordechai Dinerman, Yossi Gabay, Simon Jacobson, Shmuel Kaplan, Moshe Kotlarsky (of blessed memory), Shimon Kramer, Ephraim Mintz, Mendel Mintz, Menachem Rapaport, Yossi Rapaport, Peretz Reisenberg, Eli Rubin, Leibel Schapiro, Motti Seligson, Zalman Shmotkin, Zevi Tenenbaum, and writers Shalom Magidman and Esther Leah Tenenbaum. Special thanks to Rabbi Mendel Glukowsky for his time and wisdom. Thank you to Zeldy Stillerman for the cover design and my son Yosef Simcha for suggesting the cover photo.

The research for this book brought me to Russia and Latvia, where the Rayatz lived. I am appreciative of the Chabad *shluchim* who soldier on in these communities and facilitated my visits. Thanks to Rabbis Berel Lazar, Dovid and Mendel Moonshine, and Mendy Wilensky in Moscow; Rabbi Chaim Danzinger in Rostov; Rabbi Gavriel Gordon in Lubavitch;

Rabbis Mendel Pewzner and Chaim Shaul Brook in St. Petersburg; and Rabbis Mordechai Glazman and Schneour Kot in Riga.

My thanks to Rabbi Yehuda Krinsky and Rabbi Manis Friedman, who have been a beacon of encouragement to me, initially with my first book, *The Secret of Chabad,* and again with this biography. A special thank you to Carolyn Starman Hessel, who has dedicated her life to Jewish authors, uplifting Jewish publishing to new heights, and who has been a pillar of support for my writing.

It is a pleasure to collaborate yet again with the phenomenal professionals at Koren/Toby Press. Their devotion to Judaism expresses itself in their commitment to bringing great Jewish content to the world. My thanks to publisher Matthew Miller, Rabbis Reuven Ziegler and David Silverstein, Shlomo Peterseil, Tali Simon, Meira Mintz, Taly Hahn, Tani Bayer, Marc Herman, and all the staff.

This book was made possible by the wealth of original historical sources that have been published in recent decades in the Chabad community. Seventeen volumes of letters of the Rayatz and many of his unpublished letters from private sources are the foundation of this book. The six volumes of the Rashab's letters and the thirty-three volumes of the letters of the seventh Rebbe were also integral. The vast majority of these letters are in Hebrew or Yiddish, and a few are in other languages. In his Hebrew and Yiddish letters, the Rebbe used the Hebrew date exclusively; in other languages, the Gregorian calendar date was sometimes included. In the endnotes of this book, the letters are cited using both dates.

The original research on Chabad in Rabbi Shalom Ber Levin's series on the history of Chabad in Russia, Europe, Israel, and the US has been invaluable. I thank him for repeatedly giving of his time and insight. Other historical sources, such as the collection of over six hundred letters of Rabbi Yechezkel Feigin, secretary to the Rayatz in Europe, provided a remarkable understanding of the day-to-day activities of the Rebbe's court. Family histories and historical material published in *teshurahs,* mementos from family celebrations, were another valuable resource. Additionally, the wealth of documents in the JDC archives provides a vital contemporary record of the efforts of US Jewry to help Jews around the world. The translations of the classic Jewish texts and of the Rebbe's talks and letters are my own. If there are any inaccuracies, they are not a reflection of the original sources.

This work does not attempt to document every moment of the Rebbe's life, as that would take many volumes. It does endeavor to identify the central events and challenges that the Rebbe faced and to give them historical context.

This work also does not explore the vast Torah teachings that the Rebbe has left as a rich intellectual legacy. Two hundred works of the Rebbe's *maamarim*, talks, and letters have been published, and I encourage readers to expand their appreciation of the unique contributions of the Rebbe by studying his Torah and teachings.

In recent decades, important historians have examined the history of Jews in Russia and the US. Unfortunately, some of these historians did not have access to or were not aware of many of the above-mentioned books and documents, as many of them were only published in recent years. Coming from secular academic backgrounds, they tend to view history from that context. While acknowledging the efforts of the Rayatz, they often fail to grasp the scope of his impact. Hopefully, this work will broaden the understanding of the historic role of the Rayatz for world Jewry.

Noted historian Rabbi Aaron Rakeffet says the mission of a historian is to examine the past and to accurately portray those events. I pray that this biography lives up to that aspiration.

It is the support of my family, good friends, and warm community at Chabad Beth Meir HaCohen in Yorba Linda, California, that has enabled me to write this book over the past few years.

My six children, Yoni, Chani, Yehoshua, Naomi, Yosef, and Dina and their spouses, as well as my grandchildren, have been an inspiration to me. Over the last few years, they have been a sounding board for this book, offering their wisdom and ideas. A special thanks to my three granddaughters, Chaya, Bassie, and Ita, who brainstormed the title for this book, "Undaunted."

I would like to dedicate this book in honor of my dear wife and life partner of over half a century, Stella. Stella has enabled me to author this book with her patience and insight. Our greatest life accomplishment is that together, we have created six families who aspire to strive for the values, lessons, and teachings of the Rayatz and the seventh Rebbe. As their children – our grandchildren – begin to marry and start their own families, it brings us immense joy to see them continue passing down these ideals to yet another generation. I give my heartfelt gratitude to Stella for building our tribe.

Rabbi David Eliezrie
12 Tamuz 5785/2025
Celebrating ninety-eight years
since the Rebbe's release from Soviet prison

Preface

Rabbi Yosef Yitzchak Schneersohn, the sixth Lubavitcher Rebbe, stood at the apex of history. In his early years, he faced down the oppression of czarist Russia, and later, when he became Rebbe, the rise of the communist Soviet Union that sought to eradicate Jewish tradition. Forced out of Russia, he had to adapt Chabad Chasidism to Westernized Europe. Later, driven from Poland by the Nazis, he found a haven in America, where the Jewish community was racing down the highway of assimilation. There, he reimagined Jewish life, laying the foundation for a renaissance of tradition.

Each era presented its own unique threat to the physical and spiritual welfare of Jewish life. And in each case, the Rebbe bucked conventional wisdom. Time and again he had to start anew in a different country, and each time he successfully adapted to the challenge. He faced these obstacles head-on, despite serious health issues, limited finances, and a Jewish community that did not always share his vision.

Through all of this, the Rebbe was first and foremost rooted in deep spiritual values. While he was an activist and organizer, his true joy stemmed from the study of Torah and the teachings of Chasidism. As he once said, "Without a yeshivah there is no life." He left a rich legacy of over two hundred volumes of his profound *maamarim,* talks and writings.

We have been blessed with a glimpse into his inner world through thousands of letters, public addresses, and first-person accounts. The Rebbe's rich legacy allows his own voice to resonate in this biography.

In the following pages, we encounter his broad range of emotions, from anguish to joy, as well as boundless compassion, devotion to faith, and a desire to connect with G-d. Above all is his sense of mission, instilled by his father, Rabbi Shalom Dovber Schneersohn. From the Rebbe's courage facing down tyrants to his concern for the fate of Jews living in far-off Morocco, this biography helps us understand the remarkable life of one of the greatest Jewish leaders in an era of upheaval for world Jewry. His life reflects the trials of the Jewish people from the sunset of the oppressive rule of the Russian czars, to the totalitarianism of Communism, the struggle to implant a chasidic milieu in Western Europe, and the bounty of freedom offered by America. It is a story of determination, self-sacrifice, compassion, and vision.

With the perspective of history, it's clear that the Rebbe was one of the most consequential figures of the modern Jewish era, a godly man who created a path for a bright Jewish future in the midst of unparalleled disruption and transformation. Through every challenge, he remained – "Undaunted."

A NOTE ON TERMS:

In the chasidic community, it is common to refer to distinguished rabbis using a shortened version of their name composed of an acrostic of the letters. **Rabbi Yosef Yitzchak Schneersohn** is alternately referred to in three ways, reflecting different periods in his life.

- **Yosef Yitzchak:** From his birth until his bar mitzvah in 1893.
- **The Rayatz:** From his bar mitzvah until succeeding his father as Rebbe in 1920
- **The Rebbe:** From becoming Rebbe in 1920 until his passing in 1950. Chasidim commonly refer to the Rayatz at the Frierdiker Rebbe, Yiddish for "Previous Rebbe."

Other notable family members:

- **The Rashab:** Rabbi Shalom Dovber Schneersohn, the fifth Rebbe, father of the Rayatz.
- **The Raza:** Rabbi Zalman Aharon, brother of the Rashab and uncle of the Rayatz.
- **The Rashag:** Rabbi Shmaryahu Gurary, eldest son-in-law of the Rayatz.
- **The Ramash, the seventh Rebbe:** Rabbi Menachem Mendel Schneerson, the second son-in-law and the successor of the Rayatz. Until 1950, he is called the Ramash; afterward he is referred to as the seventh Rebbe.

See appendix 1 for a list of the seven Lubavitcher Rebbes.

Chapter One

Lubavitch

It was a bright summer day in the town of Lubavitch, a village nestled in the rolling hills and forests of White Russia. From surrounding villages and farms, people streamed into Lubavitch, doubling its population of two thousand for *yarmarka,* the two-day market in late June of 1891.[1] The streets were festive, bustling with farmers, craftsmen, and other vendors, all vying for customers.

Young Yosef Yitzchak Schneersohn, just a few weeks shy of his eleventh birthday, made his way down Shielve Street with his friend Shimon Rabinowitz. It was midday. "I was walking from school to eat lunch," he later wrote in his diary.[2] "The market was packed with farmers, horses, and buggies." As the two boys navigated the busy street, they met Reb[3] Dovid the butcher. "He was carrying a calf on his shoulders, a lamb in his arms, and a basket of chickens hanging in front of him. His face beamed as he exclaimed, 'I hope G-d will give me a decent profit.'"

Yosef Yitzchak was well acquainted with Dovid. He had been staking the butcher with microloans from his fund so that Dovid could purchase livestock in nearby farms and resell it in town. Yosef Yitzchak had launched this loan fund after earning money from studying Mishnah.

"My father gave me five kopecks for every chapter I memorized. And every day I learned a new chapter, my mother used to give me five kopecks a day." When he finally saved up one ruble, he began dreaming about buying a watch "so I could organize my day." But his father suggested that he use the money for *chesed* (humanitarian assistance), and so young Yosef Yitzchak gave the money to Reb Saadia,[4] a trustee of a free loan fund, to assist needy people. By the summer of 1891, Yosef Yitzchak had saved enough money to offer loans himself. "I had accumulated a sum of over thirty rubles ($750 today) as a reward for the study of Mishnah by heart. Following my father's suggestion, I would lend money in small amounts – from three to five rubles – to fellow Jews engaged in buying merchandise in the market and peddlers who would buy and sell bundles of flax, hides or leather, chicken, eggs, onions, and the like." As the fund grew, he set up a system. "At the direction of my teacher Reb Nissan, I kept a detailed accounting of all the transactions, and the day before and after market day, I would be occupied with distributing and receiving sums borrowed from the fund."

Among those who frequently borrowed and repaid was the butcher. "Reb Dovid was about fifty years old. He had a family of eight and he was poverty-stricken, earning a living only from the toil of his hands. No work in the world was too heavy for him to do, be it in the hot summer days or during the harsh winter snowstorms and rain. If he earned some coins for his efforts, he never complained about his bad situation and his poverty." Reb Dovid was a simple person, having attended only *cheder* (elementary school). He knew only the daily prayers. "I loved figuring out the exact time on Erev Shabbat and holidays when Reb Dovid would go home from the public bathhouse, his face beaming, his children surrounding him and running to catch up to him. An hour later, he would walk pleasantly with his children to the big study hall where he would *daven*."

The marketplace conversation between Yosef Yitzchak and Reb Dovid was brutally interrupted by a police sergeant. "Out of nowhere, the sergeant was on him, smacking Reb Dovid so hard that blood gushed from his nose. He accused him of stealing the calf [around his shoulders]." Yosef Yitzchak stepped up to his defense. "I screamed at the sergeant, called him a drunkard and a lowlife, and pushed him away."

The sergeant ordered a nearby police officer to arrest Yosef Yitzchak. "He accused me of ripping off the copper badge from his uniform and preventing him from fulfilling his duty to enforce the law." No one noticed the young Yosef Yitzchak being escorted by police down the busy streets. "There was a lot of commotion because of the crowds, wagons, horses, and livestock." After crossing the plaza in the center of the marketplace, they came to the *volost*, the local police station. Inside, a second "officer greeted me with an angry expression, gave me a dirty look, smacked me in the face, and grabbed me by my ear." He marched Yosef Yitzchak into the jail, "opened the doors of a dark cell, pushed me inside, and slammed the door on me."

Sitting alone and hungry in the cell, Yosef Yitzchak's first reaction was fright. "Great fear fell upon me." But then an idea flashed in his mind: "I am like my holy ancestors,[5] also sitting in prison! If so, I should occupy myself with words of Torah." He began to review the two orders of Mishnah he had memorized. "I started reciting them by heart. And then, since I was sitting in the dark and I didn't know the time, I hurriedly prayed *Minchah*."

Immersed in darkness, he suddenly heard something thrashing around, making him even more fearful. "My knees were shaking." He remembered that his friend Shimon had given him a box of matches earlier. "I struck a match and noticed that in the corner of the cell lay a bound calf with a muzzle on its mouth. I calmed down."

After a while, Yosef Yitzchak heard someone approaching his cell. It was the policeman who had brutally welcomed him to the jail. "Forgive me," said the officer. "I didn't know that you are the nephew of the Raza" (Rabbi Zalman Aharon Schneersohn)." He told him that the bailiff had ordered his release. "Please have mercy on me and don't tell your uncle that I smacked you and pulled you by your ear. I didn't do it out of hatred but out of habit; you didn't bleed from your nose, and your teeth didn't get knocked out, so it's not a big deal." Later it was revealed that the sergeant who arrested Yosef Yitzchak had actually stolen a calf from a local store and stashed it in the jail cell. He had attacked Reb Dovid to cover up his crime. Dovid the butcher was exonerated, and the officer was fired.

Yosef Yitzchak's father, Rabbi Shalom Dovber,[6] was out of town during this episode. When he returned to Lubavitch, his praised his son.

"It was a good thing that you did, to protect a decent, upright Jew, and if you suffered for a few hours – so what?" Lauding him for the way he passed the time in jail, he said, "Those hours were used for Torah study and prayer. This is the advantage of a human over an animal." He then awarded Yosef Yitzchak another ten rubles for his loan fund.[7]

Fearlessly standing up to others would become the motif of the life of Yosef Yitzchak Schneersohn, who, when he reached the age of forty, succeeded his father and became the sixth Lubavitcher Rebbe. This was the first of seven arrests.[8] There were four more under czarist rule and two during Communism, culminating with a death sentence at the notorious Shpalerka Prison in St. Petersburg in 1927.

Yosef Yitzchak was born in Lubavitch on 12 Tamuz 5640 (June 30, 1880) to Rabbi Shalom Dovber (known by the acronym of his name, Rashab) and Rebbetzin[9] Shterna Sara Schneersohn.[10] His father was the second son of the fourth Rebbe, Rabbi Shmuel,[11] and his parents were cousins.[12] When they married in 1875, Rebbetzin Shterna Sara moved four hundred miles from her hometown of Ovruch, Ukraine, to Lubavitch.

After five years of marriage, Rebbetzin Shterna Sara was distressed.[13] "I had not yet had a healthy child, and it bothered me. I was also quite young and distant from the home of my parents." Those feelings were compounded on Simchat Torah in 1879, when her father-in-law, Rabbi Shmuel, blessed each member of the family and overlooked her.

"I went into my room and considered my situation, that I had not yet had a child, and also the loneliness and not receiving the blessing when it was bestowed upon everyone else, and I cried myself to sleep." That night she had a vivid dream. "A Jew entered my room and asked me, 'Why are you crying, my child?' I told him all that was bothering me. He told me, 'Don't cry! I promise you that this year you will be blessed with a son.'"

The man instructed her to distribute eighteen rubles (an average monthly salary) to charity from her own money and to keep the story confidential. Then he appeared a second time. "A while later, the Jew returned with two more men, and he repeated for them what he promised me with the conditions that he stipulated, and they also agreed. All three of them blessed me and left."

Later that evening, when her husband returned from the holiday celebration, she told him about her dream. He called his father, Rabbi Shmuel, who asked Shterna Sara what the three men looked like. After she described them, he told her that they were the first three Rebbes. "The first one was my father (Rabbi Menachem Mendel, the Tzemach Tzedek),[14] and the other two were my grandfather (Rabbi Dovber, the Mitteler Rebbe)[15] and my great-grandfather (Rabbi Schneur Zalman, the Alter Rebbe)."[16]

After the holiday, Shterna Sara sold a dress she owned and donated the profits to charity. Ten months later, she gave birth to her son, Yosef Yitzchak. Her father-in-law, Rabbi Shmuel, was given the honor of *sandek* (the one who holds the baby during the circumcision). When the baby started to cry, Rabbi Shmuel remarked, "Why are you crying? When you grow up, you will be a Rebbe and say *chasidut* (chasidic discourses) with clarity."[17]

Lubavitch today is just ten miles from Russia's western border with Belarus. By the time Yosef Yitzchak was born, a century of czarist rule was firmly entrenched. More than half of the town's residents were Jewish.[18] The town was founded[19] by the holy mystic Rabbi Meir, renowned for his kindness to all, Jews and non-Jews. Some of its early residents were Jewish migrants from Poland in the fifteenth century, including refugees from the Spanish Inquisition. In centuries past, hidden *tzaddikim* (mystics) would frequent Lubavitch, its surrounding forests and rolling hills creating a sanctuary of sanctity.

The second Chabad Rebbe, Rabbi Dovber, settled in Lubavitch in the summer of 1813. The previous year, his father, Chabad's founder, Rabbi Schneur Zalman, known as the Alter Rebbe, passed away while fleeing from Napoleon's invading army. Rabbi Dovber would be the first of four Chabad Rebbes to reside in Lubavitch. For 102 years, Lubavitch was the capital of the Chabad chasidic movement. Two Rebbes and the wives of the first four Rebbes are interred there. The town's name was derived from the word "*luba*," Russian for "love," and it would come to symbolize the movement, with its message of love for every Jew. Its leaders would become known as the Lubavitcher Rebbes.

The World War I German invasion of Russia in 1915 prompted the fifth Rebbe, Rabbi Shalom Dovber, known as the Rashab, to leave Lubavitch.

With his departure, the sun set on Lubavitch as the capital of Chabad Chasidism.[20] After the Bolshevik revolution in 1917, religious life continued in a subdued fashion. The town's last synagogue was shuttered in 1936.[21] The Nazi invasion of World War II brought the Holocaust to Lubavitch, erasing the last Jewish presence there.[22] With the fall of the Soviet Union, Jews did not return to live in Lubavitch, but it became a destination of religious pilgrimage. The historic cemetery has been restored, a museum established, and the *chatzer*, the courtyard of the Rebbes' synagogue, is being reclaimed under an ongoing project to restore the area to the grandeur of a century ago. Many come to visit, to pray at the graves of the Rebbes interred there, and to absorb the rich history of the storied town.[23]

In its heyday, when the Rebbes resided there, Lubavitch was a spiritual mecca. Jews flocked there for inspiration, wisdom, and advice from each of the successive Rebbes. During Jewish holidays, the town was filled with prominent rabbis, scholars, and Chasidim from across Russia and nearby countries. Their visits to Lubavitch were an escape from the harshness of daily life under the czarist regime to an oasis of Torah and spirituality. As the Rebbe Rayatz (an acronym of his name, Rabbi Yosef Yitzchak) once explained, "The township of Lubavitch transformed people's reality and revealed their quintessential spiritual core."[24]

Professor Yehoshua Fishel Schneersohn[25] described the arrival of the chasidic pilgrims for the High Holidays in the mid-nineteenth century, during the era of the third Rebbe, Rabbi Menachem Mendel:

> You can feel the chasidic joy. The roads to Lubavitch are filled with travelers from cities and towns, Jews of all kinds – ordinary Chasidim, distinguished philanthropists, well-dressed pious businessmen, shopkeepers, and simple hard-working tradesman. The celebration would begin on the road, as wagonloads of Chasidim joyfully made their way to Lubavitch, their numbers swelling as they passed through cities, towns, and villages. Some come on wagons; others walk. Elderly Chasidim push themselves to spend one more holiday in Lubavitch. They bring along their children to absorb the passion in Lubavitch.

Schneersohn wrote that they came primarily from White Russia, but there were also guests from other regions, including "Poland, *Eretz Yisrael,* Germany, and even America." Yeshivah student Shmaryahu Sassonkin recalls the excitement he felt when he came to Lubavitch over a century ago. "As you got close to the edge of the town, you could see the rising structures of the *chatzer,* the Rebbe's court, that reached up a few stories high."

Until its days of spiritual glory were snuffed out by the First World War, Lubavitch remained a refuge of sanctity, removed from the hustle of regular life. When Russia began to build its railroad network in the mid-nineteenth century, Lubavitch was bypassed. Rabbi Menachem Mendel asked Samuel Polyakov,[26] the rail king of Russia, to change his original plans and detour around the town. "The Torah desires prayer, and a highway full of carriages will cause a distraction," he explained.[27] Instead, a rail station was built in Rudnya, some ten miles north. Wagon drivers would wait for pilgrims there and take them on the last leg of their journey to Lubavitch.

With the passing of the third Rebbe, Rabbi Menachem Mendel, in 1866, his youngest son, Rabbi Shmuel, became Rebbe in Lubavitch. His brothers set up rival Chabad courts in nearby towns: Rabbi Yehuda Leib (known as the Maharil) in Kopust, Rabbi Chaim Schneur Zalman in Liadi, and Rabbi Yisrael Noach in Nizhyn.[28] For the next half a century, Chasidim were divided between the different Chabad Rebbes.[29]

Rabbi Shmuel, known as the Rebbe Maharash,[30] emerged as an important leader of Russian Jewry. Chasidim flocked to Lubavitch for inspiration, to hear his profound *maamarim* (discourses), and to seek his advice. Rabbi Shmuel exhibited strong leadership for Russian Jewry, intervening in the capital, St. Petersburg, to avert anti-Semitic decrees. His first wife died within months of their marriage. In 1850, he married his second wife, Rivkah, a cousin who had been orphaned of both her parents.[31] They had seven children.[32] On Erev Rosh HaShanah 1882, Rabbi Shmuel told his wife, "You will rise up thirty-two steps in a physical dimension and I will rise up thirty-two steps in a spiritual way."[33] He had a chronic illness, and in the month leading up to the holidays he had become weaker. Realizing he was alluding to his own passing, Rebbetzin Rivkah burst out in tears. Two weeks later, three days after Yom Kippur

1882, Rabbi Shmuel passed away in Lubavitch at the age of forty-eight. His youngest daughter was just four years old. He had been Rebbe for a little more than sixteen years.

His passing was a shock to Chasidim, and the future of Chabad remained in doubt. There were sons, but they were still quite young, causing many to wonder if they would step into their father's place. Though still reeling from the loss, Chabad elders and rabbis convened in Lubavitch a few weeks after Rabbi Shmuel's passing.[34] They gathered in the home of Rebbetzin Rivkah with the hope that the two older sons, Rabbi Zalman Aharon, who was twenty-four, and Rabbi Shalom Dovber, almost twenty-two, would step forward to assume the leadership.

Three days later, one of the Chasidim wrote a dramatic account of the meeting.[35] Some of the most prominent rabbis had traveled to Lubavitch. They were seated at a table in the center of the room, surrounded by benches filled by Chasidim. "They prepared a place for the Rebbe's sons around that table and sent them an invitation to join the meeting." When Rabbi Zalman Aharon and his brother Rabbi Shalom Dovber arrived, they refused to join the rabbis around the table. "Instead, they sat on the edge of the crowd on benches." The message was clear: They were unwilling to take on the leadership. The mood was somber, with everyone wondering what the future of the movement would be. Then two of the senior Chasidim, Rabbis Pinsker and Kuptzar, stood up. Passionately, they spoke of the terrible loss of the Rebbe, Rabbi Shmuel, at such a young age. Then they talked of the future. "Chabad needs to continue," they said, "and one of the brothers has to accept the leadership."[36]

"Everyone began to cry – the rebbetzin, the sons of the Rebbe, and all who had gathered. There was a great sense of foreboding and darkness." Eventually the sobbing subsided, and the elder Chasidim once again implored the two sons to rise to the occasion. "They were asked to say *maamarim* and accept Chasidim for *yechidut* (private meetings for personal advice), but they refused."

The recitation of a *maamar* holds great significance in Chabad tradition. It is a deep intellectual exploration of the mystical teachings of the Torah, emanating from the tradition of Kabbalah and expanded in the teachings of Chasidism.[37] While a *maamar* is taught by anyone, an original is imparted only by a Rebbe. It is the moment the Rebbe shares his wisdom with his Chasidim.

The conversation between the elder Chasidim and the brothers continued until finally, they relented. The meeting ended on a high note with their consent to recite *maamarim,* which seemed a tacit agreement that the brothers were, to a degree, stepping into their father's shoes.

Though the two brothers had a close relationship, they were very different. The older brother, the Raza, was an urbane businessman who spoke a few languages. Chasidic historian Rabbi Yossi Paltiel notes that the younger brother, the Rashab, did not speak Russian. "His whole life was *kedushah,* engaged in spiritual pursuits." For a while, both Rabbi Zalman Aharon and Rabbi Shalom Dovber taught *maamarim* and met with Chasidim at times, but neither fully accepted the position of Rebbe. When they did teach *maamarim,* it was privately, in small groups. Rabbi Zalman Aharon said *maamarim* only for a short time. After a while, it became clear that he did not want to be a Rebbe. He deferred to his younger brother, telling the Chasidim that Rabbi Shalom Dovber had unique spiritual qualities. "My brother, the Rashab, was born a Rebbe and is a Rebbe."[38] On another occasion, he said, "I detest falsehood, but my brother loves truth. He has to be a Rebbe."[39] Eventually, he chose to relocate to Vitebsk, just fifty miles from Lubavitch, possibly to stay out of the limelight, clearing the way for his brother to emerge as Rebbe.[40] He visited Lubavitch often, maintaining a close connection to his brother, and became a major influence over his nephew, Yosef Yitzchak. But it was over a decade before the Rashab fully accepted the position of Rebbe.

Rabbi Moshe Rosenblatt[41] visited Lubavitch during this time. He met with the Rashab and presented a *tzetel,* a written request, as is customary when a Chasid has *yechidut,* a private meeting with a Rebbe. The Rashab read the note and told him, "For this, one needs a Rebbe. If there were a place where one could access a Rebbe, I would also travel there."[42]

During the period that the Rashab demurred from fully accepting the position of Rebbe, he was faced with health challenges. Earlier, at age eighteen, the Rashab had been exempted from the army draft when the medical examiner discovered he had tuberculosis.[43] The doctor, Professor Zacharov, told the Rashab's younger brother Mendel that Rabbi Shalom Dovber had just two months to live, which proved incorrect.

After his father's passing, the Rashab was absent from Lubavitch for long stretches of time seeking medical treatment in Russia and abroad for repeated health issues.[44] He made one such trip in 1884. "When he finally came home, I did not recognize him," recalled Rabbi Yosef Yitzchak. "My grandmother, Rebbetzin Rivkah, told me, 'This is your father.'"[45]

Rabbi Yosef Yitzchak described these years as "the era of decline of Lubavitch after the passing of [my grandfather] the Rebbe Maharash and the period of my father's illness."[46] The number of Chasidim visiting Lubavitch reduced to a trickle; some shifted their loyalties to the other Chabad courts. Both the town and the Rebbe's family suffered economically; with fewer Chasidim visiting, there were fewer people paying for local food and lodging.

As the grandson and son of a Rebbe, Yosef Yitzchak grew up in a rich chasidic milieu. One of his earliest memories[47] was watching the wedding of his uncle Mendel[48] from his room when he was almost two years old. "It's a joyous memory, people making motions with their hands on various instruments, and music arising from them. I was standing at the window, moving my feet, and dancing." At the time, he and his parents were living in three rooms in his grandmother's house, which was part of what was known as the *chatzer*, the courtyard. The *chatzer* contained the Rebbe's residence, a synagogue, and in later years, the yeshivah. The third Rebbe, Rabbi Menachem Mendel, had purchased the original property, and slowly it was expanded to include a large synagogue established by Rabbi Shmuel, as well as study halls and a home for the Rebbe and other family members.

Yosef Yitzchak was a sensitive child. When he was two years old, his father, the Rashab, was in the year of mourning after his father's passing and led the prayers in his study. "The room was full of printed books and manuscripts. The writing table and the rest of the furniture was still arranged the way it was when my grandfather was physically alive in this world." Yosef Yitzchak's mother would bring him into the room during prayers. "She would sit me down in one of the big chairs and instruct me to sit quietly." He was deeply moved by his father's prayers. "It would make me cry, but I would be very careful that my father not hear me cry." Years later, his mother told him that he began to ask where his grandfather was and why his father cried. His mother noticed how deeply it affected him and "from then on, she did not permit me to be there during the prayers."

Yosef Yitzchak's father, the Rebbe Rashab, took a serious interest in his son's education. "When I was just starting to speak, my father told me, 'Ask me anything you want.'" And so, when he grew a little older, he asked his father why he needed to place his hands together while reciting the morning *Modeh Ani* prayer. The Rashab told his son, "You should do it this way because you were instructed to do it this way." But Yosef Yitzchak protested, "You told me to ask you anything!"

The Rashab then called over eighty-year-old Yosef Mordechai, who helped in the house, and asked him, "How do you say *Modeh Ani* in the morning?" Yosef Mordechai responded, "I place one hand on the other, lift up my head, and say *Modeh Ani*." "Why?" asked the Rashab. Yosef Mordechai's answer was simple: "Because when I was a young child, I was taught to do it this way."

The Rashab turned to his son and said, "You see! He is doing it this way because his father taught him to do so, and his father learned it from his father, and so on, reaching back to Moshe and Avraham." The Rashab was instilling in his son one of the essentials of Jewish belief: that Jewish observance is rooted in millennia of traditions reaching back to the giving of the Torah at Mount Sinai.

The Rashab spent a lot of time with his son. "He would tell me stories from the Torah, *Ein Yaakov*, and *Nevi'im* (Prophets), and when I got a bit older, from the Baal Shem Tov, the Maggid, and the first Chabad Rebbe." The Rashab used the stories to inculcate values in his son. "My father would explain the inner messages of the stories, linking them to some lesson in *avodah* (service of G-d) and character refinement."[49]

At four years old, Yosef Yitzchak asked his father, "Why did G-d create two eyes? It would seem that one would have been enough, just like we have one mouth." The Rashab responded by pointing out that the Hebrew letter *shin* has two forms: one with the dot on the left "eye" and the other, with the dot on the right. "There are things that you should look at with your right eye, with admiration and affection. And there are things we need to view with our left eye, with hesitancy and caution." When it comes to another person, he explained, one should strive to look for good. "We need to look at our fellow Jew with our right eye."

Yosef Yitzchak later wrote, "This embedded in my heart and mind the concept of *ahavas Yisrael,* that every Jew, no matter who he is, needs to be viewed in an affectionate way."[50]

That year, in 1884, Yosef Yitzchak began his formal education. On his first day of school, his father and his uncle Rabbi Zalman Aharon were there to celebrate, tossing candies and telling him that they were coming from the angel Mikhael[51] – just as their grandfather, Rabbi Menachem Mendel, had done when they started *cheder.*[52]

Yosef Yitzchak's teacher, Rabbi Yekusiel Aizik, was a master educator. His father was a teacher and a Chasid of the first Chabad Rebbe, as was his grandfather.[53] "He taught two classes. The lower class was taught how to *daven,* and the higher class was taught *Chumash* with *Nevi'im* (Prophets) and *Ketuvim* (Scriptures)."[54]

What Yosef Yitzchak most appreciated was his teacher's storytelling. "He would tell us nice stories, which made us very excited. The children gathered around him like small sheep, all games were suspended, and any misbehavior between the students came to an end. He came alive with enthusiasm and passion as he told the story. He referred to the Baal Shem Tov and the Alter Rebbe with a deep sense of reverence, recalling stories he heard from his grandfather. He left a profound impression on us students. He was seventy years old, educating hundreds of children and instilling in them deep spiritual values."[55] He also taught the students chasidic melodies.[56]

For two years, while Yosef Yitzchak was three and four years old, his parents were away from Lubavitch most of the time seeking medical care for his father.[57] That changed in the fall of 1885, when he was five years old. "I noticed that there was a lot of activity at home. My mother was packing up my belongings in a big box." They were preparing to take their son with them to Yalta for six months. Almost one thousand miles south of Lubavitch, its warm climate would be beneficial to the Rashab. Yosef Yitzchak was apprehensive about the disruption in his life. "I loved my teacher Reb Yekusiel. I cried, 'Who will teach me *Chumash*? Who will tell me beautiful stories?' I was also going to miss out on playing games with my friends."[58] His father assured Yosef Yitzchak, "Don't worry. My cousin, Schneur Zalman Slonim,[59] will teach you."[60] Rabbi

Schneur Zalman, an outstanding scholar, had come to Lubavitch from Hebron in *Eretz Yisrael* for an extended stay.

The family's time in Yalta was an idyllic period in Yosef Yitzchak's childhood, as it allowed him to spend a significant amount of time with his parents. "I used to go walking almost every day from 1:00 p.m. until 7:00 or even 8:00 together with my parents and Rabbi Schneur Zalman. My father would find a seat and study a scholarly book that he had brought with him while Rabbi Schneur taught me for an hour and then told me to review what I had learned. Afterward, he joined my father and they studied a book together." His mother spent her time on the mountain walks reading letters, sewing, and knitting.[61]

Six months later,[62] on the way back to Lubavitch, they stopped in Kharkiv on Lag BaOmer. The local Chasidim organized a large dinner to welcome them. The Rayatz recalled, "Rabbis, prominent Chasidim, and many community members came. The room was full to the rafters. They sang soulful melodies and when my father taught a *maamar*, Chasidim crowded around to listen."

Despite the electric atmosphere, Yosef Yitzchak discovered his mother in tears in an adjacent room. When he asked her why she was crying, she responded, "You are still very young, and it's not important for you to know why."

As his father finished the *maamar*, Yosef Yitzchak made his way back through the crowd, sat next to his father, and whispered in his ear: "Mother is crying in the other room and when I asked why, she told me I am still a child and do not need to know everything."

The Rashab was taken aback and said to his son, "Go to your mother and tell her that I am feeling good, my headache is gone, and there is no pain in my heart. She can rest assured that I feel fine." The boy climbed back over the crowd, made his way to his mother, and gave her the message. "She kissed me and said, 'Wonderful!'"[63]

When Yosef Yitzchak was around seven years old, he began to study with a new teacher, Rabbi Shimshon the *melamed*. "He taught us how to learn." But he was also very strict, telling the students, "I will hit you so you know I mean business. There are no special people in my class."[64] Being the son of the Rashab did not help Yosef Yitzchak; he too was the target of his teacher's ire. Still, during the three years that he studied under him, he advanced academically. "I thrived in the study of Talmud, developed a good understanding of *Tanakh*, and during the time I studied with Reb Shimshon, I memorized two orders of Mishnah."[65]

Those were difficult years for Yosef Yitzchak. His parents continued to be absent from Lubavitch for long periods of time. Between 1887 and 1889, from ages seven to nine, he rarely saw them. "Those three years were the most difficult of my childhood. Most of the time, except for brief interludes, my father was away in medical facilities.[66] My mother traveled with him, and I suffered tremendously." That was not the only reason for his anguish. "I did not have the best of friends. Also, Reb Shimshon was very tense and he would express his anxiety with beatings and whippings."[67]

In 1888, when the Rashab was just twenty-seven and his son eight, the Rashab, deeply concerned about the state of his health, decided to write an ethical will.[68] In it, he outlined how he wished his wife to educate his son if he passed away.

Finally, in 1890, Yosef Yitzchak's parents returned. "That year was almost the first in my life that my father spent entirely at home, the greater part of previous years having been abroad."[69] But the Rashab was still in a precarious state. In December of 1890, "my father was ill with a high fever for about two months." This was heartbreaking for Yosef Yitzchak, just ten years old. "Most of the time, I sat in my room, read psalms, and cried. A dark dread fell over me. I had a father for a year and half, and now he was ill."

One night, before daybreak, as his father's fever reached its peak, ten-year-old Yosef Yitzchak decided he must act. He turned to Rabbi Zalman Lieblis, who maintained the Ohel, the gravesites of the Rebbes in the cemetery on the outskirts of Lubavitch. He convinced the man to allow him access to the cemetery, and together, they headed there to pray on his father's behalf. "It was bitterly cold and snowing heavily" as Yosef Yitzchak stumbled in the large snow drifts on the pathway to the cemetery.

When he entered the Ohel, "I saw the holy resting places covered over by fine snow." He was so overwhelmed that he could not even recite the traditional verses of Psalms. Instead, he blurted out, "My father is ill. My father, a Chasid and *tzaddik*, is lying ill in bed. My father has only one son and he has been guiding me for only a year and a half, and he is ill." Rabbi Zalman instructed Yosef Yitzchak to ask his holy forebearers to have pity and arouse Heaven's mercy. "These words made me cry out in anguish, '*Zeides,* holy *tzaddikim,* my father is ill! Ask G-d to keep him alive and make him well, and let him guide me so that I will grow up to be an upright Jew.'" By the time they finished their prayers, the morning light had begun to shine and they made their way back to Lubavitch. As they approached the Rashab's home, they were told the good news: The fever had broken. Yosef Yitzchak had told no one before he left the house, but later that day, he shared the secret with his father. "He said I had acted as I should."[70]

During the time that the Rashab was away, Yosef Yitzchak found solace in his interactions with elderly Chasidim, some of whom lived in Lubavitch and others who came to visit. He was living in his grandmother's home, where some of them stayed while they were in town.

"During that time there were two Chasidim in our home, Reb Tzvi Chanoch Hendel and Reb Meir Mordechai," he later wrote. Yosef Yitzchak enjoyed the time he spent with them. "Due to my personal distress, I became a regular visitor to the room of Reb Chanoch Hendel, many times sleeping on a bench." He describes him as "a great scholar, with deep passion for prayer and reciting psalms." He says that Reb Hendel studied chasidic texts "with enthusiasm" and that he "would cry when he recited *Tikkun Chatzot,*" the midnight prayer recalling the destruction of the *Beit HaMikdash*. Yosef Yitzchak was inspired by him, and they became very close. When Chasidim visited Lubavitch, "they would gather at the room of Reb Chanoch Hendel for *farbrengens*." Yosef Yitzchak joined them. "I began to pay attention to their *farbrengens*." He would sit with the elder Chasidim throughout the night, "at times falling asleep and waking up in the room in the morning when it was time to go to school."[71]

The Chasidim who visited Lubavitch told him stories of their past pilgrimages to his ancestors, Rabbi Shmuel and Rabbi Menachem Mendel. Many had met Chasidim who had encounters with the early chasidic masters reaching back to Chabad's founder, the first Chabad Rebbe, Rabbi Schneur Zalman. This rich oral tradition of chasidic teachings, wisdom, and lore provided the young Yosef Yitzchak with a personal link to generations past. The appreciation for chasidic lore and history was embedded in him from this young age.

Yosef Yitzchak began recording these stories at the encouragement of one of his teachers, Reb Nissan, who revealed to Yosef Yitzchak that he had been writing stories in his own journal for many years about the boy's ancestors. As a teenager, Reb Nissan had been inspired to keep a diary when he overheard Rabbi Menachem Mendel (the third Rebbe, known as the Tzemach Tzedek) telling his son Shmuel, "When I was ten, I heard from the Alter Rebbe that he would write all that he heard in Mezeritch [referring to the court of Rabbi Dov Ber,[72] the successor of the Baal Shem Tov], not only his sacred teachings but also the stories he told and the stories he heard from other senior students. That is what the [Alter] Rebbe did and that is what I do."[73] When Yosef Yitzchak heard this was a tradition of his ancestors, he resolved to record the stories he heard from elder Chasidim.[74]

Realizing that his writing skills were poor and that his handwriting was at times indecipherable, he decided to seek help. "I studied writing under Reb Hertzl *der schreiber* (the scribe). He would arrange all the affairs of the local *poritz* (landowner), having studied in the government school."[75] From then on, Yosef Yitzchak recorded stories, chasidic lore, and customs he heard from Chasidim and his father in a diary, rich with content from generations past.[76] In 1927, after leaving the Soviet Union, he began to publish his diary entries. In his public talks, he highlighted the stories that he had recorded decades earlier. In the early 1940s, the Rayatz published *The Lubavitcher Rebbe's Memoirs*, a serialized history of the origins of Chasidism, in a popular Yiddish newspaper, *Der Morgen Zhurnal*. The series was later translated into English, Hebrew, and other languages.[77]

At the age of nine, Yosef Yitzchak writes,[78] he felt like he had begun to mature. "In the summer of 5649 (1889), I became a different boy. My father showed me such closeness that I felt all the warmth of a father." With his parents back in Lubavitch, "I went to sleep with the thought that now I too had a father and a mother to whom to say good night." It wiped away the sense of loneliness he had felt for so long. "I completely forgot the bitter conditions under which I had previously lived." He also advanced in his studies. "Every Shabbat I would listen to the reading of the Torah while following attentively in the *Chumash,* and during the course of the day, I would study Rashi's commentary." Yosef Yitzchak began to comprehend the unique spiritual qualities of his father. "I was able to appreciate the great difference between my father and his brothers," who were both businessmen. He would stand at attention and listen carefully to the chasidic discourses of his father. "For over a year now, I had been listening to *chasidut* [*maamarim*], standing behind my father as he delivered his talks." This continued for years, but instead of remaining in the background, he would face his father, absorbing every word. When Rabbi Zalman Duchman came to Lubavitch to study in 1906, he witnessed the Rashab saying a *maamar.* He portrayed how Yosef Yitzchak stood opposite him: "In the middle of the *maamar,* the Rashab would stop, and they would look into each other's eyes. It was like two souls talking to each other. Each pause lasted a while and was extraordinary."[79]

That year, at the age of nine, Yosef Yitzchak fully observed the traditions of Rosh HaShanah. "I did everything as an adult. On Erev Rosh HaShanah, after immersing in the *mikveh,* I visited the resting place of my grandfathers.[80] In the evening, I listened to my father as he prayed. In the morning, I read all the prayers in the *machzor* with due deliberation. From that day, I was grown up."[81]

In April 1891, when Yosef Yitzchak was ten years old, the Rashab contracted pneumonia. He was sick for six weeks. "There were days that he was dangerously ill, yet his mind and speech were clear." At one point, the doctors attending the Rashab gave a "fearful prognosis."

A few days after the illness began, the Rashab spoke to Reb Nissan, Yosef Yitzchak's teacher. "He told him that until he regained his health, he wanted me to remain at his side." While he was sick, "my father related things that he had seen in the presence of his father, Rabbi Shmuel, and his father-in-law, my grandfather." He shared with his young son "how he conducted his life before and after his bar mitzvah. Every anecdote served to teach a lesson in having a G-d-fearing spirit and refining one's character."

At the time, Yosef Yitzchak wondered about his father's request for him to take a hiatus from school. "My father valued the time I spent with my teacher very much, and he did not need me to assist him." But years later, he understood. "At the time, his condition was critical. This is why he risked his holy life by exerting himself to relay all those recollections – particularly all their moral lessons – in order to guide me along the path of righteousness."[82]

The Rashab's personal mentoring of Yosef Yitzchak took on new depths when his son was eleven years old: He began to study chasidic philosophy with him. "A new world opened up before me."[83] The teachings of *Chasidut* helped him understand how one can master his desires. The Rashab was following the tradition of the Chabad Rebbes to deliver certain *maamarim* in the presence of their children. This was a tradition reaching back to the Alter Rebbe, who repeated *maamarim* for his grandson, the Tzemach Tzedek, who in turn said certain *maamarim* to "my grandfather, and my grandfather delivered certain *maamarim* to my father."

In 1893, several major events transformed Yosef Yitzchak's life. First was his bar mitzvah in the summer; shortly afterward, his father fully assumed the position of Rebbe. Later that year, he was assigned a new teacher who left a lasting impression on him.

Preparations for his bar mitzvah began months before his birthday. "I had to memorize and master three *maamarim*." Two of them were long; one was short. Two he repeated publicly as part of the bar mitzvah celebration, but at the time, "no one was to know of the third *maamar*." The Rashab taught Yosef Yitzchak the three *maamarim* himself. Keeping the secret that he had mastered the third *maamar* was challenging for him. As chasidic historian Rabbi Yossi Keller points out, "Young people want to share their accomplishments with others." But Yosef Yitzchak withstood the challenge, "even though it entailed a struggle with myself," he wrote. The idea of self-control is a core value in chasidic teachings and was a large part of Yosef Yitzchak's education. As he said many years later, "One should not crave the things that he spontaneously desires, and one should want things that he does not spontaneously desire."[84]

On Monday,[85] the day of his bar mitzvah, he woke at 6:00 a.m., immersed in the *mikveh,* and then, accompanied by his father, went to pray at the gravesites of Rabbi Menachem Mendel and Rabbi Shmuel. His father directed him to stand between the tombs and then declared, "Today, my son – your grandson and great-grandson – Yosef Yitzchak, the son of Shterna Sara, becomes bar mitzvah. Invoke mercy for all of us and him." Afterward, he instructed Yosef Yitzchak to recite the *maamar*, and in Yiddish he proclaimed, "Holy grandfathers, bless us."

They returned to town, and there Yosef Yitzchak said a second *maamar* after services in the presence of many guests. The bar mitzvah was a weeklong celebration, with Chasidim convening from throughout Russia.[86] The Rashab instructed Yosef Yitzchak to spend some time with the great Chasidim who had flocked to Lubavitch. Throughout the week, he listened to their stories and absorbed the teachings that they had heard from the Rebbes of earlier generations.

On Thursday afternoon, philanthropist Yeshaya Berlin invited the guests to a gathering. Yosef Yitzchak was surrounded by chasidic greats who sang melodies and shared stories and words of Torah. Rabbi Asher Grossman from Nikolaev turned to Yosef Yitzchak and said, "I heard from your teacher, Reb Nissan, that you know a *maamar* other than the one you recited earlier this week. If you can say *chasidut*, we need to hear it." Surrounded by a distinguished group of scholars, young Yosef Yitzchak repeated the *maamar* by heart. It took an hour. Three rabbis who were present recalled that they had heard Rabbi Shmuel teach the *maamar* the first time, "and they were deeply impressed, asking if I know any other *maamarim*. For a moment I thought of revealing that my father had taught me a third *maamar*, but I restrained myself. I sat and listened" as the gathering continued through the night.

In a private moment, the Rashab gave his son his personal blessing: "You should never be fearful of anything and serve G-d with love and awe. Your *gartel* should be strong like steel, you should be a Chasid with a G-d-fearing spirit, and a scholar."[87] Then he quoted the words of King David to his son Shlomo prior to his demise: "Become a man."[88] The commentaries explain this as a directive to act maturely and wisely, to be heroic, and to fear iniquity.[89] Then, remembers the Rayatz, "he kissed me on the forehead."

On Shabbat, two days later, "my father called me and asked me to repeat the third *maamar*, which I did carefully and thoroughly. Later during Shabbat, my father called me again. He went to the closet where the manuscripts were stored and took the *maamar* of Rabbi Shmuel and gave it to me as a gift." Then he blessed him again, saying, "The same blessing my father gave me I bestow on you. May G-d give you wisdom, understanding, and knowledge to serve the One above with prayer, mitzvot, a good character, and a full heart."[90] The bar mitzvah was a major turning point in the life of Yosef Yitzchak. His comprehension of concepts of chasidic philosophy reached a new level, and the blessings of his father left a lasting impression on him.

A few months later, on Rosh HaShanah in 1893, the Rashab, then thirty-two, fully accepted the position of Rebbe, becoming the fifth Lubavitcher Rebbe. He walked into services, surprising the community when he took his father's seat near the holy ark. It had remained vacant since Rabbi Shmuel's passing eleven years earlier, a few days after Yom Kippur in 1882. Although, says the Rayatz, "in the course of those years, there were periods where he taught *Chasidut* publicly, and from the year 5650 (1890), he received Chasidim for *yechidut*," the Rashab was not fully engaged in leading the movement. "He was still behind closed doors," focusing on his own spiritual and intellectual development. "Throughout that period, my father could be termed a *mitboded,* one living in solitude." That Rosh HaShanah was a turning point, says the Rayatz. "A new order began, a new path in the *avodah* of *hitgalut* (revelation)."[91] The Rashab emerged as the most influential chasidic Rebbe in Russia at the time. With his acceptance of the position, Chasidim began to flock to Lubavitch in large numbers once again. The Rayatz described the period that followed as "the era of the rebirth of Lubavitch."[92]

The third change happened a few days after Rosh HaShanah when the Rashab appointed Rabbi Shmuel Betzalel Sheftel,[93] known by an acronym of his name, the Rashbatz, to teach his son.[94] The Rayatz described him in his diary as an "exceptional" Chasid of the third Rebbe, Rabbi Menachem Mendel, and later the fourth Rebbe, Rabbi Shmuel, who "drew him close with a deep internal bond." A scholar and an intellectual, "he was a creative and intelligent person," says Chabad historian Rabbi Yossi Paltiel. The Rashbatz had previously taught Yosef Yitzchak's father at the behest of his grandfather, Rabbi Shmuel, "who shared with him his inner thoughts in regard to the education of his middle son [the Rashab]."[95]

The Rashbatz was fully dedicated to his young protege and remained his teacher until 1900. "My teacher the Rashbatz had a particular talent for clarifying and explaining a chasidic concept. For every subject he had a parable, and everything he uttered reflected a quick and clever mind."[96] He was a Torah scholar and a vast reservoir of chasidic teachings, which he shared with Yosef Yitzchak. "He stood at a high level in his personal service of G-d. He was a great scholar with a remarkable ability to impart and explain what he had learned from Chasidim of generations earlier."[97]

At the age of fifteen, the Rayatz's relationship with his father took on a deeper dimension. "In the summer of 1895, my father traveled to Bolivke." He summered with his wife in the resort town located forty-five miles from the hustle and bustle of the chasidic court in Lubavitch. The official reason for the trip was his weakened health. "But the true motive was that my father wanted to spend time with me and dedicate himself to my personal development." The Rashab devoted a large amount of time to his son. "For six years, from 5655 (1895) to 5660 (1901), from mid-Sivan (June) to mid-Elul (August), on weekdays, my father took me for walks for some two hours." Once a week, "my father would travel to Lubavitch to visit his mother and to receive visitors who had come to Lubavitch."

During those summers, the Rashab mentored the Rayatz. It had been a tradition amongst Chabad Rebbes to share with their sons and eventual successors profound teachings of Torah, Chasidism, and family traditions.[98] The Rashab now gave his son a *kiruv penimi*, a window into his own personal spiritual universe. They studied Talmud and chasidic *maamarim*. As the Rayatz describes, "It was solid and penetrating, and included commentaries by a number of *Rishonim* (talmudic scholars)."[99] The Rashab instructed his son on his *avodah*, his spiritual service. As the Rayatz explains, prayers and character development are a key pillar of Chabad philosophy. "*Avodah* signifies that one should work on himself, toiling until he becomes the definitive master over his own limbs, faculties, and senses, as well as the 'garments' of the soul: thought, speech, and action."[100] The Rashab shared personal stories with his son – tales of his youth and spiritual struggles – as well as chasidic lore. He was not only trying to share his values with his son but preparing him for the future, when he would become a Rebbe.

Clearly, that was on the Rashab's mind. In 1896, he was very ill and traveled with his wife to Moscow for medical care. According to the seventh Rebbe, the doctors' prognosis was very bleak. "There is nothing that can be done anymore," they told the Rashab, predicting that he had just months to live. Returning to his hotel, he shared the ominous report with his wife and suggested, "I think we should travel to *Eretz Yisrael*," as he wanted to spend his last days in the Jewish homeland. Alarmed, she asked, "What will be with the Chasidim?" He responded, "Our son will remain here." Despite the fact that his son was just sixteen, the Rashab was sure that he could lead the Chabad movement. Rebbetzin Shterna Sara prevailed on her husband to remain in Lubavitch, and despite the doctors' dire predictions, he recovered, living another twenty-four years.[101]

It was a summer morning as the Rashab and his son walked down the path from Lubavitch through a marsh to the cemetery and the edge of town. Rows of stones, reminders of generations past, some with inscriptions weathered from hundreds of years of winter frost, stretched toward the forest. In the middle of it all was a small synagogue adjacent to the Ohel, the stone structure surrounding the graves of Rabbi Menachem Mendel and Rabbi Shmuel. It was the Rayatz's fifteenth birthday. The night before, his father had surprised him by telling him to wake up early the next day, immerse himself in the *mikveh*, and pray, after which they would head to Lubavitch from the resort town of Bolivke. As they made the four-hour wagon ride, the reason for the trip remained a mystery to the Rayatz. Earlier that week, the Rashab had made his weekly visit to see his mother and have private meetings with Chasidim; this second trip was very unusual. Puzzled, the Rayatz asked his father, "You were just here on Monday. My grandmother will be afraid that something is amiss." His father assured him, "She won't be afraid; she knows." After they arrived in Lubavitch, the Rashab went to speak privately with his mother as the Rayatz waited. When he returned, he told him that they were going to the Ohel, the resting place of the Rebbes. "My grandmother was in high spirits and sent us off with heartfelt blessings."

They made their way to the small synagogue. Once inside, they stood on the wooden floor, light beaming from the large windows that framed the *aron kodesh*. The purpose of their visit was still unknown to the Rayatz, but it soon became clear that this moment would be a turning point in his life. "My father opened the *aron kodesh* and proclaimed: 'Today I am bringing my son to the *akedah.*'"[102] Referencing the biblical altar on which Avraham, following divine instruction, bound his only son, Yitzchak, the Rashab sought to inculcate his own son with the ideal of *mesirat nefesh,* that a Jew is willing to sacrifice his desires and even his life for the sake of Heaven. "For the *akedah,*" continued the Rashab, "there is one who binds and one who is bound. Avraham bound his son Yitzchak so that nothing would invalidate his offering, G-d forbid. In the same way, I want this *akedah* to be perfectly acceptable above."

My father "wept profusely, and I, who still knew nothing of what was transpiring, wept with him." Standing together with the ark still open, the Rashab began to review a section of *Igrot Kodesh,* a selection of letters from the first Rebbe, part of his magnum opus, the *Tanya*. The letter begins by quoting the verse in Proverbs, "*Chagrah be'oz motnehah* – She girds her loins with strength,"[103] exploring the concept of *kabbalat ol,* following the directives of the Torah without aberration. Finally, the Rashab turned to his son and said, "In the presence of our holy forbearers, I want to enter into a covenant with you." The Rayatz described the emotional moment: "He placed his holy hands on my head and said, 'As of this day, I transfer to you the sacred task of working for the public good in both material and spiritual matters." With that, the Rashab inducted his son as a Jewish leader, a role he a role that would culminate with him becoming the Sixth Lubavitcher Rebbe a quarter of a century later.

The Rashab selected that excerpt from the *Tanya* because of its powerful message, says Rabbi Paltiel. He foresaw that during his son's leadership, the Rayatz would face many challenges and need to stand up for his principles. He was telling him that "*mesirat nefesh,* self-sacrifice for G-d and His Torah, is this way and no other way, no compromises, no matter what it costs." As the Rayatz reflected fifty years later, "It was about resilience, that in matters of principle one stands firm."

They remained in the synagogue for four hours as the Rashab explained his vision for his son and his new role as a leader. "My father outlined for me the 140 years of communal work that the Lubavitcher Rebbes had conducted in the past and the present." The Rashab told his son about the first Rebbe, Rabbi Schneur Zalman, who at the age of eleven, in 1756, urged refugees coming to Russia from Prague to become farmers so as to earn a stable livelihood. That tradition of communal service continued through the five Lubavitcher Rebbes. "My father described to me the Alter Rebbe's fifty years of communal work, the period of the Mitteler Rebbe (Rabbi Dovber), and the period of the Tzemach Tzedek (Rabbi Menachem Mendel)." He described to his son how his father, Rabbi Shmuel, strove to alleviate the "bitter plight of Russian Jewry during the last ten years of the reign of Czar Alexander III." At the core of this long account was ideal of the "superhuman sacrificing toil of the Lubavitcher Rebbes for the public good."

After the long conversation, "my father rose and wished me *mazal tov*. My heart was aflame. I promised him that I would place myself at his disposal and that with every fiber of my life I would resolutely fulfill (with G-d's help) whatever tasks were entrusted to me for the public good."

Finally, they headed back to Bolivke, stopping once more to see the Rayatz's grandmother, who gave him a blessing for this new stage in his life.[104]

From that day on, the Rayatz stood by his father's side in communal affairs, acting as his personal secretary and confidant. Historian Gershon Kranzler writes that as the secretary of his father, the Rayatz was able "to watch from the inside of this tremendous organization all tasks facing the leader of all these religious, communal, and diplomatic activities."[105] A few months later, the Rashab dispatched the Rayatz to represent him at a rabbinic meeting. He asked the Rashbatz, the Rayatz's teacher, who was now in his seventies, to accompany him, telling him that despite his son's young age, he should allow him to begin to play a leadership role, and "you should mix in as little as possible."[106]

The day that father and son stood together in front of the ark on sacred ground was a turning point. Years later, the Rebbe reflected on it. "With G-d's help and in the merit of my holy forebears, I have remained faithful, despite my shattered physical condition, to the principles governing communal activity that I was taught by my Rebbe, the great self-sacrificing leader and mentor, my father, of blessed memory. With self-sacrifice I fulfill his holy testament of disseminating Torah study inspired by the awe of Heaven, by furthering authentic Jewish education and working for the welfare of the public."[107]

Says Paltiel, "This is one of the most important days in the history of Chabad." The Rashab understood that as the twentieth century dawned, the Jewish community was undergoing revolutionary transformation: "The world was about to turn upside down." The Rayatz's new leadership role would demand immense personal sacrifice. "He never had a life for himself, and now at the young age of fifteen, his father thrust him into a position of leadership."[108]

Chapter Two

Tomchei Temimim

As the Rayatz approached his sixteenth birthday,[1] suggestions for *shidduchim*, marriage proposals, began to arrive in Lubavitch. Some of the propositions were from families of means who hoped to match their daughter to the son of the Rebbe. The family matriarch, the Rayatz's grandmother, Rebbetzin Rivkah, was intrigued by these prospects. At the time, the financial condition in the Rebbe's family was difficult. One prospective *shidduch* was offering a dowry of fifty thousand rubles ($200,000 today), and a significant dowry would necessarily improve the family's situation. But the Rebbe Rashab had heard that his second cousin in Kishinev, Rabbi Avraham Schneersohn, had a daughter named Nechama Dina[2] and he was interested in hearing more about her. He asked Rabbi Asher Grossman from Nikolayev to meet the family and prospective bride. Rabbi Grossman's positive report prompted the Rashab and his wife to consider Nechama Dina as the best choice for their son. The Rayatz's grandmother still supported the prospect with the large dowry, and so the decision was left to the Rayatz.

The Rayatz told his parents, "The Torah says that Avraham looked for a bride for his only son, Yitzchak, 'from his father's house,'[3] expressing a preference for a relative." With that, the decision was made, and in June of 1896, the Rayatz became engaged to Nechama Dina in Bolivke, where the family was spending the summer;[4] the celebration lasted a week.[5] A month later, the Rayatz's mother, Rebbetzin Shterna Sara, wrote to her cousins in *Eretz Yisrael:* "The bride, thank G-d, is charming and very observant, and we are hoping that through her, all the aspirations of our holy ancestors will be fulfilled. We gave up major financial benefits [that would have come from the large doweries being offered] for the sake of selecting the most proper young woman who would be an honor for our ancestors." She added that the wedding was being deferred for a year because "she is still very young."[6] In advance of the wedding, the Rayatz completed his studies for *semikhah,* rabbinic ordination.

Chasidim streamed to Lubavitch for the wedding, held two weeks before Rosh HaShanah in 1897.[7] The Rayatz donned a *shtreimel,* the fur hat customarily worn by Lubavitcher Rebbes, and invoked the blessing of *Shehechiyanu*[8] before the ceremony. The *chuppah* was held on Friday afternoon in the courtyard of the main synagogue.[9] Afterward, the crowd escorted the young couple through the town of Lubavitch with singing and dancing. The main wedding celebration continued on Sunday evening in the large study hall known as the *zal.*[10]

In honor of the wedding,[11] the Rayatz asked his father to open a yeshivah that would integrate the study of Talmud and chasidic philosophy. The Rashab had been considering the idea for some time but was uncertain about proceeding with such an ambitious enterprise. He told his son the proposition was "*misnagdishe shtick*" (something more aligned with the non-chasidic community). Despite the initial rejection, the suggestion provoked a serious conversation between father and son, and the Rashab said he needed to deliberate over the proposal and pray at the Ohel.[12] When he returned, he informed the Rayatz of his consent to open the yeshivah. The Rayatz later referred to the yeshivah as "one of the gifts I requested for my wedding."[13]

His father warned him that opening such a yeshivah would be complicated. "You should know what you are getting into."[14] These were visionary words. In the decades to come, the yeshivah would play a central role in the Rayatz's life.

On Sunday, the day of the wedding reception, the Rashab invited fifty of the distinguished wedding guests to a meeting at which he planned to unveil the idea of the yeshivah.[15] At 2:00 p.m., the room was crowded with "scholars and leaders, amongst them prominent rabbis, important philanthropists, and people from around the country," described Rabbi Moshe Rosenblum.[16] Curiosity filled the air, as the meeting's agenda remained a mystery.

They were surprised when the Rashab announced his plan to "open a yeshivah for our youth, with proper administration, so that they can dedicate themselves exclusively to Torah study."

There was no lack of yeshivas in Eastern Europe. The modern yeshivah began with the establishment of the yeshivah in Volozhin in 1803. With time, yeshivas were established in other communities, such as Slabodka, Mir, Telz, and Novardok. These were led by world-class scholars, including Rabbis Nosson Tzvi Finkel, Naftali Tzvi Yehudah Berlin, Chaim Soloveitchik, and others. The vast majority of young Jews spent a few years in a local yeshivah, operated on an ad hoc basis by local rabbis, which varied in quality and educational standards. Few boys remained in yeshivah beyond their early teen years. Only a few exceptional students progressed to the larger, most prestigious yeshivas to continue their studies beyond a basic knowledge of Jewish tradition, law, and philosophy.

Some students from Chabad families also attended these elite yeshivas. Until the inception of the yeshivah in Lubavitch, Chabad students developed their connection to Chasidism in a less formal fashion. "They absorbed the chasidic teachings from their families," says Professor Ilia Luria.[17] They would join their parents on their visits to the Rebbe in Lubavitch. The few select senior students who did study in Lubavitch did so informally and were known as *yoshvim* (literally, "those who sit and study").[18] They wanted to be in the Rebbe's vicinity to absorb the unique spiritual atmosphere in Lubavitch.

The new yeshivah that the Rashab was proposing would be different than the others. He told those assembled, "For many years, I have been considering establishing a yeshivah for scholars of Torah who would dedicate themselves to the study of chasidic philosophy" in addition to the classic study of Talmud. "There were obstacles that stood in the way, but now is the time to create the yeshivah."[19]

Historically, yeshivas concentrated almost exclusively on Talmud study, which focuses on the legalistic tradition of Judaism. There was a modicum of attention given to the mystical dimension of Judaism. At the meeting on the day of the Rayatz's wedding, the Rashab outlined his vision for a groundbreaking educational institution whose curriculum would not only focus on Talmud but also integrate the study of Chasidism, formally and systematically.

Chasidism is not simply an intellectual exercise. Chasidic philosophy seeks to uncover the spiritual meanings behind the study of Judaism and the rituals that lead one to seek and refine a personal connection to G-d. Studying the inner workings of creation and Creator, the spiritual architecture of the universe, and subsequently meditating upon it in prayer (*avodah*, known in talmudic parlance as "service of the heart") leads one to a genuine and personal relationship with G-d and infuses one's study, practice, and even mundane activities with sacred enthusiasm. Concepts that can present a challenge to one's relationship with G-d – such as faith and trust, free choice, good and evil, and the purpose of life – are grappled with in chasidic thought and are clarified as a means of strengthening one's connection with Him. This mode of yeshivah study was a revolutionary shift, moving away from the historic approach to classic Jewish learning that had focused solely on the intricacies and nuances of Torah text or halakhic conclusions.

As modernity began to challenge traditional Judaism, some yeshivas had begun to incorporate a spiritual dimension to combat the forces seeking to lure young Jews away from observance. Some yeshivas, such as Telz, Novardok, and Slabodka,[20] instituted the study and practice of *musar*. The *Musar* movement, established by Rabbi Yisrael Salanter,[21] was based on teaching ethics and emphasized personal behavior, probity, honesty, social welfare, care for others, and meticulous observance of Jewish tradition.[22]

The difference between the character refinement of *musar* versus that which is engendered by the study of Chasidism is that *musar* centers on the individual, either by describing the lowliness of man or by discussing how great he is or can become. Chasidism, on the other hand, focuses on G-d, highlighting the idea that the purpose of man's action is not just individual perfection but connecting with G-d and drawing down godliness into this world.

When the Rashab concluded his presentation about the new yeshivah, he asked those gathered to "share their opinions and speak from the heart." Most had serious reservations, Rosenblum says. "The majority thought it was unrealistic." With the rise of the Enlightenment, Zionism, and political movements, many young people in Russia were abandoning Jewish observance. Those present at the meeting voiced little hope of countering the spirit of the times that was drawing youth away from tradition. Even those who endorsed the idea did so with reservations, saying that the yeshivah should be started on a trial basis to explore its feasibility. Rosenblum writes, "The content of the speeches was similar, each describing the present situation of the young" and concluding that "the idea was unworkable." Even those who were open to the concept "doubted it would be successful."[23]

There were three reasons for the skepticism, says Professor Luria.[24] First, "it was a departure from the traditional mode of education." For millennia, the curriculum of yeshivas concentrated almost exclusively on Talmud; elevating chasidic philosophy to the core curriculum was revolutionary. Second, many young Jews were abandoning tradition. "The majority of the younger generation was under the influence of progressive ideas." Enlisting enough high-caliber students willing to devote themselves to a serious program would be challenging. Finally, says Luria, detractors feared that "the concentration of gifted students would increase the influence of secular forces, as happened in other yeshivas." That was the case for famed Hebrew writer Chaim Nachman Bialik, for example, who was lured from observance by clandestine groups of *maskilim* (secularists) in the famed yeshivah of Volozhin.

That evening, the wedding celebration was abuzz with conversation about the new yeshivah, says Rosenblum. Those attending the meeting shared the details with Chasidim "who had come from hundreds of communities." Dancing continued into the wee hours of the morning. During the wedding feast, the Rebbe Rashab walked around, greeting his guests and offering a *lechayim* and blessings to all.[25]

The next day, late Monday afternoon, the group of rabbis and community leaders' reconvened, and the Rashab asked whether anyone wanted to comment on his announcement. The day before, they had responded with skepticism, but now they sat in silence. Though those assembled were filled with misgivings, the Rebbe himself was not. He understood that the Chasidism that would be an integral part of the curriculum was exactly what would inspire the next generation to remain steadfast in their tradition and fortify them against the temptations of the modern anti-religious influences of the day.

He addressed the crowd: "Establishing this institution will demand much from us, both materially and spiritually – the dedication of our hearts and souls." He urged them to focus not on the obstacles but on the blessing that would come from the new yeshivah. He, too, was concerned about the state of Judaism, even within the Chabad community, but he felt the yeshivah would only help. "I am deeply apprehensive and pained by the frozen and parched spiritual level of religious Jews." Their observance lacked passion, he said. "Gone is the fire and excitement in doing mitzvot; their actions are dry and frozen, and everything is done without feeling." He explained that studying the mystical dimension transforms what could be mechanical observance or a dry reading of legalistic text into a personal and meaningful relationship with G-d.

In an intriguing dichotomy, while the Chasidim expressed skepticism due to their lack of faith in the young, the Rashab had the opposite view, seeing them, as Dr. Naftali Brawer writes, "as the potential of spiritual revival." With the proper guidance, he believed, "they would be the key to the future of Orthodox Judaism."[26]

The Rashab was also disturbed by broader societal challenges. Jews were suffering from czarist oppression and anti-Semitism, and religious leadership seemed unable to develop solutions.[27] "We need to remedy this," the Rashab declared.

The new yeshivah would infuse in the students "spiritual values" and instill in them "a sensitivity to godliness." Integration of rigorous study of chasidic teachings with the standard yeshivah learning, the Rashab believed, would be transformational. "The teaching of *Chasidut* is a complete Torah that must be studied in depth" and would enrich all aspects of Jewish learning. He explained that chasidic philosophy focuses on "understanding godliness" and "elevating character traits."[28] He wanted to create a yeshivah "where the study of Torah would be done with enthusiasm," explaining that a passion for Judaism would be instilled "by the study of Chasidism in a systematic fashion."[29] This would create a new generation of leaders, self-confident and rooted in Torah values, who would restore spiritual vitality to Jewish life and mitigate the influence of the groups drawing the young away from tradition.[30]

Until the inception of the yeshivah, chasidic philosophy had been studied in an unstructured fashion. The Rebbes taught *maamarim,* which were recorded by *chozrim,* oral scribes who memorized and then transcribed them, after which they would be distributed to the chasidic community for study. Over time, the new yeshivah created a formal curriculum of chasidic philosophy based on the teachings of the early Chabad Rebbes. The Rashab enhanced the curriculum by teaching a series of *maamarim* known as *hemshekhim,* a tranche of *maamarim* following a common theme. This eventually developed into the structured syllabus that is used today by Chabad yeshivas worldwide.

In addition to studying Talmud and Jewish law for eight hours a day, the students of the new yeshivah devoted four hours daily to the study of Chasidism. They were empowered with an understanding of the classic ideas of Jewish mysticism, and they learned how to apply those ideas to life. In the conventional Lithuanian-style yeshivas, an outstanding scholar was praised as being a *gadol* (a "great" scholar). In the Lubavitch yeshivah, the goal of the students was to be a *penimi,* one who had internalized the spiritual values he studied. Identifying a person as a *gadol* was considered self-aggrandizement; instead, humility and piety in serving G-d were the central values in the yeshivah in Lubavitch.

The faculty was also organized differently than in the standard yeshivas, which were traditionally led by a *rosh yeshivah,* head of the yeshivah, who was a distinguished talmudic scholar. This new yeshivah was headed by a *mashpia* (literally, "one who influences"). It was the *mashpia's* responsibility to guide the spiritual and character refinement of the students through teaching chasidic philosophy and focusing on prayer and the service of G-d. Initially, there was no *rosh yeshivah* in Tomchei Temimim, but as the yeshivah grew, additional faculty members were added to fill that role.

Another difference between this yeshivah and others was that the study of *pilpul,* using sophistry to analyze talmudic arguments that do not always have a practical application, was not encouraged by the Rashab. Instead, he emphasized "knowing the subject being studied,"[31] analyzing talmudic arguments and their application to real life.

The day after the second meeting in Lubavitch regarding the new yeshivah, the Rashab personally selected the first group of students, many of whom were *yoshvim* studying in Lubavitch, and appointed Rabbi Shmuel Gronem[32] as their *mashpia,* with instructions regarding the curriculum.[33] The following day, on the auspicious date of 18 Elul,[34] the birthday of both the first Chabad Rebbe and the Baal Shem Tov, studies began in Lubavitch. After the holidays, the students and their *mashpia* relocated to Zembin,[35] a town of one thousand residents, most of whom were Jewish, some 160 miles west of Lubavitch. Says Naftali Brawer, "The town was smaller than Lubavitch, and it appears that there may have been fewer distractions for the students."[36] Over the course of the year, more students joined; the original group swelled to eighteen.

The Rashab suggested that the yeshivah meet all of its students' personal needs. Customarily, yeshivah students in Eastern Europe were hosted by local families for their daily meals, referred to in Yiddish as *essen teg,* literally, "eating days." One family would host a boy or two on Monday, and another on Tuesday, creating a partnership between communities and the local yeshivah. But the Rebbe's yeshivah provided in-house meals for its students, initially reimbursing the students individually for the cost of their food until it eventually had its own kitchen.[37]

After almost a year of study in Zembin, the students, accompanied by Reb Shmuel Gronem, returned to Lubavitch to absorb the unique spiritual atmosphere in the Rebbe's court during the High Holidays season of 1898. "You couldn't recognize them," the Rayatz wrote. "They had been transformed." Their academic and spiritual accomplishments brought his father "great joy," and he was impressed by their "tremendous changes."[38] The Rashab was interested in the students' individual achievements, instructing his son to meet with each one privately and then to prepare a series of detailed briefings on them.[39]

In Lubavitch, Chasidim from across Russia who had come for the holidays encountered the students of Tomchei Temimim. The cadre of young, passionate, and intellectually gifted students impressed the guests, and the skepticism that had greeted the idea of a yeshivah just a year earlier evaporated. It was replaced by enthusiasm and prompted the Chasidim to discuss the yeshivah's future and the need for strong leadership. A group of Chasidim led by Rabbi Asher Grossman of Nikolayev approached the Rayatz, then eighteen years old, and asked him to become the yeshivah's director. They felt he had the "wisdom, motivation, and energy needed to spur the growth of the yeshivah," Rosenblum writes, adding that when the Rayatz demurred, they appealed to the Rashab. When he endorsed the idea, "the Rayatz could not refuse anymore."[40] As the yeshivah entered its second year, Rabbi Yosef Yitzchak became its director.[41]

The task facing the Rayatz was complex. He was responsible for raising funds for the yeshivah's growing budget and creating a stable economic base. He had to nurture the yeshivah from a small group of exceptional students into a full-fledged institution, preserving its high academic standards while expanding the program to include students of diverse ages and backgrounds.

During the High Holidays, the Rashab announced that the yeshivah would move to Lubavitch. With time, branches of Tomchei Temimim were opened in other locations, including Doksycy, Koblitz, and Vitebsk, with the expanding network funded and administered by the Rayatz. The yeshivah was staffed by notable scholars and distinguished Chasidim who were many years, even decades, older than the Rayatz. He hired them, and at times, he discharged staff members who did not live up to expectations. As the yeshivah grew larger and new facilities were needed, the Rayatz found the significant funds necessary for capital improvements.

The Rayatz applied himself to his new role immediately, says Rosenblum, "investing all his strength and abilities." Lubavitch was filled with holiday guests, and two weeks after assuming the position of director, he convened them on the day after Rosh HaShanah. "He outlined the yeshivah's successes so far and told how they had seen how remarkably the students developed during the year." The Rayatz appealed to the guests to be the vanguard, asking that "each give according to his abilities." He enlisted them in a plan to create a broad-based fundraising campaign, asking them to become activists – "each one, in his city, should undertake to support the yeshivah."

The Rayatz spent the next few days firming up commitments. "He worked intensely and was able to secure annual pledges of 1,400 rubles (about $40,000 today)." He created an association, named Tomchei Temimim, to galvanize Chasidim from all over Russia to support the yeshivah. Members agreed to be ambassadors of the yeshivah and committed to standards of financial accountability, record-keeping, and specific procedures for transferring funds to Lubavitch. They were also asked to help recruit students. The groups bylaws stated: "If a young man requests to study [in the yeshivah], they should examine him thoroughly: his name, residence, age, qualities, character, and how he acts, as well as his family background and information on where he studied [previously]." They were to forward information about candidates to Lubavitch.[42] This comprehensive strategy, attests Rosenblum, "created many donors." Support flowed in from across Russia, and during this initial stage, "the yeshivah had no deficit."[43]

The Rayatz realized that it was crucial to enlist supporters who could donate large amounts. After the holidays, he turned to Yeshaya Berlin of Riga,[44] a noted Chabad philanthropist who was close to forty years his senior. He asked Berlin to "make a monthly or annual commitment." Berlin replied that he had heard good things about the yeshivah and shortly afterward, he met with the Rayatz and the Rashab and made a sizable pledge.[45]

Simchat Torah in Lubavitch was the culmination of the holiday season. That year, 1898, *hakafot* (the customary dancing with the Torah[46]) continued until sunrise. At approximately 4:00 a.m., as they began the seventh and last *hakafah*, the Rashab paused the singing and exclaimed: "With divine blessing, I have established a yeshivah in which both *nigleh* [the revealed part of Torah, i.e., Talmud] and Chasidism are studied." He exhorted the students to realize that embedded in the revealed part of Torah is a deeper spiritual dimension. "They should understand *Chasidut* the same way that they understand a concept in the revealed Torah." After singing a melody, he offered a prayer: "The One who gave the Torah should assist the students of the yeshivah."

The Rashab danced around the *bimah* (the podium on which the Torah is read), leading the recitation of the traditional *hakafot* verses: "*Tomekh temimim, hoshiya na. Takif la'ad, hatzlichah na. Tamim bemaasav, aneinu beyom koreinu* – Supporter of the sincere ones, deliver us. Eternally invincible One, grant us success. Perfect in His ways, answer us on the day we call." As he completed the circuit around the *bimah,* the Rashab started to dance intensely. Afterward, he returned to his place in the front of the synagogue and continued to encourage the crowd to sing and dance with great joy.

The crowd grew silent as the Rashab stepped forward to speak. "The yeshivah that was established by the grace of G-d doesn't have a name. Now I am naming it Tomchei Temimim [literally, "Supporters of the Sincere," derived from the verses he had just recited], and the title of those who learn and conduct themselves in its spirit will be *temimim* [sincere, virtuous, complete ones; *tamim* in the singular]."[47]

After the High Holidays, the Chasidim returned to their cities and towns across Russia and word spread about the new yeshivah. From around the country, Rosenblum reports, "a huge number applied." The Rayatz instituted high acceptance standards, and applicants went through a rigorous process. The candidates were subjected to multiple interviews and tests with the Rayatz and the Rashab, "to ensure that the students were only the best candidates." The Rayatz took the approach of building the yeshivah slowly and accepting only top-tier students. In the yeshivah's second year, just twenty-five finalists were accepted, and they joined only "on a trial basis, and during that time they were tested again."

Three years after the yeshivah's founding, in 1900, the Rashab laid out a mission statement. Again, he chose the night of Simchat Torah, the high point of the holiday season. Chasidim who had come from far and wide, including the students of the yeshivah, packed the synagogue. It was late at night when the Rashab turned to his son. He noted that three years had passed since the yeshivah was founded. He compared the students to *orlah,* the term for a tree's produce in its first three years; as the tree matures in those first few years, one does not eat from its fruit. "I entrusted to you the directorship of the yeshivah, making you responsible for both its spiritual and material welfare. Our vineyard, Yeshivas Tomchei Temimim, is now three years old, and it has produced fine fruits."

He asked the Rayatz to have the students rise. He addressed them: "*Temimim* [the term of endearment used for students of Tomchei

Temimim], you are like the soldiers of King David." He recalled how the ancient soldiers, renowned for their devotion to the Jewish people, would write a bill of divorce that allowed their wives to remarry in the event that they did not return from battle and their death could not be determined.[48] "You should divorce yourself from worldly concerns and make scholarship and spiritual development your priority. The study of chasidic philosophy will instill in you the passion to overwhelm the coolness of the world to sanctify it." It was the key to "standing strong" for principles and ideals of Judaism, he told them. The Rashab saw the students as the vanguard of Jewish leadership. "We are assured that the students of Tomchei Temimim, wherever they may be in the four corners of the world, will exemplify the quality of self-sacrifice for the higher purpose of creating a dwelling place for G-d in the physical world."

Rosenblum writes that the purpose of the yeshivah was not just to produce scholars. "There is no lack of great students of Torah." Tomchei Temimim's mission was to create a different kind of scholar, one rooted in profound values, "where the Giver of the Torah was embedded in them." It was to nurture a cadre of students who would be willing to stand up for Jewish principles "with all their strength and vitality." According to Luria, the Rashab viewed the yeshivah's role as "producing leaders." Most Jews were traditional, "but they were passive and lacking inspired direction." Tomchei Temimim became the institution to change that.[49]

That night, the Rashab told the students that aside from fully immersing themselves in the study of Torah, they had another responsibility: to disseminate the teachings of Chasidism. He recalled the story of Rabbi Israel Baal Shem Tov,[50] who ascended to the heavenly realms to ask the Messiah when he would redeem the world. The Messiah answered, "When your wellsprings [chasidic teachings] will be disseminated outward." The Rashab said that this was the students' mission: to spread the ideas of Chasidism to the broader Jewish world.[51]

Year after year, enrollment grew – from its first year in Zembin with eighteen students to two hundred just five years later. The Rayatz had to ensure a high caliber of students, manage the growth, and provide suitable facilities for the burgeoning student body. In 1901, he approached philanthropist Yeshaya Berlin and solicited a large gift. With his help, the study hall known as the *zal* was refurbished, and a dining room and other facilities were built. The budget also grew annually: In 1899, it was 3,120 rubles, and by 1903 it reached over twenty thousand rubles. During those first years, there were financial ups and downs, forcing the Rayatz to secure loans at times. In 1902, there was a deficit of over 1,500 rubles, but just a year later, things turned around and there was a small surplus.

The Russian government refused to recognize the yeshivah, because it didn't offer courses in secular studies or Russian language, putting it at risk of a government shutdown. The stationery of the yeshivah reflected this, referring to the institution as a seller of books and religious articles. The lack of formal recognition put fundraising in jeopardy, too. The Rashab wrote to his son that if they obtained the recognition, "our hands could be open to receive donations without any fear or concern." But a major effort by the Rayatz and others to secure government recognition proved unsuccessful.[52]

In addition to the initial skepticism the Rashab encountered from his own Chasidim, opposition arose from the competing Chabad courts in Kopust and Liadi, whose members feared that the new yeshivah would strengthen "the dominance of the Lubavitch stream in the Chabad community,"[53] says Luria. "Opposition rose from varied quarters, both internally in the Chabad community and from the progressives and Zionists."[54] Those challenges were part of the broader culture war in the Jewish community between traditionalists and the new ideas of the Enlightenment, Zionism, Bundism, and Communism. In the city of Lubavitch, *maskilim* had opened a secular school, and its director, Gedalia Weinstein, organized opposition to the yeshivah, attacking it in the Jewish media, which caused some to withhold donations.[55] Nevertheless, Luria says, it did not deter the Chabad supporters who remained loyal to the yeshivah.

Tensions with Zionist activists that had been simmering for some time took a far more ominous turn, coming to a head in 1906.[56] Berel Davzik, a teenage student of the yeshivah from Chernihiv, began neglecting his studies and became active in the local Marxist Zionist group Poalei Tzion.[57] Because he was still a minor, the Rayatz telegrammed his parents and asked them to pick him up. Until they arrived, he required him to remain on the yeshivah premises. This angered members of Poalei Tzion, who marched into the yeshivah on a Thursday night[58] to confront the Rayatz. "We came to inform you that Davzik is a member of Poalei Tzion," they declared. "We heard that you intend to send him away from here, so we have come to notify you that we won't allow this to happen." When the Rayatz rebuffed them, they pulled out weapons and threatened him. "Get out of here! I'm not afraid of your guns," the Rayatz responded. They left, but they made it clear that the situation was far from over.

Three days later, on Saturday night, they returned, again brandishing weapons. They threatened the Rayatz again, but unafraid, he ordered them, "Put aside your toys." After a tense back and forth during which the Rebbe refused to give in to their demands, the group retreated outside but threw stones at the yeshivah facility, breaking windows. Then they began shooting at the yeshivah. A bullet missed Rabbi Moshe Klatzkin, the rabbi of Romanov, by inches. As word of the confrontation spread, others joined, swelling the Poalei Tzion mob to two hundred. The yeshivah students heard the commotion and headed out to confront them. As the Rashab writes, "They came from the *zal* and drove them off. The yeshivah students wanted to attack them, but my son did not permit it."[59]

Berel Davzik left the next day with his father, but Poalei Tzion continued to stew in their grievances. Articles misrepresenting the affair appeared in Yiddish papers as far as New York, the writers accusing the yeshivah of fanaticism. They wrote outlandish tales of the burning of secular books in Lubavitch, labeling it an *auto-da-fe*. Poalei Tzion demanded that the yeshivah fire some of its staff, expel five senior students, and pay them compensation. The Chasidim responded by boycotting the stores of Poalei Tzion supporters in Vitebsk and other communities. The tensions continued to simmer for months, and at one point, the members of Poalei Tzion planned to ambush the Rayatz at the train station in Osha. From inside the train, the Rayatz spotted them. At that time, "I always carried a gun with me," the Rayatz confided to Yitzchak Goldin years later. He was traveling with Shmuel Katzman that day and told him to get out of the train to warn them. Katzman confronted the group and said, "If you think you are going to start up with the Rebbe's son, you will suffer a dreadful fate." Fearing for their lives and seeing police nearby, they fled.[60] With the continued threat of violence all too real, the Rayatz relocated to Germany until things would settle down.

In the meanwhile, the Zionists continued to make demands, but the Rashab refused to cave in. They resorted to violence again a few months later, raiding the Rashab's summer home in Bolivke. The Rashab describes the terrifying incident: "Six to eight of them came into the house and others stood outside." Brandishing revolvers, they exclaimed, "We'll show you!" The intruders destroyed furniture and ransacked the house while the Rayatz's young daughters were present with their grandmother. "The children began to cry, and my wife asked that they let them leave the house, but they stood there with guns." Eventually they left, "but they stood on the road to ensure that no police came."[61] The Rashab was forced to hire security guards. The Rashab's brother, the Raza, was living in Vitebsk, and he negotiated with the members of Poalei Tzion over a period of months. An agreement was finally reached, the crisis calmed, and the Rayatz returned home.[62]

Each of these conflicts – the besmirching of the yeshivah by Haskalah (Enlightenment) leaders and the efforts of Marxist Zionists to terrorize the yeshivah and the Rebbe's family – reflected the underlying conflicts in Russian Jewish life at the time. To the Rashab, the founding of Tomchei Temimim was the antidote to the movements seeking to lure traditional Jews away from observance. His goal was to create a cadre of strong Jewish leaders who could reinvigorate traditional Jewish life. Those who were determined to shift Jewish life away from its historic values realized this and attempted to undermine the yeshivah in any way, even resorting to violence. Luria asserts that ultimately, the yeshivah was successful. "It was able to earn community support and grow from year to year."

In 1910, the yeshivah took a major leap forward when the Rashab began to seriously consider opening a branch in *Eretz Yisrael.* From the early eighteenth century, there had been a concentration of Chabad followers living in Hebron.[63] Rabbi Dovber, the second Rebbe, had purchased a property for a synagogue there. His daughter, Rebbetzin Menucha Rochel, immigrated there in 1845. Her descendants kept up a close connection with the Rebbes in Lubavitch, traveling there regularly.

At the time, the community in Hebron was in decline, with many being drawn to nearby Jerusalem by the housing and financial support offered by various *kollels* (charitable funds) that would subsidize Torah students.[64] But Jerusalem was undergoing a demographic transition due to the influx of non-religious Zionist immigrants, who were changing the historically religious city. Hebron, meanwhile, remained a spiritual oasis still untouched by secular immigration. To bolster the impoverished community and enable its members to remain there, the Rayatz established Chevronim, a special fund to help the Jews in Hebron. (There had been local efforts to start a Chabad yeshivah, but they faltered.)

Leaders of the Hebron community turned to the Rashab to purchase a large property, known as Beit Romano.[65] It was originally owned by an affluent Jew from Istanbul who had erected a large mansion on it. Upon his passing, his children put it up for sale. Over a few years, the Rashab raised the necessary funds to purchase the property and navigated through the complicated legal steps to acquiring it. The Rayatz was intimately involved in assisting his father complete the challenging transaction. By 1908, the Rashab was the owner of the large complex and an adjacent property. Combined, this became the base for the new yeshivah and gave the Rashab a strong foothold in the city.[66]

In 1911, the Rashab sent a group of outstanding students, led by noted scholar Rabbi Zalman Havlin, to Hebron to establish the yeshivah. The new yeshivah, named Toras Emes, would be the first chasidic yeshivah in the Jewish homeland and was considered a branch of Tomchei Temimim in Lubavitch.

The yeshivah in Hebron had broader societal purposes: to invigorate the study of chasidic teachings in *Eretz Yisrael* and create a new cadre of Jewish leaders there. Many of the social changes that were occurring in Russia were happening in *Eretz Yisrael* too, and just as the Rashab hoped the graduates of Tomchei Temimim would set a new direction for Russian Jewry, he hoped the graduates of Toras Emes would do so in the holy land.[67]

The onset of World War I disrupted those plans. With Russia and the Ottoman Empire on opposite sides of the conflict, the Russian students sent by the Rashab were considered enemy aliens in *Eretz Yisrael,* which was under Ottoman rule. Along with Rabbi Havlin, they were forced to return to Russia. Before his passing in Rostov in 1920, the Rashab instructed Rabbi Havlin to return to *Eretz Yisrael* as soon as possible. In 1922, he did so and reconstituted the Toras Emes yeshivah in Jerusalem. Today it remains a flourishing center of Jewish scholarship.

The Rayatz was intimately involved in setting up the program in *Eretz Yisrael,* giving detailed instructions for the curriculum and the acceptance of students. However, he expected that Rabbi Havlin would ultimately take full responsibility. In 1913, he wrote to him,[68] "Our approach is to appoint individuals and entrust them with the management, and they are responsible for the projects given over to them." He explained that this extended to all aspects of the yeshivah, "both the spiritual and financial."

This method for establishing branches of the yeshivah and this management style were the precursors of the entrepreneurial model of management that would be emblematic of Chabad in the decades to come. The Rayatz and his successor, the seventh Rebbe, entrusted individuals with projects and gave them the autonomy to administer them.

The concept of sending selected students from the flagship yeshivah to establish a new center of learning was similarly an innovation that would be replicated in the future. In the 1930s, the Rayatz sent students from the main yeshivah in Poland to set up branches around the region. Later he did the same in the United States. The seventh Rebbe set up new yeshivas around the globe following the same model of selecting senior students to form the core of the new institutions, beginning with his dispatch of a group of elite students to Australia in 1966. Today there are some fifty Chabad yeshivas around the world, and the approach has been systematized so that senior students are sent from the central yeshivas to satellite branches for one or two years to ensure that the branches have a high level of scholarship and to serve as role models for younger students.

Yeshivas Tomchei Temimim was central to the Rayatz – first in Russia, later in Europe, and then in the United States. When his attempt at establishing a yeshivah in Riga, Latvia (after he was exiled there from Russia) was unsuccessful, he moved to Poland so he could be near the branch in Warsaw. From there, the Rayatz set up a network of yeshivas in Poland and Lithuania. He made the decision to move to the United

States only once he felt that establishing a yeshivah there was a realistic goal. During and after World War II, the Rebbe set up more yeshivas in Montreal, Israel, and Europe. He viewed the yeshivah as his lifetime mission entrusted to him by his father.

The Rayatz formally became active in community affairs at the age of fifteen in 1895, and from then on, he served as his father's private secretary. For a quarter of a century, until the passing of the Rashab in 1920, he was intimately involved in almost all of his father's communal activities. As his secretary, he managed much of the Rashab's personal correspondence with Jewish leaders on issues of communal concern.

It was a tumultuous era for Russian Jewry. In 1881, Czar Alexander ll was assassinated. His son and successor, Alexandar lll,[69] rolled back the reforms of his father and increased his oppression of Russian Jews. A year later, he instituted the May Laws, whose discriminatory polices restricted Jewish residency, stifled their economic growth and educational opportunities, and strengthened the restrictions of the Pale of Settlement.[70] When violent pogroms were perpetrated in Russia, the new czar did nothing to curtail them, and according to some historians, he even encouraged them. After his death in 1894, his son, the last czar, Nicholas ll, succeeded him and continued the anti-Jewish policies of his predecessors, claiming in a letter to his mother that the Jews were responsible for Russia's problems. "The labor strikes are organized by the Polish and Jewish engineers," he wrote. "The world accuses us of making pogroms, but I believe that the pogroms are a natural appearance. The Jews wish to dominate over Russia and over the Russian czars."[71] The Jews of Russia continued to suffer greatly under his rule, which ended with his abdication and execution in 1917.

Many Jews sought to flee the harsh reality of life in Russia. Between 1880 and 1920, two million Jews went in search of a better life in Western countries, primarily America. Others within the Jewish community advanced different solutions. Leaders of the Enlightenment championed assimilation. They believed that if Jews would only abandon their ancient traditions, they would find acceptance in Russian society. They backed the development of an educational system that would replace Torah with secular studies. In this way, they hoped to lure the youth away from observance and toward the cultural mainstream; they received support for their agenda from elements of the czarist government as well as from Jews in Western Europe. The Zionist movement offered hope for Jewry in the form of self-governance and a state for Jews in their historical homeland. BILU, one of the earliest Russian Zionist groups, sent its first settlers to *Eretz Yisrael* in 1882. Many Zionist leaders saw the new movement as replacing the foundations of Jewish identity with secular nationalism. No longer was one required to observe tradition in order to feel Jewish; it was enough to be part of the effort to build a new state. This prompted a schism between them and traditional Jewish leaders, including the Rashab, who strongly criticized Zionism.[72] Jews also gravitated to the leadership of those advocating for the revolutionary societal reforms of socialism and Communism. There was also the Yiddish movement, which wanted to replace Judaism with a new cultural identity based on language, among many more ideologies and movements.

From the time that he formally assumed the position of Rebbe on Rosh HaShanah in 1893, the Rashab began to reassert the involvement of Lubavitch in communal affairs. Government advocacy for Jews had been dominated by members of the Enlightenment, who shared the Russian authorities' agenda of assimilation. Key Jewish business leaders, such as Baron David Gunzburg, were Jewish representatives to the Russian government. The Rashab was disappointed by the role played by Gunzburg, who, as part of the Jewish elite in St. Petersburg, was disconnected from the needs of the average Jew in Russia. Prominent rabbinic figures from the non-chasidic yeshivah communities arose in the capital of St. Petersburg as advocates for traditional Judaism. The Rashab, with his son at his side, asserted leadership on behalf of the chasidic community. They drew support from the vast network of Chabad communities around Russia and key Chasidim in St. Petersburg and began to play a larger role in communal affairs.[73]

During this tumultuous time, the Rayatz was thrust into the role of leadership. He was dispatched by the Rashab on many missions, both public and secret. Already at the age of fifteen, he represented his father at a conference of Jewish religious leaders in Kovno in 1895, and again the following year in Vilna.[74] He repeatedly traveled to Russia's capital, St. Petersburg, to intervene with government authorities to mitigate anti-Semitic decrees and lobby for Jewish interests. He also traveled overseas to meet with Jewish leaders and representatives of other countries and lobby them to put pressure on the Russians to curtail the pogroms and to implement economic sanctions against them. This communal work, coupled with the Rayatz's position as head of one of Russia's most prestigious centers of Jewish learning, propelled him to the center of Jewish communal life. He met important rabbinic figures, influential businessmen, and government ministers.

Most of the activities of the Rayatz were performed covertly, in tandem with his father, and remain clouded in mystery. When either the Rashab or the Rayatz traveled outside of Lubavitch, they would continuously correspond, sometimes daily.[75] Sadly, few records of these private communications have survived, but it is clear that the Rayatz was closely involved in almost all areas of his father's communal activities, playing a key role in bringing his father's visions to reality. As his private secretary, he managed much of his personal correspondence with Jewish leaders on issues of communal concern.

One of the more dangerous missions the Rashab sent his son on found him battling state-sponsored anti-Semitism. The Rayatz was assigned to subvert the anti-Semitic plans of Pyotr Stolypin,[76] Russia's interior minister and prime minister under Czar Nicholas, who was planning to institute a decree that would have an adverse effect on the Jewish community.[77] The Rashab dispatched his son to the capital of St. Petersburg to find a way to block the measure.[78]

The seventh Rebbe recalls, "Once all other avenues did not work, it was decided to approach the Russian elder statesman Konstantin Pobedonostsev.[79] He had retired from a formal government role, and Stoypin, who was much younger, regularly sought his advice."[80] Despite Pobedonostsev's anti-Semitic attitudes, he "had respect for religious figures" because he had been the head of the Russian Orthodox Church. Pobedonostsev lived in a dacha in a suburb of the city, devoid of Jews. The only time he would meet the Rayatz was on a Friday night. At the time, Jews were not permitted to live in the capital without a special permit. As the Rayatz recalled years later,[81] "A few Jewish businessman lived in the city, but none on the outskirts."

For Shabbat, the Rayatz rented a room adjacent to a bar within walking distance of Pobedonostsev's dacha. "I gave the owner a large tip, and he agreed to escort me to the appointment." Despite the harsh weather, they navigated the forested area in the dark night. Pobedonostsev was surprised that the Rayatz actually came. "You are your parents' only son," he said. "My dogs could have ripped you apart." The Rayatz retorted, "A Jew should not fear a dog. The dog should fear the Jew." As a senior government official, Pobedonostsev had a special pass to access government offices, and the Rayatz convinced him to lend him his pass for the government ministry in St. Petersburg.

The Rayatz turned up at the ministry, surprising the guard with his special pass. It was midday, and many of the staff were out for lunch. Once inside, the Rayatz made his way to the office of the minister responsible for the unfavorable edict. Finding no one there, he entered and searched the minister's desk for the document he had prepared for approval. When he found it, he stamped it "Rejected," placed it in the outbox, and quietly exited the building.

The seventh Rebbe reflected years later, "It is difficult to imagine the Rayatz in a bar with Russian drunkards, particularly on the holy Shabbat. But he did all of this because he might revoke a decree against Jews." The Rayatz explained that this principle of putting oneself at risk for the sake of the community was instilled in him by his father. "After this incident, two prominent Chasidim, Yeshaya Berlin and Yaakov Horowitz, asked my father how he could justify sending me on such dangerous missions." The Rashab responded to them, "The mission must be achieved irrespective of the risks. The purpose of a soul coming into this world is realized when a Jew undertakes self-sacrifice for G-d, and I am confident he will live a long life."[82]

Education was the primary battlefield for the future of Russian Jewry. For many years, the Enlightenment had been pushing to secularize the educational system in Russia. In 1843, Max Lilienthal,[83] a German Enlightenment activist, orchestrated a government-backed conference in St. Petersburg to institute a plan to secularize the Jewish educational system in the country. The third Rebbe, Rabbi Menachem Mendel, played a key role in that conference, blocking Lilienthal's plans.

In 1863, the secularists set up an organization called Chevrah Mefitzei Haskalah (Society to Promote the Enlightenment), known by its acronym, Chamah. It was backed by some of Russia's wealthiest Jews.[84] Baron Horace (Naftali Hertz) Gunzburg, and later his son Baron David Gunzburg,[85] were seen by the czarist government as the premier representatives of the Jewish community; they both took leadership roles in the organization. Chamah's goal was to promote the assimilation of Jews into Russian society. Starting in the 1890s, the organization began to expand its campaign, setting up schools with minimal Jewish instruction. At first, their success was marginal, but with time they gained momentum, and by 1900, they boasted 150 schools.

They even targeted the town of Lubavitch, sending Enlightenment activist Mordechai Ben Hillel to explore the possibilities of opening a school there in 1897. He reported that because the community was the bastion of chasidic life, a school there would have a large impact. "Lubavitch is visited by thousands annually. It is important to establish a school there, as its influence will not be only on the residents of Lubavitch but on all of Russian Jewry."[86] With the support of Baron Gunzburg, the school opened with 130 students, despite the Rashab's opposition.[87] According to Luria, "The school in Lubavitch became an ideological objective." Yisrael Jacobson, who was a student in Lubavitch, recalls that shortly afterward, at a major *farbrengen*, the Rashab spoke bitterly about Gunzburg's support of the school. "I requested of him that he 'give me Yavneh' [referring to Rabbi Yochanan ben Zakkai's ancient request of Emperor Vespasian to spare the scholars of the city of Yavneh when he destroyed the Temple in Jerusalem]. At least in Lubavitch, there should not be a school [promoting assimilation]. He did not heed my request."[88]

Chamah's campaign to open schools expanded further when, in 1900, the Jewish Colonial Association (JCA) in Paris pledged 1 million francs to support the development of Enlightenment schools in Russia.[89] The Rashab, with the help of the Rayatz, organized an international lobbying effort to block the funding. They enlisted the support of prominent rabbis in Russia and France, petitioning the JCA in Paris to withhold the funds. Ultimately, they were successful in blocking a second allocation of 600,000 francs.

With the help of the Polyakov brothers, they convinced the JCA to divert the funds toward creating economic opportunities for Russian Jews.[90] The Rayatz was tasked by his father in 1901 to open a textile mill in Dubrovno, some sixty miles from Lubavitch, using funds from the JCA. The Rayatz spent a year setting up the factory, traveling extensively to get it off the ground.[91] Gershon Kranzler notes that in order to succeed in this ambitious project, the Rayatz had to "enlist support from all camps in the Jewish community," both Chasidim and *mitnagdim*. He adds that the project had a broad impact, as "it removed the social stigma from those who worked in the factories." In the years that followed, the mill – which was closed on Shabbat[92] – provided two thousand local Jews with gainful employment and "a place in the industrial economy."[93]

In 1904, war broke out between Japan and Russia over control of the Far East regions of Manchuria and Korea. Thousands of Jewish soldiers were enlisted in the Russian army and fought for two years before suffering an inglorious defeat. The Rashab was concerned about the Jewish soldiers, thousands of miles from home, with no food or matzah for Passover. With the help of the Rayatz, he launched an initiative to meet the soldiers' Passover needs, with limited success. The following year, they intensified their efforts. They faced many obstacles: an anti-Semitic regime, the need to create a broad-based Jewish coalition to lobby the government, the logistical nightmare of shipping supplies thousands of miles to the Far East, the distribution to soldiers dispersed over a broad geographical area, and securing the necessary funds. After much effort, permission was obtained from the czarist government, and Passover supplies were shipped and distributed throughout the Far East front. The Rayatz was heavily involved in the lobbying and funding, ensuring that the needs of Russian Jewish soldiers would be met.[94]

In the summer of 1905, the Rayatz participated in a covert meeting of prominent rabbinic leaders in St. Petersburg. The agenda: to create a strategy to stem the tide of pogroms that had erupted across Russia against the Jews.[95] Pressure from outside Russia was essential, Kranzler writes, and so the Rayatz was sent to Western Europe[96] to meet "famous statesman of Germany and Holland, to induce them to intervene with the Russian government." Despite his young age – only twenty-five – "the

Rayatz accomplished his mission beyond all expectations." He also persuaded foreign bankers to apply economic pressure, proving he could be "a modern *shtadlan* (advocate) on the international Jewish scene."[97]

The Russian government decided to host a conference of rabbis and community leaders to set the direction for Jewish community life and finally put to rest two major issues that had been festering for years: community leadership and education. There had been a long-simmering conflict over the position of rabbis in Russia. Starting in the 1820s, the government began to take an active role in shaping Jewish community leadership by appointing "crown rabbis." These were Russian-speaking rabbis who registered weddings and lifecycle events and served as liasons between the authorities and the Jewish community. The primary requirement for the job was the ability to read and write in Russian. They were known in Hebrew as a *rav mitaam*, a derogatory Hebrew term meaning "rabbis on behalf" (of the government). Almost anyone could qualify, and a large percentage of those appointed were not knowledgeable in Jewish tradition and were in fact poor role models of Jewish observance. The system was rife with corruption, as anyone with political connections could secure the position. Professor Antony Polonsky claims that "some crown rabbis resorted to charging high fees for their services."[98]

In the coming years, the government formalized this process, even establishing "rabbinical schools" in Vilna and Zhytomyr in 1847. These schools were heavily influenced by the Enlightenment, and their graduates were poorly regarded by the Jewish public. The schools eventually closed, but the problem of the crown rabbis still festered. Operating alongside them, at times cooperatively and at times with tension, were the true spiritual leaders, many great scholars who, while not fluent in Russian, were respected by their communities for their erudition and ethical behavior.

The double rabbinate became a flashpoint between observant Jews and Enlightenment activists. Communities saw the crown rabbis as a tool to marginalize traditional rabbis and advance the secularists' agenda backed by government authority. Judah Leib Katzenelson justified the institution of the crown rabbis in a piece he wrote for the secular paper *Voskhod*, where he maintained that the unregulated traditional rabbinate was "abnormal and required immediate and fundamental reform."[99]

He and others claimed they wanted to professionalize the rabbinate by making secular education a requirement for ordination. This proposal was met with resistance from the great Jewish scholars, including the Rashab.

The date and location for the government-rabbinic conference was set for St. Petersburg in 1910. The traditional rabbis, representatives of the crown rabbis, and community leaders were all invited to seek a consensus. There had been other rabbinic conferences in the past, but a meeting of this kind, with full government sanction, was unprecedented. The Rashab was named as one of the conference organizers. His son was at his side throughout the process.

Planning began well in advance. In October of 1908, the Rashab asked the Rayatz to organize a confidential meeting of a small group of rabbis closely aligned with Chabad to strategize a way forward and develop a consensus. There were a variety of issues to address before the St. Petersburg conference. Because of the political disruption in Russia, the czar had agreed to an election for the first time. As the Rayatz writes, they needed to strategize "the manner and extent of our involvement in preparation for the elections in the forthcoming duma (parliament)."[100]

Due to the efforts of the Rashab, in coordination with Rabbi Chaim Ozer Grodzinski,[101] Lithuania's leading rabbi, the government granted permission for a pre-conference meeting of twenty-five leading rabbis. They convened in Vilna in May 1909 with the goal of setting an agenda for the conference. The Rayatz was named secretary of the meeting.[102] Finally, in 1910, the national conference was held in St. Petersburg. Throughout the conference, the Rayatz assisted his father and spent much time with the renowned rabbis, including Rabbi Grodzinski, Rabbi Chaim Soloveitchik (the Brisker Rav), Rabbi Yisrael of Radin (the Chafetz Chaim), the Gerrer Rebbe, and others.[103]

The Rashab argued that there was no need for secular education for community rabbis. Rabbi Grodzinski said a modicum of knowledge of Russian would be acceptable. The crown rabbis and their Enlightenment supporters argued that secular education was essential. Rav Grodzinski's compromise was supported by the majority.[104] The conference concluded with a meeting between the leading rabbis and Prime Minister Pyotr Stolypin.[105] But the plans were never actualized – first because the government wavered on implementing the proposals, and then because of the revolution that brought the czarist regime to an end.

Russia's political turmoil in the first part of the twentieth century, culminating in the Russian Revolution of 1917, was imbued with anti-Semitism. As historian Eli Rubin writes, the government blamed the Jews for all their failings. "The ills of Russia were the result of the Jewish-led efforts to erode Russian nationalism, never the result of government corruption and incompetence." In 1913, this rose to a new level with the infamous Beilis affair.

Mendel Beilis,[106] a Kiev Jew, was accused of killing twelve-year-old Andrei Yushchinksy after the boy's body was discovered in a cave near the brick factory in Kiev that Beilis managed. It was a typical blood libel – prosecutors resurrected the myth of ritual murder, accusing Beilis of killing the boy to use his blood in the Passover matzahs. Government leaders sent investigators to bolster the prosecution, hoping the trial would weaken the liberal parties in the upcoming elections.[107] Their claim, according to Russian nationalist Professor Vasily Chernov, was that it was not all Jews who practiced this sort of ritual, but specifically Chasidim, "a barbarous fanatic sect that engages in ritual murder." Beilis, while not fully observant, came from a chasidic background, and prosecutors tried to link him and the alleged murder to the Chabad community because of his friendship with a man by the name of Feivel Schneersohn, who was born in Lubavitch. Rubin says, "This was the only link to the Rebbes of Lubavitch, but though he shared the same last name, he was not a known relative."[108]

The Beilis trial was a threat to all Jews in Russia and the chasidic community in particular. The Rashab dispatched the Rayatz to enlist Oscar Gruzenberg, one of Russia's leading attorneys, to spearhead the defense. Gruzenberg came from a traditional family but was not personally observant. The Rayatz brought a letter from the Rashab to Gruzenberg, urging him to defend Beilis. "It is your destiny to represent all Jews around the world and to remove these terrible accusations from over our heads," wrote the Rashab. After presenting the letter, the Rayatz told Gruzenberg about "the despair among Jewish brethren in Russia," explaining the "poisonous agitation" against the community at large.

"News of your acceptance of the defense would restore their confidence," he said. His plea was answered; after thirty minutes of deliberation, Gruzenberg agreed.

The trial sparked interest the world over. Jewish communities across the globe protested the outrageous accusations. Hundreds of reporters attended. If the prosecution could prove that ritual murder had a place in Jewish tradition, it would set the stage for a guilty verdict for Beilis. The prosecutors tried to link Beilis to the Chabad community, attempting to put the teachings of Chasidism on trial. The Rashab and the Rayatz played a major behind-the-scenes role in fighting the accusations, and they were involved in trial preparations. The Rashab considered testifying but decided against it, citing a few reasons, including that it "would draw much attention and might strengthen the other side."[109]

Describing the trial's conclusion, the Rayatz wrote, "The last public hearing in the trial of Beilis was held in one of the greatest halls of Kiev in the presence of thousands of men and women and members of the highest spheres of government." Gruzenberg orchestrated a masterful defense with the testimony of Moscow's Chief Rabbi Jacob Mazeh in a nine-hour presentation, demolishing the prosecution's case. Much of his closing argument was spent explaining the teachings of Chasidism, particularly Chabad Chasidism.[110] Gruzenberg concluded his closing arguments with a plea: "The G-d of Israel demands justice and righteousness. I, Oscar Gruzenberg, am a Jew, and from the bottom of my aching heart for the fate of the Torah and our brethren, I call upon you, this court, to look through the window of truth which the members of the defense have opened in the wall of deceit." As he finished, Gruzenberg followed the instructions of the Rashab and called out, "Mendel Beilis is innocent of this blood libel! *Shema Yisrael Adonai Eloheinu Adonai Echad* – Hear O Israel, G-d our G-d, G-d is One!"[111]

The Rayatz's energetic and far-reaching public activities, his watchful defense of the rights of Russian Jewry, and his constant fight against the local and central authorities aroused the displeasure of the czarist regime. Between 1911 and 1916, the Rayatz was arrested on four occasions. The first time was a result of accusations by leaders of the Enlightenment school in Lubavitch. The next incident was in December 1906, when the

Rebbe was investigated due to riots in Lubavitch by radical youth, who he proved were not part of the yeshivah.[112] In 1910 and again in 1916, he was imprisoned in St. Petersburg because of his efforts to exempt young men from military service. All of these detentions were brief, since government inquiries found nothing incriminating in his behavior. He was released each time with a stern warning. These incidents did not deter the Rayatz from continuing his work – on the contrary, they spurred him to even greater efforts.

In 1917 and 1918, the Rayatz again took a leading part in the assembly of rabbis and laymen in Moscow and Kharkiv.[113] For a quarter of a century, until his father's passing in 1920, the Rayatz took center stage in Jewish life. There was hardly a major concern among Russian Jewry in which the Rashab was not involved, and as his father's private secretary, the Rayatz dealt with many of these issues on a day-to-day basis. He battled anti-Semitism in czarist Russia and lobbied foreign governments and bankers to pressure Russia to curb its oppression of the Jews. He attended many key meetings of prominent rabbinic leaders, both on his own and at his father's side. From a young age, he became closely acquainted with Europe's most prominent rabbis. He worked side by side with many of the distinguished Chabad Chasidim who played leadership roles in Russian Jewry. He nurtured the yeshivah in Lubavitch from a small core of students to one of Europe's most respected centers of Jewish learning. All of this would prepare him for the challenges he faced in the years after his father's passing.

In 1914, the winds of war began to blow through Europe, ignited by the assassination of Archduke Franz Ferdinand of Austria. Germany declared war on Russia that summer and invaded the following year. The Rashab was alarmed by the German onslaught and told the Chasidim on Simchat Torah in 1915, "I know the kaiser well from the thirty years that I have been traveling outside Russia. He is an *apikores* (heretic), and under his rule I cannot dwell."

The Rayatz recalled the time that he and the Rashab had attended a public speech of Kaiser Wilhelm in Berlin. "We saw from afar that the kaiser was staring at us with a sharp look. He tilted his head to the crown prince beside him, whispered something in his ear, and the prince smirked slightly. A few moments later, police detectives approached us and ordered us to leave. My father said to me, 'Do you remember when we were in Berlin and saw Wilhelm speak, his face as white as plaster? Already then, all the plans of this war were arrayed in his mind and thoughts.'"[114]

The Rashab was alarmed by reports that the Russian government was seizing Jewish leaders near the front lines and accusing them of spying. With the Germans creeping closer, the Rashab deliberated and then made the decision to abandon Lubavitch, hoping to return at the end of the conflict. For 102 years, four Chabad Rebbes had called Lubavitch home, making it a hub for Russian Jews. Chasidim and Jews of all backgrounds flocked there to celebrate the holidays, to bask in the light of the Rebbes, and to absorb the profound teachings of the Torah. Since the founding of the yeshivah there in 1897, it had also become a center of academic excellence. Now, in late October 1915,[115] the sun set on Lubavitch when the Rashab, his son, and their families departed. The yeshivah lingered there for another two years before following suit.

The Rashab hoped the move would be temporary. As he left, he told the Chasidim, "We hope to return. With Hashem's help, we will be back before Passover."[116] The historic Chabad library was packed into thirty-five crates and placed in storage in Moscow,[117] and the Rashab took with him the collection of valuable manuscripts.

They made their way far from the invading Germans to the city of Rostov-on-Don, seven hundred miles south of Moscow. Some of the yeshivah students in Lubavitch hailed from Rostov, creating a strong connection between the communities. The Jewish leaders there offered the Rashab a safe haven.[118]

Rostov was outside the Pale of Settlement. Its community was founded by Jewish Cantonist soldiers who, after being drafted as children and serving twenty-five years in the Russian army, were permitted to reside anywhere in Russia. It was augmented by Jewish businessmen who had received permission to live in the city. Following the Communist Revolution, when Jews were granted the freedom to live anywhere in Russia, Rostov's Jewish population grew. By 1915, the number neared fifteen thousand, and the city boasted synagogues, schools, and mutual aid societies.

The capital of Chabad was reestablished in Rostov. The Rashab spent the last five years of his life there, purchasing a large building to serve as his family residence, the community synagogue, *mikveh,* and eventually, the new location for the yeshivah. Despite the tumultuous, conflict-filled time, Chasidim still made their way to Rostov to visit the Rashab.[119]

But the turmoil in Russia intensified. After the German invasion came the Bolshevik Revolution, followed by a civil war in which the Communists emerged victorious and slowly consolidated their control over the country. This raised the alarm in *Beit HaRav,* the Rebbe's household. As Zalman Havlin,[120] a member of the Rebbe's inner circle, wrote, "The idea of relocating out of Russia entirely was raised." That suggestion faded in January 1920, after the Bolsheviks took control of the city.

Not wanting to draw the attention of the new regime, the Rashab decided to curtail his public activities. He told Havlin, "Please ask *anash*[121] in my name to limit visiting me for services, *maamarim,* or *yechidut.* Only if it's a pressing issue should they come, but they should use discretion." From then on, only a small group of Chasidim joined the Rashab for services and *maamarim.*

In late February of 1920,[122] with Purim approaching, the Rashab summoned his son to discuss what he believed would be a stormy future for the Jews in Russia. The Rayatz was not aware of the meeting's agenda, nor of the fact that it would set the course of his life for decades to come.

When the Rayatz entered his father's study on the second floor of the residence in Rostov, he was struck by an "awesome sight." The study was illuminated by candles, casting an eerie light across the room. His father was "sitting with a *Pri Etz Chaim* [a classic work of Kabbalah] open on his desk." He had been studying the section explaining the mystical meaning behind the story of Mordechai and Esther, the heroes of the Purim saga. "I recall that Friday when the Rebbe [Rashab] spoke terrifying words to me," the Rayatz later wrote. His father's facial expression became very grave as he told his son that the Jewish people were entering into a period of "dark clouds that will last at least twenty-two years."[123] The Rashab understood that Communist rule would begin an oppressive period for the Jews. Still, he said, the regime would not last forever, forecasting the eventual disintegration of the Soviet Union. "A country that persecutes Judaism will eventually fall," he said, citing the words of the first Chabad Rebbe, Rabbi Schneur Zalman. The last czar, Nicholas,[124] "persecuted the Jews and Torah study, and in the end, there was a revolution and he was overthrown."

It would take seventy years before Soviet Russia collapsed. Still, says Russian Jewish historian Nissan Rupo, "After twenty-two years, the Russian government curbed its active persecution of religion." During World War II, in the early 1940s, the Russian Orthodox Church was permitted to operate publicly again. Also, says Rupo, "In 1942, a Lubavitch yeshivah opened in Samarkand."

The Rashab predicted to his son that the Communist Jews who had formed the Yevesektzia, the anti-religious Jewish section of the Communist Party, would be the greatest threat to their fellow Jews. But he also foresaw their eventual fate. "The Jewish group that combats Judaism will be broken and their leaders killed. In the meanwhile, we will suffer from their evil actions and denunciations." Their downfall began in 1930, when Stalin dismantled the Yevesektzia, killing and exiling many of its leaders and activists.[125]

The Rashab also foretold[126] the fate of prominent Communist leaders. "Lenin will die in a strange fashion. Trotsky will be exiled, and they will execute him. Stalin will follow the spirit of the time as needed, and he will be adorned with epaulets." Three and half years later, in January 1924, Lenin died at the age of fifty-three after repeated strokes and medical complications.[127] In 1928, Trotsky was banished to remote Alma Alta and deported from Russia two years later. After living in European cities, he relocated to Mexico. In 1937, he was sentenced to death in absentia in a Moscow trial and assassinated by a Stalinist agent in his home in Mexico City in 1940.

As Lenin's health deteriorated, Stalin consolidated power. He adapted his leadership to the times, presenting himself as a father to his people. He built Soviet industry and galvanized the public to fight the German invasion, using brutality without hesitation to advance his agenda.[128] During the war years, Stalin wore a military uniform adorned by epaulets. At the Yalta conference with Roosevelt and Churchill, and later in Potsdam with Truman and Churchill, Stalin wore a uniform decorated with his rank of marshal.[129] Stalin biographer Simon Montefiore says Stalin's military attire "was a deliberate strategy to cultivate the image of authority and dominance."[130]

That night in 1920, the Rashab entrusted his son with the sacred mission of combatting the Communists' plan to extinguish religious life in Russia. He commanded him, "Yosef Yitzchak, for the sake of strengthening Torah, reverence of Heaven, and support for Judaism, you will have to act with actual *mesirat nefesh* (self-sacrifice), risking your life."

Hearing these terrifying words, the Rayatz began to cry. His father consoled him. "Why are you crying? Once the month of Adar begins, we increase joy!" Then he added, "When it becomes difficult, remember my instructions to you that you must be willing to sacrifice your life to spread Torah, reverence of Heaven, and support for Judaism." The risks to the Rayatz's life would not be theoretical but real threats. Ultimately, said the Rashab, he would be successful, and the Soviet regime would collapse.

The Rayatz did not imagine that in just a few weeks, his father's passing would thrust him into a position of leadership.

Seven years later, on a trip to Moscow while being pursued by the Yevesektzia, the Rayatz reflected in his diary on the trials that had transpired so far for Jews who remained loyal to Torah. "I was shaken when I heard my father's words that we would suffer for at least twenty-two years. A tremor passes through my body over what can happen in the next fifteen years, and I cry bitter tears." Nevertheless, he writes, the words of his father endowed him with the fortitude and inspiration to soldier on in the darkest times. "Whenever something happens that causes me to feel disheartened, I envision the sacred and alarming words of my father, the Rebbe, about the new regime and the fate of its three leaders that were said to me three weeks before his passing."

The holiday of Purim had always been very joyous in Lubavitch. Distinguished Chasidim were invited to the traditional Purim dinner at the Rashab's home, and the rest of the community would crowd around the table. As Rabbi Moshe Dovber (Berel) Rivkin recalled,[131] "Almost all *anash* and the students would join them. The Rashab would teach a *maamar* and share words of Torah."[132]

The holiday celebrations of 1920 in Rostov were held under very different conditions. With a government ban on meetings and a curfew set at nine p.m., it was decided that the celebration should be more subdued.

"We all gathered at the Rashab's home," Zalman Havlin says, "and at first they told us the celebration would be brief, just for a few hours." The Rebbe's wife had notified the Chasidim that the celebration would go only until curfew, after which they would disperse, unlike in Lubavitch, where the *farbrengen* lasted through the night.

The Chasidim listened as the Rashab shared teachings and interspersed his remarks with joyous melodies. Rivkin recalls that the rebbetzin and the Rayatz asked them to keep their voices down. The Rashab, however, encouraged the singing, saying, "On Simchat Torah we danced and sang" – before the Bolsheviks took over the city – "and now we will also. And if it's a [divine] test, we will persevere." The Rashab took out some money and sent someone to purchase additional liquor. This only increased the Rayatz's alarm that the large, lively crowd might attract the attention of the police. Noticing his son's concern, the Rashab reassured him, "Yosef Yitzchak, don't worry. We're going to be completely fine."

The celebration continued through the night, only becoming more boisterous. It caused some in the crowd to become "fearful," as Havlin puts it. The Rebbe was in an upbeat mood, and no one had the audacity to leave, despite the danger. "His face was radiant, almost unworldly. He taught *Chasidut,* and it was unlike any experience we ever had with him," remembers Havlin.

Everyone's fears were realized when three Bolshevik police officers arrived. "They wanted to inspect the house," says Havlin. "The Chasidim told them that the Rashab was occupied with people and could not see them, and they should return in a few hours." To everyone's surprise and relief, they departed.

A few hours later, they came back. This time, they pushed their way toward the room where the celebration was underway. "The table was full of bottles of *mashkeh* (liquor), and there were plates full of money that had been donated." The Chasidim wanted to hide the bottles and money, but the Rashab instructed them not to move anything. "I have no fear of them," he exclaimed.

The officers entered the room and stood opposite the Rashab. "He turned his face to the Chasidim" as if the officers were not there. "We have to say *chasidut,* and they will be *batul* (nullified, as if they don't exist)." The Rashab began saying a *maamar* [133] that explored the concept of evil being a false reality, with the true essence of all creation being godly and holy. "The police stood there for a long time, gazing intently at the Rashab, and then left without saying a word."

The *farbrengen* lasted twelve hours, until the morning light. Afterward, the Rashab retired to his private study. Yaakov Landau,[134] a student and the Rashab's personal assistant, followed him and remarked, "Tonight was a time of great joy. We sat the whole night with the Rebbe and heard profound teachings of *Chasidut* that we never anticipated. Next year we should celebrate [the chasidic holiday of] 19 Kislev in Lubavitch."

The Rashab sat stoically and did not reply. Landau repeated the statement, and still the Rashab was silent. The Rashab walked into his bedroom. Surprised by the lack of response, Landau trailed behind him and repeated the statement for the third time. The Rashab turned to him and said, "G-d should help that we should be close spiritually."

Landau was confused and troubled by these words, and he shared the incident with Zalman Havlin. "Who could have imagined that two weeks later, the Rashab would no longer be with us," he later reflected.

In the coming days, Havlin saw that the Rashab was very preoccupied. He spent the week secluded his study, composing a document. Later, the Rayatz told Havlin, "I went into his office and he covered the papers with a kerchief. Now I understand that it was his will." Havlin says that "the whole week he was preparing himself in an orderly way." In retrospect, "it was astonishing."

On Friday, the Rashab began to feel unwell. "His temperature rose over Shabbat, and on Sunday the doctor diagnosed him with typhoid." As the week progressed, his condition deteriorated. "All the students and Chasidim recited psalms day and night [in the merit of his recovery]."

The following Shabbat afternoon, a week after the onset of the illness, the situation turned bleak. The Rashab asked to be moved into his study. As they carried him in, he remarked, "I am going to heaven, and I am leaving you my manuscripts." He then added, "Take me in one and we will be together," insinuating that when the Chasidim studied his teachings, they would be united with him.

These shocking words frightened the Rayatz. The Rashab, seeing the fear in his son's face, exclaimed, "*Hitpaalut? Hitpaalut? Mochin,*

mochin – Excitement? Excitement? Intellect, intellect." He was referring to the chasidic teaching that one's intellect should control his emotions.

Rivkin writes that this was a transformational moment for the Rayatz. "From that point on, he was different. He never had the natural expression of becoming anxious." In the years to come, "he approached everything with *gadlut hamochin* (guided by his intellect)." Later, even when the Rayatz was arrested and investigated, he never allowed himself to be intimidated, always maintaining control even when being threatened with bodily harm or death.

As darkness set in and Shabbat ended, the mood became foreboding. The Chasidim gathered and continued praying, fearing the worst. The Rayatz stepped into the hallway outside the room where the Rashab lay. "He was deep in thought. He recited psalms, cried intensely, and then quietly sang the [Four Stanzas] chasidic melody of the Alter Rebbe [reserved for special occasions]," says Rivkin.

Close to three a.m., the Rashab gazed at his son, attempted to lift his hands, and moved his lips. Rivkin says, "The Rayatz realized that his father wanted to bless him and asked all to leave the room, leaving just him and his family." Later, the Rayatz and his daughters told Rivkin that the Rashab had blessed each of them. "First the eldest, Chana. The Rashab gazed at her, raising his hands over her head, and they heard [him say] the [priestly] blessing of *Yevarekhekha*. Then the middle one, Mushka, and the youngest, Shaindel. He then placed his two hands on the Rayatz" and gave him a blessing.

Late that night, the Rayatz left the room again for a moment, and in the hallway, he blurted out to Rivkin in a loud voice, "*Gevald* (woe), Berel!" He cried profusely and then asked, "Berel, what do you say?" Grasping for words, Rivkin finally uttered, "G-d Himself can help."

The Rashab continued to weaken. His heart fluttering, the Rayatz called out, "*Tatte, Tatte!* – Father, Father!" The Rashab gazed silently at him. "As they heard these words, the hearts of the Chasidim broke," recalls Rivkin.

At 4:00 a.m., the Rashab's breathing became weaker. His son exclaimed again, "*Tatte, Tatte*!" The Rashab turned to him and smiled. An hour later, they realized that his passing was imminent. Havlin recalls,

"We were all standing around him in trepidation as the morning light peeked in, wondering what would become of us [without the Rebbe]." Again, the Rayatz cried, "*Tatte, Tatte*!"

"This time, the Rashab opened his eyes and we saw tears." Then they heard the Rashab whispering. It was difficult to decipher what he was saying, but they soon realized that he was reciting the words *"bekhol levavkha uvekhol nafshekha* – with all your heart and all your soul" of the *Shema* prayer. Then suddenly, "he turned to look at us and his soul ascended to heaven."[135]

Chapter Three

The Secret Covenant

"G*evald, gevald,*[1] where was my understanding of the situation? The whole winter, he clearly warned me that he would pass away, and I did not comprehend it." Late Sunday evening, the Rayatz, now age thirty-nine, confided in Berel Rivkin. It was just hours after the Rashab's burial; the Rayatz had slowly led the evening prayers in tears. Rivkin recalls, "We spoke for two hours. He cried bitterly." The Rayatz realized in retrospect that the "long conversations he had with his father during the winter were preparation for this tragic moment." In the coming months, the Rayatz would share more details with Rivkin. "During the winter of 5680 (1919–20), my father reviewed in detail the spiritual levels and characteristics of each member of *anash* (the Chabad community)."[2]

The funeral took place at the Jewish cemetery in Rostov[3] on Sunday afternoon, mere hours after the Rashab's passing late Saturday night.[4] The casket, says Rivkin, "was carried to the cemetery by the students of the yeshivah and the elders of *anash*." The crowd was massive – "all the Jews of the city were there." The German invasion had brought the Rebbe to Rostov, and the revolution and upheaval in its wake prevented his return to Lubavitch. Still, hope lingered of eventually returning and reinterring the Rebbe Rashab near his ancestors in Lubavitch. With that in mind, standing ahis father's fresh grave, the Rayatz publicly turned to three rabbis[5] and told them, "I am empowering you as a *beit din* (rabbinical court) and declaring to you that I am purchasing this grave on condition that I have the authorization to transfer my father to the cemetery of my holy forefathers in the ancestral burial ground in Lubavitch."[6]

The last day of the *shivah* (week of mourning) coincided with Shabbat, when mourning practices are suspended. Late that afternoon, as the sun was setting, the Rayatz invited Rivkin into his father's private study. The dimming light spilled into the long rectangular room adjacent to the synagogue through the bay windows facing the street, illuminating the green wallpaper and its decorative floral patterns.[7] With a broken heart, the Rayatz turned to Rivkin and said, "My father instructed me to teach chasidic discourses to the community. But who am I to do this? How can I stand in front of *anash*?"

Rivkin was taken aback by the suggestion and by the expressions of both humility and sorrow. He attempted to divert the conversation. The Rayatz was wary of reciting an original *maamar* in front of the Chasidim, and so he came up with a compromise: "I can fulfill that directive by delivering the *maamar* to you."

Together they paced the wooden floor of the high-ceilinged room. The Rayatz repeated his father's *maamar* that had been recited a few weeks earlier, on Purim, adding a few insights of his own.[8] When he finished, he asked Rivkin to keep the incident between them. "Why?" Rivkin asked. "I want to share this with others in the community." Again, the Rayatz implored him to keep it private, but Rivkin remained silent, not giving his word. Later that evening, he shared the experience with others and slowly, news spread that the Rebbe Rashab's son had delivered a *maamar*.

The Rayatz's *maamar*, though said privately, was his first step in accepting the position of sixth Lubavitcher Rebbe, succeeding his father. After the Rashab's passing, a few of those who had been close to him opened his desk, says Zalman Havlin. "We were surprised to find on the top of the drawer a will with a note attached, saying that his son should accept upon himself the position of Rebbe." Despite the dark times – being exiled from Lubavitch, the ominous threat of the growing power of the Bolshevik government – the Rashab's instruction "comforted us, [reassuring us] that the golden chain" of leadership would not be broken," says Havlin.[9] The public section of the will[10] contained a directive that the Rayatz should continue to teach and mentor the Chasidim.[11] (As the will had originally been drafted many years earlier, it also contained guidance regarding the Rayatz's education.) The section added later focused on the importance of the yeshivah, Tomchei Temimim, and requested that *anash* continue supporting it and preserving its unique focus on chasidic teachings; the Rashab specified that the executive director of the yeshivah should be "my son." The yeshivah was a revolutionary accomplishment close to the Rashab's heart. He saw it not only as the key to the continuity of chasidic teachings and observance, but also as an incubator for a new generation of Jewish leadership in a changing world.

The Rayatz revealed his reaction to reading his father's instructions that he assume the position of Rebbe. "After some time, I opened the will. My eyes darkened when I read that the leadership of the community was placed on me." He was deeply shaken with the awesome responsibility. "For many days I was overwhelmed; I made a step forward and then took a step back. I became deeply ill, but G-d with His boundless kindness restored me to life, and like a humbled servant, it is incumbent on me to follow my father's sacred instructions."[12]

As the news of the Rashab's passing traveled from Rostov to Poland and the United States, some expressed skepticism over Chabad's future. Jewish newspapers around the world reported the Rashab's passing, some with a bleak forecast. As chasidic historian Rabbi Eli Rubin writes,[13] "These did not read simply as obituaries. They predicted nothing less than the end of Chabad." Jonathan Mark opined in New York's *Yiddishes Tageblatt*,[14] "He did not leave an appropriate successor. His son hasn't the aptitude to follow in his place."[15]

The relationship between Rebbe and Chasid is voluntary and comes at the initiative and request of the Chasidim. They would select an appropriate candidate among the family members or students of the prior Rebbe and encourage him to accept the position. This was done by collectively writing a letter called a *ktav hitkashrut*, a pledge of loyalty to the candidate's leadership, which was signed by the Chasidim.

The title of Rebbe does not refer to the position that he assumes, but rather is seen as a reflection of a person's innate spiritual and intellectual qualities. The Midrash delineates the hierarchy of Jewish leadership: "A scholar comes before a king, a king before a high priest, and a high priest before a prophet."[16] It explains that kings and priests are replaceable; there is always a crown prince or an assistant high priest waiting in the wings. A scholar, however, is a status one must achieve through effort. Similarly, a Rebbe should be a person of scholarship, piety, empathy, and vision. A true Rebbe is a *tzaddik*, a deeply righteous person whose life is rooted in sanctity and spirituality. That is not something one can become overnight, like a prince who assumes the position of king. Many progenies of Rebbes were never considered for succession because they lacked the proper qualities. It's a reflection of one's essence, achieved by much effort and personal refinement. In the lexicon of chasidic philosophy, this is called "*avodah*," which connotes a service of G-d that comes through much personal struggle to reach higher levels of spirituality and the effort to root one's life in the sacred and selfless.

At times, multiple candidates for the role of Rebbe emerged, sometimes splitting a chasidic group. After the passing of the third Rebbe, Rabbi Menachem Mendel, in 1869, his youngest son Rabbi Shmuel succeeded him as Rebbe in Lubavitch. At the same time, four of his brothers established themselves as Rebbes in other towns in Russia. Those dynasties eventually petered out when there were no suitable successors. The last leader of those was Rabbi Shmaryahu Noach Schneersohn of Bobruysk (today located in Belarus, some 180 miles from Lubavitch), who passed away in 1924.[17] With time, the Chabad Chasidim from the various courts coalesced around the Rayatz.

There were also cases of candidates declining the position. The Rayatz's father, the Rashab, was only twenty-three when his father, the fourth Rebbe, Rabbi Shmuel, passed away. Despite being urged by the Chasidim to become Rebbe, he only fully accepted the position eleven years later. The Rayatz's successor, Rabbi Menachem Mendel Schneerson, also demurred; it took a year before he acquiesced to the lobbying of the Chasidim that he become the seventh Rebbe.

To be a Rebbe is an awesome responsibility of leadership. Untold numbers of people from all backgrounds visit and write, seeking advice, blessings, and inspiration. Rebbes navigate difficult social challenges and controversial communal issues. At the very core, a Rebbe is not a political leader or organization executive, but a spiritual leader steeped in Torah and sanctity. Rebbes accepted the position for life, putting aside all their own physical and spiritual needs and aspirations in order to dedicate themselves to the welfare of others.

The Rashab's passing was a shock. The illness at the end of his life was swift, and the Rayatz was deeply shaken. Writing about his father's last moments, he said, "A great sense of foreboding fell on me. The heavens were closed, our prayers not accepted."[18] A victim of the typhus epidemic, the Rashab passed away at the relatively young age of sixty-one. Now the Chasidim yearned for a new Rebbe, and the Rashab had only one son. There were no other fitting candidates from the other branches of the Schneersohn family. Since the age of fifteen, the Rayatz had been at his father's side assisting him, and from a young age, he had been entrusted with the leadership of Tomchei Temimim. The Rashab had also trusted his son to lead the Chasidim. Many years earlier, when physicians had informed the Rashab that he might have just three months to live, he pondered going to *Eretz Yisrael* for what he feared could be his last days.[19] When his wife asked him who would take care of the Chasidim if he left, he responded, "Our son." The Rayatz was then only eighteen years old.

The process of the Rayatz becoming Rebbe took a leap forward a few weeks after his father's funeral. On the first day of Passover, the Rayatz once again told Rivkin that he wanted to recite a *maamar* privately to him after the evening service, "to fulfill the instructions of my father." As before, he requested that Rivkin not tell anyone. This time, Rivkin shared the information with others in advance, suggesting they gather outside the room when the Rayatz spoke to him so that they would be able to hear the *maamar.* Rivkin and the Rayatz entered the Rashab's private study alone. After the Rayatz began saying the *maamar,* the Chasidim who were standing in the adjoining small synagogue slowly cracked open the tall double doors and listened in. The Rayatz noticed them hovering in the next room, but he continued reciting the *maamar* for almost an hour.

A week later, as Passover was coming to an end, the Rayatz again told Rivkin that he wanted to confidentially recite a *maamar.*[20] Rivkin decided the time had come to push the issue further, telling his fellow Chasidim to come inside the room immediately when the Rayatz began. The two of them were alone in the Rashab's study when the Rayatz started, but within moments, the Chasidim pushed open the doors, filed into the back of the room, and stood listening with concentration. Rivkin described the moment: "It felt exactly like it did when the Rebbe Rashab said a *maamar*."

The news that the Rayatz had said a *maamar* in front of the Chasidim uplifted the community despite the sense of loss that they all felt. The only son of the Rebbe Rashab was slowly stepping into the position of his father, though it would take some time.

On Rosh HaShanah, the Rayatz resisted blowing the shofar, which his father had done. Only after his mother requested it did he acquiesce, and even then, he blew it only once before passing it to someone else to complete the blasts. It would be a little longer until the Rayatz took the final step forward in leadership by beginning to accept requests from Chasidim for advice and blessings.[21]

The new Rebbe reached out to Chasidim in Russia and other countries via written correspondence. Before World War I, Chasidim flocked to Lubavitch for Shabbat and especially for holidays to listen to the Rashab and his predecessors. Professor David Fishman notes that the rise of Communism made such a thing impossible at this point, and so the Rebbe Rayatz sent letters "to reestablish contact with his scattered Chasidim, after years during which there had been no meetings or mail due to civil war and pogroms." There was no longer religious Jewish media, and "one of the greatest problems facing religious activists was their isolation and atomization." The new Rebbe was "seeking out his Chasidim." He initiated correspondence with them after tracking down their addresses. And he made requests of them: study Torah daily, teach classes to adults, speak before the congregants in their local synagogues, establish a school, influence community members. He also inquired about their welfare – how were they faring, materially and spiritually?[22] During his lifetime, the Rebbe composed some 100,000 letters.[23]

In the wake of the Rebbe Rashab's passing, great hardships continued to afflict the citizens of Russia. Political unrest, food shortages, and economic turmoil wracked the country, making travel difficult. The czar had been overthrown and the new regime was ushering in far-reaching change to the political and economic systems. The czarist embrace of anti-Semitism was swept away, and opportunities for Jews opened up in commerce, education, and other spheres. Jews played a major role in the emerging government. Despite making up less than two percent of the population, they comprised over nineteen percent of the staff of the newly formed justice ministry, three percent of the trade ministry, and 5.2 percent of the Communist Party.[24] The increased influence of Communist Jews did not make it easier for the observant Jews of Rostov, and with time, conditions worsened.

During the war, the yeshivah had been transferred from Lubavitch to Kremenchuk, Ukraine. As the conflict continued, many key Jewish community members abandoned the city, drying up sources of financial support. The yeshivah had so little money that the students were forced to ration their bread, eating it only every other day.[25] In the winter of 1920, with the fear of starvation becoming a reality, the yeshivah relocated to Rostov. The new Rebbe said, "I want Tomchei Temimim to be next to me."[26] Things were not much better there, but thankfully, Rabbi Shmuel Gurary,[27] a noted philanthropist who had been a long-time supporter of the yeshivah, stepped forward to help, even though the revolution had weakened his business. "He borrowed funds and sold expensive personal property" to keep the yeshivah afloat, wrote the Rebbe.[28]

With the move of the yeshivah to Rostov, Rabbi Shmaryahu Gurary (the Rashag), the fiancé of the Rebbe's oldest daughter, Chanah, was appointed executive director, and Yitzchak Goldin[29] became his assistant.

Within two weeks, about eighty boys showed up, writes Goldin. "Many were very ill and wearing torn clothing."[30] Goldin was tasked with preparing apartments for them. The Rebbe told him, "Yitzchak, the door is open for you; whenever you need, as many times as you need during the day, just enter."

The Rebbe took a keen interest in the students, observing them from his window that looked out onto the courtyard. Goldin writes, "One time he called me over and said, 'I want very much for each boy to have two uniforms [suits], one for Shabbat and one for weekdays, but what can I do that I don't have the funds? But at least the same jacket could be mended and not torn." The Rebbe wanted the students to walk the streets with a sense of dignity so as not to provoke the Communists:

"One doesn't have to needle them." The yeshivah did not have the funds to pay teachers, so senior students assumed the role of staff. The Rebbe said, "It is a time of war – mobilized soldiers become officers."[31]

With Reb Shmuel Gurary's financial support, the students were able to continue learning throughout the summer of 1920 and into the beginning of the following winter.[32] That summer, a few boys passed away. As tradition mandates, the Rebbe led the services during the year of mourning. Goldin recalls that the prayers were recited with "a loud voice and accompanied by much crying."[33]

In November 1920, the typhus epidemic intensified in Rostov. The Rebbe became ill and unable to lead evening services.[34] In the days that followed, Goldin remained next to him, administering his medicine. Shortly afterward, the Rebbe's mother, Rebbetzin Shterna Sara, and his three daughters also caught the dreaded disease.

On the Shabbat after the disease struck, the Rebbe had enough strength to say a *maamar,*[35] but then the illness intensified. His situation became grave,[36] and the doctors said that he had little chance of surviving. Professor Milsalavski told Goldin, "From a medical point of view there is no cure, but this is Rabbi Schneersohn, and because of that, you can believe that it is possible that he will heal." Yehudah Chitrik,[37] then a yeshivah student, later recalled: "The Rebbe was in critical condition. Led by Reb Itche der Masmid, we went to pray repeatedly at the Ohel of the Rashab."[38]

Finally, after some three weeks,[39] the tide turned and the Rayatz started to recover, though it would take longer to return to his full strength. Chitrik writes that the Rebbe was still too weak to stand. As he was still in the months of mourning for his father, "every day a group would come to make a *minyan*. He reclined on the bed as he led the services and recited *Kaddish*." Three months later, while observing the Fast of Esther the day before Purim, the Rebbe fainted. He nevertheless completed the fast. He asked the doctor if he could *farbreng*[40] and say a *maamar* on Purim. The doctor allowed it but instructed him to limit the *maamar* to fifteen minutes and to keep the *farbrengen* brief as well. The next day, Purim 1921, he recited a *maamar* for two and a half hours and sat afterward for more than three hours with the Chasidim.[41]

Many of the students of the yeshivah also fell ill. The epidemic added to the economic woes. The Rebbe was forced to borrow large sums to keep the yeshivah afloat and pay the mounting medical bills. Shmuel Gurary soon passed away, exacerbating the financial crisis. As the winter wore on, the financial pressures, coupled with famine and disease, prompted some students to leave the yeshivah and return home. The Jewish newspaper in Chicago reported that "the yeshivah students who have evacuated Lubavitch for Rostov-on-Don are starving."[42] Others stayed in Rostov and set out in search of ways to make a living. The grand yeshivah of Lubavitch, once one of the great centers of European Jewish scholarship, was whittled down by war, famine (1921–22), and disease to just forty students in Rostov.[43]

But all these challenges paled in comparison to the looming threat to the Rebbe and Judaism in general: the dreaded Yevesektzia.

Established in 1917 to fortify Bolshevik control over the Jewish masses, the Yevesektzia, the Jewish section of the Communist Party, began to consolidate its power and exert its influence. It remained a major force until it was dismantled by Stalin in 1930, after which many of its leaders were killed or exiled in the Great Purge. The Rebbe became its primary adversary and the focus of its persecution. He suffered much at its hands, culminating with his arrest and exile.[44]

At the time, most of Russia's Jews were traditional, many religious. Even those not fully observant came from Orthodox families and had an appreciation of tradition. They were tethered to the classic Jewish communal structure, the *kehillah* that included synagogues, schools, and *chadarim* (traditional Jewish elementary schools). Most cities boasted their own community rabbis, many of them prominent scholars. Though some one million Jews had emigrated to the United States and other countries in the previous decades, four million Jews remained in the newly established Soviet Union.[45]

The Yevesektzia's campaign was not just an attack on religion but on a way of life, writes historian Nora Levin.[46] "A Jew's religious beliefs and observances infused every aspect of his daily life and were invested with national values and feelings." Everything was centered on the Jewish community: "Family relations, work, prayer, study, recreation, and culture were all part of a seamless web." The new Communist government aimed to wipe out religion. "Religion is the opium of the people," revolutionary Vladimir Lenin famously said. Lenin promoted the belief that religion was a form of oppression.

The Communists debated how to minimize religious influence. Soviet law permitted personal observance; however, the Communists viewed organized religion as a political threat. The new Communist government launched an assault on the Russian Orthodox Church, which had been aligned with the czarist government.[47] During the famine of 1921–22, it moved to confiscate the treasures of the church "for the benefit of the hungry." Lenin ordered show trials for church leaders with death sentences that were determined in advance. The Communists initiated a strategy of divide and conquer: They backed a small group of clergy who supported their agenda, creating a new religious group, the "Living Church," to undermine the existing leadership.[48]

The same tactics were replicated in the Jewish community by creating the Yevesektzia, a Jewish group supportive of Bolshevik goals. Many of the Yevesektzia members had come from the Bund, the secular workers' party that had a paltry thirty-four thousand members in 1917. Historically hostile to Jewish religious observance and Zionism, they aggressively targeted both – at times exceeding the government policies that wavered between aggressive attacks on religion and tolerance of personal religious practice. Often, the Yevesektzia acted more zealously than the government authorities to repress Judaism.

The Yevesektzia had a staunch core of passionate activists. Few were Jewish scholars. One exception was its leader, Semyon Dimenstein.[49] Born in 1886 to a chasidic family, he attended the yeshivas in Slabodka and Lubavitch and received rabbinic ordination from Vilna's renowned scholar, Rabbi Chaim Ozer Grodzinski. This was not the first time in Jewish history that Jews took up the battle against religious observance. During the Syrian-Greek reign over Judea that led up to the story of Hanukkah, Jewish Hellenists similarly sided with their rulers to stamp out religious belief.

The members of the Yevesektzia were zealous in seeking to prove their loyalty to Communism, systematically attempting to stamp out

Judaism. Historian Zvi Gitelman says that with the Yevesektzia's negligible membership[50] and prevailing sense of insecurity, they "were determined to prove themselves more Bolshevik than Lenin."[51] The Yevesektzia's campaign exceeded the mandate given to it by the government, at times even forcing the Russian authorities to intervene on behalf of the Jewish communities in order to restrain the Yevesektzia from closing a synagogue or persecuting their brethren.

The Rebbe argued that Soviet law permitted freedom of religion and that Jewish religious life had no connection to politics. The real enemies of Jewish religious expression were the Jews of the Yevesektzia who had turned on their own.

The Yevesektzia similarly targeted the growing influence of Zionism.[52] They touted Yiddish as the language of the "Jewish proletariat"[53] and Hebrew as "bourgeoisie," abolishing the study of Hebrew culture and language as championed by the Zionism. They established a new network of state-run Yiddish schools. By 1929, there were 1,100 such schools in the Soviet Union, attended by some 130,000 students. Jewish religion, history, Hebrew, and tradition were excluded from the curriculum. Some parents saw these schools as a pathway toward integration into Communist society. Many religious parents chose to send their children to non-Jewish schools to avoid the anti-religious propaganda that was central to the Communist Yiddish schools.[54]

As part of its assault on Zionism, the Yevesektzia set its sights on the Hebrew language theater, Habima, which had been organized at the onset of the revolution in 1917, even gaining government recognition. In 1919, when the Soviet ministry of culture approved a grant to the theater, Dimenstein protested,[55] claiming they were giving in to "the whim of the bourgeoisie."[56] Dimenstein and his Yevesektzia henchmen acted more fanatically than the government when it harassed the Habima actors. In 1926, the whole troupe departed Russia on a government-sanctioned international tour. Once they left, they never returned, instead relocating to Tel Aviv.[57]

In the months following the Rashab's passing, the Yevesektzia increased its campaign against Jewish observance. As the new Rebbe was taking a larger role in opposing them, they targeted him. One morning in July

1920, while the Rebbe was still in the year of mourning for his father, three men appeared in the synagogue as he was completing his prayers. They were officers of the feared secret police, the Cheka,[58] who worked with the Yevesektzia, each armed with ammunition belts across their chests. Two of them were Jews, and one was familiar to the Rebbe; the Rebbe had lent him money during hard times before the revolution. That kindness forgotten, he was now a Yevesektzia member.

"Take off your tallis and tefillin and come with us," the familiar officer ordered harshly. The Rebbe calmly indicated that he was going to finish his prayers and only then would he accede to their request. The two Jews insolently repeated the demand, only to have the non-Jewish officer intervene and instruct them to wait until the end of the prayers. When the service concluded, they left the synagogue escorting the Rebbe like a common prisoner, one armed officer on either side and one in the rear.

At the police station, the Rayatz was brought into a large room with a long conference table in its center. The Rebbe was seated at one end with fifteen armed officers sitting along the sides and another two at the other head. This setup was designed to intimidate.

The officer sitting at the head of the table addressed the Rebbe. "We are the committee charged with reviewing religious affairs," he began. "We met with Rabbis Berman and Goldberg[59] and now we would like Rabbi Schneersohn to answer some questions for us about Judaism and Kabbalah." Clearly, the agenda was not about acquiring a better understanding of Judaism, but an attempt to intimidate the Rebbe into limiting his religious activities.

They spoke in Russian, but the Rebbe responded in Yiddish, correctly discerning that almost all the men were Jewish. Looking them squarely in the eye, he told them, "The police questioned me already twice before. I will not budge from my principles. I didn't then, and I won't now. No person who has yet been born will budge me from my ideals even one iota."

Those sitting around the table each had a gun set before them. One of the officers lifted his gun and said, "This toy eliminates principles, and its fear causes mouths to open."

The Rebbe's response was swift. Still speaking in Yiddish, he replied, "You have made a mistake. This toy only impresses those who have no faith and weakness of heart – people who have one world and many gods and who worship their desires. We, however, have one G-d and two worlds.[60] This toy you hold does not impress me, nor does it instill any fear."

They began questioning the Rebbe, asking if Judaism was based on faith or an actual knowledge that the tradition is true. The Rebbe responded that Judaism was based on "absolute knowledge" and then reproached them, "I am willing to answer your questions, but if you were interested in astronomy, would you accost a university professor on the street and ask him to explain the science? He would tell you to come to his observatory, and there he would teach you about the stars. So too here, if you really want to understand Judaism, you must come to the yeshivah and gain a proper comprehension of its complexities and teachings." With that, the interrogation ended,[61] just one act in the drama of a conflict that would play out in the coming years.

The Yevesektzia staged show trials against religion, designed to mock Judaism and intimidate its adherents. A large community venue was selected for these trials, and witnesses prepared. Levin describes the *cheder* (traditional Jewish school) on trial in Vitebsk that was scheduled for January of 1921. Five thousand local Jews came out to protest the intimidation, "shouting to stop the trial and threatening to close the cinema where the trial was being held." Thousands of others assembled in local synagogues to protest. Uneasy Yevesektzia members called off the trial after being threatened physically, but their hesitation did not last long. A short time later, they regrouped and staged a second trial in which the *cheder* was sentenced to be liquidated.

In February 1921, a similar trial was organized by the Yevesektzia against the Lubavitch yeshivah in Rostov. "They testified with lies," the Rebbe described in a letter,[62] "and forcefully demanded that the yeshivah be closed and that its students become part of the army of workers." During this time, the Yevesektzia forced their way into the Rebbe's home, where they seized household goods, clothing, and silver inherited from his father. They even took his furniture, filling three large vehicles, and imprisoned three students and his future son-in-law, Rabbi Shmaryahu Gurary.[63] For five days, they sat in a prison cell with society's worst criminal elements until the Rebbe successfully convinced the prosecutor that the allegations were utterly false. Though Gurary and the students were released, none of the property was returned.

The battle against the Yevesektzia was taking a toll. The financial pressure was immense, and the Rebbe writes that "even sources of loans had disappeared."[64] It was clear that the yeshivah had no future in Rostov.

In Poltava, 375 miles to the west in Russian Ukraine, a group of local Chabad followers were willing to underwrite the yeshivah. The famine was not as severe there, and the area boasted a strong, well-organized, diverse community[65] of some twenty thousand Jews. Twenty traditional *chadarim*, a modern Jewish school, Zionist organizations, and a wide variety of social programs were all part of community life in Poltava. The Yevesektzia was less influential there, and it was hoped that the yeshivah would be under less scrutiny. They could not obtain authorization to travel to Poltava from Rostov by train, so forty students made the four-hundred-mile trip by horse and wagon. During the summer of 1922, the Rebbe appointed Rabbi Yechezkel Feigin[66] to be the administrator of the central yeshivah in Poltava.

With time, the difficulties of Rostov spread to Poltava as well. In 1922, the yeshivah sent a letter to supporters describing the rising costs of food and the lack of basics beyond "the black bread we get daily." There too, they became a target of the Yevesektzia. After two years, they moved the yeshivah to Kharkiv for six months, and then back to Rostov.

In one form or another, the yeshivah managed to survive the next seventy years in the Soviet Union.[67] Between 1922 and 1940, it opened and closed in twenty-seven cities, at times operating in multiple locations simultaneously. Branches were even opened in remote Soviet Georgia, where the Communist rule was less overbearing. In 1936, Rabbi Elchonon Morozov wrote in a letter from Russia to his friend Rabbi Yisrael Jacobson in New York, "The yeshivah is operating in five cities and other smaller branches with three hundred students."[68]

During the Second World War, in October 1942, a branch of the yeshivah was established in the remote city Samarkand in Uzbekistan, and within a short period of time another branch was established in Tashkent. As Communism weakened, the yeshivah operated more openly. In the late 1980s, many students studied in Moscow's Marina Rosche

Chabad synagogue. The students educated during those Communist years became the nucleus that sustained Jewish life there until the fall of the Soviet Union.

As the new Rebbe fought to save Judaism in Russia, other prominent rabbinic leaders took a different approach. Some rabbis stayed put, trying their best to help their communities despite the intense anti-religious campaigns of the Yevesektzia. Most kept under the radar, valiantly trying to keep the spirit of Judaism alive locally without drawing the attention of the authorities. One of the dozens who remained was the venerable Rabbi Moshe Feinstein,[69] the rabbi of Lyuban, Belorussia, then part of the Soviet Union. Like many other rabbis, he preserved a core of observant Jews in his city as the next generation gravitated toward Communism under the relentless anti-religious propaganda. In 1937, he immigrated to the United States.[70]

The leaders of the great yeshivas of Russia – Slabodka, Slutsk, and others – fled with their students during the early years of the Communist regime. Rabbi Isser Zalman Meltzer, dean of the Belarussian Slutsk yeshivah, immigrated to Palestine after being imprisoned for teaching Torah, and his son-in-law, Rabbi Aharon Kotler, relocated the yeshivah to Kletsk in Poland. Similarly, the celebrated scholar Rabbi Moshe Soloveichik[71] moved to Warsaw, accompanied by his eighteen-year-old son, prodigy Rabbi Joseph Ber, who would later emerge as a leading rabbi in the United States. The chasidic Rebbes of Skver, Rachmistrivka, and Trish fled to Ukraine with some of their Chasidim.

Rabbi Yisrael Meir Kagan, the saintly Chafetz Chaim,[72] had transferred his yeshivah to Russia from Poland in 1915. He moved it back in March 1921, when he was in his early eighties. As he was leaving Russia, he stopped in Minsk, where he told the local community rabbi, Nissan Telushkin, in a trembling voice, "I have no strength left to battle this malicious government and the evil renegades who have arisen in our midst, who oppose us and are ready to force yeshivah students to desecrate the Shabbat."[73] It was a decision he would come to regret, later in life reflecting, "I should have remained. A Jew must be ready to sacrifice himself for Judaism. What could the Soviets have done to me, shot me to death or hung me on the gallows?"[74]

In the era of Communism, Tomchei Temimim remained the last bastion of Jewish scholarship[75] functioning in Russia, moving from one city to another to avoid persecution.

The exodus of the prominent rabbinic figures of the era was a stark contrast to the insistence of the new Lubavitcher Rebbe to remain; it represented a fundamental difference in priorities and strategies for Jewish survival. The scholars who stood at the helm of the great yeshivas of Russia felt that their most vital task was to preserve Torah study. That mission was paramount, and since, in their view, Jewish learning could not flourish in a hostile Communist regime, they departed for safer countries. The Rebbe saw things differently. Though the yeshivah was the crown jewel of his efforts, as Rebbe, he carried a responsibility for each and every Jew, not only his students. To abandon the Jews of the Soviet Union and transfer his yeshivah to a friendlier environment would hand victory to the Yevesektzia and spell certain extinction of Judaism in Russia. He chose to stay and stand his ground. Only after building an underground network that could sustain Jewish life under Communism – and faced with the threat of death – did he leave. Even then, he continued his work from overseas, funneling financial resources, guidance, and support to the underground network.

The diverse strategies between the Rebbe and the heads of the Lithuanian-style yeshivas reflected a deeper debate. It would emerge again two decades later, in the early 1940s, when some of those same scholars charted a different path in the United States than the Rebbe. They opened yeshivas as citadels of scholarship, focusing on a small nucleus of students, advocating for an insular brand of Judaism, preserving the core.[76] In contrast, the Rebbe campaigned for fundamental change in general Jewish life worldwide. He established the first network of Jewish day schools in the United States[77] and later, in the postwar era, laid the foundation for global Jewish renaissance by dispatching his Chasidim to live in Jewish communities around the world in order to rebuild Jewish life in those locations.

This division reflected a two-century-old debate, going back to the founding of the chasidic movement by Rabbi Yisrael Baal Shem Tov in 1734.[78] At the time, the yeshivas of Eastern Europe were bastions of elitism, detached from the average layman in the *shtetls*. One of the Baal

Shem Tov's unique teachings was the spiritual nobility of every Jew. Contrary to prevailing views, he taught that a simple uneducated tailor could have deeper religious piety than the greatest scholar.

And so, though most of the Orthodox leaders left to protect their circles of disciples, the new Lubavitcher Rebbe remained, becoming the dominant figure[79] of Russian Jewry.[80] As Russian Jewish historian Avraham Gershoni[81] writes, "During the greatest test to Russian Jewry, he was the only Jewish leader who acted." He adds that the Rayatz was uniquely gifted: "The Rebbe had unlimited self-sacrifice, courage, organizational capabilities, and a broad vision. He was blessed with all of these talents in an outstanding fashion and dedicated them to the welfare of the Jewish community."[82]

Many rabbis in Russia, even those from other segments of Orthodoxy, looked to the Rebbe for guidance. Rabbi Aryeh Leib Kaplan had studied at the Slabodka yeshivah and was a protege of Rabbi Baruch Ber Leibowitz. When the Communist influence grew in 1922, Rabbi Kaplan, thirty-eight at the time, decided to immigrate to Palestine. He planned to board a ship at the port of Baku in the Russian province of Azerbaijan. On the way, he stopped in Rostov, where he visited the Rebbe, who advised him to stay to help Russian Jews. Rabbi Kaplan was greatly concerned about the Jewish future in Russia, telling the Rebbe, "I want to leave for the sake of my children." The Rebbe responded, "If you protect the children of G-d, G-d will watch over your children." The next day at the train station, Rabbi Kaplan discovered that the group that had gathered in Baku was arrested by the Communist police. Instead of seeking another route, he decided to take the Rebbe's advice and moved to a community near Kiev, serving as a rabbi there until his arrest in 1939.[83] His children all survived, escaping to the West in 1946. Three went to Israel and one to the United States.[84]

The Rebbe was faced with an extraordinary challenge: a government intent on destroying religious Jewish life. The Bolshevik revolution had dismantled the institutional anti-Semitism of the czarist era, allowing Jews to live anywhere, not just the Pale of Settlement. It opened the doors of commerce and higher education, even though anti-Semitism was still prevalent in Russian culture. The freedom that Communism allowed the Jews came at the price of the elimination of religious observance and Zionism. To promote secular Jewish socialism, Stalin even created a Jewish province on the border of China, in remote Siberia, with its capital Birobidzhan. Jews began settling there in 1928. It had Yiddish street signs, but religious practice was banned.[85] Its Jewish population failed to rise above forty-five thousand.

Jews had faced religious oppression before. In ancient Israel, in 165 BCE during the Greek rule, Jews revolted because of religious oppression. In the second century, during the Roman reign in Israel, Torah study was also banned, prompting an uprising against the Romans, which sadly led to the deaths of hundreds of thousands. In later historical periods, Jews were forced to navigate the whims of despotic regimes that repressed Jewish religious observance.

In the new Communist Russia, the fight against religion was led by Jews themselves, backed by the power of a government. They targeted the youth, attempting to sever them from Jewish practice so that it would eventually die out. Visitors from overseas could find a handful of elderly Jews in a synagogue, studying Talmud in Yiddish. Teaching Talmud in Russian was banned so that younger Jews would not be able to comprehend it.

The Rebbe understood the stakes. His conflict with the Yevesektzia was a fight over the next generation, the Jewish future. Thus, while the local community rabbis could potentially survive if they stayed under the radar and did not reach the youth, the Rebbe had a much broader goal: the survival of Judaism in Russia. A local grassroots effort would not suffice. He stood his ground, creating for the first time in Jewish history a spiritual resistance movement that was not local but nationwide, and specifically targeted the youth. This secret Jewish underground operated throughout the Soviet Union, spanning eleven time zones.

A strategic plan was needed for Judaism to survive the Communist regime. The Rebbe's underground network consisted of two parallel responses to the challenge. One involved the broader Jewish community and operated discreetly. The other was a completely clandestine effort, whose details were known only to a few activists who were sworn to absolute secrecy.

The Rebbe wanted to take a strident approach; other rabbis advised against it. "For a few days, I pondered the general situation and decided that I must overcome all the obstacles, gird my soul for the sake of Torah, and ignore what others say," he wrote. What inspired him was a credo of his grandfather, the fourth Rebbe, Rabbi Shmuel, which his father had shared with him: "When you cannot go around an obstacle, you must go over it (in chasidic parlance, *lekhatchila ariber*). You must fortify yourself, not be affected by anything, and do what has to be done. When you do this, G-d helps from above."[86]

By 1922, the Rebbe was in touch with communities across the country. "There is hardly a city in Russia that I have not been in contact with about the schools, a *mikveh,* and the placement of rabbis and *shochtim.*"[87] At the same time, he initiated his first quasi-public initiative, establishing the Rabbinical Committee. In a departure from the historic model of decentralization that had dominated Jewish life in Russia, the Rebbe now convened rabbis from all over Russia. Professor David Fishman explains that the Rebbe viewed the committee as "an executive agency for all of Russian Jewry."[88] This national organization advocated politically for rabbis in their local battles against the more powerful forces of the Yevesektzia, using Soviet law that permitted religious practice as a counterweight to the Yevesektzia.

Not all of the region's rabbis agreed with the Rebbe's initiative. Rabbi Shmuel Rabinowitz of Moscow felt that holding the conference would accomplish nothing.[89] But the Rebbe forged ahead, successfully convened rabbis from across Russia, and created a new national rabbinical organization to stand at the helm of Russian Jewry, with him as its chair. Critical to its success was funding, and eventually, in 1924, the US-based charitable fund the Joint Distribution Committee (JDC)[90] diverted some of its funds to what it described as "cultural work," code for education and the religious activities of the committee of rabbis.

One of the major projects of the Rabbinical Committee was advocating for the legal status of Jewish education.[91] Rabbi Shlomo Yosef Zevin[92] was appointed secretary of the committee. He lobbied the Soviet Bar Association for clarification on the issue of religious schooling. During the 1920s, the government policy seemed to be constantly shifting, at times permitting religious activity and at other times forbidding it. The Yevesektzia, on the other hand, pursued the destruction of Judaism with zeal and were often more hostile than officially necessary. It was on this inconsistency that the Rebbe capitalized, arguing that Soviet Russia permitted freedom of religion and that the campaign against Judaism was propelled solely by the Jewish Communists exceeding their mandate.

The eventual legal ruling stated that Russian law permitted private religious instruction at home for up to six children. With this clarification in hand, the Rabbinical Committee defended the teachers who were being prosecuted by local courts. In 1923, when the People's Commiserate of Justice proposed closing the loopholes allowing religious home instruction, the Committee once again successfully lobbied to block the change. "Despite this victory," the Rebbe wrote in July 1923 to the leaders of Agudath Israel in the United States, "there is still much harassment by local authorities on religious homeschooling."[93]

Galvanizing the financial resources to sustain the growing education system and help Russian Jews was a daunting task. Some money could be raised in Russia, but other sources were needed. The Rebbe established a strong bond with Dr. Joseph Rosen, the JDC representative in Russia, who was able to direct some funds to the Rebbe for educational projects. There were also allocations to support job training in home-based industries to give Jews who had moved into cities the ability to earn a dignified livelihood. Within the Jewish community, there were some who resented the Rebbe's leadership and tried to disrupt the JDC funding. Communist officials also wanted the support to be withheld. Still, Rosen's admiration for the Rebbe helped overcome the critics, and the JDC did provide some assistance.[94]

The Rebbe's situation in Rostov was proving tenuous. Returning from meetings in Moscow in 1924, he was met outside the city by his secretary, Rabbi Elchonon Morozov, with ominous news: The Yevesektzia had searched his house while he was away. One of the Chasidim had overheard the officers saying, "When Schneersohn arrives, we'll arrest him and send him to exile." The Rebbe returned to Moscow for ten days and then traveled back to Rostov. Within hours, the house was surrounded. "They did an extensive search and asked many questions.

The search ended at four a.m., and at that point they wanted to take me to jail." Only the intervention of some influential locals prevented the search and questioning from ending in an arrest.[95]

Clearly, Rostov could not continue to provide a haven for the Rebbe, so the decision was made to relocate to Leningrad (now St. Petersburg), where there was a large Jewish community. As the historical capital of Russia, it became the center of many Jewish organizations, and its community was accustomed to representing all of Russian Jewry before the government.[96]

The Rebbe rented a large apartment in the center of the city. "The Rebbe's apartment was located on the corner of two of Leningrad's most prominent streets: Machovaya and Fantilamanskaya. The previous tenant had been a member of the nobility," described Rabbi Eliyahu Chaim Althaus. "It is, thank G-d, a spacious and beautiful dwelling, with seven windows looking onto Fantilamanskaya Street, ten onto Machovaya Street, and one overlooking the corner, at an angle. The room in which they prayed and where the Rebbe said *chasidut* was an expansive room, similar to the hall in Lubavitch." There was no official permit for prayer assemblies, Althaus pointed out. "The entire thing was sustained by a miracle."[97]

Leningrad's chief rabbi was Rabbi David Tevel Katzenellenbogen, whom the Rebbe knew well and greatly respected. The Rebbe's arrival added a new dimension to the community. As Professor Michael Beizer writes,[98] "The other main focus of Jewish religious life in Leningrad of the mid-1920s was the Chabad leader: Yosef Yitzchak Schneersohn."

The semipublic activities of the Rabbinical Committee, while they did have an impact, were clearly not enough to overcome the onslaught from the Yevesektzia. To create a long-term counterweight, a new approach was needed to operate against the government in total secrecy, something that would stand the test of time and ensure a future for Soviet Jewry.

That's where the second strategy came in.

While the work of the Rabbinical Committee gained steam, the Rebbe began to lay the foundation for a simultaneous clandestine endeavor. In November 1923, on the chasidic holiday of 19 Kislev,[99] the Rebbe spoke to his Chasidim in Rostov about the need to send emissaries to every city to "establish places of study – to gather children and hire teachers." Some of those present volunteered, and the Rebbe responded by saying that he would make a pact with them. A few months later, in the winter of 1924, the Rebbe formalized his plan. He called a confidential meeting of nine of his Chasidim in Moscow to establish a "secret covenant," applying the Hebrew term *kritat brit* that G-d used when He made a covenant with Avraham promising a unique destiny for the Jewish people. Like Avraham, this group was entering unknown and stormy territory. Avraham's mission was to bring monotheism to a world steeped in idolatry. The small nucleus of Chasidim who gathered in Moscow that winter night were attempting to preserve belief in G-d in an atheistic state that was willing to use force to impose its view.

Years later, the Rebbe described that meeting in Moscow.[100] "The decrees against Torah students and Jewish schools had begun. Nine *temimim* [students or alumni of Yeshivas Tomchei Temimim] gathered in Moscow, and I completed the quorum of ten. We swore an oath to continue defiantly fortifying Judaism under the Soviet regime, even if it reached *mesirat nefesh,* sacrificing our lives to the last drop of blood." The Rebbe went on to describe the gravity of the situation. "Classes had to be held in hiding, in cellars – not cellars like in America, but simply dungeons dug into the ground. They were cold, without fire, without windows." And the fear was palpable. "If they were caught, the teachers were cruelly tortured and exiled, the children were tormented, and others were shot."

The nine were committed to never revealing that they were part of the secret covenant. Thirty-six years later, in 1960 in Brooklyn, the seventh Rebbe turned to Rabbi Bentzion Shemtov during a chasidic gathering, and asked, "Did you make a *kritat brit,* a covenant, with my father-in-law the Rebbe, or not?" Shemtov was clearly conflicted. He felt beholden to the promise he made to the Rebbe Rayatz never to reveal the members of the secret group. Three times the seventh Rebbe asked and still, Shemtov remained silent, never breaking his solemn oath. [101]

These men became generals in the secret army that was fielded across the breadth of Russia. They led their fellow Chasidim in organizing a clandestine network of elementary schools, yeshivas, synagogues, and *mikvehs* that lasted until the fall of the Soviet Union. Funding was raised locally and funneled from abroad.

The underground operation succeeded. A confidential 1926 report[102] from Russia sent to the JDC in New York stated that some fifteen thousand children were being educated in a growing number of secret schools operated by the Rebbe's network. "In Moscow alone," reads the report, "we have three hundred children studying in small groups of three.[103] They hide in cellars, and in the summertime, they go out to the woods." The report explained that each teacher was paid thirty rubles a month, and another thirty rubles was paid to each watchman required to keep an eye out for authorities. "If a teacher is arrested, thirty rubles are needed to support his family while he is imprisoned. Though the teachers and children know the danger, they heroically take all risks for their education."

Despite the intense level of secrecy demanded by the Rebbe, the identities of a few of the original quorum are known, including Elchonon Dov Morozov, Bentzion Shemtov, and Simon Yakovshvili (Jacobson).[104]

Two had been students at the Rebbe Rashab's yeshivah in the town of Lubavitch, and the third hailed from the remote province of Georgia and studied in Rostov. None of the three came from Chabad families, though Shemtov had an ancestral connection to Chabad. Each was passionately loyal to the Rebbe and willingly put his life on the line for Judaism. Yakovshvili served a decade in Russian prisons and Shemtov spent three years in Siberia until they escaped to the West in the postwar period. Morozov, who coordinated the network after the Rebbe left Russia in 1927, was exiled to Siberia and later shot by a Russian firing squad. They each left behind large, Torah-observant families, and today many of their descendants are Chabad emissaries across the globe.

The stories of these three Chasidim represent the experiences of the rest of the members of the network.

Shemtov, the youngest of the four, was born in 1902.[105] His father was an affluent lumber merchant in Druya, northern Belorussia, where Jews made up some forty percent of the town's four thousand residents. His mother had lost multiple pregnancies and so, while pregnant with him, she traveled 180 miles to Lubavitch for a blessing from the Rebbe Rashab to bear a healthy child. The Rebbe assured her that the birth would be fine and suggested naming the child Bentzion. Winds of change blowing in Druya were promoting secularism, and to protect young

Bentzion, his mother brought him to the yeshivah in Lubavitch when he was just twelve years old, making him one of its youngest students. His subsequent siblings, who did not attend the yeshivah, did not end up fully observant.

Young Bentzion, a child from an affluent family,[106] found himself in a small town where the prime values were the pursuit of Jewish scholarship and spirituality. He developed a passionate loyalty to the Rebbe Rashab and the next two successive Rebbes. After taking the oath of the covenant with the Rebbe, Shemtov was dispatched to Volhynia, the northwestern region of Ukraine. There were few Chasidim living there, but the Rebbe was not concerned only with his followers, but with all the Jews of Russia. Shemtov visited dozens of communities and spoke in the remaining synagogues, promoting Jewish education for the youth. In numerous communities, he successfully set up schools and encouraged the synagogues to be kept open.

In March of 1927, Shemtov was in Korosten in western Ukraine. The secret police discovered his activities and his involvement in the Rabbinical Conference held there. They arrested him and transported him to Kharkiv, where he was jailed for a month, until Passover, and then released. But his freedom did not last long. Three months later, in June, on the same day that the Rebbe was arrested in Leningrad, Shemtov was detained in Kharkiv. He was held for another thirty days and grilled about the clandestine Chabad system in Russia. He never revealed any information and was eventually released pending trial.

Between arrests, Shemtov became engaged to Esther Golda Futerfus. Her brother Reb Mendel, a legendary figure in the Chabad underground, suggested the match, as their father had passed away years earlier. With the new trial looming, the wedding date was delayed.[107] Then Shemtov was sentenced to exile in Siberia for three years. In the summer of 1930, his bride made the long trek to Siberia to meet him, and finally, in September, in the small village of Yanivskiek about fifty miles from the Trans-Siberian railroad, they celebrated their wedding. Lacking a *mikveh*, Esther Golda hacked through an icy Siberian river to immerse in its frigid waters. They had no ring for the wedding ceremony, so Shemtov fashioned one out of a silver fork.[108] Rabbi Shmuel Levitin, a noted chasidic rabbi who had also been exiled to Siberia for promoting Judaism, officiated.

After being released from Siberia, Shemtov returned to central Russia, living in Kharkiv and then Moscow. After the German invasion, the couple made their way to remote Uzbekistan, settling in Tashkent. In 1947, Shemtov and his family were able to leave Russia on false Polish passports as part of the secret escape organized by Chabad Chasidim after the war.[109] In 1948, the Shemtovs were sent by the Rebbe to England, where they worked to build the Chabad community there. At the end of his life, Shemtov moved to Israel, where he established Machon Levi Yitzchak, an organization dedicated to publishing the talks of the seventh Rebbe in Hebrew. He passed away in Israel in 1975 at the age of seventy-two.

The second member of the quorum, Simon Yakovshvili, was born in 1900 and raised in Kutaisi in Soviet Georgia, some 1,200 miles south of Moscow. The local Jewish community was steeped in tradition but lacked rabbis and scholars, so in 1916, community leaders turned to the Rebbe Rashab for assistance. He dispatched Rabbi Shmuel Levitin, among other rabbis, to establish a yeshivah for the Sephardic Jews.[110] But Yakovshvili never studied in the Chabad yeshivah in his home province. His first encounter with Chabad was in Rostov.

In 1918, on his way to study in Italy, having received a scholarship for agricultural studies, Yakovshvili stopped in Rostov for Rosh HaShanah. "He was a tall, handsome eighteen-year-old," shared his grandson, Rabbi Yosef Yitzchak Jacobson.[111] "He walked into the synagogue sporting distinct Georgian dress, with yellow shoes, a white jacket, and a little bow-tie." Not knowing the proper protocol, and standing out because of his unusual garb, he annoyed some of the Chasidim by brazenly pushing his way to the *bimah* to stand near the Rebbe as he sounded the shofar.[112] The Rayatz signaled to them not to interfere. After the holiday, he had a private meeting with the Rebbe Rashab. Jacobson says his grandfather could not speak Yiddish, so the Rebbe spoke in Hebrew, telling him, "You will arrive in Italy when the right time comes. What is important for you now is to learn Torah, to know what it really means to be a Jew." Yakovshvili was moved by the conversation, and he took the Rebbe's advice. Eventually, he completed his rabbinic ordination and became certified as both a *shochet* (kosher slaughterer) and a *mohel* (circumciser).

After Yakovshvili took the oath in Moscow, the Rebbe sent him back to his home province. Russian rule in the remote province was not as oppressive, and the Georgian Jews were known for their fierce independence. Yakovshvili strengthened the existing Jewish schools and opened new ones. Unfortunately, his inspiring talks caught the attention of the authorities, and he was imprisoned and eventually freed. In a cryptic letter to friends written in rabbinic Hebrew to circumvent the censors, he said, "I had an astonishing miracle."

Yakovshvili's success alarmed Yevesektzia leader Moshe Litvakov.[113] At a meeting with fellow activists in St. Petersburg in 1927, Litvakov complained,[114] "In every part of the country – not just White Russia but even in remote provinces like Georgia and Turkistan – his [the Rayatz's] followers are there preserving religious life." He described his visit to one town in Soviet Georgia, where he was informed by local Jews that a representative of the Rayatz, referring to Yakovshvili, was residing in their town. They said that the representative spoke their language and had provided funding to repair the local *mikveh*. Litvakov lamented bitterly to his audience in Moscow, "Jewish leaders in Tbilisi presented me with a petition to reopen the local synagogue, all because of Schneersohn and his representative."[115]

Yakovshvili eventually relocated to Moscow. In August of 1937, armed men burst into his home and arrested him. He was accused of being a counterrevolutionary and initially sentenced to twenty-five years in exile. Years later, at a meeting of rabbis in Toronto in 1952, he described the harsh interrogation he endured. "They gave me a list of one hundred men, women, and children who they said were also counterrevolutionaries, telling me that if I confirmed and signed that it was true, I would go free."[116] Yakovshvili refused to inform on fellow Jews, sealing his own fate. He suffered terrible torture during the ten years he was imprisoned. He was flogged repeatedly, his wounds lasting for life. Finally, he received a death sentence. From prison he sent an appeal to Lavrentiy Beria, head of Stalin's dreaded secret police, who also hailed from Georgia. Yakovshvili hoped he would show mercy to a fellow countryman. Minutes before his scheduled execution, Yakovshvili asked for a few moments to pray. As he was uttering what he thought would be his last prayers, an edict arrived from Beria sparing his life.

For almost three years after his arrest, Yakovshvili's family had no idea where he was. His wife tirelessly searched for him. They nearly lost hope, to the point that many assumed him dead.[117] Despite this, the family held tightly to their beliefs and Jewish observance, and his two sons continued attending a secret yeshivah at night, after public school. When news finally reached them that Simon was alive, the family was joyously surprised.

After nine years in the Soviet gulag, Yakovshvili was released. His son Gershon says, "His back was broken, his beard was white. He didn't recognize me, and I didn't recognize him." Shortly thereafter, the Yakovshvili family fled Russia following the same escape route as Shemtov, masquerading as Polish refugees and changing their name from Yakovshvili to the more Polish-sounding Jacobson. In 1952, the Jacobsons immigrated to Toronto, where Simon was appointed rabbi of the local Chabad congregation. However, "he was worn out from years of suffering," says his grandson Rabbi Yosef Yitzchak Jacobson. In June 1953, he passed away at the age of fifty-three. His wife followed him two years later, leaving three orphaned boys, ages six, twelve, and fourteen.

The most well-known member of the group of ten was Rabbi Elchonon (Chonye) Morozov. When the Tomchei Temimim yeshivah was established in Lubavitch in 1897, a small select group of outstanding scholars were chosen as its first students. Morozov, born in 1877 to a religious family, was one of them. He originally studied in Minsk and then went to Lubavitch to pursue chasidic teachings. He excelled in his studies to the point that the Rebbe Rashab chose him as the personal study partner for his son, the Rayatz. He eventually joined the yeshivah faculty.

The Rebbe Rashab soon drafted Morozov as his personal secretary, and he continued in the same role for the Rayatz. This put him at the center of the Rebbe's secret campaign in Russia, and indeed, Morozov was one of the first Chasidim to be arrested and sent to Siberia for a three-year sentence in 1927. He was a role model to others, displaying great self-sacrifice. Rabbi Yisrael Jacobson quotes his famous saying about the tribulations of Chasidim in Russia: "A year in prison is an obligation; two years is a *hiddur mitzvah* (beautification of a mitzvah)."

Morozov's personal life was marred by hardship. In 1915, his wife passed away, leaving him with five children. He later married her cousin and had four more children, one of whom passed away at a young age. Two of his daughters[118] were drawn from religious observance by the lure of secular Zionism. This created tensions in the family, and at one point he told one of his daughters to leave the home, fearing that she would negatively influence the others. The Rebbe intervened, telling Morozov that it was inappropriate for a father to evict his child from her home. The Rebbe showed a special concern for this daughter by visiting her in the hospital when she was ill. Morozov's two daughters were imprisoned at the same time that he was – they for their Zionist activities and he for his work for the Rebbe. When his daughters learned that he was being mistreated, they declared a hunger strike in prison until his conditions were improved.

When the Rebbe left Russia in 1927, Morozov became the lead organizer of the secret network. But he too wished to leave Russia. At one point it seemed possible to get a visa for Palestine, but the door closed on him before the needed funds were procured. Beginning in 1930, Morozov hid from the authorities in Leningrad, using false papers that identified him as Berke Pesner. Finally, in 1938, the long arm of the secret police caught him and his son Shmuel. They tortured Shmuel, asking him to verify that his father was indeed Elchonon Morozov. He refused to answer, understanding what his father's fate would be if his true identity was revealed. Morozov cried out, "Shmuel, tell them that I am your father!" Shortly afterward, Shmuel took his last breath, and the interrogators informed Morozov that he was to be put to death.

"Your crime," the police told him, "is being a representative of the Lubavitcher Rebbe, who is G-d's representative in Russia." Morozov was murdered by a firing squad.[119]

The life journeys of the other men who took the oath, and the members of the network they began, follow similar paths as those of Shemtov, Yakovshvili, and Morozov. Many of them and their recruits were imprisoned in the Siberian gulag. Some were killed, and almost all were harassed by the secret police. Few emerged from the experience unscathed.

The Rebbe himself was constantly at odds with the Yevesektzia, acting surreptitiously to evade them. In February 1927, he had a close call while on a trip to Moscow to meet representatives of the JDC. "The plans for my trip were known only to my wife and to my confidant, Chonye

Morozov," the Rebbe wrote in his diary.[120] Arriving at the train station, he waited in the taxi until just a few minutes before the train's departure, then dashed through the station and immediately entered his compartment. He remained there for the duration of the trip so as not to draw the attention of patrols. "I heard that the Yevesektzia had requested that the GPU (secret police) monitor my travels in an attempt to find evidence against me."

But the man in the next compartment did notice the Rebbe, and the next morning, as they neared Moscow, he knocked on his door. He introduced himself as Mark Semyonovitch Bashkov, chairman of the Soviet Council of Chelyabinsk, a province in southern Russia, and a member of the OGPU (secret police).[121] He said that the Rebbe was greatly respected in his home, and they agreed to meet in three days' time at the Rebbe's hotel. When the Rebbe checked into the hotel in Moscow, he tipped the staff generously and asked them to send a message to his home in Leningrad saying that "Yosef Chaim is well" – Yosef being the Rebbe's first name and Chaim signifying life. The message indicated that the Rebbe was alive and well.

Shortly after midnight, the Rebbe heard a knock on his door but did not answer. A few minutes later, the phone rang. The hotel manager was on the line asking the Rebbe to open the door because he had something vital to tell him. "Fifteen minutes ago, a Yevesektzia official arrived at the hotel asking if Rabbi Schneersohn had checked in." The official told the hotel manager that the Rebbe had left Moscow the day before and that he had been searching for him the whole day so that he could arrest him. "I told him that citizen Schneersohn had not arrived," the manager told the Rebbe. "He gave me his phone number and told me to call him the moment he arrives."

The manager hurriedly smuggled the Rebbe out the kitchen entrance and escorted him to the Bolshoi Moskovsky Hotel, where his friend was the manager. Finally, at 3:30 a.m., the Rebbe settled in at the second hotel. The Rebbe wrote in his diary, "The manager here knows I am hiding from the Yevesektzia and gave me instructions on how to leave the hotel through a side exit."

During that visit in Moscow, the Rebbe met with Dr. Rosen, the JDC representative in Russia. They discussed the Rebbe's initiative to train

Jews for home-based industries, which the JDC was partially supporting. The Rebbe also met with chasidic activists, always careful to keep out of the public eye.

On Wednesday evening, Bashkov, the Soviet official who had met the Rebbe on the train, came to visit and shared his story. "My father was a teacher in Orsha [a city in Belorussia]," he began. His great-grandparents had been Chasidim of the Alter Rebbe, Chabad's founder. His grandfather had been an ardent follower of the Tzemach Tzedek, the third Rebbe. "He was involved with Jewish schools and he was arrested by Czar Nicholas."[122] Bashkov studied in yeshivah until the age of fourteen, but he felt that yeshivah studies were not for him, and he returned home. "Eventually, I could not accept the rules at home and left for Warsaw, where I joined the Socialists." In the years to come, he pursued an education in England before returning to Russia. There he rose to prominence, becoming chairman of the Russian Provincial Government in Chelyabinsk and a member of the board that oversaw the secret police.

He told the Rebbe that after his mother's passing, he decided to visit his father in Orsha. It had been twenty years since he had been home. When he arrived, he found his father living with a friend. "He was bent over and weak and did not recognize me." Seeing an official, his father asked, "Have you come to arrest me again? Please let me recover from my illness first." He corrected his father, saying, "It's me, your son Meir," and asked him to come to Moscow, where he would care for him. At first, his father did not even want to speak with him. Then he said, "Once, teachers were needed to instruct children. Now they are put in jail and beaten." Bashkov attempted to placate his father and offered him money, but his father refused, saying, "I have what I need."

What Bashkov did not know, the Rebbe wrote in his diary later, was that his family was active in the Rebbe's underground. "His father Shimon and his uncle Aryeh Shlomo are teachers in Orsha, and his uncle Menachem Shmuel (Ragolin) is a teacher in Yekaterinoslav. All of them receive a salary from our center."

As Bashkov was telling his story, they heard a pounding at the door. In burst three men, one a police officer, two carrying guns. One of them, named Krotov, proclaimed: "Citizen Schneersohn, you are under arrest! Do not move or we will shoot you." The Rebbe remained stoic, having endured harassment from the Yevesektzia many times. Bashkov was also silent. As they searched the Rebbe's luggage, Krotov gleefully told the Rebbe what he did to two rabbis in his hometown of Amskislav: "We harnessed them to a wagon and ordered them to pull it. The older one stumbled and died the same day, and the younger one died two days later."

At that point Krotov turned to Bashkov, demanding to search him, too. Bashkov told them that the search was illegal. Krotov exploded in rage. "I am a member of the Yevesektzia and I am responsible for the surveillance of this hotel," he said. He demanded to see Bashkov's documents. "We will find a place for you in the dungeons of Lubyanka Street [the notorious Russian prison]," he threatened.

Bashkov then presented documents revealing him to be a senior member of the OGPU. The Rebbe writes, "Krotov's face turned white. They all recoiled and stood like blocks of wood, as if thunderstruck."

The three men fled the scene. Afterward, Bashkov attempted to console the Rebbe. "This is an overreaction of young people who lack judgment." There were some officials who acted with greater consideration as Bashkov did, partly out of nostalgia for their own family backgrounds. Still, the Yevesektzia had a free hand in pushing the Soviet anti-religious policy to the edge.

After this incident, the Rebbe returned safely to Leningrad.

Throughout the Soviet Union, many Chasidim put their lives on the line to sustain Jewish life and educate the next generation. The Rebbe's unflinching efforts not only put himself at risk, but them too. How could the Rebbe put his Chasidim in danger? There are several points to consider.

First, the Rebbe viewed it as a sacred mission entrusted to him by his father just a few weeks before his passing. As he reflected poignantly in his personal diary during the Moscow visit in 1926: "Whenever I feel disheartened, I reflect on this moment. I recall that Friday when the Rebbe [Rashab] spoke terrifying words to me."[123] His father's bold message, that he would have to stand up to the Communists and put his life on the line and "that eventually the Soviet Union would collapse," remained at the forefront of the Rebbe's mind. Clearly, he felt that in order to succeed in the mission entrusted to him, it was imperative that he enlist others, despite the risk that entailed.

A second explanation is given by Rabbi Yehuda Leib Schapiro, dean of the Rabbinical College of Greater Miami. "The very future of Judaism in Russia was at stake," he says. Russia was then home to one of the largest Jewish communities in the world. Schapiro says that the Rebbe knew that if they did not act radically, Jewish religious life was doomed to die out under the Communist regime. Thus, even when some Chasidim had the opportunity to leave Russia in the 1920s, the Rebbe urged them to stay and continue their holy work.

Schapiro adds that for the Rebbe himself, this was heart-wrenching. "He had a great love toward every one of his students, and putting them at risk pained him deeply." That was made clear to Rabbi Simcha Gorodetsky[124] when he met with the Rebbe to report on a mission to cities in Russia, Azerbaijan, and Bukhara[125] in the mid-1920s. He hesitated in sharing the desperate situations of some of the Chasidim.

The Rebbe told him, "*Nu, nu,* continue. As my emissary, you must tell me everything." Gorodetsky shared the difficulties he had observed.

Suddenly the Rebbe burst into tears. Gorodetsky stood in stunned silence, witnessing the Rebbe's anguish. When he left the Rebbe's room, he met the Rebbe's mother, Rebbetzin Shterna Sara. Seeing his distraught face, she asked him, "Why do you look so pale?" He told her what had just occurred and how the Rebbe had begun to cry. She whispered to him, "I don't know what happened today, but sometimes I enter his room after *yechidut* and I see the floor soaked with tears."[126]

Third, there was historical precedent for this kind of strategy. Rabbi Mendel Gluckowsky, a member of the Chabad Rabbinical Court in Israel, points to the revolt of the Maccabees against the powerful Syrian-Greek Empire in the second century BCE. "A small group of poorly armed faithful Jews courageously stood up to the oppression, even confronting the Hellenist Jews who had accepted the Syrian-Greek culture and were working with them." Quoting a talk that the seventh Rebbe once gave to a group of children,[127] he says, "The goal of the Greeks was to get the Jews to forget the Torah. And just as the Maccabees stood up to the Greeks and the Hellenists, so did the Rebbe stand up to the Communists and the Yevesektzia."[128]

During a late night *farbrengen* in 1974, the seventh Rebbe spoke with great passion about the dilemma that the Rebbe faced.[129] "The Rebbe

[Rayatz] had actual self-sacrifice. If it was for a small thing or a larger one, no matter what, in that country [Russia], when you upheld a Jewish tradition you put your life on the line." As he spoke of the Rebbe's anguish, the seventh Rebbe cried. "When you send someone on a mission that is full of danger, it's much more difficult than putting yourself at risk. And then the person you sent is arrested and exiled." Faced with a quandary over whether to continue or to stop, the Rebbe acted fearlessly. "Then the next day you acted again with self-sacrifice and sent another who has to put *his* life on the line in place of the one who was arrested."

Rabbi Simon Jacobson's son Sholom, who was orphaned at age six because of his father's activism, insists that the Chasidim who took the oath of the Rebbe's secret covenant and the hundreds of others who joined the effort in Russia "wore it as a badge of honor." This sentiment is echoed by Rabbi Moishe Levertov in his memoir about his father, Rabbi DovBer Levertov.[130] Rabbi DovBer grew up in the Chabad underground and died in the gulags in 1947, where he was sent because of his activism. "Although my years in the USSR were full of terror and persecution, in a sense they were the most satisfying years of my life – not to be exchanged for anything in the world. Every moment had a sense of living for a higher ideal, an inspiring feeling difficult to evoke under our present conditions of plenty."

Moishe's son, Rabbi Berel Levertov, the Chabad emissary in Santa Fe, New Mexico, reflected on the life of the grandfather he never met and for whom he is named. "My grandfather never hesitated to do what was needed – *brit milah* (circumcision), kosher slaughter – no matter the great personal risk. When his children had escaped the Soviet Union and were out of danger, he redoubled his efforts. He felt that he now had nothing to fear and nothing to lose."[131]

Rabbi Berel's daughter Mussi Sharfstein was raised in Santa Fe and today is a Jewish educator in Miami Beach, Florida. She reflected on her great-grandfather's sacrifice, losing his life to Stalin's henchmen because of his commitment to the Rebbe's work in Russia. "My great-grandfather's staunch, unwavering dedication instilled in his descendants the importance of a life of Yiddishkeit and of keeping it alive for others. He refused to compromise even one iota in his Torah observance, insisting on maintaining Yiddishkeit and *Chasidut* under the most difficult conditions. This commitment still reverberates three generations later and motivates me in my life today."[132]

Based in Leningrad, the Rebbe operated throughout Russia, and for a while, the city provided a haven from the Yevesektzia. But it would not last. An initiative of Jewish communal leaders in St. Petersburg, secretly backed by the Yevesektzia, led to the Rebbe's arrest and exile from Russia.

The central Jewish communal organization at the time was the Leningrad Jewish Religious Community (LERO), formally recognized by the government in 1925. Standing at its helm was Lev Gurewicz.[133] He was a dynamic leader, an avid Zionist and active in the Enlightenment. Gurewicz's aspirations for communal leadership were not limited to Leningrad and included a plan to gain more power by uniting all of Russian Jewry in a congress.

In the summer of 1925, Gurewicz met the Rebbe for the first time[134] and suggested that he partner with him and LERO in creating a national conference the following year that would include all elements of Russian Jewish life. Gurewicz believed that this was politically achievable; the government had sanctioned a similar convention of Christian leaders in Moscow. He assured the Rebbe that although he was not personally observant,[135] he was working in cooperation with the chief rabbi of Leningrad, the renowned scholar Rabbi David Katzenellenbogen,[136] who was deeply respected by the Rebbe.

The Rebbe sat silently as Gurewicz presented his initiative. The response he offered was lukewarm: "I am sure your intentions are noble, but at first thought, I am against it." The Rebbe explained that while the issue required further contemplation, it seemed that there were too many risks[137] and, in his view, that it could cause more problems than it would solve. The Rebbe wrote to Rabbi Katzenellenbogen that "the idea of a conference needs further consideration," urging him to not act unilaterally, but to wait to consult with other rabbinic leaders.[138]

But that didn't stop Gurewicz. In the months to come, he traveled across Russia attempting to gain support for the conference, falsely claiming that he had the Rebbe's endorsement. He started with smaller communities and eventually met with the leaders of the largest community in Moscow. Some local leaders were supportive. Others were concerned that the congress, being lay-led, would ignore the concerns of the rabbis and bring about religious changes,[139] and even step into other issues of politics and economics. The Moscow leaders also resented the fact that Gurewicz had saved them for last, meeting with smaller Jewish communities first.

The fears of religious change that concerned the Moscow community leaders were valid. The intentions of LERO's leadership were exposed when a conflict erupted over local Jewish communal politics in Leningrad. The board of LERO had twenty-four members whose views split along the lines of those who wanted to retain classic Jewish education and religious practices and those who wished to modernize religion. The reformers, who were the majority, unilaterally instituted changes behind the backs of the religious minority. Their actions were exposed, creating a major schism among the members. Feeling betrayed, the ten religious members resigned in October 1926, accusing LERO of acting unethically and "secretly implementing a plan to reform Jewish education and religious practice against the Torah and tradition."[140] A few weeks later, the ten members called a meeting at the main synagogue in Leningrad and decided to apply for government recognition of a new religious organization.[141]

The actions of LERO in Leningrad substantiated the Rebbe's concerns about the national congress they wished to organize. The matter became clearer when the conference organizers met with local rabbis in Leningrad. Rabbi Eliyahu Althaus described it as a tense meeting, with the rabbis telling the organizers that the conference was unnecessary. "We don't need a conference to deal with questions about kosher and religious life," they said. "We already handle that."[142]

After a heated debate, the planners revealed the true intent behind the conference. "Our real agenda is targeting schools and education," they admitted. "We want to introduce reforms in the schools to make them relevant to the spirit of the age. The schooling we currently have is outdated. What our forefathers gave us from a bygone time is unsophisticated, with untrained teachers, and without a proper curriculum. We are living in a new age. Today we need new people, new teachers, and an enlightened, relevant Torah."[143]

The Rebbe understood that the plan for a national congress involved an even more sinister danger. More and more evidence pointed to the fact that the plan was supported by the Yevesektzia. The Yevesektzia viewed it as an opportunity to create a new communal structure that would be an alternative to their intractable foe, the Rebbe.

At this point, the Rebbe was chair of the Committee of Rabbis, which was the most influential force in Russian Jewish life. Groups like the JDC provided their funding. This new group would claim to represent Russian Jewry, diverting funds from the Rebbe's secret network of educational and religious services. It would be guided by lay people, not rabbis, many of whom wished to enact changes in education and religious practice. The new organization would render irrelevant the opposition of the rabbis who refused to compromise on their ideals; it would clear the way for the Yevesektzia to advance their agenda.

At first the Yevesektzia did not show its hand, operating in the background. If the congress succeeded, it would establish a new communal leadership that the Yevesektzia could easily manipulate. But soon, the Yevesektzia's role became obvious. In cities throughout Russia, the secret police interrogated local rabbis, asking if they supported the planned conference and warning them not to follow Rabbi Schneersohn's lead. The rabbis who endorsed the conference were encouraged to go; some were even offered compensation for travel expenses. "Then," says Althaus, "the rabbis were asked to swear, in writing, not to disclose what had been discussed with them, on the pain of death." Rabbi Binyamin Gorodetsky,[144] Chabad's roaming ambassador and liaison to the JDC in the postwar era, writes in his autobiography that the Russian authorities supported the conference. "Their sole intention was to use it as a counterweight against the Rebbe's leadership, so that he could not receive funds from American Jewry, from the JDC, and others."

Just after Passover, in April of 1927, the Leningrad community announced that the conference would take place that October, after the High Holidays. But despite the event being scheduled, Gurewicz's grand plan remained in jeopardy. Following the Rebbe's lead and seeing through the facade, the major communities in Moscow and Minsk withheld their approval of the conference. Debates for and against put many Jewish communities throughout Russia in turmoil. If the conference failed, the plan to create a new organizational structure that could challenge the Rebbe's leadership of Russian Jewry would break down.

For seven years, the Rebbe and the Yevesektzia had been battling each other from a distance. He would open a Jewish school; they would shut it down. The Rebbe would dispatch a rabbi, *shochet,* or teacher to a community, and the secret police would arrest the person. He would lobby the government to allow religious life to function, and they would try to undermine those efforts. Now the scheme to replace the Rebbe as the most influential Jewish leader in Russia was being countered. With this plan faltering, it would only be a matter of time before the Yevesektzia took drastic action against the Rebbe directly.

In the summer of 1926, a delegation of prominent rabbis, led by Rabbi Zev Kipnis, a distinguished Torah scholar, came to see the Rebbe with the idea of creating a conference of rabbis in the city of Korosten, Ukraine. The Rebbe was wary. "My personal opinion was that the conference was not necessary," the Rebbe wrote later.[145] Still, this conference was unlike the one being developed by the Leningrad community, whose agenda was to restructure Jewish life in Russia. In this case, the Rebbe felt that the intentions of the rabbis were noble, even though he was skeptical about the outcome. "I felt that the conference in Korosten would not be productive, but that it would also not cause any harm because the organizers are G-d-fearing." The organizers secured government sanction and announced the conference.[146]

On October 26, 1926, close to one hundred rabbis convened in Korosten, where half of the population of twelve thousand was Jewish. Despite his doubts, the Rebbe encouraged some of the leading Chabad rabbis to attend, including Rabbi Yosef Zevin, who was a featured speaker. He secretly dispatched Bentzion Shemtov, then just twenty-four, to work behind the scenes to ensure an agenda that would strengthen Jewish education and tradition. His efforts were successful.

The Rebbe did not personally attend, but the delegates nominated him as honorary chairman, notifying him by telegram. When the Rebbe cabled back, his message was read while all the rabbis present stood in respect.[147] "You are following the approach of the [fifth] Lubavitcher Rebbe and Rabbi Chaim Soloveitchik of Brisk, our teachers, who did not compromise," he wrote. He was referring to the principled stand of both rabbis regarding standards of Jewish tradition during conferences held decades earlier under the czar.[148]

While at the conference, Bentzion Shemtov discovered the reason that the government had sanctioned the conference: It was a strategy of divide and conquer to prepare the ground for the conference being organized by the Leningrad community. "They wanted to evaluate the strength of the more traditional elements and drive a wedge between them and the modern Jewish leaders," he wrote in his memoir.[149] "This was the same strategy they used successfully between Christian religious groups." With the hand of the rabbis weakened, they could pursue their goal of creating a new leadership structure for the Jewish community. But to the Communist officials monitoring the conference, the esteem that the rabbis showed for the Rebbe was alarming. Their primary opponent was the Rebbe, and he clearly had broad support from Russian Jewish leaders. Their scheme to use the conference to divide Russian Jewry and weaken the Rebbe's leadership had failed.

Shemtov was arrested following the conference. Government agents conducted long interrogations, and, in the process, they confirmed their intent to use the conference to weaken the rabbis' influence.[150] Rabbi Kipnis, the conference organizer, was also arrested, and the executive board formed at the conference was dissolved by the authorities.[151] Kipnis writes in his memoir: "They imprisoned me for sixteen days and told me that the Rebbe is the most dangerous person to the Communist regime, unlike other rabbis who were very passive." As part of the interrogation, the secret police threatened Kipnis, saying it had been decided on the highest level that four people would be sent to Siberia: the Rebbe, Rabbi Shimon Lazaroff,[152] Kipnis, and one other. He wrote that they planned a private trial so as not to elicit criticism from abroad. All four were indeed arrested. Kipnis writes, "It was a miracle I was freed."

The Chasidim in the vicinity of the Rebbe felt a sense of foreboding during the High Holidays in September 1926. Traditionally, before the sounding of the shofar, a series of verses are recited out loud by the cantor with great emotion. This time, before the words *"Al Ya'shkuni Ziedim* – Let the wicked not oppress me," the Rebbe cried out in a loud voice, "*Oy gevalt*!" This expression of angst by the Rebbe alarmed the Chasidim. Rabbi Eliyahu Althaus, who was standing nearby, writes that he was extremely disturbed.[153]

"The Rebbe was always vigilant with his words, even in ordinary conversation," Althaus notes, "and much more so on the first day of Rosh HaShanah." To Althaus it was clear: "This was an omen." That portentous feeling was present through the holiday of Simchat Torah,[154] normally the most joyous of occasions. "The talks of the Rebbe that night and the next day were infused with a sense of bitterness." The Rebbe asked that all congregations around the world start reciting a daily allotment of psalms that are usually recited during times of distress. Chasidim wondered if this request from the Rebbe came from a premonition that dangerous times lay ahead.

"I am permitting myself to reveal to you certain things said to me in private," the Rebbe's secretary, Rabbi Yechezkel (Chatche) Feigin, wrote in a letter to his friend Rabbi Yisrael Jacobson in the United States about that fateful Simchat Torah.[155] "After the talks at the table, the Rebbe retreated to his study." Sensing a moment of opportunity, "I took my sons into the Rebbe's room to receive a blessing. Afterward I remained alone with the Rebbe." Rabbi Feigin then changed the subject from personal matters to the hardships of recent months, requesting a blessing "to remove the obstacles to Torah study."

The Rebbe was silent. "He seemed to be in a higher world." Finally, he responded, "Chatche, there is no blessing for this! Avraham Avinu conducted himself with self-sacrifice because it had to be done. For Avraham, the self-sacrifice was part of what he had to do, because it was necessary to reveal divinity in the world. He needed to do it, so he did it."

The Rebbe then contrasted this with the self-sacrifice of Rabbi Akiva, who taught Torah despite the ban by Roman authorities in the second century. The Talmud explains that while the Romans were torturing Rabbi Akiva to death, he remarked that he had always yearned to be a martyr for G-d.[156]

"In our case," he continued, "we must strive to teach Torah, and if self-sacrifice is required, we will do it too." Unlike Rabbi Akiva, the Rebbe was not seeking martyrdom, but if it was necessary to fulfill his mission of teaching Torah, he was ready.

It seemed that the moment when the Rebbe might be required to pay the ultimate sacrifice was drawing closer. All that winter, Althaus writes, "heavy clouds hung over the Rebbe and the entire Chabad community. The atmosphere in his home was charged with dread." They discovered later that the Yevesektzia was "energetically fabricating slanderous accusations against the Rebbe."

In February 1927, they made their first public move.[157] The Rebbe's secretary Rabbi Elchonon Morozov was arrested and jailed, held with people who Althaus describes as "the worst political prisoners." Before he was taken away, Rabbi Morozov managed to secretly hand the list of underground yeshivas and schools to his eleven-year-old son, who hid it without the police noticing. Rabbi Feigin wrote that because Rabbi Morozov was a key figure in the underground, his arrest was "terrifying and ominous."[158] Rabbi Morozov had carried much of the financial responsibility for the yeshivas. His arrest created an additional financial strain on the their operations.

The shadow of the Yevesektzia loomed like an angry beast waiting to pounce at the slightest provocation. Still, the Rebbe courageously disregarded their intimidations and the very real threats. On Purim, in mid-March 1927, the Rebbe held a fiery public *farbrengen*. Rabbi Zalman Duchman, who was present, described it as "terrifying."[159] The Rebbe screamed, "Who is the Yevesektzia? A rabbi's son? A butcher's son? A villager's son? I am not frightened by them!" He brazenly urged his Chasidim to continue practicing and spreading Judaism and to defy the government opposition to the point of self-sacrifice. The Rebbe repeated over and over, "We must sacrifice our lives not to send our children to their schools."[160]

"In every conceivable way," describes Althaus,[161] "this Purim was unlike any other. The Rebbe spoke with such passion, at a level we had never heard before. It felt like he was literally pouring out his soul."

At one point, the Rebbe turned to one of his Chasidim and forcefully enjoined him, "Zalman, if they ever build a bonfire and confront you with the choice of yielding your child to their schools or casting yourself into the flames, let yourself be cast into the flames!" Everyone was acutely aware of the Yevesektzia spies present at the *farbrengen*, listening to every word spoken. Duchman writes, "Everyone was in dread." Althaus recalls, "We gazed at the agents, their faces flushed with anger. We knew that it was only a matter of time before something terrible would happen."

Rabbi Eliezer Poupko[162] was the rabbi in the Russian town of Velizh. A local Communist activist confided to him that the Rebbe would be arrested shortly. He decided to travel to St. Petersburg to warn the Rebbe. The Rebbe was unfazed by Rabbi Poupko report, addressing him in deferential third-party Yiddish, "Velizh Rav, I am ready to go on *mesirat nefesh* [to give up my life]." As Rabbi Poupko told his grandson Mordechai Dovber, "The Rebbe would not budge."

Chapter Four

Armed Men at Midnight[1]

It was a few minutes after midnight on June 15, 1927,[2] and the Rebbe and his family had gathered for a late supper in his Leningrad apartment. For the Rebbe, it had been a long day. He received people for private audiences until 11:30 p.m. and then prayed the evening service. Now he was finally sitting down for dinner with his family. He was weary.

Barely ten minutes passed, and suddenly the silence was broken by the doorbell ringing. Chana, the Rebbe's oldest daughter, went to the double doors, asking who was creating a commotion at this late hour. A loud voice exclaimed, "The *upravdom* (superintendent)." The Rebbe, realizing it was a ruse, stopped anyone from opening the door. "It's not the *upravdom*," he warned. "It's the GPU (secret police)."[3] A few moments later, two officials, followed by a contingent of armed men, burst into the dining room shouting, "We are representatives of the GPU. Who is Schneersohn and where is he?"

Tensions with the Yevesektzia had been rising for years. Their latest skirmish was over the Rebbe obstructing the conference of Russian Jewry.[4] On Purim, the Rebbe had publicly encouraged his Chasidim to resist the Yevesektzia. Since then, the Chasidim had noticed greater surveillance over the Rebbe's home. Still, the Yevesektzia hesitated. Global politics would set the stage for them to act.

Two months earlier, at the end of May, England severed diplomatic relations with Russia after discovering Russian spies in the United Kingdom.[5] The following week, international tensions rose again with the assassination of Russia's ambassador to Poland, Pyotr Voykov.[6] A Russian monarchist slayed Voykov at the Warsaw train station because of his involvement in killing Czar Nicholas. In response, Stalin unleashed a wave of oppression against his rivals, ordering the execution of former members of the nobility in Russia.[7] Historian Stephen Kotkin wrote that "Party organizations mobilized meetings at hundreds of factories to affirm the executions." Stalin empowered the GPU with "extrajudicial powers including the introduction of emergency tribunals to expedite cases." Among the targets of the crackdowns were members of the clergy. As the Rebbe wrote, "They struck out against religious leaders from all faiths, to take revenge for the assassination of their ambassador in Poland and for the expulsion from England."[8] The Yevesektzia seized the moment to go after their most fiery foe, the Rebbe.

Both arresting officers came from Chabad families who were familiar to the Rebbe.[9] One was Mikhail Nachmanson,[10] born in 1903 in the chasidic enclave of Nevel.[11] His father was a Chabad Chasid[12] who had visited Lubavitch. At the age of sixteen, Mikhail joined the Bolshevik party. He studied at Moscow's Sverdlov Communist University, where Lenin and Stalin lectured, and then law at Leningrad University. He rose in the Communist ranks, heading the regional departments of the secret police, the GPU, and its successor, the NKVD. In 1936, he was arrested for counterrevolutionary activity and sentenced to labor camp in the remote Kolyma region of Siberia.[13] Later in his life, he lived in Novgorod. Nachmanson told an interviewer in 1992, "Never, even in the most terrible days, did I separate myself from the party, still believing in it."[14] The second officer was Grigory Lulov,[15] born in Riga in 1899. He joined the secret police in 1919. At the end of 1938, he was arrested and shot by order of the Supreme Soviet.

Eliyahu Chaim Althaus describes the Rebbe's reaction to the intrusion.[16] "The Rebbe was still at the supper table when the officers arrived. Unruffled, and with a quiet smile, he remained seated. He quietly requested a cup of coffee and then some water for the ritual hand washing after the meal, and recited grace." He said grace slowly "so family members could cover incriminating documents with unimportant papers. Because of this, they did not discover information during the search that could be damaging."[17] Afterward, he rose from the table and retired to his study, where he calmly took his seat. Facing the armed men, the Rebbe remained composed, unimpressed by the show of force. "I don't know which Schneersohn you seek. If you enter someone's home, surely you know in advance who dwells there. This drama is pointless. Deliver your message and clearly state your wishes."[18]

Nachmanson ordered his assistant Lulov to join him in searching the premises. As for the Rebbe, he told him, "If you are able to continue eating, we won't disturb you," and he stationed one official in the dining room as the soldiers began conducting a thorough search of the house.

As this was unfolding, the Rebbe's future son-in-law, Rabbi Menachem Mendel Schneerson, and his daughter Chaya Mushka (known as Chaya Moussia) arrived at the Rebbe's apartment building. Seeing that the entire house was brightly lit, they understood that something was amiss. Chaya Mushka suggested that Rabbi Menachem Mendel wait outside, and if the GPU was present, she would open a particular window as a signal to him. Through the open window, one of the daughters called out, "Schneerson, guests have come to visit us!"[19]

Immediately he rushed to alert the Chasidim who were closest to the Rebbe, waking up Althaus and running to the home of Rabbi Chaim Lieberman, the Rebbe's secretary. Knocking on the window, they warned Lieberman to destroy any financial records and documents in his possession related to the secret school system. They feared the GPU would search his house next.[20]

In the Rebbe's apartment, Nachmanson continued his search, entering the room of the Rebbe's two younger daughters, Chaya Mushka and her younger sister Sheina. "Which party do you belong to?" he asked. They replied unabashedly, "We are members of our father's party, apolitical Jewish women who hold dear Jewish traditions and despise new trends." Sheina insisted that she was under no obligation to explain why this was the case. Nachmanson attempted to intimidate them. "You must consider the authority and power of the GPU that can force even the silent tongue to speak and tell what is hidden in the heart." Sheina retorted, "The entire tragedy is that you wish to accomplish everything by power and coercion, attempting to intimidate the intelligent and informed with the power of the fist and the threats of the gun."[21]

The search lasted an hour and a half. Having been informed earlier that he was at risk, the Rebbe had removed sensitive documents from his apartment,[22] giving them to Zalman Duchman.[23] Despite the long search, nothing incriminating was found. According to Duchman, the search in the Rebbe's home lasted longer than planned,[24] buying Lieberman extra time. Lieberman recalled, "Immediately I took all the mail that had been received, as well as whatever else might arouse their suspicions, and burned it all. The fire had not yet consumed everything when there was a knock on the door, and in walked the agents. As they entered, they looked at the fire and muttered to themselves, 'Everything is already burned.'" Still they arrested Lieberman.[25]

After the officers completed the search in the Rebbe's home, they requested that he sign a form indicating that the search had been conducted legally. The Rebbe refused, warning the officers, "I believe that the arrest will result in highly negative publicity, and you should proceed with caution until the truth is clarified – if you are actually seeking the truth. However, if you mean to conceal this error or libel with lies and falsehood, I am certain that you will regret it."[26] The Rebbe told them to call their superiors and share his warning, asking to be left under house arrest. They made the call, but the superior refused.[27]

The Rebbe's daughters pleaded with the officers not to arrest their father. Nachmanson threatened them, "If you speak one more word, you will be arrested too!" Chana, the oldest, stood up to him. "We speak in the language used by people who retain their humility, not in the tongue of those who have just emerged from the slime, unable to speak forthrightly and capable only of waving a revolver and threatening imprisonment." She begged Nachmanson to take her and her sisters instead of her father. She tried reasoning with him, pointing out that the Rebbe was physically weak. She asked that a doctor be consulted to see if he was well enough to go through such an ordeal. Finally, she exclaimed, "Surely you must have what the world calls ethics and decency!" and burst into tears. The Rebbe told her, "Only wishful thinking could imagine that pleas and tears could help."

The Rebbe demanded that be permitted to take his tefillin and books, and he told the officers that according to the law, he should be able to receive food directly from his family. Nachmanson agreed to the request, promising that no one would disturb him while he was praying, reading, and writing. "This very day you will return home," he added. "You will be asked a few questions by the director of the prison and then permitted to return home."

In all the commotion, the Rebbe's mother, Rebbetzin Shterna Sara, was awakened. She burst into tears and cried out, "Woe unto us, my dear departed husband! They are taking our son Yosef Yitzchak, your one and only son who sacrifices himself for others, who heeds your instruction with actual self-sacrifice. Bandits have come, slayers of innocent people. And for what purpose? Holy ancestors, they desire to extinguish your soul's flame!" She implored the officers to take her instead. Nachmanson, discomforted by her outburst, requested that the Rebbe take her to her room to calm her down. The Rebbe walked her back to her room, and they were soon joined by his wife, daughters, and the Rashag.

As they were leaving the apartment, the Rashag asked the Rebbe, "What should be done? Should we publicize the arrest, or perhaps it would be better to keep this quiet, not to provoke them with publicity?" The Rebbe said that at this point, he should use quiet diplomacy to try to gain his release. He requested that the Chasidim pray for his welfare at the graves of his ancestors.[28] "The priority above all else was to maintain the entire network of educational activities." Though the Rebbe was already under much financial strain, he told the Rashag, "If needed, borrow money to keep the programs running."

Later, the Rebbe recalled the moment in his diary: "My mother, wife, daughters, and son-in-law stood shocked, their faces white as plaster and their eyes filled with tears. At that moment, no words were to be found. They gazed at me with wonderment, hope and longing, mercy and supplication, not uttering a word."

While they were waiting for the vehicle that would take the Rebbe away, some of the Rebbe's personal belongings, including his tallit and tefillin, *sefarim*, and additional items, were packed in a travel bag that had belonged to the Rashab. Before they left the house, Lulov, who came from a Chabad family, offered to carry the Rebbe's bag. "My grandfather once carried your grandfather's bag," he said. "Chasidim remain Chasidim and I, too, will carry your belongings." The Rebbe clutched his bag and said, "Your grandfather was a Chasid of my grandfather, so he was privileged to carry those bags to the place of my grandfather's choosing. You, however, desire to carry it so that I should go to a destination of *your* choosing. This is not happening. I will not follow your way." With these words, the Rebbe took his bag and gave it to one of the guards to carry.

The Rebbe walked down the steps outside his house with the armed contingent surrounding him on all sides. Family members tried to escort the Rebbe and were rebuffed by a soldier. Finally, Nachmanson ordered the soldier to the side and the family escorted the Rebbe to the street. The Rebbe noticed a clock in a store window. It was 2:20 a.m.

The vehicle was surrounded by guards; one assisted the Rebbe with entering the vehicle. Nachmanson sat in the front of the car, and Lulov sat in the back opposite the Rebbe, brandishing a revolver. They began traveling to Shpalerka prison,[29] less than a mile away. "Chasidim were stationed on street corners acting like they were intoxicated so they could see where they would take the Rebbe," the Ramash said later.[30] On one corner the Rebbe noticed Eliyahu Althaus, quaking in fear, and nodded in his direction.

After a short drive, they arrived at the notorious six-story prison. The doors were locked, and Lulov and Nachmanson started banging on them. The guard peered through the eyehole but refused to open the door; the plan had been to bring the Rebbe before midnight, and now it was hours later. The Ramash explained, "The guard was changed at midnight, and the new one did not want to let them in." When they finally opened the door, Nachmanson told one of the guards, "Take this citizen to the investigating room." Nachmanson left hastily to join his friend Lulov. Afterward they went to arrest Lieberman. Says the Ramash, "This was the first miracle. In the meanwhile, there was time to destroy the incriminating documents."[31]

"If one is sentenced to be taken to Shpalerka," the Rebbe writes, "it is for one of two reasons. Either judgment has already been rendered, or it is for questioning – and particularly for [coerced] investigation." And so began the nineteen-day ordeal, which the Rebbe labeled "Tractate Gehinnom (purgatory)."

Intimidation tactics began immediately. While the Rebbe was still at the entrance of the prison, he asked for permission to pray with his tefillin. Nachmanson barked, "Forget that you are Schneersohn! You are now an ordinary person who is being punished!" Then, alluding to the Rebbe's refusal to bow to the Yevesektzia, he said, "Now you pay for everything." In Shpalerka, Nachmanson took on the personality of the prison. "This was a GPU official whose primary task was to frighten prisoners, confuse them, and render them submissive," the Rebbe wrote later. "I resolved to remain strong and not yield to fear, to speak clearly and to be unaffected by the intrigue in which they sought to immerse me."

Once inside the prison, instead of escorting the Rebbe, as Nachmanson had requested, the guard simply gestured with his finger that the Rebbe should walk down the length of the corridor till he reached a door that was ajar, telling him, "Once you reach it, turn to one of the recording secretaries, and she will give you a questionnaire that you will respond to in writing."

The Rebbe walked down a long narrow maze of dark, intimidating corridors lined with burly armed soldiers standing statue-like. It would be a wrong turn that saved the Rebbe from death now, for as he walked slowly, deep in thought, before approaching the open door that he had been told to find, he entered a second corridor with no guards. "I had been instructed to go forward to a door wide-open for all prisoners, and somehow I arrived here." The Rebbe understood that this was divine providence and decided not to hurry back. He sat down on a bench to rest.

In his diary, the Rebbe gives a window into his thoughts as he sat there, a new prisoner in a place designed to strike terror in the hearts of all who encountered it. He began thinking about what was going on in his home, picturing the anguish, concern, and confusion of his family, and the unknown fate of his sacred chasidic manuscripts and writings. "This vivid panorama made me emotional, and my eyes flowed with hot tears," wrote the Rebbe. But even in the most terrifying circumstances, with his life and the fate of his movement hanging in the balance, the Rebbe was able to compose himself, writing later:

> I felt the need to still this surge of thought. Like a flash of lightning there gleamed within my mind: And what of G-d? Who has done this? Who generated this entire sequence of events? Everything has its source in G-d. True, I am indeed a son, a husband, a father, a father-in-law, one who loves and is beloved. They are all dependent on me, but I – and they in turn – are dependent on G-d, who spoke and created the world. I have done all that I am capable of doing, and G-d will do according to His will, may He be blessed. At that moment, I emerged from the mire and constraints of my situation and ascended to transcendent spiritual heights, with thoughts beyond the confines of our finite, physical existence. I was bolstered by a pure faith and absolute trust in the living G-d, secure in the merit of my holy ancestors."

The Rebbe wrote that these thoughts "sustained my soul and strengthened me greatly. I was unconcerned with the present situation and sat in absolute peace."

The Rebbe continued reflecting on his situation: "I am a prisoner in Shpalerka – I do not know for what cause. In the interrogation room they will subject me to a barrage of questions, some normal inquiries for information and others startling and totally unanticipated. From my answers they will attempt to weave a net of false accusations or provide a match to ignite a blaze of revenge. I resolved to be strong and not yield to fear, to speak clearly and in no way to be affected by the intrigue in which they sought to enmesh me."[32]

While he was sitting there, the Rebbe was approached by an official who asked him what he was doing. The Rebbe replied, "I was brought here to answer some questions." The official, who was called Chimka, noted that it was a busy night at the prison, telling the Rebbe, "It's half past three, and they have already brought many people here tonight. I have been working four hours overtime."

He asked the Rebbe where he was from. "I come from a small city," he replied. "I don't know if you ever heard of it, but I was born in Lubavitch." Chimka knew it well, as he was from a town in the same region. "In Lubavitch there was the family of a saintly man," Chimka recalled. "They lived in a large courtyard close to the marketplace, and there was a well in their courtyard. I would go there to drink water, and we would bring our horses to drink too."

When the Rebbe told him which corridor he had come through, Chimka was incredulous. "From Chimka's astonishment I understood that the dark corridor through which Nachmanson had directed me to proceed to the administrative center was for serious offenders. Anyone led that way was obviously quite a criminal." Instead of going down the corridor that the guard had instructed the Rebbe to enter, Chimka led the Rebbe to the administrative office. There, he was given a number, "another step in the dehumanization process," he wrote. The Rebbe was now inmate number 26818.

He was asked to fill out a questionnaire. The Rebbe told the secretary, "I have nothing to write. I was taken here. My name is Schneersohn. I live at 22 Mochovaya Street. I will not write any answers." The confused secretary consulted with a supervisor, who attempted to convince the Rebbe to complete the questionnaire.

Finally, the Rebbe dictated to the secretary, "I am Rabbi Schneersohn, son of the celebrated Rebbe of Lubavitch, and I am preoccupied with religious study. Like all religiously observant Jews, I have no connection to politics." He told her where he was born, where he lived, his title, and where he studied. The secretary took down his statement word for word on the form, and the Rebbe signed it.

At 4:30 a.m., the secretary led the Rebbe through the corridors. "Twelve people were brought here tonight," she told him. "The majority are religious ministers: Russians, Lutherans, Germans, Poles, a Muslim, and one Jew. They were shot by a firing squad, without investigating them. We were just notified that we should record in writing that they were killed."[33] It was now apparent to the Rebbe that by not following Nachmanson's directions, he had miraculously evaded a summary execution.

She added, "You will definitely spend another few days in this fortress, and then they will investigate you." The secretary told one of the officers, "I brought *yarlik* 26818" and delivered the papers with the Rebbe's information. The officer pointed at a room and directed the Rebbe to wait there. The Rebbe demanded his personal belongings, including his tefillin. The official responded with rage, "We have no servants to concern themselves with the personal belongings of prisoners. What need do you have for your belongings? In your prison cell belongings are unnecessary. What exactly do you have there?"

"I have a bag that contains some of my necessities: tefillin, a tallit, a siddur, Psalms, and a thick green silk blanket. If you instruct one of the attendants to bring my bag, I will pay him for his efforts," replied the Rebbe. "Bourgeois customs!" exclaimed the enraged official. "Give them servants! The prisoners are too sick to carry their bags! It is forbidden to bring any kind of religious garments within the walls of the prison. In any event, the division head, in whose custody you will be placed, will confiscate all clerical garments and religious books. What difference will it make to you if they remain where they are now or in the storage chambers of the head prison official? Forget this nonsense. You must understand that you are a prisoner."

"During the two hours that I have been here," the Rebbe answered emphatically, "I have heard it repeated dozens of times that I am a prisoner. I do not know if I alone am a prisoner or if all the officials here are also prisoners. We are identical to each other. You are not allowed to move from your guard post. Just as I must obey prison discipline, similarly you must fulfill your obligations. Stop your abusive diatribes regarding religious matters that are holy to me. The law authorizes me to request my belongings, and it says that you must permit me to pray."

The Rebbe writes, "My emotional outburst had a strong enough effect to awaken the second official sitting there, and he stared at us with intense astonishment. With smoldering anger, he stroked his moustache and delved into the piles of paper resting on his desk." The Rebbe finally received his tefillin and marched to his cell. At every turn, officials and guards hurled graphic verbal abuse, describing the horrific acts they had done to others, with the goal of terrifying him. But the Rebbe maintained his composure. Walking down one hall, the Rebbe asked the accompanying officer for permission to pray, but to no avail. Realizing that he may not have another chance, the Rebbe began to lay tefillin as he walked behind the guard.

He had just barely finished donning the tefillin when the guard turned and saw what he had done. Enraged, he struck the Rebbe, pushing him down a ladder. "I realized that the metal buckle of my belt had broken and that it had apparently cut a gash into my stomach," the Rebbe wrote.

"My heart contracted with pain; I felt that in another instant I would faint." The tefillin were confiscated, but the Rebbe still had his tallit. By 6:00 a.m., the guard brought the Rebbe to his cell and pushed him inside. It contained three beds, all occupied. The Rebbe was told to sit on the floor until they decided to bring him a bed.

Later in the morning, when the prisoners were offered bread, the Rebbe demanded to speak with the prison warden. When one of the senior officers came to the cell, the Rebbe insisted that his tefillin be returned to him and also requested a visit from a doctor. The official told the Rebbe he could see a doctor no earlier than the next day, and concerning the tefillin: "Forget about that foolishness." The Rebbe responded by going on a hunger strike until his tefillin were returned.

The Chasidim gathered in the Rebbe's home early on the morning of the arrest, and by 10 a.m., the meeting moved to the Jewish Community Center. In attendance were representatives of every Jewish group except the Communists. They decided to concentrate their efforts within Russia. Tensions between Russia, Poland, and England caused them to fear that an international campaign might exacerbate the situation. Rebbetzin Nechama Dina, the Rebbe's wife, took the lead. As Althaus writes, "She decided every matter, great and small. All decisions were hers." The Rashag headed to Moscow to meet with Jewish leaders. Alter B. Metzger writes that in both Leningrad and Moscow, the Rebbe's followers "concurred that pressure from abroad might worsen the situation. If the capitalists were supporting the Rebbe, that would be even greater proof of the Rebbe's counterrevolutionary activities."[34]

On Thursday, two nights after the arrest, while the Rebbe was still fasting, the guards demanded that he remove his hat and hide his tzitzit. The Rebbe refused, telling them he was not frightened or intimidated by them. "The GPU can overcome the most obstinate person," they retorted. They brought him in for interrogation; Nachmanson, Lulov, and two others were waiting. Later the Rebbe described the scene: "The interrogators' hands rested on the weapons of destruction lying on the table, daggers in their eyes."

The setting was designed to terrorize, but the Rebbe was not intimidated. Instead, he began to tell a story of a *Maskil* (a proponent of the enlightenment) who suffered a serious illness that lasted for three months, prompting his repentance and return to observance. The message was clear to the Jewish interrogators. But instead of taking it to heart, they responded with anger, mocking the Rebbe.

The interrogator outlined the Rebbe's crimes: "You are abetting reactionary forces in the USSR and counterrevolution. You are a religious authority and rule over the Jews of the Soviet Union." He went on to accuse him of influencing Soviet Jewish intelligentsia and bourgeois Americans[35] by creating a network of Jewish educational and religious institutions and coercing religious Jews to support it, and by conducting foreign correspondence to strengthen religion in the Soviet Union, thereby opposing the Soviet government.

The Rebbe responded by saying, "Power and coercion are alien to the chasidic path. Among Chasidim, leadership implies spiritual stature that aspires to attain moral and spiritual excellence and to inspire others to follow that same path."[36] The Rebbe reminded his accusers that Soviet law does not ban the teaching of religion. The interrogation went on late into the night. As it ended, Lulov blurted out, "In twenty-four hours, you will be shot."[37]

Exhausted after fasting for seventy-two hours, the Rebbe returned to his cell. Finally, on Friday,[38] after two nights and three days, a Jewish guard brought him his tefillin and books. The Rebbe told the officer that he refused to eat the non-kosher meals provided by the prison, and he asked for food from home. The officer mocked him for his request, but just before sunset, three loaves of uncut challah from home were delivered to his cell.

The ominous news of the looming death sentence reached the Chasidim on Shabbat, and it spurred them to expand the campaign and take it out from behind the scenes. Telegrams were dispatched to Soviet President Mikhail Kalinin and Prime Minister Alexei Rykov. A delegation of Jewish leaders attempted to meet with the head of the GPU, Vyacheslav Menzhinsky, but they were rebuffed. Across the country, hundreds of thousands of Jews signed petitions for the Rebbe's release. Rabbis declared communal fasts on the Monday and Thursday following the Rebbe's arrest.[39] Jews filled synagogues for extra prayers. One Chasid remembered feeling that "we observed Yom Kippur twice in one week."

The news spread beyond the borders of Russia, sparking action. In Germany, the chief rabbi of Berlin, Dr. Meir Hildesheimer,[40] joined the city's Reform rabbi, Dr. Leo Baeck, to enlist the assistance of Dr. Oscar Cohn, a former member of the Reichstag, the German federal parliament. Hildesheimer met with the German foreign minister and then together they appealed to the Russian ambassador to Germany, who promised to do his utmost to help secure the Rebbe's release.

To the American Chasidim, the Rebbe's fate was unclear. Bits of unverified news drifted across the Atlantic, but details were sparse.[41] The Chasidim in New York[42] met to mobilize. They sent telegrams to government officials and Jewish organizations. Prominent New York attorney Sam Kramer[43] traveled to Washington, enlisting the help of Idaho Senator William Borah, among others.[44] There were some one hundred loosely connected Chabad congregations in America at the time,[45] "but many of the Chasidim had been living in the US for some years and did not understand the mortal danger the Rebbe was in," says Rabbi Yisrael Jacobson, the head of Chabad's US organization. "Nor did they feel the sense of *gevalt* (panic and crisis) that the Chasidim in Russia were experiencing."[46]

The Rebbe's oldest daughter, Chana, sent a telegram with just two Yiddish words, "*Tatte arestirt* – Father was arrested" to Rabbi Dovid Meir Rabinowitz[47] in Boston. He was a devoted Chabad Chasid who had immigrated to the US in 1896. One of his sons, Asher, was employed by the IRS in Boston, and another son, Peretz, was an attorney in nearby Springfield. Rabbi Rabinowitz directed Asher to take the train to Washington to lobby government officials to intercede on behalf of the Rebbe, and he told Peretz to go him when the train stopped at the Springfield station.[48]

Asher's work for the IRS had brought him to the nation's capital many times; he was familiar with the political landscape. The brothers decided to seek the help of the most influential Jew at the time, Justice Louis Brandeis, who had been appointed to the Supreme Court eleven years earlier. The brothers tried to arrange an appointment but were told to return in another month, after the court's session had ended. As they left the office, Justice Brandeis, who apparently knew Asher, spotted them in the hallway and asked why they were there. They informed him of the Rebbe's arrest by the Soviets on charges of counterrevolutionary activity. Brandeis said he wanted to help, calling the Rebbe "the prince of Israel."[49] Apparently, Brandeis acted behind the scenes. Within a few days, the Russians received a strongly worded protest from the US government concerning the Rebbe's arrest.[50]

With the threat of a death sentence hanging over the Rebbe's head, and little news from the prison, the Chasidim grew more anxious. The Rashag sent one of the Rebbe's close Chasidim, Michoel Dvorkin, to Nevel[51] to recruit the father of Mikhail Nachmanson, who had jailed the Rebbe. They asked him to travel to Leningrad to learn the Rebbe's fate, but the elder Nachmanson was reluctant, arguing that his relationship with his son was frayed. Pressured by the local chasidic elder, Rabbi Zalman Moshe Yitzchaki, Nachmanson finally assented and reached out to his son for a meeting. Mikhail feared that being seen in public with his religiously dressed father would put him in jeopardy, so he arranged a clandestine encounter. The father sat on a bench in a public park while his son, not even acknowledging his presence, walked by and muttered two words in Yiddish: "*Er lebt* – He is alive."[52]

According to the GPU file recovered after the fall of the Soviet Union, the questioning continued for days. On June 21, the Rebbe was again interrogated. He stood firm, insisting that he was a rabbi before and after the revolution, a teacher of chasidic philosophy, and never involved in politics. When asked about the conference for Russian Jewry being organized by the Leningrad community, the Rebbe responded that he was against it. A few days later, on Shabbat, June 25, a postcard from the Rebbe was delivered to his home. He had been beaten repeatedly and was suffering excruciating pain. Despite it all, his message was upbeat. "I am well and feel good," he wrote. The Rebbe asked his family to send him *sefarim*, including *Likkutei Torah* and a *Chumash Bemidbar*.

The Chasidim were successful in enlisting the help of the head of the Russian Red Cross, prominent human rights activist Madam Yekaterina Peshkova.[53] She was the ex-wife of writer Maxim Gorky, a supporter of Lenin, and later Stalin. The international uproar when the Russian position on the world stage was tenuous, together with the grassroots lobbying and influence of Madam Peshkova, caused the GPU to rescind the

Rebbe's death sentence. But he was still in dire straits. The GPU decided to exile him for ten years to the isolated Solovki Islands[54] located in the remote northern White Sea. On Wednesday, June 29, a government official informed Rabbi Althaus that the Rebbe's death sentence had been commuted and replaced with exile to the Solovki Islands. He was told that the family should bring him food and say goodbye. The Rebbe's family came to the prison to see him off. Word of his exile spread quickly, and a crowd gathered outside the prison.

While the crowd waited outside, the Rebbe was called for his third interrogation. New accusations were added. Lulov continued to bully the Rebbe for the next few hours, to no avail. Finally, Lulov told the Rebbe that he would suffer greatly in exile. "You can save yourself from this punishment if you issue a proclamation saying you regret your anti-conference position. Give your blessing to the conference and you will walk out of here momentarily." The Rebbe resolutely rejected his demand. "I have no regrets," he said. "You can threaten me with serious punishments, but they will not influence my decision."[55]

In the meantime, Madam Peshkova stepped up her efforts and successfully pressured the GPU to overturn its decree. Instead of being sent to the remote Solovki Islands, the Rebbe was sentenced to a three-year exile in Kostroma, a city on the Volga River.

The next day, Thursday, guards came to the Rebbe's cell and ordered him to stand to hear his sentence. He refused and was severely beaten. They returned two more times, and each time the Rebbe refused to adhere to their orders and was beaten. Finally, the guards took him to an office, where Lulov informed him that he would be released from prison and exiled for three years to Kostroma. On the desk the Rebbe noticed a document from his file. First it had been marked "Death by firing squad." That was crossed out and replaced with "Ten years in Solovki," but that too was crossed out. The third line read "Three years in Kostroma."[56] When the Chasidim heard the news, Rabbi Michoel Dvorkin immediately traveled to Kostroma to prepare for the Rebbe's arrival.[57]

Kostroma is more than five hundred miles southeast of Leningrad and was then home to a tiny Jewish community.[58] The Rebbe was told that he would be freed that very day, and he would be able to spend six hours with his family; that night he was to commence his journey to

Kostroma. The train leaving Thursday evening would arrive in Kostroma on Shabbat, forcing the Rebbe to desecrate the holy day. The Rebbe realized their intentions and much to the shock of his jailers, he refused to leave the jail until the conclusion of Shabbat.[59]

When the Chasidim became aware of the new obstacle, they rushed to Madam Peshkova and asked her to intervene. She met with Soviet Premier Alexei Rykov, who called Vyacheslav Menzhinsky, head of the secret police, who agreed to let the Rebbe remain in prison until Sunday morning, after which the authorities permitted him a short visit home.[60]

On Sunday,[61] after nineteen days of imprisonment, the Rebbe was permitted to return home for a six-hour visit. Two of his Chasidim, Zalman Duchman and Yitzchak Minkowitz, met the Rebbe in his apartment. The Rebbe asked them if they had studied *Chasidut* while he was in prison. "We recited psalms," they answered. The Rebbe told them, "I wrote *maamarim* until they took away my pencil." Inmates were given paper to roll their own cigarettes, and the Rebbe used his to write down chasidic discourses. Now he asked Duchman and Minkowitz "to please transcribe them."[62]

At eight in the evening, he was to take the train to Kostroma. After seeing his family, the Rebbe headed to the Leningrad station for the long ride.[63]

At dusk, the Rebbe arrived at the station accompanied by his mother and his wife, and escorted by agents of the GPU and a cadre of soldiers. The station was filled with people who had gathered there, despite the danger, to bid farewell. Authorities stopped all ticket sales to prevent Chasidim from joining the Rebbe on the train. "No one discussed their plans to go to the station beforehand, since they all feared arrest," Rabbi Mendel Meisel, who was there, told his grandson Avraham Zajac years later.[64] "Nonetheless, thousands came out of their concern for the Rebbe."

The Jews of Leningrad arranged themselves like an honor guard in two rows, and the Rebbe walked between them toward the train.[65] Ignoring the guards surrounding him, the Rebbe rose on the platform and gave a defiant speech to the assembled. He began by speaking of the state of Jews in the Diaspora:

> This, all the nations of the world must know: Only our bodies were sent into exile and subjugated to alien rule; our souls were not given over into captivity and foreign rule. We must proclaim openly and before all that any matter affecting the Jewish religion, the Torah and its mitzvot and customs, is not subject to the coercion of others. No one can impose his belief upon us, nor coerce us to conduct ourselves contrary to our beliefs.[66]

The Rebbe was accompanied on his journey to Kostroma by his unmarried daughter Chaya Mussia, his son-in-law Rabbi Gurary, and Rabbi Eliyahu Althaus. Rabbi Dvorkin arrived Sunday night and started preparing for the Rebbe's arrival. He repaired the local *mikveh* and opened a *cheder* for the children of the one hundred members of the local Jewish community; he also arranged housing for the Rebbe and his entourage at the home of the town *shochet*.

Roza Melamed was just twelve years old when her parents hosted the Rebbe in their home in Kostroma.[67] Her father, Yerachmiel Kugel, was the local *shochet*. The town's small wooden synagogue, built in 1907, had been closed, so their large home became the synagogue. "We had thirteen Torah scrolls housed there and many books," she remembered. "The Rebbe was an exceptionally good and kind person, with a kind soul. He really had something holy about him." She recalled him constantly studying Torah and asking the children every day how they were doing. He blessed the family with good health and "that we should never come to know the suffering he had endured. When he spoke about what he had lived through, our hair stood on end."[68]

The Jews of Kostroma flocked to the Kugel home to see the Rebbe. Despite being weakened by his ordeal in prison, "the Rebbe received anyone who wished to see him." Melamed recalled how the local watchmaker, Zelig Alekseyevich Rosenson, climbed the fence just to catch a glimpse of the Rebbe. He was awestruck by the Rebbe's appearance, telling Roza, "I don't have the right to even look upon his holy face."

The welcome from local GPU officials was much more hostile. When the Rebbe reported to them the morning after his arrival, the official harshly told him, "You are a criminal receiving punishment for your activities against the Soviet government. Remember that." The Rebbe was ordered to make a weekly appearance every Tuesday and forbidden from leaving the city.

The Chasidim continued their efforts to free the Rebbe from exile. A group in Moscow led by Madam Peshkova met with Soviet officials, who had been inundated with telegrams and messages from around the world. The head of the GPU in Leningrad, Jewish Communist Stanislav Messing,[69] opposed the Rebbe's release. At the same time that the Rebbe was arrested, other religious leaders had been detained. Messing told the delegation from Moscow, "If liberty is granted to the Rebbe, people will clamor that this entire matter is under Jewish control." He threatened to countermand any order from Moscow to release the Rebbe and to arrest him again if he came back to Leningrad.

Finally, the efforts of Madam Peshkova, coupled with the international outcry, succeeded. On Tuesday, July 12, 1927 (12 Tamuz), the Rebbe appeared for his weekly visit to the GPU headquarters in Kostroma only to be informed by the officer on duty that it was a local holiday, and the station was closed. The Rebbe asked them to note the fact that he had come as required. Another officer overheard the conversation and told the Rebbe, "We received papers that you are being freed." Rabbi Eliyahu Althaus, who was accompanying the Rebbe, was incredulous. "Are you playing with us?" he asked. To which the officer retorted, "With us there are no jokes."[70]

The telegram from Moscow granting freedom to the Rebbe was received that day; the formal document was issued the next day.[71] Chaya Moussia called the family in Leningrad and shared the news of the release, telling her older sister Chana, "We are coming for Shabbat – *bli pirsum* [it should not be publicized]."[72] In remote Kostroma, the local Jews gathered to celebrate, and to mark the day, the Rebbe taught a *maamar*.[73]

The entire Kostroma community came out to bid farewell to the Rebbe. "They gave him a grand escort," remembered Melamed. Two days later,[74] the Rebbe arrived in Leningrad, despite concerns that he could be arrested once again. News of the Rebbe's liberation could not be suppressed, and it spread quickly to Jewish communities across the Soviet Union. Rabbi Yehuda Chitrik recalled the celebration in his hometown of Kharkiv, Ukraine: "Rabbi Hillel Levin in Kharkiv received a telegram with the good tidings. Messengers spread all over town to share the news. Within hours, Chasidim had gathered in the home of Rabbi Aharon Tomarkin to celebrate. The celebration continued the next day."[75]

Even with all the pain and suffering he had endured, the Rebbe saw his imprisonment as something of a test from above. He reflected on its significance:

> Divine providence sometimes arranges special periods that change a person's character, developing his abilities and giving him a lofty perspective from which he can behold the ultimate purpose of human life on this earth. A person's spiritual progress and the development of his abilities are affected most strongly by a period rich in suffering and persecution for his diligent and passionate work for an ideal, and especially when one is struggling with and battling his persecutors and oppressors for the survival and strengthening of his religion.

He noted the exact duration of the imprisonment: eighteen days, eleven hours, and fifteen minutes.

> Considering the great spiritual value that came in its wake, it is appropriate not just to mark the days and nights, but also the hours and minutes [of arrest and imprisonment], for every hour and moment of suffering, mortification, and affliction brings tremendous reward and infinite fortitude of mind – even a weak person is transformed into the mightiest of the mighty.[76]

A year after his release, the Rebbe explained in a public letter that his release was a "festival of liberation for those who love the Torah and observe its commands, and so too for all those who merely bear the name 'Jew,' for the heart of every man of Israel [irrespective of his particular level of observance of the mitzvot] is perfectly bound with G-d and His Torah."[77] Since then, the twelfth of Tamuz is celebrated annually in Jewish communities across the world.

Stung by Moscow's overruling of its plans to end the Rebbe's life, the Yevesektzia still had its eyes on him. Only a small number of Chasidim joined the Rebbe for services on his first Shabbat back in Leningrad, during which he recited the *HaGomel* blessing[78] said after one's release from prison. A few days later, the Yevesektzia paper, *Der Emes,* demanded the Rebbe be exiled to Siberia. Clearly, remaining in Leningrad was not an option, though the Rebbe was at risk anywhere in Russia. To step away from the public eye, the Rebbe relocated to Malakhovka, a small town outside Moscow, and instructed the Chasidim to restrict their visits.

If the Rebbe remained in Russia, imprisonment or even death were real risks, but leaving Russia was a difficult step to take. The Rebbe felt personal responsibility for Russian Jewry, and the country had been the center of Chasidism for two centuries.[79] As one of the Rebbe's confidants, Rabbi Yechezkel Feigin,[80] wrote to Chabad supporters in America, the danger to the Rebbe's life was serious and "miracles do not happen every day. We must make every effort to prevent further sickness [code for prison], from which he might not return." Rabbi Althaus echoed those same anxieties ten days after the Rebbe's release. "The dread that we experienced in the past continues to hover over us in the days ahead, for who knows what each new day will bring?"[81]

As the High Holidays neared, the Rebbe pondered the idea of leaving Russia. He made his final decision after embarking on a spiritual pilgrimage to pray at the grave of his father, the Rebbe Rashab, in Rostov.[82] Though he resolved to depart, it was not done willingly. "I was forced to leave Russia," he later wrote. "My heart and soul are with the *anash* and *temimim* in our country."[83]

The Russians refused to grant the Rebbe an exit visa – even Madam Peshkova's intercession with the Russian government encountered strong opposition. Nor had any country agreed to provide a haven for the Rebbe. In addition, funds were needed to relocate the Rebbe and his family, and in Russia there was no way to secure the funds. The money would have to come from overseas.

Nearby Latvia would be the key to the Rebbe's freedom.[84] The Riga Jewish community formally invited[85] the Rebbe to become its chief rabbi. Mordechai Dubin,[86] a member of the Latvian Parliament and a Chabad Chasid, presented the letter to the Russian officials, who rejected the request. At the same time, Dr. Oscar Cohn, who had served as an attorney to the Soviet Legation in Germany, presented an invitation to

Russian officials on behalf of the Frankfurt Jewish community, asking the Rebbe to assume a post there.[87]

A friendship and commerce treaty between Russia and Latvia had been signed but still needed to be ratified by the Latvian Parliament. The agreement was important to Russia, which was still diplomatically isolated, as England had cut off ties after discovering Russian espionage, and US diplomatic recognition would not come until 1933. According to Chassidic historian Dovid Margolin the Soviets were threatened by Baltic states, "A trade deal with the Latvians, was a step towards peeling them away from the West, which was the Russians' main objective.[88] Dubin's swing vote in the parliament was crucial to the agreement, and he was able to hold it up – unless Russia permitted the Rebbe to leave. With the trade agreement at risk and international pressure mounting, the Russians capitulated.

The Russian government granted exit visas to the Rebbe and his close family. But the Rebbe demanded that other key Chasidim also be permitted to leave, including his future son-in-law, the Ramash.[89] The Rebbe also insisted that his priceless library, which included many original manuscripts, historical documents, and intellectual treasures, accompany him.[90] "It represented the historical legacy of Chabad," says Professor Michael Berenbaum of the American Jewish University.[91] Government bureaucrats initially opposed both requests, but after intensive lobbying, they relented.

The last holiday the Rebbe celebrated with his Chasidim in Russia was Simchat Torah in October 1927. It was the final opportunity for Russian Chasidim to see the Rebbe, and despite the risk of arrest, Chasidim flocked to Leningrad. Zalman Bronstein recalls, "We all wanted to see the Rebbe before he left. The synagogue, whose normal capacity was six hundred, swelled with Chasidim who packed the room. Chasidim were pushed into every corner, everyone sweltering from the overcrowding." This last visit was deeply emotional. "It was difficult for the Chasidim to separate from the Rebbe and difficult for the Rebbe to separate from his children, his beloved Chasidim."[92]

During the holiday, the Rebbe urged his Chasidim, "Don't fear anyone. Each of you should seek to influence those in your community. As the Talmud says, a person who teaches Torah to a child is considered the child's own parent." The Chasidim and the Rebbe cried, sang, and inspired each other throughout the holiday. "I will be with you," the Rebbe consoled the crowd. Summing up the feelings of many, one Chasid, Rabbi Meir Simcha Chein, broke out in tears at the last *farbrengen* saying, "The Rebbe is going, and we are left here."[93]

Zalman Duchman was at the packed train station. "The platform was black from the crowd – hundreds and hundreds of people," he wrote. Dvorah Konikov, then a young girl, was brought by her parents to see the Rebbe off. Her mother lifted her up and told her in Yiddish, "*Kuk* – Look!" She caught a glimpse of the Rebbe. "I remember his fiery reddish beard," she says.[94] Police officers had to make way for the Rebbe to get to the train. "This was the toughest moment. We all knew that the Rebbe was leaving us, and we wondered when we would see him again," remembers Yaakov Abisov. His father turned to the Rebbe in a broken voice and begged, "Bless me!" The Rebbe turned around, looking intently at Yaakov's father, and said, "Your children should remain Jews."[95]

Standing on the steps of the train, the Rebbe's anguish was palpable as he turned to his Chasidim and blessed them one more time. Rabbi Dovid Chein heard his last words. "Whoever wants a bond with me will not make any compromises," he said. "It will be very difficult, but that is the condition." Those words, Chein says, left a lasting impression on his father Yehuda, who was faced with many challenges in the coming years. Whenever it became difficult, he would say, "The Rebbe told me that whoever wants to be united with him should not make any compromises. I do not want to be separated from the Rebbe."

Zalman Duchman describes the last moments of the Rebbe's departure: "When the train started moving, it was going very slowly, and all the people were walking after the train. Then the train started going faster and the whole crowd started running. We ran alongside the train. Everybody at the station was crying – you could see the tears falling, and not one dry eye."[96] As the train pulled away from the station, the Chasidim sang together the melody "The *Beinoni*."[97]

Many Chasidim purchased tickets to travel with the Rebbe until the last station before the border. At a number of stations along the route, crowds gathered to bid farewell, and many boarded the train. As it drew closer to the Russian border, the cars rang with the sound of chasidic melodies marking the Russian Chasidim's last moments with the Rebbe.

While the Rebbe was making his way to Riga, Rabbi Yisrael Jacobson was camped out in the offices of the Kramer brothers in New York. He had been pleading with them to wire $4,000 (the equivalent of $60,000 today) to Mordechai Dubin in Riga. The Rebbe's relocation had been expensive, pressing debts lingered from his incarceration, and the operation of the underground educational system in Russia required ongoing support. In New York, Rabbi Eliyahu Simpson[98] had secured some funding, but more was needed. The Kramers, Chaim Zalman and Avraham Dov, were strong supporters of the Rebbe, but Jacobson's demands were high. At first, they agreed to send one thousand dollars, then another five hundred. They told Jacobson, "Let's wait until Monday to deal with this. It's Friday, and Shabbat is soon." Jacobson was deeply troubled, as Dubin had wired a message saying that the situation was critical. "It pained my heart. I turned to them and said, 'I am not leaving until you wire the money.'" At first they brushed him off, but when they realized that Jacobson was serious, they agreed and wired the funds.[99]

In the years to come, it would become clear that the Rebbe's seven-year ordeal under the Communist regime was but one chapter in their conflict. He continued to orchestrate and support the spiritual resistance in the decades that followed, and the battle he waged had far-reaching historical repercussions both in the Soviet Union and beyond. The clandestine system started by the Rebbe Rayatz in the early 1920s endured, despite the harassment, imprisonment, and even execution of many key activists.

In 1946, the network orchestrated the audacious escape of one thousand Chasidim across the border to Poland on false passports.[100] They and their children provided the leadership necessary to create a global Jewish renaissance, and they were an inspiration to a new generation of Chasidim growing up in the postwar era.

In 1949, future Prime Minister Golda Meir encountered the underground when she was appointed Israel's first ambassador to Russia. Meir was far from religious but felt that as a representative of Israel, it was appropriate to attend services for the High Holidays. On the first day of Rosh HaShanah, she went to Moscow's Choral Synagogue, finding only a small group of elderly Jews gathered. Disappointed, she wondered if she should return the next day. She decided to go, and as she drew near the synagogue, she was surprised to be welcomed by thousands of Jews filling the streets. Years later, she told Italian reporter Oriana Fallaci, "It was Chabad that orchestrated the welcome of thousands."[101]

Israeli Prime Minister Yitzchak Shamir discovered the network a few years after Meir. In his keynote address at a Tel Aviv memorial service for the seventh Lubavitcher Rebbe in 1994, he recalled visiting Russia in the early 1950s, when he was an operative for Israel's spy agency, the Mossad.[102] Israel had decided to reach out to Jewish communities in the Soviet Union and, using diplomatic cover, agents were dispatched to the Israeli embassy in Moscow to connect with them.[103] Shamir said, "We were surprised to discover that in every city across Russia, there was an existing clandestine Jewish network being directed by the [seventh] Rebbe in New York." Shamir's discovery evolved into a clandestine partnership between the Mossad and the Rebbe's network in Russia.

The network surreptitiously imported aid packages that included food and other goods that could be sold on the black market. Religious items, such as matzah for Passover, tefillin, Jewish books, and ink for writing Torah scrolls, were in high demand.[104] Starting in the 1960s, when tourism from the West became possible, rabbis, educators, and businesspeople were sent from abroad to secretly connect with, inspire, and educate Jews in Russia. They brought with them goods to be sold, sustaining families who lost their source of income because they had applied for exit visas.[105]

The underground was instrumental in nurturing the Russian Jewish renaissance that was triggered by Israel's victory in the Six-Day War in 1967. Inspired by the victory, young Russian Jews began to explore their heritage. Many of those seeking greater knowledge became students of Chabad rabbis, who were still educating the youth after decades of harassment. One of those young people was Yuli Edelstein, later speaker of the Israeli Knesset. As a young man in Russia, he began to explore his Jewish identity, eventually himself becoming a Hebrew teacher, for which he was sentenced on false charges to a Siberian prison camp for three years. Speaking at the International Conference of Chabad-Lubavitch Shluchim in 2015, he paid tribute to the Chabad underground in Moscow led by Rabbi Getche Vilensky and Rabbi Mottel Lipshitz, who was then the city's only *shochet* and *mohel.* "They were my inspiration on my journey to Jewish observance," Edelstein said.[106]

As Jews began leaving Russia in the 1970s, Russian Chabad activists who had been raised in Russia and educated secretly there moved to the West and created new Jewish centers for Russian immigrants.[107]

With the fall of the Soviet Union, the network emerged from the shadows. Starting in 1990, the seventh Rebbe (who was living in New York) dispatched a series of young rabbis and rebbetzins to rekindle Jewish life in Russia. They linked up with the activists on the ground, who had been operating clandestinely for decades. That year, the first public menorah lighting took place in Moscow's Red Square. In the coming years, Chabad rabbis reclaimed historic synagogues in cities across Russia, opened schools, set up social service and cultural centers, and recreated the glory of Jewish life that had existed for centuries in Russia. Today, Chabad is the premier force in Jewish life in the former Soviet Union.[108]

This fulfilled the prediction of the Rebbe Rashab that the Rayatz recorded in his diary in 1926:[109] There would be a period of "dark clouds," but Judaism would survive. "Three weeks before his passing, my father called me into his study and said, 'There will be difficult times; you will need to have *mesirat nefesh bepoel* (actual self-sacrifice). But eventually, the Communist government will disintegrate.'"[110]

Chapter Five

Exile to Riga

The train from Russia crossed into Latvia two days after Simchat Torah.[1] The boisterous send-off from Leningrad didn't assuage the heartbreak the Rebbe felt. On the train, he composed a letter to the Chasidim, writing, "The essential connection between us cannot be broken, nor does the fact that distance stands between us break that bond."[2] A few weeks later, the Rebbe shared his feelings in a poignant letter[3] about his departure. "I am parting from beloved friends, and who knows when we will see each other again and where I will go with my staff and suitcase." He wrote that thousands had filled the station, "full of emotion," surging in the direction of the train. "In amazement, I stood in the train gazing through the window." He uttered a prayer to himself: "Hashem, have mercy on Your flock, and bless their families and children. I should merit to see them with joy. Amen, Amen." The Rebbe passed the night on the train. "Eighteen hours with anguish in the heart, pain in the soul, the darkness of the night, the ringing of the wheels of the train only adding to the sense of sadness."

His spirits were lifted when just an hour from Riga, the train paused at a station, where Chasidim boarded the train for the last leg of the trip.

"Suddenly I heard a loud noise – a large crowd had gathered, singing with joy." The Latvian Chasidim had been prevented by war and revolution from visiting the Rebbe. "This was the first time we had seen each other in fourteen years." They began to sing a boisterous song, the same joyous melody Chasidim sang thirty years earlier as they escorted the Rebbe from his *chuppah* in Lubavitch. An hour later they pulled into Riga.[4] "Thousands, with no division of party, status, or type, came to see the refugees." In the train station and the large plaza outside, the Rebbe and his family slowly navigated the crowd. "We could not move. Finally, with difficulty, a way was made for us to travel to the hotel."

The Rebbe and his family were welcomed to Riga's tree-lined streets, aesthetically pleasing architecture, and relatively mild climate. After a stay in the hotel, they moved into an apartment in an upscale Jewish area, where a beautiful green park enhanced the end of the street. But the pleasant surroundings did not assuage the Rebbe's grief and sense of loss. As he wrote, "I desire to live in our country of Russia, where people are putting their lives on the line for Torah and observance in the midst of deprivation."

The Rebbe had suffered terribly in Russia. "His body was broken," says chasidic historian Menachem Zigelbaum, "but it didn't stop him from getting to work uplifting the Jewish community and spreading Judaism and chasidic teachings in Western Europe." Zigelbaum notes that the Rebbe started from scratch three times in his life: "first after the passing of his father in 1920, then when he arrived in Riga in 1927, and then again when he came to the US in 1940."[5]

Latvia was a waystation; on the Rebbe's new stationary, "Riga" was followed by the word "temporary." "I fled the bad, but I have not yet found the good," wrote the Rebbe about living in Riga.[6] "I was driven from my country and forced to separate from my beloved brothers and friends." Permanence and stability would continue to be elusive. "The Rebbe resided in Riga for six years and during that extended time, no decision was made on his permanent place of residence," wrote chasidic historian Rabbi Sholom Ber Levin.[7] While Riga was his base, the Rebbe spent much time traveling. Some trips were designed to inspire communities, others to meet with Jewish leaders to help Russian Jewry. He spent extended periods of time in Berlin, Vienna, Paris, and the spas of Marienbad to heal his chronic health problems.[8] In 1929, he made a yearlong trek to *Eretz Yisrael* and America. Even his family celebrations were not held in Riga. The wedding of the Rebbe's daughter Chaya Mushka was held in Warsaw, Poland, and the wedding of her younger sister Sheina was in Landwarow, Poland, near the Lithuanian border.

Six years after arriving in Latvia, the Rebbe relocated to Poland. But Poland too would only provide a home for a few years, until the outbreak of World War II compelled the Rebbe to escape to New York. It was only there that the wandering ended, with the Rebbe establishing Chabad's permanent base in the iconic Gothic-style building at 770 Eastern Parkway. He lived there for the last decade of his life, until his passing in 1950.

Latvia was home to eighty thousand Jews, with about half living in Riga. In 1918, the Latvians overthrew Russian rule and became independent.[9] Jews were active in politics, fielding parties in parliamentary elections. In an election held a few months after the Rebbe's arrival, Latvian Jews earned six seats in the country's parliament, divided between the religious parties,[10] the Zionists, and their mutual ideological foe, the socialist Bund.

One of the prominent Jewish members of parliament was Rabbi Mordechai Dubin. A devoted Chasid of the Rebbe, he was arguably the most important Jewish leader in Riga, being the chair of the Latvian branch of Agudath Israel[11] and a city council member. Because of the fractious nature of Latvian politics, Dubin's party sometimes cast the crucial swing vote, giving him great influence in political affairs. Dubin was also the chairman of the *kehillah*, the official government-recognized Jewish community, and he was well respected by all. Dubin helped everyone, even his ideological opponents. When (Zeev) Latski Bertoldi, editor of the anti religious newspaper Frimorgen asked him to help jailed Soviet writer David Bergelson, Dubin used all his connections to free him. Says Dovid Margolin "Latski-Bertoli had on a daily basis attacked Dubin in his newspaper, now the conversation was about saving a fellow Jew and all arguments and differences faded away."[12]

In Latvia, the Rebbe faced a new task: recreating the ethos and spirit of Lubavitch in a Western country where Jews had freedoms and rights. At the same time, he cared for the millions of Jews in Communist Russia.

Latvia was the bridge between Russia to the east and Germany and France to the west, straddling both worlds. It was in cosmopolitan Riga, then part of Imperial Russia, that Max Lilienthal, an adherent of the German Haskalah (secular Enlightenment) movement, established the first German-style Jewish secular school after arriving there in 1839.[13] From that beachhead, he attempted to transform Jewish education throughout Russia. By the time the Rebbe arrived, the influence of the Enlightenment in Riga was considerable. Most Jewish children attended secular-oriented Jewish schools, many of them using Yiddish for instruction. Some were students of the Derech Eretz School,[14] an Orthodox school that taught both religious and secular subjects, established by Rabbi Dubin.

Riga could not compare to the main centers of Jewish life in Poland and Lithuania. The Jewish European mecca was Warsaw, four hundred miles from Riga, home to 350,000 Jews. Warsaw boasted great Jewish scholars, a thriving Jewish culture, a vibrant chasidic life, Zionist activities, Yiddish and Hebrew theaters, and a variety of Jewish newspapers. According to a 1930 census, there were twenty yeshivas, five religious high schools, and 175 Jewish schools of divergent philosophies located there.[15] Not far from Warsaw resided the great chasidic courts of Belz, Gur, Novominsk, Radomsk, and others. Poland was also home to renowned yeshivas in cities like Lublin and Radom. It possessed towering spiritual leaders such as Rabbis Yisrael Meir Kagan (the Chafetz Chaim), Menachem Ziemba, and Meir Shapiro. Nearby Lithuania had historically been a center of Jewish scholarship. Vilna boasted many prominent yeshivas, over one hundred synagogues, and one of the most influential rabbinic figures of the era, Rabbi Chaim Ozer Grodzinski.[16]

While Riga had outstanding rabbis, the city had never hosted a Jewish leader of the Rebbe's stature. His arrival caused a stir, and local Yiddish papers avidly reported on his activities, travels, pronouncements, and even health updates. But the Rebbe wasn't just a local story. The Detroit *Jewish Chronicle* reported, "The Lubavitcher Rebbe had brought a great deal of activity into the life of Orthodox Jewry in Latvia. And Soviet Russia has thus, by expelling the Lubavitcher Rebbe, done a good turn to the Jews of Latvia."[17]

Latvia was not Russia, where Chabad had deep roots, and Riga was not the chasidic hub that the town of Lubavitch had been for over a century. There had been a modest Chabad community in Riga since 1878, enhanced by recent emigration from Russia; a few Chabad synagogues dotted the city.[18] But there was no yeshivah to bring a youthful spirit to the city. It was a far cry from what Lubavitch had once been, with its outstanding yeshivah and vibrant community. Lubavitch was an oasis of sanctity, a place to set aside the difficulties of the austere realities of czarist Russia and experience spiritual renewal. Riga was geographically cut off from the Russian Chasidim, who could not cross the border. There were small chasidic clusters in Poland and Lithuania, but few could travel due to financial constraints and visa restrictions.

The Rebbe's first home in Riga was a local hotel. The *Grodner Moment*, a Polish Yiddish newspaper, reported on the Rebbe's efforts to reestablish the chasidic flavor of Lubavitch in Riga: "The Rebbe sits day and night in a room designated for prayer and learning." His mornings were occupied by prayer, and in the afternoons he received visitors. "All types of Jews, traditional Jews, old-fashioned Jewish women, modern Jews – all come to the Rebbe. One for advice, another for business guidance, personal crisis, or communal affairs. One comes for a blessing, another for personal issues. The Rebbe deals with all of them and finds salvation for the plagued moods and depressed hearts." Large crowds continually flocked to the hotel. "The corridors of the hotel are packed with masses of people. They wait there to have an audience with the Rebbe."

On Shabbat, the paper reported, "the hotel loses its mundane weekday state." On Shabbat afternoons, "people flood the hotel" to hear the Rebbe recite a *maamar.* "His voice becomes stronger and more flowing, words are streaming from his mouth, quotes from the Bible, Talmud, and Zohar woven and seasoned with parables, ideas, and interpretations."[19]

"With the Rebbe's arrival in Riga, a new era for Chabad Chasidism began. It roots were in Russia, and it had been displaced from its natural home with its tradition of a century and a half; it was transplanted in a new country," writes chasidic scholar Rabbi Nachum Greenwald.[20] "It was a major crisis for a chasidic community to be forcibly moved in brutal fashion to a foreign country." A year after the Rebbe arrived in Riga, Anshel Zvogin, a Jew from Nevel, met with the Rebbe. "Why are you so despondent?" Zvogin asked. "When I came to visit you in Leningrad, you were joyful." The Rebbe answered succinctly, "They drove me out."[21] Rabbi Yechezkel Feigin described the Rebbe's situation in Riga.[22] "Spiritually, the Rebbe is suffering. There are few *anash* here." He portrayed the lack of chasidic milieu in Riga: "When the Rebbe says a *maamar*, there are not many who appreciate it. And he is troubled that he is unable to establish a yeshivah here due to a lack of resources." The financial situation was distressing. "He is burdened by many debts, causing him much concern." Chasidim in Communist Russia were unable to support the Rebbe as they had in the past. "You cannot imagine the situation in Russia. Most have lost their livelihood or have been imprisoned. Others are suffering from the lack of bread."

The move to Riga had exacerbated Chabad's financial crisis, and money was needed to support the Jews still living in Russia and to finance the underground network. Additional funds were also needed for the yeshivah in Poland, the struggling Chabad communities around the globe, the Rebbe's activities, and his increasing need for medical care.

Since the time of Rabbi Schneur Zalman of Liadi (1745–1812), Chasidim had made regular voluntary contributions called *maamad*,[23] literally, "upkeep," to support the Rebbe's court and activities. Traditionally, these were grassroots campaigns organized by the Chasidim themselves. But now the bulk of Chasidim living in Russia were undergoing severe economic disruption and they were geographically cut off from the Rebbe.[24] He had to rely on the thin flow of donations that trickled in from small groups of Chabad followers in Warsaw, other European cities, and the United States. In America there were more than eighty Chabad synagogues, but they weren't a robust source of income for the Rebbe or the movement. The members of these synagogues were Russian immigrants with a limited financial capacity, navigating a new life in a foreign country.[25] Most of them lacked a personal connection to the Rebbe, as few had visited Lubavitch or studied in the yeshivah. They retained a sentimental connection to Chabad, with a tenuous link to chasidic tradition. Few participated in *maamad*. Rabbi Feigin urged Rabbi Yisrael Jacobson in New York to enlist supporters. "The situation is very bitter," he wrote. "The Rebbe needs to visit doctors, and where are we to find the money for this?"[26]

Most Chasidim were not aware of the extent of the problem. The seventh Rebbe explained years later, "The Rebbe's household intentionally did not allow the financial challenges to be publicly known. Outwardly, they showed no indication of financial stress."[27]

The Rebbe was now operating in a new set of circumstances that posed a major challenge. The freedoms in Western countries like Latvia offered Jews choices that were unprecedented. Could they survive the influence and temptation of the outside world? Lubavitch had been a spiritual haven, sheltered from external influences. In Riga there was a diverse community, parts of which were antagonistic to traditional Judaism. Could chasidic life flourish in a Western liberal society?

This was the dilemma for Jews as countries slowly lifted the barriers that blocked them from integrating into modern society. In Europe during the interwar years, religious observance dwindled with the lure of political freedoms and contemporary ideas. Major demographic changes uprooted the historic Jewish communal structure. After the First World War, "there was a shift to urbanization," says Jewish historian Yehuda Geberer. With an increasing population living in large cities instead of small towns, there was exposure to broader society that lured many away from the classic religious lifestyle. All chasidic groups, not just Chabad, faced what Geberer calls "the great crisis." He explains, "After 150 years of a rising population of Chasidim, the numbers began to drop in the interwar years."

To shield themselves from the spiritual perils of the modern world, some religious Jews moved inward, erecting barriers and disassociating from the outside world – in a sense, creating their own society within the broader society. Others chose to integrate into the wider culture while retaining a sense of Jewish identity, still following a modicum of tradition. Some chose the path of complete assimilation, abandoning Jewish observance altogether. Others became adherents, and even leaders, of the variety of new political philosophies that had become popular.

The most successful antidote to all this was an intensive focus on advanced Jewish education. Geberer says Chabad took the lead in this arena, opening the original chasidic yeshivah. "The first who did this was the Rebbe Rashab with the opening of Yeshivas Tomchei Temimim in 1897." It was a revolutionary move, and with time, other chasidic groups followed Chabad's lead, establishing their own yeshivas to bolster their youth.[28] After relocating to Riga, the Rebbe expanded this considerably with the development of a network of yeshivas in Poland and Lithuania.

While most Orthodox groups took a defensive position, concerned with the preservation of the observant core and ignoring the outside, the Rebbe courageously went on the offensive, taking a broader, more inclusive stance, the potential dangers notwithstanding. His philosophy delicately navigated between the extremes of insularity and integration. His approach was one of "principled engagement," sharing in the bounty of the freedoms of Western society but staunchly retaining the values of Judaism as the cornerstone of life. Riga was where this unique vision and strategy for Jewish continuity, which would later keep chasidic life thriving in America, began to emerge.

What never changed, however, was the Rebbe's dedication to the Jews remaining in Russia. Even though he had left the Soviet Union, his influence still permeated the Jewish communities there, and the Russian Communist government remained strongly opposed to the Rebbe's efforts.

A year after the Rebbe left Russia, Anatoly Lunacharsky,[29] the Soviet minister of education, took direct aim at him in *The New York Times*.[30] "We shall combat the relics of the Middle Ages, the *Schneersohnovschina*."[31] The *Times* explained the term as "the religious activities of the Lubavitcher Rebbe, who is now in exile in Latvia." According to Lunacharsky, Jewish religious life would not be tolerated. "The solution to the Jewish problem in Russia lies in the fusion of the Jews in the great melting pot of the peoples who inhabit the Soviet Union."

From his exile in Latvia, the Rebbe was determined to maintain the underground Jewish network in Russia. From the moment he reached Riga, he began to reach back to the Jews in Russia and assist them through a variety of channels. His first tool was his pen. The Rebbe wrote frequently and prolifically to the Jews of Russia, inspiring the Chasidim and providing guidance to the activists, urging them to continue the struggle for Jewish values and traditions. His correspondence during that period reveals his broad involvement in activities that took place in all parts of Russia. Shalom Ber Levin writes that "within the first month, the Rebbe dispatched seventy letters to Russia, the majority to Chabad leaders to empower and encourage them."[32] Immediately after his arrival in Riga, he wrote to his followers in Russia urging them to prevent the Russian Jewish conference, organized by the Leningrad Jewish community and surreptitiously supported by the Yevesektzia. "Anyone with a G-d-fearing spirit should protest against the Leningrad conference and undermine those plotting against the values of Torah."[33] Despite all the suffering he endured for his efforts to oppose it, including his arrest and exile, he dispatched a detailed action plan to disrupt the conference.[34] Those plans were successful, and the conference was never convened.

Despite being in Riga, the Rebbe was intimately involved in activities throughout Russia. To Rabbi Simon Yakovshvili, the Rebbe wrote, "You should travel to your hometown [Kutaisi, Soviet Georgia] and study the art of *shechitah*. As for seeking a *shidduch* (a match), you should defer it for a while." He instructed him to consult with Chasidim who were already there, "Avraham Levik [Slavin] and Schneur Zalman [Altshuler]" about projects in Jewish education. The Rebbe wanted details of efforts in all cities in the region. "Report to me all the time all that you have accomplished," he wrote.[35] In another letter, the Rebbe lauded the Chasid Shimon Bliner in Moscow. "I enjoyed reading that you established classes in Mishnah and chasidic philosophy. I read the names of those involved; please share with them my blessing."[36] He sent similar letters to other Jewish communities and leaders across Russia, written in poetic rabbinic lexicon, overflowing with blessings, deep emotion, and affection.

These communications carried a risk for the recipients. In 1930, *The Detroit Jewish Chronicle* reported that sixteen Jewish leaders were arrested in Minsk for the counterrevolutionary crime of corresponding with the Rebbe. "They had been hounded by the secret police for no other reason," stated the paper, "other than being in contact with the Lubavitcher Rebbe."[37]

Two weeks after arriving in Riga, the Rebbe convened a meeting of prominent rabbis to create Vaad Magen UMekhaseh, the Committee for the Protection and Care (of Russian Jewry).[38] The first meeting included prominent leaders such as Rabbi Yosef Rosen (the Rogotchover Gaon),[39] Berlin's chief rabbi, Dr. Meir Hildesheimer, and Rabbi Mendel Zak.[40] Their efforts to help Russian Jews gained the support of renowned European rabbis, including Rabbis Yisrael Meir Kagan and Chaim Ozer Grodzinski.

The organization declared special worldwide communal fasts to plead for heavenly intervention regarding the oppression of the Russian Jews; it also included special prayers for their welfare in the Yom Kippur services the following year. In the coming months, the Rebbe dispatched the Rashag to London, Paris, and Berlin to meet with local chief rabbis and top Jewish officials to request assistance for Russian Jewry. In the summer of 1928, following that visit, the Rebbe sent a poignant letter[41] to England's chief rabbi, Dr. Yosef Hertz.[42] "It is not a time for silence or to hold back on action. We must save Russian Jewry. What will future generations say if we do not answer their call in the time of crisis? I know of twenty thousand children in the USSR who wish to study Torah and are unable to – not because of the persecution, but rather the lack of money." The Rebbe urged Hertz to exert his influence on those in England who could help provide funds.

From one perspective, being in Riga enabled the Rebbe to intensify his efforts. As he wrote to Jewish activist Professor Waldemar Haffkine,[43] "I have not given up on Russia. My residence is just outside the border so I can continue my efforts for Russian Jewry." The Rebbe could now broaden his reach, whereas "due to peculiar circumstances in Russia, it was impossible to correspond with the friends of our work outside the country." From Riga, the Rebbe said, he could be "more unbound and freer in my work on behalf of Russian Jewry."[44] The Rebbe had more ambitious ideas, attempting to enlist Haffkine's help in arranging a private meeting of Jewish leaders for the purpose of strategizing how to mitigate the "greatest danger and damage to the activities of Russian Jewry: the Yevesektzia. We have to find a solution to extinguish the power of the Yevesektzia." The Rebbe emphasized that "this must be done with the utmost secrecy."[45]

The Rebbe continued his efforts to secure support for Russian Jewry from America's primary Jewish charitable fund to assist world Jewry, the Joint Distribution Committee (JDC). While still in Russia, he had met with local JDC representatives and visiting leaders from the US. Now based in Riga, he met with representatives of the JDC in Europe, traveling to Berlin shortly after his arrival from Russia. The JDC supported the Rebbe's work for a period while he was in Russia and in Riga, but then it began to reduce its funding. Instead it supported the

Russian government's plan to relocate Jews to communal agriculture settlements.[46]

"The revolution not only shattered traditional Jewish religious and cultural life, but it shattered the old economic and social roles," says Nora Levin.[47] In that economy, Jews had been "petty tradesman and artisans, exchanging goods with peasants in hundreds of market towns." The plan to settle Jews in agricultural colonies was supposed to change the economic status of Jews in Russia. Semyon Dimenstein, leader of the Yevesektzia, advocated this in conferences held as early as 1918. The land resettlement project was launched in 1924 to "productize Jews," as Levin puts it, "and turn them into farmers." Authorities relocated Jewish families, sometimes forcibly, to farms in Ukraine and Crimea, in the hope that doing so would provide the Jews with a proper livelihood. This was part of the Communist plan to shift from private farming to communal farms.[48]

The JDC's intensions were noble, argues Professor Jonathan Sarna. "They wanted to help the Jews of Russia."[49] The Communists ended the czarist policy of government-sponsored anti-Semitism. They abolished the Pale Settlement, permitting Jews to live anywhere. In the new Soviet Russia, Jews were equal citizens, prompting many American Jews to feel optimistic about a new era for Russian Jewry.

The Rebbe felt that this strategy was deeply flawed, as the farms lacked the basic infrastructure for Jewish life.[50] There were no synagogues, schools, or other Jewish institutions. The Rebbe feared that this was yet another insidious step in the Russian government's effort to sever Jews from their tradition. While still in Russia, the Rebbe urged US rabbis to lobby the JDC to at least "provide the agricultural colonies with the religious institutions necessary for every Jew."[51] While not criticizing the JDC publicly, the Rebbe believed that it would be far more beneficial for Jews to remain in the cities near family and community. He asked the JDC to provide Russian Jews with the tools, training, and financial support necessary to establish home-based factories and small businesses. That would give them greater economic freedom and allow them the option of not working on Shabbat. The Rebbe argued that "home-based industries would provide the Jews with a respectable income and sense of dignity."[52]

The Soviet government's intent was more insidious. "They are interested in the colonization in order to realize their evil plans to break down and destroy the Jewish spirit, to realize their old, rooted hatred toward Judaism," an anonymous writer[53] said in a scathing public letter[54] titled "The New Book of Lamentations." Published in 1928 in *Hadoar*,[55] a prominent US Hebrew-language newspaper, the letter described the bleak situation in the agricultural colonies and the Yevesektzia's motives for relocating Jews to the settlements. "Our benefactors from America and Europe who think that the salvation for the Jewish people will come from Crimea, Siberia, and Amur are mistaken." It's a failed policy, he wrote. "We plow and plant with tears and harvest with despair. When autumn comes, we and our children have to seek bread."

In 1929, in the new collective settlements in the Borisov region, Jews who refused to milk cows on Shabbat were expelled as "undesirables."[56] One American visitor described how the synagogue of the communal farm town of Krivoy Rog was converted to a hall for the arts: "The raised platform – on which once reposed the Ark of the Covenant, the Torah, and the pulpit – is now bare." The synagogues that once resounded with "holy prayer" were now full of old Yiddish ballads that "mocked traditional pieties."[57]

The JDC had curtailed its funding to the Rebbe's underground educational system because it could put them at odds with the Communist regime. Now in Riga, the Rebbe would be able to meet JDC leaders more easily and restore critical funding for Russian Jewry. Some in the JDC dissented with the decision to cut funding for the Rebbe's work. Its Berlin representative, Dr. Bernard Kahn, asked the JDC headquarters in New York in 1928 to continue providing assistance for religious activities, noting that the Rebbe's network continued to operate despite the oppression of the Communists and adding that he was "the only one who gets all the information from a network of people."[58]

The Rebbe's pleas to JDC leaders in meetings in Berlin were unsuccessful. "Is it possible that our brothers in America will see the pain in the souls and bodies of their brothers?" the Rebbe wrote in January 1929[59] to JDC board member Rabbi Aron Teitelbaum of Agudas Harabonim in New York.[60] The Rebbe painted a dire picture of Jewish life in Russia. "The institutions in Russia are hanging between life and death. There are daily requests for funding." The Rebbe was taking loans to keep things afloat in Russia, for "the schools are on the verge of closing." The decision to deny funding would bring victory to the Yevesektzia and "demoralize the activists in Russia."

By late 1928, massive food shortages were impacting the Soviet Union. Stalin's plan to create state-run collectives had disrupted the food supply to Russia.[61] Rationing was instituted in Leningrad, Moscow, and other cities. In early 1929, the Rebbe began to raise the alarm on the likelihood of a matzah shortage before Passover. He had been receiving messages from activists in Russia begging for help procuring matzah. Though the Yevesektzia had successfully dismantled many Jewish institutions, most Jews in Russia still followed basic traditions, including eating matzah and abstaining from *chametz* (leavened products such as bread) on Passover.[62] Without flour, not only would they not be able to observe the central mitzvah of Passover, but many would starve from lack of food. The Rebbe knew that hundreds of thousands of people, already suffering from starvation, would put their lives at risk rather than eat bread on Passover. "You will not find even ten percent of Jews who will eat *chametz* on Passover," he wrote.

The Rebbe organized an emergency committee in Riga and reached out to other prominent religious leaders, including Rabbis Chaim Ozer of Vilnius, Yisrael Meir Kagan of Radin, and Yosef Chaim Sonnenfeld of Jerusalem.[63] They all issued public statements calling on Jews the world over to support the Rebbe's emergency campaign. These rabbis were the Rebbe's natural allies, but would major Jewish groups like the JDC in New York and the Alliance Israélite Universelle in Paris support the emergency campaign? And how would the Russians react to shipments of matzah from abroad that could embarrass them by highlighting the famine? Without the government's approval, shipping matzah would be next to impossible.

JDC leader Dr. Cyrus Adler[64] argued against supporting the Rebbe's campaign,[65] saying, "The Yevesektzia might block the deliveries. It also might embarrass the Russians; they might not even agree to allow the shipments."[66]

The Rebbe forged ahead, overcoming the multiple challenges of raising funds and securing the Russian government's permission, as well as the logistics of producing matzah. He launched a diplomatic initiative in Latvia, enlisting the help of Mordechai Dubin, who met with the Russian Ambassador in Riga. He promised to do all he could to help the shipment go through. The Rashag assisted Dubin, meeting with the Russian trade minister, and was in daily contact with the Russian Embassy for updates.[67] The Rebbe's son-in-law Rabbi Gurary also traveled to Berlin, where Rabbi Dr. Hildesheimer led a delegation (which included Leo Baeck, the leading Reform rabbi, and other influential community leaders) to a meeting with the Soviet Ambassador in Germany. The *kehillah* (official Jewish community) in Berlin allocated five thousand German marks for the emergency campaign.

At the same time, the Rebbe launched an international fundraising campaign. Dubin and Gurary were dispatched to London[68] and Paris to raise funds and meet with the chief rabbis and other Jewish leaders. Local committees were started in most European countries, including Holland, Poland, Switzerland, and Belgium. Even smaller communities became involved, including Shanghai and Harbin, China. The Rebbe enlisted key rabbinic figures in *Eretz Yisrael,* Rabbi Yosef Chaim Sonnenfeld[69] and Chief Rabbis Avraham Yitzchak Kook and Yaakov Meir, who issued public statements calling for aid.

Press reports swirled on both sides of the Atlantic with news on the status of the shipments. First the Russians approved it; then they rescinded the authorization. Gurary lamented the byzantine Russian government in a letter to Rabbi Yisroel Meisels in Tel Aviv. "You have no idea how difficult it is to deal with Russian officials. Every day they say they have no answer. Then they say I must inquire in Moscow. Then they say they have not heard back. Then they tell us the authorization must come from Riga, and then from Berlin. It's impossible to get a clear response."[70]

Finally, five weeks before Passover, the Soviet Trade representative in Riga gave Dubin the green light for the shipment with the "modest duty of five kopecks per kilo."[71] Five wagonloads of matzah were immediately dispatched by train. But then came another twist: desperate for foreign currency, the Russians changed the duty price and demanded an exorbitant two rubles (valued at sixty dollars today) per kilo, for a total of $130,000 for the shipment (valued at some two million dollars today).

The diplomatic haggling continued until the Russians finally dropped the duty by seventy-five percent, to fifty kopeks.

Production began full force in Riga, Dvinsk, and Berlin.[72] In the end, 140,000 kilos were shipped for distribution[73] and another 5,689 packages of matzah were mailed directly to families in four hundred communities. The campaign cost a total of $88,000, some $1.3 million today. The JDC did participate with an allocation of ten thousand dollars, thanks to the urging of Dr. Rosen, the head of the JDC office in Moscow. Due to the Rebbe's efforts, the Jews of Russia survived another Passover under Soviet oppression.

With that, the Rebbe achieved another significant milestone. He proved that his influence went beyond the borders of Russia, that he could marshal global support for his advocacy for Jewish affairs with or without the endorsement of the Jewish establishment. In a totally new environment, he successfully launched an international campaign. In the years to come, Chabad took a leadership role in global Jewish affairs, and the Rebbe acted decisively when it came to helping Jews or bolstering religious life. When Chabad shared goals with other major Jewish organizations, it cooperated with them, but it did not fear acting unilaterally. This streak of independence animated many of the Rebbe's initiatives in the future.

In 1921, while still in Rostov, the Rebbe received news of the opening of a yeshivah in Warsaw. He referred to this time as "days of light and days of joy."[74] At the time, the yeshivah in Rostov was being forcibly closed, and the Chabad educational network in Russia was going underground. The Warsaw branch was established with twelve students on the first anniversary of the passing of the Rebbe Rashab. A few days later, the Rebbe dispatched a detailed letter to its administration outlining a plan for its organizational structure and educational goals.[75] He instructed them to "focus on discussions of ethical behavior, instilling a G-d-fearing spirit, and acquiring good character traits." Clearly, he wanted the new yeshivah to follow the model in Lubavitch that had concentrated not only on the acquisition of talmudic knowledge but on developing the character and spiritual qualities of its students. With time, the Warsaw yeshivah expanded significantly, acquiring a large building and eventually relocating to the suburb of Otwock. It became the primary incubator for a new generation of Chasidim and Jewish communal leaders.[76] By 1927, the yeshivah had grown to 157 students. The next year, the number increased to 250.

Four months after departing Russia, the Rebbe visited the yeshivah when he traveled to Warsaw[77] for two weeks.[78] He met with the city's leading rabbis and communal leaders, deepening their awareness of the plight of Russian Jewry. He also spent time conducting *yechidut* with many of the Chasidim. The highlight was a long Purim *farbrengen* with the students that began at 3:30 p.m. and did not end until 2:00 a.m.

Warsaw was not the only city the Rebbe visited during this period. Among other cities in the region, the Rebbe traveled to Vilnius three times, where he was greeted by crowds of thousands at the train station. On his first trip in 1928, which lasted one week, he met with Rabbi Chaim Ozer Grodzinski to discuss Russian Jewry. The Rebbe also visited Rokiškis, Lithuania; Ludmir, Poland; and Glubok (twice).[79]

For the High Holidays in 1930, Chasidim from Poland and Lithuania came to celebrate with the Rebbe. A group of twenty-one Chasidim convened in the home of the Rashag, who suggested establishing Agudas Chassidei Chabad (a Union of the Chabad Chasidim) in Poland, Lithuania, and Latvia. With the Rebbe's approval, the organization took on the mandate of strengthening the Chabad community in the region.

From Riga, the Rebbe continued to connect with Chabad Chasidim and Jewish activists around the world. He wrote regularly to Chasidim across the globe, focusing on strengthening the great center of Jewish population in Poland. In the 1930s, he dispatched emissaries to fortify Jewish life in communities as far as Australia and South Africa.

The Rebbe remained deeply involved with the Riga Jewish community. Simchat Torah of 1930 was the culmination of the holiday season for the Chasidim of Riga and those who had come from nearby countries. The Rebbe had just returned a few weeks earlier from his almost yearlong journey to *Eretz Yisrael* and America.[80] On that joyous evening, the Rebbe expressed his angst over the spiritual situation in Latvia.[81] He explained that while Latvia had a Jewish population similar in size to that of Lithuania, it lacked the vibrancy of Jewish scholarship that existed in the adjacent country. "In Lithuania there are many large yeshivas," the Rebbe said. "In every town, there is a *yeshivah ketanah* (high school) and several *chadarim*. They study like they used to study." The Lithuanian community possessed an ethos of learning, while Latvia had a "culture of supporting Torah financially." They were philanthropic, with local Jews underwriting Torah study – even in other countries – but the level of actual scholarship in Latvia was weak. The Rebbe explained that this was due to the political restrictions on Latvia during the years of Russian rule, which made establishing yeshivas difficult. But that ended in 1918 with Latvian independence. "Since then, an effort should have been made to establish Torah institutions." By 1930, Latvia was dominated by secular Jewish schools; the Rebbe called the country "Jewish only in appearance." The Rebbe turned to the leaders of Tze'irei Agudath Israel,[82] charging them with the mission of bolstering Jewish education in Latvia. "You have established schools according to the ideology of *Torah im derekh eretz*, integrating secular and religious study."[83] He was generally critical of this system, explaining that his first choice of a model for Jewish education was the traditional *cheder*, "taught by an old-world *melamed* (teacher)." But understanding the challenges in Riga, the Rebbe took a practical approach. He encouraged the community to stand behind Tze'irei Agudath Israel. "You should be given every kind of help and support."[84]

The Rebbe then turned to a group headed by Rabbi Mordechai Dubin and tasked them with leading the initiative. He told them that they must become involved in strengthening Jewish education and galvanize the financial resources needed. The Rebbe's intent was clear: He expected Dubin to transform the Jewish school system in Riga, controlled at the time by secular elements. "I am giving you this mission," he said, noting the presence of witnesses to the assignment.[85] It was clear from the emotional talk that the Rebbe was disheartened by the state of Jewish life in Latvia. Yes, Latvians could support great centers of Jewish learning in nearby countries and even send their children there, but the Rebbe demanded a fundamental change locally.

It would take some time for Dubin to fulfill the task entrusted to him. He had already laid the foundation for educational change in Riga in 1920, when he established the Derech Eretz School that taught Jewish and secular studies. The opportunity to fulfill the Rebbe's mission came in 1934, when Dubin's political influence increased. It was after the Ulmanis coup, when Prime Minister Kārlis Ulmanis disbanded all political parties and the democratically elected parliament. All the Jewish parties were deemed illegal, but because of Dubin's personal bond with Ulmanis, Agudath Israel was allowed to function. Dubin orchestrated the appointment of Rabbi Chaim Mordechai Aizek Hodakov, who had been the founding dean of the Derech Eretz School when he was just eighteen years old, as chief inspector of the Jewish schools. Until then, most schools had been secular. Many were controlled by the Yiddishists, who aimed to replace traditional religious values with a Jewish identity based on Yiddish language and culture. The Yiddish movement had begun in Russia in the late nineteenth century and spread abroad.[86] Hodakov instituted major reforms, tilting the historically secular schools toward tradition. He changed curriculums, replacing the study of Yiddish writers like Sholem Aleichem with Torah lessons. Local secular Jewish leaders opposed his actions, but to no avail. One Yiddishist, Mendel Mark,[87] bemoaned the change, writing about the secular teachers being replaced by religious ones. "Prayer is now a requirement, and wearing a yarmulke is part of the dress code." Mark wrote that some of the teachers staged a strike, but it did not hinder Hodakov's plan to alter the educational philosophy of the schools.

The Rebbe was also critical of the defensive nature of the local Orthodox groups' approach to community issues. He pushed for a change in tactics, to switch from passivity to more outward-facing activism. "You need to stand on the street corners and pull Jews into a synagogue to study," he said, laying out the vision for a new, bold model of outreach that would become the symbol of Chabad in decades to come.[88]

Toward the end of that Simchat Torah evening in 1930, the Rebbe's tone turned ominous. In an uncharacteristically serious fashion, he demanded that those unwilling to lay tefillin daily or observe other basics of tradition not stay to dance with him that night. Those attending were taken aback by the Rebbe's unusually harsh tone, and some indeed left before the traditional Simchat Torah dancing. One Jewish newspaper noted with disapproval that the Rebbe was not the progressive they thought he was, and this criticism was echoed in papers as far away as New York.[89] But soon it became clear to the Chasidim what had actually occurred. It was discovered that members of the local left-wing Jewish Communist youth club, Peretz, had planned to disrupt the celebration. "They infiltrated the crowd with the intent of cutting the electricity, and they planned to violently break up the *hakafot,*" Rabbi Yechezkel Feigin wrote to Rabbi Yisrael Jacobson in the US. "When the [Peretz] leaders heard the Rebbe's strident words, they instructed their followers to leave."[90]

On Friday, two days after the holiday, Rabbi Feigin decided to inform the Rebbe of the plot they had uncovered. "I thought it was important that he be aware, even though it would cause the Rebbe distress." When he heard the details, the Rebbe said, "Now I know that I was justified in speaking that way, though at the time I did not know what pushed me to say it."

The Rebbe was making headway, and not all were pleased. Alarmed at the new effort to boost Jewish education and observance, the left-wing *Frimorgen* paper headlined a story on the Rebbe's growing influence in Riga, "The Rebbe's Court in Riga a Danger to Cultural Life," writing that when the Rebbe arrived in Riga, escaping a death sentence in Russia, he was warmly welcomed. Now that his influence was growing, he was endangering secular Jewish culture in Riga.

Riga was not just a geographic waystation but a spiritual one, where new ideas were launched and tested. It was removed from the large Jewish centers, with their rigid communal structure that could potentially stifle innovation. Despite believing that the optimal mode of Jewish education was the traditional yeshivah, the Rebbe advocated that the schools that integrated secular and religious education were better than the Yiddish schools that were Jewish in name only. The Rebbe also prodded Jewish activists in Latvia to reach beyond the walls of the synagogues. These were two new areas of innovation that the Rebbe embarked on while in Riga.

There were three others: creating a new chasidic historiography, broadening the dissemination of chasidic teachings beyond the chasidic community, and empowering women in the realm of Jewish study. In all five arenas, the Rebbe created a series of initiatives that with time would be key to reconstituting Chabad in Western democratic countries.

The ideas launched in Riga blossomed in both Europe and the US, and after the Rebbe's passing, they were expanded by the seventh Rebbe.

CREATING A NEW CHASIDIC HISTORIOGRAPHY

The Rebbe created a new literary tradition of chasidic historiography.[91] In addition to teaching Torah, the Rebbe took the stories of the chasidic world, centuries of lore, and began to present them in systematic fashion in public talks. Those talks were published in booklets called *Likkutei Dibburim*.[92] "In letters and talks, he portrays the chasidic world vibrantly," writes chasidic historian Menachem Bronfman. "He wrote with deep emotion, revealing the internal spiritual world of Chabad Chasidism through stories, and a tradition reaching back years."[93]

Uri Kaploun, who translated those talks for publication, notes, "One is struck at once by the different nature of a *farbrengen* in those years." The audience was varied; it included Torah scholars and average Jews, those who had experienced oppression in Russia and those who enjoyed the freedoms and prosperity of Western society. The mode of presentation was "deceptively simplistic. For the most part, he spurns the formality of learned quotation couched in technical terms, preferring a homely paraphrase, a pointed parable or a heartwarming anecdote." The talks are diverse, embracing "childhood memories, insightful stories, the family traditions of *tzaddikim*, and recollections of Stalinist dungeons and interrogations."[94]

These stories came from what the Rebbe himself heard as a young child from his father, grandmother, uncles, and older Chasidim.[95] "His keen curiosity first displayed itself in early childhood in the desire to hear historical tales from his grandmother," writes Professor Ada Rapoport.[96] The Rayatz would seek out the elder Chasidim during their spiritual pilgrimages in Lubavitch, listen to their stories, and then record them in his diary. Rapoport says this "developed into a compulsive interest in the personal reminiscences and oral traditions of his father and other senior figures at the Lubavitch court, whom he would interrogate about the early history of Chasidism."

"Chabad Chasidism is not just deep intellectual philosophy but a recounting of stories from generation to generation," Bronfman asserts.

The Rebbe's intent was to remind those who came from Russia of their marvelous chasidic legacy and at the same time, instill in the next generation of Chasidim, now living in urban centers in Latvia and Poland, the richness of chasidic life of the past. Bronfman explains that the Rebbe created a collective communal memory in order to bring this world to life for those who had never known it. The Rebbe was giving them a story, an identity, and showing them spiritual aspirations "as personified by the Chasidim of years earlier. The Rebbe succeeded in creating a living testimony of the heart of Chasidism and connecting the Chasidim reading those stories to a forgotten era." The stories the Rebbe told added new dimensions to what many had studied in chasidic philosophy. "This created a foundation not only to appreciate the intellectual depth of Chabad but also the deep inner spiritual world of Chasidim."[97]

BROADENING THE DISSEMINATION OF CHASIDIC TEACHINGS BEYOND THE CHASIDIC COMMUNITY

Chabad had existed for a century and half in Russia with few rival chasidic groups. After the Rebbe's exodus from Russia, the differences between Chabad and the Polish chasidic groups, who were also influential in Riga, rose to the surface. Rapoport writes, "The encounter with all the Polish chasidic courts, some of them large and wealthy, in their native environment, to which Chabad was alien, and where it wielded little power or influence, forced the Rebbe to define its identity." Chabad's focus is on personal spiritual achievement, *avodah*, in the lexicon of Chasidism. As the Rebbe wrote, "One of the fundamental principles of Chabad is that it teaches its followers to be deeply engaged in the *avodah* of Chasidism. In contrast, for the Polish Chasidim, the main point is the connection to the Rebbe, and the Rebbe uplifts all those connected to him."[98] Chabad teaches a Chasid to strive to internalize the ideals of Torah and serve G-d with his own efforts. Polish Chasidim, on the other hand, emphasize the bond with the Rebbe.

Therefore, Chabad concentrates on intellectual ideas, while the Polish Chasidim have a broad literature of the wondrous stories of *tzaddikim*. "The Polish Chasidim have focused their attention on the lives of their leader, their tales and deeds. They write down their stories of wonders. In Chabad we provide volumes of chasidic teachings, transcripts of *maamarim*."

A few weeks before the High Holidays of September 1928, the Rebbe published his first *maamar* since leaving Russia.[99] And for the first time since the eighteenth century, a *maamar* was printed not in Hebrew but Yiddish, the language understood by average Jews,[100] making the teachings of Chasidism accessible to a broader public.[101]

In the introduction to that particular *maamar,* the Rebbe reached out to a wider audience, some of whom had drifted from their chasidic roots. "My dear students and *anash,*" he wrote, "remember your historical roots, your parents and grandparents, Chasidim and Jews of outstanding spiritual character who studied Chasidism and lived up to its principles." He asked them to "instill these teachings in your children," urging parents to inculcate these ideals in the next generation, children growing up in Western Europe far from the Russian *shtetl.*

Then the Rebbe took it a step further, for the first time publishing chasidic discourses in a European language: German.[102] The Rebbe wanted to engage German Jews, many of whom lacked a strong Jewish academic background, and give them the opportunity to gain an appreciation of the concepts of chasidic philosophy.

The seventh Rebbe notes[103] that this was another step in disseminating chasidic teachings, a key principle of the founder of the chasidic movement, Rabbi Yisrael Baal Shem Tov. He explains that it was an evolutionary process.[104] "This has happened in stages, from generation to generation, the principle of disseminating Chasidism, reaching further outward." He explains that the Baal Shem Tov focused on his students, spreading his teachings to them. A second transformation point was after the freeing of Rabbi Schneur Zalman from czarist prison in 1798. At that point, the Alter Rebbe began teaching *maamarim* with deeper explanations. "This began a new stage, when the teachings went *chutzah,* outside." The next stage, says the seventh Rebbe, was the establishment of Yeshivas Tomchei Temimim in 1897. The yeshivah created a revolutionary curriculum that balanced talmudic study and chasidic philosophy. And the next step was publishing the *maamarim* in other languages. "It created a way for the teachings to be appreciated by all Jews, in their language."

EMPOWERING WOMEN IN THE REALM OF JEWISH STUDY

It was a woman, Sylvia Reinen,[105] who translated the first *maamar* into Yiddish shortly after the Rebbe came to Riga. This marked the beginning of the effort to engage women with the intellectual depth of Chabad *Chasidut*. During his visit to the US in 1929, the Rebbe paid special attention to women. Levin writes, "In every place, the Rebbe encouraged the establishment of women's organizations."[106] This empowerment of women was a new trend in the chasidic community. As Professor Rapoport writes, "There is no doubt the mobilization of women and the positive encouragement of female activism had become the pronounced policy of the sixth Rebbe."[107]

In 1931, a large group of women requested that the Rebbe speak for them during his visit to Rokiškis, Lithuania. Rabbi Feigin writes, "In the wake of the request, the Rebbe spoke to a gathering of women."[108] Historically, chasidic Rebbes only spoke before men in their public addresses; this was unprecedented. In the fall of 1935, Rabbi Mordechai Cheifetz asked the Rebbe if it was appropriate to teach women chasidic philosophy, and his answer was an emphatic yes. The Rebbe quoted his grandfather Rabbi Shmuel as saying that "amongst Chasidim there is no difference between a boy or a girl. Yet Chasidim only educate their sons in the ways of *Chasidut*; they totally neglect to educate their daughters in the ways of *Chasidut*." The Rebbe lamented, "That was said fifty-five years ago, when the light of Chasidism was burning brightly in people's homes. Now this is an even greater imperative."[109] The Rebbe instructed Rabbi Cheifetz to study *maamarim* with young women in Riga. This directive would serve as the catalyst for the formation of the women's group Achot Hatemimim (The Sisterhood of the Temimim),[110] which brought together teens and young women to strengthen their bond with chasidic tradition. The Rebbe strongly supported the group and encouraged women to set up classes on chasidic philosophy.[111] This created a gateway for them to delve deeper into the sea of Jewish mystical knowledge.

In the 1930s, the Rebbe printed more than forty discourses in Yiddish that were the "core material in this new initiative for Chabad women," says Professor Naftali Loewenthal.[112] The Rebbe added prestige to the organization by appointing three distinguished Chasidim, Rabbis Mordechai Cheifetz, Chaim Eliyahu Althaus, and Avraham Eliyahu Asherov, to serve as mentors for the women. The Rebbe encouraged them to hold their own *farbrengens,* which according to Loewenthal was a key "to the process of internalization of chasidic ethos" and also fostered "unity between the participants."

In the summer of 1938, a women's group was founded in the US, and the Rebbe wrote to them in English. "In reply to your letter advising me of your excellent resolution to interest yourselves in the study of Chasidism and to be called The Society of the Sisters of the Temimim, I was greatly gratified with your good decision."[113] As the Rebbe had done in Europe, he selected three prominent American rabbis to teach the group and advise them on format and curriculum, instructing them to set up weekly classes.[114]

The Rebbe saw women's study as an opportunity for the participants to enhance their spiritual identity. He expressed a desire for them to "comprehend the uniqueness of Chasidism, how it reveals rich spiritual depth." The Rebbe also wanted the women to become activists. Loewenthal says he tasked them with the job of "organizing the translation of discourses and disseminating them."[115] This new effort started a process of women evolving as teachers of chasidic philosophy and as *mashpios,* spiritual mentors. The Rebbe also published public letters and booklets of chasidic teachings specifically for women. In the fall of 1941, it was the members of Achot Hatemimim of Greater New York who went on to establish the Beis Rivkah schools.

The great importance the Rebbe placed on creating educational opportunities for women became clear during his second interlude in Riga in 1940. After escaping German-occupied Poland, he made few public appearances during his short stay before departing to the US. One of these was a rare public talk to Achot Hatemimim in Riga. Before the Rebbe spoke, he requested that a representative of each class review the *maamar* they were studying from memory, something radical at the time.[116] Loewenthal explains, "Recital of a discourse by heart was something for which the young men of Tomchei Temimim were well-known. Now girls were doing it as well."

Afterward, the Rebbe addressed[117] the women as he would a group of male Chasidim, Loewenthal says. The Rebbe stressed the importance of studying chasidic philosophy to develop their inner spiritual qualities while following the teachings of the Torah.[118] Loewenthal explains, "The ultimate goal was one of empowerment and activism while maintaining the conventional structure of society."

Riga was the testing ground for many of the ideas that emerged in the coming years. The Rebbe's involvement with the educational system in Riga set the tone for a similar system integrating religious and secular education that the Rebbe went on to establish in the US. While in other chasidic groups, women saw themselves as the wives or daughters of Chasidim, Loewenthal says the Rebbe empowered women in Chabad to see themselves as Chasidim in their own merit.[119] Other ideas, such as translating chasidic teachings, taking a more strident approach to outreach, and creating new chasidic literature, expanded in the years that followed.

All these initiatives point to the Rebbe's creative approach to the new challenges of Western society. Chabad adapted to a changing reality in a diverse modern world, where Jews were no longer forced inward because of outside limitations on their freedoms. While most chasidic Rebbes focused on the needs of their constituencies, the Rebbe launched ideas that transcended his community. While still in Russia, the Rebbe rejected the parochialism of the *roshei yeshivah* (heads of yeshivas) who fled the country and abandoned the wider community to protect their institutions. Instead, he created a comprehensive strategy to save Russian Jewry. And when he arrived in Riga, suffering from weakened health due to the oppression in Russia, and with no finances to speak of, he did not withdraw or back down. The Rebbe actively led the effort to support the scattered communities materially and spiritually and engage Jews in a time when Jewish communal structure was breaking down and many were drifting away from observance. Through letters, directives, emissaries, and personal visits, he sought to uplift the standards of Jewish education and observance in the Jewish communities of Russia, Latvia, and its environs, all the way to the US. This approach of taking responsibility for the broader Jewish destiny defined the Rebbe's leadership and became Chabad's unique modus operandi in the generations to come.

Riga saw the cultivation of important personalities, such as Rabbi Chaim Mordechai Aizik Hodakov[120] and Dr. Nissan Mindel,[121] who became the Rebbe's devoted Chasidim, eventually joining him when he escaped to the US. There they rose to positions of leadership: Mindel was a secretary for both the sixth Rebbe and the seventh Rebbe, and Hodakov played a key role in the Rebbe's efforts to develop Jewish education in the US in the early 1940s. Later, Rabbi Hodakov assumed the position of the seventh Rebbe's chief of staff.

Decades later, the inspiration of the Rebbe's sojourn was still felt in Riga. Rabbi Dr. Aaron Rakeffet[122] discovered its long-lasting effects when he visited Riga in 1985, when he was sent to the Soviet Union as a covert agent by the Israeli Mossad. His mission was to connect with Jews, strengthen Judaism, and help with immigration to Israel. He was surprised to find a vibrant community in Riga. At the synagogue, he discovered a group of older Jews, the nucleus of the religious life that had held on throughout Communism. After services, he was quietly told, "When they leave, we'll go upstairs." He understood that among the worshippers were government agents and that when they departed, the group would be able to speak more freely. After the services concluded, "they broke out vodka and cake, and we sat and had a *farbrengen*. We talked about the Rebbe, told stories, and shared words of Torah and inspiration. It was like we were transported to another world." The richness of tradition that they had absorbed during the Rebbe's six-year stay in Riga was still pulsating half a century later among the local observant Jews. "It's what kept them going all those years," Rakeffet attests.

Chapter Six

The Royal Wedding

Amid the darkness of oppression and displacement, a ray of hope and joy emerged. A year after the Rebbe departed from Russia, his second daughter, Chaya Mushka, was finally to be wed to the Ramash. The "royal wedding," as historian Rabbi Dr. Aaron Rakeffet labeled it,[1] would be held in Warsaw, Poland, in the fall of 1929. The celebration heralded a new era of Chabad, exiled from its birthplace in Russia and now being reborn in Western Europe, resilient, buoyant, and revitalized. This was not the first wedding the Rebbe had hosted. His older daughter Chana had married Rabbi Shmaryahu Gurary in June 1921[2] in Rostov.

At the time, a typhus epidemic had devastated the chasidic community, and famine ravaged Rostov. The yeshivah was forcibly closed by the Yevesektzia, and the Rebbe was being harassed by the authorities. Before Chana's wedding, the secret police broke into the Rebbe's home, seizing much of his property, including the wedding dress. With limited financial resources, the celebration was very modest. Zalman Gurary attended, writing in his memoir, "The famine was so acute that all that was served to the guests at the wedding were light refreshments of cake and drinks."[3]

Four years after Chaya Mushka's wedding, in 1932, the Rebbe's youngest daughter, Sheina, married Rabbi Mendel Horenstein in the city of Landwarow,[4] Poland, just over the border, not far from Vilnius.[5] Rabbi Chaim Ozer Grodzinski officiated,[6] and many Chasidim traveled to join the wedding celebrations. Horenstein's father was an uncle of the Rebbe. He was a successful businessman who operated a Jewish orphanage. Sophisticated and worldly, he sent his son to a gymnasium, a secular-style high school, giving him a broader education than most children from Chabad families. Mendel grew closer to his father-in-law, the Rebbe, slowly strengthening his chasidic tradition. After the wedding, the couple moved to Paris, and a few months later, Chaya Mushka and her husband, the Ramash, joined them. Rabbi Mendel and the Ramash studied together regularly.

With the outbreak of war, the young Horensteins and their adopted son traveled to Otwock to care for Rabbi Mendel's aging parents. Eventually they were all captured by the Nazis. Their fate was unknown for years, until finally it was revealed that the whole family was killed in Treblinka.[7]

The engagement of Chaya Mushka and the Ramash had been unusually lengthy. The young couple met for the first time in the summer of 1923 in the Russian city resort town of Kislovodsk. The Rebbe and his family were in the summer resort in the foothills of the Caucasus, some three hundred miles south of Rostov. The idea for the match was originally suggested by the Rebbe Rashab[8] years earlier. While discussing with his wife the subject of potential grooms for their granddaughter, he had remarked, "We should think of Reb Levik's son,"[9] referring to the Rashab's cousin, Rabbi Levi Yitzchak Schneerson, chief rabbi of Yekaterinoslav, the Ramash's father.

That summer of 5683 (1923), before the two met, the Rebbe confided to Rabbi Eliyahu Chaim Althaus that he wished to marry off his "precious, beloved daughter Chaya Mushka to Rabbi Menachem Mendel Schneerson."[10] The Rebbe asked Althaus to act as the formal *shadkhan* (matchmaker) to suggest the match to the Ramash's family and introduce the couple. Althaus escorted twenty-one-year-old Menachem Mendel on the six-hundred-mile trip from his hometown of Yekaterinoslav (today known as Dinipo) to the resort town of Kislovodsk, where the couple met for the first time.[11] After two weeks there, the Ramash returned to Rostov with the Rebbe, while the Rebbe's family, including Chaya Mushka, remained in Kislovodsk. A week later, the Rebbe wrote to Chaya Mushka, "My daughter, this week I studied deeply '*Hilkhot* Mendel' (the subject of Mendel), may he be well, for several hours each day."[12] He went on to say that the visit was very friendly. Alluding to the meeting that the Ramash had with Chaya Mushka, the Rebbe wrote, "He left with a pleasant impression of the Caucasus. He would like to have another excursion in the mountains," hinting that he would like to see her again.

But the progress of the match was slowed by geography – the Ramash was living with his parents in Yekaterinoslav, distant from Rostov – as well as political instability, financial constraints, and the constant oppression of the Rebbe at the hands of the Yevesektzia. In May 1924, the Rebbe moved from Rostov to Leningrad,[13] or as he described it, "I was compelled to leave by the order of the political police."[14] His family followed shortly thereafter. The Ramash visited Leningrad regularly, also attending classes at the local university.[15] The Rebbe drew the young Ramash into his affairs. The Ramash's mother recalled in her diary that the Rebbe "would not let him go and was always finding reasons to summon him. The Rebbe said he was appointing him as his 'Minister of Education.' He entrusted my son with many tasks requiring Torah scholarship and secular knowledge."[16]

At one point, the Ramash feared being detained by the Bolsheviks, and so in the summer of 1926, he found refuge in the home of Rabbi Chanoch Henoch Etkin in Luga, on the outskirts of Leningrad. Though Etkin was a rabbi, he also had regular employment, and the government did not harass him. His grandson, Rabbi She'ar Yashuv Cohen, recalls, "At the time the Ramash was engaged, the Bolsheviks began investigating him. He hid in my grandfather's home for a few months. He spent his time studying and also learned Talmud with my grandfather daily."[17]

His presence in the Rebbe's court and his participation in the Rebbe's activities were the first stage of mentoring he received from the Rebbe that would prepare him for leadership after the Rebbe's passing. His contact with notable Jewish scholars that began at this time, and which continued later in Riga and Poland, exposed the brilliant intellect of the young Ramash to the greatest rabbinic figures of the generation.[18]

Though the Ramash was naturally very reserved, the Rebbe encouraged rabbis to discuss various talmudic topics with him.

One of those rabbis was Rabbi Shlomo Yosef Zevin, secretary of the Rabbinical Committee in Russia at the time, and later one of the leading talmudic authorities in Israel. In 1950, after the Rebbe's passing, Rabbi Zevin urged the Ramash to become Rebbe. "Thank G-d, a scion has been saved from the family of our Rebbe, who was educated and mentored in the home of the Rebbe Rayatz. You were always hand in hand [with the Rebbe Rayatz], and he never withheld any good [Torah] from you."[19]

When the Russian authorities finally granted approval for the Rebbe and his family to depart Russia for Riga in October 1927, the Rebbe insisted that his future son-in-law also be permitted to leave. Russian officials challenged him. "Can't you find another son-in-law?" they asked. The Rebbe's legendary response was, "A son-in-law like him I can't find there."[20]

The Ramash's stay in Riga was brief. In December of 1927, two months after he arrived from Russia, he departed for Berlin.[21] The day after he came to Berlin, he represented his future father-in-law at a convention of Agudath Israel,[22] continuing to play a role in the Rebbe's affairs even from a distance. In Berlin he attended lectures[23] by Rabbi Yechiel Yaakov Weinberg[24] of the Rabbinical Seminary of Berlin. With Rabbi Weinberg's help,[25] the Ramash registered at Friedrich Wilhelm University and took courses in geometry, physics, and higher mathematics.[26] He spent a significant portion of the next four years, both before and after his wedding, in Berlin, periodically visiting Riga.[27]

Latvia was a free country, and now the wedding plans could move forward without government hindrance. But two obstacles still stood in the way. The first was securing permission from the Russian government for the Ramash's parents to join the celebration. The second was financial – funds were needed in order to make a proper wedding for a Rebbe's daughter. The Communist revolution had disrupted the regular flow of donations coming from Chasidim in Russia, and few Chasidim lived in Western Europe. With the time for the wedding approaching, the financial need became acute, although most were not aware of its extent.

Rabbi Yechezkel Feigin took matters into his own hands. Secretly writing to Rabbi Yisrael Jacobson in New York, he implored his old friend for help. "We must put our heads together and find a solution," he wrote. The Rebbe had not told him explicitly how serious the financial straits were, but it seemed clear to him. "In the end, a wedding must be made. But with what?" He encouraged Jacobson to speak to members of the Chabad community in the US to ask for their assistance.[28]

The Ramash's parents, Rabbi Levi Yitzchak and Rebbetzin Chana, petitioned the Russian authorities for an exit visa to attend their oldest son's wedding.[29] The government was inflexible, rejecting their application. The news was greeted with sadness in Riga. Finding no reason to delay the wedding any longer, the Rebbe set the date for 14 Kislev (November 27, 1928) in Warsaw.

Six weeks before the wedding, the financial situation was still dire. In mid-October, Feigin wrote to Jacobson again. "The chasidic community in Europe could not really help," he explained, because of the suffering they had endured in the last few years. "You can't imagine how it was," he wrote, referring to the oppression in Russia. "Finances must come from your country." He urged Jacobson to enlist Rabbi Shalom Dovber Rivkin, who had left Russia and was now in the US. He recommended that they launch an appeal. "Write to all the Temimim [alumni of the Chabad yeshivah] or telegram them." Feigin pleaded with Jacobson to act swiftly.[30]

Around the world, Chasidim initiated their own grassroots efforts. In Kharkiv, Ukraine, Yehuda Chitrik had received an invitation for the wedding. "I realized right away there were major expenses."[31] He collected a thousand rubles and sent it to the Rebbe. Chasidim in other cities did the same. Somehow, through support in the US and Europe and through loans the Rebbe secured, the necessary funds were accumulated.

Instead of hosting the celebration in Riga, the Rebbe chose to hold it in the metropolis of Warsaw. Many Chasidim, among them Rabbi Eliyahu Chaim Althaus, wondered why. As he wrote in his diary, he dared not ask the Rebbe, "but still in my heart I harbored this question."[32] The night before the wedding, Althaus solved the riddle when he entered the yeshivah in Warsaw adorned with lights, filled with prominent rabbis, chasidic Rebbes and hundreds of students, to celebrate a pre-wedding dinner with the Rebbe and the Ramash. He realized that this would have been impossible in a more remote location like Riga.

To the amazement of the crowd, the Rebbe walked in adorned in his grandfather's *shtreimel.*[33] "Those of us who were nearby stood in fear of the awe-inspiring look on the Rebbe's pure face that shone under the *shtreimel,*" wrote Althaus. Customarily, Chabad Rebbes wore a *shtreimel* only when they were in the town of Lubavitch. When the Rashab fled Lubavitch in the face of the German invasion in 1915, he ceased wearing it. Now, the Rebbe Rayatz was wearing the *shtreimel* for the first time since assuming the position of Rebbe in 1920. The message was clear: After fourteen years of wandering and persecution, the glory and spiritual grandeur that Chasidim had felt in the town of Lubavitch was being reborn in Poland. The wedding marked a new era of Chabad, the flourishing of Chasidism in a new environment and a new country.

There were also other reasons for holding the celebration in Warsaw. As the center of the Jewish world, the message that Lubavitch was resilient would resound throughout Europe. This brought a ray of hope and optimism to the Chasidim remaining in Russia; Chabad had a future. As the Rebbe wrote to his uncle Moshe Horenstein, who accompanied the groom to the *chuppah* in place of his parents, "The *chuppah* will be on the grounds of Yeshivas Tomchei Temimim. That is a reflection of the spirit of Lubavitch." The yeshivah, the spiritual heart and essence of Chabad's ideas and ideals, lived on.

Second, it was an opportunity to introduce the Ramash to the broader Jewish community. Until this point, he was relatively unknown outside of the Rebbe's closest circle of Chasidim, especially because he didn't live in Riga full-time. He was naturally reserved and did not seek the limelight. "The Ramash was characteristically an introvert," says Rabbi Yoel Kahn,[34] chief recorder of the teachings of the seventh Rebbe. He had also chosen an unusual path by pursuing secular education at Europe's top universities, causing some Chasidim to look at him warily. He kept to himself, even though he was involved with the Rebbe's affairs, and he did not flout his Torah knowledge. At his wedding, he met some of the world's greatest Jewish scholars; the Rebbe encouraged him to interact with them. One such leader was Rabbi Meir Shapiro, dean of one of Poland's most prestigious yeshivas, Chachmei Lublin. The Rebbe introduced them, and the two had a long conversation about Rabbi Shapiro's recent scholarly publication.[35] Afterward, Rabbi Shapiro remarked to the

Rebbe, "Lubavitcher Rebbe, you have taken a son-in-law who is a *gaon* (outstanding Jewish scholar)."[36]

A month before the wedding, invitations were sent in a variety of formats.[37] To the Chasidim in Russia, the Rebbe wrote a special message, addressing them as "those who are far physically, but close and connected in soul and spirit." Lamenting the barriers that prevented the recipients from leaving Russia to participate in the wedding, the Rebbe wrote, "Due to reasons that are out of our control, it will be impossible to celebrate together." Instead, he asked them to organize celebrations in their local communities. Another special invitation, sent to the alumni of Tomchei Temimim and to select Chasidim, was a copy of a handwritten letter from the Rebbe. He also sent personal handwritten invitations to other chasidic Rebbes and distinguished scholars. The general public received printed invitations.

The Rebbe invited the needy Jews of Riga to participate in special free dinners in honor of the wedding. "The Lubavitcher Rebbe, in honor of the wedding of his daughter on November 27, is providing meals for free on Sunday and Monday," read the advertisement in Riga's paper, the *Frimorgen*. The Rebbe was following the ancient custom known as *seudat aniyyim,* providing meals to the indigent so they too can feel the joy of the wedding.[38]

On the Sunday before the wedding,[39] the Rebbe departed to Warsaw. At the Riga train station, he was greeted by thousands of Chasidim, acquaintances, and well-wishers who came to see him off. Two rows of men stretching some five hundred feet stood as an honor guard as the Rebbe entered the station. To the sound of joyous song, the train slowly began to move, and the crowd followed, dancing alongside. Joining the Rebbe on the train were the groom, the Rebbe's mother-in-law, his two daughters, his son-in-law the Rashag, and his grandson Berke Gurary. The bride and her mother had traveled to Warsaw a week earlier. As the train made its way to Warsaw, large crowds gathered in the stations in Dvinsk and Vilnius to wish the Rebbe well. Eliyahu Althaus, who was on the train when it pulled into Vilnius, wrote, "I was stunned to see such a massive crowd standing at the station."[40]

Tuesday, the day of the wedding, dawned cold. Temperatures did not rise above thirty-seven degrees.[41] The weather did not restrain the enthusiasm of the Jewish community, reported *Heint*.[42] "From 3:00 p.m., crowds streamed to the yeshivah where the *chuppah* was to take place. Only those with tickets were permitted to enter. Because the crowds were so large, the doors to the courtyard of the yeshivah were sealed until more police came to clear the area." The Rebbe and the groom arrived at the hall at 6:30 p.m. Afterward, "the bride arrived in a car decked in flowers."

"The courtyard was ablaze with light, and the *chuppah* stood in its center, surrounded by five thousand people," wrote Rabbi Shmuel Zalmanov in a long account of the wedding to his friends. *Heint* reported, "The courtyard was jam-packed, and others gazed from windows and balconies." According to *Der Moment*,[43] "The crowd was very different from those of other chasidic Rebbes. You don't see *shtreimels* here; most wear European Jewish dress in the Chabad style.... During the *chuppah* it was very packed, and the pickpockets worked hard, stealing purses and wallets."

The Rebbe's uncle and aunt, Rabbi Moshe and Chaya Horenstein, escorted the groom to the *chuppah*. The Rebbe and his wife then brought the bride. The Rebbe himself conducted the ceremony and recited the traditional seven blessings.

After the *chuppah* at the yeshivah, the wedding moved to a large hall nearby for dinner. Rabbi Yochanan Gordon attended the wedding, and his son spoke of his father's recollection of that special evening. "The Rebbe was in a state of elation. He walked around like a host, with a bottle of liquor and cups," giving out a *lechaim* to his guests. Gordon says the Rebbe knew each person's needs and showered them with blessings for health, children, and livelihood. He describes the many chasidic Rebbes, adorned in their Shabbat garb, with whom the Rebbe danced. "It was beautiful."

At one point, the Rebbe came over to the students who were standing along the walls and sat in their midst. He asked the dean of the yeshivah to distribute a toast to all the students and then called out to them, "*Lechaim, lechaim,* Temimim! Torah is retained only by one who sacrifices himself for it.[44] Only through exertion can one preserve his Torah studies. And to acquire Torah one must exert himself." He went on to explain that even a student who understands a concept at the first attempt "will not reach the same depths as the individual who exerts himself," even if that person is not intellectually gifted. He added that "Torah is true wisdom. It is godliness. Even Torah's simplest teachings are divine."[45]

At 11:00 p.m., the Rebbe began teaching a *maamar.*[46] He paused an hour later for the celebratory meal. The dancing continued throughout the night, and at 4:00 a.m., the Rebbe resumed the *maamar* for another half-hour. The meal concluded at 6:00 in the morning.[47]

Around the world, Chasidim rejoiced with their own *farbrengens*. Yaakov Dubrashvili remembers the celebration in Tbilisi, Soviet Georgia. "We received an invitation from the Rebbe for the wedding, and understandably, we could not go." They rejoiced the whole night locally, and the next morning they attempted to send a congratulatory telegram to Poland. Local police suspected that it was a secret message and accused Dubrashvili of spying. Once they realized that the telegram was indeed a wedding greeting, they sent it free of charge.[48] In Tel Aviv, local Chasidim began the evening by studying the Rebbe's invitation, analyzing it and seeking its deeper meaning. Chasidim gathered in Chicago, Philadelphia, and other US cities. In remote Finland, the sole Chasid, Rabbi Mordechai Schwei, also marked the day, writing, "I shared in the joy with all the Temimim and the Rebbe."[49] The Rebbe's daughter's marriage was not just a personal moment of joy, but a time of gladness for all the Chasidim.

The most poignant celebration outside of Warsaw took place nine hundred miles to the east, in the home of the Ramash's parents in Yekaterinoslav, Ukraine. The Ramash's parents could not rent a hall for the celebration; the only place where it could be held was in their small apartment. Half of it had been confiscated, and a wall was erected to carve out a separate apartment for another family. That family, says Rebbetzin Chana Schneerson, generally kept their distance, because they were afraid of being associated with religion. "Somehow, however, our neighbor heard in town that we wanted to hold a celebration to mark the wedding. For our benefit, he broke through the wall between the apartments, opening his apartment to ours. He removed all his furniture and moved out as well, giving us the use of his apartment for as long as we would need."

Invitations were sent out to friends and relatives in Dnipropetrovsk and the surrounding region. "Guests and family members came from neighboring towns, and we received several hundred telegrams. The evening event at home was attended by representatives of the central Jewish community of our region. Every synagogue, even if it had relatively few members, sent representatives, many of them accompanied by their wives." They came despite the fact that "contact with clergy was forbidden, a crime that could cost you your job," wrote Rebbetzin Chana.

Shmuel Schneerson, the Ramash's uncle, wrote to him describing the night in Dnipropetrovsk. There were speeches until 11:00 at night, he wrote, followed by a celebratory meal and then dancing that "went on nonstop, lasting until 7:00 in the morning."[50] The evening's exuberance was tinged with sadness. "Our longing for [the Ramash] was indescribable and our anguish was felt by the community," Rebbetzin Chana wrote. "I don't wish upon anyone the experience and taste of not being present at their child's personal celebration."[51]

The marriage of the Ramash to the Rebbe's daughter also highlighted the bond between the two men, and their relationship continued to grow. The Ramash was involved, often behind the scenes, in the Rebbe's affairs while in Europe. Later, in the US, the Ramash took a more public role, spearheading vital projects in the last decade of the Rebbe's life. On a deeper spiritual level, the wedding cemented the Ramash's bond with the Chasidim. At a *farbrengen* in 1953[52] marking his twenty-fifth wedding anniversary, the seventh Rebbe discussed the significance of his wedding. Though he rarely spoke about himself, that day he made an uncharacteristically personal reflection: "Generally speaking, even regarding a private person, his wedding constitutes an all-encompassing event. For me, however, my wedding day brought me into more general and communal affairs." Then, considering the bond between himself and the Chasidim, he told those gathered that the wedding "connected me to you, and you to me."

Three days after the wedding, the family returned to Riga, where the week of *sheva brachot* (post-wedding celebrations) continued. One of the Chasidim who hesitated to join the Shabbat celebration was Noach Lulov, whose son had arrested the Rebbe two years earlier. He shared with Rabbi Avraham Goldin that when the Rebbe heard he was not coming, "he invited me personally."[53]

For the next two months, the young couple stayed in Riga. Afterward, they headed to Berlin, where they resided for three years as the Ramash continued his university education. In the spring of 1933, as the Nazi threat began to grow, they left Berlin and after a brief interlude in Riga, resettled in Paris. There the Ramash pursued a degree in engineering.[54] The Ramash was very reserved, but slowly the chasidic community began to recognize his intellectual acumen. While the Rebbe was in the US during the High Holidays of 1929, the Ramash was encouraged to lead a *farbrengen* in Riga in his absence. Rabbi Eliyahu Chaim Althaus, who was present at that Sukkot *farbrengen,* wrote a glowing report to the Rebbe. "[The Ramash] spoke for hours on end saying words of *Chasidut* with teachings from our Sages." Addressing the wariness that some Chasidim felt toward the Ramash because of his secular education, Althaus wrote, "The critics and cynics have been silenced." News of the amazing talk in the *sukkah* spread around town so that a few days later, on Simchat Torah, "a huge crowd gathered to join the Ramash for *hakafot* (traditional holiday dancing with the Torah)." Describing that night, Althaus wrote, "Rabbi Menachem Mendel sat at the head of the table and spoke for four hours straight. As people left, they were saying that they had never seen or heard anything like it."[55]

From when the Ramash arrived in Riga until the outbreak of World War II, just over a decade, the Rebbe mentored the Ramash. Though they did not live close to each other, opportunities arose when the young couple visited with the Rebbe for the High Holidays season or for Passover. Some of these visits were for longer durations. The Rebbe, in turn, visited his daughter and son-in-law in Berlin and later in Paris, as part of his travels. All through the 1930s, as the Rebbe sought medical care in Berlin, Vienna, Paris, and the spas of Marienbad, the Ramash was by his side.[56] This included a two-month stay in Berlin starting in January 1933 and a six-month stay in the West End Sanitorium in Perchtoldsdorf on the outskirts of Vienna, starting in November 1934. These times that the Ramash and the Rebbe were together for an extensive period provided more opportunities for mentorship and conversation. At times, the Ramash functioned as the Rebbe's secretary, helping him with correspondence and other affairs.

From the time he was in Riga, the Ramash began to record his interactions with his father-in-law in a detailed private diary. It included a wealth of chasidic lore, history, and customs, with anecdotes of all the Rebbes, tracing back to the founder of the chasidic movement, Rabbi Yisrael Baal Shem Tov. These notations, discovered in his desk[57] shortly after his passing, were published posthumously.[58] They are are a window into the internal exchanges between the Rebbe Rayatz and the future seventh Rebbe, reflecting a deep spiritual dialogue that occurred over the course of a decade.[59] "There were long conversations between the two men, often centering on Chabad history and customs," writes Rabbi Adin Steinsaltz.[60] Many notations in the diary refer to scholarly issues and details of the Rebbe's personal observance of Jewish tradition. In the years to come, when asked about certain chasidic traditions, the seventh Rebbe would invariably say, "I witnessed my father-in-law the Rebbe do such-and-such," or at times indicate that a certain practice was not the Chabad custom because he had not observed the Rebbe acting in that fashion.

Even when the two were not physically near each other, the relationship and mentorship continued. Hundreds of letters sent frequently between the Rebbe and his daughter and son-in-law reveal an intimate connection.[61] These included long letters sent by the Rebbe to the Ramash explaining the history and theology of Chabad. In one lengthy letter sent in January 1932, the Rebbe explores in depth the distinctive focus of Chabad on intellectual ideas and spiritual growth, as opposed to other chasidic groups, which emphasize the spiritual qualities of their Rebbes and their miraculous works.[62] The Ramash responded, "From the depths of my heart, I thank you for this precious gift."[63]

Another part of the intellectual interaction between the two was the *Hatomim* magazine. The periodical, founded in 1935, was a platform for the Rebbe to promulgate teachings of Chabad and reinforce the importance of the yeshivah, now located in Poland, as a premier center of Jewish learning. It featured chasidic teachings, history, and scholarly essays. The Rebbe asked his son-in-law to review articles for the magazine; few knew that the Ramash was assisting with the editing from his home in Paris.

The Ramash was entrusted with many missions on the Rebbe's behalf. In 1932, the Rebbe urged his son-in-law, then in Berlin, to work on attaining repatriation of the historic library that had been seized by the Russian government.[64] The Ramash also assisted the Rebbe in expanding his library. "He spent hours going to libraries on behalf of his father-in-law, searching for specific titles and manuscripts," writes Steinsaltz.[65] When the Polish government enacted currency restrictions, making it problematic to transfer funds in and out of the country,[66] the Rebbe, then in Poland, entrusted his son-in-law in Paris with much of his financial affairs, having him open accounts there and maintain records on his behalf. The Rebbe instructed donors across the globe to send their contributions directly to the Ramash in Paris.[67] The Rebbe's correspondence with the Ramash reveals extensive instructions, often written in code to maintain confidentiality, on transferring funds to the institutions and projects the Rebbe supported in Russia and other countries.[68]

While involved with the Rebbe's work from a distance, the primary goal of the Ramash was the pursuit of scholarship. In March 1940, when the Rebbe was heading to New York, the Ramash hesitated to leave Paris to join him. Yechezkel Feigin wrote to Rabbi Yisrael Jacobson, asking him to encourage the Ramash to come to the US. "He has a great ability to draw the younger generation closer to Jewish observance," Feigin wrote. The Ramash resisted the request, seemingly because he feared it would detract from his studies. Feigin told Jacobson that the opposite was true: "He has completed his secular studies and [now] can dedicate himself totally to the sacred," referring to Torah.[69]

After the German invasion a few months later, the Ramash and his wife made a harrowing escape from Paris via Vichy, France, and Portugal, arriving in the US in March 1941. At that point, his involvement in the Rebbe's affairs expanded greatly. In 1941, the Rebbe established Kehot Publication Society, a publishing house for the works of Chasidism and Judaism in general, and he appointed the Ramash as its chairman. The Ramash was also appointed executive director of another two corporations founded that year by the Rebbe: Machne Israel, Chabad's social service agency, and Merkos L'Inyonei Chinuch, its central education branch. Merkos, as it is colloquially known, took the lead in establishing the first national network of Jewish day schools and eventually began to oversee the global network of Chabad *shluchim* and institutions that continues to this day.

The Rebbe's spiritual guidance of his son-in-law, who would eventually succeed him as the seventh Rebbe of Lubavitch, is illustrated in the following anecdote.

After the Ramash joined the Rebbe in New York, he maintained an office on the first floor of the movement's headquarters at 770 Eastern Parkway, right near the study hall. Every day, the Ramash visited his father-in-law in his residence on the second floor. When he came down, yeshivah students would congregate near the elevator, hoping to hear him retell "*frisha zachen* (fresh goods)" – stories, directives, or Torah teachings that he had just heard from the Rebbe. One day in 1943, Dovid Edelman[70] and Hershel Fogelman,[71] two students ages eighteen and twenty-two respectively, were waiting at the elevator door when the Ramash exited.

"Some of the Jews who visit me in my office," the Ramash told them, "were brought up in religious environments, but sadly they didn't keep up their observance once they came to America. Some of the elder Chasidim have chastised me for not criticizing their behavior, instead warmly welcoming everyone equally.[72]

"I went to ask the Rebbe if I was acting correctly," he continued. "If it's wrong, I would stop." The Ramash told them that the Rebbe explained to him that G-d created a feeling of unlimited love in a father and mother, no matter how many children they have. And if one of the children is missing something, like a hand or a leg, the parent will naturally feel a more special, unique love for that child. "The Rebbe told me: 'G-d, too, loves every Jew completely, but if a Jew is missing something, He loves him or her even more. So if a Jew comes into your office and does not observe the commandments, we must accept him wholeheartedly; this is a precious Jew. When you greet someone who does not lay tefillin – missing a hand, so to speak – or who does not attend synagogue – missing a leg, so to speak – you must have a deeper love for him, because the more he is lacking, the greater your love must be. You should conduct yourself like G-d does."

This philosophy clearly infused the Ramash's leadership as the seventh Rebbe.[73] It is but one example of mentorship offered by the Rebbe to his son-in-law that was translated into a global Jewish renaissance. Being involved in the Rebbe's medical care, editing his Torah teachings for print, taking responsibility for his financial affairs, and spearheading the movement's outreach, all set the stage for the Ramash to assume the mantle of leadership of Chabad.

The Rebbe in his early twenties

The Rebbe and his son-in-law Rabbi Menachem Mendel Schneerson, Riga, 1929-30

The Rebbe arriving in New York for his first visit in September 1929

The Rebbe in St. Louis 1930. On the right is Nathan Harris, on the left the Rashag.

The Rebbe at the White House in July 1930. Right to left, the Rashag, the Rebbe, Hyman S. Kramer, A. Fogelman, and Asher Rabinowitz.

The Rebbe sitting in a sleigh while visiting Jews in Lithuania in the early 1930s

Poland 1930s

The Rebbe wears his *shtreimel,* as he celebrates becoming a US citizen. Right to left, Dr. Nissan Mindel, the Ramash, Rabbi Hodakov, and court representatives

Rebbetzin Nechama Dina Schneersohn recives US citizenship. Right to left, the Ramash, the Rebbetzin, the judge, Gershon Eichhorn, Rabbi Shlomi Kazanofsky, and Dr. Nissan Mindel.

Thousands surround the coffin bedecked by the Rebbe's *kapota* on January 29, 1950 (11 Shevat)

The Rebbe 1949

Thank you to Rabbis Berel Levin, Mendel Mintz, and Yossi Gabay for providing the images.

Chapter Seven

The Voyage

In Riga, the Rebbe was faced with two dilemmas: one, how to alleviate the suffering of Russian Jews, and two – this one much more personal and deeply spiritual – how to travel to the graves of the righteous to pray there. The solution to both would involve a long journey to the United States with an interlude in *Eretz Yisrael*.

As the oppression in Russia reached new heights, the primary American Jewish aid organization, the JDC, had suspended almost all its funding of the Rebbe's work in Russia and instead partnered with the Communist regime in resettling Jews in communal farms. The Rebbe had hoped that he could sway senior officials of the JDC in Berlin, but his efforts had been fruitless. He realized the real decision makers were in New York. "The disheartening news regarding the [JDC] budget compels me to travel successfully to the US to set up support for our brothers in Russia on a firm foundation." The Rebbe wrote to Yehuda Lokshin, Chabad's director in New York,[1] telling him that the financial crisis is "causing me great anguish. Hashem should bestow His mercy on me; I am very dismayed and downhearted. I have consulted with *HaGaon* Rabbi Chaim Ozer and *HaGaon HaTzaddik* the Chafetz Chaim, who encouraged me to go."[2] The Rebbe hoped that by meeting JDC leaders in the US he could convince them to support his efforts in Russia.

The Rebbe also wanted to galvanize the general Jewish community in the US to help their brethren in Russia. There had been some financial help from US Jews, but despite pleas from the Rebbe to prominent rabbis to push their communities to give more, little money was raised. Clearly, the only way to create a solid financial base was for the Rebbe to come to the US himself and appeal directly to Jewish leaders and the public. "It is essential that the Rebbe himself travel to the United States," wrote Rabbi Feigin to his friend Yisrael Jacobson in New York.[3] The trip would also serve another important purpose: The Rebbe would dedicate much time to strengthening religious life in the United States and reconnecting with Chabad Chasidim there. It would also set the stage for his relocation to the US in 1940.

The Rebbe's purpose for visiting *Eretz Yisrael* was very different.[4] Jewish tradition encourages visiting *kivrei tzaddikim,* the graves of the righteous, to seek divine blessing, especially in preparation for the High Holidays. This had been a centerpiece of the spiritual *avodah* of Lubavitcher Rebbes for generations. Traditionally, they prayed for the welfare of the Jewish community at the graves of their predecessors, placing letters and prayer requests there. Prior to resolving to leave Russia, the Rebbe visited Rostov to pray at the gravesite of his father, only then making the fateful decision.[5] In Riga this was impossible. "At this time, I am unable to travel to our country to visit the graves of my ancestors,"[6] who were all interred in Russia. "I want to travel to the Holy Land to visit the holy places." The Rebbe planned to pray at the Western Wall in Jerusalem, at the Tomb of the Patriarchs (*Me'arat HaMakhpelah*) in Hebron, and at the graves of the great Sages.

In 1929–30, the Rebbe undertook a long overseas voyage, first to *Eretz Yisrael* (then British Mandate Palestine[7]) and then to the US. The trip came a few months after recovering from a heart attack[8] and lasted just over a year. The first stop was *Eretz Yisrael,* where the Rebbe had to navigate a complicated political terrain. The influx of secular idealistic Zionist immigrants had prompted conflict between them and the traditional Orthodox community. Some advocated partnering with the Zionists and attempting to mitigate their secular nationalism, while others stood staunchly against them. The Rebbe did not want to be drawn into the debate. When he decided to visit *Eretz Yisrael,* he turned to the country's two most prominent rabbinic leaders, who represented the two sides of the dispute: Rabbi Yosef Chaim Sonnenfeld,[9] leader of the *Eidah HaChareidit,* the traditional Orthodox community in Jerusalem, and Rabbi Avraham Yitzchak (HaKohen) Kook,[10] who was appointed the first chief rabbi by the British Mandate. Rabbi Sonnenfeld argued for opposition to the Zionists and Rabbi Kook for rapprochement, but despite their disagreements, the two respected each other. The Rebbe asked them both to help him with visa arrangements, and he emphasized that the purpose of his trip was personal, "to visit the holy sites."[11]

Once the travel plans were finalized, the Rebbe wrote to Chabad leaders in *Eretz Yisrael*[12] informing them of his plans. "I hope that the Chasidim won't overburden me during the visit, due to my delicate health situation. Every possible effort will definitely be made not to mix into any political issues or political parties, etc., because my visit is of a private nature."

It was a taxing journey for the Rebbe, leaving behind his wife, family, and Chasidim in Europe. Throughout the trip, the Rebbe wrote to his wife almost daily, sharing with her the details of his travels.[13] After visiting the Jewish homeland, he continued to the US via Europe, with a stop in Berlin. Upon returning to Europe, weak and exhausted, his doctors recommended that he rest from the journey. After a visit to the spa town of Marienbad to regain his energy, plus another stop in Berlin, the Rebbe finally headed home just over a year after he left.

When the Rebbe departed Riga for his journey,[14] he was accompanied by his son-in-law the Rashag. In Berlin, his daughter Chaya Mushka and her husband, the Ramash, joined them. Together they traveled by train though Germany, Czechoslovakia, and Austria until they arrived at the port of Trieste in Italy, where they boarded[15] a ship heading south to Alexandria, Egypt. When the boat stopped at the southern Italian port of Brindisi,[16] the Ramash and his wife departed, returning to Berlin, while the Rashag continued, accompanying the Rebbe.

In Alexandria, the Rebbe was welcomed by local Jewish community leaders. A delegation of Chabad rabbis from Jerusalem came to escort the Rebbe on the last leg of his journey by train through the Sinai Desert.

At the border crossing he was greeted by British officials. As the train crossed southern *Eretz Yisrael,* Chasidim boarded at each stop, creating a festive atmosphere. The nine-day trek from Riga ended Thursday morning, August 8, with a rousing welcome from an enthusiastic crowd of five thousand – more than ten percent of Jerusalem's Jewish population – at the train station.[17] The New York Yiddish daily *Der Tag* reported, "The platform was filled with a crowd to no end. The British police created an open space for the Rebbe to walk. Outside the station the street overflowed with people."[18] *Haaretz* reported that when the Rebbe departed from the train, "A large crowd saluted him with applause, and it continued as he made his way through the plaza outside the station."[19]

Since its founding, Chabad had fostered a connection to the ancient Jewish homeland. In 1777, Rabbi Menachem Mendel of Vitebsk led the first chasidic *aliyah* and founded settlements in Tiberias and Safed.[20] His protege, Chabad founder Rabbi Schneur Zalman, escorted him on his journey until Mogilev-Podolski in southern Ukraine. He considered continuing on to *Eretz Yisrael,* but his mentor instructed him to remain in Europe and focus on spreading chasidic teachings. The chasidic community in the Holy Land remained close to his heart, and to ensure its continuity, Rabbi Schneur Zalman established the international fund Colel Chabad in 1788.[21] He raised money in Europe to distribute to families who settled in the Holy Land. Successive Chabad Rebbes encouraged world Jewry to support the growing community in Israel through Colel Chabad.

The 1808 immigration to Safed and Tiberias by students of the Vilna Gaon,[22] opponents of the chasidic movement, brought the divisions of European Jewry to *Eretz Yisrael.* Disagreements also arose within the chasidic community in Eretz Yisrael between Rabbi Avraham Karlisker, the successor of Rabbi Menachem Mendel, and Chabad community members.[23] This prompted Rabbi Schneur Zalman's son and successor, Rabbi Dov Ber, to encourage his Chasidim to relocate to Hebron, where they established a synagogue in 1823 that still stands today.[24] In the decades that followed, the Hebron community grew, bolstered by more immigrants, including the daughter and son-in-law of Rabbi Dov Ber, Rabbi Yaakov and Rebbetzin Menucha Rochel Slonim, who arrived in 1844. An additional community of Chabad Chasidim was established in

Jerusalem, led by Rabbi Eliyahu Yosef Rivlin;[25] a synagogue was founded in the Jewish Quarter of the Old City in 1848.[26] Additional congregations were established in Jaffa and other cities. During the time of the Rebbe Rashab, Chabad expanded its presence in *Eretz Yisrael* with the purchase of a large property in Hebron,[27] where it opened a yeshivah.

Though the Rebbe sought to avoid conflict during his visit in *Eretz Yisrael,* he was dragged into controversy within minutes of his arrival. At the Jerusalem train station, flyers were distributed protesting the Rebbe's plan to meet with Rabbi Kook, describing him in very disparaging terms. *Der Tag* reported, "A troublemaker dispersed the flyers,[28] and some of the crowd turned on him. His friends stood by his side. The police broke up the fight."[29] In a letter to his family in Riga, the Rebbe wrote, "The flyers were spread out by the thousands. It is unnecessary to say what kind of fire they ignited."[30] He added that his son-in-law the Rashag made a major diplomatic effort to mitigate the damage, finalizing the meeting with Rabbi Kook.

That first afternoon, the Rebbe prayed at the Western Wall, a portion of the historic wall that surrounded the Temple Mount in ancient times. The Rebbe made his way on foot through the Old City, accompanied by hundreds of people. A crowd of 1,500 eventually filled the open space in front of the Wall, which was then much smaller than the present broad plaza.[31] Hundreds more looked on from surrounding rooftops. It was a deeply emotional moment for the Rebbe. "I cried hot tears," he wrote in a private correspondence to his family.[32] "We were in a higher world. No matter how much you believe, no matter how you believe, in such a holy moment, standing next to the Wall of the *Beit HaMikdash* (the Holy Temple), everything changes. Religious or not, we completely change." The Rebbe explained that "everything is elevated as the heart beseeches G-d for mercy." Most heavily on the Rebbe's mind at that time was the welfare of the Jews in Russia. "Oceans of tears open up as I feel the plight of our dear students, the Chasidim, and their wives and families, and I ponder their spiritual and physical predicament."

In Jerusalem, he visited with Rabbi Sonnenfeld, the chief Sephardic Rabbi Yaakov Meir, and other Jewish leaders. He met with Rabbi Avraham Yitzchak Kook three times – more than anyone else. The first visit took place in Rabbi Kook's home on Friday afternoon, where he was greeted by a delegation of rabbis. The second meeting was when Rabbi Kook returned the visit to the Rebbe's hotel after Shabbat. Their final visit took place before the Rebbe's departure. Rabbi Kook's mother[33] descended from a Chabad family, and his writings reflect a great intellectual affinity toward chasidic teachings. The conversations[34] between the Rebbe and Rabbi Kook alternated between the challenges to world Jewry and profound topics in Torah. Heavy on the Rebbe's heart, as always, was the plight of Soviet Jewry. "From the moment I left Russia, I cannot stop thinking about the welfare of the Jews there, whose lives are in mortal danger," he told Rabbi Kook during their first meeting. The Rebbe explained to Rabbi Kook that funds were needed to keep the Jewish education system in Russia afloat. Rabbi Kook suggested the Rebbe meet with Supreme Court Justice Louis Brandeis, arguably the most influential Jew in the US, and he wrote a recommendation letter. "I have met him, and he fights for the oppressed," Rabbi Kook told the Rebbe. "When he understands the situation of Russian Jewry, hopefully he will help."[35]

Interestingly, Gad Frumkin merited much attention from the Rebbe. He was the only Jewish member of the British Mandate Supreme Court, and the son of a Chabad Chasid. Frumkin had drifted from observance, but the Rebbe recognized that he "had a warm heart."[36] The Rebbe welcomed him in his hotel in Jerusalem and briefly stopped at his home. Frumkin also accompanied the Rebbe in his car on his way to Tel Aviv. Along the way, Frumkin wrote later, "I shared with the Rebbe the progress in building communities in *Eretz Yisrael*."[37]

While in Jerusalem, the Rebbe dealt with a complex institutional issue. The split between the various streams of Chabad in Russia after the passing of the third Rebbe, Rabbi Menachem Mendel, in 1866, was mirrored in the community in Jerusalem. Colel Chabad had come under the sway of the Kopust branch of Chabad. In 1920 the organization's Jerusalem-based board officially decided to pledge their allegiance to the Rebbe Rashab,[38] and after his passing they reaffirmed that pledge to the Rebbe Rayatz. The Rebbe made his acceptance conditional on reforming the organization's governance and financial procedures.[39] The concerns festered due to the Rebbe's geographic distance and the differences of opinion amongst the Jerusalem board members. During his Jerusalem visit the Rebbe resolved those issues,[40] officially accepting the leadership and appointing Rabbi Shlomo Leib Eliazrov[41] as Colel Chabad's chairman. A new charter was eventually written to formalize the modifications the Rebbe requested.[42]

On Shabbat, crowds converged on Jerusalem from all over the country, and the Rebbe recited a chasidic discourse. On Sunday, the Rebbe continued his spiritual pilgrimage, first to the northern Galilee region, where he visited holy sites in Nablus,[43] Tiberias, and Safed.[44] He prayed at the graves of many great sages,[45] including Rabbi Shimon bar Yochai, Rabbi Yosef Karo, Maimonides, Rabbi Akiva, and Rabbi Menachem Mendel of Vitebsk. He prayed at each stop, at times with great emotion and tears, and read prayer requests that had been sent to him.

The most dramatic visit was to Hebron, where Avraham, the first Jew, interred his wife Sarah in the *Me'arat Hamakhpelah,* the Tomb of the Patriarchs.[46] The double cave also includes the graves of Yitzchak and Rivkah, and Yaakov and Leah. King Herod erected a massive structure over the cave during the Second Temple era that remains standing today.[47] Considered the second most sacred site in Jewish history after the Temple Mount, Hebron was where King David was crowned in 877 BCE.[48]

Jews and other non-Muslims had been forbidden from entering the *Me'arat Hamakhpelah* since 1267, eighty years after the Muslims seized Hebron from the Crusaders. Muslim authorities permitted Jews to pray only at the bottom of seven steps, outside the entrance.[49] Benjamin of Tudela visited in 1165, before the ban, and was able to enter the cave below and view the graves.[50] There were some rare instances when the ban was lifted, usually at the insistence of the Turkish sultan; such was done for the prince of Wales in 1862[51] and the Jewish US ambassador to the Turkish Empire, Henry Morgenthau, in 1914. But the Sultan's wishes were not always enough; when he requested access for Moses Montefiore in 1838, local religious leaders barred his admission.[52] Unlike Benjamin Tudela, those admitted were only given access to the large Herodian structure, not to the cave underneath where the actual burial sites are located.

"The Rebbe's visit was cause for a general celebration. The whole town turned out to welcome this distinguished guest," wrote David Shainberg, a yeshivah student from Memphis whose correspondence with his family is detailed in Yardena Schwartz's book *Ghosts of a Holy War*.[53] Shainberg was very impressed with the Rebbe. "His appearance is that of a stately king, enhanced by a shining countenance and dignified beard." He noted that the Rebbe was the leader of "thousands and thousands of Jews in the world. Unlike other chasidic rabbis, the Lubavitcher is a modern, well-dressed personage.... It was an honor to see him at close range and shake his hand."

The Rebbe stopped at the seven steps outside the tomb where Jews traditionally gathered. There, "the Rebbe prayed *Minchah* for two hours, with sobbing that could be heard in every corner,"[54] remembered Shalom Ber Goldshmidt. Eliezer Don Slonim,[55] son of the community's rabbi and director of the local bank, had a unique relationship with local Arab leaders. Upon Slonim's request, they permitted the Rebbe to enter the historic *Me'arat Hamakhpelah* structure. No other rabbinic figure had entered in centuries. The local Jewish community accompanied the Rebbe as he walked to the site, where he was welcomed by Arab notables. Six rabbis joined the Rebbe inside for the historic visit, including Rabbi Shlomo Zalman Klonski, who described the moment:[56] "The Rebbe walked with an entourage of Arabs and Jews slowly following behind him." The Arabs noted the large memorial stones that were covered with decorative tapestries over the graves of the patriarchs and matriarchs below. For the Rebbe, it was a deeply spiritual experience. The anti-Semitic mufti of Jerusalem, Mohammed Amin al-Husseini,[57] telegrammed local authorities, demanding that the Rebbe's access be blocked, but his message was received after the Rebbe finished his visit.

As the Rebbe left, he dispensed charity to the local Arab poor.[58] The Rebbe also met with Jewish leaders, had private audiences with community members, and visited local institutions and the property purchased by his father.

Tragically, just eleven days later, after the Rebbe departed *Eretz Yisrael*, Arabs attacked Jews throughout Palestine. Jerusalem's mufti incited Arab mobs, using Jewish prayer at the Western Wall in Jerusalem as a pretext. The larger issue was the growing Jewish presence in *Eretz Yisrael*. The greatest violence took place in Hebron, where sixty-four Jewish men, women, and children,[59] many of them Chabad Chasidim, including David Shainberg, were murdered in cold blood.

The Rebbe spent a second Shabbat in Jerusalem and then went on to Tel Aviv, where a large entourage followed him. "Dozens of buses filled with Chasidim escorted the Rebbe to Tel Aviv," describes Gad Frumkin in his autobiography.[60] "At the entrance to Tel Aviv, a crowd of two thousand gathered, local officials welcomed him, and large crowds converged on his hotel." From there, the Rebbe visited Petach Tikvah and Bnei Brak, and had a private evening excursion with Frumkin to the nearby agriculture settlement of Rechovot.[61]

After a whirlwind visit of two weeks, on Thursday, August 22,[62] the Rebbe began the long journey to the United States via Egypt and Europe. His visit to *Eretz Yisrael* was a magnificent success. The Rebbe had the opportunity to pray at the important holy sites. He was the only known Jewish rabbinic leader in centuries to visit *Me'arat HaMakhpelah* in Hebron. Thousands had greeted him, hundreds had private meetings, and many were inspired by his recitation of chasidic discourses. [63] He met with the country's most noted rabbis and other leaders from a wide spectrum of the Jewish community.

The visit had put the Chasidim in *Eretz Yisrael* on a spiritual high. Many had taken time off their daily activities to be part of the Rebbe's entourage as he traveled around the county. "During the Rebbe's visit in *Eretz Yisrael*, we felt a spiritual elevation and sense of sanctity," wrote Rabbi Shimon Glitzenstein. Fifteen busloads of Chasidim escorted the Rebbe from his hotel in Tel Aviv to the train station in Lod, where a large crowd waited to bid the Rebbe farewell. There the Rebbe said his last goodbyes, Glitzenstein recalls.[64] "The Rebbe was very emotional, and gave his blessing to each and every person." He then distributed a printed *maamar* so that he would depart by sharing words of Torah.

The Rebbe traveled to Cairo[65] and then took the train to Alexandria. Local Jewish community leaders came to welcome him. In 1984, when the Arabic-speaking Rabbi Shimon Elituv[66] visited the small Jewish community in Alexandria, its leader recalled with excitement the Rebbe's visit some fifty-six years earlier. "A European-looking man came to the train station to welcome the Rebbe, carrying a large platter of fruit." He explained to the Rebbe that as child he had accompanied his grandfather to meet the fourth Rebbe, Rabbi Shmuel, in Lubavitch.[67] His grandfather told Rabbi Shmuel, "During the Temple era, Jews would bring their first fruits to the Temple. Now I am bringing my first fruits to you," asking Rabbi Shmuel to bless his grandson. At the time the Rayatz was almost three years old and was playing in his grandfather's study. Rabbi Shmuel responded, "Just as you have brought me fruits, so too I bless you that one day your grandson will bring fruits to my grandson." When the man heard the Rebbe was traveling via Alexandria, he recalled the story and decided to fulfill the blessing by bringing the Rebbe a beautiful platter. In 1984, the leader of the local community told Rabbi Elituv that the Rebbe was deeply touched and responded that he remembered as a child being in his grandfather's study and hearing the blessing he gave.

On Sunday, as the ship made its way from Alexandria to Italy, news of the Arab riots in *Eretz Yisrael* and the massacre in Hebron reached the Rebbe. Grief over the terrible bloodbath caused him to become seriously ill. As he wrote to Rabbi Kook soon afterward, "I became sick from pain and anguish after hearing the distressing news." Fortunately, Dr. Moshe Wallach, medical director of Shaarei Zedek hospital in Jerusalem, was onboard and nurtured the Rebbe back to health.[68]

The Rebbe and the Rashag made their way to Berlin and France, where they were joined for the trip to the US by the Rebbe's uncle Moshe Horenstein, Mordechai Dubin, and the Rebbe's secretary Rabbi Yechezkel Feigin.[69] They arrived in New York Harbor on Tuesday, September 17, 1929. Hundreds of Chasidim and well-wishers greeted the Rebbe as he strode off the boat escorted by New York police.

During his ten-month sojourn in the US, the Rebbe traveled as far north as Boston and as far west as St. Louis. He visited most of the major Jewish population centers, including Philadelphia, Baltimore, and Detroit, also making stops in smaller towns like Milwaukee, Springfield, and Worcester. The Rebbe spent most of his time in the Crown Heights and Brownsville sections of Brooklyn, as well as three months in Chicago. He visited Washington, DC, twice: once to meet with Supreme Court Justice Louis Brandeis and once to meet with President Herbert Hoover in the White House before departing the US. In each city, the Rebbe was greeted by massive crowds.

The Rebbe was provided an apartment in Crown Heights, then an upscale Brooklyn neighborhood. It was home to the imposing Brooklyn Jewish Center, the largest Conservative Temple in the United States.

A few miles away was Brownsville, then called "Jerusalem of America," which brimmed with Yiddish speakers, many of whom remained steadfast in tradition. When the Rebbe relocated to the US a decade later, he chose to live in Crown Heights.

In 1929, the city was teeming with immigrants who were moving up the economic scale and slowly dispensing with observance. Only twelve percent of Brooklyn's Jewish children received any Jewish education in the 1920s.[70] Aside from the few yeshivas, such as Yeshivah Torah Vodaath in Williamsburg and Yeshivas Rabbeinu Yitzchak Elchonon, which had just relocated from the Lower East Side to Washington Heights,[71] there were few Jewish schools. America had yet to become a center of Jewish scholarship.

One of the Rebbe's goals was to rekindle the connection with immigrants who had a chasidic background. As Rabbi Yisrael Jacobson wrote, "The earlier rounds of immigrants were traditional Jews, most not fully observant, and few actual Torah scholars."[72] With the rise of pogroms, the disruptions caused by World War I, and the Russian revolution, more passionately religious immigrants came. In the 1920s and 1930s, there were some forty Chabad synagogues[73] in New York City, and many more across the country. Some were filled with Chasidim, while others simply had a nostalgic tie to Chabad. Many immigrants still attended synagogue, some for religious reasons, others to connect to friends from Europe.[74]

For the Chasidim, the Rebbe's visit was spiritually uplifting. For generations, Chasidim had traveled to the Rebbe in Lubavitch, and now the Rebbe had come to them in the New World. For the High Holidays, the Rebbe attended a large synagogue in Brownsville, where he prayed at great length. On Rosh HaShanah the Rebbe recited a *maamar.*[75] Years later, Yehoshua Greenberg, who was present for that *maamar,* told his grandson, "The shul was packed, and many gathered outdoors. The Rebbe's voice was booming, and even those outside heard him."[76] The Rebbe spent Simchat Torah in Crown Heights with a few thousand people who came to celebrate during the forty-eight-hour holiday. The crowd attending the *farbrengens* and listening to the Rebbe's talks was diverse. "An elderly Chasid, a rabbi with a dignified beard, a clean-shaven man with a golden chain and a ring on his finger, a non-Chasid wearing a tall hat, a beardless Rabbi, and a student, all standing, this one in this corner, and that one in that corner, and listening attentively," wrote the Rebbe to his wife, describing the people listening to the *maamar*.[77] It was a festive holiday, with dancing that lasted till 2:30 a.m. The next day the celebration continued with a *farbrengen*, singing, and dancing that lasted late into the day.

Late in the afternoon, the Rebbe was visited by Reform Rabbi Stephen S. Wise. The two entered the Rebbe's residence to speak privately as the singing of Chasidim could be heard echoing in the background. The next day, Weiss told his students in Manhattan, "It is worthwhile for you to visit the *chakham*, the wise leader of the Jewish people, in Brooklyn."[78]

The celebration continued after sunset,[79] with Jews from all over Brooklyn and Manhattan joining the *farbrengen* that lasted well into the night. "The crowd was very enthusiastic," the Rebbe wrote to his wife.[80] He gave a series of talks interspersed with singing, outlining a vision for American Jewry.[81] The Rebbe recounted the famous story of the founder of Chasidism, Rabbi Yisrael Baal Shem Tov: When his soul ascended on high[82] and encountered the Messiah, he asked, "Master, when are you coming?" Replied the Messiah, "When your wellsprings will spread to the outside," meaning, when your teachings will be disseminated. The Rebbe stated, "Now the time has come to bring the esoteric teachings of Torah to America." The Rebbe was alluding to an important Jewish mystical concept, says Rabbi Shmuel Kaplan, a veteran Chabad *shliach* in Baltimore. "Rabbi Dov Ber, the second Chabad Rebbe, explains that Torah had not been taught in what the mystics call '*kadur hatachton*,'"[83] the Western Hemisphere.

At the time, many were lamenting the spiritual state of American Jews, in particular the younger generation. The Rebbe took a more optimistic view. "I do not despair of the offspring of Chasidim who have wandered afield. Even those who have drifted have an inner spark of faith for which their parents sacrificed, and it can be awakened in them." In America, the Rebbe told the crowd, the teachings of the Baal Shem Tov would ultimately become widespread. The ground was fertile for a renaissance of Torah and spirituality. And that would set the stage for the ultimate redemption, as promised in Jewish teachings.

These talks laid out a broad vision for revelation of the deep teachings of Torah in a fertile new realm. The exile of the Jews from their homeland, first to Babylonia in the east and then Europe to the west, brought the teachings of Torah to part of the globe. Now the time was ripe to bring Torah to the Western World on the other half of the globe, the new spiritual frontier.

In America, the Rebbe forged ahead with two of his primary goals: to connect with his Chasidim and to strengthen the broad spectrum of Jewish life. On the financial front, the Rebbe managed to raise significant funds, though his efforts were hindered by the beginning of the Depression. But when he reached out to the leaders of the Jewish establishment, primarily the Joint Distribution Committee, for financial help, he did not have success. The JDC had supported the Rebbe's operations, including job training and educational activities, on and off while he was in Russia, but it had begun to curtail funding in 1925.

The senior JDC executives in Moscow and Berlin, Dr. Joseph Rosen and Dr. Bernard Kahn, each wrote to their New York headquarters, saying, "The Rebbe is the only reliable way to help Jews in Russia."[84] But JDC leaders in New York chose to ignore those recommendations, expressing concern about the legality of transferring funds to Russia for what they called "cultural work" – code for religious life. Now in America, the Rebbe would have an opportunity to meet the leadership directly. As the Rebbe wrote to Rabbi Dovid Rabinowitz in Boston, "When I was preparing for the visit to the US, I understood that it was essential to work with the JDC."[85] Upon his arrival, he attempted to set up a meeting with Felix Warburg,[86] chairman of the JDC. Warburg rebuffed the request, suggesting that the Rebbe meet with Dr. Cyrus Adler,[87] chairman of the JDC Cultural Committee, which provided funding for Jewish educational and religious programs throughout the world. Adler was a traditional Jew, educated in Orthodox schools. As a young man, he had gotten to know firsthand the plight of Russian Jewish refugees in Philadelphia.

Just after Rosh HaShanah, the Rebbe and Adler met. Dr. Joseph Hyman, director of the JDC, prepared a confidential memorandum[88] in advance of the meeting. He raised many doubts about supporting the Rebbe's projects, including the legality of transferring funds due to Russian currency regulations. Still, he asserted that the JDC could help the Rebbe. "It's possible to carry out this work on the condition that there be no publicity and no noise. No brass bands."[89] Hyman noted that the Rebbe had created a reliable mechanism to secretly transfer funds to Russia. He referred to the Rebbe as "our friend," never actually using his name.

The Rebbe was deeply impressed with Adler, writing to his wife back in Riga, "He is very serious, with a scholarly face, and great Jewish sensitivity."[90] They met again a month later. In an internal JDC memo describing the meetings, Adler notes the difficulties of religious life in Russia and the economic woes and is clearly sympathetic to the Rebbe and open to ideas on how to legally transfer funds.[91] At the second meeting, Adler assured the Rebbe that the JDC would help in a significant way, but it would be done secretly.[92] That commitment was not honored.

It was Felix Warburg, chair of the JDC, who disagreed with the Rebbe on the best strategy to help Russian Jews. Warburg was an American banker who supported the partnership with the Soviets in transferring Jews to communal farms.[93] In 1927, he traveled to Russia, meeting the Rebbe and a delegation of rabbis twice and promising help that did not materialize.[94] Warburg also visited the agricultural colonies and was impressed as he witnessed Jews lining up with farming utensils, looking like they were creating a new life. The Communists put on a good show when he toured the farm towns named after him, Warburg-4 and Warburg-5.[95] His brief, staged visit inspired him to become a champion of forced collectivization. "For a man pampered with luxury, he responded to those threadbare outposts with the glad-handing gusto of a politician in the hustings,"[96] wrote Ron Chernow, Warburg's biographer. "The settlements evolved into a bizarre hybrid of Park Avenue charity and Marxist agriculture," with wealthy Jews of New York partnering with the Communists, funding their goal of socialism. Uprooted from their friends, relatives, and community, Russian Jews were denied the individual right to choose their economic and religious path, yet some still hoped that the colonies would bring financial stability.

As early as June 1925,[97] the Rebbe wrote to the board of the JDC expressing his concerns over the project. The following year, the Rebbe dispatched a long letter to Warburg about the settlements.[98] While not expressing direct opposition, he raised important questions about the religious services and the wisdom of forcibly moving Jews to Ukraine.

He requested support to train Russian Jews with skills that would ensure their livelihoods. "In the name of thousands of Jews, take upon yourself the provision of *melekhet yad,* home-based industries for Jews." The Rebbe requested that the JDC provide three things: one, facilities and religious services in the settlements they were establishing; two, funding for Jews living in urban areas to train in home-based industries; and three, subsidies for rabbis and religious functionaries. A few weeks later, the Rebbe also wrote to JDC vice chair Sam Rosenberg, with whom he had met in Russia, "The Jewish people are looking up to you and your colleagues." The Rebbe urged the JDC to intercede with the Russian government as Jewish British leader Sir Moses Montefiore[99] had done in the nineteenth century when he traveled to St. Petersburg to meet the czar in an attempt to convince him to improve the conditions of Jews in Russia. "Likewise, today the Jewish people will be saved through your efforts and those of your colleagues."[100] The Rebbe wanted the JDC to use its influence to speak up for religious rights, support Jewish education, and provide ways for Jews to become self-sufficient. For a short time, the JDC indeed provided funding for training in home-based industries

According to historian Zvi Bauer,[101] JDC leaders did not believe there was a "specific Jewish problem in Russia anymore," as Communism had lifted the czarist restrictions on Jews. Instead, the saw the challenges to "Russian Jewry in pure economic terms" and they wantedd to help their fellow Jews. To advance these projects, in 1924 the JDC created a subsidiary corporation, Agro-Joint, to work in cooperation with the Communist regime. As Professor Michael Beizer writes, "The program remained operational for fourteen years, during which time 200,000 Soviet Jews were transformed from urban dwellers to peasants."[102] Historian Zvi Gitelman was struck by the strange coalition. "The American Joint Distribution Committee, a thoroughly 'bourgeois' organization backed by some of the most prominent bankers and financiers of the American Jewish establishment, supported the agriculture colonies."[103]

The Rebbe hoped that in America he would be able to convince the JDC leaders to rethink their Russian strategy. But as he was lobbying the JDC, an incident in Russia derailed that plan. In February 1930, a group of rabbis was arrested in Minsk. JTA, the Jewish news service, reported: "The secret police also searched the synagogues and say that it discovered documents that show that the community is a counter-revolutionary organization supplying information to anti-Soviet bodies abroad. Rabbi Pevsner was directly accused of receiving and executing instructions from Riga from Rabbi Joseph Schneersohn, the Lubavitcher Rabbi, who is now in the United States. The GPU asserts that it found at Rabbi Pevsner's home a letter in Rabbi Schneersohn's handwriting containing instructions on how to organize illegal rabbinical seminaries and Hebrew schools, and how to strengthen Jewish religious life."[104] The arrest emboldened those in the JDC, led by Warburg, who opposed funding the Rebbe's activities, ignoring cables from their Berlin office saying that Stalin had started a crackdown against the Jews.[105] Fearing that association with the Rebbe might damage their standing in Russia, they refused any more support for the Rebbe's Russian network.[106]

Some in the JDC leadership remained sympathetic to the Rebbe. Professor Cyrus Adler made personal donations and attempted to help in other ways. He believed that the JDC's unwillingness to speak out was wrong. "I am not willing to take the attitude that every vestige of Judaism shall be destroyed in Russia with our silence, which means assent," he wrote to Joseph Hyman in February 1932.[107] A few days later, Warburg wrote to Hyman, chastising Adler.[108] It was "stupidity" and "a waste of time" to support efforts to bolster religious life in Russia, he said. "Any act of ours to save the Jewish religion in Russia would have had any but tragic results."

Warburg did not believe that "youth in Russia have any interest in those things,"[109] referring to Jewish observance. He was under the illusion that there was no anti-Semitism in Russia, claiming, "Jews are treated as well as the rest of the population." This in a period described by historian Nora Levin as being filled with the "mass persecution of prominent Jews."[110] In 1932, Warburg rejected the Rebbe's campaign to send matzah[111] to Russian Jews, even though Russia was in the throes of severe famine.[112] Insisting that Jews were in possession of flour, he said, "If they wish to bake their bread in the form of *matzos* instead of bread during the holidays, they can do so." Warburg was still clinging to the misconceptions formed during his staged visit a few years earlier. In his mind, he was saving Jews by assisting in their integration into the new Soviet paradise. Warburg expressed disdain for the Rebbe, writing,

"I have no confidence in Schneersohn."[113] Lingering under the surface was his own view toward tradition. German immigrants like Warburg had abandoned observance. As Chernow writes, he would make "an appearance"[114] on Yom Kippur at Temple Emanuel, the gothic-style Reform temple in Manhattan. Bauer says that the Jewish faith and tradition "were of marginal concern" to Warburg. As a Reform Jew, he wanted to "break down the barriers between a Jew and his neighbors." In contrast, the Rebbe, while deeply concerned about the economic welfare of Russian Jews, believed that Judaism was essential.

The JDC began to wind down the Agro-Joint beginning in 1936, as the farming communities gained economic stability. They did not anticipate the wave of terror that Stalin would unleash that would bring a tragic end to the JDC-Soviet partnership. In 1937, Stalin turned his secret police on JDC workers, arresting close to two hundred of them for being associated with a "foreign organization."[115] Many were shot; some died in prison or remained in jail for long periods. The majority of those targeted were Russian. Also included were forty-one German physicians who had come to the settlements to provide medical services. Seventeen doctors were shot or died in the Soviet prison camps; others were deported. Rosen, head of the JDC in Russia, protested unsuccessfully to officials in Russia.

It took time for reports of the purges to arrive in New York,[116] and even then, the JDC remained silent.[117] News of the expulsion, imprisonment, and murder of JDC staff would have put a damper on its image.[118] Instead, they continued to paint a glowing picture of life in the Soviet Union.[119] In 1939, Hyman wrote an extensive assessment of the JDC's achievements in Russia for the American Jewish Yearbook, saying, "In less than a decade and a half, the work of the Agro-Joint helped transform Russian Jewry from a downtrodden, almost helpless ghetto population into self-reliant and productive workers of the field and factory,"[120] not revealing[121] that close to two hundred Agro-Joint staff were killed, imprisoned, or deported, or that all JDC assets in Russia were seized by the Communist regime. Instead, Hyman lauded the JDC efforts in Russia as "one of the most amazing feats of human engineering in modern history." The reality was different. "However worthy and ambitious the experiment, it had backfired," Chernow writes. The JDC did its best to hide the tragic end. "The episode was buried, forgotten, and obliterated. Most people don't know that in the 1920s, American capitalists had briefly been the largest landlord in the Soviet Union."[122]

In the coming years, the numbers of Jewish farmers dropped. As Nora Levin writes, "The last days of Jewish agriculture were tragic." By 1939, just six percent of employed Russian Jews were farmers. "Hopes for secure and lasting Jewish peasantry which might have provided a territorial base for Jewish autonomy crumbled." Those remaining on the farms came under German occupation and "Jews were massacred." After the war, some Jews wanted to return to the region, but instead "the government encouraged them to move to remote Birobidzhan."[123] In 1965, the editorial committee of *Sovetish Heymland* considered doing a story on Jewish agriculture and concluded, "The Jewish village no longer existed."[124]

According to Hyman, the JDC invested sixteen million dollars ($250,000,000 today) in the resettlement program in Russia.[125] If they had diverted even ten to twenty percent of those funds, it would have alleviated the financial stress of many families, mitigated hunger, enabled them to observe tradition, and greatly expanded the number of children receiving Jewish education.

When the Rebbe arrived in the US, he discovered indifference to the plight of Russian Jews. "The attitude here to Russian Jewry is hopelessness and coldness from both the JDC and Agudas Harabonim (Union of Orthodox Rabbis); even public opinion here was not in favor of assisting our brethren in Russia."[126] He wrote to Rabbi Dovid Rabinowitz[127] that he was deeply disappointed after his first few months in the US. "I trusted naively the words of Dr. Rosen [in Riga] that the JDC would help." The crash of Wall Street had an adverse impact, and the Rebbe's visit to Philadelphia had not yielded much support, but the Rebbe remained undeterred. "We must break down the wall [of indifference]," he told Rabinowitz. "The condition of Russian Jewy is very grave."[128]

Eventually, he sensed a slight shift in public sentiment. "After months of being here, the public is waking up slightly and is beginning to feel that something must be done."[129] He hoped to capitalize on this awareness by creating a new coalition of major Jewish groups. In late January 1930, the Rebbe met with Justice Louis Brandeis in Washington and asked him to spearhead an effort to convince the major Jewish groups in the US to help

Soviet Jews. They discussed creating a community-wide alliance to be organized on many levels. He proposed that the JDC coordinate the agricultural colonies while others facilitate emigration and back efforts to sustain religious life. The Rebbe felt this broad-based coalition should include Felix Warburg, Stephen S. Wise, and Cyrus Adler, with Brandeis as chair.

"Rabbi Schneersohn impressed me so much,"[130] wrote Brandeis after the meeting. The Rebbe had hoped he would take a public leadership role, but Brandeis limited himself to working behind the scenes, trying to orchestrate others to lead the coalition. Brandeis enlisted the help of David Bressler, a prominent leader of the American Jewish Committee who became vice chair of the JDC. Bressler attempted to create a joint initiative of the American Jewish Committee, the American Jewish Congress, and the JDC.[131] Sadly, this proposal floundered – though perhaps it could have succeeded if Brandeis had stood at the public helm of the initiative.[132] While sympathetic to the Rebbe, he felt that his "judicial duties and other limitations precluded me from doing more."[133]

With the lack of support from the JDC and other establishment groups, the Rebbe was left a solitary soldier on the field. He singlehandedly tried to marshal support to sustain Judaism under the oppressive Russian regime. He was careful never to criticize the JDC publicly, but the Rebbe's fundraising initiatives outside their framework still exacerbated tensions with them. He had arrived in the US to a hero's welcome, lauded as the rabbi who had stood up to the Soviets and escaped a death sentence. As one Jewish newspaper put it, "The Lubavitcher Rebbe is the ambassador of the two million Jews of Soviet Russia. Their suffering is his suffering. The Rebbe is a personification of self-sacrifice; his heroic battle in defense of Judaism in the Soviet Union evoked a storm around the world."[134] Until this point, the JDC had been the dominant organization on issues of Russian Jews. Now, another voice with great credibility challenged that hegemony.[135] Rabbi Yisrael Jacobson writes in his memoirs, "JDC leaders did not want the Rebbe to connect with prominent philanthropists in the US because they recognized that he would have great influence. They tried to deter potential donors from participating in the Rebbe's fundraising events for Russian Jewry."[136]

The Rebbe was also careful not to criticize the Russian government publicly,[137] or even to detail the oppression of Russian Jews. Rabbi Yosef

Landa notes, "During the Rebbe's visit to St. Louis, there is no harsh rhetoric condemning the Communist paradise or its leaders, no mention of arrests, exiles to Siberian labor camps, or executions."[138] The situation in Russia was one of life and death, and public controversy could provoke retaliation against Chasidim by the Russian government. As *The Jewish Record* wrote, "The time is not ripe to disclose publicly[139] all that the Lubavitcher Rebbe has done and continues to do on behalf of the Jews of Russia."[140]

Shortly after arriving in the US, the Rebbe began visiting the various Jewish communities in the country, beginning with Philadelphia and Baltimore. In Philadelphia, the Rebbe visited Independence Hall, where he was honored with an invitation to sit in the chair of George Washington. "I wanted to see the cradle of American democracy," he said. There he praised the American Constitution and the freedoms that were given to citizens in the US. He expressed his appreciation of the US government, saying, "It has always been supportive of us [the Jewish people] even when other major powers were not."[141] The Rebbe echoed this theme of gratitude for American freedoms throughout his US visit.

The Rebbe visited major Jewish communities in Milwaukee, Detroit, and Boston, staying in each for about a week. He spent three months in Chicago, where there was a large Chabad community. He made shorter stops in Springfield and Worcester, Massachusetts, and in other areas of New York such as the Bronx. The furthest western city that the Rebbe visited was St. Louis. He arrived there on Sunday, May 4, and stayed for ten days.

In every city, the Rebbe was welcomed by crowds of thousands thronging the train stations. The Yiddish daily *The Jewish Record* displayed a six-column banner headline over the front page announcing his reception in St. Louis. "Such a large crowd consisting of thousands of men, women, and children has never been witnessed at any reception accorded to a Jewish leader visiting our city."[142] The *Detroit Free Press* reported that when the Rebbe arrived there, "thousands thronged the lobby of Michigan Central Station and overflowed the streets."[143] From the train station, a procession of "more than ten thousand escorted the Rebbe to the Emanual Synagogue" in Detroit's Jewish neighborhood.

Chicago's *Morning Journal* described how a boisterous crowd of "fifteen thousand welcomed the Lubavitcher Rebbe in LaSalle Street Station."[144] The *Chicago Courier* noted that the crowds were comprised of "old and young, men and women."[145] It took police half an hour to make a path for the Rebbe and his entourage to exit, after which, wrote the *Morning Journal*, "a large parade of hundreds of cars accompanied the Rebbe."

The American Jewish community included many Eastern European immigrants who had a great respect for chasidic Rebbes and distinguished rabbinic scholars. The Rebbe was admired for fearlessly standing up to the Russians, and he was respected for his piousness as a chasidic Rebbe. That, together with his genuine concern for all Jews regardless of their background, made the Rebbe a figure greatly adored.

But the Rebbe himself was distressed by the honors bestowed on him. On the day of his arrival in a city where he would invariably be greeted by large crowds, he would fast, seeking spiritual refinement.[146] As he remarked to one of his close Chasidim, Rabbi Nissan Telushkin, "Honor should cause you to diminish yourself." In each city there would be banquets, major speaking events, and receptions. Late one night, after one of these gala dinners, the Rebbe wrote to his wife, "It's midnight. I just came from a banquet, I must say to you with a heavy heart. Every time I am at a banquet arranged in my honor, it brings a very *vochedik* [Yiddish: mundane] feeling.... I don't feel good or comfortable, not from the speeches which I listen to, nor from the rousing ovations which are made for me or the praises and the falsehoods which are spoken."[147]

While thousands turned out to welcome the Rebbe, in some cities the Jewish establishment stayed away. In St. Louis, *The Jewish Record*[148] editorialized about the lack of support from Jewish Federation leaders, explaining that traditional Jews, mostly immigrants, had always feared making a move "without the approval of the community establishment." The Rebbe's visit was a moment of empowerment, a "demonstration on the part of the Jewish masses that Yiddishkeit (traditional Judaism) is not lost, that the roots are healthy, even if the branches have broken off." It went on to explain the reality of the Jewish immigrants, "ordinary Jews, whose hearts throb with a strong burning love to all that is Jewish," even though some had drifted from full observance. This underscored a great schism. On one side were the suave Americanized Jews, whose origins lay in the nineteenth-century immigration from Germany. They dominated Jewish life and tended to be connected to the Reform movement, which was much less religiously observant. On the other side were the traditional European Jews, who started arriving in mass numbers much later and still felt tethered to tradition, continuing to speak Yiddish even after they settled into life in America. The paper labeled the visit a "victory for the grassroots Jews."

At each stop, the Rebbe would utilize every opportunity to inspire the local community to increase its level of observance. During his visit to St. Louis, a group of women raised concerns about the city's run-down *mikveh*. When the Rebbe entered the large sanctuary of Shaare Tzedek Synagogue, he heard a loud noise. "The Rebbe looked around, searching for the source of the commotion," says Faye Zeffren. She and other women were banging on the benches, hoping to get the Rebbe's attention. "The women called out that there was a dire need for a new *mikveh* and appealed to the Rebbe for help." Tired of the inaction of local leaders, they hoped the Rebbe would intervene. The Rebbe met with the women, including Zeffren,[149] suggesting they form a committee to oversee the construction of a new *mikveh*. He encouraged local leaders to make the project a priority. Within days, advertisements appeared in the local Jewish press for a fundraising dinner in support of the new *mikveh*; the dinner was held a week later.[150] The Rebbe gave the committee a gift of coins to distribute to anyone who contributed to the *mikveh* that was built shortly afterward. Even after returning to Europe, the Rebbe kept in contact with the *mikveh* committee.

During the Detroit portion of the Rebbe's visit,[151] Isadore Starr,[152] who came from a Chabad family, was asked to serve as translator. He later wrote that hundreds came to meet the Rebbe. "Some just wanted the honor of seeing and speaking to him. Others had various problems for which they wished to receive the Rebbe's blessing and advice." Starr recalls one woman whose son was ill and requested that the Rebbe "tell her son to recover and be well." Starr was struck with the Rebbe's compassion. "He received her with kindness, sympathy, and exercised a great deal of patience." He finally told her that he was not a "miracle worker," but his ancestors were *tzaddikim* (saintly Jews), and he would pray for them to intercede on high for her.

One individual said he would make a major donation to the Rebbe if he would visit him in his home. Starr says the Rebbe demurred, saying "he could not accept the offer, as there were many people of lesser wealth who perhaps were much more deserving and more entitled to a visit."

At one point the Rebbe made an unannounced visit to a local Chabad synagogue. The Rebbe began to talk about "the economic conditions and the deplorable fact that people who were willing to work could not find employment." The congregants were surprised by the Rebbe's grasp of the situation in the wake of the Wall Street crash. He reassured them, "Do not despair. G-d will help, and America will return to prosperity." During that visit the Rebbe also encouraged the synagogue members to set aside time for Torah study. He added that it was important to preserve a sense of community, "to maintain a friendship and friendly spirit between each other, as that too is worshiping G-d. It is the mitzvah of *ve'ahavta lerei'akha kamokha* (loving your fellow Jew), a cardinal principle of the Torah."

Lewis Boxer,[153] then twenty-five years old, had heard about the Rebbe's arrival in Philadelphia, where he was welcomed by large crowds.[154] Boxer was intrigued by all the public attention.[155] "My friends and I read these articles and wondered whether the Rebbe was actually planning to replace the Almighty. We discussed this with an official of our synagogue, and he suggested that we visit the Rebbe and ask him what he had in mind." Late Saturday night, Boxer and his friends piled into a car and headed to the home where the Rebbe was staying. Through the window, they saw the house was crowded with men. "We rang the doorbell," Boxer says, "and a dignified, bearded man came to the door and inquired what we wanted. One of us responded, 'We'd like to speak to the Rebbe. We have an important question to ask.'" The man, taking notes, told them the Rebbe needed to know the question before he could see them. "We'd like to know how he expects us to keep an old-fashioned religion in a modern country," the young man said. They were told they would have to wait behind the crowd of people who came before them. Just a few minutes later, the group was called in, bypassing the crowds. "We wondered why we had been admitted before all those people downstairs who had been there before us," Boxer said. At the top of the stairs, they found the Rebbe waiting for them. "He was tall, handsome, with gleamin bright eyes. He wore a large fur hat. His hand was outstretched in greeting." The Rebbe surprised them by saying, "This is the happiest moment I've had in Philadelphia," and started to arrange chairs for them around his desk. The young group wanted to help him, but he insisted on doing this task himself.

They sat down, facing the Rebbe, who took a long look at each one of them and said:

> You look like very intelligent young men, and therefore I must speak on your level. You are wondering about those people downstairs who were here before you. Well, here are some of the problems for which they are asking for help. One man's daughter is seriously ill. What can I do? Nothing more than he can do, provided he approaches G-d. He should be able to ask for a complete recovery. Another has a lawsuit and wants me to pray that he will win. I do not know who's right, but he can pray that G-d will give justice. There's a man who wants to buy a business and wants me to intercede to make sure it succeeds. If I could do that, I'd be a rich businessman. But if I could not answer your question, I'd have no right to be a rabbi.
>
> First, I must admit a great secret which you will most likely keep. There are 613 mitzvot; while the Lubavitcher Rebbe tries to keep them all, he finds it impossible to keep them all. So what does he do? Discard 613 mitzvot? No, he keeps as many of them as humanly possible."

The Rebbe's words touched the young men deeply. "With these few sentences, he removed the venom we had brought with us," says Boxer. "Then he asked us to try and keep as many mitzvot as we could. If we did, then we'd be doing the same thing as the Lubavitcher Rebbe!"

The Rebbe then asked for their Jewish names and the names of their mothers. "Several of the boys put their hands in their pockets, but he stopped them with a gesture, thanked them, and said he had no use for money. He wanted mitzvot – he asked us whether we donned tefillin every day." Several admitted they had given it up. He offered them tefillin so they could fulfill the mitzvah. "All of us promised to try to live up to his suggestions. He then blessed us individually, shook hands again, and we left."

The conversation made a profound impression on the group. "We stood on the porch for nearly two hours digesting the visit. Everyone agreed to pray at least once a day. One said he would give up his Saturday work as a dental technician, and some months later he even prevailed upon his employer to do the same." One member of the group, "Gabriel Lowenthal, of blessed memory, attached himself to a synagogue and taught what he had learned from the Rebbe's philosophy to many others." Decades later, Boxer wrote, "the ten minutes we spent with the Rebbe strengthened the spirit of Judaism in all of us."

It wasn't only young people. The Rebbe also challenged rabbis and community leaders. During the three months the Rebbe spent in Chicago, a prominent local Jewish scholar, Rabbi Nachman Bar,[156] went to meet with him.[157] Rabbi Bar had been a star student in the Mirrer yeshivah in Europe, immigrating to the US in 1917. By the time the Rebbe visited Chicago in 1930, Rabbi Bar was the *rosh yeshivah* at Chicago's Hebrew Theological College.[158] The Rebbe asked him a seemingly simple question in Yiddish: "*Vost tut eir* – What do you do?" He responded he was a *rosh yeshivah* and that he taught Talmud. The Rebbe repeated the question. Thinking that the Rebbe must be hearing impaired, Rabbi Bar said again, "I am a *rosh yeshivah*." The Rebbe looked at him and repeated the question in Yiddish for the third time. Rabbi Bar yelled back in Yiddish, "*Ich Reb Nachman Bar, rosh yeshivah fun Beis Midrash LeTorah*," adding that he taught boys the classic talmudic tractates to prepare them for ordination. Finally, the Rebbe said to him, "I heard you the first time, and I know you are a dedicated teacher and that this is your job, but my question is, what are you doing to uplift Judaism in Chicago?"

Rabbi Bar was surprised, later telling Chicago's Chabad leader, Yosef Katz, "I had never heard a person talk that way to anyone." Confused, he wondered if he should leave immediately or if he should attempt to answer the Rebbe. Then he realized the Rebbe would provide the answer, and he asked, "*Vus zul itch ton* – What should I do?" The Rebbe answered his own question: "I want you to gather all the men and boys who never reach the doorknob of your yeshivah, and I want you to teach them the *parashah* (portion) of the week seasoned with interesting *midrashim* (rabbinic commentaries)." The Rebbe added two caveats: "Never mention that I suggested this idea, and don't teach it in your yeshivah." Rabbi Bar assured the Rebbe, "I will try to do this." He began teaching a weekly class at Congregation Adas B'nei Israel, attracting large crowds. In 1946, Katz was traveling to visit the Rebbe in New York, and Rabbi Bar asked him to give a message to the Rebbe: "I have been teaching the *parashah* class for sixteen years, and it has been very successful. I have not become a Chasid of the Rebbe, but I am following his instructions."

The Rebbe challenged the mindset prevalent at the time in which being a good Jew was redefined as living an ethical life and being a good citizen.[159] In a *maamar* that the Rebbe presented in Baltimore[160] to a crowd of close to 1,500, he questioned this new ideology. The Rebbe underscored that the foundational key to Judaism was the mitzvah, the performance of an actual commandment. "This is the reason for their error, in that they argue against closeness to godliness through practical mitzvot, yet they admit the closeness by the way of the service of heart." He was alluding to the theology emphasizing ethical ideas rather than observance of mitzvot. The Rebbe explained, "The key to connecting with the Divine is through fulfilling the commandments. One comes close to godliness though the practical mitzvot, with physical actions." Rabbi Shmuel Kaplan, today a Chabad *shliach* in Baltimore, explains, "The new liberal philosophy rejected the observance of mitzvot, saying that the primary principle is ethics, not how we live on a daily basis." He argues that "this is the underlying failure of American Jewry. Judaism rooted in theoretical ethical ideas, instead of real action, has proven to be unsustainable."

Prior to returning to Europe, the Rebbe made a second trip to Washington, where he was received by President Herbert Hoover at the White House.[161] The Rebbe wrote to his family that he had not planned to visit the president, but at the last minute he was invited and made the trip.[162] He was accompanied by Rabbis Moshe Kramer and Chaim Fogelman, the chair and vice chair of Agudas Chassidei Chabad, and Asher Rabinowitz,[163] who served as the translator. The Rebbe saw the visit as an opportunity to express appreciation for the freedoms granted to American Jews and for the American government's assistance to Jews living overseas. Afterward, the Rebbe told his family in a letter that he was happy they met and that he felt it was a productive meeting.

After the visit to Washington, the Rebbe prepared to return to Europe. He had accomplished some of his objectives during his long sojourn in the US, but others remained elusive. His goal of raising funds was marginally successful, but some of the money was lost in a bank failure. As for the JDC, he had hoped that meeting with its leaders would inspire them to support his religious education network in Russia. While many were sympathetic, like Cyrus Adler, even offering personal support, JDC chair Felix Warburg remained opposed to funding the network.[164] These setbacks did not put a dent in the Rebbe's spirit. He continued to forge ahead, impervious to obstacles thrown in his path.

As for his second goal, the visit reinforced the bond between the Rebbe and the Chasidim in the US, who were saddened by his departure. They hoped that he would consider their proposal to relocate to the US. After the Rebbe returned to Europe, the American Chasidim expanded Agudas Chassidei Chabad, the national Chabad organization. They began working to increase the study of chasidic teachings. Rabbi Yisrael Jacobson, for example, began teaching chasidic philosophy to students in the New York yeshivas. This drew them closer to the chasidic worldview,[165] and some of them eventually traveled to Poland to study in the Rebbe's yeshivah in Otwock.

The connection between the American Chasidim and the Rebbe was also invigorated by emissaries the Rebbe sent to America. Outstanding Chasidim such as Rabbi Itche "*der masmid*" Gurewicz (literally, "the avid student")[166] and Rabbi Shmuel Levitin,[167] both exceptional role models of scholarship and piety, were sent by the Rebbe to visit the US to inspire the community there. They and others the Rebbe sent taught chasidic philosophy, led *farbrengens*, and galvanized support for the Rebbe's yeshivah system in Poland and his underground network in Russia. They became an active bridge between the Rebbe in Europe and his followers in the US.

The Rebbe's third goal for his trip to America was to invigorate Judaism there. Throughout the visit, he encouraged Jews he encountered to increase their observance. He seized every opportunity to stress the importance of Jewish education. His sense of optimism was infectious, and his visit was deeply inspirational for thousands who came in contact with him.

During the ten months the Rebbe traveled throughout America, he gained a keen understanding of the state of US Jewry. The visit led the Rebbe to adopt a different perspective on its future than the predominant view among other great European Torah scholars, who held little hope for American Jewry. The Rebbe regarded the enthusiasm that greeted him and his ideas as a reason for optimism. While in St. Louis, the Rebbe told a reporter from *The Jewish Record,*[168] "I am not pessimistic like other European Jews who visit America." Rather, the Rebbe saw great potential in the US, saying, "American youth possess a deep religious feeling." Later, in Latvia, the Rebbe reflected on his US visit. "The Jewish youth of Europe excel with the mind," he said, referring to the high level of Jewish scholarship in Europe, but "the youth in America excel in the realm of heart because they are openminded and receptive to Torah." In the last major *farbrengen* that the Rebbe held before departing the US, marking his fiftieth birthday and the anniversary of his release from Communist prison three years earlier, the Rebbe said, "The unpretentious American youth are full of wonderful potential. They can be educated and inspired." Prior to leaving, the Rebbe did an extensive interview with New York's *Der Morgen Journal,*[169] in which he stated that American youth pine and thirst for religion and lack only knowledge and education. "All the raw materials, all the components of the grand Jewish edifice, are already here in the US," he said. He told the reporter that American Jews would not only support the Jewish infrastructure in Europe, they would also build Torah centers in the US and "have institutions here."

A large crowd gathered on the pier on the day of the Rebbe's departure.[170] There he proclaimed a new vision for American Jewry,[171] saying it was time for them to redefine their role. "Until this point, you were in the role of givers, and with an open hand you endeavored to support Torah institutions in Europe. But now, "you also have to become takers. You have to adapt from the Torah centers of Europe the approach of disseminating Jewish learning and strengthening Judaism, and institute it in America." He challenged the crowd to transform the US into what few imagined possible at the time: "Make America a place of Torah."[172]

A week later the ship docked in Bremen, Germany.[173] For the Rebbe it had been a long, exhausting trip. He traveled to Berlin accompanied by his daughter Chaya Mushka and son-in-law the Ramash. The doctors had ordered the Rebbe to rest from the taxing journey, and he went to the spa at Marienbad. "I was very weak from travel and stayed there for three weeks," the Rebbe wrote.[174] After recuperating, he felt a marked improvement and finally headed home to Riga,[175] arriving a little more than thirteen months after his departure.[176]

In Riga, the train station was packed with well-wishers waiting to greet the Rebbe. As soon as the train pulled in, a loud welcome of "*Baruch haba*" reverberated in the air. The crowds were so thick that the passengers could not depart from the train. The police created a corridor, and the Rebbe's entourage navigated between rows of uniformed officers, finally entering two cars that waited outside the station. The celebration continued later in the Rebbe's large apartment, where many Chasidim gathered. Two weeks later, the Rebbe celebrated the High Holidays in Riga. Joyful at the Rebbe's return, Chasidim from nearby Poland and Lithuania flocked to join him. Even many local Jews who were not so observant participated in the festivities.

After the holidays, the Rebbe faced many questions about his next steps after the yearlong trip abroad. Those choices would set the destiny of Chabad for years to come.

Chapter Eight

Poland – Starting Anew

The Rebbe returned from his yearlong trip just before the High Holidays of 1930. As the holiday season concluded in Riga and the Chasidim returned home, the Rebbe stood at a crossroads. To the east lay millions of Jews locked behind the Iron Curtain, subject to rising totalitarianism and the beginnings of Stalin's reign of terror. To the west was Poland, the center of European religious life, with the task of reinvigorating Chabad's yeshivah system so it could birth new generations of Chasidim. Around the world there were scattered emerging Chabad communities that required nurturing. Specifically, across the Atlantic was a growing Chabad community, now spiritually invigorated from the Rebbe's visit. In the coming years, the Rebbe would face serious health challenges, and just over the horizon was the ominous rise of militarism in Germany. All of this would require major financial resources. While the visit to the US had broadened the base of support for the Rebbe's work, the impact of the Depression limited that potential.

But the most pressing question was where the Rebbe's permanent place of residence should be. Riga remained an option; it was close to Russia, enabling the Rebbe to help the Jews there more easily. An idea had been floated to establish a Chabad yeshivah in Riga, something that was dear to the Rebbe's heart. America was another option. The Chasidim there had been galvanized during the Rebbe's visit. In New York, a committee had formed[1] and requested the Rebbe to move there; the Chicago Chasidim had also extended an invitation. The Jewish future seemed to be in America, and the philanthropy of US Jews could help the Rebbe assist those still in Russia. At the same time, Chasidim in Poland were entreating the Rebbe to relocate to Warsaw, the epicenter of European Jewish life and home to the Rebbe's flagship yeshivah. The Rashab had entrusted the yeshivah to the Rebbe, and he viewed it as a sacred responsibility. It was also the key to Chabad's future. Only by inspiring a new generation of Chasidim could Chabad thrive in Western Europe. The Rebbe's close proximity to the Warsaw yeshivah would make him its spiritual anchor, raise its prestige, and enable him to mentor its students more directly.

The fear that the Rebbe might move to the US spurred the European Chasidim who had flocked to Riga for the holidays to take action. They convened Saturday evening after Rosh HaShanah to formally establish Agudas Chassidei Chabad (Association of Chabad Chasidim) of Poland, Lithuania, and Latvia.[2] The new organization's goals were to unite the Chabad community, reinforce the study of chasidic philosophy, and create a financial foundation to enable the Rebbe's relocation to Warsaw. The next day, they wrote to the Rebbe, "Our souls were deeply disturbed when we heard that *anash* in the US were requesting that the Rebbe relocate there." Asserting that Warsaw was "the most appropriate place for the Rebbe to reside," they assured him that they would do whatever was needed for such a move. They noted that the yeshivah students would greatly benefit from the "light and kindness" that would shine with the Rebbe in their midst. It would also strengthen the Rebbe's bond with his Chasidim, since many could not travel to Riga due to visa restrictions and travel costs.

For a while it seemed that the Rebbe would accept the request to come to America, but finally he resolved to remain in Europe. Writing to his US Chasidim a few weeks after the holidays, he said, "I enjoyed hearing their tremendous arousal of love and friendship, which is very precious to me, in their suggestion to relocate, with G-d's help, our residence and settle in their country." The Rebbe lauded them for their noble intentions "for the sake of Heaven and the benefit of Chasidim," and most importantly, their aspiration of "spreading of Torah in the spirit of Tomchei Temimim." Nonetheless, he informed them that he would be remaining in Europe "due to the spiritual needs of the Chabad community [in Europe], my communal duties here, and my responsibilities for the yeshivas here." Quoting the talmudic teaching, "A person may not demolish a synagogue until he has built another synagogue in its place,"[3] the Rebbe implied that coming to America now would weaken Chabad's work in Europe. The Rebbe was also concerned about "the weakness of my health." He didn't reject the idea of moving to the US outright, indicating that it could happen in the future with proper preparation "to build a stronger foundation." He encouraged the Chasidim to "unify in a stronger way and increase the study of chasidic philosophy." Ultimately, he said, the time was not ripe, as "such a thing does not happen by itself – it needs work."[4] A week later, Feigin wrote to the New York committee chair Rabbi Nissan Telushkin, "The decision to move to the US is deferred for now."

When the Rebbe did end up fleeing to the US after the 1939 Nazi invasion of Poland, he viewed it as an orchestration of divine providence. Reflecting then on his hesitation to relocate a decade earlier, the Rebbe asserted that he would not have been effective at that time. He bemoaned the attitude of US Jewish leaders who were failing to uphold classic Jewish values. "Even rabbis" rationalized making compromises, he said. "This is the way of the world."[5]

To bolster US Jewry and the Chabad community, the Rebbe dispatched a series of emissaries to the US in the 1930s. He selected inspirational role models, Chasidim of spiritual stature and scholarship, as "*shadars*," ambassadors of the Rebbe, to teach Torah, spread chasidic teachings, and raise funds. The first was Rabbi Yitzchak Horowitz, known as Reb Itche der Masmid (literally, "the diligent student"), celebrated for his remarkable devotion to Jewish learning and piety. He arrived in New York a few weeks before the High Holidays in 1933 and spent two years in the US. "His sanctity and kindness made a great impression," Rabbi Yisrael Jacobson wrote.[6] The burgeoning Chabad community in New York was so enamored with him that they decided to immediately collect a sum of five thousand dollars ($100,000 today). "We had to borrow most of the money, but we did it because we wanted to ensure Reb Itche's success in the US." During his visit, Reb Itche traveled to communities, teaching Chasidism and raising funds for the Rebbe's work in Europe. In Boston, he stayed in the home of Shmaya Krinsky, his daughter Rivkah recalls.[7] "He made a big impression on us." Then fourteen years old, it was the first time she saw such extraordinary dedication to Torah study. "We would go by his room at night, and he would never sleep. He would stand and learn the whole night with a book on the bureau." His visit was so successful that the Rebbe wanted to send him a second time, but he could not secure a visa. The Rebbe encountered the same legal barriers with other rabbis he wanted to send.

In 1938, the Rebbe dispatched Rabbi Mordechai Cheifetz to the US. The students of New York yeshivas such as Torah Vodaath were drawn to him. He led chasidic gatherings that "lasted almost till dawn," writes Jacobson.[8] Avraham Hecht, then a teenager, was captivated by Cheifetz. "He used to *farbreng* three times a week and we were swallowed up by him. He could melt a stone. He melted me."[9] Hecht says Cheifetz got everyone excited about the Rebbe. "We began to truly want to see the Rebbe." A year later, Hecht and five friends traveled to study in the yeshivah in Otwock.

When Cheifetz returned to Poland, he spent ten days with the Rebbe over the holiday of Shavuot. The Rebbe was not well. "My health is weak," he told Cheifetz, who provided detailed reports to the Rebbe about each of the US Chasidim and their families. The news bolstered the Rebbe's spirits and even affected his physical condition. "At that moment he actually looked healthy," recalled Cheifetz. "I saw that as the Rebbe looked at each name on the list, his face shone and he could see the person in his mind, He told me, 'I desire to see each one individually.'"[10]

A year later, in 1939, the Rebbe appointed Rabbi Shmuel Levitin as an emissary. Born in 1883, he had been sent by Rebbe Rashab to Soviet Georgia, where he was imprisoned for his religious activities, finally escaping Russia in 1937. Like the other emissaries, he was a model of piety and scholarship. He arrived in the US just before the High Holidays and visited communities across the country. The war's outbreak prevented

Levitin's return to Europe. Tragically, his wife was trapped there and killed by the Nazis. Levitin emerged as one of the chasidic elders, playing a major role in the development of Chabad in the US.[11]

The Rebbe also encouraged Chasidim in Europe to immigrate to the US. One Chasid, Yochanan Gordon, had three brothers who moved to America. When the Rebbe returned to Riga, he asked Gordon, "Why don't you join your brothers? They will arrange a visa for you." He responded, "I don't want my children to go off the *derekh* (stop observing the Torah)," explaining that his brothers' children were no longer religious. The Rebbe assured him, "Move to America, and I promise you that your children will remain religious Jews." This wasn't enough for Gordon. He told the Rebbe that he wanted his children to learn in the Rebbe's yeshivah. The Rebbe assured him again. "I promise you that they will learn in my yeshivas." Gordon immigrated a year later,[12] and the Rebbe's guarantee was fulfilled in 1940 when Gordon's oldest son Shalom Ber became one of the first students in the yeshivah the Rebbe opened in Brooklyn.

While in Poland, the Rebbe had bold ideas to reach out to Jews across America. In a letter to Rabbi Dovid Rabinowitz,[13] the Rebbe described his plan of sending "outstanding yeshivah students to cities across the US to teach chasidic philosophy." The idea was for them to "spend longer times in communities," with their mission being "only spiritual." The Rebbe urged Rabinowitz to find sponsors to back this ambitious undertaking. At the time, the project did not come to fruition, though it did become a reality later, after the Rebbe relocated to the US. In 1943,[14] he began sending yeshivah students to various American Jewish communities.

Even after the Rebbe made the fateful decision to remain in Europe, there was still the question of whether he would live in Poland or Latvia. A major factor was his desire was to live in proximity to Tomchei Temimim. As Feigin wrote, "He must be next to a yeshivah, which means either moving near the yeshivah in Warsaw or opening a new branch in Riga."[15] To explore the options, the Rebbe traveled to Warsaw, home to Chabad's flagship yeshivah, the summer after returning from the US.[16] The purpose, wrote Feigin, was to conduct a "deep internal review of the yeshivah."[17]

News of the Rebbe's visit electrified the Warsaw yeshivah students and those in the branches in Vilnius and Lodz. Moshe Gerlitzky,[18] then a student in Lodz, recalls, "The dean of the yeshivah permitted us to travel to Warsaw to meet the Rebbe, but only if we studied thirty *blatt* (double-sided pages) of Talmud and knew twelve chapters of *Tanya* by heart." Thirty out of one hundred students qualified, and they chartered a bus to join the festivities in Warsaw. A group from Vilnius also came.[19]

Gerlitzky joined the yeshivah students and thousands of Warsaw's Jews at the gates of the yeshivah's courtyard to welcome the Rebbe before Shabbat. It was an inspirational few days with the Rebbe. He spent much of Shabbat day in prayer, not ending till 4:00 p.m. Then the Rebbe taught two *maamarim*. Yeshivah student Aryeh Leib Kramer recalled, "This is the first *maamar* that I heard from the Rebbe. The Rebbe's speech was strong; wherever we stood we could hear his voice."[20] On Sunday evening the Rebbe led a *farbrengen* until midnight in honor of his release from prison four years earlier. On Monday and Tuesday, the Rebbe met privately with each of the students. Gerlitzky was one of them. "Each had a *yechidut* (private audience) with the Rebbe. He took a great interest in every student, specifically asking about his studies." The students from Lodz and Vilnius returned to their yeshivas, and the Rebbe spent a few more days in Warsaw before heading to Marienbad and Riga.[21] The visit gave the Rebbe "great *nachat* (pleasure)," Feigin wrote to Jacobson.[22]

The success of the visit to Warsaw motivated the Chasidim of Riga to mobilize. "The Chasidim in Riga and in Lithuania decided to establish here in Riga a Tomchei Temimim yeshivah," Feigin wrote. He added that this might cause the Rebbe to remain in Riga, but he remained skeptical. "I don't see it happening, and if the financial situation would allow the Rebbe to move to Poland, he will."[23]

The Riga yeshivah was short lived, as students were forced to leave when they were unable to secure military exemptions. Poland emerged as the top choice for the Rebbe's residence, and now the debate was whether he should live in bustling Warsaw or the quieter resort town of Otwock, on its outskirts, which would benefit the Rebbe's health. In the end, the Rebbe first chose Warsaw and later relocated to Otwock.

The move was delayed to September 1933. "I decided to wait, not to make the move until I secured Latvian citizenship. Now that this has been achieved I am going to complete the plan,"[24] the Rebbe wrote to his daughter in Paris.

The Latvian passport would later prove lifesaving when the Nazis invaded Poland. In the interim, the Rebbe would make a series of visits to Jewish communities in Poland and Lithuania.[25] Chabad Chasidim had been living in Lithuania for some time; he first visited the capital city of Vilnius in 1929, where thousands welcomed him at the train station. He met with the famed Rabbi Chaim Ozer Grodzinski, who worked with the Rebbe for many years on communal concerns. In 1931, the Rebbe toured Ludmir, Poland, and other cities in Lithuania, including Rokshitz and Glubok. He returned to Glubok a second time in June 1934 and was welcomed by thousands there, too.[26] The local Yiddish paper, *Gluboker Lebn*, claimed that the reception given the Rebbe "surpassed" those for the presidents of Czechoslovakia and Austria. During this visit, the Rebbe navigated a local conflict over a rabbinic appointment in the city.[27]

Ultimately, it was the success of the yeshivah in Warsaw that lured the Rebbe to Poland. The Rebbe confided to the Ramash:[28] "The spiritual state of the yeshivah in Warsaw is outstanding, and with G-d's help there is an opportunity for the yeshivah to expand.…When I make a personal assessment, I feel a deep inner longing to be in the *ohel* (atmosphere) of Torah, where there are scholars full of knowledge who strive to serve with *avodah*.(dedication to prayer and character refinement)." The Rebbe had been longing to be in such an environment for a while. During his visit in the US, he wrote in his diary, "I yearn to be in a small town, or even a larger city surrounded by Jews filled with *yiras Shamayim* (G-d-fearing spirit), true masters of *avodah*."[29]

Finally, in September of 1933, the move to Warsaw was completed. Two years later, in 1935, the Rebbe relocated to Otwock, twenty miles south. Many leading rabbis lived in or visited Otwock, making it a spiritual hub. Rabbi Simcha Elberg recalled that there was no city in Poland that could boast "such a great number of *tzaddikim*."[30] Professor Glenn Dynner writes that it had a "chasidic ambiance."[31] The clearer air and more relaxed environment also benefitted the Rebbe. Yeshivah student Avraham Garfinkel says, "We heard the Rebbe was not well. Otwock was a resort town – people would come from all over the world because the air was good, and it was full of pine trees."[32] Shortly afterward, the yeshivah in Warsaw followed the Rebbe there. Without the burdens of procuring a visa and incurring the cost of a journey to Riga, it was significantly easier for Polish Chasidim to make the traditional spiritual pilgrimage to the Rebbe.

But Poland presented its own unique set of challenges. As chasidic scholar Rabbi Nachum Greenwald writes,[33] "Chabad had historically been a regional chasidic movement based in White Russia, Ukraine, and nearby cities in Lithuania. It had a collective history and culture." Poland was different and had many established chasidic groups, Greenwald explains. "The Chabad style of dress was different than the Polish chasidic groups. The Yiddish accent was different." On a deeper level, the mentality and outlook of the Polish Chasidim was unlike that of Chabad. Chasidism is not just a style of dress or the study of chasidic philosophy; "it's a spiritual culture, with its own story."

Lithuania was home to a small group of Chabad Chasidim, and in Poland the numbers were also modest; it was Russia that held the largest concentration of Chabad Chasidim. Greenwald says the Rebbe was alone, almost "like a king without a people. He had to start again anew." In Russia, the Rebbe was the country's foremost Jewish religious leader. In Poland, there were prominent rabbis and many well-established Jewish groups who had a major influence on communal affairs. Significantly, it was a Western country – while at times, the government was anti-Semitic, it did not repress religious beliefs. "The leadership needed in Poland was totally different than the one [needed] in Russia," Greenwald explains. Other chasidic Rebbes had migrated from their historic homelands and were not successful in recreating their chasidic milieu in the new country. For the Rebbe to succeed in reconstituting Chabad in Poland, "it wasn't enough to establish a yeshivah." Rather, Greenwald says, "what was needed was to create a new generation of Chasidism from Polish students and instill in them the ethos of Chabad in the midst of Polish Jewish culture."

Poland was not Russia, where "the Rebbe fought like a lion to keep the flame of Judaism alive. He was the head of the Jewish underground and was even jailed and sentenced to death." He was also the recognized leader of Russian Jewry. To succeed in planting Chabad in Poland, "the Rebbe changed his leadership style."

The religious community in Poland was highly organized. Jewish groups fielded parties in the Sejm, the Polish parliament. Orthodox Jews were split between Agudath Israel, a coalition of Chareidim,[34] and Mizrachi, the religious Zionists.[35] In the Polish election of 1922, Agudath Israel earned six seats, Mizrachi won five, the General Zionists, fifteen, and a combination of smaller Jewish parties won eight. Despite representation in the parliament, Jews in Poland still felt politically vulnerable and suffered from anti-Semitism.[36]

The Rebbe, like his father the Rashab, refrained from joining Agudah or any of the religious parties. This was in stark contrast to the other chasidic leaders in Poland. Chasidic Rebbes, such as those of Ger,[37] and prominent Lithuanian yeshivah scholars were all part of this religious coalition. "Chabad is not involved in politics"[38] was the Rebbe's stance. The unwillingness of the Rebbe to encourage his followers to be active supporters of Agudath Israel created a degree of tension with other Rebbes and rabbinic scholars. They viewed Agudah as vital in representing the interests of traditional Jewry in Poland. In local communities, Agudah, Mizrachi, and other parties vied in *kehillah* (community) elections. Dynner writes, "The Warsaw *kehillah* was the de facto leader of European Jewry." Schools, yeshivas, community organizations, and representation to the government were allied to the religious political parties. By standing outside that structure, the Rebbe did not benefit from its influence.

Polish Jewry was also undergoing major changes. In 1919, seventy-five percent of Poland's Jews were Shabbat observant, but by the 1930s the numbers had dropped to fifty percent, though many were still very traditional. As Jews moved to the cities, they encountered varied ideas and cultures. As Professor David Biale writes, "The primary challenge for Orthodox Judaism and Chasidism in Poland was the abandonment of religion, especially by the young, who embraced secular movements such as Zionism and socialism in unprecedented numbers."[39]

Still, says Biale, "The twin traumas of World War I and interwar secularization did not paralyze Polish orthodoxy." He explains that they "found new ways" and strategies to response to these challenges. Glenn Dynner writes that "Polish Rebbes were making monumental internal adjustments" as the traditional Orthodox community grappled with modernity. The most important response was the creation of a vibrant educational system of schools, yeshivas, and educational programs for women.[40]

The Rebbe took an independent leadership path in Poland. He abstained from involvement in the Jewish political parties, propagated a unique educational philosophy that focused on chasidic teachings, and was concerned for all Jews regardless of religiosity. His vision was global – he was active in efforts to assist Russian Jews and remained deeply involved with the American Jewish community. The Rebbe was engaged with Jews around the world through emissaries and constant correspondence. This created a degree of uneasiness with the established Orthodox leadership.

The seventh Rebbe compared the Rebbe's period in Poland to the attitude of the sons of Yaakov toward their brother Yosef, as described in the Torah: "and his brothers envied him."[41] While the Rebbe's relationship with other major rabbinic leaders had a degree of tension, it was a strain between "brothers" who maintained a strong bond despite their different outlooks. The seventh Rebbe explains that divine providence caused his exile from Russia and ultimately created a new mission: to bring the teachings of Chasidism to Poland. "In Riga and Poland, he acted with self-sacrifice,"[42] the seventh Rebbe said, alluding to the opposition that his father-in-law encountered from other prominent rabbinic leaders.

One of the important factors fueling these tensions was the success of the Warsaw Tomchei Temimim yeshivah and its developing network of branches. Many of its students were drawn from other chasidic groups, some even from the Lithuanian yeshivas. There were those who resented losing students to Tomchei Temimim. It was a growing, thriving educational empire. In 1930, the single branch of the yeshivah in Warsaw had a small enrollment;[43] its financial foundation was shaky. On the eve of the War, in 1939, the flagship yeshivah relocated from Warsaw to Otwock, and a network of ten branches spanned Poland and nearby Lithuania. Total enrollment reached 1,440 students.[44] In addition, many of these branches spawned Chabad *chadarim*, elementary-level schools, in their communities.

The Lithuanian-style yeshivas were focused on talmudic mastery, with some also including the study of *musar*, ethics.[45] The Lubavitcher yeshivah was drawing students seeking the intellectual profundity of chasidic philosophy and spirituality. The Rebbe's view was that the study of Torah should impact the individual and not just be scholarship that might prompt a sense of self-importance. "The knowledge of Torah should cause humility and good character," the Rebbe wrote to one of his Chasidim.

In a letter[46] to the Ramash, the Rebbe described diverse types of students. "There are those who study Torah and those who let Torah instruct them. There are great scholars who are consumed with their ego, feeling above criticism, in particular if it may impact their honor." There are others who study Torah, even *Chasidut,* spending time contemplating those concepts and the idea of divinity, but their cold intellect does not permit it to have an impact on them. "This is a person who studies Torah, but it does not teach him." Even though he follows the dictates of Jewish law, such a person does not truly live as a Chasid. The Rebbe aspired for a higher level for his students: "those who allow the Torah to teach them" and who enhance its study with *Chasidut.* On that level, the person sees his fellow as someone "whose essence is good. If he sees a negative trait in another person, it is only a reflection of his own inadequacies." The Rebbe was referring to the principle in chasidic philosophy that each person has a divinely given soul and a spiritual core that is full of goodness and sanctity. The Rebbe's goal was that the Yeshivah in Otwock and its network of branches would instill these principles in a new generation of Polish yeshivah students.

A crucial component of the Chabad yeshivah was its distinctive focus on prayer. The Rebbe explained, "Prayer is the tool with which we can grasp divinity, and Torah study is the tool that lets us use godliness to understand the world."[47] This duality of focusing on both the service of prayer as a way of raising spiritual consciousness and the study of Torah to form a worldview based on Jewish values had always been central to the Chabad approach to education. This differed from the classic training of the Lithuanian-style yeshivas that dominated Poland, whose primary focus was on acquiring talmudic mastery. Even those yeshivas that had instituted classes in *musar,* the study of ethics and character refinement, originally championed by Rabbi Yisrael Salanter,[48] refrained from delving into the deep theological and philosophical issues that chasidic teachings explored. Nor did they emphasize prayer as the way to unlock a person's inherent spiritual potential.

This unique approach attracted students from throughout the broader Orthodox community, particularly from other chasidic groups. One such student, Leibel Kramer,[49] was the child of Gerrer Chasidim. The devotion to prayer of a Chabad Chasid in his hometown of Chelm inspired Kramer to travel to Warsaw with his friend Yitzchak Hendel[50] and apply to the Chabad yeshivah. With just forty spots and many more applicants, there was fierce competition. Assigned a section of Talmud to prepare, they proved their acumen and were accepted. "I was taken by the chasidic atmosphere in the yeshivah," Kramer said. On Shabbat afternoon, "one of the students would recite a *maamar*, after which they would all sing beautiful chasidic melodies." Kramer was deeply moved by the Rebbe's prayer on Rosh HaShanah in 1931, later recalling, "On Erev Rosh HaShanah he *davened* for six or seven hours,"[51] completing his prayers around midnight. Most of the students remained in the synagogue as the Rebbe prayed silently, leaning on the podium in the front of the sanctuary. "He looked like a *malakh Elokim* (a divine angel)," Kramer recalled with enthusiasm some sixty years later.

Tzvi Hirsch Kotlarsky enrolled in 1931. "My father and grandfather were Kotzker Chasidim, but the Kotzker Rebbe encouraged my father to have me study in Tomchei Temimim in Warsaw,"[52] he said. The yeshivas even attracted some of the Lithuanian yeshivah elite. Rabbi Mendel Zaks, the Chafetz Chaim's son-in-law, enrolled his son in the Chabad yeshivah in Vilnius. "I sent him there to learn about humility," Rabbi Zaks told Chaim Meir Bukiet, who also studied there.[53]

Yitzchak Hendel says it was not just the study of chasidic philosophy that attracted students. "Some were drawn by the high standards of general Torah study and others by the fact that the yeshivah was well-organized and included a dorm and food service." At the time, many yeshivas were small, mostly based in a local synagogue whose rabbi would be the primary teacher. Students had to take care of their own living arrangements and meals. Tomchei Temimim, by contrast, provided these as part of the program.

Avraham Garfinkel enrolled in 1933, encouraged by his high school principal, Rabbi Mordechai Zemel, a respected Gerrer Chasid.[54] He told Garfinkel that the yeshivah had a high level of learning. "I came for the talmudic scholarship, for the *lomdut* (deep analytical study)."[55] Garfinkel had heard that Rabbi David Tablung taught in the yeshivah. "He was one of the greatest Jewish scholars in Warsaw, and I wanted to be in his class."

The Rebbe's move next to the yeshivah in Warsaw was transformational, not just for the students, but for the Rebbe himself. Just after the High Holidays of 1933, Feigin wrote,[56] "The Rebbe returned to his old self – he said long *maamarim,* some two hours in length." A few months later, he wrote, "It is like it was in Lubavitch. The Rebbe says a *maamar* Friday night and then the students and *anash* review it during Shabbat."[57] Garfinkel recalled, "How beautiful was the image of the Rebbe walking from his home to the yeshivah on Shabbat surrounded by the elders of *anash,* Chasidim of stature, and the students. His face was radiant and bursting with joy."[58]

For the students of the yeshivah, the greatest privilege was to listen to and meet with the Rebbe. They had opportunities for *yechidut,* personal appointments with the Rebbe. Hendel remembers when his friend and future brother-in-law, Yosef Tenenbaum, had his first private audience with the Rebbe in Otwock. "The Rebbe spoke to him with great love. The endearment of the Rebbe to the students was palpable."[59] "The Rebbe was very attached to the students. He wanted to have the students around him," says Garfinkel. The Rebbe once confided that without students, "*nish kein leben*" (there's no life).

Otwock became one of Europe's great centers of Jewish learning. Garfinkel says the students were like brothers. The yeshivah's teachers were outstanding talmudic scholars and taught the thoughtful study of chasidic philosophy. All this attracted top students from throughout Europe.

"Those who excelled in their studies," Tenenbaum explained, "received special privileges." They were selected to be part of a small group of students permitted to attend the Rebbe's recitation of a *maamar* on Shabbat (the Rebbe's health prevented him from speaking to large crowds). Since the *maamarim* given on Shabbat could not be recorded, some students acted as *chozrim,* Tenenbaum among them, memorizing the Rebbe's chasidic discourses and transcribing them later. They would review them with others, including the Rebbe himself. On holidays and the occasional Shabbat, the Rebbe would lead a *farbrengen*. The *maamarim*, filled with deep esoteric and philosophical teachings based on chasidic philosophy, the *farbrengens*, and the private audiences became the glue that fortified the personal relationships between the students and the Rebbe. Some remained tethered to the chasidic groups that they came from, but in many cases, the unique educational program coupled with the opportunity to interact with the Rebbe in a personal way prompted the students to become Chabad Chasidim.

Yitzchak Hendel explains that the new students from varied backgrounds "began to realize that the study of chasidic philosophy was an essential part of the curriculum. It took them some time to assimilate that fact."[60] When Garfinkel joined the yeshivah, "I didn't yet know what a Rebbe is, I didn't yet know about Lubavitch and what it meant to be a student in Lubavitch." The turning point for him came when the Rebbe arrived in Poland in the summer of 1933. "On 12 Tamuz, the anniversary of the Rebbe's release from Soviet prison, the Rebbe came to the yeshivah and had a *farbrengen* with the students. We were so excited to see the Rebbe in person.[61] After that I began to take a strong interest in chasidic philosophy."

But chasidic philosophy did not appeal to all the students coming from diverse backgrounds. "Some of the students wanted to restructure the academic program by expanding the time dedicated to Talmud study and minimizing the study of chasidic philosophy," Hendel says. This concerned the Rebbe, as he wanted the yeshivah in Poland to mirror the original Tomchei Temimim established in Lubavitch. The Rebbe felt that the way to change these students' attitudes would be through their peers. In 1936, he invited a small group of senior students to a private meeting.[62] "The Rebbe asked the students to make a special effort to instill in their classmates a stronger connection to chasidic teachings, to share with them the unique approach of Chabad that integrated the *nigleh*, the revealed part of the Torah (Talmud study), with the *nistar*, the deeper, esoteric teachings that are the core of chasidic philosophy.

During that meeting there was a moment where the Rebbe expressed his personal angst about the challenges he faced in Poland. "In Russia I experienced self-sacrifice. Now I am experiencing it again with the move from Riga to Poland." The Rebbe did not go into detail or explain exactly what he was referring to, but the context of the conversation was the series of obstacles involved in recreating in Poland the spirit of the original Tomchei Temimim.

With time, students began to trickle in from the US too. In 1938, Berel Levy and Avraham Barnetsky enrolled, along with newly married Shlomo Zalman Hecht. The Rebbe was concerned that Americans, who were used to greater comforts, might find the more austere conditions in Poland to be challenging. But Levy felt at home, writing to his family, "We hardly felt any strangeness in our new surroundings."[63] Otwock was exciting to the young Americans. Levy describes "hundreds of students from every part of Europe and hundreds of [other] Chasidim arriving for *yechidut* with the Rebbe."[64] A year later, seventeen days before the war began, a group of six students arrived from the US. They were proteges of Rabbi Yisrael Jacobson in New York.

The Rebbe expanded from a single yeshivah to a network spanning the country by encouraging his students to open branches of the yeshivah throughout Poland and Lithuania. It would be the same system of spiritual entrepreneurship that would define Chabad activism in the decades ahead.

Rabbi Yosef Goldstein was one of the early students in the Warsaw yeshivah, enrolling as a sixteen-year-old in 1922. In 1931, now twenty-four and newly married, he visited the Rebbe in Riga for the High Holidays. In the midst of a *farbrengen,* he was surprised when the Rebbe called him up, placed his right hand on his shoulder, and urged him to open a yeshivah in Chmielnik, a town in southern Poland with a population of twelve thousand, eighty percent of whom were Jews.[65] Goldstein enlisted the help of some friends, including Rabbi Mottel Bryski, and started the yeshivah.[66] It grew to over seventy students, primarily from the region, and soon expanded to include an elementary-level program as well.[67] Chaim Meir Bukiet was just eleven years old when Goldstein opened the yeshivah. "My mother walked past the yeshivah and fell in love with it," he said.[68] She saw that though the boys were older than her son, they were excited to learn, and she wanted me to go there." Even though it was only for students above the age of bar mitzvah, "she worked it out with the administration, and I began studying there at eleven years old." Chaim Meir transferred to Warsaw and then Otwock when he was sixteen.[69]

This process was repeated in other cities. In 1931, the Rebbe sent Rabbi Zalman Gurary, who was just nineteen, to Volhynia in Eastern Poland. He sent a letter ahead to the local Chasidim, telling them that he was sending his "outstanding student to visit the chasidic communities and synagogues, to strengthen the study of Torah, and to explore the possibility of opening a yeshivah."[70] Gurary reported his welcome to the Rebbe. "They all laughed, saying that there is no one to enroll and no place for a yeshivah."[71] They told him that Novardok[72] had already made a failed attempt to open a yeshivah there. But Gurary persevered and was able to overcome the initial skepticism when the community understood that the goal was to create a yeshivah for local students.[73]

The Rebbe empowered his students to be his *shluchim*, his emissaries. They would either return to their hometowns or be dispatched to cities around Poland and Lithuania to work with the local communities to establish yeshivas. By the eve of the war, a broad system of yeshivas spanned Poland and nearby Lithuania.

The period of the yeshivah in Otwock was the golden era of Tomchei Temimim in Poland.[74] The Rebbe's presence there made it the spiritual center of Chabad until the Nazi invasion in 1939. Tragically, many of the students lost their lives in the Holocaust. The network of Yeshivas Tomchei Temimim was an incubator for a new generation of Chabad followers. Those who survived the Holocaust emerged in the postwar era as leaders of the worldwide Jewish renaissance that the Rebbe initiated and the seventh Rebbe later expanded.

When the Rebbe relocated to Warsaw in 1933, eighteen-year-old Moshe Gerlitzky was given the task of unpacking the Rebbe's library with a few friends. The extensive collection had been shipped from Riga in twelve large crates. The Rebbe directed Gerlitzky to handle the books with care as they were unpacked and placed in bookshelves.[75] "The students did their work, studiously refraining from looking into the books, some of which were original manuscripts and priceless first editions," writes chasidic historian Dovid Zaklikowski.[76] At one point, the students discovered a booklet of private correspondence from the Gerrer Rebbe, the Sfas Emes (Rabbi Yehuda Leib Alter, 1847–1905) addressed to the Rebbe Rashab. The Gerrer Rebbe was the leader of the largest chasidic group in Poland. Their curiosity was piqued, says Gerlitzky. "*Nu,* as young Polish lads, we wanted to see at least something from there." As they crowded around to peek, the Rebbe himself walked in and caught them in the act. "We almost fainted," Gerlitzky remembers. The Rebbe smiled, telling them, "Just don't look into it."

The Rebbe had been an avid bibliophile from a young age, creating his own personal library. As he wrote[77] to Peter (Peretz) Wiernik,[78] editor of New York's *Morning Journal,* "As I told you, my dear friend, I am a collector of books." The Rebbe requested copies of Wiernik's works, which included a Jewish history of the US. "I would like to enrich my library with your publications." In 1904, at the age of twenty-four, the Rebbe wrote to Rabbi Yaakov Yosef Slonim, a distant relative in Jerusalem, in his pursuit of antiquarian books.[79] He asked him to search for unique collector's volumes in Jerusalem, specifically early edition books. Five months later, he offered to pay Rabbi Slonim's travel expenses to the northern town of Safed for the purpose of searching for historic books and manuscripts. "It may be possible to find books and antique manuscripts from well-known scholars." He asked him to "be sensitive to the price because my budget is still limited." The Rebbe also requested that Slonim search *genizah,* storage rooms for discarded holy books (because Jewish law prohibits their destruction), in historic Hebron and Jerusalem. He wished to procure manuscripts from chasidic masters, particularly the Mitteler Rebbe,[80] and thought that Chabad Chasidim who had emigrated from Russia a century earlier could have brought such manuscripts with them. "This is a top priority."[81]

When the Rebbe evacuated Lubavitch in 1915, he combined his personal collection with that of his father, and the bulk of it was placed in storage in Moscow. They retained some priceless manuscripts, including valuable chasidic writings dating back centuries, and a select number of books, taking them to Rostov. With the fall of the czarist government, the books stored in Moscow were seized and eventually transferred to the Russian National Library in 1924. Even before the passing of his father, the Rebbe Rashab, in 1920, the Rayatz began the effort to have the library returned. Authorities agreed to repatriate the library but then reneged, first in 1921[82] and again in 1925.[83] The Rebbe made repeated attempts to have the library returned while he was living in Russia, Latvia, Poland, and the US. While in Riga, the Rebbe approached the Russian ambassador to Latvia with a request for his help in returning the library.[84] He also encouraged the Ramash, who was studying in Berlin, to lobby the German government for its help. "It is causing me great anguish that the library is being held in Moscow," the Rebbe wrote. He felt it was a tragedy "that the books that the holy Rebbes studied and wrote annotations in should be imprisoned."[85] The Rebbe looked for every opportunity to pressure the Russians to release the library. He never gave up hope that it would be returned to him. The seventh Rebbe continued the effort after the Rebbe's passing. As the Soviet Union weakened, he established a committee of prominent Chasidim to work on securing the return of the library.[86]

The historic library in the town of Lubavitch had been reserved for the use of the Rebbes and a few select scholars. While still in Russia the Rebbe began a new initiative to increase the collection. In 1925, he acquired a large private collection[87] comprised of some five thousand items including valuable, rare, and antique volumes. Ironically, the new Bolshevik government helped expand the library. During the czar's rule they had seized two copies of every book. "There were millions of books. During the first years of the Communist regime, they needed money, but they didn't need Yiddish (Jewish) books, so they sold many of them off for use as paper. I was able to procure many,"[88] Rabbi Chaim Lieberman recalled. In 1927, when the Rebbe left Russia, he took the library with him to Latvia, overcoming the Russian government's opposition.[89]

In Riga, a broader vision began to develop – the idea of creating a formal world-class library. Rabbi Lieberman, who was appointed the librarian, said the process began in the summer of 1928. "There were enough books for the Rebbe's personal use," but the Rebbe had a bigger idea. "He wanted to create a public library, not for lending but for research, like the British Museum that is open to scholars." This was an ambitious project. "Thousands of books were needed, and we weren't sure if we could find the finances to acquire them." He explained that in the town of Lubavitch the Rebbe's library had been simply stored on some shelves in the Rebbe's home. But this undertaking would necessitate a suitable facility, with an area for researchers and a proper catalogue. The Rebbe told Lieberman, "Let's try. We will advance this project over a period of a few years, adding more books every year."[90]

The Rebbe cast a wide net in his quest to develop a world-class research library. In letters to Chasidim around the world, he urged them to source books in their home countries. The Rebbe even included secular publications, calling them "the left side of the library."[91] He sought all books published in Hebrew and also stocked selections in other languages of Jewish importance.[92] The Rebbe even requested "names of book sellers in Yemen, Australia, Africa, France, and Italy."[93]

In his drive to expand the collection, the Rebbe and his librarian Chaim Lieberman requested that authors and publishing houses donate a copy of their publications to the library. In 1934, Lieberman turned to Rabbi David Solomon Sassoon in London, requesting a donation of his book *Ohel David*. "Many authors send their publications to us as a gift." Lieberman also placed advertisements in prominent Jewish publications requesting that authors gift their works to the *Bibliothek Lybubawithc*. Feigin asked Rabbi Eliyahu Simpson in New York to spread the word that "the Rebbe would be very happy to receive books from authors as a token for the library."[94] A month later, the Rebbe thanked Simpson for books he had sent, writing, "I am interested in books published from the earliest Hebrew publishing in America," noting that this included books from the pre-revolutionary period.[95] Feigin asked Shanghai's Chief Rabbi Meir Ashkenazi to look into whether there were historical Jewish books in "Japan, China, and other remote countries."[96]

Year after year, the Rebbe's library continued to grow from purchases, gifts from authors and publishers, and donations from Chasidim around the world. By 1928 it had already made a name for itself. The London Jewish newspaper *HaOlam* reported,[97] "It is a treasure of Jewish artifacts," noting that the collection included "one of the oldest *siddurim* ever printed, from the year 1475, [and] 950 Haggadahs translated from many languages from across the world" as well as "the siddur of the Baal Shem Tov." The paper heralded the library as "an important source for research."

The Rebbe wrote to the Ramash enthusiastically about the library's progress.[98] "In the span of one month, two hundred publications were added." He said that Lieberman was "happy" with this development and was in the process of creating a catalog. The library had three sections: one, "sacred," referring to Torah volumes; a second, "secular," referring to Hebrew-language publications that were not necessarily religious in nature; and third, "foreign languages." The Rebbe hoped the catalog would be completed soon and translated into various languages. "Then we will know what we have and what we lack."

When the Rebbe fled to America at the onset of the war, he tried to secure the transfer of the library to the United States as well. The majority of the collection arrived in 1941 via Stockholm. Some of the collection became lost during the war, eventually being placed in the Polish National Library. It was discovered in 1983,[99] and five years later, it was repatriated to the Chabad Library in New York.

The Rebbe's library, inaugurated in Russia and nurtured in Latvia and Poland, ultimately blossomed into one of the largest Jewish libraries in the world. Today it is located in a large facility adjacent to Lubavitch World Headquarters in Brooklyn and is open daily for research. Its exhibition hall features historic publications, artifacts, and manuscripts.[100] The collection boasts close to 300,000 items, with more than three thousand manuscripts, including great treasures like the siddur used by Rabbi Yisrael Baal Shem Tov, marked with his personal notations.[101] Its online catalog is translated into five languages.[102]

But the Rebbe's greatest priority was the fate of Russian Jewry. He started organizing support for them from the communities in Poland during his visits there before he made the actual move in 1933. As he had in Riga, he established a committee of community leaders and prominent rabbis to raise funds and awareness.

Soviet agriculture was disrupted by collectivization and other factors, prompting shortfalls in food production. Between 1931 and 1933, some six million Russians died of starvation. As historian Nora Levin writes, "The famine of the winter of 1932–33 affected especially southern Ukraine, where many Jewish colonists perished."[103] Writer Boris Pasternak visited the colonies and described "inhuman, unimaginable misery."

During this time, the Russian government intensified its anti-religious campaign, says Professor David Fishman. "The situation took a dramatic turn for the worse in the early months of 1930."[104] The government was targeting religious functionaries. "Numerous practicing rabbis were stripped of their civil rights and branded "*lishentsy,* (disenfranchised people)." Homes were confiscated and "rabbis were levied with excessive taxes, which forced them to sell their personal belongings, or face arrest and deportation." The rabbinate, which had until then continued to function to a degree, faced disintegration. No longer was the Committee of Rabbis established by the Rebbe after the rise of Communism able to distribute funds in Russia for religious education. The rabbis themselves were barely surviving, at times leaving their hometowns to escape harassment.

In 1930, eleven rabbis from Leningrad were arrested, including the head of the community, Rabbi Shimon Lazaroff.[105] Secret police files uncovered by Russian historian Irina Osipova[106] reveal that the indictment was because he was "the head of the religious association Tzemach Tzedek, organizing unlawful yeshivas and *chadarim* for which he received money from foreign capitalists." Rabbi Lazaroff was sentenced to ten years and died in 1933 in a prison camp. There were more arrests throughout Russia. Despite this constant harassment by the government, the underground educational system had remarkable resilience. When a yeshivah was closed in one town, it would pop up in another.

After the Rebbe's departure from Russia, his secretary Rabbi Elchonon Morozov coordinated the network. Wanted by the secret police, he evaded capture by acquiring false papers in 1931. For almost a decade, he found sanctuary in the home of Raskin family in Leningrad. Sara Raskin, who was a child at the time, recalls, "Rabbi Elchonon came to live with us, and our apartment was transformed into a veritable headquarters. Through him, the Rebbe maintained contact with Chasidim inside Russia."[107] Raskin remembers that Rabbi Morozov would say, "While there are yeshivas, our flag will not be lowered even in the hardest times."[108]

In 1930, the Russian government dismantled the Yevesektzia,[109] as the Rebbe Rashab had foreseen.[110] Until this point, the Rebbe and the Committee of Rabbis had been able to play government officials against the Yevesektzia, arguing, many times successfully,[111] that religion was permitted in Russia and the Yevesektzia was overly zealous. After its closure, the state itself pursued the policy of suppressing religion, Judaism as well as other faiths. In the purges of the 1930s, Stalin's regime turned on many of its own activists, including Yevesektzia leader Semyon Dimenstein, who was killed by the Soviets in 1938. Editors of the Yevesektzia paper *Der Emes* were targeted; Moshe Litvakov was executed in 1937 and Esther Frumkin was arrested a year later. She died in a prison camp in Kazakhstan.[112]

Jews who resisted moving their farms from private ownership to Communist-run collectives, and those who refused to buckle to anti-religious oppression, suffered greatly. They had difficulties finding employment, made worse when it came to Shabbat observance. The poverty in the rural areas continued to be a catalyst for Jews moving to urban areas. Religious Jews in particular gravitated to larger cities, where their lifestyle and dress did not draw as much attention as it did in smaller towns.

The bleak news emanating from Russia aggrieved the Rebbe. Feigin wrote[113] of the Rebbe's emotional state, "What gives him no peace are the reports from expulsions in Moscow, Leningrad, and Kharkiv." The Rebbe's spirit was broken, he said, as "the situation in Russia affects the essence of his soul."

New legislation introduced in Russia in 1929 created another major economic stumbling block for Shabbat-observant Jews. If they were not officially employed, they were liable to pay five to ten times as much for rent. The law targeted clergy of all religions, curbing their ability to serve congregations in Russia. Reports of growing hunger and food shortages trickled out from Russia, alarming the Rebbe. He attempted to arrange food shipments, such as had been done in 1929 when he sent matzah for Passover. But this time the Russians would not authorize large, organized shipments.

The intensified oppression weakened the Rebbe's network in Russia. Still, the underground built on the self-sacrifice of the Rebbe's Chasidim was resilient and continued to operate clandestinely.[114] During the 1930s, yeshivas opened and closed in a variety of cities, including Kyiv, Zhytomyr, Chernihiv, Machovka, Novikov, and Kursk. For a while, there was a yeshivah in Kutaisi in Soviet Georgia, which was distant from Moscow and subject to less intense scrutiny.[115] After the war, yeshivas opened in Uzbekistan. Despite harassment from the secret police, and despite the expulsions and murder of rabbis, the secret system set up by the Rebbe starting in 1920 operated in the Soviet Union until its collapse.

Faced with fresh challenges, the Rebbe created a new strategy, writing to Peter Wiernik in New York, "According to reports we are receiving from there [the Soviet Union], their situation is severe and they are hungry for bread."[116] He proposed that packages with food and clothing be sent directly to Jews in Russia, "as if from one relative to another." The Rebbe explained that observant Jews did not work on Shabbat and were therefore not entitled to ration cards, but even if they had received bread via ration cards, "they were lacking many other staples such as sugar." The Rebbe's plan was to create a network of Jews in Europe, the US, and other countries who would send packages on a regular basis to individuals in Russia. Their "relatives" from overseas would help those who were suffering. This campaign operated covertly, as exposure could cause the Soviets to block the shipments. As the Rebbe wrote to one of his followers, "the fundraising could not be done publicly."

The Rebbe's son-in-law, the Rashag, took the lead on this project, contacting Jewish communities around the world to ensure that it appeared to be a grassroots effort. "The Rebbe feels it imperative to inspire Jews to send packages to their brothers in Russia," he wrote to Rabbi Yehuda Leib Horowitz, one of the Chabad leaders in Boston in 1931.[117] "This will keep people alive," he emphasized. The crisis was more acute for observant Jews, "who are not members of the Workers' Party and do not have the right to get food from government stores." He appealed to Jewish leaders as far as Cape Town. "The Rebbe has ascertained that the best way to help our fellow Jews in Russia is by sending food packages via the postal service." He asked that a campaign be organized in South Africa to support the effort. Jews could send packages directly from South Africa or they could sponsor packages being sent from Riga. "I am sending you a list of packages that can be sent from here in Riga, which is close to your friends and relatives in Russia."

While in Paris for medical care, the Rebbe also organized a committee to spearhead a similar effort based in France. Local Jewish leaders including prominent rabbis such as Rabbi Moshe Eisenstadt worked with the Rashag, also placing ads in newspapers in *Eretz Yisrael* so families there could sponsor packages for their loved ones.[118] The Rebbe also appealed to the JDC and other Jewish organizations to sponsor shipments, telling JDC officials that the rabbis being oppressed by the Communists were "on the verge of expiring from hunger."[119]

And it was not only packages. With the help of the Rashag, the Rebbe arranged the direct transfer of funds to Jews in Russia. Money sent to Soviet citizens from overseas could only be exchanged at official rates. Desperately needing foreign currency, the Russians kept the exchange rate artificially low. Russia and nearby Latvia were strong trading partners, so the Rashag worked with businessmen in Riga who operated in Russia. He provided the Latvians with US dollars or other currencies, and through associates in Russia, they converted the funds to rubles and transferred them to needy Jews. As he explained to Rabbi Yitzchak Horowitz in Boston, if the money was sent through official means like the post or a bank transfer, the addressee would get less than two rubles per dollar. But "if we send the funds in an illegal fashion, they get five rubles. I have done this successfully many times, to all parts of Russia." Discovery by the Soviets could result in imprisonment for the Jews in Russia, but the threat of starvation outweighed the risks. Quietly, word went out to Jews around the world that there was a way to move funds to friends and relatives in Russia.

Within a few years, the operation had grown so much that four Russian refugee Chasidim were busy full-time running an office in Riga that took orders from Jews around the world and dispatched packages to Russia. The four Chasidim, Rabbis Moshe Gurary, his brother Shmaryahu (Shmerel), Dovber Chaskind, and Yosef Rosenblum, were alumni of the yeshivas in Lubavitch and Kremenchuk. As Russians themselves, they understood the difficulties faced by those still in the country and were devoted to the mission entrusted to them by the Rebbe.

One late night in November of 1935, Latvian police raided all four of their homes simultaneously.[120] Shmerel Gurary's daughter, who was just seven years old at the time, remembered the police search many years later. "They didn't permit us to move," she said. "I stood in the house wondering what they were looking for." All four were hauled off to jail; with great difficulty, they were released on bail. As Russian citizens – not Latvians – their legal predicament was dangerous. Finally, authorities gave them a choice:

a long prison sentence or expulsion from Latvia. The Rebbe advised them to immigrate to British Mandate Palestine.[121] In Tel Aviv they recreated the operation, continuing to ship packages to Russia, and eventually opening branches in Petach Tikvah, Haifa, and with time, New York.[122]

Since the Bolshevik revolution in 1917, the US had refused to recognize the new regime in Russia. In 1933, the newly elected Franklin Roosevelt was determined to change that policy. US recognition was important to Russia, and so Russian Foreign Minister Maxim Litvinov traveled to Washington to personally negotiate with US officials.[123] As with so many other Communist officials, Litvinov was Jewish, born as Meir Finkelstein in 1876 in Bialystok, Russia.[124]

The Rebbe viewed this as a historic opportunity. He launched a global campaign to pressure the US to make the religious freedom of Russian Jews a perquisite for formal diplomatic recognition. The campaign was broad, galvanizing international Jewish leaders to appeal[125] to Litvinov on behalf of world Jewry. It included leaders from across the spectrum, from prominent European rabbis such as Chaim Ozer Grodzinksi[126] to the head of the Jewish Agency, Nahum Sokolow. The Rebbe turned to prominent US Jews, including Rabbi Eliezer Silver, leaders of the JDC, and others, urging them to use their connections to US officials. "The representative of the Soviet Union is coming to the US to establish formal relations," he wrote. "It's important to use this moment to benefit Russian Jews."[127] The Rebbe also reached out to his contacts in the US government, including US Senators William Borah of Idaho and William King of Utah.[128] He encouraged them to intervene with the Roosevelt administration to condition the recognition of the Soviet Union on lifting the restrictions on religious life in Russia.

Following his approach of many years, the Rebbe worked quietly behind the scenes.[129] "In my experience in years of efforts in Russia, both when I was there and after I departed, much more can be accomplished by secret diplomacy than demonstrations."[130] The Rebbe added, "Having influential people lobbying can be very effective." Still, word leaked to the press, and a London Jewish paper[131] reported on the letter from world Jewry requesting that the "Soviet Union cease its policy of closing synagogues, allow Jewish schools to operate, and permit Russian rabbis to emigrate."

Unfortunately, the US government, eager to strike a deal with Russia, did not acquiesce to the Rebbe's requests. The Russians agreed to one concession: US citizens visiting Russia would be free to practice their religion as they pleased.[132] There was one more concrete achievement with Litvinov. Twenty-three Chabad Chasidim, caught secretly crossing Russia's southern border on their way to *Eretz Yisrael,* had been arrested and sentenced to labor camps. Reb Itche der Masmid was in the US on behalf of the Rebbe and lobbied Litvinov for their release. The two met in Washington, and as a result, the Russian government freed the group from prison, though they were not permitted to emigrate.[133]

As the Rebbe was marshaling the support of world leaders to lobby US government officials for religious freedom in Russia, he created a separate parallel push to repatriate the Chabad library. He turned to some key US Chasidim to request that the US government urge Litvinov to return the library. Rabbi Avraham Axelrod from Baltimore reached out to the secretary of state. It was a much more subtle effort and clearly calculated not to undermine the more important initiative to relieve the suffering of Russian Jews.[134] Ultimately, this initiative failed. Under Secretary of State William Phillips wrote to Axelrod, "Rabbi Schneersohn is not a citizen of the United States and this government is not in a position to take any formal steps to induce the Soviet government to return the books."[135]

Aside from his work on behalf of Russian Jews, the Rebbe continued to reach out to communities across the globe during the 1930s. Many Jews had emigrated from the chasidic heartland in Russia to new communities around the world. Some were ardent Chasidim; others merely had a nostalgic connection to Chabad. With those the Rebbe knew personally, he kept a correspondence, sending letters, *maamarim,* and *likkutei dibburim* (published talks and chasidic lore). Many of those immigrants arrived in locations where religious life was just setting down roots. As time went on, their connection to Chabad and observance in general weakened. In America, Agudas Chassidei Chabad was established in 1924, but in other countries, Chabad was not formalized. In some regions, the Rebbe's Chasidim were community rabbis. He encouraged them to expand their vision, to take responsibility for all Jews, and to reach out to those on the periphery of the Jewish community. He praised Rabbi Meir Ashkenazi in Shanghai, "I received great pleasure that you have initiated educational classes for the public." Ashkenazi had previously reported to the Rebbe that the Ashkenazi and Sephardi communities in Shanghai operated independently. The Rebbe urged him to bridge those gaps. "When it comes to bolstering Jewish life, it is preferable to unify."[136] The Rebbe told Rabbi Yisrael Zuber in Stockholm,[137] "The purpose of being a student of Tomchei Temimim is to brighten the spiritual darkness,"[138] lauding him for organizing classes and *farbrengens*.

The Rebbe kept in touch with Chasidim across the globe. He wrote to a follower in Montreal about the bond between a Rebbe and a Chasid: "The affection and love is a foundation of chasidic life, and that feeling is not broken by borders and distance." It is a deep spiritual connection, he wrote, "a bond of soul to soul, enhanced by Torah study."[139] In another connection that withstood geographic distance, the Rebbe advised Moshe Feiglin,[140] the first Chasid in Australia, on how to ensure that his children would live by his chasidic values. "Each member of *anash* must relate to his children his memories of his ancestors so they will understand their background." The Rebbe quoted his father's dictum, "Just as it's an obligation to lay tefillin daily, so too a parent must invest an hour each day to instill in his children spiritual values."[141]

To connect with the newly established communities and to energize them, the Rebbe renewed the concept of sending personal envoys, *shluchim*. One of those was Rabbi Zelig Slonim,[142] who started traveling the globe as the Rebbe's emissary in the 1920s. Slonim was born in Hebron in 1897 and orphaned of his father a year later. His mother trekked to Lubavitch to enroll him in the yeshivah when he was just fifteen. A direct descendant of the Chabad Rebbes, he excelled in his studies and was devoted to the Rebbes, first to the Rebbe Rashab, then his son the Rayatz and the seventh Rebbe. His first formal mission was to England in January 1926.[143] The Rebbe was in Russia at the time, locked in spiritual combat with the Yevesektzia but still concerned with the welfare of Chasidim in other countries. He wrote to the community in London,[144] "I am sending you my outstanding student to teach chasidic philosophy and to inspire the *anash* and strengthen Jewish learning and observance." While Slonim was there, the Rebbe corresponded with him regularly, asking for "detailed descriptions of each Chabad synagogue, its leadership, and their addresses."

In England and later in other countries, Slonim was instructed to find positions for Chabad rabbis, *shochtim*, and others. Through the 1930s, the Rebbe was constantly searching for ways to help his Chasidim and others leave Russia, but it was difficult for Russian Jews to get visas to other countries. In 1924, the US Congress instated severe immigration controls.[145] One of the ways to facilitate emigration from Russia was to arrange employment overseas.

The Rebbe tasked Slonim with ensuring that Rabbi Mordechai Gutnick,[146] who had studied in Lubavitch, would be appointed rabbi of the Nusach Ari (Chabad) synagogue in London. The congregation split between those who wanted a classic Chabad rabbi and those who advocated for a candidate with academic degrees. Slonim argued that the synagogue had been founded by Chasidim and those traditions should be upheld. As the opposition rose, he wrote to the Rebbe in frustration, "The synagogue leaders are giving me all kinds of excuses, but their opposition in not based on reason." The Rebbe shared an idea to bypass the recalcitrant leaders: "Organize a meeting of all the members and speak to them about the need to have a chasidic rabbi for all *anash* in England." Slonim prevailed, and Gutnick was hired. Later the Rebbe commented, "Zelig knows how to get things done."

Slonim spent a year in England, visiting Scotland and Ireland. This would be the first of a series of missions. After he went home to Jerusalem, Slonim visited the Rebbe, who had relocated to Riga. In 1928 and again in 1929, the Rebbe dispatched Slonim to Scandinavia and other European countries, requesting detailed reports about each community he visited. The Rebbe encouraged Slonim to seek every opportunity to inspire others, instructing him, "Don't act judgmentally toward them." The Rebbe wanted him to use a positive approach. "Share memories of what you studied in your time in Lubavitch."

In 1929, after a short interlude in *Eretz Yisrael*, the Rebbe sent Slonim to South Africa.[147] Yechezkel Feigin wrote to him on behalf of the Rebbe, "I have been asked to inquire if you are willing to accept a mission to South Africa," adding that some Chabad Chasidim were there, but "we have little knowledge of what is happening in the country." It would be a long journey. Slonim's mission was to connect to the immigrants, strengthen Jewish life there, and find employment for Chasidim. "I am turning to you on behalf of the Rebbe to ask you to explore employment opportunities for rabbis and *shochtim*," wrote Feigin. Slonim spent over two and a half years in South Africa visiting communities and nearby Rhodesia. In subsequent years, he was involved with Chabad in Jerusalem, visiting the Rebbe in Europe periodically.

In 1939, Slonim went on his final long mission, this time to Australia. He traveled throughout the country and nearby New Zealand.[148] While there, he was involved in a host of projects, such as the building of a *mikveh* in Brisbane. Seven months after the outbreak of the war, in March of 1940, Slonim headed back to *Eretz Yisrael* on a long, dangerous trip that departed from Perth on Australia's western coast and finally arrived in Suez in British-controlled Egypt.

The missions were not always easy. Slonim encountered rabbis[149] who compromised Jewish law, due to pressure from community members. He had to navigate local politics in his effort to inspire others and remain true to his mission. Throughout his visits, Slonim maintained a regular correspondence with the Rebbe on a wide variety of issues.

Slonim's missions and those of other Chasidim invigorated the connection of the Rebbe to those with a historical link to Chabad. Traveling as official *shluchim* of the Rebbe carried an element of prestige. Slonim himself was an outstanding Torah scholar and full of enthusiasm. The Rebbe took a deep personal interest in the reports that Slonim and other emissaries sent him about the Jews they met and the challenges faced by their communities. For many immigrants who had drifted from the fully observant lifestyle, the arrival of a *shliach* of the Rebbe rekindled the spiritual identity that they knew from the "*alter Heim*," the rich religious life that Jews had in Europe. It also sent them an important message that the Rebbe was deeply concerned with their welfare. All of this would serve to revitalize their Jewish identity in a new country with little Jewish infrastructure.

In September of 1930, the Rebbe returned to Europe from his long trip abroad. Instead of going directly home to Riga, he made a stop. "I was weak from the trip and traveled to Marienbad."[150] This resort[151] with kosher hotels was visited by many prominent rabbis. During the Rebbe's break there, he met with the Belzer, Aleksander, and Gerrer Rebbes.[152] After three weeks he headed home to Riga. His speech began to slowly change. "The tempo of my speech altered, but I did not pay attention to it," he wrote. This was the beginning of the series of health challenges that the Rebbe suffered from for the rest of his life. "The Rebbe's condition raises much concern," Feigin wrote in the fall of 1932.[153] "As you know, the sickness in his foot has improved, but he is very weak." Feigin went on to say that they were using a local physician in Riga. "He comes daily and is very dedicated, but he is not an expert physician." Describing the deterioration in the Rebbe's speech, Feigin said, "There is a heaviness in his speaking."

The Rebbe also recognized the change. "After two years, the weakness in speaking became apparent, and I decided to seek medical help." The doctors in Riga suggested he travel to Berlin, where there were vastly superior medical resources. Starting in January of 1933,[154] the Rebbe spent two months in a clinic. The doctors did not have a clear diagnosis. "The medical experts, including the renowned Professor Leve, came to a conclusion that they do not know the actual sickness. However, they do recommend that I should be under medical supervision."[155]

The doctors' consensus was that the Rebbe was weak from years of suffering. "You cannot imagine how much I have endured in the last five and a half years since I was exiled [in 1927]," he said. The Rebbe wrote that he was distraught from the hardships of his Chasidim and disheartened that despite major efforts his fundraising success had been marginal. To help the Rebbe rest, Feigin withheld correspondence.[156] "Daily, a large number of letters arrive with all the *tzarot Yisrael* (Jewish suffering), and this gives the Rebbe no rest."[157] The Rebbe agreed, writing, "Due to the weakness of my health, the physicians have prohibited me from receiving correspondence and exerting myself." The Rebbe was not alone in Berlin. "My son-in-law, Rabbi Menachem Mendel, comes daily to visit."[158] In the years to come, the Ramash took the lead in assisting the Rebbe with his medical care, spending extensive time with him in Marienbad, Berlin, and later in Vienna and Paris.

The underlying medical condition causing the Rebbe so much discomfort remained a mystery for almost two years.[159] His condition continued to decline, and in the summer of 1934, the Rebbe traveled to Marienbad for a month, accompanied by the Ramash. In November that year, the Ramash traveled with him to Vienna to consult with medical experts. "The doctors were able to determine the sickness, but they had no medicine to cure it, the Rebbe later wrote.[160] He was diagnosed with multiple sclerosis,[161] an autoimmune disease that even today has no real cure. It afflicted him for the rest of his life. The doctors in Vienna offered varied opinions on how to mitigate the illness, creating much confusion. Finally, they met Dr. Max Gerson, a German Jewish doctor who had fled the country with the rise of Nazism. His approach was fundamentally different, prescribing a "regimen of diet and injections." It was not a conventional medical approach and was rejected by other practitioners. As Rabbi Chaim Miller writes, "Gerson's holistic approach viewed the patient body as an organism whose various parts, including the mind, are interconnected." This appealed to the Rebbe.

Still accompanied by the Ramash, he moved into Gerson's Westend Sanatorium located in Purkersdorf, a town not far from Vienna. The Rebbe arrived there in December 1934 and left a few days before Passover. Gerson's daughter, Charlotte, who was twelve at the time, recalled[162] many years later that the Rebbe was a "distinguished figure. He was the *wunder* rabbi (miracle rabbi), and we children admired him from afar." When Dr. Gerson moved to France, the Rebbe traveled there for treatment. Between 1933 and 1939, the Rebbe spent some twenty-two months[163] away from his home in medical facilities, primarily the sanatoriums in Berlin, Purkersdorf, and Paris.

The constant need for medical care and travel put a severe financial burden on the Rebbe. Feigin tried to ameliorate the situation by orchestrating a fundraising effort by Chasidim. In the summer of 1936, he wrote to Alter Simchovich in Jerusalem that the Rebbe planned to go to Paris for treatment, but he had pushed off the trip "due to a lack of funds." He explained that the treatments in Vienna "had caused a small improvement," but the illness was unique and required the attention "of world-class medical experts." Feigin told him that Reb Itche Horowitz was "in London and raising money for *maamad* (support of the Rebbe)." The plan was to send him to Ireland; Feigin asked Simchovitch to secure a letter of recommendation from Rabbi Isaac Herzog, the previous chief rabbi of Ireland who had just been appointed chief rabbi of *Eretz Yisrael*. "If he will write a letter, since he was the chief rabbi of Ireland it will definitely help."[164]

In the sanatoriums, free from some of his usual day-to-day tasks, the Rebbe dedicated much time to writing and correspondence, producing a series of long letters on chasidic history and lore. These included a letter of more than one hundred pages[165] on the early history of Chasidism, written in Yiddish to his daughter Chaya Mushka in Paris. Translator Shimon Neubort describes it as "a glimpse into the lives of several early Chasidim who were instrumental in spreading chasidic teachings and the chasidic way of life."[166] The letter is full of "rich prose" and offers the reader a "graphic portrait of the spiritual rhythms of life in the shtetl and what inspired the Jews of the era."

When the Rebbe moved to Poland in 1933, he came with few Chasidim and limited resources. The well-established chasidic courts of Ger, Belz, and others had hundreds of thousands of followers and dominated religious life in Poland. The Rebbe realized the future was the youth. He began with one yeshivah with 157 college-age students in 1929. It moved to Otwock and emerged as one of the leading centers of Jewish scholarship in the world, growing to a network of yeshivas in ten more cities. By the eve of the war there were 1,500 students in eleven yeshivas.[167] In many of those communities the yeshivas spawned *chadarim* (elementary schools) and *mesivtas* (high schools).

The Rebbe was nurturing Chasidim in a new country, people who lacked the ethos and memories that the Chasidim in Russia had lived with for two centuries. He introduced the study of Chasidism and used his prolific pen to create a literary culture, bringing alive the stories of Chasidim from generations past. He gave those drawn to Chabad a historic identity as lived by the Chasidim who had experienced the greatness of the Rebbes of earlier generations. All this time, the Rebbe strived to remain in close contact with his geographically diverse community. He visited chasidic enclaves in Lithuania and Poland, and he dispatched emissaries to cities in Europe and around the world. The Rebbe encouraged his Chasidim to take up leadership in Jewish communities, setting the stage for the emergence of Chabad around the world in the postwar era.

Constantly weighing on the Rebbe's heart was the fate of Russian Jewry. During this period, he sustained the Jewish underground network that kept the flame of Judaism alive in Russia, despite the unwillingness of major groups to support his efforts. The Rebbe unsuccessfully lobbied the United States to pressure the Russian government to relax restrictions on religious freedom in Russia. He was in constant contact with his Chasidim in Russia, funneling money, food, and other assistance in a variety of ways. He also worked to help Chasidim immigrate to the West.

It was the personal fate of his Chasidim that was his deepest concern. One Chasid, Moshe Binyamin Kaplan, fled Russia during the Great Escape in 1946. When he arrived in a DP camp in Germany, he wrote to the Rebbe, then in Brooklyn. "I don't know if the Rebbe remembers me, but I learned in the underground yeshivas in Russia from 1934 to 1939," he said. "My father was known as the Ksavrov Rabbi, and he met the Rebbe several times. I wonder what kind of bond I can have with the Rebbe since I never met him." The Rebbe responded, "I remember him very, very well." Writing in poetic rabbinic Hebrew, he said, "The bond between us is when you learn my Torah," referring to the Rebbe's *maamarim*, "or the Torah I am learning." Years later, Rabbi Shalom Ber Levin discovered among the Rebbe's possessions a picture of Moshe Binyamin Kaplan. It was taken in Russia around 1935, when he was about eighteen. It was common at the time for students in the underground yeshivas in Russia to take pictures of themselves and send them via third parties to the Rebbe in Poland. All those years, first in Poland and later in the US, the Rebbe kept his picture and would gaze at it from time to time.[168]

Just as the Rebbe's life changed dramatically when he was exiled from Russia, it was transformed yet again with the advent of World War II. The German invasion of Poland shattered the Rebbe's world again, destroying the magnificent network of yeshivas and communities that he had built in Europe after he departed from Russia. The invasion put the Rebbe in mortal danger and set the stage for a miraculous escape from Europe to America – where, yet again, he would start from nothing and adapt to a totally new set of challenges.

Chapter Nine

The World Is Shattered

When Rabbi Yisrael Jacobson entered the Rebbe's study on Saturday night, he had no inkling that five days later, the war would engulf Poland.[1] He had escorted six students from New York to the yeshivah two weeks earlier, and now he was preparing to return home. That night the primary topic of discussion was the idea that had been brewing for a decade: the Rebbe's relocation to the US. The Rebbe had finally resolved to make the move, telling Jacobson, "I wrote Rabbi Shmuel Levitin asking if a Lubavitcher yeshivah could succeed in the US, and he responded yes." That assessment was affirmed by the success of the US students at the yeshivah in Otwock.[2] When the first group came in 1938, yeshivah administrators feared the pampered Americans might not adapt, but they had done well. The Rebbe told Jacobson, "From the students that you have brought I see there is no problem – we can have a fine Yeshivas Tomchei Temimim in America." Jacobson assured the Rebbe that the community would support his work. The Rebbe's decision was firm. "Arrange everything systematically and on a solid basis. In about half a year, with G-d's assistance, we will come to America."[3]

The Rebbe wasn't just going to move, he was going to change his focus. He told Jacobson, "I am entering my sixth decade. The last time I was in the US [referring to his 1929–30 visit], I was involved in strengthening traditional Judaism, and thank G-d, I was successful. This time my intentions are to teach Chasidism and take care of the Chasidim."[4] The Rebbe's sixtieth birthday was ten months away, and he was weakened by his ordeal in Russia and Poland as well as acute health challenges. "I want to be a Rebbe for Chasidim, not a Rebbe for the whole world," he said.[5] In America, the Rebbe's goal would be to open a yeshivah and focus inward on the chasidic community.

The Rebbe told Rabbi Jacobson not to linger in Otwock; he wanted him to leave the next morning. Jacobson was scheduled to sail later that week on the Queen Mary, departing from France. But with the border now closed, Jacobson was forced to take a roundabout route via Hungary, Yugoslavia, and Italy, only reaching Paris ten days later and missing the departure of the Queen Mary. By then, Germany had invaded Poland. Jacobson was desperate to get home, realizing that only US intervention could save the Rebbe. Finally, he secured a berth on a ship leaving for the United States, which turned out to be a cot in the ship's swimming pool locker room, as it was overcrowded with Americans fleeing Europe. They celebrated Rosh HaShanah at sea with Rabbi Jacobson leading the services on deck, finally arriving in New York more than two weeks after the war had started.

Jacobson immediately sprang into action, launching a campaign to save the Rebbe. It would involve Chabad activists in Brooklyn, government officials in Washington, Chasidim in Riga, diplomats in Berlin, the Abwehr (German naval intelligence service), and soldiers from the Wehrmacht – many of Jewish background. They would have to overcome the overt anti-Semitism of US officials who objected to Jewish immigration, and evade the Gestapo, who saw the Rebbe as a high-value target. They would have to discover the Rebbe's whereabouts in war-torn Poland and transport him, his family, and key followers across the border through Nazi Germany to Latvia, and eventually to refuge in the United States. Throughout all this, the Rebbe endeavored to help as many of his students as possible escape Poland, and he continued to reach out to other Jews, attempting to help them find an avenue of salvation from the Nazi onslaught.

Thursday nights in Chabad yeshivas are traditionally reserved for late-night study review. At times, a chasidic *farbrengen* is held, which can last the entire night. The evening before the world was devastated by war[6] was no different. In Otwock, Avraham Garfinkel[7] spent the night with his fellow students at a *farbrengen* marking the yeshivah's founding thirty-two years earlier. As the students sang melodies and listened to words of Torah and chasidic stories, none of them imagined that their world of camaraderie, Torah study, and inspiration would be shattered at daybreak. The celebration finished as the sun began to rise that Friday morning. They were unaware that at 4:45 a.m., a German battleship began shelling Gdańsk. Shortly afterward, led by columns of panzer tanks, a million and a half German solders invaded Poland. At 8:00 a.m., as the students were getting ready for morning prayers, German planes began bombing Otwock.

"Thunderous sounds were suddenly heard," recalled Garfinkel. The students ran outside to find people screaming, "Don't you see? It's war!" Avraham Hecht, one of the six recently arrived American students, described the shock. "It was a pleasantly warm summer day with a cloudless sky and mild sunshine. My attention was once again interrupted by the disturbing sound of airplanes streaking across the sky."[8] Outside, Hecht saw German bombers raining death and destruction on the town. In an instant, the world changed forever. "A deafening explosion rocked our building and shattered its window."

The war came as a surprise, says Garfinkel. "At first, we didn't want to believe it." There had been some talk of war, but there was much skepticism. "Many thought that in the months leading to the conflict, Hitler was conducting a war of nerves and was in fact not prepared for actual war," wrote Rabbi Pinchas Hirschsprung, who lived in the small Polish town of Dukla.[9] "The prevailing thought was that Hitler's threats were designed to win more concessions, and Jews held on to the hope there would be no war."

That was the Rebbe's view too. Earlier that summer, some of the parents of US students planning to come to Otwock expressed concern about traveling to Poland. The Rebbe responded to one of the boys, Mordechai Fisher, "You have nothing to fear."[10] With that assurance, they boarded[11] the Isle de France with Rabbi Jacobson, arriving at the yeshivah just seventeen days before the conflict started. The day the war broke out, the Rebbe told the American students, "I did not foresee it."[12]

Hecht says they were "bewildered by the horrendous chain of events." They reached the American Consul, who advised them, "Germany just issued an official declaration of war. I strongly advise you to travel immediately to Warsaw, and we will arrange your return to safety." They verified that travel to Riga, capital of neutral Latvia, was possible. Shortly after noon they headed out, stopping off at the Rebbe's residence before they departed.

Avraham Hecht[13] vividly remembers that moment. "We entered the study where the Rebbe was sitting regally, already dressed in his silk Shabbat garments." The Rebbe bid them farewell. Since they had American passports, they had freedom of movement, and the Rebbe directed them to travel as soon as possible to neutral Latvia. "I'm sending you to my Chasidim in Riga, Latvia," he said, telling them to remain calm. "Reb Mordechai Cheifetz will make arrangements for you." The Rebbe asked one of the students, Meir Greenberg, to relay a request to Mordechai Dubin in Riga "to arrange that the Latvian government should request a permit for the Rebbe to leave Poland with his family, since the Rebbe and his family are Latvian citizens." The American students would be traveling in a war zone. One of the students asked the Rebbe, "What should we do if we need to desecrate the Shabbat?" The Rebbe quickly responded, "The merit of the two *tzaddikim* whose birthdays fall out on Chai Elul,[14] the Baal Shem Tov and Rabbi Schneur Zalman, is sufficient that you will not need to transgress this Shabbat."

The Americans first went to nearby Warsaw where, according to Mordechai Altein, "The US Consulate refused assistance because they were chasidic Jews." A JDC representative saw the stranded Americans outside the consulate and intervened, suggesting they go to the Hotel Britannia. "He got a wheelbarrow and helped us move our stuff," Hecht remembers. By then it was after nightfall, but the hotel owner refused them accommodation unless they would sign the registration form. The students debated what to do. Shloma Zalman Hecht insisted "that since the Rebbe said they won't have to desecrate the Shabbat, they shouldn't sign the form."[15]

That turned out to be fortuitus. A religious Jew found them a haven in a small, ramshackle guesthouse a short distance away. There, Greenberg met a classmate from New York's Yeshivah Torah Vodaath. He asked Greenberg if the group could take a large sum of money to America – the exact amount needed for train tickets to Riga. On Sunday morning, Greenberg's friend purchased the tickets[16] to Riga, where they were welcomed by the Chabad community. Greenberg was able to get the message to Dubin to bring the Rebbe to Riga. A month later, the students traveled back to the US.

The bombing continued that Friday morning in Otwock, snuffing out the lives of ten children in the Jewish orphanage.[17] The new yeshivah building was also struck, but there was no loss of life. As night fell, the Jews of Otwock ushered in Shabbat. "The police issued an order prohibiting the lighting of any fire or light," remembered the Rashag.[18] The Rebbe's home was blanketed in an "eerie atmosphere. Small Chanukah candles were lit," providing somber, subdued lighting. "The windows were covered tightly," so as not to let out any light. They did not have enough gas masks for everyone, "so the Rebbe's family kept glasses of soda water and cotton to shield against gas." The Rebbe insisted that the Shabbat meal not be disturbed and celebrated in a traditional manner. During the meal, a siren signaled another air raid. The Rebbe and his family had no choice but to "leave the Shabbat meal and descend into an underground shelter, where we sat for two hours."

After the conclusion of Shabbat, plans were made to transfer the Rebbe and his family to nearby Warsaw. Before the war, dozens of trains ran daily between Otwock and Warsaw, but "now there was nothing," says the Rashag. The roads were under bombardment, and travel was dangerous.

From Warsaw they intended to head to Latvia, which still was neutral and could be a base from which to assist in the rescue of others. "My grandfather decided quickly to get to a place where he could organize [efforts] to save Polish Jews," remembered Berke Gurary, the Rebbe's grandson.[19] On Monday, the Latvian Embassy sent a car with diplomatic plates to transport the Rebbe and his family to Warsaw. "Since it carried license plates of a foreign country, there was no worry of it being stopped," the Rashag explained. The car made the trip twice: Chaim Lieberman left with some members of the Rebbe's family on Monday, and the Rebbe followed the next day. The Rebbe took along with him valuable historic manuscripts, leaving the bulk of his library behind in Otwock.

A large crowd gathered to bid the Rebbe farewell. Yosef Wineberg recalled the tearful scene. The Rebbe's face was etched with sadness, and he cried profusely as he blessed the crowd. "A king guards his subjects. You Jewish children, may G-d guard you where you will be, and us, wherever we will be."[20]

The drive to Warsaw was harrowing. German planes overhead continued to terrorize them, dropping bombs. All along the way there was death and destruction. As the planes attacked, other travelers abandoned their cars, finding shelter along the road. The Rebbe told those with him not to fear. "There is no need to run and hide because Father [the fifth Rebbe, the Rebbe Rashab] is interceding on our behalf."[21]

As the Rebbe's entourage neared Warsaw, some feared that Jewish neighborhoods were being targeted by the Luftwaffe and thought it might be safer to stay in a non-Jewish area.[22] The Rebbe rejected this, saying he wanted to be with the Jews no matter what the risk. "Our brethren are in the greatest danger, and you want me to separate from them and hide in another neighborhood?" Hundreds of thousands of Jews lived in Warsaw, and the Rebbe was emphatic: "My lot will be with theirs." The Rebbe was determined to help as many students and Chasidim as possible escape the Nazi onslaught.

The Rebbe moved into an apartment in the heart of Jewish Warsaw owned by Zalman Shmotkin.[23] When they first arrived, says Wineberg, "Nobody in the city knew just how serious the situation was." A day later, a German bombing raid hit the building across the street.[24] The Rebbe instructed his Chasidim to search the rubble for survivors. Ominous news began to trickle in. "Only on Wednesday did we learn that the Germans were rapidly advancing toward Warsaw." The Latvian Consulate would be a safer shelter, but officials rejected the Rebbe's request for refuge. Finally, a few days later they agreed, but by then it became too dangerous to move around the city.

A week later was the eve of Rosh HaShanah.[25] The Rebbe provided funds to Zalman Shmotkin to ensure that the students of the yeshivah remaining in Warsaw had food. That day, "at five in the afternoon, bombs struck Shmotkin's building, and it burst into flames." The Rebbe and his family escaped to the other side of the street, finding shelter in an archway. Wineberg says all the residents of the building were packed together. "Women and children were wailing." Wineberg and a few other students stood next to the Rebbe, guarding him. "His face was awesomely grave. He sat whispering prayers in an undertone the entire time."

The German bombing was relentless. "Suddenly, a horrifying scream was heard. A bomb had exploded nearby, and the powerful blast threw the Rebbe and his family from one end of the yard to the other," says the Rashag.[26] The blast had filled the air with smoke. Thinking the worst, "they began screaming, 'Gas!' The Rebbe's daughter Chana applied a wet cloth across her father's mouth, but quickly they discovered that it was only dust."

With the sun setting soon and Rosh HaShanah about to begin, the Rebbe's daughter Chana and his sixteen-year-old grandson Berke insisted that the Rebbe move to a safer location. After a tremendous effort, a Jewish wagon driver agreed to take the Rebbe and family[27] to a nearby medical clinic. It was risky, as he could be arrested for transporting private passengers, but he was still willing to help, saying, "If it befits the Rebbe to be in danger, it befits me too." Others walked alongside as they made their way to 8 Gegrnitche Street.

That night, the Rebbe prayed without a *minyan*. His grandson recalls that on Rosh HaShanah, "normally he would spend three to four hours in *Maariv*," his prayers filled with tears, but that night it took just a half an hour. "He was totally exhausted and could not stand." Everyone was worried as the bombs continued to rain down. "The Rebbe was reassuring everyone around him, a remarkable strength of character for a man who could not move for physical reasons."[28]

The next day, Jews streamed from around Warsaw to be near the Rebbe. One account sets the number of those gathered at one thousand. It was unlike any other High Holiday. "Services began at the crack of dawn and were not drawn out so that the shofar could be sounded early, before the Germans began their daylight bombing," says the Rashag. The day after Rosh HaShanah, a bomb fell on the building occupied by the Rebbe. "In one room, half a wall fell down, and all the windowpanes were blown out. Debris sprayed into the room where the Rebbe was sitting and studying Torah." Fortunately, he was unscathed.

After the bombing, they moved yet again, this time to Nalevki street. That too became the target of German bombing, and the Rebbe crowded into a shelter with hundreds of others. Not only were bombs falling from above, but as German troops drew closer to Warsaw, an artillery bombardment of the city began. During the attacks, says Wineberg, "The Rebbe would sit in the room writing *maamarim,* and his hand would shake from the bombing. He would tell those around him, 'I am not afraid.'"

Two days before Yom Kippur,[29] the Rebbe moved back to Shmotkin's apartment. As the holiday was about to begin, "The Rebbe was unusually grievous," Wineberg says. A small group prayed with the Rebbe. "As the Rebbe recited *maftir Yonah,* everyone's hearts overflowed. There were thunderous explosions. The calmness in the Rebbe's voice kept everyone from hysteria and flight." The final service of Yom Kippur was prayed hastily, and the shofar sounded before nightfall, "to ensure everyone could leave before further bombing." Wineberg stayed with the Rebbe; they broke the fast with a bowl of soup. The Rebbe's mood had changed, and soon, as Warsaw was being bombarded and everyone was sitting in the corridor, the Rebbe's daughter Chana started humming a tune from a chasidic melody. "The Rebbe told us to sing that song, and he accompanied the song with his holy hands with a strong motion of elevation. In the background, the deafening sounds of explosions mingled with our singing."

Four days later,[30] just a few hours before the holiday of Sukkot was about to begin, the Polish army in Warsaw surrendered to the Germans. Still, skirmishes raged around the city. As sunset neared, the Rebbe requested that a sukkah be erected by the building manager. Quite surprised by the request, he asked the Rebbe how he could sit in a sukkah in the middle of a war. The Rebbe replied, "Never once have I missed sitting in the sukkah, and I won't this year." Wineberg remembers, "The Rebbe said that we have to do what we have do, and G-d will do what He has to do." Late that night, a sukkah was erected, and the Rebbe was able to recite the traditional blessings inside it.

They had found refuge in the home of Herschel Gurary, a distant cousin of the Rashag. The family had heard that "the SS was looking for Schneersohn," recalls Berke Gurary. The apartment was not near the main Jewish area, and the Rebbe stayed there for a few weeks. While chaos reigned outside, the Rebbe was always productive. "He would sit at the dining room table to write *maamarim*."[31]

The Rebbe remained hidden in Warsaw as the Germans extended their reign over the city. On October 5, just over a month after the German invasion began, Hitler arrived in Warsaw. He was welcomed with a military parade as thousands of Nazi soldiers strutted down the main avenues of Poland's capital.[32] The Jews had been surprised by the power of the German blitz; they could not have imagined the Holocaust lurking on the horizon. Indeed, the German occupation of Poland in World War I had been benevolent to the Jews. Now, some Polish Jews sought sanctuary in nearby Russia, while others feared the anti-religious Communists more than the Germans. This attitude changed quickly as Germany's true face of anti-Semitism was quickly exposed.

In Dukla, Pinchas Hirschsprung saw the cruel hand of the Germans revealed right away. Jews were immediately forced into labor battalions and compelled to keep their stores open on Shabbat. On Rosh HaShanah, they feared that sounding the shofar might provoke the Germans. Finally, they blew it, concealed behind the closed doors of the synagogue. By the holiday of Sukkot, just three weeks after the war started, "the town was on edge," Hirschsprung says. "People were being snatched off the streets and taken to work." His friend Mendel Shuss had run away from nearby Przemysl. "He barely escaped with his life. In Przemysl six hundred Jews had been slaughtered."[33] Still, even with the foreboding signs, few would have believed the Nazis' plans to annihilate every Jew in Europe.

Most of the students of the Lubavitch yeshivah were Polish citizens, so Latvia was not open to them. The Rebbe urged them to leave immediately for Vilnius, which had now been declared the capital of nearby Lithuania. It was still neutral, and the Chabad yeshivah there would provide refuge. Moshe Feder was one of the students looking for refuge. "I had in mind to go to Romania or Hungary," he says. But he did not want to leave without consulting the Rebbe. "I heard the Rebbe was staying with Herschel Gurary in Warsaw." The Rebbe told him, "It's good you came" and instructed him to go to Vilnius. "The Rebbe gave me money and saved my life," Feder says.[34]

Yosef Kramer says the war disrupted communication. "Under German occupation there was no way to be in touch with the Rebbe."[35] His friend Yosef Rodal, who had already crossed the border to Lithuania, was able to get a message to him with the Rebbe's instruction to come immediately. He did, and it was a harrowing journey. Joined by other students from Warsaw, Kramer crossed the frozen Bug River into Soviet-controlled territory, where he was arrested by Russian soldiers in the town of Radum. Local Jews bailed him out, and finally he made his way to nearby Lithuania.

Yosef Goldstein in Chełmiec received a postcard with a coded message written in Polish: "Grandfather is asking that all his grandchildren come."[36] He understood that the Rebbe was imploring his students to leave Poland. Some students made the trek. Chaim Meir Bukiet got a similar message relayed by his fellow student Menachem Greenglass. The border had been closed, but smugglers helped him cross in the middle of the night. "It was terrifying," says Bukiet. He was surprised to discover that he was not in Lithuania. "Finally, a local farmer told us we had reached Russian territory." He made his way to Brisk, where he met up with other students, finally finding a haven in Vilnius.

But many never got the notification. "I sent many letters to the students," Greenglass recalled. "Chaim Meir Bukiet was an only son. It was difficult for his parents to part with him. Still, he followed the Rebbe's instructions."[37] But many of the yeshivah students did not make the journey to Lithuania. Dispersed throughout Poland and with communication limited, some never received the Rebbe's instructions or were unable or unwilling to take the risky trip across the border. Others got there too late to cross the border. "Almost all of those who remained in Poland were killed," Greenglass lamented.

As the Rebbe was dodging bombs in Warsaw, a campaign to save him was gaining steam in the US. Rabbi Jacobson had finally arrived back in New York on September 18. He was told that during the first days of the war, the Chasidim in Riga had been in contact with the Rebbe. Lately, they had heard nothing; the Rebbe's fate was unclear. Jacobson believed the key to saving the Rebbe was American intervention, but it seemed an impossible feat. Chabad in America was tiny, basically a one-man operation in Brooklyn with Jacobson at the helm. He did not have any political or financial clout, but he had one asset: determination.

Jacobson enlisted Samuel Kramer,[38] an attorney and son of the founder of Agudas Chassidei Chabad in the US. Within days, Jacobson and Kramer recruited the help of prominent New York politicians. On the eve of Yom Kippur, New York Senator Robert Wagner wrote to Secretary of State Cordell Hull, telling him that leading New York Jews had contacted him about the Rebbe's fate. Asking Hull "whether there is some way by which the whereabout of Rabbi Joseph Isaac Schneersohn of Poland might be ascertained."[39] Within a few days, Congressman Sol Bloom,[40] chairman of the House Foreign Affairs Committee, replied to Wagner that communication with Poland had been disrupted. "The department will endeavor to advise you when communication with Poland is reestablished."

Late into his first night back in the US, Jacobson was "sitting and worrying," wondering what else he could do. "I remembered that the lawyer Asher Rabinowitz had arranged for the Rebbe to meet President Hoover when he visited in 1929." Despite the late hour, Jacobson called Rabinowitz, telling him, "Come to New York at once." Asher's father, Rabbi Dovid Rabinowitz, was a prominent Lubavitcher follower in Boston and a confidant of the Rebbe. Asher had extensive Washington connections thanks to his work in the IRS. The next day, Asher and his brother Peretz from Springfield, Massachusetts, met with Jacobson, who told them, "Go to Washington immediately. Don't leave until you find a way to contact the Rebbe. Let nothing deter you, not even Shabbat or Yom Kippur. Find a way to get the Rebbe out of Poland."[41]

The Rabinowitz brothers took a train to Washington and headed to the Supreme Court to see Justice Brandeis, who had met with the Rebbe twice during his year-long visit a decade earlier. Brandeis enlisted the help of Benjamin V. Cohen, a senior official in the Roosevelt administration. Surprisingly, he would become the key inside man, spurring the government bureaucracy to save the Rebbe. Born to a German immigrant family, Cohen grew up in Muncie, Indiana with a modicum of observance of Jewish holidays. According to his biographer William Lasser, "Cohen more strongly identified as an American than as a Jew."[42] After he graduated from the University of Chicago, he met Felix Frankfurter, who was appointed to the Supreme Court in 1939, and through him, Judge Julian Mack and Justice Louis Brandeis. After practicing law in New York, Cohen moved to Washington in 1933, where he rose in government ranks. In 1938, *Time* magazine[43] featured him on the cover as the architect of the New Deal and a member of Roosevelt's "Brain Trust." During the war years, Cohen rebuffed requests from Jewish leaders to lobby Roosevelt to relax restrictions on Jewish immigration or to bomb Auschwitz. But when it came to the Rebbe, despite not having a strong connection to tradition, Cohen used all his influence to ensure the Rebbe's safety. His uncharacteristic zealousness for the Rebbe may have been due to his close friendship with Brandeis, or perhaps it was based on a feeling that as a Jew, he could make a difference. Lasser says he cared about the Jews in Europe "and wanted to do something – Cohen liked to operate in the background and make things happen."[44]

In the US, Jacobson was growing more concerned. Mordechai Dubin in Riga had cabled him, "Every hour is becoming more dangerous." The next day, Dubin cabled again, proposing that an effort be made to contact the Rebbe "through neutral countries." Jacobson and Kramer weren't reaching out only to US government officials for help; they also enlisted the support of the Rebbe's longtime friend Dr. Joseph Rosen, head of the JDC in Europe. He, in turn, implored the US Ambassador in Riga, via cable, to intervene with Latvian authorities. "I urge you to do your utmost to effect his protection and removal to Riga."[45]

One Shabbat, as Jacobson was trying to save the Rebbe, ten-year Yisrael Gordon and his father Yochanan stopped by to visit. "Suddenly, the phone started ringing," Yisrael Gordon recalled years later.[46] "Not everyone had a phone, and it never rang on Shabbat." Jacobson jumped up and turned to young Yisrael. "Pick up the phone," he ordered. Yisrael was confused – picking up the phone would be transgressing Shabbat. "I glanced at my father. He shot me a look that said, 'Do it.' Instantly, I picked up the phone, and it was exactly what Rabbi Jacobson had thought, a government official calling about the Rebbe." Once it was clear that it was about saving the Rebbe, Jacobson took the phone.

The Rebbe's whereabouts were unclear to Chasidim around the world. On the first night of Rosh HaShanah in Tel Aviv, Rabbi Michoel

Dvorkin bellowed in an anguished voice as he came to the words of the prayers "The deliverance of the righteous is from the Lord." His friend Pinchas Althaus explained, "From the beginning of the war, we don't know where the Rebbe is, and that's why he is crying out."[47] The Israeli paper *Haaretz*[48] reported from London that the Rebbe had perished. Two days later,[49] the paper relayed a dispatch from Vilna that the Rebbe was alive. Apprehension was heightened by the fact that the Rebbe was a high-value target for the Gestapo.

Finding a way to extradite the Rebbe from war-torn Warsaw was a daunting challenge. The Chasidim in the US assessed potential routes of escape, such as heading north to Latvia, or south via Italy and from there to the US. Latvia could be very risky. Russia was in control of half of Poland and was setting its sights on seizing Latvia. If Russia invaded,[50] the Rebbe would be at grave risk. Clearly, Latvia could only be a temporary haven. The only true solution was to find a way for the Rebbe and his family to leave Europe entirely and find refuge in the United States.

To prod the wheels of the government forward, Jacobson and Kramer enlisted the support of prominent Washington attorney Max Rhoade.[51] Rhoade was born in Poland in 1898, and his family immigrated to the US in 1901. In 1929, he was appointed the Washington representative of the Zionist Organization of America, developing relationships with many prominent Jewish leaders, including Justice Louis Brandeis and Reform Rabbi Stephen S. Wise. Well-connected in government circles,[52] Rhoade was a passionate Jew with deep ties to key Jewish leaders. He would be a compelling advocate for the Rebbe's rescue.

Rhoade faced the challenge of strict US immigration regulations that had been tightened in 1924. But there were exceptions to the quotas, including one that allowed religious ministers to be admitted to the US on special visas if they had a position waiting for them at an American congregation.[53] Jewish groups successfully used this opening to save European rabbis. Still, the barrier of bias by State Department officials loomed large. Breckinridge Long,[54] the assistant secretary of state appointed by President Roosevelt in 1939, supervised the issuance of visas in US embassies worldwide, and he used his power to deter Jewish immigration. In June 1940, Long wrote a memo to State Department staff. "We can delay, and effectively stop, for a temporary period of indefinite length, the number of immigrants into the United States."[55] He suggested that US representatives overseas "put every obstacle in the way" of refugees and "postpone and postpone and postpone the granting of the visas."

Further complicating Rhoade's efforts was that Chabad was just a small organization with little political clout. Though there was a network of some 150 Chabad-associated congregations established by immigrants, there were few actual practicing Chabad Chasidim. Most of the congregations' members were linked by a sentimental connection to Chabad. Agudas Chassidei Chabad led by Rabbi Yisrael Jacobson was established in 1924[56] to strengthen the bond between these congregations. It had made some strides forward but had not yet matured into a major national Jewish organization. Jacobson was devoted to the Rebbe, but his managerial talent was marginal and his financial resources were limited.[57] But what he lacked in organizational skills he made up for in enthusiasm and passion for the cause. Ultimately, his fiery commitment and willingness to overcome any obstacle would be the keys to saving the Rebbe.

Rhoade began to reach out to his connections, and Jacobson and Kramer kept up the pressure. Congressman Bloom enlisted the support of Democratic kingmaker Postmaster General James Farley. Dr. Joseph Rosen, head of the JDC in Europe, turned to the US Ambassador in Riga, urging him to do the utmost to help the Rebbe escape Warsaw. This coalition of congressmen, senators, key administration officials, and Justice Brandeis, all clamoring for the US to help find the Rebbe's whereabouts and save him, slowly broke down the wall of indifference that surrounded the State Department.

Benjamin Cohen personally appealed to Robert T. Pell, head of the State Department's Division of European Affairs. On October 2, Cohen and Pell had an extensive phone conversation strategizing on how to save the Rebbe.[58] Cohen impressed on Pell the Rebbe's unique value to Jews globally. "He is one of the leading Jewish scholars of the world," he said. Pell replied that the State Department had received requests from "many prominent Jews" to help the Rebbe. Cohen was a senior White House official, very close to the president, and it seems that it was this call that finally stirred Pell to act.

Cohen told Pell that he was pessimistic about the ability of the Latvians to intervene. Despite being neutral at the time, they did not have the capability to search for the Rebbe in Warsaw. He then proposed a novel idea. He was aware that during the 1938 Evian Conference on the plight of Jewish refugees,[59] Pell had befriended Helmuth Wohlthat, a senior German diplomat. Cohen also knew that Wohlthat had assured Pell that if there was any specific case in which America was particularly interested, he would try to find a solution. In the past, Wohlthat had quietly helped US concerns. Cohen suggested that Pell ask Wohlthat to find a way to save the Rebbe. In 1939, German leaders still expected the war to be over soon and wanted to be in the good graces of the United States, still neutral at the time.

A day after getting the endorsement of Secretary of State Cordell Hull, Pell telegrammed the senior secretary at the US Embassy in Berlin, Raymond Herman Geist,[60] telling him that he was inundated with requests for help, including from influential members of the administration.[61] He asked Geist to explore the possibility of the German military providing safe passage for the Rebbe to Riga.[62] He instructed Geist to act with discretion, suggesting he contact Wohlthat. "Inform him as from me, in view of our previous relationship, the interests of the country in this particular case."

Geist was the longest-serving American consular official in Berlin, having arrived there in 1929. Time and again, he bent US visa regulations to benefit German Jews under threat. He had intervened with senior Nazi officials to expedite the emigration of Sigmund Freud and other prominent Jews. Well placed and well connected, Geist would also play an essential part in prevailing on elements in the German government to help save the Rebbe.

Wohlthat had been a soldier in World War I and later joined the Nazi party. He attended Columbia University in 1929–30, earning a degree in economics. By 1939, he was in the senior echelon of the Nazi government, serving as chief economic advisor to Hermann Goering, the second-highest Nazi official in Germany. Pell made a shrewd decision in directing his request to Wohlthat instead of Germany's foreign minister Joachim von Ribbentrop,[63] a known anti-Semite. Pell expected Wohlthat to use his discretion and knowledge of the upper levels of Nazi politics to expedite the Rebbe's evacuation from Warsaw.

Wohlthat agreed to help and turned the rescue over to Admiral Wilhelm Canaris, head of the Abwehr, Germany's naval intelligence. Goering himself may have very well endorsed Wohlthat's efforts. German historian Professor Wilfred Meyer says, "I think Goering knew about the rescue operation since Wohlthat was one of his closest associates."[64] Rabbi Yisrael Jacobson wrote that Goering gave his approval.[65] According to Meyer, Goering and Canaris had a mutual interest. "They wanted to prevent the war against Poland from becoming a world war." Two days after the German invasion of Poland, Britain declared war, but it did not dispatch troops to help the Poles, and Meyer explains that Goering and Canaris wanted to find favor with the US administration. "They hoped that President Roosevelt would arrange talks between the Germans and the British in order to save peace." Because of this, he says, "they were glad to do the American government a favor by rescuing Rabbi Schneersohn."

Canaris was a decorated career military officer, having served in World War I on a surface vessel and as a U-boat commander.[66] He was an early supporter of Hitler, thinking he would rebuild the country and its military. He joined the Nazi party in 1933 and in 1935 was appointed head of the Abwehr, which brought him into regular contact with Hitler. But Canaris was becoming disillusioned with Hitler. He confided to Paul Frankenheim, a German Jew he assigned to spy in Palestine, that he was distraught over the atrocities he witnessed in Warsaw.[67] Quietly, Canaris helped some Jews escape Germany and employed soldiers of Jewish background on his staff. In 1943, he attempted to negotiate a ceasefire with the allies, meeting in Spain with the heads of US and British intelligence. Later in the war, Canaris was implicated in a plot to kill Hitler. He was hanged on April 9, 1945, just a few weeks before the war's end.[68]

A military unit in Warsaw was needed to discover the Rebbe's whereabouts and transfer him to a neutral country. "The only force that would be able to do anything was the military intelligence, since Warsaw was occupied by the German troops," Meyer says. Canaris recruited Lt. Colonel Ernst Bloch, a World War I veteran who earned two Iron Crosses for valor. Bloch's daughter Cornelia says her father "was a professional soldier and in the military for most of his life."[69] After World War I, he attended Friedrich Wilhelm University in Berlin, earning a doctorate in economics, and continued to serve in the Wehrmacht. In 1935, Canaris appointed Bloch as head of the Foreign Economic Intelligence Department at the naval intelligence. Bloch's father was Jewish but, his daughter says, he had little connection with his father's religious background. The Nuremberg Laws,[70] instituted in 1935, segregated Jews and limited their rights as German citizens, including banning them from serving in the military, but Bloch dodged the issue because of a special clause that afforded Hitler the discretion to declare a person of mixed Jewish blood an Aryan. In 1939, after Canaris personally interceded with Hitler, he declared Bloch an Aryan.

Bloch headed to Warsaw to find the Rebbe and his family. Joining him for this secret mission were other soldiers of Jewish descent.[71] Much of Warsaw had been severely damaged during the bombing. The Chasidim in Latvia could not locate the Rebbe's whereabouts. Neither could the American Embassy in Warsaw, with whom Pell was in contact.

Bloch witnessed the oppression of Warsaw Jews by the occupying German troops. Some were forced into labor battalions, others subject to beatings or shot with little cause. Jews were required to wear a yellow star, and they were subjected to numerous regulations whose punishment for violation was death. The Jews in Warsaw were living in fear, wondering what would happen next. Adding to the suffering was the shortage of food. Yosef Wineberg was able to secure a few kilos of rice for the Rebbe's family in hiding. "When I brought the rice, there was such joy," he said.

Throughout October, Bloch and his soldiers searched the Jewish sections of Warsaw, looking for the Rebbe. They tried asking local Jews if they knew his whereabouts. The Rebbe was well-known, and no doubt this inquiry alarmed those they asked, who could not imagine anything but nefarious intent. Bloch tried visiting Jewish gathering points and asking for the Rebbe, to no avail. Finding the Rebbe in a city of millions, much of it ruined and its residents fearfully secretive, would be difficult.

Bloch and his group continued to scour the city. They were given an address and reported back that it was completely demolished and they were unable to determine if the Rebbe was still alive. News was relayed in a long, convoluted route, from Bloch in Warsaw to his commanders in Berlin, and then to Germany's embassy in the US. They cabled Pell and other US officials in Washington, who informed Max Rhoade and Chabad representatives. Two days later,[72] a second message came from German authorities, who had obtained a new address for the Rebbe. The reports were unclear to Rhoade, who immediately requested that Pell ask Wohlthat to confirm that this address was not the "demolished building" and to notify Sam Kramer.[73]

Then some news leaked from Warsaw to Riga that gave hope but heightened the urgency. Rabbi Chaim Lieberman escaped Warsaw, making his way to Riga. He wrote to Rabbi Jacobson, "We have received word of the Rebbe in Poland. The situation is indescribably horrible."[74] He went on to say that besides the concerns about the Rebbe's health, they were alarmed about the German atrocities. "We know they are under pressure of real terror, for the Germans are inflicting terrible tortures, particularly on rabbis." A few days later, Lieberman sent a cable from Riga to the US with news from Warsaw. "Rabbi healthy, situation gross, awfully dangerous. Begs enable immigration," the message included an address, "Bonifraterska 29."[75] Asher Rabinowitz telegraphed Justice Brandeis: "Received cable from Latvia advising me that Rabbi Schneersohn can be found at home of Gurary, Bonifraterska 29, Warsaw." The message was passed from Brandeis to Cohen in the White House, from Cohen to Geist in Berlin, and eventually to Bloch, who was leading the search in Warsaw.

Back in Warsaw, the constant inquiries from German soldiers about the Rebbe's location became known to the Rebbe's family. According to the Rashag, at one of the places the Rebbe had once stayed, soldiers challenged the residents to reveal where the Rebbe was. They had answered truthfully that they did not know, at which point they were threatened with death. When the Rashag heard about the incident, he became alarmed, fearing they wanted to harm the Rebbe. The Rebbe was unafraid, declaring, "I have never hidden and I will not hide now, no matter what happens."

Bloch continued the search for the Rebbe in Warsaw, especially near the address he had been provided. He met an elderly Jew outside one building who claimed that the Rebbe was not there. Chaim Lieberman says that some of residents knew the Rebbe was in fact in the building, but "they feared saying anything because they feared that the soldiers had evil intent."[76] When the information reached the Rebbe that the Germans were searching for him again, he responded as before, that he had never hid and would not do so now.

Suspecting the Rebbe was in the building, Bloch and his soldiers returned, forcing their way into the apartment. The Rebbe's grandson Berke, sixteen at the time, later described the pandemonium inside. "They pushed the door open. We were surprised when the Germans marched in. They ordered everyone to stand up, and we thought we were going to be shot." Through all of this, "the Rebbe was calm and controlled. He was a very strong personality. He always knew what he was doing." Then, to everyone's surprise, the soldiers announced that they had come to save them and handed out exit visas and travel papers.[77]

At first the Rebbe did not want to leave Warsaw. As Dr. Nissan Mindel writes, "It was only after he realized that there was nothing more that he could do that the Rebbe finally consented to heed the urgent requests of his many followers in Warsaw and abroad, particularly in the United States, to leave the shattered and charred ruins of the Polish capital and make his way to the United States." Two days later, on November 27, Pell reported to Rhoade that the German soldiers had found the Rebbe alive and that he was now under the protection of a German staff officer. Rhoade informed Sam Kramer, and the news reached the Chasidim in the United States. They were overjoyed, but they knew the ordeal was far from over.[78]

Despite being under the protection of the special unit of German soldiers, the Rebbe was still in mortal danger in Nazi-controlled Warsaw. The SS could still try to seize the Rebbe if they became aware that he was in German custody. Tensions between the Abwehr and the SS reached up its highest echelons. Heinrich Himmler doubted Canaris's loyalties and resented his authority. The revelation of this mission could have been used by Himmler as an excuse to undermine Canaris.

The Rebbe and his family required transport to a neutral country. The Rebbe's Latvian citizenship made it the most obvious destination, but there was a legitimate fear that the Russians could pounce any moment and seize Latvia, putting the Rebbe at serious risk. The US was still not willing to provide refuge for the Rebbe. The visa division of the US State Department, known for its unwillingness to help Jews, had not approved the Rebbe's immigration to the US. The road to safety was complicated and still very treacherous.

Bloch had to transport the Rebbe and his family to safety. It seemed the best option was to depart from the functioning train station at the edge of Warsaw to Berlin and then on to Riga, though this meant heading west and doubling back east to reach Riga. The whole journey would be incomprehensible to bystanders: German soldiers escorting religious Jews into the heart of anti-Semitic Germany in the midst of the war. It was a risky move.

Back in Washington, Max Rhoade expressed doubts about the intended itinerary.[79] He suggested a few other options, south via Italy or directly north to Stockholm. The anxieties about the fate of Latvia were heightened when Russia invaded Finland at the end of November. Rabbi Schneur Zalman Gurary arrived in New York a few days later and shared his assessment with Chabad leaders[80] that the Russians were poised to invade "in three or four weeks." He believed that "it would be extremely dangerous for the Rebbe to go to Riga." The Rebbe had escaped a Russian death sentence in 1927; if the Communists got hold of him again, it could be disastrous. In the end, it was the Germans on the ground who made the final determination. The Rebbe and his family would go to Riga via Berlin, and from there they could transit to Stockholm.

Just over two weeks after Bloch discovered the Rebbe's whereabouts, on the last day of Chanukah, December 14, 1939, the convoy departed. Warsaw's central train station had been bombed during the German attack. According to the Rebbe's grandson, "Bloch secured a truck and a wagon to take us to a station on the outskirts of the city." Bloch told the Rebbe that he might have to act disrespectfully to him if they encountered the SS or other German military groups. "The trip was through a military area of German soldiers thirsty for blood,"[81] Chaim Lieberman described. Soldiers could have tried to detain the group of obviously religious Jews at any moment. Lieberman says about Bloch, "There was a Jew[82] from the German army with impressive medals on his uniform who traveled with the Rebbe." German soldiers whose suspicions were raised by the strange sight of Jews with a military escort tried to intervene and stop the Rebbe and his family. "Bloch stood up to them unflinchingly, telling the soldiers, 'They are my responsibility, and I must escort them to Berlin safely.'" Still, the Rebbe's appearance was drawing attention. The Rashag recalled,[83] "The soldiers escorting the Rebbe wanted the Rebbe to cover his face so as not to draw additional attention. He refused, declaring, "A Jew should not be embarrassed of his appearance." At one checkpoint, soldiers aimed their rifles at the Rebbe. Bloch shouted at the officer that he was under the command of Admiral Canaris, and he would have him arrested if he continued to interfere. They were challenged again at the train station, and Bloch defused the confrontation. The train ride took a full day, and finally they arrived in the Berlin, where they were taken to the Jewish Community Center, staying overnight before moving into a hotel for Shabbat.[84]

On Sunday, they boarded the train in Berlin for the five-hundred-mile trip to Riga, this time in first class. The route led them through Lithuania, where Chasidim greeted the Rebbe at the Vilnius train station. In Kovno, the Yiddish paper *Dos Vort*[85] reported that the train station was filled with Chasidim straining to catch a glimpse of the Rebbe. "They began to sing boisterously" as the train pulled into the station. A non-Jewish observer remarked, "The Jewish emperor is arriving." Some of the Chasidim joined the train, where the celebration continued to the next station, with chasidic tunes and toasts of *lechaim*. The paper's correspondent, Eliyahu Vad, remained aboard and managed to interview the Rebbe. "What is the state of the Jewish nation today?" he asked. Finding a silver lining, the Rebbe responded that during this time of tragedy the inner goodness of the Jewish people was shining. "There is a great feeling of camaraderie and caring." He described his experience in the cellar in Warsaw. "Sitting in a dark cellar, while bombs were flying overhead, we – both young and old – didn't eat or drink. Still, they did not lose their faith and confidence. They prayed and said *Avinu Malkeinu*." The Rebbe explained that the true beauty of the Jewish people could be seen in these circumstances. "Not a physical beauty, but a spiritual one, a deep feeling of unity and common destiny, that all, religious and not religious, sensed the *pintele Yid* (a Jewish consciousness)."

Shortly afterward, they arrived at the Latvian border. The Rebbe's grandson describes the mood as they finally escaped the Nazi regime.

"We were very quiet," he said, but inside the emotions were soaring: "We were very, very happy." At that point, Bloch and his soldiers departed from the train.[86] The Chasidim traveled without an escort for the last one hundred miles from the border to Riga, where a large crowd welcomed the Rebbe.[87]

That night, a telegram arrived in New York: "The Rebbe is free." Yisrael Jacobson ran outside and "did handsprings on the sidewalk, shouting with delight." He could not contain his joy; there was a huge *farbrengen* in his house that night. The next day he placed a transatlantic call and spoke to the Rebbe, who thanked him for the unprecedented effort of the Chabad community in the US on his behalf.[88]

It had been a terrible ordeal. "It is not in the human imagination to describe in words all that transpired in the close to four months," wrote Yechezkel Feigin to his brother-in-law in the US.[89] "For the first month, we were under terrible strain, and as battles raged in the cities, we were under siege and suffered from hunger. More than once, we had to move to seek safety. All the personal possessions of the Rebbe were destroyed. Only with compassion showered on us from Above and with self-sacrifice were we able to save the precious manuscripts of the Rebbe." The Rebbe's fragile health had been gravely impacted as well. Feigin wrote to one of the Chabad leaders in Chicago a few days later, "Because of all that the Rebbe endured, he will need to rest in the sanatorium."[90]

In Riga, the Rebbe and his family waited for US visas. The Atlantic Ocean stood as a moat between freedom in the US and chaos in Europe. The Chasidim in the US were gravely worried, fearing a Russian invasion. It was a race against the clock, and Max Rhoade took the lead in this difficult task. Since the enactment for restrictive immigration laws in 1924, it had become more difficult for European Jews to gain entry into the US. The State Department was full of bureaucrats whose mission seemed to be to put up as many barriers as possible in front of Jews seeking refuge in the US. Immigration quotas remained unfilled due to the obstruction of State Department officials and the unwillingness of President Roosevelt to help Jews in war-torn Europe.

Upon the urging of Benjamin Cohen, Robert Pell had managed to get the US to intervene with the Germans to search for the Rebbe in Warsaw. But as head of the European division, Pell had little influence on the visa process. On November 4, while Bloch's troops were scouring Warsaw for the Rebbe, Rhoade implored Cohen in the White House to urge Secretary of State Cordell Hull to intervene. "It seems logical if the State Department went out of its way in one phase of this matter, it might just as well complete the job."[91] Despite the lobbying, things were moving very slowly.

At first, Rhoade tried making use of the immigration exemption for clergy who were invited to lead religious institutions in the United States. That clause required applicants to have an American sponsor with at least five thousand dollars ($100,000 today) as security, so as not to become a public charge. A different congregation would be needed to employ each member of the Rebbe's entourage. For this, Rhoade needed information from Jacobson on the structure and finances of Chabad in the United States, which was easier said than done. Jacobson operated his ad hoc organization from his synagogue in Brownsville, Brooklyn. It served as a loose confederation of the immigrant synagogues, each its own entity. There simply was no well-structured national organization, but Rhoade needed facts and figures, detailed bookkeeping, and an understanding of the Chabad organization in the United Sates. This resulted in a culture clash between the professional lawyer, well-schooled in business and finance, and the old-world Chasid.

In December, with the Rebbe now in Latvia, the issue took on greater urgency. One of the Chasidim, Judah Gurary, came up with a novel idea. "The Rebbe was the world leader of Chabad, which had been first headquartered in Russia and then Poland," he wrote to Jacobson. "Now that these centers have been destroyed, we the Chabad Chasidim in America want our leader, together with those who helped him, to come and establish the headquarters in America." Instead of having to prove that each member of the family was employed by a different synagogue, they argued that the Rebbe and his entourage represented the leadership of one of the most important segments of world Jewry. This also solved another problem: A member of the clergy applying for permission to enter the US was required to show that he had been a religious leader in an existing congregation for the past two years. The Rebbe and his family members, while leaders of Chabad, were not connected to a specific synagogue in Europe. Rhoade framed the issue to government officials: "If the Vatican wished to find refuge in the US, would the US provide them refuge as part of a religious hierarchy?"

Immigration visas were issued in overseas embassies. On Rhoades's instructions, Jacobson cabled the Chasidim in Riga to immediately meet with the US consul to accelerate the process. He wrote that it was decided to "bring the entire hierarchy to Chabad for reestablishment [of the] world seat," saying they should inform the consul that "Chief Rabbi Schneersohn is indispensable to American Chabad congregations" and that funds had already been deposited as a guarantee.[92] That same day, Rhoade pressured the State Department again, writing to Pell that the Rebbe and his entourage were in "grave danger by the spread of Russian control over Latvia. They are regarded as counterrevolutionaries by the present Soviet regime."[93]

Frustrated by the lack of progress with the visa department, Rhoade again turned to Cohen, hand-delivering a letter. "Even Pell, a high department official, is disappointed with the result of his efforts. It is obvious that some special further channel is necessary."[94] Rhoade explained that everything was wrapped up "with a lot of hyper-legalistic red tape, and visas are something over which Pell unfortunately has little jurisdiction." He desperately asked Cohen to intervene again, saying, "We have now stuck a snag on the very brink of deliverance." He explained that because of Cohen, they had been able to facilitate the "miraculous evacuation to Riga," and they now needed his help "to have the job completed." If the Russians invade,[95] "Rabbi Schneersohn and the other rabbis of the Chabad hierarchy are subject to execution by Soviet Russia."

Just after New Year's, there were signs that the lobbying was having an effect. The visa department finally sent a memo acknowledging the principle that Chabad might be considered a religious hierarchy. "Exemption from quota restrictions is being requested by applicants on that basis as a group." They assigned an investigator to meet with US Chabad leaders to evaluate their request. A week later, two senior officials of the visa section met Chabad leaders in New York. They received a detailed briefing on the history of Chabad, its structure in the US, its finances, and its network of synagogues.[96] In Riga, Chasidim continued to pressure the local consul, and at the same time, other public officials continued to urge the State Department to approve the visas. Just over a month later, on February 13, 1940, the visas were finally issued by the US Consulate in Riga.[97]

Not included were two of the Rebbe's daughters and their husbands, Rabbi and Mrs. Mendel and Sheina Horenstein, and Rabbi Mendel and Chaya Mushka Schneerson. Eventually, the Ramash and his wife Chaya Mushka were able to escape Paris after the German occupation, arriving in Vichy, France. From there they made their way to neutral Spain and arrived in the US in March 1941. Tragically, the Horensteins were captured by the Nazis and lost their lives in Treblinka.

Within a few hours of arriving in Riga, the Rebbe composed two letters. The first was addressed to Jews worldwide. "It is indescribable what has happened to the Jews under siege in Poland and in Warsaw."[98] He wrote that "many perished with bullets of death, [while other were] burned alive and their homes became their graves when they could not escape" the bombardment. He added that those who were injured "may carry those wounds for life." The economy was also devastated. "All sources of income have been disrupted. Most businessmen, and even the affluent, are now poverty-stricken." The Rebbe urged Jews around the world, "Irrespective of political party or personal philosophy, raise funds for Polish Jewry and transfer the funds to the JDC." The second letter was addressed to the global Chabad community. The Rebbe described the conditions of the Chabad community in Warsaw as "terrifying and shocking."[99] He requested that Chabad Chasidim around the world extend help to their brethren in Poland, describing it as a situation of "saving lives and redeeming captives" and asking for support to help save Chasidim under Nazi rule.

The Rebbe wrote to the JDC leaders directly asking them to ameliorate the suffering of Polish Jewry. He repeatedly wrote to Morris Troper, head of the JDC European office in Paris. "Having witnessed the cruelties and horrors of the war and its aftermath, I feel it is my scared duty to give you firsthand information." He lauded the JDC as "the only Jewish institution in Warsaw now working in aid of our unfortunate brethren there." He urged the JDC to mount a "vast campaign to relieve the dreadful distress" in Poland. In the Rebbe's view, the JDC needed to help Jews escape Poland. He implored the organization "to include in its relief work a provision for emigration," asking the JDC to facilitate emigration "to Palestine or elsewhere." He asked that the JDC first focus on the "most urgent cases," saying the next stage should be "the wholesale immigration of Polish Jewry to a quiet place under the sun, where they can live a normal Jewish life."[100]

While the Rebbe urged Jews around the world to work together to help the Jews in Poland through the JDC, he also felt a great sense of personal responsibility to save the lives of his Chasidim and the students of his yeshivas. The efficacy of this two-track approach became clear in late February when Chabad leaders in New York met with leaders of the JDC.[101] They offered limited funds but would not provide any financial subsidies to Jews immigrating to the US, citing US law. Nor would they assist the yeshivah in Vilnius. The Rebbe would have to rely on his own resources to aid Chasidim still suffering in Poland, help them escape Nazi rule, and sustain the yeshivah in Vilnius.

Within a few days of arriving in Riga, the Rebbe began working on saving the students of the yeshivah in Vilnius, telegramming Rabbi Yisrael Jacobson to find an avenue of rescue for the students. The Rebbe followed up with letters to Jacobson and the Kramer family, as well as other prominent rabbis such as Dr. Leo Jung, asking for help in arranging visas and financing to transport the students. "The students are in grave danger," he told Jung. Similarly, the Rebbe urged Jacobson "to work as fast as possible "to arrange transport to safety for the students."[102]

The Rebbe was also concerned about the fate of his precious library. The most valuable manuscripts had stayed at his side during the siege in Warsaw, but the bulk of the collection was still in Poland. Feigin asked Jacobson to arrange the transfer of the library that remained in Otwock. "There are 127 cases of books and three cases of handwritten manuscripts," he wrote. These were priceless treasures from great chasidic masters and rabbinic scholars. Feigin pressed Jacobson to intervene with the US officials to see "if the US consul in Warsaw will take them under his control."[103] This library was a national Jewish treasure, and the Rebbe felt a great responsibility to preserve this historic legacy.[104] Jacobson's efforts were partially successful, as a portion of the collection did reach the US embassy in Warsaw and eventually the United States in June of 1941.[105]

The Rebbe spent ten weeks in Riga waiting for the issuance of the visas. The ordeal in Warsaw had impacted his fragile health, and he rested in a nearby sanatorium. While in Riga, the Rebbe made repeated attempts to secure visas for Rabbi Yechezkel Feigin and other Chasidim. He also wrote to leaders in *Eretz Yisrael* asking them to expedite certificates that would permit immigration there. At this point, there was no way for the students in the yeshivah in Vilnius to gain visas to the US. In the coming months, when a route to survival opened up via the Far East, the Rebbe strongly encouraged his students to seize that opportunity, and he provided vital funding for their travel.

In Riga, the Rebbe fell and broke his hand.[106] "For three weeks I had a cast, and then in the fourth week a regular bandage," he wrote to his daughter in Paris.[107] The injury was difficult for the Rebbe. "I was unable to write until a few days before our departure." The Rebbe's mother, Rebbetzin Shterna Sara, also faced a health challenge during those weeks in Riga. Because of a stomach ailment, "she had a twelve-hour operation. Everything went well. She is moving around and healing." The Rebbe told Yehoshua Wolosow, who also was headed to the US, "I can't travel now, because the rebbetzin [referring to his mother] is recovering."[108]

From Riga, the Rebbe was in contact with Jews throughout the world. He wrote a series of letters to thank those who had helped save him and his family, and he wrote other letters about a host of communal issues. He was also in communication with the students of the yeshivah in Lithuania and the US. He expressed a strong interest in the educational programs for women in both Latvia and the US, sending letters and meeting members of Achos Hatemimim, the young women's organization he had established ten years earlier, encouraging them to progress in their studies.

During the interlude in Riga, the Rebbe had an opportunity to hold *yechidut*, private meetings, with many Chasidim, some of whom even traveled from Lithuania to see him. One of those was Shraga Feivel Zisman and his son Leibel, who came from Kovno. "Hundreds were milling around and waiting to see the Rebbe," Leibel recalls. The Zismans were finally admitted at 2:00 a.m. "My father told me that one never sat in front of the Rebbe." Shraga Feivel exchanged a few words with the Rebbe and then asked him to bless Leibel. "At that moment, the Rebbe looked at me. He had a powerful stare, his eyes boring into a person as if seeing the core of his soul. I felt his eyes going through me. I was scared." The Rebbe remained silent. Leibel heard his father ask a second time, "Rebbe, bless my child, bless my child," starting to cry. "It seemed like time stopped still, my father sobbing, me shaking, and the Rebbe staring with x-ray eyes. But then finally, the Rebbe pronounced his blessing." Leibel always wondered why the Rebbe hesitated. He and his brother Berel, who had received a blessing from the Rebbe on an earlier occasion, were the only family members to survive the Holocaust. Leibel was sent to Auschwitz and immigrated to the US after the war.[109]

The Rebbe had been contemplating a move to the United States for years, but as he had confided to Rabbi Yisrael Jacobson on the eve of the war, he wanted to focus inward.[110] "Before I left for America, my spirit was anguished, exhausted by forty-five years of difficult public service, my body shattered by life-threatening experiences," he said a few years after his arrival. "I had a yearning to find myself in a tent of Torah and derive tranquil pleasure from the sounds of Torah study."[111] But after witnessing the destruction in Poland, the Rebbe keenly felt a new sense of purpose in moving to the US.

He shared these feelings at a farewell gathering the Saturday evening before his departure. It was a deeply emotional evening, the room filled with "elder Chasidim." Some of them had been followers of the Rebbe's father and grandfather. One had even met his great-grandfather, the third Rebbe, seventy-four years earlier. The Rebbe told them that the move was a divine mission and not of his own making. "I am not going because I want to go, but because I am being compelled to go." Ever since he had assumed the position of Rebbe in 1920, he had been forced to keep relocating. "I was compelled to move from Rostov to St. Petersburg,[112] and I relocated to Riga not because I desired it but rather because I was compelled. I went from Riga to Warsaw because it was required. Similarly, from Warsaw to Otwock, and from Otwock to Riga, and now the trip to America. I am going because I am compelled to do so." The Rebbe was going to have to start again in the new world. "Sensing my anguish about what I was undergoing, they said, 'We are sure that it is not you who is traveling to America, but G-d who is leading you there, whether you desire it or not. G-d is leading you to do arduous work, and He will richly bless you with success. You carry the spiritual merits of your holy forbearers, the Rebbes that preceded you.'" Instead of seeing the US as a sanctuary where he could step back from communal concerns, the Rebbe believed that the move to America was for a vital purpose. "The ultimate mission of a soul down here is to do a fellow Jew a favor materially and spiritually."[113]

On March 4, thousands gathered for a large sendoff. A local paper reported, "The Jewish community of Riga bid farewell to the Lubavitcher Rebbe. The Rebbe blessed the Jewish community, and he blessed the Latvian government and its president before departing."[114] Leibel Zisman recalls the emotional parting. "Everyone was crying, fearful they would never see the Rebbe again. It was very chaotic." Many people begged the Rebbe to stay. When it was time to leave, "an ambulance pulled up to take the rebbetzin [the Rebbe's mother] on a stretcher." Zisman's father organized a human chain to hold back the massive crowds to allow the departure of the Rebbe's family.[115]

Parting from the Chasidim in Europe was heartrending for the Rebbe. Earlier in the day, the Rebbe sent an encyclical letter to all Chabad Chasidim in Europe and *Eretz Yisrael*. "The love and bond are not divided by barriers and the borders of countries. We are together with an intrinsic love."[116] At the airport before takeoff, it was impossible to address the large crowds. The Rebbe asked Rabbi Mordechai Cheifetz to share a message: "Tell the Jewish community that the great ocean is not a barrier but a connector. It binds together those on one side of the globe and those on the other. Tell them I am with all of you as one, and you are one with me."

The Rebbe boarded the plane with his entourage of eleven family members and assistants.[117] The Rebbe discovered that there were an additional seven empty seats. He refused to depart, exclaiming, "I cannot leave, I need to save others."[118] The flight was held up until the seats were filled. They flew the 275 miles to Stockholm, where Rabbi Yisrael Zuber welcomed the Rebbe. The group traveled by train to the port of Gothenburg, where three days after leaving Riga, on March 7, they boarded the SS *Drottningholm*.

The ship filled with refugees was the only ocean liner still operating between neutral Sweden and the US. Ahead lay a treacherous trip across the Atlantic, crossing the path of warships of Britain and Germany. On the side of the ship, "Sverige" (Sweden) was painted in large letters. Due to mechanical problems, it was held up for a night at the port of Bergen, Norway. The passengers were not aware that German submarines patrolled underneath, preparing for the invasion of Denmark that would occur a month later. Once the ship broke free from the North Sea, it headed across the wide expanse of the Atlantic. Twice, Germans submarines stopped them and sailors boarded the ship searching for military supplies. The sight of Germans created a wave of anxiety, particularly for the Jews on board. The Rebbe's grandson says that for him, this was the most terrifying moment of the whole experience.[119] "There was a conversation with the Germans, after which they let us through." And it wasn't just the Germans. British warships also stopped the ship three times. Each time, they were allowed to proceed.[120]

The twenty years since the Rebbe had assumed his position in 1920 were tumultuous. He faced a death sentence at the hands of the antireligious Soviet regime, rebuilt Chabad in Riga and Poland while sustaining the underground religious network in Russia, and escaped the Nazis. But his independent leadership and activism would not stop there. Ahead lay America, a country where Jews were redefining their religion. In their minds, America was different, and Judaism could be recreated in a new American style. Inspired by the concepts of personal empowerment and American individualism, Jews were abandoning religious observance. The immigrant generation rooted in tradition was aging, and they watched their children head down the path to assimilation.

As the ship crossed the Atlantic, the Rebbe was preparing to launch a major initiative to transform US Jewry. He was undaunted by the exhaustion he felt from years of community service, physical ailments, and a lack of financial resources. Unlike in Russia or Poland, there were few actual Chabad Chasidim in the US who would stand by his side, as chasidic life had little American history or roots. In the US, the Rebbe would start from scratch, rebuilding Chabad yet again. He would transcend his own milieu, undertaking a greater vision, and alter the trajectory of American Jewry.

Chapter Ten

America Iz Nisht Andersh

Hovering offshore in New York Harbor on a balmy March morning[1] was the Swedish liner *Drottningholm*, worn from her journey across the North Atlantic. The ship had pulled in the night before, after a harrowing ordeal, stopped at several points along the way by British warships and German submarines. According to port regulations, the weary passengers, the Rebbe and his family among them, would have to wait until the morning to disembark.

For the passengers, America was a refuge from war-torn Europe. For the Rebbe it was a new spiritual frontier with immense potential. He wanted to create a robust, self-assured Jewish life, and reinvigorating Jewish education was the foundation of his strategy to remold American Jewry. He intended to go on the offensive, motivated by his pride in uncompromising standards of Judaism. This was, he believed, his next mission, orchestrated by divine providence.

A delegation of US Chabad leaders motored to the vessel to welcome the Rebbe. Joyously, they boarded the ship and entered the Rebbe's stateroom. The Rebbe greeted them warmly but quickly turned their focus to practical matters. "The suffering I endured in prison in Russia does not compare to the torments of the twelve weeks I spent under their [Nazi] rule. Now we will quickly take care of the formalities and get to work immediately. Our work is Torah and Yiddishkeit. As for the contention that we are weak physically, that we have no strength, Hashem is, after all, *hanoten laya'eif koach* (the one gives strength to those who are weary)," he said, quoting from the morning prayers. "It is written *al kol neshimah veneshimah tehallel Kah* – we must give thanks and praise to G-d for every breath."

When the Rebbe finally disembarked, a crowd of thousands welcomed him. Among them was sixteen-year-old Yitzchok Groner. Early that morning, his father woke him. "You're going to miss a day at Yeshivah Torah Vodaath. Today we're going to the port – the Rebbe is arriving."[2] Thirteen-year-old Risya Kazarnovsky also rose early that morning, too excited to sleep the night before. Before sunrise, she dressed in a special outfit, a camel-colored coat with brown buttons and a broad-brimmed hat to match.[3] By dawn she stood on the pier with her father, Rabbi Shlomo Aharon Kazarnovsky, one of the prominent Chabad rabbis in the US who played a key leadership role in Chabad's growth. Also at the dock was Eliezer Shoen, an observant Jew, though not a Chasid. He recalled years later, "There were many traditional Jews, not fully observant, who came to welcome the Rebbe." His miraculous rescue touched a chord, and the Rebbe inspired many people to reembrace the traditions they had left behind in Europe, Shoen said.[4] At the dock, historian Gershon Kranzler saw Jews of all types. "Young and old, rich and poor, bearing the traditional kaftan, black hats, beards and *peyos*, or the most elaborate creations of Parisian courtiers, they pushed and jostled each other to get closer and have a look at the man in the round fur cap and reddish grey long beard."[5] For Groner and Kazarnovsky, the impact would be much more personal.[6] They did not realize that the Rebbe's arrival would be a turning point, propelling their lives in a direction they could not have imagined.

New York's Yiddish daily, *Der Tog*, wrote that the rabbinic group Agudas Harabonim could have held its annual convention at the pier.[7] Young Yitzchok Groner remembers encountering a massive security presence. His father had VIP status, so "he got a pin and was permitted to stand in the front." Yitzchok wasn't so lucky. He was pushed further back in the crowd.

The Rebbe did not march off the ship as he had done on his visit to America eleven years earlier. He came down the gangway in a wheelchair, guided by one of the ship's officers, bedecked by a *shtreimel,* which is customarily worn on Shabbat and holidays. His countenance made an impression on those present. Kranzler says, "His very presence seemed to electrify the large crowd." The *Brooklyn Eagle* reported that he had a "reddish gray beard and a face stern and luminous as if from another epoch, from the era of the Geonim." He looked "*malchusdik,*" like spiritual royalty, says Avraham Hecht, the American student who fled Poland when the war broke out. The *Herald Tribune* described the Rebbe as "a man of striking appearance." Shoen says "many broke out in tears."

When the crowd saw the Rebbe coming down the gangway, they cried out, "*Shalom aleikhem*!" Cantor Shmuel Kantaroff joyously began to sing the *Shehechiyanu* blessing. Seized with excitement, the crowd burst into a lively chasidic tune. Risya Kazarnovsky says the singing was a moment of personal affirmation for her, a girl who went to public school whose family always seemed different from those of her peers. "These were the Chabad melodies I heard at home," she says. Groner strained to get a glimpse of the Rebbe. "I gave a jump, and I saw the Rebbe."

On the dock, at the bottom of the gangway, a reporter approached the Rebbe asking why he came to America. He replied, "*Altz iz hashgacha prutis, gekumen machen America a makom Torah* – Everything is by divine providence. I came to make America a center of Torah." The reporter responded with skepticism. "You will see hair on my hand before America will become a center of Torah." The Rebbe rebuffed his doubts. "I don't know about hair, but America will become a center of Jewish learning." Rising from his wheelchair, the Rebbe was emphatic. "*America iz nisht andersh* – America is no different. It will become a center of Torah."[8]

The Rebbe was wheeled to the nearby reception area, and the crowd ebbed and flowed as everyone strained to see him. Government officials greeted the Rebbe, and he thanked everyone for the warm welcome. The Rebbe's voice was low, though "occasionally his determination [overcame] his fatigue and his voice would grow stronger," reported the *Brooklyn Eagle*. Hundreds climbed tables and benches to see and hear the goings on. "Tears ran from the eyes of Chasidim hanging from the stage," reported *Der Tog*.[9] The Rebbe addressed the crowd, the fate of Polish Jewry weighing heavily on his heart. "It's painful for me to shatter the sense of joy," he said in an anguished tone, "but we can't be silent in the face of the agonizing cry of our brothers and sisters and my students in yeshivah in Poland." He urged the crowd to act. "We must do all that we can to save those in the Polish inferno."[10]

From the port, the Rebbe headed to the Greystone Hotel on Manhattan's Upper West Side. It would be his base for the next few months until a permanent home was purchased. Services were conducted in the Rebbe's apartment and in the hotel's ballroom. Later that day, the Rebbe addressed the large crowd that congregated in the hotel, again highlighting the crisis of Polish Jewry and the need to save them. He connected it to the broader theme of *ahavat Yisrael,* the Torah commandment of love and concern for another, reminding the crowd of its importance as a foundational Jewish ideal. "The love of G-d and the love of another are intrinsically bonded together," the Rebbe said. "One who loves G-d also loves his fellow Jews, and the person who is concerned with the welfare of others will rise in his devotion to G-d. We cannot, and we dare not, forget the predicament of our brothers overseas. We must do everything possible to give them the support for whatever they need." The Rebbe implored the crowd to support them and assist in their escape from the clutches of the Nazis.

The Rebbe also outlined his broad vision for American Jewry. "It is time to fortify Jewish education in the US," he said. He began to implement his plan immediately. "Tomorrow, in the Oneg Shabbat Synagogue, Yeshivas Tomchei Temimim Lubavitch will open in America."[11] Earlier, the Rebbe and local leaders had met in the hotel and resolved to start the yeshivah.

The same day, the Rebbe issued a statement to the press urging American Jews to stand behind the work of the JDC, "whose exemplary activity for Polish Jewry is well known." He also asked for support toward a "rescue fund to enable the evacuation of the students [of Yeshivas Tomchei Temimim] from Poland."[12] He called for a new direction for US Jewry, explaining that Poland had been the center of Jewish scholarship, and that America, blessed with peace, "must now become the Torah center of the Jewish people. I am willing to work with all of those interested in furthering religious education." The Rashag told the press that that Rabbi Hodakov, the overseer of Jewish schools in the Latvian Ministry of Education, was going to spend six months organizing day schools in the US.[13]

This was a marked contrast from the intentions the Rebbe had voiced to Rabbi Yisrael Jacobson during a private meeting in Otwock just days before the war started.[14] "I am entering my sixtieth year, my Shabbat years," the Rebbe told Jacobson. He explained that he wanted to "focus inward on the chasidic community, rebuild his yeshivah, and refrain from being involved with broader communal issues." He said, "I want to be a Rebbe for my Chasidim, not for the whole world. "A few months after arriving in New York, the Rebbe quoted Proverbs, "Many thoughts are in the heart of man," saying that now that he was turning sixty, he had hoped that G-d would grant him "the good fortune of a peaceful life." The war dashed that dream.

The voyage from Riga had been a time for personal reflection. "The ten days from Riga to New York were my Ten Days of Penitence and decision-making about the kind of life that I would have to undertake on the site of my new *shlichut* (mission)." In the Rebbe's eyes, that duty was "the task of bringing to America the *mesirat nefesh* (self-sacrifice) for unadulterated Torah study that my revered father implanted in Tomchei Temimim."[15] The goal was for America to replace Europe as a center of Torah. As the *Young Israel Viewpoint* wrote, "With his arrival the center of gravity of Jewish life shifts from the old world to the new." The Rebbe's long US sojourn a decade earlier had prepared him. As historian Rabbi Dr. Aaron Rakeffet explains, "The Rebbe came knowing the lay of the land and he would have a broad vision that impacted US Jewry. Other leaders would act defensively, taking care of their own needs."[16]

Years later, the seventh Rebbe explained[17] that there were three distinct periods of the Rebbe's leadership between 1920 and 1950. There was the first decade, in Russia, when the Rebbe risked his life standing up to Communism. The second period was in Latvia and Poland, where Rebbe attempted to establish the unique approach of Chabad Chasidism, despite skepticism, envy, and criticism from others. Finally, the last decade was in the US, where the Rebbe wanted to wake up American Jewy and change its trajectory. He arrived "as a refugee, depending on the kindness of the country that received him graciously." Despite this, the Rebbe sought to change American society, announcing in his first proclamation that the reason he was settling there was to transform the United States – challenging the very idea that America was a "new world" where all things, including Judaism, were done differently.

This new vision worried some of the Rebbe's closest supporters. Later that first evening, two of them met privately with the Rebbe. "I was visited by two notable individuals, veteran Americans and my most devoted friends." The Rebbe recounted their warning in his diary: "We must tell you that your noble desires are not feasible in America, no matter what exertion is invested."[18] They felt "duty bound" to save the Rebbe from "a catastrophic disappointment and shameful failure." One cautioned, "America is a land that devours good people. It gobbles up the greatest of newly arrived distinguished men." The second advised, "America is a land of fleetingly fiery enthusiasm and of endlessly cold-blooded interference. Many famous Torah scholars received warm welcomes. In the end, these highly esteemed rabbis have been forgotten, shunted off the side like outcasts." Referring to what he had heard from his "dear friends," the Rebbe wrote bitterly in his diary, "Endless tears of disappointment accompanied my first bedtime *Shema* on American soil."

Kranzler had the same feeling when he saw the excitement portside. "I thought to myself that after the novelty has worn off and the curiosity is stilled, the rabbi too will be forgotten."[19] Avraham Hecht was on the organizing committee for the Rebbe's welcome. "Most saw the Rebbe as an *erliche Yid*, a sincere Jew, but they did not take him seriously. They laughed at him." The Rebbe's proposals seemed improbable; in the US he would be starting over again from nothing. "Anyone else would have retired at this point. But in reality, the Rebbe was just starting his work at the age of sixty."[20] Hecht grew up in an immigrant community in Brooklyn. "Some had run away from the [Russian] army, others were simple tradesman. There was little Jewish learning and few Torah scholars." When the Rebbe set up shop in the Greystone Hotel, he had few followers. "A few of us would cross the bridge from Brooklyn. We used to walk two, three hours on Shabbat to ensure the Rebbe had a *minyan*."

It was a period of decline for Orthodox Jewry, writes historian Jonathan Sarna. Starting in 1924, the flow of immigrants dried up as the US established quotas for European immigrants. "With the end of immigration, its supply of pious newcomers was shut off at the very moment when the children of the those who immigrated years earlier seemed to abandon the movement's teachings."[21] A 1935 survey found that seventy-five percent of New York Jews had not attended synagogue in the previous year. In 1938 in San Francisco, only eighteen percent were affiliated with a congregation. When they did attend, many chose the new American styles of Jewish observance that were gaining steam. The Reform movement was already well entrenched, rooted in nineteenth-century German immigration. When Russian and Polish immigrants from Orthodox backgrounds came in large numbers starting in the 1880s, they loosened their ties with tradition and joined the growing Conservative movement. At the time of the Rebbe's arrival, that was the fastest-growing segment of the Jewish community.[22] Orthodoxy was in free fall. Jewish sociologist Marshal Sklare described its decline as "a case study in institutional decay."[23]

There was a small core of rabbis and community members working tirelessly to kick-start traditional Judaism in the US. Yeshivah Torah Vodaath,[24] led by the visionary educator Rabbi Shraga Feivel Mendlowitz,[25] was fostering a new generation of Jews dedicated to the classic yeshivah-style learning. Rabbi Mendlowitz was a Hungarian immigrant with a chasidic background, devoted to developing a European-style yeshivah in a new land. The yeshivah blended chasidic warmth and traditional Lithuanian scholarship. As historian Jeffry Gurock writes, "The Hungarian-born Mendlowitz came from an environment in which the teachings of Rabbi Moshe Sofer still loomed large," Rabbi Sofer being "the foremost arch resister in Europe to any Jewish concessions with the changing secular world."[26] Rabbi Mendlowitz did make some compromises with modernity, but they "were subtle ones." Other yeshivas were slowly sprouting, including Chaim Berlin and Mesivta Tiferes Yerushalayim.

At the same time, Rabbi Dov Revel was developing an institution with a new approach in Manhattan. Originally named Yeshivah College, later rebranded Yeshiva University, its goal was to integrate high-level Jewish study with college-level secular studies. Rabbi Mendlowitz was advocating insularity, while Rabbi Revel, who was himself an outstanding scholar and graduate of the great yeshivas of Europe, wanted to prod Orthodoxy into the cultural mainstream. As Sarna writes, American Orthodox Jews looked at Rabbi Revel's achievements "as a symbol that simultaneously reflected and legitimated their own quest to uphold and maintain Judaism and to adapt it to their new homeland."[27]

Other important Orthodox institutions emerged.[28] The Orthodox Union, founded in 1898, united many Orthodox synagogues and began to centralize kosher supervision in the US. Young Israel, founded in 1912, lured younger Jews back toward observance and was expanding its network of congregations. Mizrachi, the religious Zionist organization, was launched in 1914, and the more traditionalist Agudath Israel was established by Rabbi Eliezer Silver in the 1930s.

By the time the Rebbe arrived, there was a cornucopia of rabbinical groups. Agudas Harabonim[29] unified rabbis with backgrounds in the European yeshivas. The Rabbinical Council of America[30] linked graduates of Yeshiva University. America did not boast world-class Jewish scholars like in Europe, but Rabbis Silver and Eliyahu Henkin were shining exceptions. In the years leading up to World War II, some notable Torah scholars immigrated to the US,[31] including Rabbis Moshe Feinstein,[32] Joseph Soloveitchik, Yaakov Kamenetsky, and Joseph Breuer. Other prominent rabbis[33] found sanctuary in the US when the war broke out in Europe. It took time for their influence to grow, but ultimately, the immigration of these rabbis contributed to establishing the US as a center of Jewish scholarship.

The primary strategy of the time was defensive, to shore up the small core of observant Jews and stem the Orthodox attrition that would not abate for years. That mindset was echoed in the speech of Rabbi Moshe Soloveichik at the ordination ceremony at Yeshiva University in 1940. He called on the newly minted rabbis to "resist the onslaught" and to "expand and increase the study of Torah." He urged them to "salvage what was left and continue the long legacy for which our ancestors gave their lives."[34]

The Rebbe's strategy was the opposite; he chose to go on the offensive. His proclamation, "*America iz nisht andersh* – America is no different," challenged the prevailing attitude. He didn't want to just bolster the small religious community, but to fundamentally change the direction of American Jewish life.

Nineteen-year-old yeshivah student Herschel Fogelman was at the pier when the Rebbe disembarked. He describes the mentality of the small Orthodox world overwhelmed by attrition, struggling to balance the freedoms of America with loyalty to tradition. "We, the students of Torah Vodaath, felt like pioneers in a wagon train on the prairie surrounded by Indians. The Rebbe's arrival was like the calvary had finally come to save us. But the Rebbe didn't just want to chase off the Indians, he wanted to conquer the whole continent."[35]

In America, the Rebbe would have to start again from scratch – for the third time – in a totally different environment. Immense sums of money were needed to help Jews stranded in Europe and to transform Judaism in the US, but the Rebbe lacked affluent supporters. Rabbi Adin Even-Israel Steinsaltz explained the difficulties the Rebbe faced. "There were Jews who were sentimental to traditional Judaism, but unfortunately, they did not have financial resources. Those who had money did not have that sense of longing for traditional Judaism," nor did they perceive the urgency of the threat in Europe. Steinsaltz says that during this period, every contribution was vital. The Rebbe even wrote "a personal letter to someone who made a donation of fifty dollars."[36]

Though large crowds had turned out to welcome the Rebbe, the actual number of Chabad Chasidim was small. Only a handful of Chasidim lived in the upscale Crown Heights neighborhood where the Rebbe would soon set up his headquarters. Steinsaltz notes that when he settled there, it was still hard to get a *minyan* in the middle of the day. "There were so few Chabad members that someone would stand on the street to recruit the tenth man for afternoon prayers."[37]

The Rebbe had announced the founding of the American Yeshivas Tomchei Temimim on his first day in the US. Mordechai Fisher, one of the yeshivah's original students, says the Rebbe told Rabbi Jacobson that day, "If you do not promise me that you will open the yeshivah, I will not go to bed to sleep tonight." The next morning, Jacobson began enlisting students. "He spoke to me and to this one and that one, and we all decided to volunteer to become the nucleus of the new yeshivah." Studies began a week later in Congregation Oneg Shabbat in the East Flatbush section of Brooklyn; its members had converted a house into a shul. Avraham Hecht recalls the modest start: "Benches and tables were dragged down to the basement. A kitchen was speedily constructed in the homey yeshivah hall, transforming a dingy cellar into a room fit for use."[38]

The first group of students was made up of Americans who transferred from other New York yeshivas and gravitated to Chabad.[39] A few students who had studied in Otwock, such as Hecht, also joined. Rabbi Mordechai Mentlik, one of the outstanding Polish scholars, was appointed dean of the yeshivah, a position he held until his passing in 1987. The group was very small, Hecht says. "There was just a *minyan*."

On the day the studies started, the Rebbe addressed the students.[40] "Today is the seventh day since divine providence brought me to America to transform America into a haven for Torah."[41] The Rebbe spoke of the unique purpose in life that each individual has and emphasized the importance of Torah study. He reminded them that in Europe the yeshivah student was "recognizable by his outward appearance. They were not embarrassed and didn't hide their distinctness." By contrast, in America some rabbis and yeshivah students "hide their distinguishing face" and are wary of being outwardly Jewish by "wearing tzitzit, *peyos,* and a beard." Steinsaltz says, "Shaving one's beard was emblematic of modernity. If Jews wanted to fit in, they would have to look the part. The Rebbe demanded that the students in the yeshivah grow beards. At the time it was like he asked them to grow tails. No young people wore beards."[42]

For the first few months in America, the Rebbe resided in the Greystone Hotel in Manhattan, except for an interlude for the holiday of Passover in Lakewood, New Jersey. The Chasidim began searching for a permanent home for the Rebbe in the summer of 1940.[43] Hecht says some of the Chasidim thought the most appropriate location would be a suburban town, such as Lakewood. There a yeshivah could operate with fewer distractions, less "opposition and ridicule." But the Rebbe rejected this proposal. "He wanted to transform the religious topography of American society. This could only be accomplished if his chasidic movement was visible to the public eye."

Instead of settling down in Brooklyn's religious hub, Brownsville, known as the "Jerusalem of America," the Rebbe selected prestigious Crown Heights. A three-story brownstone[44] was purchased on the main thoroughfare of Eastern Parkway.[45] "It is a beautiful residence in a wonderful location," described Rabbi Shmuel Levitin, "with room for the Rebbe's needs, including offices, a library, and synagogue like there was in Lubavitch that will be renovated and that will welcome all of *anash*."[46] Chasidim began to refer to it simply as "Seven-Seventy" after its address. With time, its iconic profile would become a symbol of Chabad and replicas would be constructed around the world.[47]

Around the corner was President Street, lined with mansions owned by the Jewish nouveau riche. Down the block loomed the Brooklyn Jewish Center, the largest Conservative congregation in the US, known as the "shul with a pool." Its rabbi and other community leaders opposed the Rebbe planting his headquarters in their midst. Hecht says, "They lobbied city hall and local congressmen to block the Rebbe from moving to Eastern Parkway." That didn't faze the Rebbe. "He was unimpressed by those who wanted to disrupt his plans." At the time, there were only three Chabad families living in the neighborhood, but Crown Heights would become a base to reach out to all kinds of Jews, secular and religious.[48] "For a chasidic Jew, in particular a Rebbe, to move into Crown Heights at that time was like something from a different planet," says chasidic scholar Michoel Seligson.[49]

Just after Chai Elul (September 22, 1940), the birthday of Rabbis Yisrael Baal Shem Tov and Schneur Zalman, the Rebbe moved into his newly acquired home.[50] The Chasidim were delighted that the Rebbe finally had a permanent residence. "I cannot describe the happiness and joy that we saw on the faces of everyone," says Avraham Pariz.[51] Avraham Hecht says the enthusiasm of the crowd embodied "the hopes and dreams for Chasidism in America."[52] But the joy was tinged by anxiety over the war. "While Europe was being consumed by merciless flames, a new reality was taking place. Destruction and construction were occurring simultaneously in two distant lands."

It was this destruction that preoccupied the Rebbe as he planted roots in the US. His attention was on the fate of the Jews in Europe, both those in Poland and Russia. Though there was anxiety over the fate of European Jews under German rule, few imagined that Germany would soon embark on a policy of Jewish genocide. As the Rebbe reflected after his arrival, "G-d dispatched us here with a dual mission to American Jewry, to their rabbis and lay leaders. The first mission is to urge them to do whatever is possible to sustain and save the Jews abroad." Strides had been made, "however, all of this is far from enough." The Jews in Europe were suffering acutely. "Their spirits are so crushed by the cruel bondage that they have not the strength to cry out." The Rebbe called for direct assistance to the Jews in Europe and to "increase the possibilities of immigration."[53]

"The second mission which divine providence has placed upon me," the Rebbe continued, "is the furtherance of G-d-fearing Torah study and proper Jewish education." As historian Shalom Ber Levin writes,[54] "From the moment the Rebbe escaped from Warsaw, this became a life's purpose: not to forget, or rest, until he could save his students." It would be an almost impossible task. Immigration to the US had slowed to a trickle after Congress supported the Johnson-Reed Act in 1924. The State Department, its hallways filled with bureaucrats with little sympathy, if not outright hostility, to Jews in Europe, heavily regulated immigration. While still in Poland, the Rebbe had instructed his students to flee to nearby Lithuania.[55] Afterward, during his brief interlude in Riga, he turned to major Jewish groups asking them to help save the Jews still stranded in Poland. The Rebbe looked for any avenue to rescue those still in Europe.

America was still neutral and would not enter the war until the attack on Pearl Harbor in December of 1941. Hopeful that the US would provide sanctuary, the Rebbe tried securing visas and raising large sums of money to transport the students. From Riga, before departing to the US, he urged Rabbi Yisrael Jacobson to "act expeditiously and as soon as possible"[56] to lobby the State Department for visas. After landing in the US, the Rebbe addressed the "Jews of America" in a letter, imploring them to rescue the students in Europe from "a great threat to their lives.

Help me save the students!"[57] The Rebbe turned to friends across the globe to find avenues of rescue. He wrote to Jewish leaders in Palestine, including Chief Rabbi Yitzchak Herzog, asking for help with procuring immigration affidavits to *Eretz Yisrael*. In June 1940, the Rebbe contacted Shanghai's chief rabbi, Meir Ashkenazi, about the possibility of escape via Russia and China. "When you receive the names of the students, can you arrange transit visas for them?"[58] He explored options in countries as far away as Paraguay and Cuba.

Meanwhile, the route to safety via the Far East was discovered when two yeshivah students in Lithuania realized there was no visa requirement to travel to Curacao.[59] Jan Zwartendyk, the Dutch honorary consul in Kovno, agreed to stamp the students' passports, "No visa required to enter Curacao." Based on this, Chiune Sugihara, the Japanese consul in the Lithuanian capital, started to issue transit visas for Jews via Japan. Skepticism on the success of this route reined amongst the yeshivah students in Lithuania. Some were fearful that sending students via Communist Russia could be dangerous.[60] Earlier, the Rebbe had instructed his students to seek the advice of the Amshinover Rebbe, Rabbi Shimon Kalish, should communication with him be interrupted.[61] Rabbi Kalish instructed the students to flee east via Russia, and when the Rebbe was notified, he endorsed the plan.

At first, the Rebbe secured US visas for fifty-two students. The plan was for them to come directly to the US, but as the war intensified, travel across the Atlantic became impossible. The only way open was eastward, through Russia and Japan. The Chabad students did not hesitate. Chaim Meir Bukiet recalls, "It was the students of Tomchei Temimim who broke the ice." The Russian official responsible for permitting travel via Russia was named Schlossberg. He was a Communist, but his father had been a Chabad Chasid. When he saw the bearded students, he realized they were from the Lubavitcher yeshivah. "We were terrified," Bukiet recalls. But Schlossberg reassured them and told them not to worry. He arranged visas and asked them to get a tallit for his father.[62]

One of the students, Herschel Fuchs, says, "The Russians wanted to show the world they were not so terrible and were permitting the transit of students throughout Russia."[63] He adds that they needed foreign currency; the Russians demanded about five hundred dollars per student ($10,000 today). The Rebbe had to secure the funds quickly, before the window of escape closed.

The Rebbe sent appeals and emissaries to collect money across the US. He emphatically petitioned Rabbi Dovid Rabinowitz in Boston: "It's an emergency. We have no idea what will happen tomorrow."[64] Despite the difficulties, the Rebbe couldn't ignore the pleas for help. "What can I do? They are turning to me from every side." The fate of the students impacted his own fragile health. "Saving the students is causing me pain and anguish. I sent a large amount of money," he wrote. He pleaded with Moshe Starkenstein, a philanthropist in Detroit, "The cost is $430[65] per student. I am trying to save at least fifty of them. We cannot wait, it's *pikuach nefesh* – we are saving the lives of great scholars, the best of the Jewish people." A month later, the Rebbe turned to Wichita, Kansas, businessman Tzvi Hirsch Gore in desperation: "I received a telegram from the students in Vilnius. The Soviets are demanding another $5,040 ($100,000 today), and the transit visas are only valid for a short time. Please have mercy on my students and provide a meaningful amount now."[66]

The Rebbe even appealed to Moshe Zalman Feiglin in far-off Australia. "I've secured US visas for one hundred students and fifty families with a cost of upward of $500 each."[67] The Rebbe wrote that funds had already been transferred to save thirty students, but he was unable to find the money for the rest. "I am in great pain and disheartened that we are unable to save these students." When the Rebbe could not raise the funds in time, he borrowed them. He told a supporter in Pittsburgh, "We are seeking a loan. They have visas and if we don't cable the funds in four days, they could lose permission to travel. This is on top of the five thousand dollars we sent last week and the previous payments that were made."[68] The debts were weighing on him. He confided to one of his followers that he was taking out one loan to pay another.[69]

The students headed east by train to Moscow, where they expected to receive their visas at the US Embassy. Tzvi Kotlarsky says that until that time, only individuals had trickled through Moscow; they were the first large group. "The US ambassador had never had a request for such a large number of visas." Indeed, few people ever left Russia. "He said it was impossible to process them in the three short days we were in Moscow."[70] Instead he suggested they obtain the visas at the US embassy in Tokyo, since they were traveling to the US via Japan. The Russians put them up in upscale hotels, and the students spent a few idyllic days in Russia's capital.[71] From there they took the trans-Siberian railway to Vladivostok and then to an ocean crossing to Japan. Avraham Garfinkel recalled, "The trip took two weeks across Siberia, and then we stayed three days in a hotel in Vladivostok." When they finally arrived in Kobe, Japan, the small Jewish community there opened its doors to them. They had established a synagogue in 1912, and by the onset of the war there were one thousand Jews in Kobe.[72] The first group of Chabad students arrived in early 1941.[73]

At the US embassy in Tokyo, they discovered that US policy had changed. Their visas were revoked, and unable to travel to the US, they were stranded in Japan. In New York, the Rebbe reached out to unsuccessfully to other countries, such as Paraguay, Canada, and Palestine, to provide them refuge.

Others took the route to Kobe, including two hundred students of the Mir Yeshivah led by their *rosh yeshivah,* Rabbi Chaim Shmuelevitz.[74] Seven months later, in August, the Japanese government relocated all the yeshivah students from Kobe to the international city of Shanghai.[75] It had a substantial Jewish community, founded by Sephardic Jews lured by business opportunities in the nineteenth century and augmented by refugees from Russia and other European countries. Rabbi Meir Ashkenazi, a Chabad Chasid, was the Ashkenazi chief rabbi. He arranged for the large Beth Aharon Synagogue, built in 1927,[76] to be assigned to the Mir Yeshivah. The Chabad yeshivah with just some forty students rented another location, continuing its classic mode of study[77] as in Poland.

Unlike the Mir Yeshivah, whose staff had come along, the Chabad students were isolated, as no teachers or administrators had joined them. Communication with the Rebbe in New York was nearly impossible, especially after the attack on Pearl Harbor.[78] Cut off from the Jewish world, they had to fend for themselves. One of the students, Chaim Sapochinksy, recalls, "It was hard for us, the Lubavitcher students in Shanghai, because we were without a Rebbe or *maggid shiur* (teacher). But we were Chasidim… we tried to strengthen ourselves."[79]

The war years in Shanghai were grueling. Initially, Jewish refugees were permitted to live anywhere in the city, but in 1943 the Japanese created a Jewish ghetto in the Hongkou district. The Japanese rule was cruel[80] and food was scarce; there were times when the students were barely surviving. To help, the US-based Agudas Harabonim organized a rescue committee, the Vaad Hatzalah,[81] which launched a national fundraising campaign to support the students. They sent funds to the Mir Yeshivah and some additional smaller yeshivas but intentionally excluded the Chabad students from the life-saving disbursements, even as many donations came from the chasidic community.[82] "Telegrams from the Vaad Hatzalah in New York were sent to Shanghai instructing that the money be given to all students of Torah except Chabad," says Chaim Bukiet.[83]

After a fundraiser in Chicago raised a large sum, many of the donations coming from chasidic donors, the Rebbe pleaded for a portion of the funds to be used to help the Chabad students in Shanghai, but his fervent request went unheeded.[84] The Rebbe had received a report via Stockholm that described the refugee situation as "catastrophic. We must save them from hunger and sickness."[85]

"We were in a very serious physical condition," recalls Bukiet. "Our clothes were in tatters and we had barely anything to eat except for a bit of rice every day." The transfer of funds to Shanghai was very challenging with the city under Japanese occupation. Sending money from the US was illegal, considered "trading with the enemy."[86] There was great risk that the Japanese would arrest someone for receiving funds from the US. Bukiet says the Vaad Hatzalah was one of the few that found a way of moving money through neutral countries such as Switzerland and Uruguay.[87] In 1943, the Vaad Hatzalah was able to convince Henry Morgenthau, secretary of the treasury, to make an exception to US law and permit the transmission of funds to the students in Shanghai.[88]

The war prevented communication between the students held in enemy-controlled Shanghai and Chabad in New York. After the Japanese surrender, contact was reestablished, and only then did the hardships endured by the Chabad students become clear. The students sent a heartbreaking letter[89] to the Rashag detailing Vaad Hatzalah's conduct. The letter explained that in December of 1942, all funds to Chabad were cut off by the Vaad Hatzalah. Afterward, "with great difficulty, and after experiencing shame and embarrassment, small amounts were given to us from time to time when they saw our situation was critical and we had nothing to sustain ourselves." One of the students, Shimon Goldman, recalled, "While the students of Mir and other yeshivas received generous stipends to help them eat and buy clothes, the students of Tomchei Temimim had to fend for themselves."[90]

Bukiet recalled a miraculous story about how the hunger was somewhat alleviated. Aryeh Leib Brailovsky, a local Jew who was originally from Russia, told Rabbi Ashkenazi about an enigmatic dream that he had. "A rabbi came to me and told me, 'My children are hungry for bread.'" Ashkenazi showed him a picture of the Rebbe. Bukiet says, "Brailovsky was startled. He told Ashkenazi that this was the rabbi he had seen in his dream." This astonishing occurrence motivated Brailovsky to raise funds from friends and to make significant personal donations toward sustaining the yeshivah." According to Fuchs, Brailovsky eventually became fully observant.[91]

Rabbi Chaim Shmuelewitz, disturbed by the policies that he was instructed to follow by the Vaad Hatzalah, quietly assisted the Chabad students. Bukiet recalls, "He would try to give us some money when he could." Trying to get around the ban of using the funds for Chabad students, Shmuelewitz invited them to join his yeshivah. Wanting to retain their unique approach to Torah study, they didn't accept his offer.

The Vaad Hatzalah policies created a controversy that remains an open wound.[92] Goldman wrote in his memoir, "We had suffered at the hands of the Poles, the Germans, the Americans – and now we suffered at the hands of religious Jews like ourselves." Members of the Vaad Hatzalah claimed that the Rebbe had a fund for *pidyon shvuyim* (redemption of captives) which was set up to secretly help Jews in Russia.[93] The Rebbe asserted that Vaad Hatzalah were reaching out to all segments of the community, including Chasidim, claiming to take care of all yeshivah students under siege. The Shanghai students believed that the Vaad Hatzalah policy was a continuation of the enmity of the *mitnagdim* toward Chasidim that reached back to the time of the Vilna Gaon.[94] This caused the Rebbe great anguish. In 1962, in a rare moment of candor and criticism, the seventh Rebbe confided to Rabbi Chaim Gutnick[95] that the actions of the Vaad Hatzalah members "caused my father-in-law to weep."[96]

In 1941, Canada allotted a small number of visas for Polish Jewish refugees in neutral countries. The Canadian Jewish community had to make the gut-wrenching decision of whom to save. Rabbi Oscar Fasman of Ottawa pleaded with the Canadian Jewish Congress to prioritize Jewish scholars. "We are saving not merely people, but a holy culture which cannot be otherwise preserved."[97] When they agreed, the Rebbe[98] dispatched Rabbi Yisrael Jacobson to Canada to urge Jewish leaders to include the Chabad students.[99]

In September 1941, visas were designated for eighty yeshivah students, including nine from Chabad. With war looming on the Pacific, passage to Canada was difficult to secure. Space was found for them on a US ship sailing from Shanghai to San Francisco. Rabbi Ashkenazi asked the students to stay in Shanghai through the holidays. The route would take them across the international date line on Yom Kippur, raising questions on when they should fast and causing some to consider waiting for the next ship.[100] But the Rebbe insisted they depart as soon as possible, telegramming Rabbi Ashkenazi, "Please make every effort to secure berths for travel on the first ship."

Hearing this directive, the Chabad students booked passage immediately. They were joined by some of the other students of the Mir Yeshivah, but the majority decided to wait. Yitzchak Hendel took the first ship. "From the eighty students who received visas, only twenty-nine actually left.[101] Tragically, most of those who stayed spent the war years in Shanghai."[102] In San Francisco, the refugees were escorted by US officials to Chicago by train, and then on to Canada. They reached the Montreal train station on Friday, October 24, and the community welcomed them with open arms.

Rabbi Yisrael Jacobson was also at the train station, sent by the Rebbe with instructions for the students. "He told us that we were to establish a yeshivah," recalled Tzvi Hirsh Kotlarsky.[103] On Saturday night, at a community reception for the students, Rabbi Jacobson surprised the crowd by announcing the opening of Yeshivas Tomchei Temimim the very next day.[104] Jacobson's unilateral announcement sparked a debate in Montreal. Local leaders had envisioned opening one yeshivah for all the students, not two separate ones. Judah Albert, president of Montreal's Chabad synagogue, asserted, "Lubavitch has its own principles, be it in learning and teaching, be it in their general outlook to Judaism in their chasidic way of life."[105] Two yeshivas opened, Tomchei Temimim and Mercaz HaTorah.[106] Both flourished, transforming Montreal's Jewish community.

To survive, the new yeshivah needed financial support. Hirsch Wolofsky, the opinionated editor of the Yiddish newspaper *The Canadian Eagle*, asked Samuel Bronfman, Seagram's owner and Montreal's leading Jewish philanthropist, "Are you going to help the new yeshivah?" Bronfman responded indignantly, "I'll give them six thousand dollars ($100,000 today) to move to Toronto." Wolofsky met with the nine students to convince them to take the offer and leave town. In response, Yitzchak Hendel says, "We told him that with time we will get to Toronto,"[107] implying that one day they would open a branch of the yeshivah there. But for now, "We're staying and fulfilling the Rebbe's directives." Wolofsky continued arguing with the students. Finally, they told him, "If you have complaints, take it up with the Rebbe in New York." Wolofsky accepted their suggestion and met with the Rebbe. "We don't know what the Rebbe said to him, but from then on he stopped all criticism of Lubavitch," Hendel recalls.

Jacobson returned to New York, and the Rebbe sent Rabbi Shmuel Levitin to Montreal to nurture the new yeshivah through its early stages. In the months to come, the Rebbe gave Levitin detailed instructions regarding the yeshivah's curriculum, organizational structure, and educational philosophy.

The first Jews who came to Montreal were Sephardic, establishing the Spanish and Portuguese Synagogue in 1768. European, mostly Russian, Jews came in the twentieth century, and by the early 1930s there were over sixty thousand Jews in Montreal, the vast majority of them Yiddish speakers. The Labor Zionist Jewish People's School opened in 1928 as the first Jewish day school in Montreal.[108] The Yiddish Peretz School started as an afternoon program and opened a day school in 1941. These schools were a continuation of the Yiddish movements in Europe that rejected conventional Torah study and religious observance. Their curriculum consisted of Yiddish language, culture, and Zionism, and by 1941 there were 426 children enrolled in these schools.[109] The vast majority of local Jewish children, over ten thousand, attended Protestant-run public schools.[110] Just thirty-six percent of Jewish children in Montreal attended a supplementary program such as a Talmud Torah.[111] The two yeshivas founded by students from Shanghai were the first Orthodox day schools in Montreal.

The Rebbe's vision was broad: that the yeshivah should elevate Jewish life in Montreal. He challenged the students to look beyond their personal academic achievement, directing them to reach out to the community and enroll children in the yeshivah and other programs.

"The primary act of *tzedakah* (kindness) is to go from street to street and from house to house, and gather the lilies, the pure children, and bring them to learn Torah,"[112] the Rebbe wrote to his followers in Montreal. The students fanned out in the city looking for students. Avraham Gerlitzky says, "If we saw a mezuzah on the doorpost of a home, we would knock and ask if they perhaps had a young child that they could send to the yeshivah."[113] The first day, the yeshivah had seven local students in addition to the Shanghai boys. Within two months, two dozen were enrolled.

The Rebbe's objective was clear. He viewed the influx of the yeshivah students to Montreal as divine providence. Instead of bringing them to New York to solidify the yeshivah there, they would be a beachhead for Yiddishkeit in Montreal.[114] There were few young religious Jews in Montreal; the appearance of bearded yeshivah students was revolutionary. Like in the US, Jewish immigrants to Canada were slowly moving away from tradition. Hendel recalls they were shocked to see the level of religious observance. "In Vilnius there was an occasional Jew whose store was open on Shabbat. Here in Montreal, it was the majority." Even some of the children of rabbis opened businesses on Shabbat. "They came to Montreal fully observant, and they did not believe that their children could follow this in the new country." They mostly attended Orthodox synagogues, but their children received minimal Jewish schooling. The opening of the yeshivah was a turning point for Jewish education in Montreal. Now there were authentic yeshivah students in their midst, full of spirit and passion, role models for the younger generation. They initiated a variety of programs with full day and afternoon schools. They inspired many, including Arnold Dalfen. "Within two years," he remembers, "there were 250 students learning daily in various locations."[115] In the summer of 1942, the yeshivah students opened a summer camp.

The yeshivah continued to grow. By 1943 it was clear that a proper facility was crucial. The Rebbe sent a series of letters encouraging the local leaders to purchase a building. With the help of many, including Sam Bronfman,[116] who by now saw the value of the yeshivah, a former orphanage was acquired. Montreal's Chief Rabbi Yehoshua Hirshorn wrote, "Montrealers should be proud of Tomchei Temimim," adding that December 12, the day of the building's dedication, "should be a *Yom Tov* (holiday) in the city."[117]

The students, ranging from their late teens to early twenties, were alone in Montreal without parents or relatives, the fate of their families in Europe uncertain. Yosef Rodal, the oldest of the students, reminisced to his son Shmuel, "The Rebbe was like a father to us. We students had lost our whole families. We didn't have anybody, no cousins, nothing." Shmuel's mother told him, "The Rebbe would send Rabbi Shmuel Levitin to give *chizuk,* encouragement, to the students and see how they were."[118] In 1942, Rodal was the first of the Shanghai students to get married.[119] As a refugee, he had few resources for a wedding. "The Rebbe knew my mother was a Canadian girl and that they were used to getting diamond rings," says his son Shmuel. "So, the Rebbe gave my father money to buy a diamond ring so that my mother would be happy." Yitzchak Hendel asked the Rebbe if he should pursue a match that had been recommended to him. The Rebbe replied, "The suggestion requires review,"[120] telling Hendel to wait a bit. He turned to Rabbi Shmuel Levitin to inquire about the family and the young lady. After receiving a positive report, he told Hendel to look into it. Upon their engagement, the bride traveled to New York to meet with the Rebbe personally and receive his blessings. The Rebbe sent a delegation of Rabbis from New York to the wedding.

As they grew older, most of the group stayed in Montreal; a few moved to New York. They each married and put down roots. Rabbi Hendel would become a prominent member of the city's rabbinical court. Leibel Kramer would direct the yeshivah. Others became teachers and community leaders.

The Rebbe was also gravely concerned about the fate of his two daughters and their husbands stranded in Europe.[121] They were included in the visas granted to the Rebbe and the Chabad hierarchy; regulations dictated that those visas had to be issued directly to them by a US consul in Europe. His younger daughter, Sheina, and her husband Menachem Horenstein had relocated from France to Poland to care for his elderly parents.

As Polish citizens, the Horensteins were not permitted to enter Latvia, so they were unable to join the Rebbe in Riga. Their file bounced between consulates in Europe as bureaucratic obstacles kept blocking their way. Aside from the issue of the visas, the Horensteins could not secure exit permits from Poland. Eventually, they lost touch with the Rebbe, and for many years their fate remained unknown. After the war, a survivor of the Treblinka death camp confirmed that Mendel Horenstein, his mother, his wife Sheina, and their adopted son[122] were killed in the fall of 1942.[123]

The Ramash and Chaya Mushka were in Paris when the war broke out, it seems that initially, when the war broke out, the Ramash hesitated to leave Europe.[124] That changed when the Germans invaded France. The Ramash and Chaya Mushka fled south to Vichy, France, after the Nazis occupied Paris. First they tried to secure visas from the US Consulate in Nice, but officials there were openly antagonistic to Jews. Ultimately, they succeeded at the consulate in Marseille. The couple's plan was to head overland to neutral Spain and Portugal and from there to the United States. Acquiring the transit visas was problematic, but at the last minute, they received permission. On June 12, 1941, they boarded a ship in Lisbon and made the Atlantic crossing, arriving in the US eleven days later.[125]

The night before the Schneersons disembarked, Yitzchok Groner and his father Mordechai were waiting for *yechidut*, a private meeting with the Rebbe.[126] Rabbi Yisrael Jacobson burst out of the Rebbe's study and turned to them with excitement. "Reb Mordechai," he said, "the Rebbe said the whole yeshivah should go welcome his son-in-law! He is a *gaon*[127] (Torah prodigy) who knows all of Talmud Bavli and Yerushalmi, with the commentaries of Tosfot, Rashi, and Ran, and all the printed chasidic thought."

The welcome the next day for the Ramash and Chaya Mushka at the port was more subdued than the one the Rebbe had received a year earlier. A small crowd of Chasidim and some forty yeshivah students waited on the dock. Yitzchok Groner recalls, "Down came a youngish man with a black beard, a white creased hat, and a short brown-grey suit." The couple was welcomed by the elder Chasidim. "Then he walked over to the forty students, greeting each one personally and asking their name." Groner recalls being touched by both the Ramash's personal warmth and his sense of humility.

The Ramash's arrival meant the start a new stage of the Rebbe's work in the US. The Rebbe set up three new organizations that would become the institutional pillars of Chabad: Merkos L'Inyonei Chinuch (Central Organization for Jewish Education), which developed educational programs and eventually operated the global Chabad network; Kehot Publication Society, which evolved into one of the largest Jewish publishers; and Machne Israel, the social services branch of Chabad to bolster religious life. It also created a program to reach out to Jewish farmers, "whose distance from Jewish centers is likely to make them removed also from Jewish life."[128] The chairman of these three entities would be the newly arrived Ramash.[129]

As the war progressed, engulfing the world and threatening the Jews of Europe, the Rebbe looked to Jewish tradition for inspiration to cope with the crisis. Judaism teaches that during difficult times, the Jewish nation must look inward for spiritual renewal, seek G-d's help from above, and reorient their lives toward sanctity. The Rebbe believed a proper response would not only be temporal, but spiritual, based on millennia of Jewish teachings. Historically, the prophets called on the Jews to repent when they were faced with threats of annihilation, such as the prophet Yoel, who called for the Jews to "return to the Lord your G-d."[130] We find the notion of a spiritual response throughout Jewish history. Faced with annihilation in ancient Persia, Mordechai gathered the Jewish children to study Torah so as to invoke divine mercy.[131] As the Talmud states, "If a person sees that suffering has befallen him, he should examine his deeds."[132] Maimonides enshrines this ideal in the *Mishneh Torah*, his code of Jewish law, writing, "It is a divine command to cry out [to G-d] and sound trumpets when tragedies occur to the Jewish people."[133] The Rebbe's worldview, rooted in the teachings of Kabbalah and Chasidism, taught that the physical world is a façade for the spiritual universe, which is the true reality. As the chasidic dictum states, "Just as the soul fills the body, so too G-d fills the world."

The Rebbe believed that self-reflection, repentance, and spiritual transformation would invoke a divine blessing on the Jews and all of mankind during this unprecedented worldwide conflict. He turned to the public with a call: "*L'alter leteshuvah, l'alter legeulah* – Immediate repentance will prompt redemption." He emphasized the need to take spiritual stock and look inward, as that repentance would be a catalyst for salvation, blessing, and ultimately the redemption though the Messiah. He issued public statements urging all Jews to reaffirm their commitment to observance. To amplify this message, the Rebbe began publishing a magazine, *HaKriah VeHaKedushah*, starting in late 1940.[134] It was published monthly until the war's end.[135] The primary language of the magazine was Yiddish, though starting in April 1941, a small English section was added. Its central message was that Jews should rededicate themselves to observance, as the prophets of earlier eras had demanded, with the hope that this would cause G-d to send deliverance.[136]

The Rebbe wanted American Jews to empathize and identify with their brethren in Europe, even on a personal level. Rabbi Leibel Groner recalls his teacher, Rabbi Zalman Gurary, coming into his classroom and telling the teenage students that "the Rebbe wanted us to experience in a small way the suffering of the Jews in Europe." Gurary asked each of the students to undertake something that would remind them of the pain of the European Jews. Some of the children decided to cease attending movies. Groner resolved not to eat chocolate. Gurary made a list of the students' decisions and reported them to the Rebbe.[137]

When he landed on American soil, the Rebbe said the most important issue was saving European Jews. But he discovered that numerous barriers stood in the path of rescue. US government policy was actively blocking immigration, and leaders of the American Jewish establishment were hesitant to publicly pressure the Roosevelt administration to issue more visas. While the miraculous salvation of the Rebbe had been successful, it did not translate into political influence in Washington for Chabad.[138] The Rebbe's circle of Chasidim was quite small and comprised almost entirely of first-generation immigrants without political connections or financial resources.[139] As Rabbi Herschel Feigelstock[140] says, "There were barely ten real Chasidim" who were fully dedicated to the Rebbe. Additionally, the Rebbe suffered from a chronic disease that became more acute with time. His speech was impaired, making it difficult to understand him, and he was constrained to a wheelchair. His efforts were severely limited by a lack of major donors, placing the Rebbe under constant financial strain. Most American Jews with means were not Orthodox or sympathetic to the causes the Rebbe championed. Few understood the real risks of life and death that the Jews were facing in Europe. The Rebbe had struggled to secure the funds needed to facilitate the escape of just a small number of yeshivah students from Lithuania via Russia. Major Jewish groups would not support the rescue effort. He appealed to Jews across the country, borrowing funds when he fell short. All these factors dramatically inhibited the Rebbe's ability to organize the rescue of his own Chasidim and others.

Major Jewish groups like the American Jewish Committee, the Anti-Defamation League, and the American Jewish Congress controlled Jews' access to Washington. These organizations were dominated by Jews, many from Germany, who had immigrated to the US in the mid and late nineteenth century. By the 1940s they had attained financial success and assimilated to a large degree. Despite their success, they were apprehensive about being fully accepted in US society, fearing the anti-Semitism that had driven them and their ancestors to American shores. Professor Jonathan Sarna describes the Jews of the time as "an anxious subculture."[141] They would not tolerate Orthodox Jews taking a leadership role, concerned that they might be just a bit "too Jewish," tarnishing the image of good citizens who looked like all other Americans. Their religious garb might provoke anti-Semitism, and they might be too parochial with their demands. The number of Orthodox Jews was small and most were European immigrants whose first language was Yiddish. They had no real political power or connections to American political leaders.[142] Their financial resources were meager, and to a large degree, the Orthodox were excluded from the broader Jewish communal power structure. It would take decades before they developed the self-confidence and organizational influence to strike out on their own and assert their views.

The preeminent Jewish leader of the time was Reform Rabbi Stephen S. Wise.[143] He stood at the helm of a conglomerate of key Jewish groups, including the American Jewish Congress, the American Zionist Organization, the Jewish Institute of Religion rabbinical school, and a prominent congregation in New York. It was unprecedented for one person to so dominate Jewish life in the US. As America entered the war in December of 1941, the prevailing attitude was that the plight of Jews would be resolved once overall victory had been achieved. Leaders like

Wise feared making the war a Jewish issue, apprehensive that it would create a wave of anti-Semitism. He was a loyal apologist for President Roosevelt, and was wary of confronting the president, or the "chief," as he called him. As historian Rafael Medoff says, "Roosevelt glad-handed Wise." Wise did lobby quietly to help the Jews, but he was unwilling to confront the leaders in Washington or muster American Jewry to protest US inaction to help European Jews.

It was Peter Bergson,[144] an immigrant from Palestine, who galvanized grassroots support in the Jewish community for European Jewry. He placed large ads in the major papers and staged productions lamenting their fate. He also orchestrated the Rabbis' March on Washington in 1943. Wise opposed him, appalled by what he called his "theatrics." He did everything he could to ostracize Bergson, refusing to allow major Jewish groups to cooperate with him and blocking his political access to Washington. Weiss told Bergson, "You are endangering American Jewry."[145]

Forced to bypass the Jewish liberal leaders, the Rebbe turned to the Quaker-led American Friends Service Committee,[146] which arranged an appointment with First Lady Eleanor Roosevelt.[147] In March of 1941, the Rashag led a delegation of Chabad leaders who met her in the White House. They implored Mrs. Roosevelt to intervene with the Russian government to permit the emigration of the Bobover Rebbe, Rabbi Benzion Halberstam, as well as prominent Chabad Chasidim[148] who were Polish refugees in Russia and Soviet-controlled Latvia and Lithuania. But her attempt to seek the assistance of US and Russian officials was unsuccessful. The Bobover Rebbe fled to Russian-controlled Lvov; the Germans invaded in July 1941, and the Rebbe was beaten to death by German soldiers.

The Chasidim in Riga were killed after the German invasion of Latvia. Assistant Secretary of State Breckinridge Long, who oversaw US immigration policy, did his utmost to block Jewish immigration. Each country was allotted a quota for immigration, and Long ensured that those quotas were not filled. Medoff says, "Two hundred thousand more Jews could have entered under the existing law than actually did."[149] US officials refused the pleas of Jewish leaders to divert warplanes by just a few miles to bomb Auschwitz.[150] Between the hostility of Long, the apathy of Roosevelt, the silence of the media, and the unwillingness of

Jewish leaders to challenge the administration, there was little hope for the Jews being systematically exterminated in Europe.

This caused the Rebbe much despair. In March 1943, he wrote a long, anguished letter[151] to Dr. Jacob Klatzkin,[152] a noted Jewish philosopher and activist. Klatzkin had corresponded with the Rebbe, suggesting the time had come for "Jews to march with Torah scrolls adorned with a tallis to speak out about the murder of thousands of Jews."[153] He hoped this dramatic action would wake up the public. There had been some protests in New York, but none had taken on the religious nature Klatzkin was suggesting.

The Rebbe responded that tragically, no one was interested in the plight of European Jews. The media "are sitting behind a shade," ignoring the suffering. Newspapers like *The New York Times* relegated their sparse reports of Nazi atrocities to the back pages.[154] Political leaders, the Rebbe lamented, were unwilling to act. "Their ears are closed to hearing our cries, and their eyes are shut to our rivers of tears." The Rebbe argued that throughout Jewish history, the "kindness of the nations of the world had protected the Jewish people." But even countries who had acted benevolently to the Jews in the past were oblivious to the present misery. "Now their ears are shut and their eyes are closed to the spilling of Jewish blood." The Rebbe noted that legions of diplomats were telling Jewish leaders, "'Once the war is over, we will see what we can do." He added pointedly, "There are organizations who defend the abuser of animals, but none defending the Jewish people."

The Rebbe felt that the Jewish community was sleeping, its leaders failing. Those with access to levers of power in Washington were unwilling to speak up. Instead of saving European Jews or bolstering Jewish education, they were engaged in interfaith activities. "The priests invite the rabbi to conduct a Passover Seder in their place of worship and in return the rabbi invites the priests to hear the shofar blowing and *Kol Nidrei* in the synagogue."

With all the doors closed, the Rebbe told Klatzkin that the time had come for "Jews to turn to G-d with prayer and supplications.... We must call every Jew, irrespective of party or perspective, to fasting and prayer."

The Rebbe noted to Klatzkin that members of other religions in the US were responding to the war in a spiritual manner as well. "We are living in a time when believers of faith, men, women, and children, gather at their houses of worship and turn to G-d with prayer to remove the darkness from the world." Other faith leaders had put out a call for "a day of prayer for victory." The time had come for Jews to do the same, he said, and "gather in synagogues and study halls to pray to our Father in heaven." The Rebbe quoted the High Holidays prayer, "The decree can be reversed with repentance," saying that prayer and repentance would prompt the fulfillment of G-d's promise to send the Messiah, a redeemer who would transform the world into a place of sanctity and peace.

Seven months after writing Klatzkin, the Rebbe supported the Rabbis' March on Washington, the only Jewish demonstration held at the Capitol during the war years. It was orchestrated by Peter Bergson in conjunction with Vaad Hatzalah and Agudas Harabonim three days before Yom Kippur in 1943. More than four hundred rabbis, all Orthodox, many bearded and wearing the traditional rabbinical garb, gathered at the Capitol and marched to the White House. The Rebbe, unable to travel,[155] personally selected[156] a delegation of four distinguished Chasidim to represent him. They included two of his secretaries, Dr. Nissan Mindel and Rabbi Eliyahu Quint; his close confidant and *rosh yeshivah* of the yeshivah in Brooklyn, Rabbi Zalman Gurary; and Rabbi Binyamin Levitin,[157] his personal assistant and son of Chabad elder Rabbi Shmuel Levitin.[158]

The demonstration was a dramatic move. There had been rallies for European Jews held in New York and other cities, but never had Jewish leaders marched on the White House. At the time, the Orthodox community had no organized arm for political activism or a presence in the nation's capital. Most of the rabbis who took part in the march were Yiddish-speaking European immigrants who had lived in countries where protest would bring swift government retribution.

Washington was the exclusive domain of the liberal-dominated Jewish establishment, whose leaders were opposed to the march. Samuel Roseman, a senior White House advisor and important leader of the American Jewish Committee, advised the president not to meet with the rabbis, claiming that they were "not representative of the most thoughtful elements of Jewry." Roseman also told the president that he had tried "to keep the horde from storming Washington." Reform Rabbi Stephen S. Wise publicly derided the march as an "Orthodox rabbinical parade" and a "painful and even lamentable exhibition." Ridiculing the organizers as "stuntists," he accused them of offending "the dignity of [the Jewish] people."[159] It was these types of leaders the Rebbe had chastised since his arrival in the US for their unwillingness to stand up for Jewish values, calling their behavior a "lack of Jewish pride and courage."[160]

Seven months earlier, in his letter to Klatzkin, the Rebbe had questioned the value of demonstrations – "For whom, and for what purpose?" – expressing skepticism about their effectiveness. Chasidic historian Eliezer Zaklikowski explains that despite his general wariness of demonstrations, the Rebbe supported this march because he felt that "it was a positive, constructive event with clear-cut goals and a strong expression of Jewish pride." The Rebbe also respected Rabbi Eliezer Silver, one of the prominent rabbis who led the march. "He was a fearless Jewish leader. And the rabbis were attempting to influence US policy at the highest level. They planned to see the president with a list of requests."

Dr. Mindel retained a firsthand account of the march in his personal archive. "They marched from Union Station to the Capitol, where they were met by Vice President Henry Wallace and members of Congress." Rabbi Silver read the petition, bursting out in tears in the middle. "Millions have already died, sentenced to fire and the sword," he cried. "How can we pray on the holy day of Yom Kippur knowing we have not fulfilled our responsibility? So we came brokenhearted on the eve of the holiest day, Yom Kippur, to ask President Roosevelt to form a special agency to rescue the remainder of the Jewish nation in Europe."[161] *Time* magazine reported that Wallace was uncomfortable[162] at the meeting and made no mention of rescuing any Jews.[163] From the Capitol, wrote Mindel, "they walked to the Lincoln Memorial, where they prayed for the welfare of the president."

From there, the rabbis walked to the White House. Mindel records their surprise and subsequent disillusionment when they were refused a meeting with the president. "When the rabbis reached the gates of the White House, they were stunned to be told that the president was unavailable to meet with the delegates. What the rabbis did not know was that FDR's top Jewish advisors, Wise and Roseman, told him to avoid the rabbis. FDR left the White House by a back exit. The rabbis were very disappointed." With bitterness, Mindel concludes, "It was a tragic day."

There was a silver lining. The president's refusal to meet with the rabbis created a media storm, and the attention helped raise public consciousness about the plight of European Jews. In the wake of the march, Congress held hearings calling for a US government initiative to save European Jews.[164] That prompted Roosevelt to finally act. Three months after the march, in January 1944, the president signed an order creating the War Refugee Board.[165] It saved many Jews, particularly those in Hungary. But it was too late for the more than five million Jews who had already been killed.

The Rebbe continued to work to find a way for Jews in general and his Chasidim in particular to reach places of refuge, be it the United States or other countries.[166] A few Chasidim found an avenue to the US, but the majority remained stranded in Latvia, Poland, and Lithuania, including the Rebbe's secretary Rabbi Yechezkel Feigin and Rabbi Mordechai Dubin. In June of 1940, the Russians invaded Latvia, creating additional barriers to escape. The Rebbe worked on every front to obtain visas and to assist those still in Europe. Packages and funds were smuggled from nearby neutral countries to help those who were trapped to survive.

The Rebbe seized every opportunity to help refugees. In 1940, when he learned that the Dominican Republic had become one of the few countries to open its doors to European Jews, he reached out to help.[167] When a group of Jewish youth and teens from Germany were interned[168] in camps in Canada in 1941, the Rebbe urged the newly arrived students in Montreal to make efforts to free them.[169] In 1944, when close to one thousand Jewish refugees arrived in a camp in Oswego in upstate New York, the Rebbe sprang into action.[170] Ten days after the refugees arrived, the Rebbe sent a prestigious delegation, including Rabbis Hodakov and Kazarnovsky and Dr. Mindel, to meet them and evaluate their situation. In the coming months, Chabad provided their religious needs, as well as offering educational programs and general assistance. When they were released in 1945, a group of the children enrolled in the Chabad yeshivah in Brooklyn. When the Rebbe discovered that several German Jews, including the son of the Kapischnitzer Rebbe, were being held in a refugee camp in Australia, he urged his Chasid there, Moshe Zalman Feiglin, to intervene and assist him.[171]

During the war years, the Rebbe focused on what he called his "second mission in America," transforming US Jewry. His goal, the reorientation of Jewish life toward tradition, was ambitious and unprecedented. As the seventh Rebbe pointed out some years later, "Despite his persistent medical condition, he widened his efforts to help others."[172]

At the time, Jewish education rooted in classic Torah values was limited to a small group of yeshivas centered primarily in New York. The Rebbe believed that developing a national network of Jewish schools with a curriculum of both Jewish and secular subjects[173] was essential to nurturing Jews who would have a fidelity to tradition. Those schools would not only educate children but influence their families and communities. As he made his way across the Atlantic, the Rebbe had long discussions with Rabbi Chaim Hodakov, superintendent of the Jewish schools in Latvia,[174] to design a comprehensive plan to revamp Jewish education in the US.[175] Hodakov's extensive experience in Latvia[176] would help the Rebbe establish the first national Jewish educational network in the US and Canada, upgrade Hebrew schools, and create new dynamic youth programs.

Until now, day schools and yeshivas had been local grassroots initiatives, mostly located in New York. Hebrew schools were run by local congregations with few standards of instruction. They needed a formal curriculum and trained teachers. The majority of Jewish children at the time received little to no Jewish education. In 1940, only eight thousand children attended Jewish day schools and yeshivas. There was a network of Talmud Torahs, Hebrew schools, and *chadarim* serving as supplemental educational programs for children who attended public school. These supplementary schools were populated by immigrant children. Many teachers were untrained Yiddish speakers who lacked teaching skills. They could quote the Talmud they had studied in Europe, but they had abandoned observance in the US. Instead of instilling a love for Jewish tradition, they did the opposite. "They were *maskilim*, secularists, who denied the basic principles of Jewish belief," says Avraham Hecht. The Rebbe described these schools as *treif*, nonkosher.[177]

There were initiatives for educational reform, curriculum upgrades, teacher training, and educational resources. Most of these efforts were designed to modernize Jewish education, discarding traditional values and reorienting the programs toward Jewish culture, Zionism, and history. Instead of infusing children with a love of Torah, these so-called state-of-the-art schools attempted to create a new style of Jewish identity based on culture and Jewish nationalism.[178]

In a talk to Jewish community leaders during his 1942 visit to Chicago, the Rebbe reasserted his belief that Jewish education was the key to the future.[179] "The entire religious state of the Jewish people depends on the nature of education and the guidance provided in the Talmud Torah and the yeshivah," he said. It was vital that the educators and administrators themselves be examples of Jewish observance. "Matters of Torah and Jewish education must be entrusted to steadfast G-d-fearing people." The Rebbe said that educators who are not role models "are leading children to an active rejection of their faith." He told the Chicago rabbis to exert leadership in the sphere of education. "When it comes to checking the kosher status of what may be put into kosher saucepans, there are plenty of supervisors, but when it comes to checking what may be put into the heads of little Jewish children, there are no supervisors and no stamps of approval. You rabbis bear the full responsibility for the current state of education" – which, he said, was "deplorable."

Avraham Hecht says the European-born, Yiddish-speaking rabbis "were in a haze. They had no idea how to solve the problems in America." Many of their own children did not remain observant, and they were daunted by the challenge of finding their way in a new world. "They didn't know how to make a living, they didn't speak English, they didn't understand American Jewish life."[180] The Rebbe attempted to prod the rabbis to adapt and take responsibility for the Jewish education in their communities.

While the Rebbe challenged the rabbis to assert their leadership, at times using harsh, direct language, to the teachers his tone was filled with affection. In Chicago, he told Hebrew school teachers, "You need to constantly keep in mind what treasures have been entrusted to your hands. Material treasures, gold, gems, and jewelry, are all worthless next to the priceless G-d-given gifts that the parents of these children have entrusted to your hands."[181] The Rebbe compared the role of a teacher to someone planting an orchard. "An orchardist works long and hard for many long years until he lives to see that his tender sampling has grown in a strong and healthy tree." He explained that as teachers, they were working in G-d's orchard and their responsibility was to instill proper values in their charges. "In return, the greatest moral and spiritual gratification will be yours when you see that our frail little plants have grown into big, sturdy, thickly branched trees that yield delicious fruit and beautify G-d's own orchard."

By prodding Jewish community leaders and rabbis, the Rebbe attempted to reform existing afternoon Hebrew schools. He also launched a network of Hebrew schools in New York and other cities, developed the curriculum, and expanded the ranks of teachers.

The Rebbe realized that many children would not attend yeshivah or Hebrew school, so he began an array of other programs. The largest was Released Time, a weekly after-school program, which was complemented by Mesibot Shabbat clubs and other youth programs. He published a monthly children's magazine, *Talks and Tales,* and encouraged the creation of educational materials and curriculums. The Rebbe believed that every method should be used to teach the youth. As Gershon Kranzler wrote, "everything, textbooks, fiction, magazines, even comics, whatever the other world was using to lure the Jewish child away from Jewish heritage, had to be drawn into this service." During the 1940s, more than two million items – a vast collection of books, magazines, and educational materials – were published.[182]

To implement his ambitious agenda of boosting education, the Rebbe needed manpower: teachers and educators with leadership skills who could build institutions and rabbis who could inspire. They would need the courage to stand up for Jewish values in the face of the opposition they would encounter from the Jewish establishment. A tiny group of young Americans and a few Europeans took the lead. They were the students of the burgeoning Tomchei Temimim yeshivah in New York and the young women in the Chabad community. In total, they did not amount to a more than a few dozen, but they became the Rebbe's vanguard. The immigrant yeshivah students from Poland spoke little English, had a European look, and were swimming against the cultural mainstream. The small group of Americans who had joined the yeshivah had been educated in an era in which Jews instructed their children not to flaunt their heritage. Altering the mindset of his students and Chasidim to be more strident with their Jewish identity was not easy.

The Rebbe inspired the young chasidic men and women to dedicate themselves to the mission of Jewish education. In talks, letters, and teachings, the Rebbe time and again spoke of the importance and obligation of caring for one's fellow Jews. He wrote to the yeshivah students that they must spread Jewish learning. "As you know, I require from the students of my yeshivas that they infuse the homes of Jews with the light of Torah."[183] To the students, the Rebbe was a powerful role model, having almost lost his life in Russia for sustaining a Jewish educational network under the Soviets. Avraham Hecht said, "We looked at the Rebbe like Daniel in the lions' den." They were awed by his determination and the way that nothing fazed him. "The Rebbe didn't stop."

The Rebbe's objective was to motivate the young rabbinical students to break out of their traditional role of pursuing personal academic excellence and instead become communal activists. To motivate his students, the Rebbe highlighted the mitzvah of *ahavat Yisrael* (loving one's fellow Jew) as the paramount ideal. The Rebbe modeled this in the love he showed to others and the endearment he expressed to his students. Secondly, he empowered the students to be leaders, providing them with broad directives while giving them the space to operate in their own creative fashion, expecting them to think for themselves and apply their own ingenuity to the challenges facing each community. Thirdly, he told them to seek inspiration from the students of Tomchei Temimim in Russia, who were putting their lives on the line under great oppression to sustain Jewish life there. Finally, the Rebbe reminded them that their efforts could very well be the tipping point in Jewish transformation and be the catalyst for the ultimate redemption through the coming of the Messiah.

In the early 1940s, traditional Judaism was still in fortress mode: preserve the core, guard the fort, and keep outside influences at bay. The Rebbe was taking a totally different strategy, going on the offensive with confidence.

It would be an uphill battle to change attitudes amongst his own Chasidim and in the greater Orthodox community. The younger generation being nurtured in the Rebbe's yeshivah in Brooklyn were being instilled with this idealism. However, there was an undertone of dissent amongst some of the elder Chasidim. They had grown up in Europe, where the lines between secular and religious were stronger. Some had family members who had abandoned observance, replacing it with devotion to socialism, Zionism, Communism, or other ideologies.[184] In the US, these Chasidim had children, family members, and friends who chose to assimilate. They had sacrificed everything to preserve their faith, and it rendered them defensive and somewhat insular. The Rebbe was now prodding them to look outward and engage Jews who were not observant. This was a fundamental change in mindset, and just as the Rebbe had to contend with the insecure in the broader Orthodox community, he had to overcome similar attitudes among his own Chasidim.

The Rebbe acknowledged the difficulties with the Chabad community, sharing his feelings in a poignant letter in 1943.[185] "My heart is greatly pained by *anash* who are not helping in my work – not in establishing Torah classes, the study of chasidic philosophy, the yeshivah, or the work of Merkos L'Inyonei Chinuch [organizing educational programming]. We were exiled from Lubavitch and afterward wandered from city to city and country to country." He lamented leaving a rich spiritual culture in Europe. "Close to three years ago, I left a place full of life, filled with Torah, mitzvot, and a radiant chasidic life." He contrasted that with the United States, where he said Jewish observance was superficial: "Everyone is focused on earning a livelihood." For generations, Chasidim had dedicated themselves to Torah with self-sacrifice for Jewish principles. In the US, this was proving more challenging. "Whom do I have here, and what do I have here?" the Rebbe wrote. "I fell into this sea of ice, which lacks sanctity, pureness, and an open heart. There are those who are sincerely interested in my situation, but not fully willing to help me fulfill the mission that I have in this world." He ended on a note of optimism. "Hopefully, soon my dear friends in *anash* will awaken to fulfill the responsibility they have, since G-d has brought them to this country."[186]

It was the students in the yeshivah who would take the lead. One night, they were discussing how to implement the Rebbe's vision. Avraham Hecht, just twenty years old and so bashful that he had not spoken at his own bar mitzvah, resolved to act. A week later he found himself standing at a podium in a large Brooklyn congregation, urging its members to enroll their children in a Jewish school. "The Torah teaches us that a parent must teach his child how to swim," he said. "Learning Torah gives a child the ability to navigate his way in the world. It's essential to sign up your child in a yeshivah."[187] Hecht was proud of his debut and begin going from shul to shul to spread the message.

The Rebbe dispatched yeshivah students to cities in the northeast to enroll more children. In 1940, Meyer Greenberg, a twenty-year-old American who had studied in Otwock, walked into a Scranton, Pennsylvania, synagogue and announced: "If you have children whom you would like to send to yeshivah, we will take them, tuition free. Meet me tomorrow at the train station at noon." One Hungarian immigrant, Tzipora Gross, was there with her two sons, ten-year-old Elye and nine-year-old Berel. They joined the yeshivah and celebrated their bar mitzvahs in Brooklyn.[188]

The Rebbe began to send rabbis and yeshivah students to open schools in cities outside New York. Avraham Hecht recalls, "I wanted to remain in the yeshivah and study, but the Rebbe wanted to revolutionize Jewish education elsewhere."[189] They were going into unknown and uncharted territory – never before in US Jewish history had a rabbi dispatched a cadre of young rabbis and educators to communities to set up schools. They weren't always welcome. Most Jewish parents were not interested in parochial schools. The trend was to assimilate into American culture, and the ticket to success was public school, which offered a path toward higher education and a successful career. Afternoon Hebrew schools were considered the optimal mode of Jewish education. There was little sympathy for full-time Jewish schools, which many believed would lead to greater insularity. The goal was to become mainstream Americans.

Mordechai Altein[190] was single and just twenty-two when he was summoned to the Rebbe's office on a Saturday night in December 1941.[191] The Rebbe had received a letter from the president of the Nusach Ari Congregation in Pittsburgh asking for help in finding a new rabbi. "I want you to go there tomorrow morning," the Rebbe told the surprised Altein. "Can't it wait a week until after the nineteenth of Kislev?"[192] Altein asked. "No," said the Rebbe. "Leave immediately. I will send them a message that you are coming." The next day was Sunday, December 7. On the train, Altein heard the news of the Japanese attack on Pearl Harbor. No one at the congregation knew he was coming. A few days later, he discovered the Rebbe's unopened telegram in the synagogue.

Altein took a trolley across town to the home of the synagogue's president to introduce himself. He thought Altein was a fundraiser and was astonished to learn that his letter to the Rebbe had prompted the appearance of this young bearded rabbi, ready to work. A debate was raging about the congregation's future. The neighborhood had changed, and most Jews had moved out. The president was considering relocating the congregation to a new area and possibly following the trend of the time, affiliating with the Conservative movement. Altein reported the controversy to the Rebbe, resulting in his intervention. The Rebbe wrote to Yaakov Schiff, one of the synagogue's religious members, "I have sent my student Rabbi Altein to examine the situation closely and explore options such as moving to another area."[193] Not only did the Rebbe want the synagogue to remain Orthodox, he also had bigger ideas. He instructed Altein, "Once you settle the issues with the synagogue, you should begin to consider establishing a *yeshivah ketanah* (elementary-level yeshivah)."[194]

By Chanukah, Altein had opened a Hebrew school and enrolled some of the local children. In the coming months, the Rebbe directed the establishment of a local branch of Agudas Chassidei Chabad to plot a new direction for the synagogue.[195] Altein continued to expand the programs, starting a Mesibot Shabbat club for children on Shabbat afternoons. With time, Altein returned to New York, where he was instrumental in setting up other schools, including a yeshivah in the Bronx.

In 1943, matters took a leap forward when the Rebbe sent Rabbi Sholom Posner[196] to Pittsburgh. Posner was a Russian refugee who had studied in the yeshiva in Lubavitch. After marrying, he moved to Palestine and then to the US in 1930, settling in Chicago, where he served as the sexton in a local synagogue. A business opportunity arose, and he traveled to New York to seek the Rebbe's advice.[197] The Rebbe had other ideas, telling him, "There's so much work to be done in America and I have so few people to do it. Better go to Pittsburgh and set up a school."

Posner was forty-two. His mother tongue was Yiddish, his English was sparse, and he had no experience in running a school.[198] Leaving his wife Chaya and children in Chicago, he headed to Pittsburgh. Noticing his absence, a synagogue member asked his wife where he'd gone. She responded that he was in Pittsburgh to open a yeshivah. Surprised, the man told her, "Hair will grow on my palm before there is a yeshivah in Pittsburgh."

Jewish leaders in Pittsburgh were not very welcoming. "We already have shuls and kosher businesses," they said. "Why should we open a yeshivah in Pittsburgh when there are bigger cities without one?" Local Orthodox rabbis were opposed, fearing the new yeshivah would draw children away from their congregational Hebrew schools. The Jews of Pittsburgh were rushing down the road of assimilation. They were not interested in a rabbi adorned in European chasidic garb who reminded them of the world they had left behind. When Chaya Posner joined her husband, they had a hard time renting an apartment in the Jewish neighborhood. "People [Jews] did not want to rent to a religious Jew with a beard," she recalled.

Unfazed, Posner hit the streets, going door to door to register students. He later recalled this as "the most difficult part." With his long rabbinic coat and his European look, he found it difficult to attract the of the local Jews. He wrote to the Rebbe repeatedly about his difficulties. He responded, "You dig a hole and plant seeds, and I will water it with my tears."[199]

Posner's planting and the Rebbe's tears began to bear fruit when, finally, Posner was able to enroll five children. One was Kehos Weiss, whose parents were impressed with Posner's sincerity. "My parents agreed – not only because they wanted a Jewish education [for me], but because they admired Rabbi Posner's persistence," Weiss said. The children were of different ages and in five different grades. Posner put them in one class and taught them all on assorted levels. By the end of the year, there were twenty-seven students. With this growth came the need for money. Posner had never raised a dime in his life. "There was no financial support from New York. I had teachers to pay, and for three months I hesitated to fundraise." With no choice, he began to ask local Jews for help. With time, Posner cultivated supporters, and the yeshivah continued to grow. They soon purchased a home to house the small school. By 1950, it boasted one hundred students.[200]

Avraham Hecht and his five brothers[201] were also part of the first cadre of activists the Rebbe drafted. They were American boys, brash, outspoken, and articulate. Avraham graduated from yeshivah in 1942.

He wanted to study longer, but "the Rebbe wanted us to go out to open yeshivas." The Rebbe told him, "In wartime, even a private can become a general. When the general gets shot, the private steps up."

At twenty, Avraham was sent to Worcester to start a yeshivah. "We met with the local rabbi and used his shul. Things were rough in the beginning. We started with just one kid." Shortly afterward, in 1942, his newly married brother Moshe and his bride Rivkah[202] came to Worcester as well. She grew up in Boston, where she was the only religious girl in the city, and graduated from the Hebrew Teachers College there. She recalls, "I was pushed right into education. We knew the Rebbe was not going to sit still and whatever the Rebbe said, we were going to get it done."[203]

The Rebbe continued to send out his students. At times there was a local request; other times the rabbi would simply arrive and drum up support. Except for Posner, they were all young men in their early twenties who had studied in Brooklyn. They were full of passion, empowered by the mission the Rebbe entrusted them with.

In Buffalo, Hershel Fogelman started a school with just a few children. The same story happened in Rochester, Philadelphia, and a dozen other cities. Young women were enlisted to teach. As the young rabbis married, their wives shared in the leadership of the schools. Yitzchok Groner was sent to Buffalo, Tzvi Shusterman to Rochester, and Hershel Fogelman soon moved to Worcester. In city after city, the Rebbe opened one yeshivah after another. Alongside the yeshivas, girls schools were opened.[204] When the Rebbe received a request to open a school in California, he responded that he hoped to reach that area in the future.

Rivkah Hecht says, "We were the pioneers."[205] After a few years in Worcester, she and her husband Moshe moved to New Haven, Connecticut, where they started a school with just four students. "The locals knew little of Yiddishkeit. There were shuls with old Yiddish-speaking European rabbis who could not connect to American Jews." The Rebbe was sending the opposite: young American rabbis. "Our arrival was a turning point for the community." Moshe "had a beard but he spoke in English. He wowed them." And it wasn't just the families; "students from Yale also came." The Rebbe was concerned with their progress and "wanted to know how everything was getting on." He corresponded regularly with the Hechts. "I have tons of letters," Rivkah said.

The Rebbe supported Released Time, the program that permitted public school students to leave school for one hour a week for religious instruction. The program had been active in many states since 1914, but it was only approved in New York in 1940.[206] Rabbi Chaim Tzvi Konikov observed Christian groups offering religious instruction for public school children for an hour a week, and he started a program of his own for Jewish children in his Brooklyn synagogue. Konikov informed the Rebbe, who seized on the idea, viewing it as an opportunity to reach out to Jewish children who were not receiving any Jewish education.[207] The Rebbe directed the newly established Merkos L'Inyonei Chinuch to organize the program for students in New York public schools. "A law has been established that one hour a week, on Wednesdays, children are released from school at 2:00 p.m. instead of 3:00 p.m. to attend religious instruction."[208] He detailed the conditions: Instruction was not permitted to take place on public school grounds, so the children needed to be transported to nearby synagogues. Parental permission was required, and the teachers were responsible for the children getting home afterward.

Merkos created a special division, the National Committee for the Furtherance of Jewish Education (NCFJE), to coordinate the program. The youngest Hecht brother, Yankel, was one of the first teachers at age eighteen – and he soon became the program's director. Within a year, three thousand children attended weekly. Three years later, the number doubled to six thousand, and the National Committee announced its goal of reaching ten thousand. Students and volunteers from yeshivas and Jewish high schools were enlisted to teach. It was a daunting administrative challenge to coordinate the hundreds of teachers at multiple venues throughout the five boroughs. Teachers' Guides were created with lesson plans that included stories from our sages, Torah, history, and traditions. The National Committee hosted large fundraising dinners to cover the costs.

Until this point, only Christian groups had operated Released Time programs. The Rebbe's creation of a Jewish program sparked opposition by New York's Jewish leaders. *Jewish Life* reported, "Orthodox groups feared it would undermine the already low standard of Jewish education."[209] Critics complained that just one hour of religious instruction a week would have limited impact. Some rabbis worried that parents might abandon synagogue Hebrew schools, an important source of members and income, because of the free one-hour-a-week program. Liberal Jews were staunchly opposed to what they considered a breach of the separation of church and state. Reform leaders declared that it would "jeopardize the very basis of American life."[210] The American Jewish Congress lamented that Released Time "creates antagonism among students of various faiths and violates the principle of separation of church and state."[211] Jewish groups, such as the ADL, American Jewish Congress, and the American Jewish Committee, didn't just issue press releases; they backed a lawsuit against Released Time.[212] But the US Supreme Court rejected their arguments that government was supporting religion, ruling in favor of Released Time.[213]

The Rebbe was unbothered by the critics. To him, the burning issue remained the large numbers of Jewish children who were still receiving little or no Jewish education. As the Rebbe wrote to the organizers of Released Time, "Thousands of Jewish children could have been lost to Judaism, but you have brought the warmth of Yiddishkeit into thousands of homes, to parents and to children."[214] Certainly, the Rebbe would have preferred that all Jewish children attend full-time Jewish schools, but understanding that this was unrealistic, he created multiple options for children at all levels of observance.

In 1942, Yitzchok Groner and Moshe Kazarnovsky were asked to organize a children's parade on the intermediate days of Passover in Crown Heights. Rabbi Hodakov told them that the children should hold placards urging people to observe Jewish traditions. They did so, leading three hundred children down busy Eastern Parkway, which was lined with tall apartment buildings full of Jewish residents who often sat and socialized on the benches that adorned the broad parkway. "The benches were packed with Jews," Groner remembers. The Rebbe watched the parade from his second-floor window as it passed by his residence. The Ramash told Groner that the Rebbe was enthusiastic about the parade's success.[215] This parade represented a change in mindset: Judaism should not be limited to the synagogue or home, but celebrated publicly. The Passover parade was a precursor to the Lag BaOmer parades that the seventh Rebbe began in the early 1950s. They have now become the norm in Jewish communities worldwide.[216]

The Rebbe's educational strategy was innovative, part of a new paradigm that would mold Chabad in the decades to come. First, the Rebbe inspired young men and women to dedicate their lives to securing a Jewish future, placing his full confidence in these young Jewish leaders. This was far different from the Russian experience, where his Chasidim were steeped in decades of rich religious tradition as graduates of the intellectual and spiritual experience of the yeshivah in Lubavitch. In Russia, they were fighting to preserve tradition. In the US, they were going against the mainstream that promoted assimilation. The Rebbe pushed his students to be outgoing, positive, self-confident, and innovative. He had great trust in the young. The Rebbe once remarked about two of the Hecht brothers, "With Avraham and Yankel, I can take over all of America."[217] He believed in his students and empowered them to become Jewish leaders.

Secondly, the Rebbe insisted that each school develop its own base of local supporters. He saw his young emissaries as entrepreneurs, building partnerships with local Jews. The Rashag, based in Brooklyn, was director of the yeshivah system. He did offer some funds, but it wasn't enough to cover the growing budgets in over a dozen cities. Chabad's system of fundraising, encouraging partnership between the *shliach* and his local community, was starting to form.

Thirdly, the Rebbe was not deterred by critics. He was an innovator. When others said, "That's not the way we do things" or "We must not cross the separation of church and state," the Rebbe forged forward. When it came to saving Jewish youth from assimilation, he remained focused on the goal.

Finally, the Rebbe would not change tradition to suit the whims of the time. His motto, "America is no different," asserted that traditional Judaism could flourish in the new world, a concept that ran counter to the dominant mentality. The liberal Jewish movements were experiencing their greatest growth as they made changes to Jewish tradition, modernizing Judaism. The Orthodox were in free fall, losing members; the timid leadership was anxious about saving its core. The Rebbe described America as a "*medinah shel chesed*," a county of kindness, grace, and opportunity. He believed that you did not have to give up your identity to succeed. You could simultaneously be a proud Jew and a proud

American. He urged his students not to discard their traditional appearance – to grow beards, dress as Chasidim, and celebrate their unique traditions – and at the same time take part in the society that offered them freedom and opportunity.

Few grasped the broad vision of the Rebbe. The small, insecure Orthodox world would take decades to develop self-confidence and place outreach as an important value.[218] Rivkah Hecht, one of the Rebbe's pioneers, noted, "We knew the Rebbe was not going to sit still. The Orthodox world could not understand him."[219] In time, Orthodox communities would come to see the success of his path and emulate it. One of those first steps was in 1944, when Torah Umesorah, a new Orthodox initiative led by Rabbi Shraga Feivel Mendlowitz, took the first tentative steps toward opening day schools. Instead of being upset by the "competition," the Rebbe was pleased that others were waking up to the value of such endeavors.

Encouraging the yeshivah students and young women to become activists contrasted with the approach of the Lithuanian-style yeshivas in the US. They argued that the pursuit of Jewish knowledge was the highest ideal, while the Rebbe prioritized arresting the trend of assimilation. These differing approaches for securing a Jewish future reflected the different strategies taken two decades earlier in Russia. When Communism attempted to destroy religious life, the Lithuanian yeshivas abandoned the country to preserve Jewish scholarship. The Rebbe, however, remained in Russia, putting his life on the line for the welfare of all Jews. Now again in the US, the same debate emerged. Underlying it was the question of how Jews should respond to the freedoms of modernity: Was it better to withdraw into insular communities or to engage the broader society? Chasidic philosophy argues that the purpose of a Jew is to reveal the potential sanctity in the world around him. In contrast, the yeshivas[220] stressed protecting oneself from negative influences. In the decades to come, these varied ideologies would each offer its vision for the future of traditional Judaism in the US and around the world.

Unfortunately, liberal Jewish communities, which dominated the American Jewish landscape in the midcentury, failed to see the value of Jewish day schools for many years. They resisted investing communal funds in schools and ardently opposed government funding of any sort, claiming it would infringe on the separation of church and state. The opposition was rooted in the belief that the key to Jewish success was integration into society, and the public school system was the avenue for that aspiration. Yeshivas and day schools would only push Jews inward and limit their options for higher education and employment opportunities. The Rebbe rejected all those ideas and created a model that would be emulated in time by all segments of the Jewish community.

At this point, Chabad was a sideshow in Brooklyn, its numbers small and its influence negligible. Few could imagine that the network of schools and educational programs the Rebbe launched during the war years would be just the first steps in a broad vision to change the course of US Jewry. After the Rebbe's passing, his successor, the seventh Rebbe, would take his vision to new levels in the second half of the twentieth century. The foundation for the change that would blossom into a global Jewish renaissance was the Rebbe's pioneering of Jewish education in the early 1940s. There is no question that many other Orthodox groups made important contributions to the rebirth of traditional Judaism in the US. But it was the Rebbe's declaration of "*America iz nisht andersh*" when he stepped foot on US soil that was the turning point. He reversed the course of Orthodox defensiveness, instead going on the offensive. He was an innovator, doing things that others thought were impossible but later ended up emulating.

Between 1940 and 1950, ninety-seven Jewish schools opened in the US, a dramatic increase from the twenty-eight that had opened in the previous twenty-two years.[221] One-third of these ninety-seven schools were started by the Rebbe,[222] mostly during the war years. His pioneering efforts showed that schools could flourish not just in the bastions of Orthodoxy in Brooklyn, but also in less traditional and smaller communities. His efforts also revealed that families could be swayed to leave public schools. Additionally, the Rebbe's system of developing local financial support showed that American Jews were willing to invest in day school education.

When it came to revitalizing Jewish life, the Rebbe was not only focused on advancing the work of Chabad. His scope was far-reaching; he sought to encourage any group that could enhance tradition. At times he challenged other organizations to broaden their horizons, even stepping in to help when they faced moments of crisis. This began immediately with the Rebbe's landing on US shores. On Purim, less than a week after he disembarked, the Rebbe appealed to Rabbi Dr. Leo Jung[223] to help complete a new *mikveh* in Manhattan. Rabbi Joseph Lookstein had visited the Rebbe a few days before and told him the project had stalled. The Rebbe asked Jung, who had previously championed creating ascetically pleasing *mikvehs* in the US, to help. "Everything must be done to finish the *mikveh* as soon as possible," he wrote. "You will be blessed with much goodness, physically and spiritually."[224]

At times, the Rebbe even intervened to assist those who could be seen as his competitors.[225] During the war,[226] America's flagship yeshivah, Torah Vodaath, faced a major financial crisis. Salaries were late, the yeshivah was in debt, and the mortgage was in arrears. The bank gave the yeshivah a deadline: It had three weeks to bring the payments current or the property would be seized, rendering the yeshivah homeless. This threat was a breaking point for Rabbi Shraga Feivel Mendlowitz. He simply saw no way to obtain the funds before the deadline.

Years later, in a speech at Torah Vodaath in 1958, the *rosh yeshivah*, Rabbi Shmuel Kuselewitz,[227] described the looming catastrophe.[228] Mendlowitz, who had dedicated his life to the yeshivah, was distraught and keeping the gravity of the situation to himself. "He felt that because of him, Torah Vodaath was going to be closed." He placed appeals in newspapers, but little money came in, and the deadline was getting closer. One day, he was surprised to receive a phone call from the Rebbe's office inquiring about the situation.[229] "I didn't want to share the yeshivah's precarious state with anyone," Mendlowitz disclosed years later.[230] "I dismissed the Rebbe by saying that everything was in order." A few hours later, the Rebbe's office rang again, and the secretary insisted that he reveal the true gravity of the crisis. "I had no reason to think the Lubavitcher Rebbe's financial state was better than mine. I certainly didn't think he could help me. Finally, after the secretary's repeated requests, I told him of the yeshivah's plight and about the contents of the letter I received from the bank." The Rebbe's secretary relayed a message of encouragement from the Rebbe: "In my day, no yeshivah will be closed – not in Russia and not in America." As the deadline neared, the Rebbe's office called repeatedly for updates.

Things remained bleak. The funds were due on a Monday, Mendlowitz recalled. "The Friday before, the Rebbe's secretariat called again, asking to whom the money had to be paid and how. I was utterly appalled by this meddling, but out of respect I gave them all the information they requested." On Monday, Mendlowitz says, "I sat hopelessly in my office, resigned to the fact that in another few hours the bank officials would arrive and close the yeshivah." That's when he heard a knock on the door. Standing there was the Rebbe's emissary with an envelope. Rabbi Shmuel Kuselewitz recalled the words of the messenger:

> The Rebbe asked that before I give you this envelope, I advise you of some facts: When he was in Russia, he had to fight against the strongest country in the world so that the Torah would not be extinguished. The biggest tyrant in the world was Joseph Stalin, and the Rebbe paid no attention to him. Whoever needed help in order to strengthen Torah, he helped them. He didn't ask if the recipient was Chabad or not. Whatever they needed – a *mikveh*, a kosher butcher, a teacher – he tried to supply it. He did whatever he could so the light of Torah would not be extinguished. His emissaries were caught, shot, and killed, and he then supported their orphans and widows. And still he would send another person to replace the one who perished. And now divine providence has brought him to the United States of America where there is freedom of religion, and he is pained to learn that a major yeshivah with thousands of students is going to be closed – not because Stalin in Russia wants to get rid of Judaism, but because the Jews in America don't care. This the Rebbe cannot abide. He is willing to put his own movement in danger – because he also has debts to repay – but he is giving you a check for the whole amount you need, in order that the Torah not be extinguished. Please repay it as soon as possible, because everything the Rebbe has built up is now in danger.

The money was eventually repaid, but as Kuselewitz pointed out, "When he gave it, he could not have been sure that that would happen. That's real self-sacrifice."

This was not the only time the Rebbe interceded to save a Jewish school from financial woes. In 1946, the Hebrew Parochial School faced a financial crisis. Established in 1942 in Chicago's West Side, it would evolve into one of the city's premier Jewish schools, the Arie Crown Hebrew Day School.[231] When it opened, the Rebbe urged his Chicago followers to support the new school. He also sent "the pedagogical expert with extensive experience in the field of education, Rabbi Chaim Hodakov" to help organize the school.[232] Chabad rabbis including Zalman Posner taught there. Just a few years after it opened, there was no money to pay the mortgage, and a board meeting was called to discuss closing the school. Yankel Katz, a Chabad follower, was on the board. Two years earlier, the Rebbe had written to him, "You should use your influence to benefit the school."[233] The idea of giving up and closing troubled Katz, who told his fellow board members that the Rebbe had supported the school. "We can't do anything without first contacting the Rebbe. I will call him." There was no phone in the meeting room, so Katz collected quarters from the board members and headed outside to the nearest payphone. Avraham Reese, another board member, says the Rebbe asked how much money was needed, what time the meeting had started that night, and what the address of the school was. He then instructed Katz: "Set a meeting for tomorrow night at the same time and everything will be taken care of." The board members "were confused, wondering what's going to happen tomorrow." Despite their skepticism, they agreed to come back again. The next night, as Reese opened the gate to the building, he was surprised to see a group of obviously affluent people waiting there. Thinking they might be attending another event in the building, he asked, "Why are you here? Is there a wedding happening tonight?" They answered, "We came for the meeting." They explained that they had been contacted by the Rebbe and asked to help. "The Rebbe called in his favors," they said. The meeting started, and "within a couple of minutes the problem was solved" as they pledged the funds needed.[234]

The Rebbe even intervened to bolster institutions whose worldview differed from his own. He worked behind the scenes to ensure that Rabbi Yosef Dov Soloveitchik[235] would be appointed *rosh yeshivah* of Yeshiva University.[236] In 1941, Rabbi Moshe Soloveichik passed away, having served as *rosh yeshivah* since 1929. A leading candidate to succeed him was his son Rabbi Yosef Dov, then a rabbi in Boston. He had graduated from the University of Berlin with a degree in philosophy and was considered a world-class talmudic scholar. The young Soloveitchik and the Ramash became friends[237] when they studied together in Berlin.[238] The Rebbe became acquainted with Soloveitchik when he visited his daughter and son-in-law in Berlin.[239]

The board of Yeshiva University was divided on this appointment. Rabbi Dr. Aaron Rakeffet, Soloveitchik's biographer,[240] says, "It was the Rebbe who sealed the deal." The Rebbe wrote a letter[241] to officials at Yeshiva University saying, "It is my hope that the great, excellent, and renowned *gaon,*[242] Rabbi Yosef Dov Soloveitchik, be selected to sit in his father's position." His appointment would "restore the school's former glory." His son, Dr. Haym Soloveitchik, says,[243] "The Rebbe was the deciding factor in my father getting the job." One of the board members was Abraham Mazer, a supporter of the Rebbe. "The Rebbe called him to ask him to support my father." Once the board appointed Soloveitchik, the Rebbe sent him a long letter of congratulations in which he recalled the bond between his grandfather, Rabbi Chaim Soloveitchik, and the Rebbe's father, the Rashab.[244]

The Rebbe encouraged other Jewish groups to raise their horizons and expand them. The Rebbe met the leadership of Young Israel, the budding network of synagogues targeting younger Jews, just before the holidays in 1942. A few weeks later he wrote to them, encouraging them to push ahead on a project "to increase programs for younger people in cities beyond New York." When Young Israel's president, Irving (Simcha) Bunim, lamented to the Rebbe about the difficulties of Jewish leadership, the Rebbe responded with a long, inspiring letter. "G-d has given you the opportunity to be involved in communal leadership," he wrote. The Rebbe told him he should not complain, but rather approach the challenges "with a heart of happiness and joy," adding that "G-d will give you success in the material and spiritual."[245]

In a long personal missive to Palestine's Chief Rabbi Isaac Herzog, the Rebbe advised him to remain above politics. "My deeply honored friend should not stand with any political party. He should express the opinion of the Torah in all his statements." The Rebbe encouraged Herzog to stand up for Jewish spiritual values for Jewish people the world over. At the time, most Zionist leaders in Israel were secular and antagonistic to traditional Judaism. The Rebbe cautioned Herzog "that it is painful to see the desecration of the sacred" and warned him about being manipulated due to his "deep humility."[246]

The Rebbe intervened in Jewish affairs both in the US and globally. He did not fear raising his voice if Jewish values were being trampled on or if Jews were at risk. When the Rebbe discovered the poor quality of prayer books used by American soldiers, he created a new prayer book with English translation. Even seemingly smaller things would prompt the Rebbe to speak up. When he became aware that the Jewish Welfare Board organized a non-kosher Purim party at a US military base, he strongly protested.[247]

Other issues had broader implications. In 1943, more than one thousand Polish refugee children arrived in Palestine. Known as the Children of Tehran, they were primarily from religious families, had made the long trek overland via Russia, and ended up in Iran.[248] From there, they were brought to *Eretz Yisrael* by the quasi-government Jewish Agency, controlled by the Mapai (Labor Zionist) Party. Mapai leaders like Yaakov Uri saw these children as future supporters. As he said, "these children are not only an object of rescue, but also one of the cornerstones of our future" – a future that was secular and socialist. Mapai ensured that they would abandon their religious roots by placing them on secular kibbutzim without religious teachers, kosher food, or Shabbat observance. According to a 1950 Government Commission of Inquiry,[249] "The youth leaders were not religiously observant. They showed no interest in developing a religious aura and lifestyle."[250]

The forced secular indoctrination of the children alarmed Orthodox leaders. The Gerrer Rebbe[251] requested that the Rebbe raise the alarm amongst American Jews. The Rebbe immediately requested that Orthodox groups publicly call "to transfer the children to a proper educational environment."[252] Two weeks before Passover 1943, the Rebbe issued a letter printed in Jewish newspapers protesting the actions of the Jewish Agency.[253] Zionist officials refused to budge.[254] Chief Rabbi Herzog cabled US rabbis, writing, "For two months I have waged a bitter battle against Jewish Agency."[255] The Rebbe organized a petition of over four hundred American rabbis in support of Rabbi Herzog.[256] The Jewish

Agency was intractable, rejecting calls to transfer the children to a religious environment. In August, the Rebbe convened US rabbis and outlined a series of proposals including an international ban of donations to the Jewish Agency and public denunciation in all synagogues, "unless the Jewish Agency agrees to the request of Chief Rabbi Herzog."[257] In some countries,[258] rabbis indeed began the boycott. With mounting controversy, the Jewish Agency acquiesced, permitting the children to transfer to religious schools.[259]

In 1942, the JDC began assisting Polish Jewish refugees who had fled the German invasion into Russia.[260] The US and Russia had become allies, and sensing an opportunity, the Rebbe turned to the JDC to include Russian Jews. "Nothing is being sent to help Russian Jews for Passover,"[261] he wrote to them, requesting that the organization allocate $100,000 ($2,000,000 today) for Passover needs. The JDC was uniquely poised "as a nonpartisan group whose purpose is for all Jews, irrespective of party or affiliation." The Rebbe suggested a two-track approach: First, create a coalition of all US Jewish groups to urge the Russian ambassador in Washington, Maxim Litvinov, "that American Jews wish to help their brethren in Russia." Second, he wanted to lobby US officials who had close ties to the ambassador.[262] He believed that Litvinov could be swayed to prevail on the Russian government – "because he values their opinion" – to permit humanitarian aid for Russian Jews. Despite pressure from the Rebbe, the JDC chose not to lobby Washington officials or create a coalition. Instead, they sufficed with sending a telegram directly to Moscow asking for permission to aid Russian Jews. When Moscow rejected the request, the Rebbe bemoaned the situation, saying the perfunctory Russian refusal "was just an excuse" and claiming that if he had approached the Russian ambassador in Washington, he could have secured permission. With Passover coming and nothing accomplished, the Rebbe wrote bitterly to one of his close followers, "It pains me when I see that all the efforts will not bring any result,"[263] adding that the JDC had failed its mandate as the global Jewish responder and was "an embarrassment to the Jewish people."

Europe was flooded with refugees in the postwar period. The Rebbe worked in partnership with the JDC to assist the families, encouraging the organization to provide kosher food in camps in Italy and other locations.

In 1947, the JDC sponsored twenty-seven Chabad *shochtim* (certified kosher slaughterers) who were sent to Ireland to create a kosher meat production plant to provide kosher meat to refugees in Europe.[264]

The Rebbe's health had been precarious for some time. After the High Holidays in 1944, he began to feel discomfort around his heart.[265] The Rebbe was visited regularly by a cardiologist, who instructed him to curtail his schedule and take time to rest. A few days later, the Rebbe wrote, "I am suffering from pain around the heart and my speech is difficult." The doctors ordered more rest. The Rebbe followed the doctors' orders, writing in his diary, "I have been resting for four hours, a shame the waste of time. May G-d send me a full recovery." Despite the discomfort, the Rebbe continued to answer letters and receive visitors. In the coming weeks, the Rebbe wrote of pain and exhaustion, further curtailing his activities. The Rebbe confided to Rabbi Yaakov Yisrael Twerski, "The doctors have ordered me to absolute rest." Still, his spirits were up as he saw "phenomenal success in spiritual matters."[266] On November 10, the Rebbe issued a brief letter to the general Chabad community, in which he wrote, "Upon the orders of physicians to rest from receiving people, I will answer only by correspondence."[267]

Despite these precautions, two days later the Rebbe suffered a heart attack,[268] triggered by receiving a letter that detailed how the Nazis had murdered the Jews of Riga.[269] Among those killed were some of the Rebbe's closest Chasidim, including Reb Itche der Masmid, Rabbi Mordechai Cheifetz, Rabbi Yechezkel Feigin, and others. According to the report, they were locked in a synagogue and burned to death.[270]

For the next three weeks, the Rebbe rested and slowly regained his strength. Writing to his Chasidim the day before Chanukah, he said, "I would like to thank G-d above for His abundant goodness." He explained that he had suffered "greatly in the last few weeks," but the worst was over. In beautiful poetic prose, the Rebbe thanked his Chasidim and dear friends for their "prayers, efforts to spread Torah, and good wishes." He ended the letter with a prayer for "our brothers and sisters at war in the air, sea, and land, who need the mercy of Heaven to protect them."[271]

After a further period of rest, the Rebbe slowly returned to his regular schedule. By late December, he was feeling better. "After a break of six weeks that I was ill, I was able to sit in my office and review books. I am still feeling weak. May G-d give me the strength to have success in my work in spreading Torah and instilling a G-d-fearing spirit, strengthening Judaism with proper education, teaching chasidic philosophy, and recording my memoirs."[272] Many of the letters he sent during the winter months were dictated to his secretary and signed "in the name of the Rebbe." The Rebbe also wrote chasidic discourses during this period and spent more time in Torah study. "I spent four hours today learning. From 7:00 p.m. till now, I was involved in composing the *maamar Lech Lecha*," he wrote in his diary.[273]

During the winter months, as the Rebbe was slowly recovering, he wrote a long letter[274] to the teachers and rabbis in the network of schools and yeshivas. The missive was designed to inspire them to the "highest degree of *mesirat nefesh* (self-sacrifice) to disseminate the study of Torah." Always a storyteller, the Rebbe included the stories of three Chasidim and contrasted their modes of divine service: The first was Rabbi Nachman Zalman, who in the nineteenth century would make a spiritual pilgrimage to Rabbi Menachem Mendel in Lubavitch and spend his entire day, from early morning to late at night, in Torah study, prayer, and meditation. The other two Chasidim were Rabbis Yosef Hillel and Shmuel Chaim. Yosef Hillel had been taught by the elder Chasidim that an individual's goal should be to inspire others. Rabbi Shmuel Chaim had been sent by the Rebbe's grandfather, Rabbi Shmuel, to the town of Lutzin, where he "excelled in his educational task" and after a few years "transformed the local townsmen." The Rebbe explained that his father had told him about these Chasidim, and he contrasted the service of Reb Nachman Zalman, "which focused on the individual," with that of Yosef Hillel and Shmuel Chaim, "which focused on the public." Each mode has its advantages, but the Rebbe appealed to the educators and rabbis to emulate the approach of Yosef Hillel and Shmuel Chaim. He explained that each person needed to create a "vessel" for blessings in his life. "That vessel is *mesirat nefesh*. After all, the true meaning of a Chasid is the ability to forgo one's own spiritual ego for the sake of another's welfare."

The worldview articulated in the letter represented the Rebbe's effort to create a paradigm shift in the attitudes within the Chabad community and beyond during the war years. He urged the rabbis and educators to be role models. "If his personal conduct is upright and springs from positive character traits such as *ahavat Yisrael* (love of others), the merits of the public are attributed to him," he wrote. Other voices in the Orthodox community were arguing that the key to changing America was by creating a small cadre of outstanding scholars who would have a trickledown effect on the broader Jewish community. The Rebbe, while giving great value to Jewish scholarship, felt that the crisis of assimilation was extremely acute and more proactive measures were needed. This mirrored the teachings of Rabbi Israel Baal Shem Tov, the founder of Chasidism, which highlighted the innate value of every single Jew. The Rebbe wanted to reach out to the simple Jew, uplift him, and reconnect him to his heritage. This, he believed, was the best strategy to transform American Jewry.

Slowly, the Rebbe's vision was gaining steam. In 1945, Harold Berman wrote in the *Toronto Hebrew Journal* that the dominant force in US Jewry had been the Conservative and Reform movements. "Both accented Americanism and the need for a thorough integration with it."[275] Berman attended the fifth anniversary dinner for the Chabad yeshivas "at the fashionable Hotel Plaza in the heart of the city of New York." He sensed that the event represented a change in direction for American Jewry when he saw the hotel's "swank lobby filled with a type of guest new to them." He explained that in the past, one could expect that the Yiddish-speaking religious Jew would come to America and slowly lose his identity, that those who remained Orthodox were just in a "transition period phenomenon, and that outer husk would gradually be peeled away." Berman says the advent of Chabad obligates us "to reckon with a changed perspective." He wondered what kind of American Jewy would exist in the next century. That elegant evening in the hotel was a "glimpse at that ecstatic gathering, a Poland in miniature, transplanted on American soil." He forecasted that the Rebbe's approach of recreating old-world Judaism on American soil was the "secret of Jewish survival written in large letters."

With the war coming to an end and peace on the horizon, a new set of challenges loomed. As the allies liberated the concentration camps, the full horror of the Holocaust was coming to light. Jewish refugees were emerging from the conflict, looking to restart their lives, many seeking to flee Europe for America, *Eretz Yisrael*, and other countries. In the postwar era, Jews became even more comfortable in America. The anti-Semitism of the 1920s and 1930s was fading as Jews fought alongside their fellow citizens, boosting their sense of belonging in the US. Postwar Jewry also began a massive shift to the suburbs, leaving behind the close-knit Jewish community that flourished in Brooklyn and other cities. As these new communities developed, they sparked a boom in the liberal movements; the newer generation loosened their ties with Orthodoxy even more than their parents had. In Palestine, the struggle for independence presented a new set of challenges as conflict with the British Mandate heated up and refugees made their way to *Eretz Yisrael*. Behind Russia's Iron Curtain, millions of Jews, including thousands of the Rebbe's Chasidim, were still being denied the freedom to live full Jewish lives. Weary of decades of Communist oppression, they yearned to escape the harsh regime.

The Rebbe, still suffering from frail health, would have to adapt to the emerging patterns and set the direction for his community and the Jewish people in a world that had been rocked by over half a decade of global conflict. In the postwar era, the Rebbe would broaden his horizons again, setting new sights and laying the foundation for the global rebirth of Jewish life.

Chapter Eleven

A Global Vision

It was May 1945. The war had finally ended in Europe, and the Japanese would surrender four months later. Word of the magnitude of the tragedy that had befallen Europe's Jews was beginning to cross the ocean as people discovered the scope of the Nazis' final solution. In his office, the Rebbe sat gazing at pictures of his Chasidim whose lives had been snuffed out by the Nazis. They included some of his most devoted followers, Rabbis Yechezkel "Chatche" Feigin, Yitzchak "Itche der Masmid" Horowitz, and others. Uncontrollable tears flowed from the Rebbe's eyes as he looked at their faces. And these were just the people whose deaths were known – the fate of his daughter Sheina and her husband was still a mystery. Alarmed at her father's heartbroken weeping, the Rebbe's daughter called Rabbi Shmuel Levitin. He tried to console the Rebbe, but his efforts proved fruitless. Then Rabbi Moshe Chaim Yehoshua Schneersohn-Twerski[1] was summoned. A distant relative and a close confidant of the Rebbe, as well as a naturally upbeat, joyous person, he was finally able to lift the Rebbe's mood.

The postwar ushered in a whole new series of challenges for the Rebbe. Around the globe, survivors and refugees were looking to restart their lives. Their families and communities were in shatters. Poland, the prewar heart of European Jewish life, was now a graveyard, Jewish homes and businesses seized by the Poles. When Jews returned to reclaim their property, the Poles lashed out with brutality. A year after the war, a group of Poles killed forty-two Jews in a vicious pogrom in Kielce. The message was clear: Jews were not welcome back. Refugees began searching for a haven in other European countries, the United States, Canada, South America, and even far-off Australia. The Statue of Liberty beckoned many, while others were lured by the hope of Jewish independence in Israel.

Since the Rebbe had disembarked on American shores in 1940, he had successfully created a beachhead of traditional Judaism in the US. Now, in the aftermath of the war, as refugees started to reimagine their lives, the Rebbe broadened his scope, believing the refugees could create Jewish revitalization on a global level. His Chasidim scattered throughout the DP camps in Europe, and the students in his yeshivas in Shanghai, the US, Canada, and Israel became the Rebbe's foot soldiers to realize his vision. This infused the survivors with a new sense of purpose. The Rebbe wanted them to see the reestablishment of their lives as not just a new personal start, but as part of the mission to create a global Jewish renaissance.

The refugee yeshivah students who had spent the war years in Shanghai finally made it to the US in 1946. They had fled Poland to Lithuania at the onset of the war, and from there made the long trek through Russia and Japan, forcibly relocated to Shanghai. There they had faced isolation, starvation, and other hardships. At the war's end they learned that almost all their relatives had perished in the Holocaust. Now, after a year of waiting for visas, they were finally arriving on American shores.

In a poignant letter,[2] the Rebbe empowered the students and laid out a new vision, explaining that the purpose of every soul is to infuse the world with sanctity "by the striving of man to serve G-d." He charged them with the goal of bolstering Jewish life, telling them that their long odyssey from Poland, China and now the US was part of a larger plan. "The reason that divine providence has brought you here is to warm up the tepid America with reverence of Heaven and chasidic passion. Proceed on the mission, with graciousness and warmth – as the famous saying goes, look for the positive qualities in others and the deficiencies in yourself." He warned them to stay focused and not be overwhelmed by the bounty of America: "Don't get sidetracked by the nonessential." The Rebbe summed up his goals in a letter to Rabbi Yosef Wineberg, who was helping refugees with relocation. There should be "in every community and in every country, a student of Tomchei Temimim, a beacon of the Torah light in the ways of Chasidism."[3]

This strategy had been percolating for a few years. In 1941, students from Poland's Telz Yeshiva[4] who had British passports, including twenty-year-old Chaim Gutnick,[5] fled east.[6] It was a long and hazardous journey by train through Russia and Japan, and then by ship to Brisbane, Australia, where the Commonwealth County provided safety. Australia had many synagogues, almost all of them Orthodox, stately places for Shabbat services where rabbis wore top hats and dared not challenge the weakening religiosity of their members. Australia had no yeshivas or day schools. Local Jewish leaders were anxious that an influx of young idealistic yeshivah students could challenge the communal status quo. Their solution was to sponsor their tickets to the United States. Faculty members[7] of the Telz Yeshivah who had already found refuge in the US secured their visas. The students gratefully accepted the offer to have their travel expenses covered and joined the reconstituted Telz Yeshivah in Cleveland, Ohio.

Gutnick was the only Chabad follower of the group.[8] He wrote to the Rebbe in Brooklyn, asking him to arrange his admission to the US. But the Rebbe instructed him to remain in Australia, charging him with a mission to prepare for refugees who would come after the war. "Man's steps are ordained by G-d, and since Providence has guided you to Australia, this is your place," the Rebbe told him. "Prepare the ground for the arrival of Jewish refugees so that it will be a place of Torah, where G-d can be found."[9] It was early 1941, and Germany reigned supreme in most of Europe. The US would not enter the war until the attack on Pearl Harbor in December. It was a dark time, an Allied victory was uncertain, and the idea of Jewish refugees immigrating to Australia at the war's end seemed improbable. "This was the vision of a true Jewish leader," Gutnick said years later.[10]

The Chabad refugees came in two waves: The first to come were those who had survived the war in Europe, Shanghai, and other locations and were looking to restart their lives; afterwards came some one thousand Chasidim who made an incredible escape from Russia in late 1946 and 1947. Most of the first group had lived through the Holocaust. Some survived death camps; others were hidden from the Nazis in Europe or had found a haven in other countries. The second group consisted of Chasidim who had withstood almost three decades of anti-religious oppression in the Soviet Union and who had educated their children in underground yeshivas. Many were imprisoned in Siberia for their Jewish devotion, and some had family members who had never returned from that ordeal. These two groups, known as the "*Poilisher*" and the "*Rusisher*," the Poles and the Russians, would be the Rebbe's vanguard. The Polish students of Tomchei Temimim who had been in China brought with them a youthful vigor.[11] The Russians who persevered under Communism served as powerful symbols of Jewish self-sacrifice to their counterparts educated in Western countries with little adversity. Both groups were role models of chasidic values and scholarship.

Until now, the pool of manpower available to the Rebbe had been limited. That changed with the arrival of the two sets of refugees – they built the foundations for a dramatic revolution in the last five years of the Rebbe's life. They filled key leadership positions in the postwar era, and their children would fill the ranks of the seventh Rebbe's army of emissaries, eventually transforming the landscape of Judaism across the world.

When the war began, many Russian Chasidim fled to remote Uzbekistan, two thousand miles from Moscow. Far from the invading Nazis, they clustered in Samarkand and Tashkent. Russia's focus on repelling the German invasion and the remoteness of the province permitted a degree of religious freedom. The local community's connection to Chabad reached back to the turn of the century, when the Rashab dispatched emissaries to inspire and educate. Clandestine yeshivas operated with little government intrusion, and Chasidim experienced a sense of freedom not felt in decades. But as the war ended, the harsh hand of Communism slowly began to reassert itself. At the same time, an avenue to freedom opened when Russia permitted Polish citizens and their families who had found a haven in Russia during the war to be repatriated back to their homeland.

With Polish passports, Chasidim could cross the border to freedom. Polish passports of refugees who had died or who desired to remain in the Soviet Union were available on the black market. The names were inscribed in ink, making it possible for a skilled forger to modify details. Azriel Chaikin, who was a teenager at the time, describes the confusion. "Some were trying to marry Poles. There were rumors you could buy papers."[12] A few Chasidim dared to make the crossing. One of the first to go was Michoel Lipsker. "He was a man of action," recalls Chaikin. "He took his family and left." As word of the successful escapes of Lipsker and others filtered back to the Chasidim in Russia, they began to wonder if they too could cross the border to freedom.

There were many obstacles to overcome. Most of the Chasidim were living in faraway Uzbekistan, requiring them to travel over 2,500 miles west to the border town of Lvov. There, they would need housing, food, and documents as they waited for transports, at times for a few months. The sudden appearance in the city of large number of religious Jews could spark the interest of the authorities. They would have to stay under the radar – not easy for men sporting beards. They would have to acquire Polish passports on the black market and then forge the names of additional family members. Crossing the border posing as Poles without knowing any Polish would be very perilous. They would have to remember their new names and ensure that their children did not accidentally reveal their identities. Large amounts of money were also needed to cover travel, housing, and bribes. It was very risky. Success meant a life of freedom, but capture could bring possible death in Soviet prison.

The Chasidim in Russia did not want to undertake such a dangerous journey without the Rebbe's accord, but communication from Uzbekistan to Brooklyn was almost impossible. A message intercepted by the Russian authorities could have dire consequences. Cryptic messages were relayed via third parties. In New York, Rabbi Shmuel Levitin informed the Rebbe that he had received a message from his son-in-law Binyamin Gorodetsky in Uzbekistan, asking in code if they should leave. The Rebbe responded that because the situation was still unclear, it would be best to wait.[13] The Rebbe's exact words were too dangerous to relay, so Rabbi Levitin sent a telegram to Uzbekistan saying, "Grandfather says it's better to stay put."[14]

The situation continued to be fluid, with a few more Chasidim crossing the border successfully. An update was communicated to the Rebbe, who responded in code: "It is not good to be in a place with no *shalom bayit* (domestic peace). Better to be in a place of *shalom bayit* and to wait for another opportunity." The Chasidim understood that the Rebbe was giving them the green light to escape, but not to remain in Poland, where rabid anti-Semitism made it unsafe.

At the time, Poland was under Russian control, and some Chasidim were unsure whether they could make their way to the West from there. But more Chasidim were successfully crossing the border, and that information was relayed to the Rebbe. Just before Passover, Gorodetsky received a letter from Levitin with the Rebbe's approval (in code), provided there was the possibility of going from Poland to Germany to the DP camps under American control.[15]

Gorodetsky himself was already under police scrutiny in his hometown of Samarkand. Fearing arrest, he secretly decided to depart. At midnight, he and his family climbed out a window in the back of his apartment and headed to Tashkent, 170 miles away, by car.[16] He left in the nick of time, as just a few hours later, the secret police came looking for him. The Gorodetskys hid with relatives for Shabbat, and on Sunday the family headed to Moscow by train. Afraid of a long journey with multiple identity checks, Gorodetsky himself secured a seat on a flight to Moscow with the help of a black marketeer. From Moscow, they made their way to the border town of Lvov. People heading to Poland were loaded onto freight trains for the trip over the border that lasted through the night. Gorodetsky was questioned by officials who suspected that he was not Polish, but he managed to convince them otherwise. Finally, they arrived in Cracow. From there, he notified the Rebbe of the full details of the situation, and the Rebbe arranged a payment of two thousand dollars (thirty thousand dollars today) to smuggle the Gorodetsky family to Czechoslovakia. As Gorodetsky writes, the Rebbe "gave full consent for our people to leave Russia." He updated the Chasidim in Russia about the Rebbe's unequivocal approval, telling them that they could receive up to three thousand dollars per family for travel expenses, if needed.

News of the Rebbe's approval and reports of the success of individual escapees spread amongst the Russian Chasidim. Some of the elders worried that if all the Chasidim departed, there would be no one left to direct the Jewish educational underground. In the end, single students were given a green light while others were told to make their own choice. Many decided to try, and from all over the country, Chasidim began streaming to Lvov, the departure point for transports to Poland.

In Samarkand, Tzemach Gurewicz applied for an exit permit for his family[17] using doctored Polish passports. Tzemach's daughter Yehudis recalls, "He escaped from prison during the war, so he was afraid that they were looking for him." Once they received the permit, they kept it a secret, fearing informers who knew their true identities. "We could not trust our neighbors and sometimes even family." Departing in the middle of the night, her mother took the children and just a few personal items stuffed into backpacks. "No one knew we were leaving. We climbed out of a back window and scrambled into a truck and boarded the train."

In the meanwhile, Tzemach followed his daily routine, "acting like nothing was happening." On board the train, Yehudis's mother worried as it began to move and Tzemach had still not joined them. At the last moment, "he caught up to the train." The 2,500-mile trip to the border took a few weeks, with stops in the forest to forage for food. As they got close to the border, they were instructed to keep quiet. "If we spoke Russian, we would be shot. We were given new names. Mine was Abramowitz." The train picked up speed as it crossed the border. "Forty-three of us were standing in the cattle car." Once in Poland, the mood changed: "My father was smiling." From Poland, the family was smuggled to Czechoslovakia with the help of the Brichah,[18] and then into Germany. "We walked and walked," Yehudis remembers. Finally, they arrived in a German refugee camp.

As more and more Chasidim tried to secure passports to make the trip, concerned that the window of opportunity would soon close, the community decided to coordinate logistics in an organized fashion. A small Sanhedrin,[19] a rabbinical court of twenty-three distinguished rabbis, convened secretly in Lvov to set guidelines for the project. All the Chasidim would pool their money and possessions into a central fund for the benefit of everyone. Professional counterfeiters would be engaged to modify and manufacture passports to be presented to Ovir, the government agency issuing exit permits. Money was designated for bribing officials. As large numbers of religious Jews in Lvov could draw the attention of the authorities, the bearded Chasidim were ordered to remain hidden in apartments. Young girls and women, who were less conspicuous, were tasked with the job of being messengers, moving money, documents, and people to hiding places. The most audacious escape in Soviet history was underway. It became known as "the Great Escape." In total, one thousand Chasidim, men, women, and children, crossed the border in a series of transports via cattle cars that moved slowly between Lvov in Russia and Poland.[20]

During the summer and fall of 1946, more and more families arrived illegally in Lvov, hiding out in apartments around the city. As they waited, tensions rose, as discovery would bring arrest and imprisonment. Most had disposed of all their possessions and were living in limbo, waiting for documents, exit permits, and the unpredictable announcements of train departures. Before the High Holidays in 1946, the Chasidim became aware that government officials had increased surveillance at the train station. For over a month, families sat in their apartments fearing for their lives, not even venturing out to attend Yom Kippur services. With tensions high and money and resources diminishing, a small group decided to make a run for it. To evade agents posted in the Lvov station, they boarded the train a few stops ahead of the city. The train passed through Lvov without incident, and they successfully crossed the border.

One of those who crossed the border was Rebbetzin Chana Schneerson, mother of the Ramash. She was placed in a German DP camp and finally made her way to Paris. Her husband was jailed and exiled in 1939 to a remote village in Kazakhstan near the Chinese border. She followed him and was at his bedside when he passed away in Alma Ata in 1945. In 1947 the Ramash traveled to France to be reunited with his mother after twenty years of separation. He remained in Paris for three months, arranging her US immigration and eventually escorting her to New York.

During his visit in Paris, he led a farbrengen marking Lag BaOmer.[21] The Ramash recounted what the Rebbe in New York was doing while a large group of Chasidim, including his mother, crossed the border between Russia and Poland on December 2, 1946.[22]

"That day, the Rebbe's nurse, Manya, came to give the Rebbe his daily injections. She knocked on the Rebbe's door and did not hear a response. Entering, she discovered the Rebbe sitting, not acknowledging her." Alarmed, the nurse called for the Rebbe's wife, who came running. Frightened when the Rebbe didn't respond to her either, she summoned the Ramash. "I ran quickly and entered the Rebbe's room. I drew close to the Rebbe and heard him saying the words of the prayer *Az Yashir* [sung by the Jews at the crossing of the Red Sea, Exodus 15]. I told everyone that everything is fine." The Rebbe remained seated but motioned with his feet as if he were walking. When he finished reciting the prayer, he repeated it again. Suddenly, he exclaimed, "They got through, they got through." Then the Rebbe began to respond to those around him. Shortly afterward, a telegram arrived from the group of escapees that read, "We have crossed the border and we are in Przemysl."

The crossing had been frightening. The train was delayed at the border for two hours while the Russians removed all the passengers and inspected their papers. "Terrible tension filled the air. We feared discovery that we are Russian citizens," recalled passenger Efraim Sudakevitch. Finally, all were permitted to reboard the train except for Rabbi Berel Gurewicz, who was arrested. The Ramash told the group in Paris, "It was during those exact two hours when they were held up at the border that the Rebbe said the prayer *Az Yashir*." On that day, fifty families, totaling 232 men, women, and children, escaped Russia.

Six days later, the Rebbe sent the group a letter[23] overflowing with joy, greeting them warmly: "Blessed is the Lord, our G-d and the G-d of our forefathers and our rabbis, who saved you and your family members." The Rebbe assured them that they would not be alone: "All of our brothers and sisters will help you with love and affection to find a livelihood and education for your children." He expressed the hope "that soon we will meet face to face." To support the refugees, the Rebbe appointed Rabbi Binyamin Gorodetsky as his European representative. He wrote to him[24] the same day asking him to establish an office in Paris[25] to "assist them in France and other countries for now" and facilitate their future permanent resettlement. He asked Gorodetsky to create a detailed questionnaire about the refugees and "to send pictures of each family member with their names and ages on the back.[26]

In early 1947, the Great Escape came to an end when Chasidim still camped out in Lvov attempted to cross on a passenger train.[27] Secret agents circulated onboard and arrested Chasidim, including escape leader Rabbi Mendel Futerfas, at the border.[28] The arrests were the first stage in a roundup that entrapped many Chasidim, including Sara Katzenelenbogen, another organizer.[29] With the authorities closing in, the Chasidim in Lvov fled deep into Russia to evade the secret police.[30]

Berel Gurewicz's wife, who had made it out of Russia, wanted to return to try to free her husband, who had been arrested for trying to escape and locked up in a local jail in Lvov. The Rebbe advised her against going. "It is preferable that he come here rather than her going there," he said. Gurewicz and two other Chasidim, Berke Chein and Tzipa Kozliner, had been detained by local police who did not realize they were part of the large-scale organized escape. Local police were more susceptible to bribes, and this presented an opportunity. The Rebbe advised Chasidim Zalman Serebryanski and Yitzchak Goldin to remain in Poland "and help their brothers."[31] He wrote that Goldin "should stay and arrange things in conjunction with my son-in-law the Rashag." They linked up with Chasidim still in Russia in order to make connections with the jailers. Finally, a coded message from Russia arrived: The jailers had a contact in Vilnius who was willing to accept a bribe on their behalf. "Please send the medicine to the city of Rabbi Eliyahu [the Vilna Gaon] that I understand will help with all kinds of illnesses [those jailed]." The Rebbe provided seven thousand dollars ($112,000 today) to pay the bribe.

After the payment was received, conditions of the prisoners in Lvov improved, and eventually their sentences were reduced. Tzipa Kozliner was released from jail and received permission to leave Russia in 1970. Berke Chein's death sentence was commuted, and after three years, he was freed. He immigrated to Israel in 1961.[32] Berel Gurewicz continued to assert that there had been a mistake in his papers and he was a Polish citizen. The bribed officials included him in a prisoner exchange between Russia and Poland. Just before Passover of 1948, he was freed in Poland. He secretly crossed the border to Czechoslovakia, and with help of Vaad Hatzalah, he traveled to Paris and was reunited with his family.[33]

A total of one thousand Chasidim escaped in the unprecedented secret exodus. They were dispersed among refugee camps, with over five hundred placed in a converted American air force base in Pocking, Germany. There they would remain in limbo for the next year or so, many eventually making their way to Paris and from there relocating to other countries. In the camps, Chasidim restarted their lives, setting up a yeshivah and a synagogue. Young couples got married and babies were born.

The Russian Jews had endured terrible oppression under Communist rule, preserving Judaism in an anti-religious atheistic state. They had secretly educated their children in underground yeshivas, circumcised their sons, dipped in underground *mikvehs,* and observed Shabbat and holidays despite harassment by the Russian secret police. They were interrogated, tortured, and jailed, some for long terms in Siberian prison camps. Their friends and relatives were killed by Stalin's henchman. Now for the first time, they tasted freedom. Finally, they could live their lives in peace, with no restrictions on their religious observance.

Shula Kazen was a twenty-five-year-old chasidic mother who escaped Russia with her husband Zalman and their three children, making it to the Pocking refugee camp in Germany's US-controlled zone. She recalls that the Rebbe challenged the refugees to think beyond their own needs. When the Chasidim set up a school in the camp for the Chabad children, the Rebbe asked them to also enroll other children, both religious and secular. "The Chasidim were surprised by the Rebbe's request," she says. In the camp, the Chasidim were mocked by the non-religious Jews for their stubborn adherence to tradition. Now the Rebbe was demanding that they reach out to them. Kazen says it was a difficult request to digest. "Exhausted by the long journey and barely processing the trauma of the Soviet Union, we did not know whether we could fulfill the Rebbe's directive." Yehudis Groner, who lived in Schwabisch Hall Camp with her family, says they were "broken Jews with nothing. The Rebbe wanted us to spread Yiddishkeit. He wanted us to make yeshivas to educate the kids."[34] In Poking, despite their misgivings, the Chasidim decided to try to reach out to others, and to their surprise, their efforts succeeded. Kazen recalls, "It evoked a largely positive response."[35]

The Rebbe dispatched a series of emissaries to Europe to help the refugees. The first was the Rebbe's secretary, Dr. Nissan Mindel, sent to England a few months after the war's end in September of 1945. His mandate was to "collect detailed information on the economic and spiritual status of our fellow Jews in liberated Europe"[36] and to explore options to expand Chabad's educational programs to the United Kingdom.

As the Russians crossed the border, the Rebbe sent Rabbi Yisrael Jacobson, who flew to Paris and then to Prague in the summer of 1946. A few of the Russians had reached Czechoslovakia, but many were still stranded in Poland. Jacobson organized a clandestine escape across the border with the help of the Brichah. From there they secured papers to permit the refugees to move to Germany's American zone.[37] Jacobson was followed by other emissaries, including the Rebbe's son-in-law, the Rashag. They provided the Rebbe with firsthand information on the conditions the refugees faced, and they strengthened the bond between the Rebbe and his Chasidim. They assisted the Chasidim who arrived in the DP camps with setting up schools, synagogues, and other Jewish services.

The primary concern of the refugees in DP camps was where to eventually settle: the United States, Canada, Israel, or elsewhere. They turned to the Rebbe for his guidance and blessing. The refugees yearned for tranquility, but the Rebbe had a different agenda. He wanted them to become the vanguard of change for world Jewry. Like a maestro leading an orchestra, the Rebbe choreographed the settlement of his Chasidim around the globe.[38] Some remained in France, creating the nucleus for a Chabad community that would evolve in the coming decades to become the largest Jewish movement in France. A large number went to Israel, many moved to the US, and some went to Canada, emboldening the nascent communities. At times the Chasidim would turn to the Rebbe with a list of possible destinations based on family connections, job prospects, or the opportunity to acquire visas. The Rebbe would either endorse them or propose alternative destinations, be it in Europe, South Africa, South America, or Australia. He prodded many to accept positions as rabbis, ritual slaughterers, teachers, and other community roles. The theme underlying every suggestion of destination was that the refugees were not coming to these places just to find a safe haven, but to effect positive change. Those with leadership qualities were appointed to initiate projects around the world.

One of those was Bentzion Shemtov, who was one of the nine Chasidim who took an oath with the Rebbe in 1924. Shemtov was sent to establish a Chabad in London.[39] The Rebbe appointed Rabbi Simon Jacobson (formally Yakovshvili), who had spent a decade in Soviet prisons, as roving ambassador to visit Jewish communities throughout Europe.[40] Jacobson reported to the Rebbe on the challenges they faced and the opportunities to develop and embolden Jewish education and tradition as these communities attempted to rebuild themselves. In the US, the Rebbe sent yeshivah students and young rabbis to visit communities. He selected Rabbi Shmuel Dovid Raichik, one of the Shanghai students, as a roving ambassador in the US, eventually sending him permanently to Los Angeles. Concerned about the spiritual welfare of Jewish students on college campuses, in 1949, the Rebbe dispatched two of his students to Brandeis University, telling them, "The time has come for us to reach out to college students."[41]

Six Chabad families were encouraged to immigrate to Australia.[42] The Rebbe asked Moshe Feiglin, a Chabad follower there, to help his fellow Chasidim acquire visas. They would be part of the influx of Holocaust survivors that would boost Australian Jewry. Their mission began even before they docked in Melbourne. The Rebbe instructed Nachum Zalman Gurewicz to begin outreach on the long boat ride from Europe to Australia. "During the trip you should endeavor to influence the others on the voyage, in particular the young, to study Torah."[43] In Melbourne Gurewicz discovered an anemic community with limited Jewish education, lamenting the state of affairs in a report to the Rebbe. The Rebbe responded emphatically: "The time has come that he, along with his fellow Chasidim, should work with zealousness and joy to improve the situation." In the Rebbe's view, this was the reason they relocated to Australia. "This is a mission that the divine providence has brought you there [to fulfill]."[44]

The Rebbe was seeking to transform the mindset of his Chasidim. Instead of seeing themselves as refugees who finally found a sanctuary, he prodded them to step forward and take on leadership roles, infusing them with a new sense of purpose. In Russia, the Chasidim had persevered to preserve Jewish life under an adversarial regime. The Western societies into which the Rebbe was dispersing his Chasidim were vastly different from Russia, with a new culture, language, and way of thinking. Now, in countries offering freedom, the Rebbe demanded that they pivot from defense to offense.

He encouraged Reb Betzalel Wilshanski, one of those sent to Australia, to become an activist. He was known for his scholarship; as a teenager he had studied in the yeshivah in Lubavitch. Now at age fifty-two, he was learning to adapt to a new world. The Rebbe exhorted him to reach out to Australian youth. "Even those who apparently don't want to study, you should draw them closer by giving them reading material in their language. Don't get disillusioned in your efforts to influence them."[45]

Tzemach Gurewicz had made it out of Russia, but he was unable to secure an American visa. He took his family to Cuba in the summer of 1948 with the hope of finding a way to get from there to New York. He had endured five years in a Russian prison and longed to finally see the Rebbe and his relatives in the US. But the Rebbe wanted him to boost the community in Cuba. He wrote[46] to Gurewicz's uncle, Rabbi Moshe Leib Rodshtein, who was trying to secure visas to the US, "I do not understand why he is rushing to come here to this country. So much can be done there in the sphere of spreading Torah and boosting Jewish education." Only after Gurewicz had set up educational programs in Cuba did the Rebbe finally tell Rodshtein, "Now is the time for Tzemach to come."[47]

The Rebbe also urged others to remain in their positions of leadership. Rabbi Meir Chaikin was appointed as a rabbi in Stockholm, Sweden. Disillusioned with the lackluster religious community, he wanted to relocate. The Rebbe rejected that idea. "You should consider your arrival in Stockholm a great honor that divine providence has chosen you to illuminate with the light of Torah in an unplanted field," the Rebbe wrote to him. In the merit of this "devotion in fulfilling the mission of your soul, G-d will bless you and your family with goodness."[48]

Rabbi Yirmiyahu Aloy, a Chabad Chasid, immigrated to South Africa from Lithuania before the War. In 1948, he met with the Rebbe in New York. The Nationalist Afrikaner Party had just been victorious in the elections. "Everyone thought it would be disastrous for the Jews. They anticipated another Holocaust,"[49] recalled his daughter Winnie Gourarie. Apprehensive, Aloy asked the Rebbe in a private meeting if he should leave. The Rebbe laughed and responded in Yiddish, "*Fuhr aheim* (go back home)." Winnie says, "There was nothing to talk about, so he went home." With time, Aloy emerged as one of the country's most prominent rabbis, taking a leadership role in the community's prestigious rabbinical court.

While the Rebbe wanted his Chasidim to take on communal roles, he also wanted them to seek employment and become financially self-sufficient. Many Chasidim transferred from the refugee camps to France, where the JDC generously supported them. This dependence on charity concerned the Rebbe, who told community leaders[50] that the time had come for the Chasidim to become self-sufficient. He wrote to the community, "My cherished *anash* and students of Tomchei Temimim, who are dear to my heart: It is inappropriate what you are doing, nor is it the way of Chasidism, to sit with folded hands and depend on the support of the JDC." The Rebbe added that the support was a good thing on an interim basis. "When you come to a new place, a foreign environment, you need help for a short time." But he emphasized that it should not become a permanent arrangement. "Each one of you must make an effort to earn a livelihood, each person in his distinctive way. Exert yourselves and move quickly, be it in an institution of Torah, business, or employment. Each person will be guided along the path that is best for them."[51]

It was not only his own Chasidim whom the Rebbe urged to move to smaller religious communities. Hungarian Holocaust survivor Herman Kohen had Australian relatives who sponsored his relocation there. On the way, he stopped in New York to bid farewell to his family.[52] With doubts about the move, he consulted his rabbi from Budapest, Rabbi Yonason Shteif, who had moved to Brooklyn. He told him to remain in New York. "There is no Yiddishkeit in Australia. Stay here in the US and live in our community." Conflicted, Kohen decided to seek the guidance of the Rebbe, who advised him to see this as an opportunity. "You say there is no Yiddishkeit there – you will make there Yiddishkeit." In Melbourne, Kohen became an integral part of the resurgence of traditional Jewish life.[53]

The Rebbe's dispersion of Chasidim around the world created multiple challenges. They had to adapt to the norms of Western society, quite different from their experience in Russia and Poland, and at the same time remain true to their mission of implanting traditional Judaism. The

Rebbe exhorted his Chasidim to transfer the ideals of self-sacrifice to a new paradigm in Western democracies. Instead of government oppression, they faced assimilation, indifference, and movements that wanted to alter basic Jewish ideas to create a new version of Judaism. In Western countries, Jewish communal leadership had shifted from the European model, where rabbis held sway, to a structure dominated by lay leaders. Boards hired and fired and dictated to rabbis what they should do and how to observe. The Rebbe's goal was to reassert the role of rabbis in communal governance. Instead of a board of well-intentioned Jews deciding the standards of tradition and communal priorities, he wanted the rabbis, rooted in scholarship, to assert leadership. These refugees were not longtime residents with local roots. Rather, communities had opened their hearts to welcome them. The Rebbe was instructing his Chasidim to challenge the norms in the very communities that provided them with a chance to restart their lives.

That was the very dilemma that faced Rabbi Nachum Zalman Gurewicz in Melbourne.[54] He started a business with a great desire to help the new yeshivah. Every Sunday he would visit local Jews in their homes to seek financial support. One week, he went to the home of Victor Smorgon, a successful immigrant who had built a major meat business in Australia. Smorgon challenged Gurewicz's old-world style. "Why do you insist on wearing a beard in twentieth-century Melbourne?" he asked. Gurewicz retorted, "Stalin could not get me to remove it and surely you won't." Deeply offended by the question and the condescending tone, Gurewicz walked out of the house. Smorgon was surprised and ran after him to apologize. They became lifelong friends after that, and Smorgon became a key supporter of the yeshivah.[55]

The Rebbe showered his Chasidim with blessings about the nobility of dedicating their lives to others. Many of them, tired from years of oppression in Russia and having suffered from the chaos of war, craved a life that was not so challenging. They yearned to live in communities with others who shared their values. Instead, the Rebbe urged them to be agents of change in existing communities, to create communal infrastructure in cities that lacked the basics of Jewish observance. The shift in mindset for both the Russians and the Poles was a daunting transition.

Despite the Rebbe's exhortations there was resistance to the change in mentality. The transition would take time, gaining momentum when the children of the refugees became yeshivah students during the era of the Rebbe's successor, the seventh Rebbe. He would expand the vision of his father-in-law of creating a global cadre of *shluchim* that would transform world Jewry.

The Rebbe was deeply concerned with the spiritual and material welfare of *Eretz Yisrael*. Chabad had been active in Israel since the eighteenth century. Colel Chabad, the oldest charitable organization in the country, was established in 1788 by Chabad's founder, Rabbi Schneur Zalman, to support the early chasidic immigration from Europe.[56] There were Chabad yeshivas and a network of synagogues, but their focus was inward, toward the needs of the Chasidim. To create opportunities for the refugees and to refocus Chabad in Israel to a wider role, the Rebbe established Kfar Chabad, a village on the outskirts of Tel Aviv.

The idea crystallized when Zionist leader Zalman Shazar[57] met with the Rebbe in late 1947.[58] Shazar stemmed from a Chabad family, and as a young man he became a devoted Zionist activist. Despite drifting from observance, he retained a sentimental connection to his roots.[59] He played a central leadership role in the new state, serving as the education minister, the chairman of the Jewish Agency, and two terms as president of Israel. In November of 1947, Shazar was in New York to ensure that the United Nations[60] would ratify the establishment of Israel.[61] The UN vote was slated for Friday, and that morning, Shazar received an unexpected phone call in his hotel. "The Rebbe's son-in-law, the Rashag, was calling," he recalled. "He said the Rebbe[62] wanted to know the details of the situation." The Jewish delegation had been trying to round up votes, but things weren't looking good, and they feared failure. Shazar was despondent, confiding to the Rashag, "The situation is very bleak. We need heavenly mercy." The Rashag told Shazar to wait on the line. After a long stretch of silence, he relayed a message from the Rebbe: "You will win with extra votes. G-d will help." The Rashag asked that the Rebbe be notified of the results. The vote was deferred to Saturday night and the Rebbe's prediction proved true.[63] Shazar told Rabbi Shmuel Cheifer,[64] a prominent Chabad leader in Israel, "The Rebbe was happy with the results of the vote."

Three days after the vote, Shazar traveled to Brooklyn, where he joined[65] the Rebbe's *farbrengen* marking the anniversary of the release of Rabbi Schneur Zalman from czarist prison.[66] That evening, the Rebbe spoke[67] of Rabbi Schneur Zalman's "self-sacrifice for *Eretz Yisrael*" during the first *aliyah* of Chasidim in 1777. "He supported the rabbis and their families who settled in *Eretz Yisrael*." Shazar met privately with the Rebbe, and they discussed[68] the establishment of a Chabad agricultural community.[69] He proposed that it be located near the northern town of Meron, known for its mystical history. The Rebbe rejected that idea. He wanted a central location so that "the Chasidim could have a positive impact on the new state."[70] The Rebbe wanted an assurance that the new government, which was dominated by secular socialists, would not disturb the classic mode of yeshivah education. He told Shazar he was willing to establish the town "if the government will give a commitment not to interfere with the education of the community." Shazar told the Rebbe, "I am only one member of my party [Mapai], and it's just one of many parties. How will my guarantee help?" The Rebbe responded, "For me your guarantee is enough." Years later, retelling the story to the Chasidim in Paris, Shazar ended by saying, "When the country was established, I was appointed minister of education," giving him the power to follow through on his promises to the Rebbe. "Chasidim will surely say this was a *mofet* (a miracle)."

Encouraged by the Rebbe, Chabad Chasidim in Europe began to immigrate to the newly established Israel. To absorb them, Kfar Chabad was established just ten miles outside Tel Aviv in 1949.[71] The Rebbe dispatched his son-in-law the Rashag to Israel to secure government funding. Chicago philanthropist Shlomo Palmer was also instrumental in helping to get the town on its feet. The Chasidim, raised in Russian cities, now became farmers. "Chabad members refused all offers of help from religious and political organizations; they insisted on going on the land," reported *The Jewish Observer*. "[They are] adapting themselves to modern agricultural methods. To them it was a point of honor to live as they were taught. This meant subsisting only on what they earned by their own toil."[72] The Rebbe emphasized to the new settlers that "each one of you should be a candle to illuminate the darkness."[73] He hoped that the new residents would "have an independent and honorable mode of livelihood through the settlement."[74]

As Zionism emerged in the late nineteenth century, activists in Russia created BILU[75] to galvanize Russian Jews to immigrate to Palestine. Its name was inspired from Isaiah's prophesy, "O house of Jacob, come and let us go."[76] The organizers, influenced by Marxist teachings, had omitted the last two words of the verse: "in the light of G-d." The Rebbe recalled that his grandfather, the fourth Rebbe, Rabbi Shmuel, had told his father, the Rashab, that he would have brought a hundred thousand Jewish families to *Eretz Yisrael* "if only they had completed the verse with its last two words. I too would have made the journey.[77]

The omission of G-d was intentional and represented the core of the debate around the goals of Zionism. Should the envisioned state be rooted in Jewish tradition, or should it develop as a new society based on secular nationalism? For many Zionist thinkers, the state they imagined was based on a replacement ideology. Religious observance was diasporic to them. They wanted to create the "new Jew," self-reliant and sovereign. Their religion was secular nationalism. As the early Zionist writer Nachman Syrkin wrote, "The new Zionist Judaism stands in complete contrast to the Judaism of exile. Zionism uproots religious Judaism in a stronger way than Reform or assimilation."[78] These ideas resounded amongst the Zionist pioneers. The poet Chaim Nachman Bialik supported the substitution of the classic works of Jewish law with a new Zionist literature.[79] The denial of the classic beliefs of Torah and its substitution with a secular brand of nationalism – at times rooted in Marxism and socialism – alarmed leading rabbinic figures in Europe. The Rashab spoke out against Zionism, and the Rebbe followed the approach of his father.

When Shazar met the Rebbe after the UN vote, he complained bitterly about Chabad's opposition to Zionism in the past. According to Shazar, the Rebbe responded, "That was then, now is now, and I have no regrets. Then indeed it [the establishment of an agricultural settlement in Israel] was not an option; now it is."[80] The seventh Rebbe echoed this change in attitude: "From 5708 (1948), when my father-in-law, the Rebbe, established Kfar Chabad, a new objective was added to the activities of Chabad Rebbes." He went on to explain that the effort to transform *Eretz Yisrael* should not be only in spiritual pursuits such as Torah study and prayer. Those sent to Kfar Chabad "were not just the elderly or yeshivah students, but families" who were engaged in agriculture.[81]

The establishment of the State of Israel in 1948 posed a new reality, prompting major theological questions.[82] For millennia, Jews had yearned for a return of sovereignty over their homeland with the arrival of the Messiah.[83] The Holocaust was a fresh memory, and the new state became a haven for Jews.[84] Now that the country was established, the traditional Jewish community grappled with the new reality. Three major schools of thought[85] emerged on how religious Jews should respond to the new state.[86]

Mizrachi,[87] the religious Zionist movement founded in 1902 by Rabbi Yitzchak Yaakov Reines, nurtured by the teachings of Israel's first chief rabbi, Avraham Yitzchak Kook, was an active partner with the broader Zionist movement. He attempted to mitigate its secularism and imbue the movement with spiritual direction. Mizrachi viewed Israeli independence as the first step in the redemptive process, as reflected in a prayer for the state composed in 1948 identifying it as the "first flowering of our redemption." Mizrachi believed that the state was infused with an element of sanctity, and it was incumbent on all Jews to live there. With time, the movement established a network of Hesder yeshivas that integrated miliary service and Torah study, the ideal of Jewish scholarship merged with sharing in the burden of defending the land.[88] Its adherents became full-fledged members of the new Israeli society while retaining their fidelity to Jewish observance.

On the other side of the debate, much of the Chareidi (traditional Orthodox) community regarded the state with great apprehension. The aspiration of Zionism was to create the new Jew. Chareidim had seen this firsthand – many had friends and family members who had abandoned observance, lured by the idea of the new nationalistic Jew. Religious groups and Zionist leaders had clashed for years over issues of education, communal leadership, and the role of Judaism in society. Many Zionist leaders came from religious homes, embracing the new movement and discarding Jewish tradition.[89] Some retained a respect for tradition, while others, driven by their personal rejection of Judaism, were openly hostile. This animated their policy decisions, exacerbating tensions with traditional Jews. Fresh in everyone's minds were the memories of the forced secularization of the "children of Tehran," the group of Polish refugee orphan children, primarily from religious homes, who had traveled by land to Iran in 1943. Sadly, in the early years of the state, there was similar grossly anti-religious behavior against Jewish immigrants from Yemen, Morocco, and other countries.

Fearing that the power of government would be used to impose secular values, Chareidim turned inward. They created their own society within a society, forming an autonomous community within the new state that lived according to its own values and ideals. Just a few miles from bustling secular Tel Aviv is Chareidi Bnei Brak.

The Chareidim demanded that the new state defer to them and the weight of thousands of years of Jewish history and tradition that they carried.[90] In the years to come, large segments of the Chareidi community encouraged its members to spend their lives in Torah study, supported by their wives, families, and philanthropic funds. The vast majority of Chareidim do not serve in the military.[91] To preserve their way of life, Chareidim became politically active, establishing parties in the Knesset (at first just Agudath Israel, later also Shas and Degel HaTorah) to represent their interests. Each of these parties has a council of prominent Torah scholars that sets their policies.

Chabad took the middle ground, believing that the historic land of Israel is sacred but not endorsing the ideology of Mizrachi, which says that the state is imbued with sanctity. Chabad believes in the timeless promise of Jewish redemption through the Messiah, who will rebuild the holy Temple and create a society based on holiness and spirituality. It does not see the state as the first step in that process.[92] Still, Chabad views Israeli military victories, such as in 1948, the Six-Day War, and others, as miraculous. Chabad also differed from the Chareidi community's policy of insularity; the Rebbe encouraged his followers to be active members of society. Kfar Chabad was built as an agricultural community, not necessarily one of exclusive Torah study. Chassidim were urged to attend yeshivas, after completing their studies seek employment, join the army and participate in the in the country's economy. Chabad did not separate itself from Israeli society but instead struck the middle ground of engaging with society while retaining its own unique approach to life. Further, Chabad would attempt – in a peaceful and nonpolitical fashion – to imbue society with Torah and tradition through education and outreach.

When the IDF was being formally organized, a group of Chasidim asked the Rebbe if they should enlist. He answered affirmatively. "It's essential for everyone to share in the defense."[93] In January of 1949, when Israel held its first elections, the Rebbe told his Chasidim to participate. "It is certainly a responsibility to vote."[94] The Rebbe instructed Chabad to be apolitical, not to create its own party[95] or endorse[96] any party in elections.[97] Chabad Chasidim voted as individuals, each making their own choice in the ballot box. This differed from almost all segments of Israel's Orthodox community, which align with one of the religious parties.[98] Chabad's political neutrality gives it a moral authority that other religious groups lack. It has become the voice of tradition to the broader society, serving as a bridge to Judaism for all.

The educational system in Israel was initially set up along political lines: the secular system, aligned with Mapai (labor Zionists); the Dati Leumi (religious Zionist) schools run by Mizrachi; and Chinuch Atzma'i, an extension of Agudath Israel.[99] There was intense pressure on Chabad to join one of these political alliances. Here too, Chabad took an independent line, refusing to affiliate its schools with any political party.

The seventh Rebbe was a strong advocate for a vigorous defense of Israel, criticizing efforts to relinquish territory for promises of peace and arguing that Jewish law forbids such actions, because it would endanger the security of the country's citizens. He encouraged investment in and strengthening of the economy. Israel's government leaders, political and military, flocked to Brooklyn to meet with the seventh Rebbe, including six of Israel's prime ministers.[100]

Kfar Chabad remains the center of Chabad in Israel. Its primary industry is no longer agriculture, but education. Thousands of students from Israel and abroad attend its schools, yeshivas, and seminaries. Chabad plays a unique role in Israeli society, straddling the secular and religious divide. Today there are close to a thousand Chabad institutions in Israel. There is hardly a town or city in the country, large or small, that does not have a significant Chabad presence.[101]

The Rebbe's concern transcended the Chabad community, extending to Jews the world over. When he became aware of a need, he made an effort to help. Despite his physical limitations, his *ahavat Yisrael* knew no bounds. When European refugees in the Dominican Republic turned to him for help, he responded immediately with detailed questions about the community and the state of Jewish affairs there.[102] When a non-Chabad rabbi in Santiago, Cuba, was struggling, the Rebbe encouraged him to soldier on. "The icy reception you are getting from some members of the community is only their outward expression. Deep down, there is good in every Jew."[103] The Rebbe then asked a Chabad refugee in Havana, Cuba, Tzemach Gurewicz, to help this rabbi and "investigate what is going on in Santiago."[104]

When Jews began to immigrate to Israel from North Africa, the Rebbe was gravely concerned about the plans to place them in secular educational programs. He wrote to Jewish leaders including Rabbi Eliezer Silver,[105] "The children were educated with traditional Jewish values by religious families and are being placed in non-religious programs with no Torah and Judaism. Their excuse is that the religious programs have no space." He implored Silver to act quickly and please "inform me on what has been done."

He dispatched his representative in Europe, Rabbi Binyamin Gorodetsky, to reclaim Jewish children who had been placed in non-Jewish orphanages and convents during the war.[106] In 1947, news that thousands of Jews in refugee camps in Italy did not have kosher food and provisions for Passover prompted a major initiative by the Rebbe to prod major Jewish organizations, in particular the JDC, to assist them.[107] He also turned to US government officials, including President Truman, encouraging them to assist Jews in refugee camps across Europe.[108]

The Rebbe used his influence to help other segments of Israel's religious community, even when he had differences with them. When the state was established in 1948, the new education ministry, led by Zalman Shazar, wanted to impose standards on the Chareidi schools. For their part, the Chareidi schools wished to retain educational autonomy, fearing that government involvement would undermine their religious values, and they lobbied to prevent implementation of this policy. When their efforts failed, the Brisker Rav, Rabbi Yitzchok Zev Soloveitchik,[109] instructed Knesset member Menachem Porush to meet with the Rebbe in New York. He hoped the Rebbe could use his influence with Shazar to obtain educational independence for Chareidi schools.

At that meeting, Porush recalled that his father had welcomed the Rebbe to Riga in 1927. He told him that he came on the behest of the Brisker Rav and explained the challenge they were facing.[110] The Rebbe instructed Porush to visit Shazar as soon as he got back and tell him, "The Rubashov family in Israel should not do anything that will embarrass the Rubashov family from Russia." Rubashov was Shazar's original family name before he Hebraized it, as many other Zionist leaders had. The Rebbe was pointing out Shazar's family's long chasidic tradition reaching back generations. Shazar had always maintained a loyalty to his chasidic roots, and the Rebbe was subtly telling him to consider his historical legacy in his decisions.[111] Porush was confused by the Rebbe's words. "I did not understand what the Rebbe meant, but I knew I must convey the message." The day he arrived in Israel, Porush headed to the Knesset, where he encountered Shazar speaking with Prime Minster David Ben-Gurion. He turned to Shazar and told him, "I have a mission for you from the Rebbe." Ben-Gurion asked, "You were actually with the Rebbe?" Porush answered affirmatively and conveyed the message. Upon hearing the Rebbe's words, Shazar became very serious. Porush says he understood the significance of the message – and he soon granted educational autonomy to the Chareidi schools.

Just a week after the Rebbe stepped onto US soil, he held a Purim celebration at the Greystone Hotel in Manhattan. "The place was packed. There were people standing on the chandeliers," remembers Yitzchok Groner.[112] The Rebbe sat on a stage, adorned in his *shtreimel*, looking regal. The Greystone, says Groner, was "a very ritzy hotel" with an affluent clientele. He was in the back of the ballroom when he observed three aristocratic ladies "wearing minks" take a peek inside. They had noticed a large crowd and were curious. One of the women, sporting gold-rimmed glasses, drew a bit closer. Groner overheard her as she gazed in wonderment at the Rebbe and murmured to herself, "Oh, an angel, an angel."

Yankel Hecht was a teenager when he attended the gathering in the Greystone Hotel that day. At the time, he says, "there weren't many Chasidim, and no young men with beards. We heard the Rebbe speak but we did not understand one word." However, he realized that the Rebbe embodied the commitment to sacrifice everything for Judaism. "We saw his self-sacrifice." For Hecht and his friends, it was a transformational moment. "This is what we American kids saw when we took a look at the Rebbe on that Purim. This is what captured American youth."[113]

The day the Rebbe stepped into New York Harbor in 1940 was a turning point in American Jewish life. The Rebbe would establish the first major chasidic court[114] in America.[115] Until this point, historian Jerome Mintz writes, Chasidim "had come as individuals, leaving behind their Rebbe."[116] The Rebbe established in the new world the vibrant chasidic life that had been the fixture of Europe. He was a spiritual magnet for Jews seeking inspiration and a deeper connection to spirituality.

After six months in Manhattan's Greystone Hotel, the Rebbe took up residence in the second story of 770 Eastern Parkway. There he recreated the spirit of Lubavitch in the midst of America's largest city. Just outside, the subway raced underground to Manhattan. Large apartment buildings filled with Jews lined the leafy parkway. Metropolitan New York bustled with first- and second-generation immigrant Jews striving to make it.

A synagogue was carved out of the ground-floor rooms, and during his first years there, the Rebbe would occasionally come downstairs for services or to recite a *maamar*.[117] With his mobility constrained and his health precarious, he mostly remained in his second-floor apartment.[118] There he took part in services, accepted visitors for *yechidut* (private audiences), and led *farbrengens*.[119] Chasidim, yeshivah students, and Jews of all backgrounds would jam the stairways leading up to the apartment, hoping to be admitted to a service or *farbrengen* with the Rebbe.[120] They came for advice, to be comforted, receive blessings, hear the Rebbe's teachings, and some just to catch a glimpse of the saintly figure.

His pen was his greatest tool of communication. Letters arrived daily to the Rebbe from around the world filled with requests for help, advice, and blessings. Each letter was numbered, and the Rebbe would systemically review them individually.[121] The Rebbe's empathy filled the pages of his responses; his concern for Jews knew no bounds. He was in constant contact with Jewish leaders and deeply engaged with Jewish communal life around the world.

Sara Esther Winter was just eleven years old when she wrote to the Rebbe the first time in 1942. The year before, he had sent two yeshivah students to visit her hometown of McKeesport, Pennsylvania, to drum up support for Jewish education. The students, Mendel Feldman and Mordechai Altein, promised to come to her parents' home for Shabbat lunch. "That day, it started pouring," recalls Sara. She thought the rain would deter them, but they made it. Surprised, she asked, "How did you manage to come?" They responded, "When you do a mitzvah, you walk between the raindrops." Inspired by the passion of the yeshivah students, Sara and her sister started a Mesibot Shabbat club for kids. She wrote to the Rebbe about her initiative, and he responded with a letter in Yiddish, attaching an English translation to ensure that she would understand.[122] She was deeply touched that the world-renowned chasidic Rebbe would take the time to respond to a young girl in McKeesport, so she joined her father and sisters on a later trip to New York. Her father was able to take them to the Rebbe's *farbrengen*. "I was a young girl who was very short. I was not able to see anything despite trying to stand on my tippy toes," Sara recalled. One Chasid noticed the girl blocked by the crowds. "He swung me up and I was able to see the Rebbe. And he saw me. He gave me the broadest, most beautiful smile, and I knew the Rebbe cared."[123] Afterward, she accompanied her father to a private audience with the Rebbe. She continued to write to him, and the Rebbe would respond, advising her on how to inspire other children. "The Rebbe said we should talk about the beauty of nice behavior." He instructed her to tell other children to be careful in observing Shabbat, to "love and respect their parents, and study diligently." Sara wrote to the Rebbe about her studies, and he encouraged her to strive further. "The Rebbe would always give me a *brachah* for the next level." The Rebbe was so impressed with Sara and her sister that he wrote to Rabbi Shlomo Zalman Hecht from Chicago, "If two girls from McKeesport can organize Shabbat clubs, can't you do it in Chicago?"

Sara kept up the correspondence throughout her teenage years. The Rebbe became intimately involved in making her *shidduch*, her match, with Herschel Feigelstock, an Austrian refugee who studied in the yeshivas in Montreal and New York. When he started looking for a bride in 1946, he sought the Rebbe's advice at every step. Asked about one suggested match, the Rebbe urged him not to pursue it. Another time, he left the decision up to him, "to explore and see if his heart is in that direction." Years later, Feigelstock reflected that even when the Rebbe endorsed a prospect it seemed lukewarm. That changed with the suggestion of Sara Winter. This time, the Rebbe responded enthusiastically. "The recommendation of Sara Winter is a good proposal and you should look into it."[124] She was nearing her eighteenth birthday at the time, and her parents worried she might be too young. The Rebbe reassured them, "It is good idea."

With the Rebbe's encouragement, Herschel and Sara met. But geography made dating a challenge, as she was living in Pittsburgh and he in Montreal. They corresponded regularly and after about six months, she wondered if Herschel was the one. Again, she wrote to the Rebbe. This time the Rebbe told her that ultimately, she would have to decide for herself. "You have to clarify it for yourself, the truth, what it is, and come to a good decision." One year after they first met, in November of 1949, the two married, with the Ramash conducting the ceremony. Afterward, the Rebbe appointed Herschel to the administration of Chabad in Montreal, and Sara became a prominent educator. Together they raised ten children.

The Rebbe met with people of all backgrounds in *yechidut*, private audiences. These were scheduled for three times a week: Sunday, Tuesday, and Thursday, from 8:00 to 11:00 p.m.[125] They were occasionally suspended when the Rebbe had health complications. Appointments were arranged by the Rebbe's secretary, Rabbi Eliyahu Simpson. He or another secretary, Rabbi Chaim Lieberman, and occasionally Rabbi Moshe Leib Rothstein, would also accompany many of the visitors into their meetings during the last decade of the Rebbe's life.[126] At that point, the Rebbe's speech became more difficult to understand due to his stroke.[127] The secretaries would facilitate the conversation between the Rebbe and the visitor.

Yechidut was the time when a Chasid would meet with the Rebbe to take an assessment of his spiritual life and seek direction and blessing. It wasn't only Chasidim who met with the Rebbe. Jews of all stripes would flock to him for his advice and blessings; visitors included young brides and grooms before their wedding, bar mitzvah boys, businesspeople, yeshivah students, rabbis, and community leaders. The Rebbe also met leaders of major Jewish organizations. He kept his finger on the pulse of issues affecting Jews the world over. They came with questions on personal issues, business opportunities, requests for blessing for good health and success, and more.

When Chasidim met with the Rebbe, they would prepare their questions on a note, known as *pan,* which stood for *pidyon nefesh,* a petition for the soul. The Rebbe would sit at his desk, wearing a hat, and at times a *shtriemel.*[128] Azriel Chaiken[129] described the scene. "On the desk he had a small *Shas* (a full edition of the Talmud). There were shelves that turned from all sides." They were filled with Jewish classics. "He would turn and take out a *sefer.*" The Rebbe "took the note with his hands, he opened it, read it, and spoke to me." For some, the meetings were brief – the Rebbe would respond to the questions on the note and give a blessing. For others, there were longer conversations.

Countless people shared their personal troubles and anxieties with the Rebbe. The Rebbe's wife, Rebbetzin Nechama Dina, disclosed the toll it took on him. "I went into my husband's office after he had completed an evening of *yechidut* and discovered him weeping. 'Why are you crying?' I asked, and he replied, '*Ich ken nisht ois'halten* – I can't continue to carry the troubles of the Jewish people!'"[130]

But the Rebbe carried on. Gershon Kranzler observed,[131] "I have watched innumerous people enter his office, tense, worried, and tortured by conflict. Then I have seen them leave with a glow of inner happiness and ease, radiating joy from the extraordinary experience." He said the Rebbe had the "capacity of probing their hearts and finding the kind of words and type of answer that loosened their tightness and transformed it into the dynamic certainty of conquering problems." Yisroel Horowitz says, "When you met the Rebbe, you were in awe. It was like you were going into a king – you couldn't forget his face."

Chaya Rosenfeld went to see the Rebbe with her father just before her wedding in 1949. "You looked at him and you knew he was a *tzaddik,* you didn't have any questions in your mind," she says. Chaya was so overwhelmed by the experience that she began to cry. Seeing her upset, the Rebbe tried to calm her by giving her a compliment: "The bride is a *baal daat* (an intelligent, well-reasoned person.)" Her father responded, "Yes, she is a *baal daat,* she chose Peretz [Hecht as a groom]." The Rebbe gave a hearty laugh, and her father joined in. "That made me feel comfortable," she says.[132]

Tzivia Lipsker went with her family to meet the Rebbe when she was twelve years old. "He looked like an angel; he had this beautiful white beard," she remembers.[133] But he was practical. Tzivia's father had been one of the Chasidim who escaped Russia, and the Rebbe advised him to purchase a farm in nearby New Jersey. "Buy a copy of the *Morgan Journal* [Yiddish newspaper] and look at the ads. You'll find a farm." Lipsker did locate one in New Jersey and was able to reestablish himself in the US.

Zalman Posner was fourteen and his brother Leibel a year younger when they met the Rebbe privately before Passover in April 1941. They were heading home to Chicago by bus after a year in yeshivah in New York. Zalman was surprised when the Rebbe asked him, "How long will you be on the bus?" Zalman replied that it was a 24-hour ride. "Is it warm on the bus? What are you going to eat? How will you *daven*?" Zalman says, "Not even my mother asked these questions. This was the special sensitivity of the Rebbe." They continued to meet the Rebbe before returning home each year for Passover. The first time, he inquired about their upcoming journey, but from then on, he focused on their spiritual progress, asking, "What are you learning? What have you accomplished since I saw you last?" During one meeting, the Rebbe told them of the experiences of their father, who studied in Lubavitch decades earlier. At the end of another, he expressed his inner feelings: "You are to me like children."[134] He then began to cry, repeating, "You are my children. You are your parents' physical children, but my spiritual children." He ended the meeting by blessing them, "Travel *gezunterheit* (in good health)."

Indeed, all of the Rebbe's students were like children to him. Just a few minutes before the onset of Yom Kippur in 1949, Rabbi Mordechai Mentlik, dean of the yeshivah in 770, received a summons from the Rebbe. He rushed up the stairs and discovered the Rebbe prepared for *Kol Nidrei,* adorned in a *tallit* and white *kittel.* But his mind was occupied with an earlier event he had just heard about: A student in the yeshivah, whose parents were farmers, had been set to be engaged to a girl from the Borough Park section of Brooklyn. "The bride's grandfather was a well-known scholar from a famous family from Europe," recalled Herschel Chitrik,[135] "but when he met the groom and his parents and saw the father wearing large boots and with rough hands, he stood up and walked out, feeling that such a family was beneath him. His whole family followed him, breaking the match."

The Rebbe was distressed upon hearing the story. He told Mentlik, "After you break the fast tomorrow night, go immediately to the family in Borough Park and tell them that anyone who learns in Tomchei Temimim is my son. I am the *mechutan* (the family of the groom)." Right after Yom Kippur ended, Mentlik took a taxi to Borough Park to meet the family. After hearing the message from the Rebbe, the grandfather reconsidered and exclaimed, "If the Rebbe himself is becoming my *mechutan,* we are proceeding with the *shidduch* and will start planning the wedding immediately."

Dovid Tennenhaus's chasidic parents had immigrated from Romania to Montreal in 1938. He was drawn to the yeshivah students who arrived from Shanghai in 1941. In 1946, he met the Rebbe for the first time and was overwhelmed by the Rebbe's piercing eyes. At their second meeting, in 1948, the Rebbe wanted to know why Dovid, who was then twenty-seven, wasn't married. He replied, "I have a checklist of what I am looking for in a wife, and I am waiting to find someone with those qualities." The Rebbe then asked to see the list, which contained some twenty items, and Dovid obliged. The Rebbe smiled and told him, "This checklist describes someone who is perfect. Since you're not perfect yourself, you should throw it away." When he walked out of the room, Tennenhaus tore up the list. A few weeks later, he met Chana Faust, and shortly afterward they were married.[136]

The Rebbe was prone to strong emotion. He would often break into laughter at receiving good news and tears at painful tidings. His years of suffering left a deep impression in his soul. Chasidic historian Rabbi Yossi Paltiel recalled the story of a woman who visited the Rebbe regularly, taking up an inordinate amount of his time. At one point, the Rebbe's secretary, concerned about his schedule, attempted to interrupt a meeting. The Rebbe motioned him away. Afterward, the Rebbe explained why he gave her so much attention. "She has a broken heart and I have a broken heart, and our souls come from the same spiritual source."[137]

In 1946, Berel Zisman, then seventeen, and his brother Leibel, sixteen, arrived in the US after surviving the Holocaust in ghettos and then concentration camps. When the Rebbe heard that the two boys were in New York, he invited them for a visit immediately, even though it was not a regular night for *yechidut*. Berel says he wanted to know their plans and where they were staying. The Rebbe's greatest concern was their family's fate, says Leibel. "We told the Rebbe we were the only ones who had survived from the whole family" – their four siblings and parents had been murdered. The Rebbe asked about other family members and their hometown of Kovno. "He was very much interested in what happened." The boys told the Rebbe all they knew. "Then the Rebbe looked at my brother and looked at me, and I recognized the same look he had given me in 1940 in Latvia." Before the war, the Rebbe had met both boys and blessed them with long life. Now in New York, "the Rebbe put down his head and began to cry." Zisman says, "When the Rebbe laughed, his whole body laughed, and now, when he was crying, his whole body was shaking." Watching him, the two boys were shaken. "The Rebbe was crying and crying, and we too began to cry."[138]

Many people who met with the Rebbe discussed important communal concerns. Snippets from the Rebbe's diary and correspondence reflect the wide range of those encounters:[139] One visitor was Rabbi Mentlik, who spoke with the Rebbe about the welfare of the yeshivah students. Another was Chaim Palmer, a Chicago businessman whom the Rebbe sent to Israel and Paris to explore ways to assist the refugees. The Klausenberger Rebbe visited to discuss the status of Jewish education in newly established Israel.[140] Communal leader Irving Bunim came to discuss the expansion of Young Israel. The Rebbe followed up on the meeting, writing him, "In continuation of our meeting, I was pleased to hear of your enthusiasm in strengthening Judaism."[141]

At one point, the Rebbe considered suspending the meetings, remarking to Rabbi Simpson, "When the Alter Rebbe [Chabad's founder] established the idea of *yechidut* it was for people to request assistance in spiritual matters. Now, since I arrived in the United States, those who come to *yechidut* ask primarily about material affairs." Simpson was alarmed, and together with Rabbi Shmuel Levitin, they convened a meeting of yeshivah students. "A new system was set up to help the students prepare spiritually for the private audiences with the Rebbe," remembers Yehudah Leib Groner, one of the students. They changed their focus and began asking the Rebbe his advice on their spiritual growth and studies. Groner says, "The Rebbe reconsidered, and continued *yechidut*."

The Rebbe conducted *farbrengens* in his second-floor apartment in 770. Rabbi Yehuda Krinsky was thirteen when he participated in his first *farbrengen* in 1946. Chasidim would stand on the staircase leading up to the second floor, hoping to be admitted to the Rebbe's study, where the *farbrengens* were held. Krinsky was still too young to officially be permitted entry, but Rebbetzin Chaya Mushka opened the door for him. "I was able to get into the room where the Rebbe was leading the *farbrengen*," he remembers. Krinsky saw some fifteen people sitting around the table. "At the head of the table was the Rebbe wearing a *shtreimel*. To the left was the Ramash and to the right was the Rashag." There were another thirty to forty people sitting and standing around the room. "Everyone was, of course, looking at the Rebbe. It was something like paradise. It was not earthly; it was something beyond comprehension. I was taken by it."[142]

Mottel Zajac,[143] a yeshivah student from Brazil, attended the *farbrengens*. He describes the Chasidim sitting around the table, including Rabbi Shmuel Levitin, the Rebbe's grandson Berke, and elder Chasidim. On the Rebbe's two sides were his sons-in-law, the Rashag and the Ramash. "If you wanted to see what *bittul* (humility) means, it was the way the Ramash would sit at the Rebbe's table. He did not move. When the Rebbe took a spoon, he took a spoon. When the Rebbe took a fork, he took a fork. It was *moredik* (astonishing) to see the reverence of the Ramash for the Rebbe." The Rebbe was prone to emotion. At the Rebbe's last *farbrengen* before his passing,[144] Zajac recalls the Rebbe crying a lot. "But we also saw moments of joy." The Rebbe had a sense of humor. "The Rebbe liked to make a joke," Zajac says. One Purim, the Rebbe was passing out glasses of spirits for a toast of *lechaim*, and one of the Chasidim hesitated to drink. Another said to him, "Don't worry, it's water," and the Rebbe had a good laugh. "The Rebbe's *farbrengens* were much briefer than those of the seventh Rebbe. There was no *maamar,*[145] just *sichot* (talks)."[146]

Uri Kaploun, the English translator of the Rebbe's talks, says they were "spiced with candid and outspoken remarks on a wide range of sensitive topics." Talks from the early 1940s, Kaploun writes, "resound with an urgent call to American Jews, firstly to sensitize them to the realization that European Jews are under mortal threat." According to Kaploun, the Rebbe "urged his listeners to feel the pain of their brothers and sisters and do whatever could be done to alleviate it." The Rebbe also expressed his concern for the trajectory of American Jewry, at one point saying, "American Jews have jumped onto a ship and have landed in a very nice country, where they have fallen asleep without realizing the danger." It was a call to action, says Kaploun. "The Rebbe looks each of us straight in the eye and leaves us with a bold challenge: What action are we taking in our days to stem the tsunami?" With the end of the war, the Rebbe's talks reflected his deep distress over the plight of Jewish refugee children in Israel. He spoke out strongly against "the secular indoctrination of those children from observant European homes."[147]

The Rebbe also focused on the inner spiritual lives of his Chasidim, using stories of Chasidim of old who modeled a life of spirituality. Kaploun says the Rebbe "includes the oral traditions of early chasidic history, verbal portraits of memorable Chasidim." A Chasid is one "who appreciates the light of Torah, an *oved,* one who toils in the service of G-d (prayer)." The Rebbe asserted that prayer opens the heart to "the light of Torah." His talks strike a balance between a "high regard for scholarship, together with a soft spot for the unlettered."[148] He writes that they are "a veritable symphony of diverse but harmonious themes, inspirational teachings, chasidic expositions, candid (but loving) pointers to personal growth, historical jottings, portraits of vintage Chasidim, heartwarming narratives, family traditions, and pungent comments on the Jewish world of the time."[149]

Two days after Purim in 1949,[150] a delegation of attorneys and government officials visited the Rebbe in his home to officially grant him and his family American citizenship. Congress had passed a special bill to accommodate the Rebbe, permitting immigrants to receive citizenship in a private home. He greeted them bedecked in a *shtreimel*, representing the significance and joy of the moment. Led by attorney Sam Kramer, they administered the oath of citizenship to the Rebbe. The Rebbe told the delegation, "After all the wanderings from place to place, from country to country, now by divine providence I have found a place where I can disseminate the teachings of Torah and Chasidism, here in America." Often the Rebbe would refer to America as a *medinah shel chesed*, a country of kindness and grace. Later that day, he inscribed in his diary, "How good it is in this country, and how pleasurable it is for its inhabitants."[151]

A few weeks after the High Holidays of 1950, the Rebbe invited the newly married Yitzchak Levy for a meeting.[152] Levy was a Sephardi rabbinical student whose parents had fled Iraq for Shanghai, immigrating to the US after the war. Half a million Jews lived in Morocco, Tunisia, and nearby counties, and the Rebbe was interested in their spiritual welfare.[153] Levy explained to the Rebbe that "there are many Sephardi Jews who are observant, but when it comes to Jewish scholarship, they are weak. They study Tanach (Bible) but lack a proficiency in Talmud." The Rebbe asked, "Why is the level of scholarship so low? Are there teachers there? Aren't there scholars there?" Levy replied that the few students from Morocco who were more advanced in their studies had come to learn in the Mir Yeshivah in New York. "Would they be willing to travel back there to teach?" the Rebbe asked. He then pointed to himself. "We are willing to underwrite the expenses." Levy didn't think they wanted to return, explaining that they had come to the US to find better opportunities. Despite Levy's pessimism, the Rebbe instructed him to try to enlist Mir students from Morocco or other Sephardi backgrounds to teach in North Africa.

Levy did not have success in recruiting rabbis and teachers to travel to North Africa. The Rebbe decided that Chabad would have to create an educational system and provide teachers. He instructed the Ramash to implement the program. He recalled, "A few weeks before his passing, the Rebbe told me that in North Africa there is a large concentration of Jews, thousands of boys and girls, and because of the level of poverty, it seems a great percentage are not receiving any education, despite the fact that they are G-d-fearing. We must begin working there." Ten days after the Rebbe's passing, the seventh Rebbe wrote[154] to Michoel Lipsker in Paris, asking him to help fulfill the Rebbe's directive. Schools opened in Morocco[155] and then expanded to Tunisia with support from the JDC. This was the last major initiative of the Rebbe before his passing. It encapsulated his entire life's work of seeking to improve the spiritual and physical welfare of Jews all over the globe. The *mellahs* of Morocco were vastly dissimilar to the chasidic town of Lubavitch, but to the Rebbe, the wellbeing of the children in Morocco was just as important.

The last week of the Rebbe's life was filled with activity. He dispatched letters across the globe. One letter encouraged Paris yeshivah students to seek employment serving the Jewish community. "You should carefully consider any suggestion that will be a benefit to others," he wrote. In another he instructed Rabbi Binyamin Gorodetsky to "act decisively to help the [Russian] children in the refugee camps in Marseille." To Holocaust survivors in Montevideo, Uruguay, he wrote, "I am unable to provide ongoing support for your schools, but I have arranged a grant of fifty dollars [six hundred dollars today] for two months." The Rebbe wrote to Rabbi Yosef Zevin and Chabad leaders in Israel instructing them to ensure that Chabad institutions in the country received an allocation from funds designated by the JDC and the Jewish Agency for yeshivas. He wrote a letter of blessings for success to Jewish activist Yosef Palmar in Chicago, as well as a letter of support to Rabbi J.J. Hecht for the annual dinner benefiting the Released Time program.[156] He directed Rabbi Yosef Wineberg in Canada to continue his efforts to help the Chabad refugees in Europe "secure entry visas for *anash*."[157]

In the days before his passing, the Rebbe spent hours meeting with Jews from a variety of backgrounds. On Sunday, a group of yeshivah students who had escaped Russia and finally made it to the US met with the Rebbe. On Thursday, he conducted *yechidut* again.[158] Rhoda Friedland and her husband were escorted by Rabbi J. J. Hecht into the Rebbe's study that night. Rhoda recalls, "As soon as you entered the room, you felt a radiance." Rabbi Hecht outlined their situation: They were having trouble having children and were considering adopting. The Rebbe asked, "Did they go to doctors?" The couple answered that the physicians with whom they consulted had pronounced Rhoda infertile. The

Rebbe surprised them with a joyous laugh and a promise: "They'll have children. They'll have healthy children."[159] When they left the Rebbe's office, Hecht, confident in the Rebbe's guarantee, slapped Rhoda's husband on the back and joyfully exclaimed, "I will be the *sandek* (the one honored with holding a baby at his circumcision)!"[160]

Others also met the Rebbe that night. One businessman lamented his dire financial situation, to which the Rebbe instructed him with a spiritual response. The Rebbe was reunited with Rabbi Yitzchak Dubov,[161] who had studied in Lubavitch and had been sent by the Rebbe to Manchester, England, over twenty years earlier. "How is the Rebbe feeling?" Dubov boldly asked. The Rebbe replied, "We need to be content. Hashem should bless us with good news." In another meeting that night, Gedalia Segal told the Rebbe he had come from Australia to visit his mother, to which he responded, "Visting your mother fulfills the mitzvah of honoring your father and mother, and it states in the Torah that the reward is long life. You will live many years."

Terry Wertheim was nineteen and a soon-to-be bride, with her formal engagement to Avraham Weingarten set for the following Saturday night.[162] In advance of the joyous moment, Avraham and his parents met with the Rebbe on Thursday evening, after which Terry entered the Rebbe's study separately with her parents.[163] They were among the last people who met privately with the Rebbe.[164] Later that night, the Rebbe's secretary, Rabbi Moshe Rodstein, called Terry's parents with a message. The Rebbe was concerned that the family might be offended because he had not formally wished them mazel tov during their meeting. Rodstein clarified in the Rebbe's name that mazel tov was only wished after an engagement.[165]

Their joy was dampened by the events that occurred two days later, on Shabbat morning. At 7:45 a.m., the Rebbe suffered a heart attack. He had endured major medical challenges for years, but this time it would be fatal. Rabbi Shmuel Levitin, the Ramash, and Dr. Avraham Seligson were hastily called, and police officers rushed in with respirators. At 7:50 a.m., the Rebbe passed away.

Filled with anxiety over the news filtering down to them from the second floor, yeshivah students in the ground-floor synagogue started reciting psalms. One student, Elya Gross, overheard a departing police officer say, "He is gone."

The community was filled with incredulity. Later that afternoon, the Ramash remarked to Dr. Seligson, "I cannot believe the *shver* (father-in-law) has passed away." Rabbi Leibel Groner says that while it was still Shabbat, the Ramash did not display any emotion. "During the whole Shabbat, we witnessed no signs of mourning. Right after Shabbat ended, the Ramash wept bitterly."[166]

Moshe Lazar arrived in 770 after Shabbat ended. "Older Chasidim were sitting and crying like babies," he remembers. The yeshivah students had divided themselves into a rotation to recite psalms in the Rebbe's room, where his body rested. Lazar was given the last watch, from 6:00 to 8:00 a.m., during which the door opened and the Ramash entered. Deep anguish was etched into his face. Lazar says it was a sight that he could never forget. "It was hurt – something so deep, I can't describe it."[167]

The next day, Sunday, Jews from throughout New York and beyond thronged to Eastern Parkway. As the Rebbe's casket was carried out of the front doors of 770, dark clouds hovered overhead, and a light snow sprinkled down. The casket had been hastily constructed from the wood of the Rebbe's *shtender* (lectern). It was now bedecked by the Rebbe's black *kapota,*[168] a dark sign on a dark day.

Eastern Parkway was blocked, jam-packed with thousands of people. Aaron Lichtenstein, then sixteen, remembers that the large crowd filled the parkway. "They stopped the traffic."[169] Students from all of New York's yeshivas attended. Lazar says, "There weren't yet many chasidic Jews in New York. Still, everybody was there." Gershon Kranzler described the crowd: "Massed there were famed figures and plain Jews, Chasidim and non-Chasidim. There were rabbis, Rebbes, yeshivah *bachurim,* college students, workers, and professionals. They came in sleek Cadillacs and dilapidated Fords, by subway or trolley, by railroad, buses, or planes, the rich and poor, women and children." The mood was somber. "Mute mourning gripped the thousands of Jews from all walks of life that crowded into the large area. United by a common loss, they gathered to pay their last respects to the man who had stood out in our days as a veritable giant of another, greater generation of leaders of whom none are left."[170]

The plan was to continue on foot to the yeshivah on Bedford Avenue, but the massive crowd made that impossible. Instead, the casket was placed into a vehicle and after a brief stop at the yeshivah, it was escorted to Old Montefiore Cemetery.[171] The Rebbe was interred near his mother, who had passed away eight years earlier.

The news of the Rebbe's passing sent shock waves around the world. For the Russian refugee Chasidim clustered in Europe, it had a chilling effect. "It was devastating," says Rabbi Yossi Paltiel. "So many who survived Hitler and Stalin dreamed of just looking at the Rebbe." Now his passing made that impossible. In the home of Moshe Feiglin in Shepperton, a small farming town one hundred miles from Melbourne, a large portrait of the Rebbe fell, the glass shattering. "I realized that something ominous had happened," Feiglin says. That portentous feeling was confirmed a few hours later when a telegram arrived from New York.[172]

A week later, in Havana, fourteen-year-old Yehudis Gurewicz brought her father a copy of New York's Yiddish paper, *Der Morgen Journal*. Excitedly, she told her father, "Look, the Rebbe's picture is on the front page!" She hadn't read the article, but when her father Tzemach saw the headline announcing the Rebbe's passing, he let out a scream. "*Oy! Oy vei iz mir*, the world has ended!" He fell on the bed, crying.[173]

Today, with the passing of over seven decades since the Rebbe's death, we can appreciate the far-reaching impact of his life.

The Rebbe's life spanned just sixty-nine years. He lived through one of the most tumultuous and challenging periods in Jewish history. Born under czarist rule in the town of Lubavitch, he endured the state-sponsored anti-Semitism of the Russian monarchy. As the forces of modernity shook the foundations of Jewish identity, he stood at the forefront of the struggle to retain traditional Jewish values, first standing at the side of his father and later as the lone soldier facing down Communism. After his expulsion from Russia, he undertook the integration of the mores of Chasidism into Western Europe. Escaping from the Nazi regime, he finally arrived in America, where he resolved to remake and rebuild Jewish life in the face of assimilation. In the postwar years, he expanded that agenda internationally to lay the foundation for a global Jewish renaissance.

Through all these trials, the Rebbe's greatest joy was teaching Torah, particularly the profound ideas of chasidic philosophy. He left a rich intellectual legacy of two hundred volumes of chasidic *maamarim* and talks.

His prolific pen was his primary means of communication, especially in his later years. It is estimated that he composed over 100,000 letters in the course of his lifetime, of which 6,760 have been published in seventeen volumes.[174] They are an invaluable firsthand account of a historical era filled with hardship. The letters burst with rabbinic wisdom, personal guidance, inspiration, profound teachings, and chasidic lore.[175] The Rebbe created a new milieu of chasidic historiography, bringing to life the richness of tradition from previous centuries. He recorded stories that unveiled the spiritual essence of Chasidism, providing an important chronology for the origins of the chasidic movement with life lessons for the modern Jew.

After founding the Tomchei Temimim yeshivah with his father the Rashab, the Rebbe nurtured it for decades, expanding the yeshivah. Today there are over fifty branches the world over. Its unique approach to Torah study fusing chasidic philosophy with classic Talmud study has created thousands of Jewish leaders and generations of Jews rooted in tradition.

The Rebbe's theme of "*America iz nisht andersh* – America is no different" challenged the mindset that Judaism must change in order to thrive in the US. He was a pioneering force in Jewish education in America, creating the first national Jewish network of day schools, complemented by supplementary programs, youth clubs, and educational curriculums.[176] He instilled new pride in Jewish tradition, changing the trajectory of American Jewry. After his passing, the seventh Rebbe took the baton and brought Chabad to new heights. In the US and Canada, Chabad is the fastest growing Jewish organization, with over one thousand centers. According to a study by the Pew Research Center, thirty-eight percent of US Jews are active in Chabad.[177]

With the establishment of the State of Israel, the Rebbe seized the middle ground between secularism and tradition, rejecting the model of insularity put forth by segments of the Chareidi community, while still refusing to comprise on observance. He encouraged his Chasidim to be active members of society while retaining their chasidic identity and also bringing others closer to the path of Torah, positioning Chabad as a bridge between the secular and religious worlds.

The underground Jewish network that the Rebbe established in Russia in the 1920s sustained Judaism during the darkest of times. As the Soviet Union disintegrated, as predicted by the Rebbe Rashab, Chabad activists emerged from the shadows and sparked a Jewish rebirth. Today, Chanukah menorahs shine in Red Square and tens of thousands of children attend Jewish schools. Chabad has become the backbone of Jewish communal life in the former Soviet Union.

In the international arena, by sending his Chasidim around the world in the postwar era, the Rebbe planted the seeds for the growth of traditional Jewish life that flourishes till today. In the countries to which the Rebbe sent emissaries, the far-reaching impact is obvious. Australia, once void of Jewish education, has become one of the most successful Jewish communities in the world, with eighty percent of children attending Jewish schools, low intermarriage rates, and strong support for Israel. The vast majority of the country's synagogues are led by Chabad rabbis; the same is true in South Africa. In France, Chabad is the largest Jewish movement in the country, with an extensive network of centers. In the UK and much of Europe, close to fifty percent of synagogues are led by Chabad rabbis. In China and much of the Far East, Chabad operates most of the Jewish communal structure. Globally, Chabad has emerged as the largest Jewish organization in the world.[178]

In an unprecedented epoch of Jewish history, the Rebbe's leadership towers. His love of Jewish learning and his vision, tenacity, determination, bottomless love, and compassion reshaped the destiny of global Jewry.

"He was a visionary and pragmatist," says Rabbi Yossi Paltiel. "He was so capable of making things happen and until the moment of his passing, his strength never waned."[179] At his core, the Rebbe was animated by a love for his fellow and a willingness to sacrifice all for others. He laughed when he felt the joy of another and cried when he sensed his pain.

The Rebbe summarized his life's work as standing up for Jewish principles. "I am my father's disciple," he said. "He endeavored for forty years never to compromise on even the minutiae of Jewish ideals."[180] At his core was his concern for the welfare of every Jew, whether locked behind the Iron Curtain, living in the *mellahs* of Morocco, or beginning anew in America. "I am a Jew who was instilled with *ahavat Yisrael* (love for a fellow Jew) and the idea that we must put our lives on the line for Judaism and for another Jew."

Afterword

A *Maamar* in Brooklyn

It had been a year since the shocking passing of the Rebbe. Chasidim flocked to 770 in Brooklyn to mark the first yahrzeit (anniversary of his passing) with a *farbrengen*. The question on everyone's mind was whether the Ramash would succeed his father-in-law by becoming the seventh Lubavitcher Rebbe. Unlike the Rashab, who left instructions that his son succeed him, the Rayatz had left no clear directive. In the immediate wake of the Rebbe's passing, there had been some jostling within the chasidic community. Some Chasidim felt that the eldest son-in-law, Rabbi Shmaryahu Gurary, should be the next Rebbe. With time, however, his support faded, and Chasidim gravitated toward Rabbi Menachem Mendel Schneerson, the Ramash.

For the last twelve months, Chasidim from around the world had sent letters to New York urging the Ramash to become Rebbe, signing a *ktav hitkarut,* a pledge of loyalty to him. Until now, the Ramash had repeatedly rebuffed these entreaties. According to chasidic theologian Rabbi Yoel Kahn, "The Ramash was very reserved, a private person. Public leadership was the opposite of his character."[1]

A few weeks before the yahrzeit, a distinguished group of New York Chasidim met with the Ramash. They presented him with a letter signed by Chasidim throughout the US declaring him the new Rebbe. When the Ramash read the first line, he broke down in tears, telling them, "This has no connection to me."[2]

Despite the Ramash's unwillingness to assume leadership, the Chasidim were still determined that he become the next Rebbe. They had witnessed the years of mentorship that the Rayatz had given the Ramash. Since his arrival in America in 1941, the Rayatz had entrusted him with important projects and responsibilities. They had also observed the Ramash's phenomenal deference to the Rayatz. Chasidim would often say that the Rayatz had only one real Chasid: the Ramash. He had been leading *farbrengens* regularly in Brooklyn, impressing the Chasidim with his warm spirit and his encyclopedic knowledge of Torah. It seemed only fitting.

The real test would come on the yahrzeit: Would the Ramash give in to the will of the Chasidim and say a *maamar,* thereby accepting the position of Rebbe, or would he continue to reject their request? Many say it was his wife who propelled him to his final decision, imploring, "If you don't become Rebbe, the work of my father will have been for naught."[3]

The small synagogue in 770 was packed to the rafters when the Ramash finally entered at 9:45 p.m. for the *farbrengen.* The Chasidim sang a melody, after which the Ramash began to speak about strengthening the bond between the Rebbe and his Chasidim. "Each of us must continue the task the Rebbe entrusted us with." He then explored the concept of *ahavat Yisrael,* the central mitzvah of the responsibility to love every Jew.

The crowd grew restless. The question was on everyone's mind: Would the Ramash say a *maamar* as his predecessors did when they became Rebbe? Suddenly, Rabbi Sender Nemtzov, one of the chasidic elders, rose. He was over eighty years old and had been a student in the yeshivah in Lubavitch and a rabbi in Manchester, England, for many years. Surprising the crowd, he proclaimed, "We want the Rebbe to say *chasidut* [a *maamar*]!"

Absolute silence filled the room as the crowd held its breath, all eyes on the Ramash. To everyone's delight, the new Rebbe broke the silence and began his first *maamar*. He started by referencing the last *maamar* the Rayatz had published on the eve of his passing. "My father-in-law, the Rebbe, of blessed memory, writes as follows in the *maamar* that he released for the day of his passing, the tenth of Shevat 5710 (1950), [based on the verse in Song of Songs]: 'I have come into my garden, my sister, my bride.'"[4]

He then expounded on the themes of his father-in-law's *maamar*.[5] When the new Rebbe finished the first part of the *maamar*, he paused and asked everyone to say *lechaim* (a toast). Nemtzov surprised the crowd again. Despite his advanced age, he leaped onto a table and called out, "Chasidim, we have a Rebbe!" before loudly proclaiming *Shehechiyanu* (the blessing for good tidings).[6]

This would become the motif of the seventh Lubavitcher Rebbe: Just as the theme of his first *maamar* was based on the teachings of the Rayatz, in his tenure as Rebbe, he built on the foundation established by the Rayatz, expanding Chabad into the largest Jewish movement in the world. Time and again, he referred to the teachings and directives of his father-in-law as his guiding light.

Forty-two years later, in 1994, when the seventh Rebbe passed away,[7] he was interred alongside his father-in-law. Today, hundreds of thousands flock to pray at this holy site every year. The two graves are enveloped by stone walls that rise up to the open sky. Two simple granite headstones mark the resting place of the two great leaders of modern Jewish life who transformed Jewish destiny and created a spiritual renaissance that continues to reach every community in the world.

Special Acknowledgment

We are deeply appreciative to **Rabbi Shalom Ber Schapiro**, who provided documents from the **archives of Rabbi Nissan Mindel**.

Rabbi Mindel served both Rabbi Yosef Yitzchak Schneersohn and his successor, Rabbi Menachem Mendel Schneerson, for over fifty years in the capacity of personal secretary, among his other duties.

The **Nissan Mindel Archives** are an authentic collection of priceless historical documents and artifacts that offer a glimpse into the recent history of Chabad. The reader will notice the occasional endnotes in the book that refer to these important archives.

Appendix 1

THE SEVEN LUBAVITCHER REBBES

Rabbi Schneur Zalman of Liadi, the Alter Rebbe (Yiddish for "old Rebbe"), 1745–1812

Rabbi Dov Ber, the Mitteler Rebbe (Yiddish for "middle Rebbe"), 1773–1827

Rabbi Menachem Mendel Schneersohn, the Tzemach Tzedek (the title of his classic work on Jewish law), 1789–1866

Rabbi Shmuel Schneersohn, the Rebbe Maharash, 1834–82

Rabbi Sholom Dovber Schneersohn, the Rebbe Rashab 1860–1920

Rabbi Yosef Yitzchak Schneersohn, the Rayatz or Frierdiker Rebbe (Yiddish for "previous Rebbe"), 1880–1950

Rabbi Menachem Mendel Schneerson, today known as "the Rebbe" (1902–94)

FOUNDERS OF THE CHASIDIC MOVEMENT

Rabbi Yisrael Baal Shem Tov, 1700–60

Rabbi Dovber, the Maggid (preacher) of Mezeritch, d. 1772

PUBLICATIONS OF RABBI YOSEF YITZCHAK SCHNEERSOHN

Some two hundred volumes of the Rebbe's teachings have been published. A full catalogue is available at kehotonline.com. English publications are available at chabad.org/3574953.

TIMELINE OF THE LIFE OF RABBI YOSEF YITZCHAK SCHNEERSOHN*

1880 (5640): Birth of the Rebbe in Lubavitch, Russia, on July 12 (12 Tamuz).

1895 (5655): Begins communal work as the personal secretary of his father.

1897 (5657): Marries Nechama Dina Schneersohn on August 22 (13 Elul).

1898 (5658): Appointed head of Yeshivas Tomchei Temimim.

1901 (5651): Travels to Vilna, Brisk, Lodz, and Koenigsberg to establish the Dubrovna factory.

1902 (5662): Travels to St. Petersburg for communal matters.

1905 (5665): Participates in organizing a fund to provide Passover needs to Russian troops in the Far East.

1906 (5666): Travels to Germany and Holland and persuades bankers there to use their influence to stop pogroms.

1908 (5668): Participates in organizing the Vilna Conference.

1909 (5669): Travels to Germany to confer with communal leaders.

1910 (5670): Involved with preparing for the Rabbinical Conference. Between 1902 and 1911, he is arrested four times in Moscow and St. Petersburg due to his activity.

1920 (5680): After the passing of the Rebbe Rashab in Rostov, accepts position of sixth Lubavitcher Rebbe.

1921 (5681): Arranges program to strengthen Judaism in Russia, establishes Yeshivas Tomchei Temimim in Warsaw.

1924 (5684): Forced to leave Rostov and relocate in St. Petersburg. Intensifies efforts to strengthen Jewish life in Russia. Establishes Agudas Chassidei Chabad in the United States.

1927 (5687): Establishes yeshivas in Bukhara, Russia. Arrested, sentenced to death, exiled to Kostroma, and forced to depart Russia for Latvia.

1928–29 (5688–89): Campaigns to have matzah sent to Russia.

1929–30 (5689–90): Visits *Eretz Yisrael* and the United States.

1934 (5694): Moves to Warsaw, Poland.

1935 (5695): Begins publication of *Hatomim* journal.

1936 (5696): Moves Yeshivas Tomchei Temimim and his residence to Otwock, Poland.

1940 (5700): Arrives in New York after escaping from Poland. Settles in Brooklyn and establishes Yeshivas Tomchei Temimim.

1941 (5701): Begins publication of the journal *HaKriah VeHaKedushah,* founds Machne Israel.

1942 (5702): Establishes Yeshivas Tomchei Temimim in Montreal; establishes yeshivas in Newark, Worcester, and Pittsburgh; establishes Kehot Publication Society.

1945 (5705): Establishes relief office for refugees with a branch in Paris; establishes Shaloh for religious instruction for public school children; launches outreach program for Jewish farmers.

1948 (5708): Establishes Kfar Chabad in Israel for Russian refugees.

1950 (5710): Lays the foundation for a Jewish educational network in North Africa. On January 28 (10 Shevat), passes away and is interred in New York.

* The corresponding Jewish year given in parentheses is based on the timeline in *HaYom Yom* (New York: Otzar Chasidim).

Appendix 2

Below is a timeline of the Rebbe's travels from the time of his return to Riga in 1930 until his departure for the United States in 1940. It is based on a variety of historical sources, but there may be slight inaccuracies due to the difficulty in tracking every one of the Rebbe's travels. Thank you to Yoel Shernofsky for compiling this timeline.

1930 (5690): Returning to Europe after the trip to America

The Rebbe departs from the United States on Thursday, July 17, 1930 (21 Tamuz 5690), arriving in Breman, Germany, on July 23 (27 Tamuz). From there he travels to Berlin for Tisha B'Av on August 3. Before returning to Riga, he stops in Marienbad for two weeks to recover from the long and arduous overseas trip. He then heads home, stopping in Berlin for a few days, and arrives in Riga on September 8 (15 Elul).

1930–31 (5691)

He stays in Riga for most of the year. From Wednesday, February 18, 1931 (Rosh Chodesh Adar) until February 26 (9 Adar) the Rebbe visits

Rakshik in Lithuania. The purpose of this visit was to give an opportunity for the Chasidim in the surrounding area to visit the Rebbe. On Wednesday, June 24 (9 Tamuz), the Rebbe departs from Riga. He heads to Warsaw for two weeks to survey the situation of the yeshivah there and explore the possibility of relocating there himself. He spends Shabbat July 4 (13 Tamuz) in Otwock. On July 8 (23 Tamuz), the Rebbe travels to Marienbad, departing back to Riga on August 13 (Rosh Chodesh Elul). He makes a short stop in Berlin, arriving home on August 20 (7 Elul).

He travels to Poland for the holidays, departing Riga on September 4 (21 Elul).

1931–32 (5692)

The Rebbe remains in Poland, dividing his time between Warsaw and Otwock until October 21 (10 Cheshvan), when he returns to Riga.

On March 8, 1932 (30 Adar Alef), the Rebbe travels to Lithuania, visiting the communities of Glubok and Pastov, among other townlets. He returns to Riga on March 17 (9 Adar Bet).

The Rebbe departs Riga a few days before the holiday of Shavuot, June 10–11, and travels to Landvarov, Poland, to celebrate the marriage of his youngest daughter, Sheina, to Mendel Horenstein. The wedding takes place on June 14 (10 Sivan). A few days after the wedding, the Rebbe travels to the town of Druskenig, where he stays for about two months for medical treatment for his feet.

On August 24 (23 Av), the Rebbe heads out to Ludmir, stopping along the way in Brisk and Kovel. On August 30 (28 Av), he heads back to Riga. He stops in Warsaw and Vienna along the way, saying a *maamar* in each city. He arrives home in Riga on September 10 (9 Elul).

1932–33 (5693)

On January 10, 1933 (12 Tevet) the Rebbe travels to Berlin for medical care, remaining there approximately two months.

In March (exact dates unknown), the Rebbe travels to Paris, retuning to Riga on March 21 (23 Adar).

On July 4, the Rebbe leaves Riga. At this time, he is leaving Riga permanently, though that has not been announced publicly. On July 5, the Rebbe stops in Warsaw and leads a *farbrengen* in the yeshivah before departing for Marienbad, where he arrives on Friday, July 7 (13 Tamuz). The Rebbe stays in Marienbad until August 21 (29 Av) and then travels to Warsaw, his new permanent residence.

1933–34 (5694)

The Rebbe is now officially living in Warsaw. He visits Riga from February 27–March 7, 1934 (12–20 Adar) and then returns to Warsaw. During his visit in Riga, the Rebbe says a series of *maamarim* and speaks to the women of the community.

On Sunday, June 3, the Rebbe leaves Warsaw. He travels to Glubok in Lithuania, stopping along the way in Vilna. He remains in Glubok till Tuesday, June 19 (6 Tamuz). This was a very inspiring visit for the Chasidim of the region. He returns to Warsaw, traveling on July 5 (22 Tamuz) to Marienbad.

On July 27 (15 Av), the Rebbe visits Prague on his way back to Warsaw, returning on July 30 or August 1 (18 or 20 Elul).

1934–35 (5695)

On November 13 (6 Kislev 5695), the Rebbe travels to the West End Sanitorium in Perchtoldsdorf (located right outside Vienna) to be treated for health-related issues by Dr. Max Gerson. The Rebbe remains there for almost half a year.

On December 30 (4 Tevet), the Rebbe *farbrengs* in Vienna in the home of Reb Klonimus Kalman Poppenheim.

Before returning to Warsaw, the Rebbe spends a few days in Vienna, meeting local Jews and conducting communal affairs. He returns to Warsaw on April 15 (12 Nisan), just before Passover.

During the summer months of 1935 (starting in late June/Sivan), the Rebbe stays in the countryside next to Warsaw in the Otwock area. He returns to Warsaw in mid-August (around Rosh Chodesh Elul). On Thursday, September 19, (21 Elul) the Rebbe relocates permanently to Otwock. The main yeshivah in Warsaw is also transferred there.

1935–36 (5696)

On January 12, 1936 (17 Tevet), the Rebbe returns to the sanatorium in Perchtoldsdorf for medical treatment. He returns to Warsaw on February

17 (24 Shevat), attending the bar mitzvah of his grandson, Shalom Ber (Berke) Gurary, on February 18–19 (25–26 Shevat).

On Sunday, June 28, the Rebbe travels to Paris for medical treatment, staying in the Sanitorium in Ville-d'Avray, a suburb right outside Paris. He remains in Paris until the end of August. Before departing, he says a *maamar* in the chasidic community in Paris on August 26 (8 Elul).

On the way back to Otwock, the Rebbe stops in Vienna for about a week and then Perchtoldsdorf for a few days. He returns to Otwock on September 9 (22 Elul).

1936–37 (5697)

On Sunday, December 27, the Rebbe departs Otwock for Vienna (Perchtoldsdorf) for medical treatment, remaining there about a week. The Rebbe then travels to Paris, arriving on January 4, 1937 (21 Tevet) and staying till February 18 (7 Adar). The Rebbe then returns to Perchtoldsdorf, traveling home to Otwock on Tuesday, March 23 (11 Nisan).

On June 15 (6 Tamuz), the Rebbe travels to Perchtoldsdorf for medical treatment, staying until August 26 (19 Elul). He returns to Otwock for the holidays.

1937–38 (5698)

On December 28 (24 Tevet), the Rebbe returns to Perchtoldsdorf, stays until March 9 (6 Adar Alef), and then departs for Paris. Three days after his departure from Austria, the Germans annex Austria. In Paris, the Rebbe stays at the Sanitorium in Ville-d'Avray until April 13 (12 Nisan), returning to Otwock in time for Passover.

1938–39 (5699)

The Rebbe is in Otwock for most of the year. He travels to Riga for health reasons, staying there from January 24, 1939 (4 Shevat) until March 31 (11 Nisan).

A few days after the war breaks out, on September 5 (21 Elul), the Rebbe leaves Otwock for Warsaw.

1939–40 (5700)

The Rebbe is rescued by the German Army and departs Warsaw on December 14 (21 Kislev), arriving in Riga on Sunday, December 18 (25 Kislev). He departs Riga on March 4, 1940 (24 Adar Alef) for Stockholm, Sweden, boarding a ship in Gothenburg on March 7 (27 Adar Alef) and finally arriving in the United States on March 19, 1940 (9 Adar Bet).

Endnotes

Among the notes that follow are many citations of the *Igrot Kodesh,* the collections of published letters of the Rebbes of Chabad. When a note mentions the name of the book alone, the reference is to the *Igrot Kodesh* of the Rayatz. Otherwise, the name of the Rebbe is specified.

CHAPTER ONE

1 That summer, there was a two-day *yarmarka,* market fair, on June 29–30.

2 *Hatomim,* issue no. 7 (Israel: Kehot Publication Society, 1971).

3 "Reb" is a title of respect, similar to "mister."

4 The notebook of the Malbish Arumim of Lubavitch (society of clothes for the poor), extant in the Lubavitch Library of Brooklyn, documents loans extended by Reb Saadia the son of Yehuda Leib.

5 Chabad Rebbes were repeatedly imprisoned for standing up for Judaism in oppressive Russia, starting with the arrest of Chabad's founder, Rabbi Schneur Zalman of Liadi, in 1798.

6 Rabbi Shalom Dovber Schneersohn (1860–1920), the Rashab, was the second son of Rabbi Shmuel, the fourth Rebbe.

7 *Hatomim,* issue no. 7 (Brooklyn, NY: Kehot Publication Society), 701–3; Rabbi Dr. Alter B. Metzger, trans., *The Heroic Struggle* (Kehot Publication Society, 1999), 189.

8 The second arrest (1902) was due to accusations from teachers at the secular school in Lubavitch. The third (1906) occurred as a result of a conflict with Poalei Tzion in Lubavitch. The fourth (1910, St. Petersburg) was due to an informer in connection with the planning for a rabbis' conference. The fifth (1906, St. Petersburg) was due to the Rayatz's efforts to exempt rabbis from military service. The sixth (1920, Rostov) resulted from accusations of the Yevesektzia, the Jewish section of the Communist Party. The seventh (1927, St. Petersburg) was when the Rebbe was sentenced to death and eventually freed due to pressure from world Jewry. *Igrot Kodesh* 3:79, letter dated 17 Iyar, 5434; *Nesi'im BeMaasar* (Kiryat Malakhi, Israel: Mekhon Ohali Tzaddikim).

9 "Rebbetzin" is an honorific title for the wife of a distinguished rabbi. Many rebbetzins played a prominent role in community affairs.

10 For more on the rebbetzin's life (1860–1942), see "From Lubavitch to New York: The Little-Known Story of Rebbetzin Shterna Sarah," available at: https://www.soulwords.org/video/from-lubavitch-to-new-york-rebbetzin-shterna-sarah/.

11 Rabbi Shmuel, known as the Rebbe Maharash (1834–82), was the youngest of the seven sons of Rabbi Menachem Mendel Schneersohn. At the age of twenty-one, he became involved in community affairs in Russia upon the instruction of his father. Later, in 1866, he succeeded him as the fourth Lubavitcher Rebbe. He was a great Torah scholar; twenty volumes of his teachings have been published by Kehot Publication Society. For more, see "The Rebbe Maharash," available at: chabad.org/626953 and "Biography & History of the Rebbe MaHaRaSh, by Rabbi Yossi Paltiel, 5767," recording available at: https://www.youtube.com/watch?v=Q58fDqw7bv8.

12 As a young child, the Rashab spent much of his time in his grandfather's home. In 1865, the Rashab's cousin Shterna Sara visited Lubavitch from her hometown of Ovruch. Seeing his two grandchildren standing together in his home, Rabbi Menachem Mendel declared, "Bride and groom!" That year, when they were both still young children, their parents wrote a *tena'im,* an engagement contract. Shterna Sara's parents were Rabbi Yosef Yitzchak (1822–76) and Chana Schneersohn; Rabbi Yosef Yitzchak was the brother of Rabbi Shmuel, the Rashab's father. The contract appears in Rabbi Zalman Hertzl, *Nisuei HaNesi'im,* vol. 1 (Brooklyn, NY: 2012).

13 Rebbetzin Shterna Sara Schneersohn retold the story in Rostov to Rabbi Rafael Kahn. See *Shemuot VeSippurim,* 1st edition, vol. 1.

14 Rabbi Menachem Mendel (1789–1866) was the third Lubavitcher Rebbe. He was the grandson of Chabad's founder, Rabbi Schneur Zalman of Liadi, who raised him from the time of his mother's passing when he was three years old. Rabbi Menachem Mendel was the author of numerous scholarly works, including some of the great classics of chasidic thought, such as *Ohr HaTorah* and *Derekh Mitzvotekha.* He is known by the title of his talmudic commentary and halakhic responsa, *Tzemach*

Tzedek. He was a strong advocate for Jewish interests to the czarist government, a staunch opponent to the Haskalah, the secular Enlightenment, and he was revered by Jews throughout the country. As Haskalah leader Mordechai Aharon Ginsburg (1799–1846) wrote, "In all my travels I did not find a town or hotel where the Jews did not recite psalms daily, where the housewife did not tell two or three wonderous stories of the Lubavitcher Rebbe. A sense of respect and awe for the Rebbe is embedded in the depth of their souls, and they mention the Rebbe constantly. If it is in financial matters or spiritual affairs, he is sacred to them, and they will follow his guidance with self-sacrifice." See Rabbi Elyashiv Kaploun, *Lubavitch: The City of Chabad Chasidim* [Hebrew] (Lubavitch, Russia: Irgun Lubavitch), chap. 9. For a more complete biography, see Rabbi Sholom Dovber Avtzon, *The Rebbeim Biography Series: The Rebbe, the Tzemach Tzedek* (Brooklyn, NY: 2012) and Rabbi Chanoch Glizenstein, *Sefer HaToldot: Rabbeinu Tzemach Tzedek* [Hebrew] (Brooklyn, NY: Kehot Publication Society).

15 Rabbi Dovber (1773–1827) was the second Lubavitcher Rebbe, known as the Mitteler (literally, "middle"). He was the oldest son and the successor of Rabbi Schneur Zalman. See Rabbi Sholom Dovber Avtzon, *The Rebbeim Biography Series: The Mitteler Rebbe, Rabbi Dovber of Lubavitch* (Brooklyn, NY); "The Mitteler Rebbe," available at: chabad.org/4246230; and "The Life of the Mitteler Rebbe – Various Series," audio lectures available at: https://insidechassidus.org/series/mitteler-rebbe/.

16 Rabbi Schneur Zalman of Liadi (1745–1812), known as the Alter Rebbe, was the founder of Chabad and the first Lubavitcher Rebbe. A child prodigy, he became a member of the inner circle of Rabbi Dovber, the successor of Rabbi Israel Baal Shem Tov. Rabbi Schneur Zalman was the author of the great classic the *Tanya* and *Shulchan Arukh HaRav*, his code of Jewish law. See "Rabbi Shneur Zalman of Liadi, the Alter Rebbe," available at: chabad.org/110437.

17 Rabbi Yosef Yitzchak Schneersohn, *Reshimat HaMaasor, Likkutei Dibburim*, trans. Uri Kaploun, 4:1,235 reads: "You will be a Chasid," but in a talk delivered by the seventh Rebbe on 14 Shevat, 5710, he said that in the original *Reshimat HaMaasor* in his father-in-law's handwriting, he wrote that his grandfather said only, "You will be" (with an empty space after those words), but that Chasidim who were at the circumcision quoted the Rebbe Maharash as saying, "You will be a Rebbe."

18 In 1880, there were 2,040 residents; 1,289 were Jewish. By 1896, the population had risen to 2,592, including 1,660 Jews, and in 1910 there were 3,376 residents, including 2,325 Jews. See Kaploun, *Lubavitch*, chap. 18.

19 For a history of the origins of Lubavitch, see Rabbi Joseph Isaac Schneersohn, *Lubavitcher Rabbi's Memoirs*, trans. Nissan Mindel (Brooklyn, NY: Kehot Publication Society, 2004).

20 The Rebbe and his family departed Lubavitch on October 25, 1915 (17 Cheshvan, 5676). The yeshivah remained in Lubavitch for another two years. The Rashab

never returned; in 1922, the Rebbe Rayatz came to Lubavitch for the final time to pray at the graves of the Rebbes who were interred there. See Kaploun, *Lubavitch*, chap. 25.

21 The synagogue in Lubavitch was closed by Communist authorities in 1936 after the passing of Rabbi Yosef Leib Beriya, a scholar respected by Jews and non-Jews alike. See Kaploun, *Lubavitch*, chap. 19.

22 The Nazis seized Lubavitch on July 21, 1941 and set up a ghetto that September. On November 4 of that year, 483 Jews were murdered and the ghetto was destroyed. The *Hebrew Standard of Australia* reported on May 25, 1944 that due to Lubavitch's history as the center of Chabad, its town residents were targeted with extreme brutality by the Nazis: "The horrors revealed in Lubavitch supersede anything the Red Army committee investigating Nazi atrocities have thus far come across." For details on the extermination, see Kaploun, *Lubavitch*, chap. 26. Only one Jewish resident remained in Lubavitch until the early 1960s.

23 In recent years, the cemetery has been refurbished, and the historic synagogue and the homes of the Rebbes have been rebuilt, bringing back their former glory. Additionally, a museum has been created to teach the history of Lubavitch, and thousands of Jews come to the visitors center annually. For more on visiting Lubavitch, see Cnaan Liphshiz, "A Tiny Russian Village of Chabad Fame Dreams of Becoming Jewish Pilgrimage Site," available at: https://www.timesofisrael.com/a-tiny-russian-village-of-chabad-fame-dreams-of-becoming-jewish-pilgrimage-site/.

24 Uri Kaploun, trans., *Sefer HaSichos*, 5701 (Brooklyn, NY: 2016).

25 Professor Fishel Schneersohn (1888–1958) was a grandson of Rabbi Shalom Dovber Schneersohn, the founder of the Kopust branch of Chabad and son of the third Rebbe, Rabbi Menachem Mendel. Fishel was an observant Jew and a psychiatrist who lived in Europe and the United States before moving to *Eretz Yisrael* in 1938. His autobiographical novel *Chaim Gravitzer*, published in Yiddish and then in Hebrew, provides a description of Lubavitch during the years of the third Rebbe. See *Chaim Gravitzer: The Odyssey of a Hasid* (Machon LeSefer). For an excerpt in English, see https://ingeveb.org/texts-and-translations/chaim-gravitzer.

26 Samuel (Shmuel) Polyakov (1837–88) was one of three brothers who were financiers and built railroads in Russia. As a young man, he visited Rabbi Menachem Mendel, who predicted he would have great wealth. Polyakov told non-Jewish author Stanislav Ukrieze, who visited Lubavitch in 1862, about the blessing that he had received a few years earlier: "The Rebbe told me I would be wealthy and live in Petersburg in a time when Jews were banned from residency there, and that I would be given honorary titles. At that moment, I could not imagine this happening. Now I am very affluent, I live in Petersburg, and they honor me with titles." See the Hebrew translation of the story published by Ukrieze in December 1905, as it appeared in *Kerem Chabad*, issue no. 2, p. 81.

27 When the Rayatz visited Moscow in 1899, Eliezer Polyakov shared with him this story (Machon LeSefer) he heard from his brother Samuel. *Sefer HaSichos*, 5701, *Acharon shel Pesach*, 108. The Polyakov family had a long connection with the Rebbes. Their father brought them to the Rebbe as children. Yaakov Polyakov and his wife met with the Rebbe on November 23, 1865 (5 Kislev 5626), seeking advice for business ventures. See Yaakov Polyakov's diary from November 1865, available at: https://blog.nli.org.il/en/the_brothers_polyakov/.

28 Rabbi Menachem Mendel had seven sons:

1. Rabbi Baruch Shalom (1805–69) did not become a Rebbe in his own right; he chose to remain in Lubavitch and become a follower of his youngest brother. Rabbi Menachem Mendel Schneerson, the seventh Rebbe of Chabad-Lubavitch, was his great-great-grandson.
2. Rabbi Yehuda Leib Schneersohn (1808–66), also known as the Maharil, settled in Kopust a few months after the death of his father, where he founded the Kopust branch of Chabad. He died two months later. He had three sons who were Rebbes in Kopust, Rechytsa, and Bobruysk.
3. Rabbi Chaim Schneur Zalman (1814–80) was Rebbe in Liadi. After his father passed away, he founded the Liadi branch of Chabad. He was succeeded by his son, Rabbi Yitzchak Dovber (1835–1910) of Liadi.
4. Rabbi Yisrael Noach (1815–83) of Nizhyn founded a branch of Chabad. Although officially a Rebbe, he had only a small following and no successor. His son Rabbi Avraham Schneersohn lived in Kishinev, and his daughter, Nechama Dina Schneersohn, married Rabbi Yosef Yitzchak Schneersohn, the sixth Rebbe.
5. Rabbi Yosef Yitzchak (1822–76) was a Rebbe in Ovruch. He founded the Ovruch branch of Chabad. He was the maternal grandfather and namesake of Rabbi Yosef Yitzchak Schneersohn, the sixth Rebbe of Chabad-Lubavitch.
6. Rabbi Yaakov (1808–76) lived in Orsha and did not assume a rabbinic position.
7. Rabbi Shmuel Schneersohn (1834–82) was also known as the Maharash. His youngest son succeeded him as the fourth Lubavitcher Rebbe. He was the father of the Rebbe Rashab.

29 With the establishment of Yeshivas Tomchei Temimim in Lubavitch, many Chasidim from other Chabad streams began sending their children to Lubavitch. In 1923, the last of the breakaway Chabad dynasties came to an end with the passing of Rabbi Shmaryahu Noach Schneersohn of Bobruysk. At that point, all Chabad Chasidim accepted Rabbi Yosef Yitzchak as the sole Chabad Rebbe.

30 "Rabbi Shmuel, the Rebbe Maharash," available at: chabad.org/110466.

31 Rebbetzin Rivkah Schneersohn (1834–1914), the granddaughter of Rabbi Dovber, the second Rebbe, grew up in Lubavitch. Her father passed away in 1837. Her mother remarried in 1843, and they relocated to Kremenchuk until 1846. When her mother passed away, the family returned to Lubavitch. Rivkah married Rabbi Shmuel upon

the suggestion of his father, Rabbi Menachem Mendel. She emerged as a respected elder in the Chabad community and had a significant influence on her grandson Rabbi Yosef Yitzchak. When he established the first Chabad girls' school in the United States in the early 1940s, he named it Beth Rivkah in her memory. See Eli Rubin, "In Lubavitch a Rose Bloomed," available at: chabad.org/6273881.

32 The children of Rabbi Shmuel were Devorah Leah, Schneur Zalman Aharon (the Raza), Shalom Dovber (the Rashab), Mendel, Avraham Sender (d. 1874, age eight), and Chaya Mushka.

33 The rebbetzin told this story to her grandson the Rayatz, who said, "My grandmother told me the story in 5668 (1907). At the time, I did not understand the story. Only after her passing in 5674 (1914), thirty-one years after her husband's passing, did I grasp its significance." *Torat Menachem: Reshimat HaYoman,* 17 Cheshvan, 5693 (Kehot Publication Society, 2009).

34 The meeting took place on Shabbat, October 21, 1882 (8 Cheshvan, 5643, *Parashas Lekh Lekha*). Participants included prominent rabbis such as Rabbi Zalman Pinsker of Kherson, Rabbi Dan Tumarkin of Rogatchov, Rabbi Dovid Tzvi Hirsh Chein of Chernigov, and Reb Chaim Yaakov Viderevitz of Moscow.

35 A report of the meeting may have been authored by Rabbi Avraham Kalisker (Ashkenazi), the rabbi of Rudnia (since he writes in the letter: "from here, Rudnia"). The written report is part of the archives of Rabbi Zelig Slonim, who studied in the yeshivah in Lubavitch. See Rabbi Yehoshua Mondshine, *Migdal Oz* (Kfar Chabad); Kaploun, *Lubavitch,* chap. 13.

36 Rabbi Shloma Majeski, "Rebbe Rashab – Acceptance of Leadership," available at: chabad.org/140518.

37 A *maamar* (literally, "statement" or "teaching") usually begins with a query on a verse in the Torah, a section of Talmud, Kabbalah, or a chasidic text. Then it explains important concepts in Jewish mystical thought and delves into the challenges of life and the purpose of human existence. See "What Is a *Maamar*?" available at: chabad.org/2905524.

38 Chaim Shalom Yosef Schneersohn (1880–1954) asked the Raza, "You are older than your brother. Why didn't you accept the position of Rebbe?" The Raza responded that the Tzemach Tzedek had *ruach hakodesh,* as did his father, the Maharash. *Ruach hakodesh,* literally, "holy spirit," is the concept that *tzaddikim,* the righteous, can be endowed with an insight from G-d regarding future events. The Raza told Chaim Schneersohn, "I can put away my initial thoughts and objectively give advice, but it could cause a loss of life," meaning that because he did not have *ruach hakodesh* he might cause someone harm through his advice. There are numerous documented stories of the various Lubavitcher Rebbes and other chasidic rebbes who gave advice that was prophetic. For the complete remarks of the Raza, including

sources, see Yisrael Barda, *The Raza: A History of Rabbi Chaim Schneur Zalman, Son of the Rebbe Maharash* (Lod, Israel: Makhon HaSefer, 2022), chap. 5.

39 Kaploun, *Lubavitch*, chap. 13.

40 The exact date of this move is unclear, though it is assumed to have been some time in the summer of 1893. Another reason for his relocation may have been financial difficulties. See Barda, *The Raza*, chap. 6.

41 He lived in the town of Zembin. Later he was appointed as an instructor of chasidic philosophy in Yeshivas Tomchei Temimim. He died in 1914.

42 Zalman Duchman, *LeSheima Ozen*, 1990 edition, 250.

43 A copy of the certificate of exemption granted to Rabbi Shalom Dovber due to medical reasons appears in Rabbi Shalom Dovber Levine, *Treasures of the Chabad Library* (Brooklyn, NY: Kehot Publication Society, 2009), 13.

44 *Torat Menachem: Reshimat HaYoman*, 334.

45 Ibid., 278.

46 *Igrot Kodesh* 3:386.

47 From a personal memoir written in Yiddish by the Rebbe titled *Reshimot Lubavitch*, apparently written to his daughters in the 1930s, possibly in Riga. The documents were seized by the Russian army after it invaded Latvia in 1941 and later discovered in the Russian National Library.

48 His father's younger brother.

49 Uri Kaploun, trans., *Sefer HaSichos*, 5701 (Brooklyn, NY: 2016), chap. 14.

50 Schneersohn, *Likkutei Dibburim*, vol. 5, chap. 39, Simchat Torah 5691; *Sefer HaSichos*, 5688–5691 (Brooklyn, NY: Kehot Publication Society, 2002).

51 There is a tradition to throw candies at a child on his first day of school to teach that the Torah is sweet.

52 *Sefer HaMaamarim*, 5710, 83–84.

53 Rabbi Eliyahu Yochanan Guraryeh, *Otzar Chasidei Chabad*, vol. 4 (Israel: 2023), 142–3.

54 *Torat Menachem: Reshimat HaYoman.*

55 *Reshimot Lubavitch.*

56 *Sefer HaMaamarim*, 5711, 299 (personal diary of the Rebbe).

57 In the summer of 1883, they traveled to Odessa and Yalta. From August 1884 until early April 1885, they were in Scheveningen, Holland, and France. See Barda, *The Raza*, 103–4.

58 *Sefer HaMaamarim*, 5711.

59 Schneur Zalman Slonim (1862–1936), born in Hebron, was the grandson of Rebbetzin Menucha Rochel Slonim, the daughter of the second Rebbe, Rabbi Dovber. In 1885, Schneur Zalman traveled to Lubavitch, where according to the Rebbe Rayatz, "he was a resident scholar" (*Likkutei Dibburim*, vol. 1). There he developed a close relationship with his distant cousin, the Rebbe Rashab. After he returned to *Eretz*

Yisrael in 1886, he headed Yeshivah Magen Avot. In 1900, he was appointed the rabbi of the Chabad community in Yaffo, where he served until his passing in 1936.

60 Rabbi Sholom Dovber Avtzon, *The Rebbeim Biography Series: The Rebbe Rashab, Rabbi Sholom Dovber of Lubavitch* (Brooklyn, NY: 2020), chapter on Yalta.

61 *Likkutei Dibburim* (English edition), vol. 4, chap. 37.

62 May 1886.

63 *Likkutei Dibburim* 4:1,376.

64 Glizenstein, *Sefer HaToldot*, chap. 4.

65 *Reshimot Lubavitch*.

66 It is difficult to ascertain the exact dates that the Rashab was absent from Lubavitch for medical care. Still, it's clear that for some ten years, he and his wife spent much time away from home. The primary information is based on recollections of the Rebbe Rayatz years later and do not include all the details. Rabbi Avtzon writes that the cities that the Rashab visited for medical care included Yalta, Vienna, Berlin and Wurzburg in Germany, and Paris and Menton in France. The Rashab also spent time in health spas, including Marienbad. See Avtzon, *The Rebbe Rashab*.

67 *Reshimot Lubavitch*.

68 It was published in 1943 under the title *Chanokh LaNaar*. The will is based on the verse "Educate a child in accordance to his way so that even when he grows old, he will not depart from it" (Prov. 22:6). Rabbi Eliezer Danzinger, trans., *Chanokh LaNaar* (Brooklyn, NY: Kehot Publication Society).

69 *Likkutei Dibburim*, vol. 2, chap. 7.

70 *Likkutei Dibburim*, vol. 3, chap. 37.

71 *Reshimot Lubavitch*.

72 Rabbi Dov Ber (d. 1772), known as the Maggid, the preacher of Mezeritch, was the successor of the founder of the chasidic movement, Rabbi Israel Baal Shem Tov. The Alter Rebbe, Rabbi Schneur Zalman, was one of his most outstanding students. See "A Brief Biography of Rabbi Dov Ber, the Maggid of Mezritch," available at: chabad.org/110433.

73 *Sefer HaMaamarim*, 5711, diary entry dated 4 Tishrei, 5654, 294.

74 In chasidic tradition, the actions of the Rebbes of previous generations are important precedents for behavior. The fact that Reb Nissan showed a written account of what he had overheard from the third Rebbe about his interaction with his grandfather the Alter Rebbe seems to have had a powerful effect on Yosef Yitzchak.

75 *Sefer HaMaamarim*, 5711, 167 (personal diary of the Rebbe, winter 5710).

76 A portion of that material has been retained.

77 Published by Kehot Publication Society, English translation by Dr. Nissan Mindel. Also available on Spotify.

78 Apparently, the Rebbe wrote his personal recollections of his childhood as a memoir for himself in Riga around 1928. It was part of an addendum to a memoir on

his arrest in 1927. This was published posthumously under the instructions of the seventh Rebbe. See *Likkutei Dibburim*, vol. 4, chap. 37. Additional material from the memoir was published recently in *Sefer HaSichos*, 5680–5687, 4th printing (Brooklyn, NY: Kehot Publication Society, 2020).

79 Rabbi Zalman Duchman, *As I Heard Them: Stories, Sayings and Memories from Lubavitch of Yesteryear* (Brooklyn, NY: Wellspring Press). See the section on the Rebbe Rashab.

80 It is a Jewish tradition to pray at the graves of the righteous, in particular before the High Holidays.

81 *Likkutei Dibburim*, vol. 4, chap. 37.

82 Uri Kaploun, trans., *Sefer HaSichos*, 5700 (Brooklyn, NY: 2015), chap. 30.

83 *Likkutei Dibburim*, vol. 1, chap. 4b.

84 Ibid.

85 Tamuz 5653 (June 26, 1893).

86 Rabbi Yossi Paltiel, "The Rebbe Rayatz's Early Life – Part 1," audio lecture available at: https://insidechassidus.org/the-rebbe-rayatz-early-life-part-1/.

87 It was a tradition of the Chabad Rebbes that on the occasion of the bar mitzvah, the father would gift his son a *gartel*, a cloth belt worn during prayer to separate the upper and lower body, the more physical vs. the more intellectual parts of a person. Yosef Yitzchak's grandmother, Rebbetzin Rivkah, made him a *gartel* and then told him to ask his father about its significance. When Yosef Yitzchak posed the question, the Rashab became very emotional; his father had given him a gartel at his bar mitzvah, and his predecessors had done the same. Historically, the *gartel* was only given to the boy who would be the successor of the Rebbe. In the case of the Rashab, only he, the middle son, received one from his father, Rabbi Shmuel. The same had happened with Rabbi Menachem Mendel, who gave a *gartel* only to his youngest son and future successor, Rabbi Shmuel. For this and other recollections, see the Rebbe's private memoir of his bar mitzvah, published posthumously: *Sefer HaSichos*, 5688–5691, *Reshimot Zikhronei Zemanei Chinukh VeBar Mitzvah Sheli* (Brooklyn, NY: Kehot Publication Society, 2002).

88 I Kings 2:2.

89 See Radak, Targum, and Ralbag on I Kings 2:2 and Rashi on Exodus 15:3.

90 *Reshimot Zikhronei Zemanei Chinukh VeBar Mitzvah Sheli.*

91 *Likkutei Dibburim*, vol. 1, chap. 5b.

92 *Igrot Kodesh* 3:386.

93 Rabbi Shmuel Betzalel Sheftel (1828–1905) grew up near Vilna. He came from a non-chasidic background and drew closer to Chabad after being impressed by Chasidim of the Alter Rebbe whom he encountered as a young man. In 1848, he traveled to Lubavitch, to Rabbi Menachem Mendel, the third Rebbe, and spent seven years studying there. In 1869, he was appointed as a *shadar* (special emissary)

of Rabbi Shmuel, the fourth Rebbe. In 1884, he relocated to Bulharkov with his family. In 1893, the Rashab invited him back to Lubavitch, where he became the teacher of the Rashab's son Yosef Yitzchak until 1900. Afterward, he served as *mashpia* (spiritual mentor) of the yeshivah in Lubavitch. For more, see "Rashbatz," available at: chabad.org/85430; *Hatomim*, issue no. 1, Tamuz 5695.

94 *Likkutei Dibburim*, vol. 3, chap. 20.

95 *Sefer HaMaamarim*, 5710. 160 (personal diary of the Rebbe, winter 5710/1950).

96 *Likkutei Dibburim*, vol. 2, chap. 16.

97 *Likkutei Dibburim*, vol. 2.

98 Decades later, the Rayatz did the same with his son-in-law, Rabbi Menachem Mendel Schneerson. See chapters 4–6 of this book.

99 *Likkutei Dibburim*, vol. 3, chap. 20.

100 *Likkutei Dibburim*, 3:27.

101 *Farbrengen*, 12 Tamuz 5616 (1956).

102 Genesis 22:1–19.

103 Proverbs 31:17.

104 Fifty years later, the Rebbe recalled this as a turning point in his life. See *Sefer HaSichos*, 5705, chap. 29, 32; *Sefer HaSichos*, 5704 [Yiddish] (Brooklyn, NY: Kehot Publication Society), 144.

105 Gershon Kranzler, *The Lubavitcher*, Mindel Archives.

106 Rabbi Chaim Mordechai Perlov, *Stories of the Rebbe Rayatz* (*Likkutei Sipurim*), Jerusalem, 5762.

107 *Sefer HaSichos*, 5705 [English], chap. 20.

108 Interview conducted by the author.

CHAPTER TWO

1 It was the tradition in the Rebbe's household to marry early.

2 Nechama Dina Schneersohn was born October 24, 1881 (17 Tishrei, 5642) and died January 7, 1971 (10 Shevat, 5731).

3 Genesis 24.

4 Since the bride's family had limited financial means, the Rebbe Rashab undertook all the wedding expenses. On Erev Yom Kippur 1896, the Rebbe Rashab asked his mother for forgiveness for not following her advice on looking for an affluent match. She responded, "I wish that G-d would forgive all of us the way I forgive you completely." *Shemuot VeSippurim*, 2nd edition (Kfar Chabad: 5736), 1:69–71.

5 The *tena'im* (engagement) was signed on June 9, 1896 (28 Sivan, 5646) in Bolivke. Copy available in *Nisuei HaNesi'im*, vol. 1, chap. 8.

6 Letter dated 1 Elul, 5646 (September 1, 1896) to Rabbi Mordechai Dovber and his son Rabbi Schneur Zalman Schneersohn, who lived in Hebron. She also requested that "when you will be at the holy places to pray before Rosh HaShanah, please pray for our welfare." The reference here is assumed to be the *Me'arat HaMakhpelah*. See *Igrot Kodesh – Rashab* 1:194; Rabbi Shalom Dovber Levine, *Treasures of the Chabad Library* (Brooklyn, NY: Kehot Publication Society, 2009), 117.

7 September 10, 1897 (13 Elul, 5657).

8 This blessing is recited when purchasing something of value, reaching a milestone in life, or eating a new fruit: "Blessed are You, L-rd our G-d, King of the Universe, who has granted us life, sustained us, and enabled us to reach this occasion."

9 It was the custom for the Rebbe to conduct a *chuppah* on a Friday.

10 *Zal* is the Russian word for "hall." Today, students in many Chabad yeshivas refer to the *beit midrash* (study hall) as a *zal*.

11 It is unclear whether this happened just before the wedding or on the day of the celebration dinner, Sunday, September 12, 1897 (15 Elul, 5657).

12 The seventh Rebbe explains his use of the plural "founders of Tomchei Temimim" when he refers to the creation of the yeshivah: "It was my father-in-law [the Rebbe Rayatz] who suggested to the Rashab to establish the yeshivah." *Likkutei Sichot* 2:484.

13 The Rayatz shared this with his son-in-law, Rabbi Menachem Mendel Schneerson, known as the Ramash, in 1934 (5694) while staying in the health resort in Marienbad; see *Reshimat HaYoman*, 335. Starting in 1928, the Ramash began to write notes about his conversations with the Rayatz, filling more than five hundred pages with chasidic lore, scholarly insights, and history. Publishing posthumously, they are a remarkable documentation of intimate conversations between the Rayatz and the Ramash over a period of many years. See *Torat Menachem: Reshimat HaYoman* (Brooklyn, NY: Kehot Publication Society, 2009).

14 *Reshimat HaYoman*, 335.

15 The day of this meeting (September 12, 1897/15 Elul, 5657) is considered the day that Yeshivas Tomchei Temimim was founded. See the Rayatz's letter as published in *Hatomim*, issue no. 1 (Warsaw, 1935), page 23; *Igrot Kodesh* 10:365.

16 In 1909, Rabbi Moshe Rosenblum, a distinguished scholar, was appointed secretary of the yeshivah. During the following year, he wrote an account of the early history of the yeshivah called *Divrei Yemei HaTemimim* ("The Annals of Yeshivas Tomchei Temimim"); he had access to the original protocols of the meeting, and the Rayatz shared with him many details of the history of the yeshivah in its early years. The account of the wedding in *Divrei Yemei HaTemimim* was published by Rabbi Yehoshua Mondshine, Jerusalem, 2017, and in *Kerem Chabad* (Kfar Chabad: 5747), 3:11–14.

17 Professor Ilia Luria, *Milchamot Lubavitch: Chasidut Chabad BeRusia HaTzarit* (Jerusalem: Machon Shazar, 2018), chap. 2.

18 The Rayatz writes that in 1896–97, there was a group of sixteen or seventeen students whose chasidic families had sent them to Lubavitch, but it was not a formal yeshivah. This group would become the foundation of Tomchei Temimim. The tradition of young Chasidim studying in Lubavitch near the Rebbe's court reached back to the time of the third Rebbe, Rabbi Menachem Mendel. *Igrot Kodesh*, vol. 2, August 7, 1928 (7 Av, 5688).

19 For a letter (not dated) describing the founding of Yeshivas Tomchei Temimim, see *Igrot Kodesh* 10:365; *Hatomim*, vol. 1 (Tamuz 5695).

20 Yeshivas Knesses Yisrael was founded by the legendary Rabbi Nosson Tzvi Finkel in the town of Slabodka in 1877 as a kollel for married men to learn Torah. Within a few years, it became a regular yeshivah for young students. It instituted the study of *musar* in a systematic fashion, which prompted a major controversy between those who argued that the study should focus exclusively on Talmud and those who supported teaching ethics. Those opposed to the study of *musar* opened their own yeshivah, Knesses Beis Yitzchak, in Slabodka in 1897, and in 1904 they hired Rabbi Baruch Ber Leibowitz to be *rosh yeshivah*. In 1921, Rabbi Boruch Ber moved the yeshivah to Vilna, and in 1926 he moved it to Kamenitz.

21 Rabbi Yisrael Lipkin (1809–83) is known as "Salanter" after the town he lived in during his earlier years. He was a brilliant scholar who popularized the teaching of *musar* as a response to the Enlightenment.

22 Rabbi Berel Wein, "The *Musar* Movement" (jewishhistory.org, no. 61); Rabbi Simcha Zissel Ziv, *Chakhmah UMusar* (New York: 1957), 50 [quoted in *Sefer She'eilos UTeshuvos Avnei Chen*]. For a detailed historical review of the state of the yeshivas and the debate over the study of *musar*, see Nathan Kamenesky, *The Making of a Godol*, revised edition (Jerusalem: 2004).

23 *Divrei Yemei HaTemimim*, 11–14.

24 Luria, *Milchamot Lubavitch*.

25 Talk delivered by the Rebbe Rayatz on the last day of Passover 5701 (1941), published in *Sefer HaSichos*, 5701, 106 (English translation: p. 149).

26 Naftali Yosef Brawer, "Resistance and Response to Change: The Leadership of Rabbi Shalom Dovber Schneersohn" (University College London), part 3.

27 Nine years later, on the last day of Passover 5666 (1906), the Rebbe Rashab described his feelings during the year that proceeded the establishment of the yeshivah: "My soul bled from what I observed, and every time I prayed at the holy gravesites of my ancestors, the Rebbes, I would pour out my embittered heart regarding the situation of Chasidim and *Chasidut*. During the summer of 5656 (1896), I visited the gravesites of our teacher the Baal Shem Tov [in Mezibuzh], our teacher the Maggid of Mezeritch [in Anipoli], the Alter Rebbe [in Hadyach],

and the Mitteler Rebbe [in Nizhyn], and when I came back to Lubavitch, I went to the gravesites of my holy grandfather [the Tzemach Tzedek] and my holy father [the Maharash], and with their holy blessing I established the yeshivah." See *Sefer HaSichos*, 5701.

28 *Igrot Kodesh* 10:365.

29 Rabbi Menachem Greenglass, chap. 7; Rabbi Zalman Hertzl, *Nisuei HaNesi'im*.

30 "The Rashab saw the yeshivah as a solution and a barrier to the rise of the negative influences of the Haskalah." *Igrot Kodesh*, vol. 2, letter to Shlomo Roster dated 7 Av, 5688 (July 24, 1928).

31 Rabbi Shalom Dovber Schneersohn, *Kuntres Etz HaChayim* [English translation] (Brooklyn, NY: 1946), chap. 27, available at: chabad.org/144473. See also the Rayatz's introduction to his father's *Kuntres HaTefilla* (Brooklyn, NY: 1941).

32 Rabbi Shmuel Gronem (1852–1921) was the first *mashpia* of Yeshivas Tomchei Temimim. He educated a generation of Chasidim.

33 See the Rayatz's letter as published in *Hatomim*, issue no. 1 (Warsaw, 1935), p. 23; *Igrot Kodesh* 10:366–67.

34 September 15, 1897.

35 *Hatomim*, issue no. 1; *Igrot Kodesh*, 367.

36 Zembin was in western Russia; today it is part of Belorussia. Its Jewish population was annihilated during the Holocaust. Brawer, "Resistance and Response."

37 Rosenblum, *Divrei Yemei HaTemimim* 3:17–18. Some of the students mentioned here are well known; for the possible identification of others, see Yisrael Barda, *BaMerchav* (2018), 95–96.

38 *Reshimat HaYoman*, Sivan 5692 (1932); see the letter from the Rayatz to the Ramash as published in *Hatomim*, issue no. 1, spring 1935.

39 See the Rayatz's letter as published in *Hatomim*, issue no. 1 (Warsaw, 1935), p. 24; *Igrot Kodesh* 10:366–67.

40 *Divrei Yemei HaTemimim*, chap. 4.

41 The Rayatz assumed the position on 24 Elul, 5659 (September 11, 1898). See *Divrei Yemei HaTemimim*.

42 *Igrot Kodesh* 1:4. "Guidelines for Tomchei Temimim" outlines eleven bylaws for its members.

43 *Divrei Yemei HaTemimim*, chap. 7.

44 Yeshaya Berlin (1852–1907) was a successful businessman who was close to Chabad Rebbes. His wife was a granddaughter of the third Rebbe, Rabbi Menachem Mendel. They lived in Riga and had no children. Berlin was involved in community affairs with the Rashab.

45 *Divrei Yemei HaTemimim*, chap. 6.

46 Simchat Torah is the final celebration of the annual holiday season that begins with Rosh HaShanah; it marks the conclusion of the annual cycle of Torah reading. It

is customary to dance with the Torah both in the evening and the daytime. The dancing is divided into seven *hakafot,* circuits, and a series of poetic prayers are recited before each dance. The Rashab took the name of the yeshivah from the fourth line in the prayers recited during the seventh *hakafah.*

47 Until today, it is customary to use the term "*tamim*" as an honorific title for a student or alumnus of Tomchei Temimim. It has become so embedded in the communal culture that it is used as a title on tombstones of alumni. *Hatomim,* issue no. 1, p. 24; *Igrot Kodesh* 10:3–4, 367–68.

48 The divorce was a conditional one, stating that it would only be effective if they did not return by a certain future date. This enabled women to remarry if their husbands did not return from battle, even if there was no proof of death.

49 Luria, *Milchamot Lubavitch,* chap. 2.

50 Rabbi Israel Baal Shem Tov (1698–1760) was the founder of the chasidic movement. He described the story of his soul elevation in a letter to his brother-in-law. See "The Chamber of Mashiach," available at: chabad.org/380401.

51 *Sefer HaSichos,* 5702, chap. 30–31 [Hebrew], 130; *Likkutei Dibburim* [Hebrew] 4:1560–90.

52 *Toldot Chabad BeRusia HaTzarit* (Brooklyn, NY: Kehot Publication Society, 2010), chap. 122. *Hosafot,* Tevet 5655, Establishment of Chevra Yavne, supplement to *Sefer HaMaamarim,* 5665 (Kehot Publication Society, 1982).

53 Luria, *Milchamot Lubavitch,* chap. 2. See also a letter that the Rayatz wrote to Rabbi Schneur Slonim on 21 Tevet, 5660 (December 11, 1899) [according to the Julian calendar then in use in czarist Russia], published in *Igrot Kodesh* 1:9–10, where he alludes to opposition from the breakaway Chabad courts.

54 Luria, *Milchamot Lubavitch,* chap. 2.

55 Weinstein attacked the yeshivah in the Russian-language newspaper *Voskhod* with a wide variety of allegations, including that the students were not trained for employment. See Luria, *Milchamot Lubavitch.*

56 There were already tensions between Zionist leaders and the Rashab. In 1899, the Rashab wrote a letter that was highly critical of Zionism, denouncing its proponents who advocated replacing Jewish identity rooted in Torah and tradition with secular nationalism. *Igrot Kodesh – Rashab,* vol. 1, letter 86.

57 Poalei Tzion united Zionism with Marxism and socialism, rejecting traditional Judaism. One of its earliest centers was Vitebsk, near Lubavitch. It was inspired by the writings of Ber Borochov, who consolidated the party in 1906. For more, see Samuel Kassow, "Po'ale Tsiyon," available at: https://yivoencyclopedia.org/article.aspx/poale_tsiyon.

58 The confrontation took place on March 22, 1906.

59 *Igrot Kodesh – Rashab* 4:137.

60 Personal Memoirs of Yitzchak Goldin, Geniza #17, 5754/2024; Rabbi Sholom Dovber Avtzon, *The Rebbeim Biography Series: The Rebbe Rashab, Rabbi Sholom Dovber of Lubavitch* (Brooklyn, NY: 2020).

61 *Igrot Kodesh – Rashab* 4:154.

62 *Divrei Yemei HaTemimim*, translation by Rabbi Boruch Werdiger available at: https://www.merkazanash.com/pdf/Perspectives20.pdf.

63 The Chabad community was founded in Hebron in 1823 by Chasidim who had immigrated earlier to Safed and Tiberias. See *Challenge: An Encounter with Lubavitch-Chabad in Israel* (Lubavitch Foundation of Great Britain, 1973).

64 Colel Chabad, the central Chabad charitable fund in *Eretz Yisrael* set up by the first Chabad Rebbe, was based in Jerusalem and was, to a large degree, under the sway of the competing Chabad courts in Kopust and Liadi. The Rashab was displeased with the direction of the Colel. Instead of focusing on its historic mission of supporting Jewish scholars, it was diverting funds to other areas.

65 Mussi Sharfstein, "Site of New Hebron Neighborhood Was Purchased by Chabad in 1909," available at: https://www.lubavitch.com/site-of-new-hebron-neighborhood-was-purchased-by-chabad-in-1909/.

66 Shlomo Zalman Havlin, *HaMashpia: The History of Rabbi Zalman Havlin* (Jerusalem: 1982); *Igrot Kodesh – Rashab* 1:388–93.

67 In a long letter to Rabbi Havlin and his "dear students" dated November 24, 1911 (3 Kislev, 5672), the Rayatz outlined the purpose of the yeshivah in Hebron. See *Igrot Kodesh*, vol. 1.

68 *Igrot Kodesh*, vol. 1, letter to Rabbi Havlin dated 3 Kislev, 5674 (December 3, 1913).

69 Alexandar III (1845–94) assumed the position of czar in 1881 following his father's assassination. In response, he was more repressive than his father, enacting the May Laws in 1882 and expanding them in 1885. Among other provisions, these laws prohibited Jews from leasing land outside the Pale, restricted high school and university attendance, and limited mortgages on land. These laws were a major catalyst in Jewish emigration from Russia to the United States and other countries.

70 Originally established by Catherine the Great in 1791, the Pale of Settlement decree was finally terminated in 1917. Its borders shifted over time – at its height, some five million Jews were restricted to the area, which included much of western Russia as well as parts of Ukraine and Crimea. Some Jews, primarily those with university degrees and members of certain guilds, were given permission for residency outside the area. The word "pale" is derived from the Latin word "*palus*," meaning a stake or area. See John Klier, "Pale of Settlement," available at: https://yivoencyclopedia.org/article.aspx/pale_of_settlement.

71 See "Nicholas II Regarded Pogroms as Natural," JTA, August 7, 1928, available at: https://www.jta.org/archive/nicholas-ii-regarded-pogroms-as-natural.

72 *Igrot Kodesh – Rashab,* vol. 1, letter dated 10 Tamuz, 5659 (July 22, 1899); Rabbi Avrohom Bergstein, "An Overview of the Chabad Attitude to Zionism and the State of Israel" (JLI Machon Shmuel, 2017).

73 Luria, *Milchamot Lubavitch,* chap. 4. The other Chabad courts played a limited role in community affairs. Lubavitch took on a major role during the leadership of Rabbi Menachem Mendel and his successor, Rabbi Shmuel. After his passing in 1882, Lubavitch's role was minimal. Much of the influence lay with business leaders such as Baron David Gunzburg; Luria asserts that at times, the rabbis attempted to cooperate with them.

74 Rabbi Nissan Mindel, *Biography of Rabbi Yosef Yitzchak Schneersohn, The Four Worlds* (Brooklyn, NY: Kehot Publication Society, 2006).

75 An example of this is a series of letters written over a period of days from the Rashab to the Rayatz in 5664 (1904) about a variety of communal concerns. See *Igrot Kodesh – Rashab* 4:40–44.

76 Pyotr Stolypin (1862–1911) served as interior minister and prime minister in the czarist government of Nicholas II from 1906 until he was assassinated in 1911.

77 The nature of the decree is unknown today.

78 This must have occurred sometime between Stolypin's appointment as interior minister and prime minister in July 1906 and the demise of Konstantin Petrovich Pobedonostsev in March 1907.

79 Pobedonostsev (1827–1907) was a distinguished lawyer and an influential advisor to three Russian czars. He was a member of Council of the Empire and chief procurator of the Most Holy Synod, the operating head of the Russian Orthodox Church. He was involved with the institution of the May Laws that limited Jewish residency and economic activity in Russia. He also supported Jewish colonization in Argentina.

80 *Likkutei Sichot* 6:287 (Brooklyn, NY: Kehot Publication Society, 2000).

81 Talk delivered on Simchat Torah, *Sefer HaSichos,* 5708 (Brooklyn, NY: Kehot Publication Society, 2001).

82 *Sefer HaSichos,* 5708.

83 Max Lilienthal (1815–92) founded a secular Jewish school in Riga and befriended Russia's education minister, Count Sergei S. Uvarov. With Uvarov's backing, in 1843 Lilienthal organized a conference to revamp Jewish education in Russia. His plans were blocked by Rabbi Menachem Mendel. Afterward, Lilienthal immigrated to the United States, where he became right-hand man to Isaac Mayer Weiss, the founder of the Reform movement in America. For more on the 1843 conference, see Mordechai Rubin, "The 1843 Battle Over Jewish Education," available at: chabad.org/5999330; *The Tzemach Tzedek and the Haskalah Movement: From the Diary of Rabbi Yosef Yitzchak of Lubavitch* (Kehot Publication Society).

84 These included Baron Joseph Gunzburg, the organization's president, his son Horace (Naftali Hertz) Gunzburg, the vice president, Abraham Brodsky, Lev Rosenthal, and others. See Brian Horowitz, "Society for the Promotion of Culture Among the Jews of Russia," available at: https://yivoencyclopedia.org/article.aspx/Society_for_the_Promotion_of_Culture_among_the_Jews_of_Russia.

85 For more on the Gunzburg dynasty, see Lorraine de Meaux, *The Gunzburgs: A Family Biography* (Halban Publishers, 2019).

86 Luria, *Milchamot Lubavitch*, chap. 4. Luria cites a letter from the documents of the Chevrah Mefitzei Haskalah in the Russian National Archives in St. Petersburg.

87 A series of letters from the Rashab to Baron Horace Gunzburg lamented the negative influence of the Enlightenment schools. The letters refer to meetings between the two men, apparently in 1896 and again in 1899, in St. Petersburg. The Rashab's letters are in Hebrew, which Gunzburg understood. See *Igrot Kodesh – Rashab* 1:190, 192; Luria, *Milchamot Lubavitch*, chap. 4; and "Guardian of Jewish Education: The Rebbe Rashab's Mission," *Perspectives Magazine*, issue no. 21, available at: https://www.merkazanash.com/perspectives-magazine.

88 *Farbrengen* on 19 Kislev, 5699 (December 3, 1898). See *Zikhron Livnei Yisrael – Memoirs of Rabbi Yisrael Jacobson: 1907–1939* [Hebrew] (Brooklyn, NY: Kehot Publication Society, 1996), chap. 4; Rabbi Rafael Kahn, *Lubavitch VeChayalehah* (Kfar Chabad, Israel: 1983), 37.

89 *Perspectives Magazine*, issues no. 22 and 23, available at: https://www.merkazanash.com/perspectives-magazine.

90 Avtzon, *The Rebbe Rashab*, chapter titled "Battling the Maskilim."

91 Rabbi Menachem Mendel Schneerson, *HaYom Yom* (Brooklyn, NY: Kehot Publication Society, 2005).

92 "Dubrovno," available at: https://www.jewishvirtuallibrary.org/dubrovno.

93 Gershon Kranzler, *The Lubavitcher*, Mindel Archives.

94 Eli Rubin, "The Chinese Matzah Campaign of 1905," available at: chabad.org/2174130; *Hosafot, Sefer HaMaamarim*, 5665; Schneersohn, *HaYom Yom*.

95 A report of the meeting appears in *Igrot Kodesh* 6:393. The 1905 meeting was also mentioned years later at a 1943 meeting of rabbis about refugee children in *Eretz Yisrael*; participants were said to have included the Rashab, Rabbi Chaim Brisker, Rabbi David Katznellenbogen, and others.

96 Schneersohn, *HaYom Yom*.

97 Historically, a *shtadlan* would advocate with government and business leaders on behalf of Jewish interests. In monarchies, the *shtadlan* had little real political power, unlike lobbyists in modern representative democracies. They had to rely on persuasion and diplomacy. Kranzler, *The Lubavitcher*.

98 Antony Polonsky, *The Jews in Poland and Russia: 1881–1914* (London: The Littman Library of Jewish Civilization, 2010), vol. 2, chap. 8.

99 *Voskhod*, no. 6 (1904).

100 *Likkutei Dibburim*, vol. 1, chap. 5b.

101 Rabbi Chaim Ozer Grodzinski (1863–1940), was the *dayan* (chief judge) of the rabbinical court of Vilnius. Universally respected as one of the leading rabbis of the world and a great scholar and community leader, he represented the traditional yeshivah community. The Rashab and the Rayatz had great esteem for Rabbi Chaim Ozer and worked closely with him on communal issues.

102 For a detailed review of the conference, see *Rabban Shel Kol Benei HaGola* (Jerusalem: 5881), chap. 13.

103 Rabbi Chaim Soloveitchik, known as Reb Chaim Brisker (1853–1918), was a great scholar. Rabbi Yisrael Meir of Radin, known as the Chafetz Chaim (1838–1933), was one of the leading Lithuanian rabbis in Europe. The fourth Gerrer Rebbe, Rabbi Avraham Mordechai Alter, known as the Imrei Emes (1866–1948), was one of the leading chasidic Rebbes in Poland.

104 In the wake of the meeting, the Rashab with the help of the Rayatz decided to lobby government authorities in St. Petersburg to advance their more conservative position. With the outbreak of war and the eventual revolution, however, those efforts became moot.

105 The prime minister treated the rabbis disrespectfully. First, they were forced to wait in a room with no seats for over two hours. During the meeting itself, Stolypin blamed the rabbis for the uprising of the Bund (the secular Jewish socialist party) against the government. He did not respond to their requests for legislation to improve the condition of Jews in Russia. There were nine participants in the meeting, including the Rashab, Rabbi Chaim Ozer, Rabbi Chaim Soloveitchik, Baron David Gunzburg (the conference chair), and Eliezer Polyakov. The Rayatz was not at this meeting. For a detailed review of the meeting including news reports, see Rabbi Dovid Kamenetsky, *Rabbeinu Chaim Ozer: Rabban Shel Kol B'nei Yisrael* (Jerusalem: 5781), chap. 15.

106 Mendel Beilis was born in 1874 and died in 1934.

107 Marina Kigel, "The People of Kiev Made Him a Target and Imposed the Suffering on All Jews: The Beilis Case – The Last Blood Libel," available at: https://www.anumuseum.org.il/blog/beilis/.

108 Eli Rubin, "The Tsar's Scapegoats: Beilis, the Chassidim and the Jews," available at: chabad.org/2335459.

109 The Rashab was also concerned that he might have to elucidate obtuse theological concepts in "modern terms." See *Igrot Kodesh*, vol. 16, letter to Shmuel Treinin dated 17 Elul, 5763 (September 19, 1913).

110 "In Defense of Chassidism," available at: chabad.org/2363483.

111 *Igrot Kodesh,* vol. 13, letter to the arrangements committee for the memorial for attorney Oscar Gruzenberg, dated December 12, 1942 (7 Tevet, 5003). The English translation of the letter is available in the Mindel Archives.

112 This arrest took place after the 1905 revolution, when political tensions were high.

113 Rabbi Nissan Mindel, *Biography of Rabbi Yosef Yitzchak Schneersohn.*

114 *Sefer HaSichos,* 5680; Eli Rubin, "Purim in Petrograd, 1917," available at: chabad.org/3605206.

115 They departed on 16 Cheshvan, 5676 (Sunday, October 24, 1915).

116 *Zikhron Livnei Yisrael,* chap. 11.

117 The library was stored in the warehouse of one of the Chasidim, Zelkin Persitz, and later seized and transferred to the Russian National Library. Despite major efforts by Chabad to repatriate the collection, it remains there until today. The manuscripts, including the priceless siddur of Rabbi Yisrael Baal Shem Tov, were saved and eventually brought to the United States by the Rayatz.

118 Rabbi Elyashiv Kaploun, *Rostov-on-Don* (Israel: Chish Publishing), chap. 9.

119 Following the fall of the Soviet Union, Chabad returned to Rostov, reclaimed the building owned by the Rashab, and refurbished the Ohel at his grave. Today there is a flourishing community with a synagogue, school, and community programs; see https://www.jewishrostov.com/.

120 Letter from Zalman Havlin to Dovid Shifrin dated 19 Adar, 5684 (March 7, 1923) as published in Havlin, *HaMashpia,* 89.

121 A term used to refer to fellow Chabad Chasidim.

122 The meeting took place on Friday, February 27, 1920 (8 Adar, 5780). While on a mission to Moscow, he was harassed by the Yevesektzia. In a diary entry dated 10 Adar Alef, 5787 (February 12, 1927), he writes that he woke up at 3 a.m. feeling troubled by events in Moscow. After reflecting on this meeting with his father, "I went back to sleep, and my soul was relaxed." *Sefer HaSichos,* 5680–87 (Brooklyn, NY: Kehot Publication Society, 1992), 132; *Likkutei Dibburim,* vol. 6, chap. 63.

123 The Rashab stated "at least twenty-two years," implying that it could be longer. Indeed, the Soviet Union lasted seventy years, disintegrating in 1990. Perhaps the fact that the Rayatz heard this prediction from his father about the end of Communist Russia spurred him on to confront the Communists, knowing that their regime would end and Jewish life would be restored.

124 Nicholas II (1849–1917), the last czar of Russia, incited pogroms against the Jews. The Beilis blood libel trial also took place during his reign.

125 Nora Levin writes, "A whole generation of Jewish Communists involved in Jewish affairs were liquidated in massive purges." Professor Nora Levin, *The Jews of the Soviet Union Since 1917* (New York University Press), chap. 14.

126 The Rayatz recalls the 1920 meeting in his diary from February 1926; it may have also been recorded at an earlier date, but we do not have diaries from 1920. By 1926,

Lenin had already died, Trotsky had not yet been exiled, and Stalin was consolidating power. It is remarkable to note the accuracy of these predictions, as well as those about the downfall of the Yevesektzia in the 1930s and the eventual collapse of the Soviet Union.

127 Gina Kolata, "Lenin's Stroke: Doctor Has a Theory (and a Suspect)," available at: https://www.nytimes.com/2012/05/08/health/research/lenins-death-remains-a-mystery-for-doctors.html.

128 Stalin died on March 5, 1953, five days after Purim. At the Purim *farbrengen* that year, the seventh Rebbe alluded to the death of the czar; when the news of Stalin's stroke and passing emerged, Chasidim claimed there was a connection to the Rebbe's remarks.

129 In June 1945, the Supreme Soviet elevated Stalin to the highest military rank, generalissimo, but he rejected the new uniform and continued to refer to himself as a marshal, wearing that uniform. See https://www.rbth.com/arts/2014/08/21/stalins_distinctive_military_wardrobe_37711.

130 Simon Sebag Montefiore, *Stalin: The Court of the Red Tsar.*

131 Moshe Dovber Rivkin (1891–1976) was born in Zintsi, Ukraine, where his father, Reb Bentzion, was a renowned scholar and the town's rabbi. Moshe Dovber was a child prodigy who began studying Talmud at age five. In his early years, he learned in Yeshivas Tomchei Temimim in Lubavitch. He became a senior yeshivah student who was intimately involved in *Beit HaRav*, the Rashab's household, and bore witness to the last period of the Rashab's life and the beginning of the leadership of the Rayatz. At the time, he wrote a personal account of the period titled *Ashkavta DeRebbe*, though he only published the first edition in 1963. It is a remarkable personal historical memoir filled with great detail and scholarly notations. While yet unmarried, Rabbi Rivkin was invited to become *rosh yeshivah* of Tomchei Temimim in Russia. He immigrated to Palestine, where he was appointed *rosh yeshivah* of Toras Emes in Jerusalem. He was invited to join the faculty of Yeshivah Torah Vodaath in Brooklyn in 1928, where he remained until his passing in 1976. See Rabbi Moshe Dovber Rivkin, *Ashkavta DeRebbe* (Brooklyn, NY: 1976), available at hebrewbooks.org.

132 Rivkin writes that the Rashab celebrated Shabbat and holidays privately with his family. "Three times a year, on Simchat Torah, 19 Kislev [celebrating the liberation of the Alter Rebbe from prison], and Purim, he would eat a public meal. These special events were very joyous; the Rashab was always in an uplifted mood.

133 Rabbi Shalom Dovber Schneersohn, *Sefer Maamarim*, *"Reishit Goyim Amalek,"* Purim 5680 (Brooklyn, NY: Kehot Publication Society, 1989).

134 Yaakov Landau (1893–1986) later became the chief rabbi of Bnei Brak. Havlin, *HaMashpia*; Rivkin, *Ashkavta DeRebbe.*

135 Ibid.

CHAPTER THREE

1 A Yiddish idiom expressing shock, similar to the English expression "woe."

2 Rabbi Moshe Dovber Rivkin, *Ashkavta DeRebbe* (Brooklyn, NY: 1976), 109.

3 In 1940, the city of Rostov planned to destroy the old Jewish cemetery and build a sports complex in its place. They banned the removal of any remains. Local Chasidim were alarmed at the planned desecration of the grave of the Rebbe Rashab, and they communicated their concerns to the Rayatz, who approved the transfer of his father's grave to a new Jewish cemetery in Rostov. The renowned kabbalist, Rabbi Levi Yitzchak Schneerson, father of the seventh Rebbe, Rabbi Menachem Mendel Schneerson, gave detailed instructions to a group of ten Chasidim on how to transfer the remains of the Rebbe Rashab. The Chasidim prepared themselves spiritually, including fasting that day, and despite the real danger of discovery by local police, they removed the grave late at night and reinterred it. Remarkably, though twenty years had transpired since his passing, the Rebbe's body remained whole and intact. The grandfather of Rostov resident Marina Kuleshova was part of the group that night and confirmed this detail. He told Kuleshova that when they discovered this, it shocked them. Her account of what she heard from her grandfather can be viewed at https://www.youtube.com/watch?time_continue=324&v=dyoARqOacro&feature=emb_logo. Additionally, a letter from one of the ten Chasidim, describing the details of the reinterment and the fact that the body was still whole, appears in *Ashkavta DeRebbe*, 151.

4 Out of respect for the deceased, Jewish law mandates that funerals be performed as soon as possible.

5 A *beit din* consists of a minimum of three rabbis. Jewish tradition prohibits the relocation of the deceased unless it was stated at the funeral that the interment is being done on condition that the body be moved in the future. As no instructions from the Rashab to inter him in Lubavitch were discovered, he remained buried in Rostov.

6 There was an ominous sign that the era of Lubavitch serving as the center of the movement was coming to an end. A month before the Rebbe Rashab's passing, the synagogue and the home of the Rebbe there were destroyed in a fire. The town of Lubavitch would never regain its prominence; the Holocaust wiped out the city's final Jewish residents. Though the Rayatz would eventually move to St. Petersburg, Russia; Riga, Latvia; Warsaw and Otwock, Poland; and Brooklyn, New York, he and his successor would forever be known as "Lubavitcher Rebbes" after the small village that was the center of the movement for more than a century.

7 Rivkin, *Ashkavta DeRebbe*, 109.

8 Rabbi Yosef Yitzchak Schneersohn, *Sefer HaMaamarim* 5680–81, "*Reishit Goyim Amalek*" (Brooklyn, NY: Kehot Publication Society).

9 See the letter from Zalman Havlin to Dovid Shifrin dated 19 Adar, 5684 (March 7, 1923) as published in Havlin, *HaMashpia: The History of Rabbi Zalman Havlin* (Jerusalem: 1982), 89. For another account, see Rivkin, *Ashkavta DeRebbe.*

10 "The Ethical Will," available at: chabad.org/149881.

11 See chap. 1 of this book.

12 *Igrot Kodesh*, vol. 14, 10 Shevat, 5682 (February 8, 1922).

13 For newspaper reports about the Rashab's passing, see Eli Rubin, "Giving Chabad New Life," available at: chabad.org/4693692, footnote 1.

14 *Yiddishes Tageblatt*, July 23, 1920.

15 Seven years later, Mark praised the new Rebbe in his book *Gedolim Fun Unzer Tzeit – Great Jewish Leaders of Our Times* (New York: 1927).

16 Midrash Rabbah, *Parshat Naso.*

17 After his passing, his Chasidim gravitated to the Rebbe Rayatz. During the tenure of his father and grandfather, there were competing courts of Chabad Chasidim. These varied groups were loyal to the sons of Rabbi Menachem Mendel, the third Rebbe, and their descendants. At this point, with the passing of the last of those Rebbes, Chabad Chasidim who followed the other groups united behind the new Rebbe. The seventh Rebbe said at a *farbrengen* in 1953, "As the Rebbe, my father-in-law, explained to descendants of Chabad Chasidim of Kopust and Bobruysk that in past years, there had been divisions. This one goes to Kopust, this one to Bobruysk, and this one to Lubavitch. Today, all come together in Lubavitch, including those from Kopust and Bobruysk." *Farbrengen*, 12 Tamuz, 5703 (1953).

18 Letter dated February 8, 1922 (10 Shevat, 5782).

19 He recovered, living another twenty-two years.

20 *Sefer HaMaamarim.*

21 Rabbi Yehudah Chitrik, *Reshimot Devarim* 5745 (Brooklyn, NY: 1995), 2:135.

22 David Fishman, "Rabbi Joseph I. Schneersohn: The Making of a Jewish Religious Leader in the Soviet Union," in Nadia Kizilova and Alex Agadjanian, eds., *Religion and the Russian Revolution* (Bloomington, IN: Indiana University Press, 2023).

23 Between 1983 and 2011, seventeen volumes of these letters were published by Kehot Publication Society, edited by Rabbi Shalom Ber Levin. Each volume has an introduction that provides an overview of the letters and the historical events of the time period of the volume. The earliest volume contains letters dated from 1897, when the Rebbe was just seventeen years old; the ensuing volumes cover the span of his lifetime. They are a rich treasure house of the insights and advice of the Rebbe and an important historical record of his life and contemporary Jewish events. The majority of these volumes are written in Hebrew, some in Yiddish, and a few in other languages, including Russian and English.

24 Nora Levin, *The Jews in the Soviet Union Since 1917* (New York University Press, 1988), chap. 3. Jews had a literacy rate of over seventy percent, higher than any other Russian ethnic group. Many young Jews were activists in the revolution.

25 In a letter signed by Rabbi Elchonon Dov (Chonye) Morozov, a close confidant of the Rayatz as well as his secretary, the Rayatz writes that in the beginning of the winter of 1920, "we did not yet know that it is good even when there is a slice of bread once in two days, G-d forbid, and it still seemed that one must eat every day." *Igrot Kodesh* 14:73.

26 Unpublished memoirs of Reb Yitzchak Goldin, quoted in Rabbi Shalom Ber Levin, *Toldot Chabad BeRusia HaSovietit, 1917–1950* (Kehot Publication Society, 1989), 244.

27 Rabbi Shmuel Gurary (d. 1921) was a student in Lubavitch during the time of Rabbi Shmuel. He was a successful businessman and philanthropist and an ardent Chasid and financial supporter of both the Rashab and the Rayatz. He was originally buried near the Rashab and transferred surreptitiously to the new Jewish cemetery, where he was once again interred next to the Rashab.

28 *Igrot Kodesh*, 175.

29 Reb Yitzchak Goldin (1900–68) came from a Chabad family and studied in Lubavitch. He assisted the Rebbe during his illness in Rostov. In 1932, he was arrested for his activities in the Chabad educational underground. Initially he was sentenced to death, but his sentence was commuted to exile in Kazakhstan. He escaped Russia in 1946, eventually moving to Brooklyn.

30 Levin, *Toldot Chabad BeRusia HaSovietit.*

31 Ibid. These students included Shlomo Chaim Kesselman, who later became a legendary *mashpia.*

32 *Igrot Kodesh*, 175.

33 Levin, *Toldot Chabad BeRusia HaSovietit.* He notes that this was particularly the case when it came to the prayers of *Refa'einu* ("May we be healed") and *Shema Koleinu* ("Hear our voice").

34 On Monday night, November 8, 1920 (28 Marcheshvan, 5681).

35 It was Shabbat *Parshat Toldot*, November 13, 1920 (2 Kislev, 5681). *Sefer HaMaamarim*, 5681.

36 As the Rebbe wrote in a letter signed by one of his students (Yehoshua Rosenblum) during the summer of 5681 (1921), published in *Igrot Kodesh* 13:55.

37 Chitrik writes that a rabbinical court convened, asking the students to donate time from their lives for the Rebbe. "The students presented the court with written pledges. Some committed six months of their lives, others a year or two years." In the 1980s, Chaim Lieberman, secretary and librarian of the Rebbe, located the list of the years pledged and found that it added up to thirty years – the number of years the Rebbe lived after his recovery (heard at the time by Rabbi Yossi Keller). There is a precedent

for this in the Torah: The Zohar (I 168a) states that the patriarchs and Yosef HaTzaddik each gave up years of their lives for King David, so that he could live a full life (see "Donations for David," available at: chabad.org/379756).

38 Goldin telegrammed Chabad Chasidim in Lubavitch, Nizhyn, and Hadyach to pray at the graves of earlier Lubavitcher Rebbes.

39 In the letter that the Rayatz sent out with Rabbi Morozov's signature (*Igrot Kodesh* 14:175), he states that the improvement began on 19 Kislev, 5682 (November 30, 1920). That Hebrew date marks the release of Rabbi Schneur Zalman from czarist prison in 1798, representing a divine vindication of his teachings. The day is known as the New Year of Chabad Chasidism and continues to be celebrated in Jewish communities worldwide.

40 Lead a chasidic celebration.

41 Yehuda Chitrik, *Reshimot Devarim* (Brooklyn, NY: 1981), 1:187–88. Also see the 2009 edition, 404.

42 *The Sentinel*, August 9, 1921.

43 The other major yeshivas had all left or were in the process of departing Russia, though there remained some local study programs. Later, in 1957, at a time when Russians showed a bit of tolerance, a small government-sanctioned yeshivah opened in Moscow's Choral Synagogue. By 1962, it had just six students.

44 Goldin writes about the Yevesektzia's first attempt to disrupt the yeshivah in Rostov: "On Shavuot, the Yevesektzia brought orders to the boys that they should go work. At that time it was obligatory for the local citizens to clean the streets for two or three days when it was one's turn. I approached the Rebbe to ask what we should do, and he said, 'What connection do we have with them? Today is the giving of the Torah – we have to receive the Torah! We have no connection to them!' Then he added: 'This is true in general. Regarding this particular issue, approach the officer in charge and tell him that today is Shavuot, and if he needs something, you will take care of it.' I immediately went over to the officer in charge. I noticed that his wife was sick and that he needed wine in order to heal her, but he didn't have any means to get it. I gave him the message and I got for him what he needed, and because of this he absolved all the boys from participating in public works." See Levin, *Toldot Chabad BeRusia HaSovietit*.

45 *American Jewish Yearbook*, 1920–21.

46 Levin, *The Jews in the Soviet Union Since 1917*, 70–71.

47 Richard Pipes, *Russia Under the Bolshevik Regime* (Vintage Books, 1995), chap. 4.

48 When it came to Islam, the Communist government acted with restraint. As Pipes writes, "The Muslims fared relativity the best. Their comparatively lenient treatment was due entirely to political considerations, namely the fear of alienating the colonial nations whose support was critical to the strategy of the Communists. Sultan Galieve, the leading Communist expert on the subject, cautioned Moscow that anti-religious

propaganda among Muslims had to be conducted in a circumspect manner, not only because of their strong attachment to the faith, but also because they regarded the Muslim community as an undivided whole and a perceived attack on one as an attack on all." Pipes, *Russia Under the Bolshevik Regime*, 367.

49 Dimenstein was born in Sebezh, today in Belorussia, in 1886. He was considered the representative of Russian Jews of the Soviet Authorities. Like many other leaders of the Yevesektzia, he was killed during the purges of Stalin in 1938.

50 Dimenstein himself admitted this. See Yehoshua Gilboa, *A Language Silenced: The Suppression of Hebrew Literature and Culture in the Soviet Union* (Herzl Press), chap. 4.

51 Zvi Gitelman, *A Century of Ambivalence: The Jews of Russia and the Soviet Union, 1881 to the Present*, 2nd edition (Indiana University Press, 2001), chap. 2.

52 For a detailed account of the Yevesektzia campaign against Zionism, see Gilboa, *A Language Silenced.*

53 Gitelman, *A Century of Ambivalence*; Gilboa, *A Language Silenced.* At the June 1919 Yevesektzia conference in Moscow, the First Jewish Educational Council was established, and one of its decisions was that Hebrew and Bible would not be taught in elementary schools. *Der Kommunist* published in Kharkiv in January 1922, "We have closed down all Hebrew courses." A year later, *Der Emes* reported in August 1923 that there were five hundred Yiddish books in the Bichov library in the Homel region, and that the Hebrew language ones had been removed. Cited by Gilboa, *A Language Silenced.*

54 Gitelman, *A Century of Ambivalence*, chap. 3.

55 In response to Dimenstein's protest, a public debate was held in Moscow in 1920. Writer and theater critic Prince Serge Wolkowski described the core issue in his memoir, writing that the Habima Theater represented the "aspirations of some Jews to set up a state of their own in Palestine." That was anathema to the Jewish Communists, who were intent on building their own version of utopia in the new Soviet Union. See Gilboa, *A Language Silenced.*

56 The Rebbe argued time and again that the driving force behind the harshness of the anti-religious campaign was the Yevesektzia, not the Soviet government. Though the Communist authorities wanted to rid Russia of religious expression, they were more tolerant, and Soviet law technically allowed freedom of religion. The fact that the government awarded grants to the Habima Theater while Yevesektzia leaders such as Dimenstein strongly opposed these actions is an indicator that at times, there was disagreement between the Yevesektzia leaders and government officials. Later, in the 1930s, after the Yevesektzia was disbanded, government actions against synagogues and religious leaders became harsher. For more on the extremism of the Yevesektzia, see Yehuda Geberer, "Treacherous Brothers: The Yevsektsia

Destroys Jewish Life in Russia," available at: https://jsoundbites.podbean.com/e/treacherous-brothers-the-yevsektsia-destryoys-jewish-life-in-russia/.

57 Gilboa, *A Language Silenced*, chap. 6. In 1958, Habima became the official national theater of Israel.

58 The secret police was established in December 1917 by the Communists. In 1923, it became the GPU, later the OGPU, NKVD, and finally the KGB in 1954.

59 Local Rostov rabbis.

60 The core principles of Judaism include the belief in the absolute oneness of G-d and the promise of an afterlife. See Maimonides's Thirteen Principles of Faith.

61 A few weeks later, on August 8, 1921, the Cheka issued a document attesting to the release of the Rebbe. See Menachem Zigelbaum, *Sippur shel Chag* (Kfar Chabad: 2011), 45.

62 The letter from the Rebbe was signed by his secretary Rabbi Chonye Morozov and dated December 12, 1921. *Igrot Kodesh* 14:175–76.

63 Rabbi Rafael Kahn, *Lubavitch VeChayalehah* (Kfar Chabad, Israel: 1983), 120.

64 *Igrot Kodesh* 14:175–76, letter dated December 12, 1921.

65 "Poltava," available at: https://www.jewishvirtuallibrary.org/poltava.

66 Rabbi Yechezkel (Chatche) Feigin (1895–1941) was a student of the yeshivah in Lubavitch until 1911, when he was one of the outstanding students sent by the Rebbe Rashab to establish a yeshivah in Hebron. He returned to Russia in 1914, where he became an organizer of the underground network of Tomchei Temimim yeshivas in the Soviet Union. Prior to serving as administrator of the yeshivah in Poltava, Rabbi Feigin was a teacher in the yeshivah in Homil. Starting in 1927, he served as a secretary to the Rebbe and accompanied him on many of his travels. He escaped Warsaw with the Rebbe, arriving in Riga in 1939. Due to issues with his passport, he was unable to travel to the United States with the Rebbe. All efforts (even those of the Rebbe) to help Rabbi Feigin immigrate failed. In December 1941, the Nazis brought most of the city's Jews to a synagogue and set it on fire with everyone inside, forcing other Jews to watch the spectacle. According to some reports, Rabbi Yitzchak Gurevitz removed the Torah scroll from the holy ark and danced with Rabbi Feigin as they burned alive along with the rest of the Jews inside, in sanctification of G-d's name. When the Rebbe received a letter about their deaths in 1945, he fainted from grief.

67 For a detailed history of Yeshivas Tomchei Temimim in Russia in Communist times, see Levin, *Toldot Chabad BeRusia HaSovietit*, chap. 51–98.

68 Levin, *Toldot Chabad BeRusia HaSovietit*, chap. 87.

69 Rabbi Moshe Feinstein (1895–1986) became the dean of Mesivta Tifereth Jerusalem in the United States. Commonly known as "Reb Moshe," he was one of the greatest Jewish legal scholars of the twentieth century. His rabbinical responsa on contemporary issues are considered foundational. Reb Moshe recalls in an

autobiographical insert in his classic *Igrot Moshe* that while in Russia, he asked a delegation from the Rebbe who had come to invite him to a rabbinical conference, "What do I have to do with Lubavitch?" The Rebbe sent a message explaining his family connection to Chabad. Reb Moshe recalled, "my father's grandmother, Rochel, was an outstanding student and lived in Liozna. Her father went to the first Chabad Rebbe asking for advice to help his intellectually precocious daughter. He suggested that she join the *cheder* class of his grandson, Rabbi Menachem Mendel [who later became the third Rebbe, known as the Tzemach Tzedek]." The great-grandmother of Rabbi Moshe Feinstein was therefore a classmate of the Tzemach Tzedek, one of the leading Jewish scholars of nineteenth-century Russia. See Rabbi Shimon Finkelman, *Reb Moshe* (ArtScroll Publications, 2006); *Igrot Moshe, Orach Chayim*, section 5, *Yoreh De'ah*, section 4 (New York, NY: 1996).

70 He was granted an exit visa as a result of lobbying on his behalf by relatives who lived in the United States.

71 David Fishman, "Preserving Tradition in the Land of Revolution," in Jack Wertheimer, ed. *The Uses of Tradition* (New York: Jewish Theological Seminary, 1992).

72 Rabbi Yisrael Meir Kagan (1838–1933) was also known as the Chafetz Chaim, the title of his classic work on Jewish ethics. He was one of the leading rabbis of Europe, respected greatly for his piety, scholarship, and integrity. Among his numerous works is the *Mishnah Berurah*, a running commentary on the *Shulchan Arukh*. He established a yeshivah in Radin, Poland in 1869, which he transferred to Russia at the beginning of World War I. He was one of the leaders of Agudath Israel.

73 Moses M. Yoshor, *The Chafetz Chaim* (Mesorah Publications, 1984), vol. 2, chap. 55.

74 Yoshor, *The Chafetz Chaim*, chap. 67.

75 For a brief time, the Novardok yeshivah continued operating in the Soviet Union. Rabbi Yosef Yozel Horwitz (1847–1919), the Alter, instructed his students to leave Russia for Poland, where Novardok developed an impressive network of yeshivas.

76 A strong argument can be made that this strategy bore many elements of success. In Lakewood, New Jersey, where Rabbi Aharon Kotler pioneered this approach, there are more than five thousand students studying today. The influence of the yeshivah community is felt in religious communities across America. But beyond the Orthodox community, its role is marginal, not reaching the majority of American Jews who have little connection to the yeshivah community. Chabad's approach of sending *shluchim* to build centers of Jewish life, which become an integral part of those communities, has had a vastly greater impact.

77 Merkos L'Inyonei Chinuch, Chabad's central organization for Jewish education, was founded by the Rayatz in 1943. Other national Jewish organizations such as Torah Umesorah came later.

78 The Baal Shem Tov began to publicly teach the ideas of Chasidism in 1734, at the age of thirty-six. See Peretz Golding, "The Baal Shem Tov – A Brief Biography," available at: chabad.org/1208507.

79 "The new Rebbe had become a symbol of resistance to the Soviet System." David Biale et al., *Hasidism: A New History* (Princeton University Press, 2018), 593. The renaissance of Jewish life in Russia today is a direct result of the secret underground organized by the Rebbe Rayatz and has proven the success of the strategy he initiated a century ago.

80 Most Jewish historians have failed to document this fully for a variety of reasons. As secular academics, they view the history of Soviet Jewry through their own prism, such as the Enlightenment, Zionism, and Yiddish culture. Much of their research was done while the Soviets were still in power, as was the case for noted historians like Nora Levin (*The Jews in the Soviet Union Since 1917*, published in 1987) and Zvi Gitelman (*A Century of Ambivalence*, published in 1988), among others. As Professor David Fishman writes, "Most of the historiography on Soviet Jewry between 1917 and 1930 has paid scant attention to the rabbis, on the assumption that they were insignificant historical players. Instead, the focus has been on secular Jewish elites."

These histories were published prior to the fall of the Soviet Union, when Chabad was still operating illegally in Russia and maintained a policy of absolute secrecy about its activities. There were no public records of the clandestine work in Russia in the postwar era that was orchestrated by the seventh Rebbe, who was at that time living in New York. Much of the instructions sent by the Rebbe to secret emissaries in Russia were given in private face-to-face meetings of which there were no written records. There were many private meetings between the Rebbe and members of Lishkat Hakesher, the secret department that Israel's prime minister established to handle Russian affairs. Not even members of the Rebbe's staff were aware of much of the covert work done in Russia. When Chabad activists immigrated to the West in the late 1940s, they did not speak of their activities so as not to endanger those still in Russia.

In one example of the extreme secrecy surrounding these activities, Rabbi Binyomin Katz returned to New York from a yearlong mission to Russia and Israel in 1965 that resulted in six hundred Jews leaving Russia covertly. Later, while participating in a public lecture in the United States about Chabad, an audience member asked him about Chabad's efforts for Soviet Jewry. Katz responded cryptically, saying, "The Rebbe is helping Russian Jews," without adding any details. Afterward, Rabbi Chaim Mordechai Aizik Hodakov, the Rebbe's chief secretary, chastised him, saying that even that short comment revealed too much.

When written material did appear, such as the book *Subbota* published in 1979 about Rabbi Lazer Nanes' twenty-year ordeal in Siberian prison, it was heavily redacted, removing anything that could be used to identify activists and activities still underway in the Soviet Union. The author even used a pseudonym.

Only in recent years has some source material come to light, including the thousands of letters of the Rebbe Rayatz that Professor David Fishman calls a "rare and unusual treasure trove" and detailed historical records in Rabbi Shalom Ber Levin's *Toldot Chabad BeRusia HaSovietit (History of Chabad in Soviet Russia)*. That information has been supplemented by a series of memoirs penned by activists and their families. Some of the members of Israel's secret service, such as Nehemia Levanon, have revealed details of their meetings with the seventh Rebbe. Still, much of what Chabad did in Russia remains a mystery, with many of those who played a role having passed away.

More recent works by academics such as David Fishman and Illia Luria have shed light on this era. There have also been important articles and books published by writers in the Chabad community such as Dovid Margolin, Zushe Wolfe, and Boruch Werdiger. Finally, Chabad publications such as the magazine *Derher* and the proliferation of *teshurahs* (wedding mementos, often featuring unpublished historical materials) have revealed much original historical information.

81 Avraham Eliyahu (Romanov) Gershoni, who was born in Russia and immigrated to Israel, is one of the few historians to document religious life in Russia during the Communist regime in a detailed, thorough fashion. He wrote two seminal works, both in Hebrew: The first, *Yahadut BeRusia HaSovietit*, published in 1961, covers the period until 1930. The second, *Yehudei Brit HaMo'atzot*, published in 1970, covers the era after 1930. These volumes are crucial to understanding the history of Jews in the Soviet Union. They include many firsthand interviews and in-depth information on the period. They are different from the works produced by American historians who did not live in Russia under Communism and who did not have access to the Hebrew-speaking immigrants in Israel who could share firsthand historical information. These historians tend to view history through a secular perspective and lack a nuanced understanding of religious life in Russia during this time.

82 Gershoni, *Yahadut BeRusia HaSovietit*, 157.

83 He was deported to the remote province of Uzbekistan. A recently discovered NKVD file documenting his arrest reported that on the train to Uzbekistan, he met Rabbi Levi Yitzchak Schneerson, father of the seventh Rebbe, who was also being exiled there. They were banished to small villages thirty miles from each other and remained in contact. Rabbi Kaplan was killed on Yom Kippur in 1943 by anti-Semitic thugs. Rabbi Levi Yitzchak Schneerson passed away in 1944 and is buried in Alma Ata. Author's interview with Rabbi Kaplan's grandson, Rabbi Nachum Kaplan.

84 Rabbi Kaplan placed his children in underground yeshivas run by Chabad in Russia. His son Elimelech grew up to become the senior rabbi of Lod, Israel, and his son Moshe became a rabbi and businessman in New York. His two daughters both married noted Jewish scholars. Today, many of his descendants are Chabad *shluchim* around the globe. Interview with Rabbi Nachum Kaplan.

85 With the fall of the Soviet Union, Judaism finally came to Birobidzhan. In 2002, Rabbi Mordechai Scheiner became the community's rabbi, opening a synagogue and Jewish school and reviving Jewish religious life. See https://fjc-fsu.org/centers/russia/birobidzhan.

86 In a long letter from Riga dated November 10, 1927 (15 Cheshvan, 5688), the Rebbe detailed the struggle in Russia. *Igrot Kodesh,* vol. 1.

87 Ibid.

88 Fishman, "Preserving Tradition in the Land of Revolution."

89 *Igrot Kodesh,* vol. 1, letter dated November 10, 1927.

90 The American Joint Distribution Committee, known as the Joint or the JDC, was established in 1914 as a merger of a variety of American Jewish groups, becoming the primary agency of American Jewry dedicated to helping Jews overseas. The Rebbe and Chabad had a long relationship with the Joint that continues till today. In the early 1920s, it was a vital partner to the Rebbe's work in Russia. In the 1920s and 1930s, despite the Rebbe's pleas, it partnered with the Communist regime in establishing agricultural colonies. In the postwar era, it was instrumental in helping Jewish refugees the world over, in particular Chabad Chasidim who had escaped Russia. Starting in the 1950s, it partnered with Chabad in creating a Jewish school system in Morocco and Tunisia, as well as other projects in Israel and throughout Europe. More recently it has worked in cooperation with Chabad in Russia and Ukraine.

91 Levin, *Toldot Chabad BeRusia HaSovietit,* chap. 7.

92 Rabbi Shlomo Yosef Zevin (1888–1978) was born in Kazimirov, near Minsk. He studied in the Lithuanian Mir Yeshivah and then in Bobruysk under the chasidic influence of Rabbi Shmaryahu Noach Schneersohn, leader of the Kopust Chabad branch. He served as a rabbi in Kazimirov, Klimovo, and Novozybkov. From 1924–34, he was the secretary of the Rabbinical Council of Russia under the leadership of the Rebbe Rayatz. In 1934, he immigrated to Palestine, becoming a leading rabbinic scholar and editor of the Talmudic Encyclopedia.

93 *Igrot Kodesh,* vol. 1, letter dated July 12, 1923 (28 Tamuz 5763).

94 *Igrot Kodesh,* vol. 1, letter dated November 10, 1927.

95 Ibid.

96 Debate about the Congress of Jewish Religious Communities in the USSR in 1925–26, Michael Beizer and Anatoli Karasev, published by Jews in Russia and Eastern Europe, summer 2003, Hebrew University of Jerusalem.

97 The apartment had belonged to the baron from Kass, the governor of the Bessarabia region. In his own handwriting, the baron signed over the dwelling and much of its furniture to the Rebbe. In June 1924, the baron was compelled, according to Soviet law, to leave Leningrad and was banished to one of the remote cities of exile. A letter written by Althaus, dated May 1928, appears in Rabbi Dr. Alter B. Metzger, trans., *The Heroic Struggle: The Arrest and Liberation of Rabbi Yosef Y. Schneersohn of Lubavitch in Soviet Russia* (Kehot Publication Society, 1999), 286–87. Althaus wrote, "Until this day many of the baron's furnishings remain in the Rebbe's dwelling."

98 Beizer notes that the other objects of focus were Lev Gurewicz, the leader of LERO (Leningrad Religious Community), and the city's rabbi, David Tevel Katzenellenbogen.

99 The nineteenth of the Jewish month of Kislev is the anniversary of the founder of Chabad, Rabbi Schneur Zalman, being liberated from czarist prison in 1798. The day is celebrated in Jewish communities worldwide. The *farbrengen* of 19 Kislev is described in the memoirs of Rabbi Michael Yehuda Cohen, cited in Levin, *Toldot Chabad BeRusia HaSovietit*, chap. 10. Also see *Sefer HaSichos*, 5680–87 (Brooklyn, NY: Kehot Publication Society, 2020), 55–58.

100 Levin, *Toldot Chabad BeRusia HaSovietit*, chap. 10; *Sefer HaSichos*, 5702, 154.

101 Author's interview with Rabbi Yehudah Leib Schapiro, who witnessed the interaction between the seventh Rebbe and Rabbi Shemtov.

102 "Aide-Memoire About Religious Education in Russia," confidential, July 3, 1926, JDC Archives.

103 The report focused on children and noted that there were additional older students in secret yeshivas in eight cities, including remote Kutaisi in Soviet Georgia, a clear result of Simon Jacobson's activities. Jacobson was one of the nine *temimim* at the Rebbe's meeting in Moscow.

104 A fourth whose identity is known is Rabbi Yerachmiel Binyaminson, who was the rabbi in the town of Shchedrin and later Zlobin.

105 Unpublished biography of Rabbi Bentzion Shemtov.

106 His parents had given him a jacket with beautiful buttons that each hid a diamond. Realizing that the yeshivah needed financial support, he gave the diamonds to the Rebbe. Author's interview with Rabbi Kasriel Sudak, grandson of Rabbi Shemtov.

107 She went to live with her uncle in Moscow until Shemtov was paroled. Interview with Esther Golda's daughter, Fradel Sudak, available at: https://www.youtube.com/watch?v=zRjSI2CUDco.

108 Interview with his grandson, Rabbi Kasriel Shemtov of Jerusalem.

109 In late 1946 and early 1947, Chabad Chasidim in Russia organized an audacious escape of some one thousand Chasidim. See chap. 11 of this book; David Eliezrie, *The Secret of Chabad*, chap. 4.

110 The Rebbe sent Rabbis Shmuel Levitin, Avraham Slavin, Nachum Sasonkin, Mordechai Perlow, and Yisrael Zuber, among others, to the region. Today, many rabbis in the Georgian community are educated in Chabad institutions. For more information, see Rabbi Zusha Wolf, *Admorei Chabad VeYahadut Bukhara* (Lod, Israel: Machon LeSefer, 2016).

111 Interview with Rabbi Yosef Yitzchak Jacobson available at: https://jewsyoushouldknow.libsyn.com/episode-137-the-truth-sayer-rabbi-a-conversation-with-yy-jacobson.

112 The high point of Rosh HaShanah is the sounding of the shofar. The Rebbe's shofar blowing was a profoundly spiritual moment, and Chasidim attempted to stand as close as possible to experience it personally. Shemtov biography, unpublished.

113 Moshe Litvakov (1875/80–1939) was the editor of the Yevesektzia newspaper, *Der Emes*. He was killed in the purges of Stalin. For more, see Gennady Estraikh, "Litvakov, Moyshe," available at: https://yivoencyclopedia.org/article.aspx/Litvakov_Moyshe; Zvi Gitelman, *Jewish Nationality and Soviet Politics* (Princeton Press, 1972), index, "Levitikov."

114 Levin, *Toldot Chabad BeRusia HaSovietit*, 76.

115 Yakovshvili's impact, together with the yeshivas that had been opened earlier, lasted for decades. When Georgian Jews began immigrating to Israel in the early 1970s, many chose to join communities established by Chabad in Lod and Kiryat Malachi. While maintaining their unique traditions, many of them remain dedicated Chabad Chasidim. Today, the synagogues and Jewish schools in the former Soviet province are operated by Chabad. In 2019, a forty-thousand-square-foot educational center was dedicated to serve the needs of the province's four thousand Jews. See http://www.oravner.ge/ (Or Avner school); https://www.timesofisrael.com/tbilisis-jewish-community-keeps-active-with-israeli-tourists-and-chabad-meal (Times of Israel); and http://www.5tjt.com/chabad-dedicates-jewish-educational-complex-in-tbilisi-georgia/ (5 Towns Jewish Times).

116 Shemtov biography, unpublished.

117 "The Life and Legacy of Gershon Jacobson," video available at: https://www.youtube.com/watch?v=5gC3YI8MAYs.

118 His daughter Rachel was born in Lubavitch in 1906; her younger sister was Sara. They both escaped the Soviet Union in 1946 and moved to Israel. Although they were not personally observant, they maintained a close relationship with their family.

119 Barbara Bensoussan, "Tunisia's Russian Jewish Leader," available at: chabad.org/1163700.

120 *Likkutei Dibburim* (English), vol. 6, chap. 63; excerpt from the Rebbe's diary from Adar, 5687, February–March 1927, printed in *Sefer HaSichos*, 5680–87, 128–58;

"Appendix: Moscow, 1927" from the diary of Rabbi Yosef Yitzchak of Lubavitch, available at: chabad.org/2221.

121 This would make him the equivalent of a governor of a US state and apparently a member of the executive committee of the OGPU, the Soviet secret police.

122 Nicholas I of Russia was czar from 1825–55. In 1827, he instituted the Cantonist system of up to twenty-five years of compulsory military service for Jewish children. He aligned himself with the leaders of the Haskalah (secular Enlightenment), challenging the traditional Jewish educational system in Russia.

123 Diary entry dated 10 Adar Alef, 5787 (February 10, 1927). While on a mission to Moscow, he was harassed by the Yevesektzia. He writes that he woke up at 3 a.m. troubled by events in Moscow. After reflecting on this meeting with his father, he writes, "I went back to sleep, and my soul was relaxed." *Sefer HaSichos*, 5680–87 (Brooklyn, NY: Kehot Publication Society), 132.

124 Simcha Gorodetsky (1903–1984) studied in the yeshivah in Rostov and Kherson. As a young man, he was an emissary of the Rebbe in Russia; after his marriage in 1926 he was sent to remote Bukhara, where he opened Jewish schools. He was arrested and sentenced to twenty-five years of hard labor in the artic in 1946. He was released in 1956 after the death of Stalin and permitted to leave Russia in 1964. His family joined him two years later.

125 Hillel Zaltzman, *Samarkand: The Underground with a Far-Reaching Impact* (Brooklyn, New York: Chamah, 2015), chap. 4.

126 Ibid.

127 Rabbi Menachem Mendel Schneerson, *Likkutei Sichot* (Kehot Publication Society, 1982), 20:480.

128 Interview with the author.

129 *Farbrengen*, 10 Shevat, 5734 (February 2, 1974). An excerpt of the talk can be found in *Likkutei Sichot* 18:304.

130 Moishe Levertov, "The Man Who Mocked the KGB," available at: chabad.org/312429.

131 Interview with the author.

132 Interview with the author.

133 Lev Gurewicz (1876–1943) graduated from the University of St. Petersburg with a law degree. Michael Beizer writes that during Gurewicz's high school years, he was carried away by the ideas of the Enlightenment and subsequently by Zionism as well. He served as chairman of the Zionist Organization of Russia and was arrested in 1929. See debate about the Congress of Jewish Religious Communities in the USSR in 1925–26, Michael Beizer and Anatoli Karasev, published by Jews in Russia and Eastern Europe, summer 2003, Hebrew University of Jerusalem.

134 Rabbi Eliyahu Chaim Althaus (1870–1941) was a devoted Chasid of the Rebbe Rayatz who studied in Lubavitch and was killed by the Nazis in Riga. He wrote

a long account of the conflict over the proposed Leningrad Jewish Conference in a series of letters to family members in 1928. He participated in many of the meetings and presents a remarkable firsthand description. Reprinted in *Likkutei Dibburim*, vol. 6 (Brooklyn, NY: Kehot Publication Society, 2012). Excerpts available at: chabad.org/82517. The Hebrew original is printed in Levin, *Toldot Chabad BeRusia HaSovietit*, 79–93.

135 Rabbi Althaus writes that Gurewicz had a limited Jewish education, attended secular high school, and earned a law degree. He describes him as "vehemently anti-religious."

136 Rabbi David Katzenellenbogen (1850–1930) was a student of Rabbi Yisrael Salanter, founder of the *Musar* movement. In 1908, he became rabbi of St. Petersburg's Choral Synagogue, and he also helped open more synagogues in the city. He was a great scholar but not a Chasid. The Rebbe had a profound respect for him and, according to Rabbi Althaus, until the conflict over the conference, they were of "one opinion on any matter involving religion." At the time, he was seventy-five, and Rabbi Althaus speculates that age had weakened him, and he put too much faith in other people who may have attempted to mislead him.

137 According to the Althaus account of the meeting, the Rebbe did not mention the specific risks. It could be that he was referring to the fact that Gurewicz wanted to change the communal structure the Rebbe had developed by replacing the rabbis who were currently at the helm with lay leaders who were not tethered so strongly to tradition. Second, perhaps the Rebbe was concerned that this group would be more easily manipulated by the Soviet government that wanted to undermine Jewish observance. This would also create competing interests for overseas support for Russian Jewry, creating communal politics over the allocation of financial resources.

138 Unpublished personal handwritten letter from the Rebbe to Rabbi Katzenellenbogen dated 23 Cheshvan, 5687 (November 21, 1926), Rabbi Dovid Kamenetsky Archives.

139 Report by Rabbi Yosef Zevin on the congress; debate about the Congress of Jewish Religious Communities in the USSR in 1925–26, Michael Beizer and Anatoli Karasev, published by Jews in Russia and Eastern Europe, summer 2003, Hebrew University of Jerusalem.

140 Levin, *Toldot Chabad BeRusia HaSovietit*, letter from Rabbi Althaus.

141 They also sent a three-man delegation to Rabbi Katzenellenbogen, still under the sway of Gurewicz, who considered the conflict as just another disagreement between Chasidim and *mitnagdim*, who had been debating various details of Jewish practice for two centuries already. The delegation told the rabbi that this was false and in truth, it was a disagreement between those who wanted to change Judaism in an attempt to modernize it and those who wanted to retain its traditional character. Katzenellenbogen insisted they rejoin LERO and follow the majority.

Despite the fact that they held the rabbi in high esteem, they refused, telling him that the leaders of LERO had misled him. The next Shabbat, the ten men who had resigned from LERO spoke in synagogues throughout Leningrad. A few days later, they held a large community meeting, and it was decided to create a new community. At the time, Soviet law permitted any religious group of twenty to petition for recognition as a community.

142 Althaus account, *Likkutei Dibburim*, vol. 6.

143 Ibid.

144 Rabbi Binyamin Gorodetsky (1907–95) came from a Chabad family in Bobruysk, Russia. He was an activist in the Chabad underground in Russia, escaping in 1946. He established the Chabad bureau in Paris and served as a *shliach* for the Rayatz and the seventh Rebbe. He was instrumental in establishing Chabad's educational network in Morocco as well as founding institutions in Europe and Israel. See Rabbi Binyamin Gorodetsky, *Light in the Darkness* (New York: Shengold Publishers, 1986).

145 *Igrot Kodesh* 1:628.

146 For a detailed historical background, see Levin, *Toldot Chabad BeRusia HaSovietit*, chap. 20. See also *Igrot Kodesh*, vol. 1, letter dated November 10, 1927.

147 In addition, the Rebbe sent the conference two letters. He wrote of the difficulties of Jews throughout Jewish history: "In every generation and in country after country, when there were decrees to destroy us, great Jewish scholars and leaders stood up." *Igrot Kodesh* 1:543–48.

148 The Rebbe writes that he was surprised by the honor. "Suddenly, without any advance knowledge, I received an express telegram that the conference of rabbis had unanimously chosen me as honorary president." *Igrot Kodesh* 1:549.

149 Levin, *Toldot Chabad BeRusia HaSovietit*, 91.

150 Shemtov writes that he learned this during the long days of questioning by the interrogators.

151 Memoir of Rabbi Kipnis, reprinted, chap. 20; Levin, *Toldot Chabad BeRusia HaSovietit.*

152 A prominent rabbi and leader of the Chabad community in Leningrad. He studied in the yeshivah in Lubavitch, was arrested in 1930, and died in a prison camp three years later. Rabbi Shalom Ber Levin, *Toldot Chabad BeRusia HaSovietit*, index, "Lazaroff."

153 *Likkutei Dibburim*, chap. 66.

154 This festive holiday celebrates the completion and restarting of the annual cycle of Torah reading. It comes two weeks after Yom Kippur and is celebrated with dancing many times through the night and the day. It concludes the annual season of the Jewish High Holidays in an upbeat, joyous way.

155 Letter from Rabbi Feigin to Jacobson dated 17 Iyar, 5687 (May 19, 1927).

156 Rabbi Akiva, one of the greatest talmudic scholars, was killed by the Romans in 135 CE in a time of anti-Semitic oppression. The Talmud says that when faced with martyrdom, he told his students: "All my days, I was troubled by this verse, 'with all your soul' (Deut. 6:5), meaning, 'even if He takes your soul.' I said to myself: When will the opportunity come that I may fulfill this verse? And now it has come to my hands" (Brachot 61b).

157 Rabbi Morozov was arrested on February 23, 1927, initially accused of attempting to smuggle the Rebbe's books abroad. He was jailed with common criminals and suffered greatly. His daughters Rachel and Sara had been arrested a few weeks earlier, on February 9, for Zionist activities and were accused of belonging to the Zionist organization Dror. In prison, they became aware of their father's plight and declared a hunger strike; on the fifth day of their strike he was moved to a cell with Zionist prisoners. That May, he was indicted for helping Jews cross the border illegally, sentenced to three years in exile, and deported to Krasnoyarsk. Irina Osipova, *Hasidim: Saving Thy People*, trans. Malcolm Gilbert, chap. 1.

158 Letter from Rabbi Feigin to Jacobson dated 15 Iyar, 5687 (May 17, 1927).

159 Rabbi Zalman Duchman, *As I Heard Them: Stories, Sayings and Memories from Lubavitch of Yesteryear* (Brooklyn, NY: Wellspring Press).

160 Ibid.

161 Althaus account, *Likkutei Dibburim*, vol. 6.

162 Jem Oral History Project.

CHAPTER FOUR

1 The account in this chapter is based to a large degree on the memoirs of the Rebbe, the Rebbe's diary, and letters from Rabbi Eliyahu Chaim Althaus written at the time. The material can be found in Rabbi Dr. Alter B. Metzger, trans., *The Heroic Struggle: The Arrest and Liberation of Rabbi Yosef Y. Schneersohn of Lubavitch in Soviet Russia* (Kehot Publication Society, 1999). Also see "Arrest & Liberation," available at: chabad.org/3382365.

Another important source is *Di Yisurim Fun Lubavitcher Rebben in Soviet Russland (The Lubavitcher Rebbe's Ordeal in Soviet Russia)*, first published in Yiddish by an anonymous writer in 1930 in Riga. The late Rabbi Yehoshua Mondshine identifies the author as the Riga journalist Elimelech Josselsohn, a religious Zionist who studied in Jerusalem before returning to Riga, where he wrote for the *Frimorgen* newspaper. This narrative provides important historical context, and as translator Uri Kaploun writes, "It photographs the mood and climate of that turbulent era." It was translated into English for the first time in *Likkutei Dibburim*, vol. 6 (Brooklyn, New York: Kehot Publication Society, 2012).

For a more detailed historical background in Hebrew, see Menachem Zilgebaum, *Sippur Shel Chag* (Kfar Chabad, 2011). The book is supplemented by original material (provided by Rabbi Yifrach Abramov) from file no. 898 of the OGPU (United Government Political Administration), managed by chief investigating officer Varenberg in Leningrad. The original questionnaire filled out on behalf of the Rebbe was partially printed (in English translation) in Metzger, trans., *The Heroic Struggle*, appendix 8, 315–16, under the caption "Excerpt from Interrogation of Witnesses/ Investigator's name: Lulov."

2 June 14 and the beginning of June 15 (14 Sivan, 5687).

3 Naftali Hertz Klotzkin, the Rebbe's assistant, was present. He later recalled the details to Zalman Duchman; see Duchman, *LeSheima Ozen*, 1963 edition, 155–56 (1990 edition, p. 191).

4 The Jewish Telegraphic Agency (JTA), the US-based Jewish news service, described the arrest as being caused by the controversy over the planned conference. Their report made no mention of the Yevesektzia's efforts to support the conference by pressuring rabbis to attend. On September 22, 1927, the JTA reported from Riga (full report available at: https://www.jta.org/1927/09/22/archive/riga-hears-sensational-report-on-cause-of-lubowitscher-rebbes-arrest): "Well-informed circles in Moscow, according to the reports received here, trace the arrest of Rabbi Schneursohn to a serious party conflict within Russian Jewry and place the responsibility for the course of the events upon certain Jewish leaders. The controversy centered around the proposed conference of Jewish kehillahs in the Union of Socialist Soviet Republics, which is to be held in Leningrad on October 21, with the permission of the Soviet government.

"Rabbi Schneursohn and the group of rabbis associated with him voiced their opposition to the holding of this conference at the present time. They contended that in view of prevailing conditions it would be impossible to elect a truly representative body of Russian Jewry and that is why the committee which might result from this conference would not be endowed with the power to carry on the work and have the religious authority required. This attitude of the Lubowitscher Rebbe called forth resentment among the initiators of the Leningrad conference. To remove his opposition they decided, it is stated, to discredit him in the eyes of the Soviet authorities, an action which resulted in his arrest."

5 Diplomatic relations between the UK and Russia were severed at the end of May 1927 after a police raid on the All-Russian Co-operative Society in the UK. Conservative British prime minister Stanley Baldwin presented the House of Commons with deciphered Soviet telegrams that proved Soviet espionage activities, available at: https://api.parliament.uk/historic-hansard/commons/1927/may/24/prime-ministers-statement.

6 Pyotr Voykov (1888–1927) was Jewish. He was born in Ukraine and attended high school in Yalta. Later he studied in Geneva, where he met Stalin and eventually

became active in the Bolshevik party. The new Soviet Union attempted to appoint him ambassador to Canada, but the Canadians refused to certify him, because of the allegations of his participation in the assassination of the czar. Later he was sent as an ambassador to Poland, where he was assassinated.

7 Stalin claimed the monarchists were part of a foreign network with ties to England. Stephen Kotkin, *Stalin: Paradoxes of Power* (Penguin Publishers, 2014), 635.

8 *Igrot Kodesh*, vol. 2, letter dated May 19, 1928 (19 Iyar, 5688).

9 Metzger, trans., *The Heroic Struggle*, chap. 1.

10 Many Jews were drawn to Communism by the promise of the eradication of the systematic corruption and anti-Semitism that was rampant under the czarist regime. During the czar's rule, Jews were regulated to living in the Pale of Settlement, and pogroms were frequent and supported by the government. There were barriers to higher education and economic opportunity. Some Jews supported Communism in the hope of gaining equality.

11 Located about 120 miles from Lubavitch, Nevel had a vibrant Chabad community. In 1897, its Jewish population reached 5,897. At the time of the Rebbe's arrest, there was a yeshivah in Nevel, but it was shut down by the authorities a year later. (See the JTA's report: https://www.jta.org/1928/11/02/archive/russian-yeshiva-in-nevel-subsidized-by-americans-closed.) The local Jewish population was annihilated by the Nazis during the Holocaust.

12 How did two young men, Lulov and Nachmanson, both from Chabad families, turn against their parents? Historian Nissan Ruppo, today the rabbi in Kostroma, grew up as a Communist Youth leader in Russia. He says this was part of the culture – put the ideals of the party over those of the family.

13 Nachmanson was arrested on his birthday, September 9, 1936, and transferred to Lubyanka Prison in Leningrad. He was never tried but was subjected to an extrajudicial sentence of five years. He was released in 1941, arrested a second time in 1950, and freed in 1953, after Stalin's death. He eventually received amnesty in 1956 (available at: https://base.memo.ru/person/show/1550682). After being freed, he lived in Novgorod, Russia. Toward the end of his life, he benefited from the Hesed, the Jewish soup kitchen operated on behalf of the US JDC for indigent Jews in the post-Soviet period. For a detailed timeline on Nachmanson's life, see Mikhail Gorelik, "Rabbi and Chekist," available at: https://lechaim.ru/ARHIV/238/gorelik.htm.

14 The interview conducted in Russian in Novgorod in 1992 details Nachmanson's long tragic life, including repeated arrests and long prison sentences. Still, he remained a staunch Communist as the Soviet Union was disintegrating. There is no reference to the Rebbe's arrest in this interview. Rabbi Nissan Ruppo of Kostroma says, "Few Communists like Nachmanson would tell of nefarious

activities done decades earlier." Interview available at: https://vgulage.name/books/nahmanson-m-s-pereryv-v-partstazhe-lit-zapis-smirnov-v/.

15 Grigory Nikolaevich Lulov (1899–1940) joined the Communist party in 1916 and the Cheka secret police three years later. He became a member of its successor, the GPU, in Leningrad. He was awarded the Order of Lenin (1937) with a badge reading "Honorary Worker of the Cheka-GPU." Lulov was arrested at the end of 1938 and executed by verdict of the Supreme Soviet of the USSR on January 21, 1940. V. Abramov, *Jews in the KGB: Executioners and Victims*; M. Yauza, *Eksmo* (2005) [Russian].

16 *Likkutei Dibburim* (English), 6:170; Metzger, trans., *The Heroic Struggle*, 301.

17 Rabbi Avraham Weingarten, *Nitzutzei Or* (Brooklyn, NY: 2007), 241–44.

18 Letter from Rabbi Eliyahu Chaim Althaus dated 24 Iyar, 5688 (May 13, 1928); Metzger, trans., *The Heroic Struggle*, appendix 7.

19 There are varied reports about this incident. According to Rabbi Rafael Kahn, *Shemuot VeSippurim*, 3:220, Chaya Mushka opened the window. Althaus writes only that it was "one of the daughters." Yeshivah student Avraham Weingarten said that he heard from the Ramash that it was the oldest daughter, Chana, who "reported what was happening." Weingarten, *Nitzutzei Or*, footnote 147; Boruch Oberlander and Elkanah Shmotkin, *Early Years: The Formative Years of the Rebbe, Rabbi Menachem M. Schneerson* (Kehot Publication Society), 477.

20 *Likkutei Dibburim* (English), 6:170–71; Metzger, trans., *The Heroic Struggle*, 301–2.

21 Metzger, trans., *The Heroic Struggle*, 29–30.

22 Yisrael Aryeh Leib Schneerson (1906–52), the brother of the Ramash, was attending university in Leningrad at the time. He had befriended some Jewish Communists and was able to glean information that they were planning to act against the Rebbe. He shared that information with the Rebbe, who realized that it was imperative to remove any documents from his home that could be used to incriminate him. Interview with Asa Paz, a relative of Aryeh Leib's wife, JEM Oral History Project.

23 According to Duchman's grandson Rabbi Shalom Ber Lipskar, who says that his grandfather never examined the documents.

24 Duchman, *LeSheima Ozen*, 205.

25 The building's doorman told the GPU officers that someone had come to the property late that night. During Lieberman's interrogation after his arrest, they wanted to know who that was. "I told them they were two drunkards who forgot their address and thought my house was theirs." Afterward they abandoned that line of questioning. *Kfar Chabad*, issue no. 108 (25 Av, 5743), 13; Rabbi Shalom Ber Levin, *Toldot Chabad BeRusia HaSovietit*, 339, footnote 24.

26 Metzger, trans., *The Heroic Struggle*, 31.

27 *Likkutei Dibburim* (English), 6:172; Metzger, trans., *The Heroic Struggle*, 304.

28 Since biblical times, when Calev visited the Ma'arat HaMakhpela, the Tomb of the Patriarchs in Hebron, to pray for success in his mission of scouting the Land of Israel, it has been a Jewish custom to pray at the graves of the righteous. The Rebbes of Lubavitch traditionally brought notes with prayers and requests to the graves of their predecessors. The seventh Rebbe visited the grave of the Rayatz regularly, spending hours reading prayer requests from thousands of Chasidim.

29 The prison was originally built during the reign of Alexander II of Russia, in the years 1871–75, on 25 Shpalernaya Street. During the Communist regime, it was notorious for its harsh conditions and the use of torture. Famous dissidents such as Alexander Solzhenitsyn were held there. Today it continues to function as a prison.

30 Weingarten, *Nitzutzei Or.*

31 Ibid, 242.

32 ibid Mezger.

33 Apparently, some nine thousand people were arrested across Russia at that time. For a detailed historical timeline of the night of the arrest, see *Haaros UBiurim, kovetz* 1101, page 147, available at: http://haoros.com/archive/.

34 Metzger, trans., *The Heroic Struggle.*

35 The reference to the Americans probably hinted to the Rebbe's connections to the JDC, which provided funding for his programs, and to his correspondence with Jewish leaders in the United States.

36 *Reshimat HaMaasor,* section 6.

37 Metzger, trans., *The Heroic Struggle,* chap. 8.

38 Friday, June 17, before sunset.

39 Jewish tradition teaches that in times of crisis, Jews should fast and add extra prayers. Communities will sometimes declare a public communal fast in response to impending calamity. See Maimonides, *Mishneh Torah, Hilkhot Taanit* (Laws of Fasting).

40 Rabbi Dr. Meir Hildesheimer (1864–1934) was the chief rabbi of the Orthodox community of Berlin. Reform Rabbi Leo Baeck (1873–1956) was the head of the Reform community in Berlin. The fact that they joined together to lobby on behalf of the Rebbe reflects the gravity of the issue. In later years, Hildesheimer stood by the Rebbe's side in his efforts to help Soviet Jews.

41 *Zikhron Livnei Yisrael – Memoirs of Rabbi Yisrael Jacobson: 1907–1939* [Hebrew] (Brooklyn, NY: Kehot Publication Society, 1996), chap. 25.

42 Established in 1924 to unite the Chabad synagogues in North America, Agudas Chassidei Chabad was still in its infancy.

43 Sam Kramer was the son of Max Kramer, one of the founders of Agudas Chassidei Chabad, the world headquarters of the Chabad movement.

44 Jacobson, *Zikhron Livnei Yisrael,* chap. 25.

45 These synagogues were established by Russian immigrants who had an ancestral connection to Chabad. Many were called Nusach Ari, after the prayer book used in Chabad synagogues. The congregations created religious and social bonds that linked Jews in the new world with their friends and family. Rabbi Shalom Ber Levin, *Toldot Chabad BeArtzot HaBrit 1900–1950 (History of Chabad in America)* (Brooklyn, NY: Kehot Publication Society, 1988), chap. 26.

46 Jacobson notes in his memoir that because at that time, he had only been in the US for a short period, and his political connections were therefore minimal; he was just getting to know the US scene. "I was only there a year and half. I couldn't do much – I just cried."

47 Rabbi Dovid Rabinowitz (1863-1943) was originally a follower of the Rebbe Rashab and was devoted to the Rebbe. He visited the Rebbe in Poland and helped save him from Europe. He assisted the Rebbe in numerous projects and had an extensive correspondence with the Rebbe. Chasidim referred to him as the Radam. He came to the US in 1896, serving as a Rabbi in Boston and pioneering traditional Judaism and Jewish education.

48 As told by Rabbi Dovid Edelman, who served as a *shliach* in Springfield, Massachusetts from 1950 until his passing in 2015. He was a close friend of the Rabinowitz brothers and heard this story from them many times. The Chabad community in Springfield refers to the celebration of the Rebbe's release as "The miracle in Springfield." For more, see: https://collive.com/the-miracle-in-springfield/.

49 Rabbi Edelman always wondered how Brandeis, who came from an assimilated background, knew of the Rebbe and referred to him in such a distinguished fashion. One historical connection, though tangential, may give us a clue: One of the major influences on Brandeis's support of Zionism was Aaron Aaronsohn, who lived in Zichron Yaakov, then in Palestine, and visited the US a few times. Aaronsohn was one of the organizers of the NILI Spy Ring that worked for the British against the Turks during World War I. His assistant and secretary was Lyova (Levi Yitzchak) Shneerson, a cousin of the Rebbe, who received an invitation to the wedding of the Rebbe's daughter in 1929. Could Aaronsohn have introduced Brandeis to his secretary during his visit to Palestine in 1919? One can only wonder. For more, see Jonathan Sarna, *Louis D. Brandeis: Zionist Leader,* available at: https://www.brandeis.edu/hornstein/sarna/americanjewishcultureandscholarship/Archive4/LouisD.BrandeisZionistLeader.pdf and Marcy Oster, "Wedding invitation of Lubavitcher rebbe discovered at National Library of Israel," JTA, available at: https://www.jta.org/2019/06/05/israel/wedding-invitation-of-lubavitcher-rebbe-discovered-at-national-library-of-israel.

50 In 1929–30, when the Rebbe visited the United States, he stopped in Springfield and thanked Peretz Rabinowitz for his role in saving his life, presenting him with a cigar as a token of appreciation. After Peretz's passing, his family gave the cigar

to Rabbi Dovid Edelman, who bequeathed it to his children; they still have the cigar in their possession today. In 1930, Asher Rabinowitz accompanied the Rebbe when he met with President Hebert Hoover in Washington (see chap. 7 of this book).

51 Duchman, *LeSheima Ozen*, 201.

52 Rabbi Mendel Futerfus, a close confident of Rabbi Zalman Moshe Yitzchaki, recounted the events years later. Menachem Zigelbaum, *Sippur shel Chag* (Kfar Chabad: 2011).

53 Madam Yekaterina Peshkova (1887–1965). She was active in helping prisoners under the czars, and later the Communists. She had many political connections and even earned the trust of Lenin.

54 A monastery was constructed in the Solovki Islands in the fifteenth century. In 1921, it was converted into the first Soviet prison camp for political prisoners, operating until the onset of war in 1939. S.A. Malsagoff, *An Island Hell: A Soviet Prison in the Far North*, trans. F.H. Lyon (London: 1926), available at: https://archive.org/details/1926AnIslandHellMalsagoff/mode/2up?view=theater.

55 Metzger, trans., *The Heroic Struggle*, 60, 145–46.

56 Ibid., 146–47.

57 As related by Rabbi Michoel Dvorkin in a *farbrengen* in the home of Rabbi Binyamin Gorodetsky, June 18, 1947 (Rosh Chodesh Tamuz, 5707). Chronicled in the unpublished memoir of Rabbi Avraham Weingarten.

58 In recent years, the Jewish community in Kostroma has undergone a rebirth. "Kostroma Synagogue Celebrated 110th Birthday," FJC, available at: https://fjc-fsu.org/kostroma-synagogue-celebrated-110th-birthday/.

59 The Rebbe told his jailers that he would not leave that day because the train journey might cause him to transgress Shabbat. They responded that if he chose to remain, they might decide to keep him imprisoned after all. He replied that he was prepared to stay in prison a long time rather than risking violating Shabbat. This raises a serious question: Jewish law states that one can transgress Shabbat to save a life. Clearly, the Rebbe's life was in danger, in particular because of the threat that the imprisonment would be extended. The seventh Rebbe analyzed this question and answered that an argument can be made that the Rebbe would have been justified in leaving the prison; it would have been "a more pragmatic response to immediately leave the prison and then formulate strategies to avoid the Shabbat journey." But he adds that had the Rebbe traveled on Shabbat, even though it might have been lifesaving, it might have been perceived by many as a capitulation to those whose intentions were to destroy religious life. Even in areas not connected to Jewish observance, "the Rebbe resolved that he would act steadfastly in any matter." For full analyses, see *Likkutei Sichot* (Brooklyn, New York:

Kehot Publication Society), 28:124; Metzger, trans., *The Heroic Struggle*, appendix 9.

60 Zigelbaum, *Sippur shel Chag*, chap. 12.

61 July 3, 1927 (3 Tamuz, 5687).

62 *Sefer HaMaamarim* mentions the names of two *maamarim*. One begins "*Anokhi Hashem Elokekha*," and the second starts "*Meheikhan zakhu Yisrael*," noting in the footnote that "they were written while in prison, and they have not been found." *Sefer HaMaamarim*, 5687, 4th edition (Brooklyn, NY: Kehot Publication Society). Also see Duchman, *LeSheima Ozen*, story 102; author's interview with Yosef Minkowitz, grandson of Yitzchak Minkowitz.

63 During his hours at home, he met with Chasidim and informed them of the causes for the arrest: 1) He is the leader of all Chasidim in the world; 2) He establishes *chadarim* and yeshivas and fosters various religious activities in the country; 3) He is the authority of the Orthodox community in the entire land, and he also has an influence over the intelligentsia and the bourgeoisie both in Russia and abroad; and 4) Through his efforts, sizable sums arrive from abroad for those who study Torah.

64 Author's interview with Rabbi Avraham Zajac.

65 Duchman, *LeSheima Ozen*, 194.

66 Metzger, trans., *The Heroic Struggle*, chap. 10.

67 She passed away in Beer Sheva at the age of 99 in 2014. She said that the Rebbe blessed her with long life. Dovid Margolin, "Roza Melamed, 99, Last Witness to Sixth Rebbe's Soviet Exile in Kostroma, Russia," available at: chabad.org/3382868.

68 Excerpt from interview with Jewish Educational Media, available at: chabad.org/1558543.

69 Some accounts claim Messing came from a chasidic family. He was shot in 1937.

70 "R. Elye Chayim Althaus' Eyewitness Report of the Arrest of 1927," available at: chabad.org/3382524; Zigelbaum, *Sippur shel Chag*, 288.

71 See Zigelbaum, *Sippur shel Chag*, 290, for a copy of the telegram informing the GPO headquarters in Moscow of the unconditional release of the Rebbe.

72 Deposition of Chaya Moussia Schneerson, November 12, 1985, p. 36.

73 The *maamar* was based on Psalms 118:7, "G-d aided me, and I shall see [revenge taken] on my enemies." The *maamar* was said on the day the Rebbe received the news of his release. It focuses on the concept that G-d helps man in his efforts; when a person stands up for principles of Torah, a spiritual light emanates from above that automatically causes evil to dissipate. The next day, in honor of his actual release, the Rebbe said a second *maamar*, "*Barukh HaGomel*," based on the blessing one makes when he is saved from prison or illness. *Sefer HaMaamarim*, 5687–88 (Brooklyn, New York: Kehot Publication Society, 2022).

74 July 14, 1927.

75 Yehuda Leib Chitrik, *Reshimot Devarim* 1:195.

76 *Igrot Kodesh*, vol. 3, letter dated May 7, 1934 (17 Iyar, 5694); Metzger, trans., *The Heroic Struggle*, appendix 3.

77 *Igrot Kodesh*, vol. 2, letter dated June 3, 1928 (15 Sivan, 5688), available at: chabad.org/2333919.

78 The traditional Jewish prayer of thanksgiving recited after being released from prison, surviving a major illness, successfully crossing the ocean, or escaping from a dangerous situation. Customarily, it is said after the Torah reading.

79 Rabbi Yisrael Baal Shem Tov (1698–1760) was the founder of the chasidic movement. He lived in Medzhybizh, Ukraine. His successor, Rabbi Dovber, the Maggid, lived in Mezeritch, also in Ukraine. The Alter Rebbe, the founder of Chabad, lived in the town of Liadi in Russia, and his son Rabbi Dovber, the Mitteler Rebbe, moved to Lubavitch, where the movement was centered for 102 years. Later, the fifth Rebbe, the Rashab, moved to Rostov because of the German invasion during World War I. The Rayatz lived there and then relocated to St. Petersburg (Leningrad).

80 Letter from Feigin to Rabbi Eliyahu Simpson and Rabbi Yisrael Jacobson dated 27 Menachem Av, 5687 (August 25, 1927). Feigin's letter carries a great sense of urgency, imploring them to act quickly. He writes cryptically, "He must get out of his sickness, he requires expert doctors, and he needs to travel to Mordechai. The illness created expenses that you cannot imagine." This was code for the fact that the Rebbe was still in mortal danger, and he must relocate to Riga, the residence of Mordechai Dubin. There were major expenses connected to fighting to free the Rebbe from prison, keeping the institutions afloat, and relocating outside Russia.

81 "R. Elye Chayim Althaus' Eyewitness Report of the Arrest of 1927," available at: chabad.org/3382524.

82 He was accompanied by his daughter Chaya Mushka. Oberlander and Shmotkin, *Early Years*, 208–9.

83 The letter was addressed to "my dear friends *anash* and the *temimim* in the country of my birth, Russia." In the letter, the Rebbe refers to Russia as "our country" and recounts the persecution of the Yevesektzia because of his efforts to strengthen Torah. *Igrot Kodesh*, vol. 2, letter dated 19 Kislev, 5687 (December 13, 1927).

84 For a detailed description of the efforts to secure an exit visa, see Dovid Margolin, "The Chassidic Member of Parliament Who Stood Up to the Soviets," available at: chabad.org/5995678.

85 On the 23 Menachem Av, 5687 (August 21, 1927).

86 Rabbi Mordechai Dubin (1889-1957) was the head of the Jewish community of Riga and a member of the Latvian Parliament. He was a Chasid of the Rebbe and assisted him in communal affairs. For more, see Avraham Godin, "Latvian-Jewish Statesman, Chassid and Martyr: Mordechai Dubin," available at: chabad.org/3995713.

87 Behind the scenes, Dubin in Latvia and Cohn in Germany coordinated their efforts. At one point, Dubin told Russian officials that Latvian Jews would be offended if the Russians allowed the Rebbe to go to Germany. Margolin, "Chassidic Member of Parliament," chabad.org/5995678.

88 Latvia was one of the few countries that had officially recognized the Communist country. The trade agreement between Russia and Latvia was vital to the Russian economy. Dovid Margolin writes: "On June 2, 1927, Latvia signed a trade deal with the Soviet Union. Though economically, Latvia needed this deal much more than the Russians did, the Bolsheviks had their own reasons for seeing the deal through. Yet, due to well-founded fears of Soviet encroachment on Latvia – after all, the country had been a Russian territory for some 150 years prior to the revolution – there was strong internal Latvian opposition to the deal, and it still needed to be ratified by the Saeima (Latvian parliament)." Dubin's party at that point held two seats in parliament. Margolin, "Chassidic Member of Parliament," chabad.org/5995678.

89 When asked by authorities why he couldn't simply find another son-in-law overseas, the Rebbe reportedly responded, "Such a son-in-law cannot be found."

90 Eventually this library became the core of the library of Agudas Chassidei Chabad in New York. Today, it contains over 300,000 items and is considered one of the premier Jewish libraries in the world. For more about the library's history, see: https://chabadlibrary.org/about-e.pdf and chap. 8 of this book.

91 Author's interview with Berenbaum.

92 Interview with Zalman Bronstein, a student in the Nevel yeshivah whose family lived in Nikolaev. He joined his father in Leningrad for the Rebbe's last Simchat Torah in Russia. Zigelbaum, *Sippur shel Chag*, 316.

93 As told by his grandson Dovid Chein, who was in Leningrad at the time. Zigelbaum, *Sippur shel Chag.*

94 Author's interview with Konikov. Her family relocated to the US, and in 1946 she married Yitzchok Groner. They went on to spearhead the Chabad expansion in Australia.

95 Zigelbaum, *Sippur shel Chag.*

96 Duchman, *LeSheima Ozen*, chap. 2.

97 Composed by Reb Aharon Charitonov, the Rebbe cherished this song and would sing it at *farbrengens* with his Chasidim. Available at: https://www.youtube.com/watch?v=4I37Gk-1GLS.

98 Rabbi Eliyahu Simpson (1889–1976) was one of the key figures in the development of Chabad in the United States. He studied in the yeshivah in Lubavitch, where he became one of the *chozrim* (those who memorized and transcribed the *maamarim*) of the Rebbe Rashab. In 1923, he immigrated to the United States, where he served as the rabbi of the Chabad synagogue in Boro Park. After the arrival of the Rebbe Rayatz in 1940, he became a secretary to the Rebbe.

99 Jacobson, *Zikhron Livnei Yisrael,* chap. 25.

100 David Eliezrie, *The Secret of Chabad,* chap. 4.

101 Author's interview with Ambassador Yehuda Avner, who was with Prime Minister Meir when she met a group of soldiers during the Yom Kippur War in the Golan Heights. It had been a brutal battle with the Syrians, and one of the soldiers asked Meir, "Is it worth it to keep fighting for a state?" She responded with the story about the crowd at the synagogue in Moscow, explaining that she was deeply touched by the show of Jewish solidarity and insisting that Jews should stand together. Avner was also with Meir when she was interviewed by Fallaci. In that conversation, she added the detail that Chabad had orchestrated the massive crowds of people in Moscow on the second day of Rosh HaShanah. Avner said that Meir also told Fallaci that she was inspired by the outpouring of Jews on the streets, and "this was the one time in my life that I considered becoming religious."

102 As heard personally by the author at the event.

103 Lishkat Hakesher, a division of the Israeli Secret Service directly controlled by the Office of the Prime Minister, was first headed from 1953–70 by Shaul Avigur. Its mission was to strengthen Jewish life in Russia and assist with immigration to Israel. The Israelis worked closely with the Chabad secret system in Russia. Its activities in Russia were terminated in the wake of the Six-Day War in 1967, when Russia broke diplomatic relations with Israel. After the Six-Day War, Lishkat Hakesher became the key orchestrator of the worldwide campaign for Soviet Jewry, including public demonstrations against the Russian government. The seventh Rebbe disagreed with the policy of public confrontation with the Soviet Union, feeling quiet diplomacy would be more effective. In recent years, Lishkat Hakesher has been reconstituted. Today it functions as Nativ, which helps Jews from the former Soviet Bloc immigrate to Israel. On the cooperation of Chabad and Lishkat Hakesher, see Eliezrie, *The Secret of Chabad,* chap. 9.

104 In the 1970s, the Soviets banned a matzah shipment organized by American Jewish groups. Afterward, those groups publicized the ban, embarrassing the Russian government. Simultaneous Chabad shipments got through the Iron Curtain because they were kept from the public eye.

105 When the famed Chasid Rabbi Mendel Futerfas left Russia in 1963, he asked the Rebbe if he should have stayed to continue helping Russian Jewry. The Rebbe told him to help from afar. Futerfas gathered some of his Russian refugee friends in New York, including Rabbi Moshe Levertov, and they established the organization Ezras Achim (literally, "assisting brothers") for just that purpose. In the coming years, they sent thousands of packages of food, religious items, and goods to be sold on the black market to sustain the Russian Jews, many of whom had lost

their jobs because they dared apply to emigrate or were openly observant. Often, Ezras Achim sent these packages with Westerners posing as tourists or businessmen who were on secret missions to Russia to help Soviet Jews.

106 Video of Edelstein's remarks available at: https://www.torahcafe.com/mr-yuli-edelstein/greetings-at-the-kinus-hashluchim-banquet-5775-video_c428e54ae.html.

107 Most major Jewish communities have Jewish centers catered to Russian Americans that are directed by Chabad *shluchim* who are themselves Russian. For instance, Rabbi Yosef Zaltzman directs the Jewish Russian Community Center of Ontario. He was educated in a secre Ezras Achim t Jewish school in Samarkand, Uzbekistan in his youth. See https://www.jrcc.org.

108 David Biale et al., *Hasidism: A New History* (Princeton University Press, 2018), 595; Eliezrie, *The Secret of Chabad*, chap. 10.

109 *Sefer HaSichos*, 5680–5687, 2nd edition (Brooklyn, NY: Kehot Publication Society, 2004), 132.

110 See chap. 3 of this book.

CHAPTER FIVE

1 They arrived on October 21, 1927. "Lubawitscher Rebbe Now in Latvia with Family," JTA, available at: https://www.jta.org/1927/10/24/archive/lubawitscher-rebbe-now-in-latvia-with-family.

2 *Igrot Kodesh*, vol. 1, letter dated 24 Tishrei, 5688 (October 24, 1927), "written during the journey on the train."

3 In a very forthcoming letter to Baruch Rizik in Rostov, the Rebbe shared his inner thoughts about leaving Russia some six weeks earlier. *Igrot Kodesh*, vol. 17, letter dated 10 Kislev, 5788 (December 4, 1927).

4 It was 7:00 a.m. on 25 Tishrei, 5688 (October 21, 1927).

5 Author's interview with Zigelbaum.

6 *Igrot Kodesh*, vol. 2, letter dated 12 Iyar, 5688 (May 9, 1928). The long letter details the Rebbe's ordeals in Russia.

7 Ibid., Introduction, 22.

8 Later, after the Rebbe's trip to the United States, he would be diagnosed with multiple sclerosis, but there were also earlier indications of his weak health.

9 Latvian independence lasted until the German invasion in July 1941. In 1945, Soviet troops seized Latvia, making it part of the Soviet Union. It regained its independence in 1991.

10 Mizrachi (the religious Zionists) and Agudath Israel.

11 World Agudath Israel (the Agudah) was established by Jewish religious leaders at a conference held in Katowice, Poland in 1912, as a response to the secularization of Jewish life and the opposition of Zionism to traditional Judaism. It unified many of the chasidic groups with the Lithuanian yeshivah community. Chabad did not join the Agudah.

In the years to come, the Agudah created branches in many European counties. In Latvia, Agudath Israel became a major influential party. It ran candidates in the national elections in 1922, winning two seats in the first *Saeima* (parliament). It retained both seats in the second *Saeima* after the 1925 elections but was reduced to one seat in the 1928 elections. The 1931 elections saw the party win two seats in the fourth Saeima. However, after the 1934 Latvian coup d'état, multi-party elections were not held again until 1990.

Today, Agudath Israel is an important religious party with seats in the Israeli Knesset and a major presence in the US and European countries. In 2019, it organized the Siyum HaShas, the celebration marking the completion of the cycle of Talmud study, at MetLife stadium in New Jersey with some ninety thousand in attendance.

12 Chabad.org/3995717.

13 At the time, there were less than a thousand Jews in Riga. According to Ilja Lensky, director of the Jewish Museum in Riga, the community invited Lilienthal because they wanted a secular Jewish school. This may have been partially due to the Russian government pressuring for a less religious education system.

14 For an overview of Jewish religious life in Riga at the time, see Abraham Godin, "Jewish Traditional and Religious Life in Latvian Communities," available at: https://www.jewishgen.org/yizkor/latvia1/lat217.html.

15 Adam Dylewski, "Jewish Education in the Second Polish Republic, part 1," https://sztetl.org.pl/en/tradycja-i-kultura-zydowska/historia-zydow-w-polsce/szkolnictwo-zydowskie-w-ii-rp-cz-1-warszawa.

16 Rabbi Chaim Ozer Grodzinski (1863–1940) was the *av beit din*, chief rabbinical judge, of Vilnius. He led the umbrella organization Vaad HaYeshivos (Council of Yeshivas). He was a world-class scholar and universally respected as one of the greatest rabbinic leaders of his time.

17 "The Lubavitcher Rebbe," February 10, 1928, available at: https://digital.bentley.umich.edu/djnews/djc.1928.02.10.001/4.

18 In the Jewish ghetto, there was a Chabad synagogue with three adjacent sanctuaries in the same structure, for Chasidim adhering to the varied Chabad groups of Lubavitch, Liadi, and Kopust.

19 *Grodner Moment*, January 10, 1928. This Yiddish daily newspaper was published in Grodno, Poland, between the World Wars.

20 *HaRav*, ed., Rabbi Nachum Greenwald (Machon HaRav, 2015), 125.

21 Duchman, *LeSheima Ozen*, 291.

22 Letter from Feigin to Rabbi Eliyahu Simpson and Rabbi Yisrael Jacobson dated 17 Iyar, 5689 (May 28, 1929). Feigin explains that the historic sources of income for the Rebbe in Russia were nonexistent in Riga, and he urged them to set up a fundraising program in the US Chabad community.

23 The second Rebbe, Rabbi Dovber, known as the Mitteler Rebbe, and his disciple Reb Aharon Horowitz organized the annual collection known as *maamad*. In 1948, the Ramash wrote that this tradition followed the talmudic teachings of supporting a Torah scholar, making the Chasidim partners in the Rebbe's work. "Giving *maamad*," available at: chabad.org/2281850. Rabbi Yisrael Jacobson, who organized the *maamad* in the US at the time, provides a historical overview reaching back two centuries. See *Zikhron Livnei Yisrael – Memoirs of Rabbi Yisrael Jacobson: 1907–1939* [Hebrew] (Brooklyn, NY: Kehot Publication Society, 1996), 160.

24 Their philanthropy supported the establishment of Yeshivas Tomchei Temimim and the communal work of the Rebbe Rashab. With the advent of the Russian revolution, much of that funding ended. Those major donors included Yeshaya Berlin, a lumber merchant who passed away in 1908, Menachem Monoson and Shmuel Trainin, who were both involved in the ice cream business in Russia, and Shmuel Gurary, who passed away shortly after the Rashab and is interred next to him in Rostov. Jacobson, *Zikhron Livnei Yisrael*, chap. 1.

25 The earlier waves of immigrants were Jews who were somewhat traditional but not highly educated in Judaism. The synagogue of their hometown in Russia was Chabad, sometimes called Nusach Ari after the Chabad tradition in prayer. In America, these immigrants wanted to feel a sense of home, so they attended a synagogue like the one they had in Russia. Many congregants adapted to the US, slowly abandoning their observance. With the rise of Communism, there were more immigrants who were committed Chasidim, but still, their numbers were small, and few succeeded financially in the US. See Jacobson, *Zikhron Livnei Yisrael*.

26 Jacobson, *Zikhron Livnei Yisrael*, 161.

27 *Torat Menachem* 5717, 3:157–58.

28 Yehuda Geberer, "Crisis Management: The Great Crisis of the Chassidic Movement," available at: https://tachlismedia.com/podcast/crisis-management-the-great-crisis-of-the-chassidic-movement/.

29 Anatoly Lunacharsky (1875–1933) was a Marxist revolutionary who was appointed as the first education minister of the Soviet Union in 1917 and served in that position until 1929. Afterward he was the delegate to the League of Nations and then appointed ambassador to Spain.

30 *The New York Times*, October 21, 1928.

31 *Schneersohnovschina* ("Schneersohnists") refers to followers of the Rebbe. During Communists times it was common for Russian authorities to accuse Chasidim who were arrested of being Schneersohnists. This accusation was cause for imprisonment.

32 Rabbi Shalom Ber Levin, *Toldot Chabad BePolin, Lita, VeLatvia (History of Chabad in Poland, Lithuania, and Latvia)* (Brooklyn, NY: Kehot Publication Society, 2011), chap. 11.

33 *Igrot Kodesh*, vol. 1, letter to Rabbi Shlomo Yosef Zevin dated 4 Cheshvan, 5688 (October 30, 1927).

34 The plan focused on nine key cities, including Moscow, Leningrad, and even remote Kutaisi in Soviet Georgia, with lists of contacts and instructions to the Chasidim in Russia on how to undermine the convention. See the chart of each city with detailed instructions. *Igrot Kodesh* 1:100, letter dated Cheshvan, 5688 (October 1927) (only the month is given).

35 *Igrot Kodesh*, vol. 16, letter dated 8 Cheshvan, 5688 (November 3, 1927).

36 *Igrot Kodesh* 16:113, letter dated 11 Cheshvan, 5688 (November 13, 1927).

37 *The Detroit Jewish Chronicle*, April 23, 1930, available at: https://digital.bentley.umich.edu/djnews/djc.1930.04.25.001/3.

38 Rabbi Shalom Ber Levin, *Toldot Chabad BeRusia HaSovietit*, chap. 24. The first meeting was held November 15, 1927 (20 Marcheshvan, 5688); see *Toldot Chabad BeRusia HaSovietit* for a protocol of the meeting that includes a comprehensive plan to seek the support of major Jewish groups such as the JDC, the Alliance Israélite Universelle in France, and other countries.

39 Rabbi Yosef Rosen (1858–1936) was known as the Rogotchover after his birthplace; his family was part of the Kopust branch of Chabad. Rabbi Rozin was the rabbi of Dvinsk and one of the most prominent talmudic scholars of the twentieth century. He was particularly known for his photographic memory.

40 Rabbi Mendel Zak (1873–1941) was the chief rabbi of Riga who established a yeshivah there in 1921. He studied in the yeshivas of Brisk and Volozhin. He and his family were killed in the Holocaust.

41 In the letter the Rebbe thanks Rabbi Hertz for the "warm welcome given to my son-in-law, Rabbi Gurary." He goes on to implore Rabbi Hertz to help Russian Jewry. *Igrot Kodesh* 16:200, letter dated 21 Tamuz, 5688 (July 9, 1928).

42 Rabbi Dr. Yosef Hertz (1872–1946) was the chief rabbi of Britain from 1913 until his passing.

43 Waldemar Haffkine (1860–1930), born in Odessa, was a noted scientist who created vaccines for cholera and the bubonic plague. He was a strong advocate for Jewish causes and became observant in the latter part of his life.

44 *Igrot Kodesh*, vol. 2, letter in German to Haffkine from Riga, dated December 24, 1927. Mindel Archives.

45 It seems that the suggestion of creating a private meeting of prominent Jews did not prove successful. *Igrot Kodesh,* vol. 2, letter in German to Haffkine from Riga, dated January 19, 1928. Mindel Archives.

46 Before they ended their support in 1938, the JDC invested sixteen million dollars ($238 million today) in helping the Communists forcibly move Jews to agricultural settlements.

47 Nora Levin, *The Jews in the Soviet Union Since 1917* (New York University Press, 1988), chap. 6.

48 Originally, much of the land had been owned by the peasants following the emancipation of the Russian serfs in 1861. The new policy forced the creation of collectives to farm, which meant a loss of personal incentive. Productivity dropped; this was one of the causes of the famine in the Soviet Union.

49 Author's interview with Jonathan Sarna.

50 Despite his reservations, in 1925 the Rebbe did write a letter with a qualified endorsement of the agricultural communities. "It was gratifying to hear from Dr. Rosen about the establishment of the agricultural colonies." However, the Rebbe raised concerns about the "lack of attention to religious institutions, *mikveh,* teachers, *shochtim,* rabbis, synagogues – none of these are a component of the program of the establishment of the colonies." He added, "Your support in establishing the colonies is to be lauded. However, what about the thousands who cannot work in agriculture, or move from their homes, and struggle to make a living?" He encouraged the JDC to help them. The letter was addressed to the leaders of the JDC in New York, translated into English, and read at the JDC board meeting. *Igrot Kodesh,* vol. 1, letter dated 25 Sivan, 5685 (June 25, 1925).

51 Letter to the Agudas Harabonim (the New York-based Union of Orthodox Rabbis) dated 10 Cheshvan, 5686 (October 28, 1925).

52 *Igrot Kodesh,* vol. 16, letter to the Board of the JDC dated 10 Cheshvan, 5686 (November 10, 1925).

53 While the writer is anonymous, he seems to have been involved with JDC activities in Russia.

54 The disturbing twelve-page public letter addressed to Dr. Rosen, the head of the JDC in Moscow, is a heartbreaking description of the condition of Russian Jewry. The letter criticized the JDC policy that supported the resettlement of Jews to farms in Ukraine. The financial support of the JDC facilitated the goals of the Yevesektzia to destroy religious observance. The letter claims the policy was not even helping the families economically; it documents hunger, a lack of clothing, and harsh winters. It describes the show put on for foreign visitors: Farmers would claim that all was well when in truth they were suffering from hunger, cold, and religious oppression. The reference to foreign visitors apparently meant JDC officials such as Felix

Warburg, who visited the farms in Russia. The letter was translated into English by JDC staff in New York and forwarded to Dr. Cyrus Adler and Louis Marshall. JDC Archives, folder no. 425.

55 *Hadoar,* March 23, 1928. *Hadoar* (Hebrew for "The Post") was a Hebrew-language periodical published from 1921 to 2005 in the United States by the Histadruth Ivrith of America. *Hadoar* was described by the Jewish Telegraphic Agency as "one of the best Hebrew-language magazines in the world" in its day.

56 Levin, *The Jews in the Soviet Union Since 1917,* vol. 1, chap. 10.

57 Ibid.

58 As Dovid Margolin explains, this letter was part of an unsuccessful effort to persuade the JDC leadership in New York to support the Rebbe's religious underground in Russia. It is difficult to speculate regarding the past, but one has to the wonder if the more secular leadership of the JDC did not have a proper appreciation for the primary role of Jewish learning and religious life. They also seemed swept up by the agenda of the Soviets, spurred on by the Yevesektzia, that promised economic independence in the communal farms. Some JDC leaders began to question if they were being duped by the Russians, as Cyrus Adler wrote in 1932, "These people are trying to defraud us of 6,600,000 rubles ($169,950,000 today)." JDC Archives, folder no. 475.

59 *Igrot Kodesh,* vol. 16, letter dated 19 Shevat, 5689 (January 30, 1929).

60 When the JDC was created in 1918, it united diverse groups to provide Jewish assistance. Teitelbaum represented the Orthodox Central Relief Committee. He was also a member of Agudas Harabonim, the Union of Orthodox Rabbis established in 1901. Its members were mostly European-born rabbis, many of them notable Torah scholars. At the time, Agudas Harabonim was influential in the US.

61 Production dropped significantly under the forced plan of communal farms. Richard Pipes, *Russia Under the Bolshevik Regime* (Vintage Books, 1995), 370–72.

62 Dovid Margolin, "The Soviet Jews Who Risked Persecution for the Sake of Matzah," *Mosaic,* April 28, 2016, available at: https://mosaicmagazine.com/observation/religion-holidays/2016/04/the-soviet-jews-who-risked-persecution-for-the-sake-of-matzah/.

63 Many others also backed the Rebbe, including Rabbi Dr. Meir Hildesheimer in Berlin, Rabbi Yechezkel Lifshitz of Kalish, Rabbi Avraham Dovber Kahane Shapiro of Kovno, and Rabbi Menachem Zak of Latvia. The chief rabbis of England, France, Holland, and Belgium joined the effort as well. *Igrot Kodesh* 16:16.

64 JDC Archives, folder no. 478, letter from Cyrus Adler to Joseph Hyman dated January 28, 1929.

65 Dovid Margolin, "The 1929 Struggle to Send Matzah into the Soviet Union," available at: chabad.org/4353455.

66 It took a while, but eventually there was an undercurrent of regret in the JDC. Cyrus Adler, who had argued against funding the matzah shipment, later became more supportive of the Rebbe's approach. In a letter written in 1932 to Dr. Hyman, head of the JDC in New York, Adler wrote, "I feel this is up to me to do something to help the Jews in Russia have matzah for Passover. I am not disposed to take the attitude to completely surrender all Jewish religious practice in Russia to the Soviets, whether they be Jewish Soviets or other Soviets." JDC Archives, letter dated February 2, 1932.

67 Letter from the Rashag to Rabbi Yisrael Meisel dated April 16, 1929. Meisel had been a rabbi in Kiev before immigrating to Tel Aviv, and he had a longstanding connection with Chabad Rebbes. The Rashag's correspondence goes into great detail about the campaign. Meisel may have assisted with fundraising in *Eretz Yisrael*; perhaps that is why he received a such comprehensive report from the Rashag. The letter was discovered in the National Library of Israel by chasidic researcher Rabbi Zalman Berger. National Library of Israel, Jerusalem, file ARC 4-1827.

68 In the Rashag's letter to Rabbi Yisrael Meisel, he writes that Chief Rabbi Hertz made a major public announcement and was extremely helpful. In Paris, he writes, there was a concentration of Russian immigrants who made large donations. France's Chief Rabbi Levi was also supportive.

69 Rabbi Sonnenfeld was the head of the Charedi community in *Eretz Yisrael,* and Rabbis Kook and Meir were chief rabbis appointed by the Zionist movement. While they respected each other, they stood apart on many issues. The fact that leaders from varied sectors of the community made a public request for the campaign reflects the broad endorsement that the Rebbe received.

70 Ibid Letter Rashag to Meisel.

71 A kopeck is equal to one cent; there are one hundred kopecks in a ruble. It would amount to less than a dollar per kilo in today's currency.

72 The Manischewitz company was willing to ship matzah from the US. For a while, this idea was considered, but because of the delay in receiving permission to ship the matzah, it was ultimately untenable. Margolin, "The 1929 Struggle to Send Matzah into the Soviet Union."

73 Ibid Margolin.

74 Levin, *Toldot Chabad BeRusia HaSovietit,* 84–85.

75 The Rebbe established a board of five members to oversee the yeshivah. He appointed three of its members, Rabbis Shraga Zalmanov, Dov Moshe Shmotkin, and Schneur Zalman Shmotkin, and told them to select another two members. They had all studied in the yeshivah in Lubavitch and understood the unique approach of Tomchei Temimim.

76 Some of the students survived the Holocaust, and some found refuge in remote Shanghai, China. These made up an important portion of the new generation of

Chabad rabbis in communities across the world in the postwar era. See chap. 10 of this book.

77 See Levin, *Toldot Chabad BeRusia HaSovietit*, chap. 15, for a detailed description of the Warsaw visit.

78 The Warsaw community wrote to the Rebbe after he arrived in Riga from Russia, inviting him to relocate there. He responded to them shortly afterward, saying, "Their request could not be fulfilled for various reasons." While there are no reasons stated in the letter, it might have been because of difficulties procuring visas or citizenship. The Rebbe added that he hoped to have the opportunity to see them soon in their country. See *Igrot Kodesh*, vol. 1, letter dated 2 Cheshvan, 5688 (October 28, 1927).

79 For a detailed description of the Rebbe's travels during his interlude in Riga, see Levin, *Toldot Chabad BePolin, Lita, VeLatvia*, chap. 9.

80 See chap. 7 of this book.

81 *Sefer HaSichos*, 5688–91 (Brooklyn, NY: Kehot, 2002), 151–69. This talk was given after the Rebbe's return from his visit to the US.

82 The young adult division of Agudath Israel.

83 The ideology of Torah with *derekh eretz* was advocated by Rabbi Samson Raphael Hirsch (1808–88) of Germany, who believed that Jews should play a larger role in their host culture while fully following traditional Judaism. Many rabbinic scholars, primarily from Eastern Europe, opposed this integration into broader society.

84 In a 1931 talk to young Jewish leaders during a visit to Rokiškis, Lithuania, the Rebbe lamented that the standards of Jewish scholarship had been lowered. It used to be, he said, that "Jews were dedicated to scholarship and knew that the study of Torah was primary." He expressed reservations about the modern schools that integrated secular and religious studies. "It saddens the heart to envisage what kind of people are going to grow up out of the children who are now attending the modern *chadarim*. Not only is today's modern education not capable of providing us with devout Jews (and obviously not Torah sages), but in addition, it is withering the spiritual potential of its pupils, leaving them barely equal to their age-mates." He praised the "old-style *cheder* with teachers imbued with spiritual Jewish refinement" who would be role models to children and the "yeshivas filled with the voices of Torah and imbued with *yirat Shamayim* (G-d-fearing spirit)." The Rebbe also criticized the new approach of "*Ivrit BeIvrit*," using modern Hebrew as the language of instruction, saying, "The approach lacks awe of Heaven and is very weak." The Rebbe well understood that government regulations mandated a program of secular studies and that these schools were a response to that requirement. "After all, what could be done? When there is compulsory schooling, there have to be secular curriculums." He also drew a contrast to the secular Yiddish schools. "Of course, these schools are better than those Yiddish schools which unfortunately bear the epithet 'Jewish,'" he said, referring to the schools set up

by the secular Yiddish movement. *Sefer HaSichos*, 5688–91 (Brooklyn, NY: Kehot Publication Society, 2002), *reshimah* 2, 192.

85 *Likkutei Dibburim*, vol. 5, chap. 39, Simchat Torah 5691; *Sefer HaSichos*, 5688–91.

86 The Yiddish movement believed that using Yiddish would be a barrier to assimilation. It was a secular philosophy that rejected classic Jewish beliefs and religious observance. At the Czernowitz Conference in September of 1908, the leaders declared Yiddish to be the "glue to hold Jewish life together." In the early years of the movement, some of its schools followed a strong anti-Zionist approach, but with time, almost all became supportive of Zionism. Yiddish schools were established in Russia and other countries in Europe, and with Jewish immigration to the US and Canada, the same happened in those locations. Yiddish schools were frequently called "Peretz Schools" in memory of Yiddish writer I.L. Peretz. By the early 1970s, most of them had closed. Today there is one full-time Yiddish day school in the world, located in Melbourne, Australia. Founded in 1935 as I.L. Peretz Sunday School, today it is called Sholem Aleichem School and has some three hundred students. It describes its educational philosophy as "fostering awareness of all aspects of Jewish life with a particular emphasis on the promotion of Yiddish language and literature, Hebrew and Jewish culture, *veltkhe yiddishkayt* – a secular approach to Jewish history, traditions and customs, ethics and values." For a history of the Yiddish movement, see David Fishman, *The Rise of Modern Yiddish Culture* (University of Pittsburgh Press, 2005).

87 M. Marks, *Di Yiddish-Veltliehke Shul in Leitland*, 260–65. In 1935, the New York JTA news agency reported that the secular Jewish Parents Union had been disbanded and all educational programs were put in the hands of Agudath Israel. The conflict over the educational philosophy of the schools in Latvia was part of a broader culture war between traditional Jewish education and attempts to create a secular Jewish identity, untethered from Torah teachings and free of religious observance. In the US, groups like Der Arbeter Ring (The Workmen's Circle) were established with Yiddish language and culture as their foundation. With time, the Yiddish movement faded, as its central idea – that language alone could be a bond powerful enough to sustain Jewish life – didn't hold up.

88 This represents a fundamental shift in strategy for Jewish continuity. Instead of waiting for a Jew to walk into a synagogue, the Rebbe demanded outreach, even on the street. This was the beginning of a new paradigm in the battle against assimilation. In the decades to come, this strident outreach strategy of Chabad became commonplace, with menorahs gracing public squares and mitzvah tanks parked on street corners with Chasidim asking Jews to come aboard to do a mitzvah. In Russia, in a community where tradition was dominant and government oppression limited freedom of expression, this was never done. Now in a Western country where there was greater freedom, the Rebbe struck out in a new direction that, with

time, would prove to be a game changer. The Ramash was present on that Simchat Torah in Riga, when the Rebbe demanded that Jews go out into the streets. Years later, once he became the seventh Rebbe, he initiated public mitzvah campaigns. The first was the tefillin campaign launched in the weeks prior to the Six-Day War in 1967, which entailed Jews donning tefillin even in public venues.

89 *The Forward*, known for its hostility toward religion, was one paper that criticized the Rebbe for his severe tone that Simchat Torah.

90 *Sefer HaSichos*, 5688, 167, footnote 84. Letter from Feigin to Jacobson dated 26 Tishrei, 5691 (October 18, 1930).

91 In Poland, this expanded with the publication of *Hatomim*, the journal from Yeshivas Tomchei Temimim that began publishing in 1935. It included articles on Jewish scholarship, chasidic philosophy, and history, and has been republished in a two-volume set by Kehot Publication Society. For an overview of the history of *Hatomim*, see "A Light from Lubavitch: Hatomim – Our History, Heritage, and Scholarship," available at: https://derher.org/wp-content/uploads/78-Adar-I-5779-overveiw-on-hatomim.pdf.

92 *Likkutei Dibburim* (literally, "A Collection of Talks") includes the Rebbe's talks between 1929 and 1950. They were first published first in Europe as booklets and eventually as volumes of a series, with the original language a mix of Hebrew and Yiddish. The six-volume set translated into English by Uri Kaploun was published by by Kehot Publication Society in 2012.

93 https://www.alysefer.com/rebberayatz/.

94 *Likkutei Dibburim*, vol. 1, Translator's Introduction (Brooklyn, NY: Kehot Publication Society, 2012).

95 At times there are inconsistencies in the accounts that the Rebbe wrote, such as a slight difference in dates regarding events that happened decades earlier. The seventh Rebbe documented a series of these in an appendix to *Chanokh LaNaar*, an essay by the Rebbe Rashab on education. Some secular historians have argued that these inconsistencies call into question the Rebbe's historical narrative. The seventh Rebbe profoundly disagreed; while acknowledging the discrepancies, he put his full faith behind the narrative. See *Chanokh LaNaar* [Hebrew] (Brooklyn, NY: Kehot Publication Society), 56.

96 Professor Ada Rapoport-Albert, *Hasidic Studies: Essays in History and Gender* (Littman Library of Jewish Civilization, 2018), chap. 4.

97 https://www.alysefer.com/rebberayatz/.

98 *Igrot Kodesh* 4:398, letter dated 18 Av, 5698 (August 15, 1938).

99 Known as *maamar kinyan hachaim*, its central themes are spiritual renewal and prayer. It was published for the first time as a booklet in September 1928 in Riga and reprinted in *Sefer HaMaamarim – Kuntresim* (Brooklyn, NY: Kehot Publication Society, 1962).

100 Author's interview with Rabbi Eli Rubin.

101 For an overview of translating chasidic teachings into other languages, see Eli Rubin, "A Linguistic Bridge Between Alienation and Intimacy: Chabad's Theorization of Yiddish in Historical and Cultural Perspective," available at: https://ingeveb.org/articles/a-linguistic-bridge-between-alienation-and-intimacy.

102 In October 1929, the Rebbe wrote to Rabbi Meir Munk in Berlin, asking him to arrange for a translation of a *maamar* into German. Later, in 1936, the Ramash arranged for the translation of a *maamar*. See Zusha Wolf, *Admorei Chabad VeYahadut Germania* (Jerusalem: Heichal Menachem), part 3; *Igrot Kodesh*, vol. 16, letter dated 24 Tishrei, 5789 (October 8, 1929).

103 *Likkutei Sichot* (Brooklyn, NY: Kehot Publication Society), 35:294.

104 The seventh Rebbe refers to the historic letter sent by Rabbi Yisrael Baal Shem Tov to his brother, in which he describes a remarkable spiritual event that took place on Rosh HaShanah of 1746. The Baal Shem Tov says that using kabbalistic secrets, his soul rose to heaven. There he asked the Messiah, "When will you come?" He answered, "In the time when your teachings will become public and revealed in the world." The Baal Shem Tov's letter was published for the first time in 1781 by one of his disciples. This principle lies at the heart of the Chabad mission of disseminating the teachings of Chasidism to the world. For a copy of the letter, see "The Chamber of Mashiach," available at: chabad.org/380401.

105 In a letter to Alexandar Sender Reinen, the Rebbe wrote: "A special blessing to your wife for her efforts translating the discourse… It will be a great merit that those who don't understand another language are able to study it." *Igrot Kodesh*, vol. 16, letter dated Tzom Gedalia, 3 Tishrei, 5689 (September 28, 1928).

106 Rabbi Shalom Ber Levin, *Toldot Chabad BeArtzot HaBrit* (Brooklyn, NY: Kehot Publication Society, 1988), chap. 26.

107 Rapoport, *Hasidic Studies*, chap. 7.

108 *Sefer HaMaamarim – Kuntresim* (Brooklyn, NY: Kehot Publication Society, 1962), 1:306.

109 *Igrot Kodesh*, vol. 3, letter dated 9 Kislev, 5696 (December 5, 1935).

110 The exact date of the founding of the organization is difficult to determine. What is clear is that the Rebbe actively supported the group. By 1937, it was active in Riga, and branches were established in other cities as well. See Levin, *Toldot Chabad BePolin, Lita, VeLatvia*, chap. 13.

111 Sarah Schenirer (1883–1935) pioneered Torah study for women by founding the first Bais Yaakov school in 1917 in Poland. The school focused on giving women basic skills in Jewish literacy, traditions, and history. However, those schools did not place an emphasis on chasidic theology. The Rebbe's support of Achot Hatemimim promoted the serious study of chasidic texts and discourses like the Tanya. This was a revolutionary change in Jewish women's scholarship. In modern Chabad

women's schools, chasidic philosophy is an integral part of the curriculum. The seventh Rebbe took this further by encouraging women to study Talmud.

112 Naftali Loewenthal, *Hasidism Beyond Modernity: Essays in Habad Thought and History* (London: Littman Library of Jewish Civilization, 2020), chap. 7.

113 *Igrot Kodesh* 4:362, letter dated 27 Sivan, 5698 (June 26, 1938).

114 The Rebbe appointed a committee of three prominent Chabad rabbis, Yisrael Jacobson, Yisrael Kazarnovsky, and Yochanan Gordon, to teach and advise Achot Hatemimim in the US. As in Riga, the Rebbe selected prestigious scholars, a clear indication of the great value he saw in developing educational opportunities for women. *Igrot Kodesh*, vol. 4, letter dated 27 Sivan, 5698 (June 26, 1938).

115 Loewenthal, *Hasidism Beyond Modernity*, chap. 7.

116 For a young teenage girl to review a *maamar* in front of the Rebbe must have been a very intimidating experience. Clearly the Rebbe was attempting to empower these young women with the courage to pursue serious Jewish learning.

117 *Sefer HaSichos*, 5696–5700 (Brooklyn, NY: Kehot Publication Society, 2012), 401.

118 This was a period where few women were immersed in serious Jewish intellectual study. The initiative to promote the study of chasidic philosophy, started by the Rebbe in Riga and continued in the US, was an unprecedented innovation of Jewish learning for women.

119 Loewenthal, *Hasidism Beyond Modernity*, 294. Loewenthal quotes one teacher in the chasidic group of Ger: "You know, after all, that there are no women Chasidim, right? There are only daughters and wives of Chasidim."

120 Rabbi Hodakov was born to a Chabad family in the Russian town of Beshankovich on January 12, 1902. His family moved to Riga when he was two years old, and he was educated there by Rabbi Yoel Barantchik of the Novardok *Musar* movement. He excelled in his studies and religious devotion. When the Rebbe arrived in Riga in 1928, Rabbi Hodakov became an ardent Chasid. During this time, he met the Ramash. In 1934, Rabbi Hodakov was named chief inspector of the Jewish schools by the Latvian Ministry of Education. He eventually accompanied the Rebbe to America in 1940, assisting the Ramash in an effort to establish the first national Jewish school system in the US. After the passing of the Rebbe Rayatz, Rabbi Hodakov became the chief of staff and secretary of the seventh Rebbe. In this role, he oversaw the growth of Chabad around the world. He passed away on April 23, 1993.

121 Dr. Nissan Mindel was born in Riga in 1912. As a young man, he met the Rebbe when he arrived from Russia. Mindel received a master's degree from the University of Manchester and a doctorate in Semitic languages from Columbia University. Prior to World War II, he served as a secretary for the Rebbe in Otwock and accompanied him on the ship to the US in 1940. Mindel continued in that capacity,

and when the Rebbe Rayatz passed away, he transitioned to working as a secretary for the seventh Rebbe. Mindel also served on the boards of the central organizations of Chabad, Merkos L'Inyonei Chinuch and Agudas Chassidei Chabad. He translated the chasidic classic, the *Tanya*, into English and wrote many important works on chasidic history and philosophy. He passed away in 1999.

122 Author's interview with Rakeffet in Jerusalem in 2019. Rakeffet is a protege of Rabbi Joseph Soloveitchik, and is one of the most authoritative historians of Orthodox Jewish history and a prolific author. For a detailed description of his missions to Russia on behalf of the Mossad, see *Kuntres Rakafot Aharon* (Jerusalem, 2019), vol. 4, chap. 5.

CHAPTER SIX

1 "The Royal Wedding," Rabbi Dr. Aaron Rakeffet, available at: https://www.yutorah.org/lectures/834665/Jewish-History-#24-%E2%80%93-.

2 Sivan 5681 (June 17, 1921).

3 Rabbi Zalman Gurary, *BeKhol Beiti Ne'eman Hu* (Kfar Chabad Israel, 2009), 25–26.

4 At the time, Landwarow was under Polish rule. Today the city is known as Lentvaris and is located some fifteen miles from Vilnius in Lithuania.

5 The Rebbe wrote in 1938 that they chose this city for the wedding location because of visa issues. See *Igrot Kodesh* 4:370. Rabbi Zalman Gurary remembers sleeping on a bench in a local synagogue because all accommodations had been taken by Chasidim visiting for the wedding. Gurary, *BeKhol Beiti Ne'eman Hu*, 67.

6 Also participating in the wedding were several noted scholars, including Rabbi Baruch Ber Leibowitz, *rosh yeshivah* of the Kaminetz Yeshivah. JEM Oral History Project interview with Mottel Sharfstein, who heard this from Rabbi Baruch Ber's student Rabbi Yudel Gershoni. He recalled that at the wedding, he and Rabbi Baruch Ber had a scholarly discussion with the Ramash. Gershoni told Sharfstein, "He had knowledge of everything in Shas (the Talmud)."

7 Sheina was killed on the second day of Rosh HaShanah 5703 (September 13, 1942) and Rabbi Mendel was killed almost two months later, on 25 Marcheshvan, 5703 (November 5, 1942). Their nephew Yaakov Yosef Liss (the son of Mendel's sister Sara), whom they adopted, was also killed by the Nazis in 1942. (The couple adopted Yaakov Yosef when his mother died a few days after giving birth to her second child.) In 1950, the seventh Rebbe wrote that he received information from a Treblinka survivor who described the details of their fate. Elkanah Shmotkin,

Rebbetzin Sheina Horenstein: A Brief Biography (Brooklyn, NY: Kehot Publication Society, 2021).

8 The Ramash and the Rebbe Rashab never met. The Ramash's younger years were a period of great disruption, first by war and later by the Russian revolution. Travel from Ukraine to Lubavitch and later Rostov was very difficult and even dangerous. The seventh Rebbe once remarked to his secretary Rabbi Leibel Groner, "I never met the Rashab, so I did not have the difficulty of shifting my allegiance from one Rebbe to another." He was alluding to the challenge that some Chasidim face when they are close followers of one Rebbe and then need to attach themselves to his successor after his demise. Reb Leibel Groner, *The Mazkir: The Rebbe's Personal Secretary* (Malchut HaKeter, Israel), vol. 1.

9 Zalman Duchman, *LeSheima Ozen.*

10 Letter from Althaus to the Rebbe dated 24 Tishrei, 5690, quoted in Boruch Oberlander and Elkanah Shmotkin, *Early Years: The Formative Years of the Rebbe, Rabbi Menachem M. Schneerson* (Kehot Publication Society), 112.

11 They met on 17 Tamuz, 5683 (July 1, 1923). Oberlander and Shmotkin, *Early Years,* chap. 2.

12 *Igrot Kodesh,* vol. 15, letter dated Erev Shabbat *Parshat Pinchas,* 23 Tamuz, 5683 (July 7, 1923). This was not the first visit of the Ramash to the Rebbe. He had traveled to Rostov and met the Rebbe for the first time on Sukkot 1923. See Rabbi Zalman Hertzl, *Nisuei HaNesi'im,* vol. 2, 3rd edition (Brooklyn, NY: 2016), 22, footnote 26.

13 St. Petersburg was renamed Leningrad after the death of Lenin in January 1924.

14 *Igrot Kodesh,* vol. 13, letter dated 19 Tamuz, 5700 (July 24, 1940).

15 For more details on the Ramash's time in Leningrad, see Oberlander and Shmotkin, *Early Years,* chap. 3. During this time, the Ramash met some of the great Jewish intellectual luminaires, including Rabbi Yosef Rosen and Rabbi Shlomo Yosef Zevin. He was also privy to many of the challenges that the Rebbe faced.

16 *A Mother in Israel: The Life and Memoirs of Rebbetzin Chana Schneerson* (Brooklyn, NY: Kehot Publication Society), 4–45; "Memoirs of Rebbetzin Chana – Part 1," available at: chabad.org/1638271.

17 Rabbi She'ar Yashuv Cohen (1927–2016) was the chief rabbi of Haifa. Once, in a meeting with the seventh Rebbe, the Rebbe recalled to Rabbi Cohen the time he spent in his grandfather's home. *Kfar Chabad,* issues 827 and 889; *Nisuei HaNesi'im,* 36–37.

18 The Rebbe once sent the Ramash to Rabbi Chaim Ozer Grodzinski with a request to sign a public call to assist Russian Jewry. When the Ramash arrived at the study hall adjacent to the rabbi's office, some of the students decided to challenge his scholarship for sport. They assumed, as many Lithuanian yeshivah students generally did, that as a stereotypical Chasid, he lacked comprehensive talmudic expertise. They

posed deep talmudic questions to the Ramash, but he remined silent and refused to engage. When the Ramash entered Rabbi Grodzinski's office, he reviewed the conversation with him and refuted their points one after another. Rabbi Grodzinski, who had overheard some of the conversation outside his office, asked the Ramash why he didn't respond to the students while they were challenging him. He answered, "They were jesting, and I saw no point. However, I was entrusted with a mission from the Rebbe and feared you might not take me seriously if I did not have talmudic acumen. Because that could have endangered the mission, I felt I had to respond to you." Rabbi Baruch Ber Lebowitz, dean of the prestigious Kaminetz Yeshivah, and Rabbi Shaya Shimonowitz, later dean of Yeshivas Rabbeinu Yaakov Yosef in New York, witnessed this encounter. Rabbi Lebowitz later entered into a long talmudic discussion with the Ramash and, impressed by the depth of his knowledge, told him, "Come to Kaminetz and I will mentor you to be the next *gadol hador*, the next great leader of the generation." The Ramash demurred. In 1966, Rabbi Shimonowitz told this story to Rabbi Yossi Krupnick, a student of his whom he reprimanded for coming late to class because he had attended a *farbrengen* of the seventh Rebbe that had concluded very late the night before. Author's interview with Rabbi Yosef Krupnick; Oberlander and Shmotkin, *Early Years*; JEM Oral History Project.

19 *Yemei Bereishis* (Brooklyn, NY: Kehot Publication Society, 1993), 202.

20 *A Mother in Israel*, 34.

21 For a detailed account of the Rebbe's time in Berlin, see Oberlander and Shmotkin, *Early Years*, chap. 4 and 5. Also see Joseph Telushkin, *Rebbe: The Life and Teachings of Menachem M. Schneerson, the Most Influential Rabbi in Modern History*.

22 In a report that the Ramash sent the Rebbe about the convention, he wrote a detailed description of the conference and the people he met, lauding the organizers. Indicative of his reserved personality, the Ramash wrote, "I am hesitant to approach the directors of the conference more closely, lest my presence be used as a premise to draw the Rebbe into this." Past Chabad Rebbes were not members of Agudath Israel (see chap. 2); perhaps the Ramash's presence could be interpreted as a more formal participation. "I sufficed with being introduced to them. For this reason as well, I did not go to the dinner that was arranged for all the participants," he wrote. The Ramash appears to prefer playing a quiet role, staying in the background. See Oberlander and Shmotkin, *Early Years*, 269–70, for the complete text of the Ramash's report translated into English. The Hebrew original appears in Zusha Wolf, *Admorei Chabad VeYahudut Germania*, 233–35.

23 Rabbi Yosef Dunner, a student at the yeshivah at the time, later remembered seeing the Ramash at Rabbi Weinberg's classes. "Pini Dunner – Unknown Picture of the Late Lubavitcher Rebbe, c. 1930s," *The Seforim Blog*, March 31, 2008, available at: https://seforimblog.com/2008/03/pini-dunner-unknown-picture-of-late/.

24 Rabbi Yechiel Yaakov Weinberg (1884–1966) was a distinguished scholar and the author of the *Seridei Eish*. Born in Poland, he attended the yeshivas of Mir and Slabodka and settled in Germany after the outbreak of World War I. He fled Germany in 1939 and was imprisoned by the Germans in the Warsaw Ghetto. He survived captivity and spent his last years in Switzerland.

25 The rabbinical seminary issued a letter facilitating his registration at the university. According to Rabbi Chaim Nachman Kovalsky, who was a student in the yeshivah in Berlin at the time, the Ramash requested a letter of certification in Torah scholarship from Rabbi Weinberg. When Rabbi Weinberg asked him what he should write as the sphere of Jewish learning in which the Ramash was proficient, the Ramash responded, "Whatever you would like." Rabbi Weinberg then gave the Ramash a copy of his new work, a complex fifty-seven-page Jewish legal essay. The next morning, Rabbi Kovalsky says, "the Ramash knew every point by heart." See "Entry Exam," video available at: chabad.org/748972. The Ramash wrote notes on Rabbi Weinberg's essay in *Reshimot* 127 and 128.

26 Oberlander and Shmotkin, *Early Years*, 343–45.

27 During these four years, the Ramash met many notable Jewish scholars, such as Rabbis Joseph Soloveitchik, Yitzchak Hutner, and Abraham Joshua Heschel, and the Belzer Rebbe, Rabbi Yissachar Dov Rokeach.

28 Letter dated August 14, 1928. A copy of the letter appears in *Nisuei HaNesi'im*, 68.

29 *Igrot Kodesh* 16:198. In a letter dated June 15, 1928 (26 Sivan, 5688), the Rebbe tells Rabbi Levi Yitzchak Schneerson that he is waiting to hear if they can procure passports to travel to the wedding. He asks to be updated so they can set a date. When the new Jewish year approached, it became clear that the Russian government was not going to grant permission to travel, and they therefore would have to set a date regardless.

30 Letter dated Rosh Chodesh Cheshvan, October 18, 1928. A copy of the letter appears in *Nisuei HaNesi'im*, 78. Rivkin had been secretary of the Rebbe Rashab and was also close to the Rayatz (see chap. 3).

31 Yehuda Chitrik, *Reshimot Devarim*, 440.

32 There are a number of different accounts of the wedding. Rabbi Althaus wrote a long, detailed description of the wedding for his fellow Chasidim who could not attend. He had a unique perspective because he accompanied the Rebbe from Riga and was tasked with taking care of the Ramash once they arrived in Warsaw. Segments can be found in *Early Years*, chap. 5. Another detailed account was written by Rabbi Shmuel Zalmanov, and there were also several newspaper articles. See *Nisuei HaNesi'im*.

33 A fur hat that is worn on special occasions, the particular style of *shtreimel* worn by Lubavitcher Rebbes is known as a *spodik*. The Rebbe had inherited it from his father, who had received it from his father, the fourth Rebbe, Rabbi Shmuel. After wearing

it in honor of the wedding, Rebbe continued wearing the *shtreimel* on Shabbat, holidays, and other special occasions, such when he received US citizenship on March 17, 1949 (video footage available at: chabad.org/471239). Other chasidic groups, such as Belz and Ger, have a tradition that men wear a *shtreimel* after marriage.

34 Author's interview with Rabbi Yoel Kahn (1930–2021). Born in Russia, he immigrated to Palestine in 1935. In 1950, he arrived in New York shortly after the passing of the Rebbe Rayatz. He became the primary *chozer,* the person tasked with memorizing and transcribing the talks of the seventh Rebbe.

35 It seems the Ramash was quite reticent to enter scholarly discussions. In a 1971 *farbrengen,* the seventh Rebbe remarked that he had wanted to "evade" the conversation with Rabbi Shapiro but felt compelled by his father-in-law, "who was very fond of [Rabbi Shapiro]." *Farbrengen, Parshat Tzav,* excerpted *Nisuei HaNesi'im,* 203.

36 Account of Rabbi Shmuel Zalmanov, who witnessed the encounter at the wedding. According to Dr. Nissan Mindel, the Rebbe responded to Rabbi Meir Shapiro, "I know, but I wanted you to know too." *Nisuei HaNesi'im,* part 2, 204.

37 The basic text was the same, with some additions depending on the specific recipients. Nine variations have been found, some with minor changes and others with more significant ones. See *Nisuei HaNesi'im,* 84–87 for a detailed description, including copies of many of the invitations. Years later, in 1953, the seventh Rebbe explained the history and special attention that the Rebbe gave to the invitations to his wedding. "Before the wedding of my sister-in-law [Sheina, in 1932], my father-in-law instructed that the text for her invitations be copied from our invitation. In response to my question, the Rebbe explained that this was the text used in his own wedding invitation. His, in turn, was copied from earlier ones. The text of the invitation includes four paragraphs, and the first letters of each spell out the word *ahavah* ('love')" (*Torat Menachem,* 5724, p. 198). Today it is customary for Chabad wedding invitations to use the same wording.

38 *Nitei Gavriel, Hilchos Nissuin* 4:3: "Many have the custom to provide a meal for the poor for a day or two days before a wedding."

39 November 25, 1928 (12 Kislev, 5689).

40 Oberlander and Shmotkin, *Early Years,* 381–84 (letter written by Rabbi Eliyahu Chaim Althaus).

41 Weather report printed in *Neir Platz* newspaper, November 27, 1928, temperature converted to Fahrenheit. Years later, in 1951, when someone suggested moving a wedding ceremony inside due to cold weather, the seventh Rebbe remarked, "My wedding was in the winter, outside under the heavens, and I am very happy with the *shidduch* (match)." *Nisuei HaNesi'im,* 181.

42 *Heint (Today)* was a Yiddish daily published in Warsaw. November 28, 1928 (15 Kislev, 5689).

43 *Der Moment* was a Yiddish daily published in Warsaw. November 28, 1928 (15 Kislev, 5689).
44 Berakhot 63b.
45 Oberlander and Shmotkin, *Early Years*, chap. 5, Zalmanov letter.
46 The *maamar* was based on the wedding blessing, "He who created joy." *Maamar Asher Bara Sasson VeSimchah, Sefer Maamarim* 5689, 86–94.
47 Oberlander and Shmotkin, *Early Years*, chap. 5, Zalmanov letter.
48 *Nisuei HaNesi'im*, 231–36.
49 Letter from Schwei to Zelig Slonim dated 16 Tevet, 5690 (January 16, 1930), *Nisuei HaNesi'im*, 236.
50 Letter from Shmuel Schneerson, *Nisuei HaNesi'im*, 228.
51 *A Mother in Israel*, 6; "Memoirs of Rebbetzin Chana – Part 10," available at: chabad.org/1708351.
52 Shabbat, November 21, 1953 (14 Kislev, 5714).
53 For the week following a wedding, there are daily celebrations called *sheva brachot*, at which seven special blessings are recited in honor of the bride and groom. Lulov's son Grigory, who had become a Communist, arrested the Rebbe two years earlier in Russia. Rabbi Avraham Goldin was in Riga at the time; years later, he recounted that Lulov told him that the Rebbe invited him personally to the *sheva brachot* celebration on Shabbat. Clearly, the Rebbe made this gesture to Lulov because he realized the distress and embarrassment he must feel over his son's actions. Recording of Goldin available at: https://col.org.il/news/127931.
54 Chaim Miller, *Turning Judaism Outward* (Brooklyn, NY: Kol Menachem), chap. 7.
55 Letter from Althaus to family and friends, excerpted in "Of Heart and Quill," available at: https://derher.org/wp-content/uploads/50-Cheshvan-5777-06.pdf.
56 See appendix 2 of this book. The Ramash spent months at time with the Rebbe during his various medical treatments in Berlin, Vienna, Paris, and Marienbad.
57 "1994: Discovery of the 'Reshimot,'" available at: chabad.org/62186.
58 The notations were published as *Torat Menachem*: *Reshimat HaYoman* (Brooklyn, NY: Kehot Publication Society, 2006). The book is printed in two parts. The first is written in the exact wording that the Ramash used at the time, and the second contains context, translations from Yiddish to Hebrew, and scholarly footnotes with sources added by the editors. The first notation is dated December 18, 1928 (5 Tevet, 5689). Most of *Torat Menachem* was written in Europe before World War II, but there are also small sections written in Brooklyn in the early 1940s.
59 Excerpts of the *reshimot* with English translation available at: chabad.org/1210901.
60 Rabbi Adin Even-Israel Steinsaltz, *My Rebbe* (Jerusalem: Maggid Books, 2014), 38.

61 See *Igrot Kodesh*, vol. 15. The volume includes 303 letters spanning 1926 to 1946, mostly during the years the Ramash and his wife lived in Berlin and Paris. It omits additional letters of a more personal nature or those dealing with the details of the Rebbe's health and personal financial issues. See introduction to volume 15 by Rabbi Berel Levin for a historical overview.

62 *Igrot Kodesh* 2:361, letter dated 24 Tevet, 5692 (January 3, 1932). For the English translation see "Supplement B: Letter by the Previous Rebbe," available at: https://www.sie.org/templates/sie/article_cdo/aid/2347628/jewish/Supplement-B-Letter-by-the-Previous-Rebbe.htm. This letter was later published in *Hatomim*, vol. 2.

63 In that correspondence, the Ramash writes that he is still "puzzled" because "again and again, I hear people say, 'In Chabad, we have no interest in miracles' and the like. I found this same sentiment expressed in your letter." Clearly, the intergenerational conversation continued on this and many other topics. See "Supplement C: The Rebbe's Response to Previous Rebbe's Letter," available at: https://www.sie.org/templates/sie/article_cdo/aid/2347629/jewish/Supplement-C-The-Rebbes-Response-to-Previous-Rebbes-Letter.htm.

64 *Igrot Kodesh* 15:117. In later years, the seventh Rebbe continued the effort. With the collapse of the Soviet Union, he appointed a committee of leading *shluchim* and librarians of the Agudas Chassidei Chabad Library to recover the confiscated books and arrange its repatriation. That effort continues until today.

65 Steinsaltz, *My Rebbe*.

66 In 1936, the Polish government withdrew from the "gold block" and instituted currency restrictions. Polish Jewish tourists in Palestine in 1936 also suffered from this when the Polish bank limited the transfer of funds to their accounts. "Polish Currency Curbs Forcing 1,000 Tourists to Quit Palestine," JTA, May 5, 1936, available at:
https://www.jta.org/1936/05/05/archive/polish-currency-curbs-forcing-1000-tourists-to-quit-palestine.

67 *Igrot Kodesh* 15:216.

68 *Igrot Kodesh*, vol. 15, Introduction.

69 *Igrot Kodesh*, vol. 15.

70 Private transcript of a conversation between Rabbi Dovid Edelman and his son Rabbi Yisroel Edelman. Rabbi Dovid became a *shliach* of the Rebbe in the 1940s and eventually moved to Springfield, Massachusetts, where he headed the Lubavitch Yeshivah Academy until his passing in 2015. For more, see Menachem Posner, "Rabbi Dovid Edelman, 90, Educator and Longtime Chabad Leader in Massachusetts," available at: chabad.org/2817283.

71 In the mid-1940s, at the behest of the Rebbe, Rabbi Hershel Fogelman founded Yeshivah Achei Temimim Academy in Worchester, Massachusetts, serving as its leader until his passing in 2013. For more, see Menachem Posner, "Rabbi Hershel

Fogelman, Trailblazing Educator, Builder of Communities," available at: chabad.org/2261879.

72 It took some years before this perspective on non-observant Jews became mainstream, even among those in the Chabad community. During the 1950s and 1960s, the concept of *shlichut,* becoming an emissary of the Rebbe, was not supported by all in the Chabad community. It was revolutionary for a couple from an Orthodox home to be sent to live in a community lacking basic religious infrastructure. Rabbi Shlomo Cunin, sent by the Rebbe in 1965 to California, recalls Chasidim in New York telling him that he would not last long on the West Coast and insinuating that he was only going because he could not get a job close to home. Much of the religious world had been decimated by the abandonment of observance, and this prompted many to look at the irreligious community with disdain. Today, however, even in the most insular segments of the Orthodox community, people are open to outreach. For more, see David Eliezrie, *The Secret of Chabad.*

73 When the great rabbinical scholars took their students and left Russia at the onset of Communism, the Rebbe remained because he believed he had a responsibility for all Jews. When he visited America in 1929–30, he prioritized reaching out to those who were not observant. Even before setting foot on US soil, while still on the ship fleeing the Nazis in 1940, he directed Rabbi Chaim Hodakov to prepare a plan for a national network of Jewish education to stem the tide of assimilation. In the postwar era, he sent his Chasidim to live in communities around the world to set the stage for global Jewish renewal. In 1948, he established Kfar Chabad, the Chabad village in Israel, and instructed that its focus should be to reach beyond religious Jews to all Israelis. His final endeavor was the establishment of a Jewish educational network for Jews in Northern Africa (referring to them as "Our Brethren of Sephardic Jewry"), a project set in motion by the Ramash just a week after the Rebbe's passing.

CHAPTER SEVEN

1 Lokshin was the director of Agudas Chassidei Chabad in New York. Before immigrating to the US, he had studied in the yeshivah in Lubavitch. This letter (*Igrot Kodesh,* vol. 16, dated 20 Shevat, 5689/January 31, 1929) was the first indication of the Rebbe's plans to visit the US. The chasidic community was informed a few months later.

2 The Rebbe corresponded regularly with Rabbi Chaim Ozer, who apparently discussed the issue with him while visiting the Chafetz Chaim in Radin (*Igrot Kodesh,* vol. 16, letter dated 4 Cheshvan, 5689/October 18, 1928). The Rebbe detailed his efforts to secure funding from the JDC in a letter to Rabbi Aharon Milovski (*Igrot Kodesh,* vol. 16, dated 4 Tishrei, 5769/September 18, 1928).

3 Letter to Jacobson dated 26 Shevat, 5689 (February 6, 1929). In the letter, Feigin tells Jacobson about the financial difficulties and health challenges that the Rebbe is facing. He asks Jacobson to make an effort to unite the Chabad community in the United States to prepare for the visit: "Leave behind the differences of opinion between you [and] make an effort to come together."

4 The Rebbe Rayatz was the only Lubavitcher Rebbe to actually visit *Eretz Yisrael.* He considered a second visit in 1935 to pray at the graves of the righteous, but that plan did not come to fruition.

5 Throughout his leadership, the seventh Rebbe continued the tradition of previous Lubavitcher Rebbes and visited the grave of the Rebbe Rayatz on a regular basis, standing for three or four hours on average in the summer heat and winter cold to read prayer requests from people all over the world. He fasted on the days he went to his father's grave, and he also visited the *mikveh* before going to the cemetery. He often responded to requests for blessings with the assurance that "I will mention this at the *tzion* (grave) of the Rebbe." This was his way of invoking spiritual blessing.

6 "While I lived in the land of my birth, I would visit from time to time the graves of our righteous fathers, the righteous [spiritual] fathers and rabbis, and invoke mercy on ourselves, for our students, the community of *anash* in the midst of all of the Jewish people. At this time, it is impossible to travel to the land of my birth, and I have decided to visit the Holy Land, with G-d's help, to visit the sacred sites." *Igrot Kodesh*, vol. 2, letter to Rabbi Shimon Glizenstein dated 1 Tamuz, 5689 (July 8, 1929).

7 In 1929, the Land of Isael was part of the Palestinian Mandate, ruled by the British government. In World War I, the British had liberated it from the hands of the Ottoman Empire that controlled it for some five centuries. In 1948, it became formally known as the State of Israel after its declaration of independence. The seventh Rebbe asserted that that the historical name, *Eretz Yisrael,* would be more appropriate. *Igrot Kodesh – Lubavitcher Rebbe,* vol. 25, letter to President Zalman Shazar dated 12 Tamuz, 5739 (June 28, 1969).

8 Dovid Rotenberg, *Masa HaRebbe BeEretz HaKodesh (The Travels of the Rebbe in the Holy Land)* [Hebrew] (Kfar Chabad, Israel: Sifriat Ashel, 1999), 19.

9 Rabbi Yosef Chaim Sonnenfeld (1848–1932) was a student of the Ktav Sofer, Rabbi Binyamin Sofer of Pressburg (now Bratislava), Slovakia. He immigrated to *Eretz Yisrael* in 1873 and worked closely with Rabbi Yehuda Leib Diskind, the rabbi of the Ashkenazi community. Upon Rabbi Diskind's passing in 1898, Rabbi Sonnenfeld became the head of the Ashkenazi community. In 1921, he formalized the Eidah HaChareidis, the traditional Orthodox Chareidi community that exists to this day. Rabbi Sonnenfeld was a strong opponent of the efforts to secularize the Jewish community in Jerusalem led primarily by Zionist immigrants.

10 Rabbi Avraham Yitzchak Kook (1865–1935) was born in Russia. His father was a student of the Volozhin yeshivah, and his mother came from a Chabad family. In 1904, he moved to *Eretz Yisrael* and became the rabbi of Jaffa. In 1929, with the establishment of the Chief Rabbinate, he assumed the position of chief rabbi. Kook strongly supported the Zionist efforts. He was renowned for his scholarship, his concern for all, and his efforts to create bridges between Jews of all backgrounds.

11 Rotenberg, *Masa HaRebbe BeEretz HaKodesh,* chap. 2; *Igrot Kodesh,* vol. 2, letter to Rabbi Yosef Chaim Sonnenfeld dated 2 Tamuz, 5689 (July 10, 1928).

12 *Igrot Kodesh,* vol. 2, letters to Rabbi Schneur Zalman Slonim and Rabbi Shlomo Eliazrov dated 3 Tamuz, 5689 (July 11, 1928).

13 Much of the Rebbe's correspondence with his wife, who was living in Riga during the Rebbe's US visit, was seized by Russian forces after their takeover of Latvia in 1940. Eventually the letters were transferred to the Russian National Library. A selection of the letters (written primarily in Yiddish) was made available to this author.

14 They departed on Tuesday, July 30, 1929 (23 Tamuz, 5689). Rotenberg, *Masa HaRebbe BeEretz HaKodesh,* chap. 4.

15 They boarded the ship on Friday, August 2, 1929 (25 Tamuz, 5689).

16 The ship stopped at the port on Sunday, August 4, 1929 (27 Tamuz, 5689).

17 According to the British Census of 1922, there were 39,971 Jews living in Jerusalem. By the census of 1931, that number had reached 51,200. The 1922 census is available at: https://archive.org/details/PalestineCensus1922/page/n15/mode/2up.

18 Cited in Rotenberg, *Masa HaRebbe BeEretz HaKodesh,* 68.

19 *Haaretz,* August 9, 1929, cited in Rotenberg, *Masa HaRebbe BeEretz HaKodesh,* 67.

20 *Challenge: An Encounter with Lubavitch-Chabad in Israel* (London: Lubavitch Foundation, 1973), chap. 1.

21 The fund was formally named Colel Chabad in 1817. Today, Colel Chabad remains the oldest organized charity in Israel, with a budget of over $140,000,000 a year. Colel Chabad is the largest provider of food security in Israel and partners with the government in that arena. It runs soup kitchens, wedding halls for indigent families, health clinics, and a wide variety of social service projects in locations throughout Israel. For more, see colelchabad.org.

22 Rabbi Eliyahu of Vilna (1720–97), known as the Vilna Gaon (great scholar of Vilna), was one of the most influential Jewish scholars of the eighteenth century. He opposed the chasidic movement, issuing a *cherem,* a ban of excommunication, in 1777 and again in 1781. After his passing, his students orchestrated accusations against Rabbi Schneur Zalman that prompted his imprisonment by the czar.

23 Rabbi Menachem Mendel passed away in 1788. His successor, Rabbi Avraham Karlinsker, also a student of Rabbi Dovber the Maggid, differed with the Chabad

founder on a variety of issues. See Rabbi Shalom Ber Levin, *Toldot Chabad BeEretz HaKodesh* (Brooklyn, NY: Kehot, 1988), chap. 1–5.

24 "The History of Chabad in Hebron," available at: http://en.hebron.org.il/history/996.

25 Rabbi Rivlin's father was a Chasid of the Alter Rebbe. In 1847 he settled in Jerusalem and became rabbi of the Chasidim there. His great-great-grandson is former Israeli president Reuven Rivlin. See "Israel's President Rivlin Makes a Wish," available at: www.lubavitch.com/israels-president-rivlin-makes-a-wish/.

26 Land was purchased in 1850, and a building was erected with help from Sir Moses Montefiore. It is known as the Tzemach Tzedek Shul, named after the third Chabad Rebbe. A second story was added in 1879, and the plaque dedicated by the Sassoon family of Mumbai remains prominently displayed till today. This was the only synagogue in the historic Jewish Quarter of ancient Jerusalem that was not destroyed by the Jordanian occupation between 1948 and 1967. After the Six-Day War in 1967, the first Jew to return to live within the walls of the Old City, Moshe Zvi Segal, took up residence there, despite the building being heavily damaged by the Jordanian occupation. The building was refurbished and today is a vibrant center located on Chabad Street in the Jewish Quarter.

27 Mussi Sharfstein, "Site of New Hebron Neighborhood Was Purchased by Chabad in 1909," available at: https://www.lubavitch.com/site-of-new-hebron-neighborhood-was-purchased-by-chabad-in-1909/.

28 The Rebbe wrote that the flyer stated: "If the Rebbe is meeting with this *rasha* [liberally translated as 'evil person,' referring to Rabbi Kook), it is because the Rebbe does everything for the good of *Klal Yisrael* (the Jewish people)." It was signed "Chabad Chasidim of Jerusalem." According to the report in *Der Tag*, those distributing the flyers were "Charedi extremists with views that are more zealous than Rabbi Sonnenfeld and Agudath Israel." It is doubtful if they were true Chabad Chasidim.

29 Quoted in Rotenberg, *Masa HaRebbe BeEretz HaKodesh*, 68.

30 Letter written by the Rebbe from the New Central Hotel upon his arrival in Jerusalem.

31 For centuries, the Arabs permitted Jews to pray only in a small area in front of part of the Western Wall. During the British Mandate, Jews were forbidden to blow shofar at the Wall. In 1967, after the liberation of Jerusalem, the area in front of the Wall was cleared, and the broad plaza that is there today was created. The Wall stretches through the Old City; much of it still blocked today by existing structures. Its total length is 1,601 feet.

32 Letter written by the Rebbe from the New Central Hotel upon his arrival in Jerusalem.

33 Zlata Perl Kook was 86 at the time of the Rebbe's visit. She asked the Rebbe for a blessing, and the Rebbe responded by blessing her with long life. She had given her son, Rabbi Kook, a yarmulke that belonged to the third Rebbe, Rabbi Menachem Mendel, the Tzemach Tzedek. Rabbi Kook told the Rebbe that he usually wore it on the High Holidays, but he wore it that day in honor of the Rebbe's visit. Rotenberg, *Masa HaRebbe BeEretz HaKodesh*, 86.

34 Rotenberg, *Masa HaRebbe BeEretz HaKodesh*, chap. 9.

35 Ibid.

36 Entry in the Rebbe's diary dated 13 Av, cited in Rotenberg, *Masa HaRebbe BeEretz HaKodesh*, chap. 21.

37 Gad Frumkin, *Derekh Shofet BeYerushalayim*, cited in Rotenberg, *Masa HaRebbe BeEretz HaKodesh*.

38 Colel Chabad minutes, Tevet (January) 1920. It was decided that "everything would be under the instruction of the Lubavitcher Rebbe," referring to the Rashab. See Shalom Ber Levin, *Toldot Chabad BeEretz HaKodesh*.

39 The Rebbe viewed Colel Chabad as "a sacred obligation." However, he insisted on having a proper understanding of the finances. "I want to assist in raising the Colel to new heights." *Igrot Kodesh*, vol. 16, letter dated 13 Elul, 5688 (August 29, 1928).

40 Much of the monies of Colel Chabad were received by post from overseas. The new guidelines included procedures to ensure that all monies were properly recorded, financial statements submitted to the board, etc.

41 Rabbi Shlomo Leib Eliazrov (1863–1952) was the grandson of Rabbi Yaakov and Rebbetzin Menucha Rochel Slonim (son-in-law and daughter of the Mitteler Rebbe, Rabbi Dovber of Lubavitch). Rabbi Shlomo Leib served as the chief rabbi of the Ashkenazi community in Hebron. He traveled overseas on at least six missions to raise funds for the community in Hebron. These trips brought him to Bukhara in Southern Russia, where he served as rabbi for a few years. He also visited the Rebbe Rashab in Lubavitch numerous times and developed a strong relationship with the Rebbe Rayatz. He assisted the Rebbe Rashab in the purchase of Beit Romano, a large property in Hebron. He moved to Jerusalem after World War I, becoming the rabbi of the Chabad community there. He was instrumental in the establishment of the Toras Emes yeshivah in Jerusalem.

42 The charter was formalized in 1933. A copy is printed in Levin, *Toldot Chabad BeEretz HaKodesh*, 282.

43 The ancient city of Nablus (Shekhem) is the site of the grave of Yosef HaTzaddik, son of the biblical patriarch Yaakov. This is noted in Joshua 24:32: "The bones of Yosef, which the children of Israel brought up out of Egypt, were buried in Shekhem." Christian pilgrims as early as Itinerarium Burdigalense in 333 CE note Shekhem as the location of Joseph's Tomb. Many Jewish pilgrims, including Benjamin

Tudela, who writes about his visit in 1160, tell of Jews making a spiritual pilgrimage to Shekhem.

44 In the fourteenth and fifteenth centuries, Safed became a center of Jewish learning, particularly of the mystical teachings of the Kabbalah.

45 During the first and second centuries, the center of Jewish scholarship moved to Israel's north after the Temple's destruction in 70 CE. Many of the Sages of the Mishnah, which was edited around the year 180 in the north, are buried in the area.

46 Genesis 23.

47 There is a massive building covering the entrance to the double cave, where the founders of the Jewish faith are interred. According to most historical accounts, it was erected by Herod over two thousand years ago. (Some historians claim it is of Hasmonean origin, which would put it at 150 years earlier.) See "Secrets of the Tomb of the Patriarchs in Hebron," available at: https://www.youtube.com/watch?v=o__ZgeqxaPA.

48 II Samuel 5:3: "All the elders of Israel came to the king in Hebron, and King David sealed a covenant with them in Hebron before G-d, and they anointed David as king over Israel." See Oded Avishar, ed., *Sefer Chevron* (Jerusalem: Keter Publishing, 1970) for a historical overview.

49 "The Seventh Step at the Tomb of Machpela, Hebron, 1913," available at: https://www.youtube.com/watch?v=X2cEDTMV8X8&feature=emb_logo.

50 Benjamin Tudela (1130–73) originated from Tudela, Spain and traveled the Jewish world, providing a remarkable account of Jewish life in his time. Tudela describes his visit to the grave in Hebron:

> If a Jew comes, however, and gives a special reward, the custodian of the cave opens unto him a gate of iron, which was constructed by our forefathers, and then he is able to descend below by means of steps, holding a lighted candle in his hand. He then reaches a cave, in which nothing is to be found, and a cave beyond, which is likewise empty, but when he reaches the third cave, behold there are six sepulchers, those of Abraham, Isaac, and Jacob, respectively facing those of Sarah, Rebecca, and Leah. And upon the graves are inscriptions cut in stone. Upon the grave of Abraham is engraved "This is the grave of Abraham"; upon that of Isaac, "This is the grave of Isaac, the son of Abraham our father"; upon that of Jacob, "This is the grave of Jacob, the son of Isaac, the son of Abraham our father"; and upon the others, "This is the grave of Sarah," "This is the grave of Rebecca," and "This is the grave of Leah." A lamp burns day and night upon the graves in the cave. (Excerpt from *The Itinerary of Benjamin of Tudela*, critical text, translation, and commentary by Marcus Nathan Adler, 1907)

51 On rare occasions, non-Muslim visitors were permitted inside the structure, including the Marquis of Bute in 1866, the Crown Prince of Prussia in 1869, and the sons of the Prince of Wales in 1882. At times, Jews, particular women, would dress as Muslims in order to gain entry. In 1935, the Gerrer Rebbe, Rabbi Avraham Mordechai Alter, attempted to visit, but crowds of Muslims blocked his access.

52 Moses Montefiore (1784–1885) was one of the most prestigious leaders of British Jewry in the nineteenth century and a confidant of Queen Victoria. He visited Palestine seven times, the first in 1827. His wife Judith Montefiore wrote in her memoir of their attempt to visit in 1838: "A turbulent throng of Mussulmans was collected in the interior of the mosque, and they were soon joined by the raving dervish. But the rage of the Turks and the howling of the dervish now became more violent than ever, and we decided that it would be prudent to retire without attempting a further entrance."

53 Yardena Schwartz, *Ghosts of a Holy War* (Union Square, 2024).

54 Interview with Sholom Ber Goldschmidt, survivor of the 1929 massacre, available at: https://www.youtube.com/watch?v=cNMyTE5l9vw&list=PLeyXYN5APcrjxsVQWDE6dx8sYGgGTDu90.

55 Slonim was a grandson of Rebbetzin Menucha Rochel. He was killed the following Saturday during the Arab riots.

56 Avishar, *Sefer Chevron*, 261.

57 Mohammed Amin al-Husseini (1897–1974) was appointed mufti of Jerusalem by the British Mandate. He was a fierce opponent to Zionism. He organized riots in Palestine in 1920 to protest the Balfour Declaration, instigated the massacre in 1929, and led the 1936 Arab Revolt. With the onset of World War II, he went to Berlin, where he met with top German officials including Hitler and encouraged the Holocaust.

58 Interview with Shalom Ber Goldschmidt. See also "Sholom Ber Goldshmid: Child Survivor Continued Family Legacy," available at: http://en.hebron.org.il/history/507.

59 "In Memoriam: Full List of the Victims of the 1929 Hebron Massacre," available at: http://en.hebron.org.il/history/520.

60 Cited in Rotenberg, *Masa HaRebbe BeEretz HaKodesh*.

61 They visited the developing community of Rechovot some sixteen miles from Tel Aviv. Frumkin says that unfortunately, by the time they arrived it was dark, and the Rebbe could not see much of the community.

62 Av 5689.

63 For the Rebbe's *maamarim*, some of which are extant, see *Sefer HaMaamarim*, 5689 (Brooklyn, NY: Kehot, 2022).

64 Rabbi Shimon Glitzenstein, *Diary of the Visit of the Rebbe to Eretz Yisrael*, excerpted in Rotenberg, *Masa HaRebbe BeEretz HaKodesh*, 212.

65 The Rebbe spent a night in Cairo. During the night, he went to visit the pyramids in Giza. Rotenberg, *Masa HaRebbe BeEretz HaKodesh.*

66 JEM Oral History Project, transcript of Rabbi Shimon Elituv. He traveled to Egypt in 1984 at the Rebbe's request to conduct a ceremony in the home of Maimonides in Cairo in honor of the conclusion of the study of Maimonides's *Mishneh Torah.* During the trip, he spent a few days in Alexandria visiting the Eliyahu HaNavi synagogue, where he heard the story from the leader of the community. Elituv says, "He told the story over with great emotion, describing what he saw when he accompanied his father to welcome the Rebbe in 1929." Prior to World War II, there were more than twenty-seven thousand Jews in the city; with the establishment of the State of Israel in 1948, the vast majority left. The Eliyahu HaNavi synagogue was built in 1354 and refurbished by the Egyptian government in 2020.

67 It seems this incident happened in 1882, shortly before the passing of Rabbi Shmuel.

68 The Rebbe suffered from pain in his kidneys and spent most of the trip immobilized in his room. Dr. Moshe Wallach (1866–1957) had immigrated to *Eretz Yisrael* from Germany in 1890. He was a religious Jew known for his piety and unusual dedication to his patients. He founded Jerusalem's Shaarei Zedek Hospital in 1902, establishing a protocol of Shabbat observance and respect for Jewish tradition. Today it is one of the premiere medical centers in Israel. The Rebbe was very impressed by Dr. Wallach's sensitivity and care and wrote about him in laudatory terms, calling him "a wise man with fear of Heaven." *Igrot Kodesh*, vol. 2, letter to Rabbi Kook dated 21 Elul, 5689 (September 26, 1929).

69 Horenstein and Dubin would return to Europe after a few months; Feigin would remain with the Rebbe in the US.

70 Most of the Jewish schools were supplementary. Most Jewish children attended public school; very few went to yeshivas or day schools. Jonathan Sarna, *American Judaism*, 2nd edition (Yale University Press, 2019), 225.

71 Yeshivas Rabbeinu Yitzchok Elchonon was founded in 1896, becoming Yeshivah College in 1928 and later Yeshiva University. Yeshivah Torah Vodaath started in 1918 in Williamsburg. Serious Jewish scholarship was still based in Europe, and until the onset of the war in 1939, students who wanted to pursue higher levels of Jewish learning traveled to Poland, Lithuania, and *Eretz Yisrael.*

72 *Zikhron Livnei Yisrael – Memoirs of Rabbi Yisrael Jacobson: 1907–1939* [Hebrew] (Brooklyn, NY: Kehot Publication Society, 1996), chap. 22.

73 A 1943 report explains that the synagogues also played a social role, as they created opportunities for immigrants to see friends from the old country. They also established social welfare institutions and burial societies. The small national Chabad organization Agudas Chassidei Chabad, founded in 1924, was still in its infancy and

attempted – with moderate success – to connect to these synagogues. Levin, *Toldot Chabad BeArtzot HaBrit* (Brooklyn, NY: Kehot Publication Society, 1988), chap. 26.

74 With time, many of these immigrant congregations closed or merged as Jews moved from the inner city to the suburbs and drifted from traditional observance.

75 *Sefer HaMaamarim – Kuntresim, "Zeh HaYom Techilat Maasekha"* (Brooklyn, New York: Kehot Publication Society), 1:69.

76 Interview with his grandson, Rabbi Heschel Greenberg.

77 *Sefer HaSichos*, 5688–91 (2021 edition).

78 Jacobson, *Zikhron Livnei Yisrael*, 176.

79 According to Jewish law, a holiday celebration can continue into the evening, past the time that the holiday actually ends, if the participants have not prayed the evening services and made *Havdalah*. Others who had formally ended the holiday traveled to join in the Rebbe's *farbrengen*. Also present were reporters from the local Jewish press.

80 In a letter to his wife, the Rebbe described the crowd: "The crowd was very enthusiastic. At the *farbrengen* there were editors and correspondents from the media, reform rabbis, and well-educated people, as well as Temimim (Yeshivah alumni) and [other] Chasidim. There was great enthusiasm and joy." *Sefer HaSichos*, 5688–91 (2021 edition).

81 Originally published in New York in a booklet after the *farbrengen*. A second version with edits and additions was published in 1937 and was printed in *Likkutei Dibburim*, vol. 2. An English version appears in *Likkutei Dibburim*, (Brooklyn, NY: Kehot Publication Society, 2021), 2:227. For the original Yiddish of the second version, see *Sefer HaSichos*, 5688–91, 84.

82 According to a letter written by the Baal Shem Tov to his brother-in-law, this occurred in 1746 (5507). See "The Chamber of Mashiach," available at: chabad.org/380401; Levi Haskelevich, "Baal Shem Tov: When is Moshiach Coming?" available at: https://www.sefaria.org/sheets/90076?lang=bi.

83 Chasidic thought refers to the Western hemisphere as *kadur hatachton*, literally, the bottom half of the world. It is explained that as Jews spread through the world, they unleash its spiritual potential by studying Torah and observing the commandments. As Jews settled in the Western hemisphere, they revealed the inherent "sparks of holiness" that had been embedded there after creation. Rabbi Eliyahu Wolf, "*Chetzi Kadur HaTachton*" [Hebrew], available at: https://col.org.il/news/139305.

84 From December 1927 to October 1928, there was extensive correspondence between JDC leaders in the US and Europe. Rosen and Kahn, the JDC's European senior staff, recommended working with the Rebbe. But American Jewish leaders were reluctant, as Joseph Hyman writes in a memo dated October 13, 1928: "While Rabbi Schneersohn might have the simplest and most practical method of handling it, it might involve some of the rabbis and expose them to danger." The absurdity of

this assertion is that their very practice of Judaism under the Communist regime and the oppression of the Yevesektzkia put them in danger. Support of American Jews might make it easier to avert that danger. If more Jews could be trained for home-based handicraft industries, that would make them self-sufficient. Louis Marshall, who was also from a German Jewish background and founded the American Jewish Committee, wrote to Adler (who was sympathetic to the Rebbe) a few months earlier, in August 1928. While referring to the Rebbe as the "indefatigable Schneersohn," Marshall went on to say that after consultations with European Jewish groups, they "unanimously decided that the risks attendant on carrying out the program of Schneersohn was too great as to forbid our undertaking in any way to cooperate. However, there was a general feeling of distrust of Schneersohn." It was a strange dichotomy: The JDC staff on the ground who knew the Rebbe repeatedly asserted that working with him was the most reliable way to help Russian Jews. And yet Jewish leaders in the US, many of them assimilated German Jewish immigrants, sought reasons not to support him. Clearly, the issues here are deeper. Jewish leaders in the US cared about Jews around the world, but they did not see the preservation of Jewish tradition as an important goal; on a personal level, most had abandoned observance. For the Rebbe, on the other hand, Torah, tradition, and spirituality were the central mission of his life. The arguments that Hyman, Marshall, and others used as reasons for not supporting the Rebbe were justification for a deeper ideological opposition to the ideals he espoused. See JDC Archives, correspondence between Adler and Marshall.

85 *Igrot Kodesh* 11:108, letter dated 2 Adar, 5690 (March 2, 1930).

86 Felix Warburg (1871–1937) was a member of the German Jewish banking family. He immigrated to the US at the age of twenty-three and married Freda Schiff, the daughter of one of the most affluent Jews in America, German-born banker Jacob Schiff. For more, see "Felix M. Warburg Dead at 66," JTA, Oct. 21, 1937, available at: https://www.jta.org/1937/10/21/archive/felix-m-warburg-dead-at-66.

87 Dr. Cyrus Adler (1863–1940) was born in Arkansas; his family moved to Philadelphia to be closer to the Jewish community. He was greatly influenced by Orthodox Rabbi Sabato Morais. Adler was the first American Jew to earn a doctorate in Semitic languages. He was the founder of Dropsie College for Hebrew and Cognate Learning (Philadelphia) and served as chancellor of the Jewish Theological Seminary from 1915 to 1940. (At the time, it was far more traditional than it is today.) He was close to the many prominent Jewish philanthropists and had a much greater affinity for tradition than other JDC leaders, most of whom came from the German Jewish community in the US.

88 Confidential Memorandum from J.C. Hyman to Dr. Cyrus Adler, October 7, 1929, JDC Archives.

89 Hyman notes that religious life is not outlawed. What is illegal are schools with more than three children under the age of 18. Transferring funds to Russia for religious programs was restricted by Russian regulations that limited foreign currency in Russia. Hyman wrote that the Rebbe was able to create a mechanism to overcome this problem by providing the funds to Jews in Riga who could not transfer assets beyond the borders of Russia, and then getting rubles from them in Russia.

90 Letter to the Rebbe's wife.

91 Memorandum of Dr. Cyrus Adler on the meeting of October 9, 1929. JDC Archives.

92 *Igrot Kodesh*, vol. 11.

93 "Warburg Pledges $1,000,000 to Fund," *New York Times* archives, available at: https://www.nytimes.com/1928/04/25/archives/warburg-pledges-1000000-to-fund-will-be-used-to-establish-jews-on.html?auth=link-dismiss-google1tap.

94 *Igrot Kodesh* 1:516. In a long letter, the Rebbe describes the history of his efforts for Soviet Jewry. He discusses the meeting with Warburg on page 534.

95 "Felix M. Warburg is Honored by Jewish Colonists in Russia," JTA, May 18, 1927, available at: https://www.jta.org/1927/05/18/archive/felix-m-warburg-is-honored-by-jewish-colonists-in-russia.

96 Ron Chernow, *The Warburgs: The Twentieth-Century Odyssey of a Remarkable Jewish Family* (Vintage Books, 2003), 294.

97 *Igrot Kodesh*, vol. 1, letter to "philanthropists of the Joint" dated 25 Sivan, 5685 (June 17, 1925).

98 *Igrot Kodesh*, vol. 1, letter to Warburg dated 27 Iyar, 5686 (May 11, 1926).

99 In 1846, Montefiore, an observant Jew and a confidant of Queen Victoria, met with Czar Nicholas I in St. Petersburg to urge him to improve conditions for the Jews. This was one of a series of trips across the world that Montefiore undertook to assist his brethren. He also visited Romania, Rome, and Morocco, and went to Russia for the second time in 1876. David Sorkin, "Montefiore and the Politics of Emancipation," available at: https://jewishreviewofbooks.com/articles/174/montefiore-and-the-politics-of-emancipation/.

100 *Igrot Kodesh* 1:527–28.

101 Yehuda Bauer, *My Brother's Keeper: A History of the JDC, 1929–1939* (Jewish Publication Society, 1974)

102 Michael Beizer, *Relief in Time of Need: Russian Jewry and the Joint, 1914–24* (Bloomington, IN: Slavica Publishers, 2015), 233–34.

103 Zvi Gitelman, *A Century of Ambivalence: The Jews of Russia and the Soviet Union, 1881 to the Present* (Indiana University Press, 2001), chap. 3.

104 "Leaders of Minsk Kehillah Arrested by G.P.U.; Charged with Counter-revolution," JTA, Feb. 17, 1930, available at: https://www.jta.org/1930/02/17/archive/leaders-of-minsk-kehillah-arrested-by-g-p-u-charged-with-counter-revolution.

105 A month before the Minsk raid, the JDC office in Berlin sent a disturbing cable to headquarters in New York warning that the Russian government was targeting Jews: "Stalin is working in a ruthless fashion." Chernow, *The Warburgs*, 295.

106 They failed to realize that the Soviet regime at the time was desperate for foreign currency, its status on the international stage still precarious. The US would not recognize the country until 1933. If JDC leaders had used their influence, they might have mitigated, even partially, Stalin's anti-religious agenda.

107 Letter dated February 2, 1932, JDC Archives. Adler also suggests in the letter that the Russians are attempting to defraud the JDC.

108 Letter from Warburg to Hyman dated February 5, 1932. The letter is filled with a sense of privilege, entitlement, and disdain for Jewish tradition and the Rebbe personally. This despite the support of Dr. Rosen, the JDC director in Russia, who repeatedly told leaders in New York that the Rebbe was the sole address to connect to the Jews in Russia, and time and again attested to his reliability.

109 Ibid.

110 Nora Levin, *The Jews in the Soviet Union Since 1917* (New York University Press, 1988), chap. 12.

111 In 1929, the JDC had provided a grant of $10,000 for the Rebbe's matzah campaign.

112 There had been a famine in Russia in 1931–33, prompted by the unsuccessful farm collectivization. It is striking that Warburg, the chairman of the Joint, was not aware of the crisis in Russia, or if he knew, that he was so dismissive of the need to provide matzah for Russian Jews. Stephen Kotkin, *Stalin: Waiting for Hitler, 1929–1941* (Penguin Press, 2017).

113 Warburg was also blustery and harsh with others. His relationship with Chaim Weizmann, for example, was marked by both close camaraderie and acrimonious debates. Warburg supported efforts to build Hebrew University and settlements in Palestine, but he did not share Weizmann's goal of Jewish sovereignty. See Chernow, *The Warburgs*.

114 Ibid.

115 Mikhail Mitsel, "The Final Chapter: Agro-Joint Workers – Victims of the Great Terror in the USSR, 1937–1940." This publication includes a list of close to two hundred Agro-Joint staff who suffered a terrible fate in Stalin's reign of terror, available at: http://catalog.nypl.org/search/o830123542.

116 One could argue that information from Russia was limited, and the JDC officials at the time did not understand exactly what was happening thousands of miles away.

117 Mitsel writes that "comprehension of the USSR and Stalin's regime by JDC officials in New York, especially Rosenberg, chairman of Agro-Joint trustees, was to remain naive and idealistic."

118 Publicity about the forced shutdown of its program and the expulsion, imprisonment, and murder of many of the staff would have been a PR disaster, undermining community confidence and negatively impacting JDC fundraising. Instead, the JDC kept silent and apparently attempted to cover up the extent of the catastrophe that befell its organization and its workers in Russia.

119 One might make the argument that Jews in the US at the time did not feel the sense of security and political empowerment that they feel today, and they were therefore wary of raising the issue. But the JDC board was composed of very influential and wealthy Jews who must have had connections to leaders in Washington. The chairman of the JDC at the time was Paul Baerwald, a German Jewish immigrant who was an influential banker. In 1938 he was appointed to President Franklin Roosevelt's Advisory Committee on Political Refugees, and he was a close friend of New York Governor Herbert Lehman. Clearly, connections to senior government officials were in place. However, it seems they never used them to attempt to help their staff suffering in Russia.

120 American Jewish Yearbook, 1939–40 (Jewish Publication Society), 41:156–61.

121 The story of these JDC staffers was regulated to two sentences in Bauer's history of the JDC. "This was the sum total of the eviction of the Agro-Joint and the arrest and death of most, possibly all of its Russian Jewish officials. There were achievements and there were disasters." The real story of those who suffered under the purge remained a distant memory until Mikhail Mitsel, who is today the JDC historian, published in Kiev in 2012 a long account of this tragic episode in Russian. Later, a shorter version was published in English: "The Final Chapter: Agro-Joint Workers – Victims of the Great Terror in the USSR, 1937–1940," available at: https://kehilalinks.jewishgen.org/Colonies_of_Ukraine/The_Final_Chapter_Agro-Joint_in_the_Yea.pdf.

122 Chernow, *The Warburgs*, chap. 21.

123 In the 1930s, Russia attempted to set up a Jewish province in Birobidzhan in remote Siberia. The official language was Yiddish. A few thousand Jews still live there today.

124 Levin, *The Jews in the Soviet Union Since 1917*, 238, 858, note 58.

125 American Jewish Yearbook, 1939–40.

126 *Igrot Kodesh*, vol. 2, letter to Rabbi Mendel Rothstein dated 28 Shevat, 5690 (February 24, 1930).

127 *Igrot Kodesh* 11:108, letter to Rabbi Dovid Rabinowitz dated 2 Adar, 5690 (March 2, 1930). The Rebbe expresses great disappointment over the repeated broken promises.

128 Ibid.

129 *Igrot Kodesh*, vol. 2, letter to Rabbi Mendel Rothstein dated 28 Shevat, 5690 (February 24, 1930).

130 *Igrot Kodesh* 11:115, letter from Justice Louis Brandeis to Israel Thurman dated March 9, 1930. Israel Thurman (1884–1982) was a brother-in-law of Rabbi Dovid Rabinowitz, a follower of Chabad. He graduated from Harvard and was a leader in the Reform movement and the American Jewish Congress. He was a close friend of Brandeis, who addressed him in a letter as "My dear Thurman."

131 Letter from Israel Thurman to the Rebbe dated March 11, 1930. In the letter, Thurman details the efforts to create a unified communal initiative to support the Rebbe's work in Russia. This is especially noteworthy because the American Jewish Committee, which represented the secular German Jewish leaders and which did not actively endorse Zionism, and the American Jewish Congress, which was made up of grassroots traditional Jews who supported Zionism, were at times at odds with each other. Still, according to Thurman, they actively discussing the proposal to create a joint effort with the JDC.

132 The Rebbe asked Thurman to encourage Stephen S. Wise to travel with him to Washington to try to influence Brandeis to take a more public role. *Igrot Kodesh* 11:115.

133 Ibid.

134 *The Jewish Record*, May 2, 1930.

135 This attitude persisted. When Professor Cyrus Adler wanted to help the Rebbe personally, he wrote to Joseph Hyman, the JDC director. "I have signed a letter to Rabbi Schneersohn; if you do not consider it objectionable from the point of view of the JDC, please let it go. You will notice I have written it on Dropsie College paper." Letter from Adler to Hyman dated February 2, 1932, JDC Archives.

136 Jacobson, *Zikhron Livnei Yisrael*, 184.

137 At times, the Rebbe even lauded the Communists. During a visit to Baltimore in January 1930, the Rashag, acting as the Rebbe's spokesman, said, "Religious Jews in Russia are grateful to the Soviets because the government has consistently repressed anti-Jewish pogroms" (*The Baltimore Sun*, January 13, 1930). However, in the same article, the Rashag is quoted as saying, "The economic status of the religious Jew in Russia is deplorable." The article also detailed the Rebbe's arrest and release due to international pressure, and noted that the "policy and legislation of the Soviet government is anti-religious."

138 Yosef Landa, "The Historic Visit by the Sixth Rebbe of Chabad to St. Louis," available at: chabad.org/3715920.

139 This discreet approach was continued by the seventh Rebbe until the fall of the Soviet Union. He strongly opposed the public demonstrations that were covertly orchestrated by Israeli Secret Service division Lishkat Hakesher. He asserted that public pressure and intimidation would only cause the Russian government to double down on its

policies and be more resistant to permitting Russian Jews to emigrate. Eli Rubin, "Soviet Jewry: Quiet Diplomacy, Covert Activity," available at: chabad.org/2619818.

140 May 9, 1930.

141 *The Yiddish Velt*, December 16, 1929 (14 Kislev, 5690); Levin, *Toldot Chabad BeArtzot HaBrit*, chap. 14.

142 *The Jewish Record*, May 9, 1930.

143 *Detroit Free Press*, April 28, 1930.

144 February 10, 1930.

145 *Chicago Courier*, February 11, 1930, reprinted in Levin, *Toldot Chabad BeArtzot HaBrit*, 67.

146 Jacobson, *Zikhron Livnei Yisrael*, 181. Jacobson notes that the Rebbe lost weight during these visits.

147 Letter dated May 11, 1930.

148 *The Jewish Record*, lead editorial, May 16, 1930.

149 Faye Zeffren recalls that when the women met with the Rebbe, he reminded them that although according to Jewish law, nail polish must be removed before immersing in a *mikveh*, women were encouraged to reapply nail polish and makeup after immersion. "It is important for Jewish women to look good," she recalls the Rebbe saying. Yosef Landa, "The Historic Visit by the Sixth Rebbe of Chabad to St. Louis," available at: chabad.org/3715920.

150 At the dinner, held on May 18, 1930 at Congregation B'nai Amoona, the plans for the new *mikveh* were unveiled. Each attendee was given a card with a picture of the Rebbe and a coin the Rebbe had given for supporters of the *mikveh*.

151 The Rebbe visited Detroit from April 27 to May 4, 1930. On April 28, the *Detroit Evening Times* reported, "More than ten thousand persons thronged the Michigan Central Railroad Station... to welcome Rabbi Schneersohn, world leader of Chasidim and head of Orthodox Jewry. A police escort was called to conduct the Lubavitcher Rebbe to his car."

152 "If the Rebbe Comes to America, America Will Come to Him!" available at: https://anash.org/if-the-rebbe-comes-to-america-america-will-come-to-him/.

153 Lewis Boxer (1904–90) was a resident of Philadelphia. In the decades that followed his meeting with the Rebbe, he remained connected to Chabad and supported its work in his city. His article describing the encounter appeared in *The Jewish Press*.

154 The Rebbe spent a month in Philadelphia, arriving December 15, 1929. Local newspapers covered his arrival avidly; the Rebbe was greeted by crowds of thousands. See Levin, *Toldot Chabad BeArtzot HaBrit*, chap. 14.

155 Local Jewish philanthropists Nathan and Jennie Faggen hosted a major fundraising dinner to benefit the Rebbe's institutions, raising over fifteen thousand dollars (more than $250,000 today) despite the stock market crash two months earlier.

See Dovi Safier, "Mother of all Yeshivos: Uncovering the Forgotten Legacy of Mrs. Jennie Miller Faggen," *Mishpacha*, issue no. 956, April 3, 2023.

156 Upon immigrating to the US, Rabbi Bar lived in St. Paul, Minnesota. He moved to Chicago in 1925, teaching in the yeshivah until 1947.

157 Interview with Benjamin Katz, JEM Oral History Project.

158 Hebrew Theological College/Beis HaMidrash LaTorah was founded in 1919 and remains a major center of Jewish learning to this day. For more information, see www.htc.edu.

159 The Pittsburgh Platform, an 1885 document listing the founding principles of the US Reform movement, repudiated classic Jewish beliefs, the divinity of the Torah, and the obligation to observe mitzvot. The Conservative movement, which began as a reaction to the Reform movement moving away from historic Jewish beliefs, was itself beginning to struggle with the same ideas. While still tethered to tradition to a degree, it also advocated for the centrality of ethics and slowly deemphasized the observance of commandments.

160 The Rebbe spent three weeks in Baltimore, starting January 12, 1930. As in other cities, he was welcomed by a large crowd – it numbered three thousand, according to *The Baltimore Sun*. During his visit, he was presented with the key to the city by the mayor, and he met with Maryland's governor, Albert Richie.

161 "Lubawitscher Rebbe Received at White House by President," JTA, July 13, 1930, available at: https://www.jta.org/1930/07/13/archive/lubawitscher-rebbe-received-at-white-house-by-president. The Rashag also thanked the president for his support of Jews in *Eretz Yisrael*.

162 *Sefer HaSichos*, letter dated 14 Tamuz, 5688 (July 12, 1930), 105.

163 Asher was the son of Rabbi Dovid Rabinowitz of Boston. He had lobbied Justice Brandeis to encourage the US government to protest when the Rebbe was arrested in 1927 (see chap. 6). He would also play an instrumental role lobbying the US government to intervene to save the Rebbe in war-torn Poland (see chap. 9).

164 The JDC's response changed in the years that followed. In the 1930s, it supported the network of yeshivas that the Rebbe developed in Poland, and in the postwar era, it actively assisted Chabad refugees who escaped Russia. Starting in the 1950s, it partnered with Chabad to support school systems in Morocco and Tunisia. It also supported Chabad projects in Europe and Israel. Today, the JDC works with Chabad in the Former Soviet Union.

165 Jacobson, *Zikhron Livnei Yisrael*, chap. 29–30.

166 Rabbi Gurewicz was renowned for his commitment to learning and scholarship. He served as an emissary of both the Rebbe Rashab and the Rebbe Rayatz. He was burned alive by the Nazis in the synagogue of Kherson, Ukraine, in November 1941.

167 Rabbi Shmuel Levitin (1883–1974) was sent by the Rebbe in 1938 and remained in the US, unable to return to Europe due to the war. He was a prominent scholar and a devoted Chasid who played a key leadership role in the US Chabad community until his passing. "Shmuel Levitin, 91, Lubavitcher Figure," *The New York Times*, Aug. 31, 1974, available at: https://www.nytimes.com/1974/08/31/archives/shmuel-levitin-91-lubavitcher-figure.html.

168 *The Jewish Record*, May 16, 1930.

169 *Der Morgen Journal*, July 16, 1930, reprinted in "America Is No Different: A Selection of Vintage Film Clips of Rabbi Yosef Yitzchak of Lubavitch in the United States," JEM, 1999.

170 July 16, 1930 (20 Tamuz, 5690).

171 *Zikhron Livnei Yisrael*, 185; *Sefer HaSichos*, 5688–91 (2021 edition), 72.

172 *Kovetz Lubavitch*, year 2 (5705), 74–75; *Sefer HaSichos*, 5688–91, 133.

173 Wednesday, 27 Tamuz, 5690 (July 23, 1930).

174 *Igrot Kodesh* 2:256, 11:143.

175 The Rebbe arrived on Sunday, 14 Elul, 5690 (September 8, 1930).

176 Vilner Radio, September 14, 1930: "A few days ago, the Rebbe of Lubavitch returned to Riga from America, where he spent almost a year"; *Frimorgen Journal*, September 18, 1930.

CHAPTER EIGHT

1 The first meeting of the New York committee took place in June 1930, while the Rebbe while still in the US.

2 The meeting was held in the Rashag's home in Riga. See Levin, *Toldot Chabad BePolin, Lita, VeLatvia* (Brooklyn, NY: Kehot Publication Society, 2011), 76–77, for a copy of the letter sent to the Rebbe by the group of Polish Chasidim who had been in Riga for the holidays.

3 Bava Batra 3b. According to the Talmud, if a synagogue is destroyed with a plan to rebuild a new one, unforeseen circumstances might make the reconstruction impossible, leaving the community with no place to pray. Also, there may be no other place to pray during the period of construction.

4 *Igrot Kodesh*, vol. 2, letter to "My friends, *anash*," dated 18 Cheshvan, 5691 (November 9, 1920). The Rebbe's long letter to US Chasidim brims with emotion and affection, emphasizing the pleasure the Rebbe had from his visit with them. He noted that much needs to be done to prepare for the transition of the center of Lubavitch from Europe to America. "Each thing needs preparation. Something like this needs a spiritual and practical foundation, and it cannot come about from itself. It demands effort to organize in a structured fashion." He says that it is indeed possible, "since nothing can restrain a person's will." In a second letter written the

same day to the US Chabad Committee, he instructs them to implement three practical suggestions: to unify and increase the study of chasidic philosophy, to support the network of Chabad yeshivas in Europe, and to strengthen the tradition of *maamad,* the ongoing support by Chasidim of the Rebbe's work.

5 *Igrot Kodesh,* vol. 6, letter to Rabbi Shmuel Levitin dated 26 Cheshvan, 5702 (November 11, 1941).

6 *Zikhron Livnei Yisrael – Memoirs of Rabbi Yisrael Jacobson: 1907–1939* [Hebrew] (Brooklyn, NY: Kehot Publication Society, 1996), chap. 33.

7 Author's interview with Rivkah Krinksy.

8 Jacobson, *Zikhron Livnei Yisrael,* chap. 36.

9 Author's interview with Avraham Hecht.

10 Letters from Cheifetz to Jacobson, reprinted in Jacobson, *Zikhron Livnei Yisrael,* chap. 36.

11 "Shmuel Levitin, 91, Lubavitcher Figure," *The New York Times,* Aug. 31, 1974, available at: https://www.nytimes.com/1974/08/31/archives/shmuel-levitin-91-lubavitcher-figure.html.

12 Yochanan Gordon immigrated at the end of 1931 (Chanukah 5692), and his family followed in August 1934. It was common for immigrants to the US to come alone and establish themselves before bringing their families.

13 *Igrot Kodesh,* vol. 4, letter dated 18 Tamuz, 5698 (July 17, 1938).

14 This program continues on a global level today. See https://www.merkosshlichus.com/about.

15 Letter to Jacobson dated 15 Av, 5691 (July 29, 1931).

16 9 Tamuz, 5691 (June 24, 1931).

17 Letter to Jacobson dated 15 Av, 5691 (July 29, 1931).

18 Moshe Eliyahu Gerlitzky (1914–2020) was originally from Lodz and studied in Chabad yeshivas in Poland, Lithuania, and Shanghai. He was one of the nine students who founded the Chabad yeshivah in Montreal in 1941. Mordechai Lightstone, "From Lodz to Montreal: The Life of Rabbi Moshe Eliyahu Gerlitzky," available at: https://www.lubavitch.com/from-lodz-to-montreal-the-life-of-rabbi-moshe-eliyahu-gerlitzky/.

19 *Igrot Kodesh,* vol. 2, letter to Dovid Helman of Bern from Marienbad, 5 Menachem Av, 5691 (July 19, 1931).

20 *Kfar Chabad,* issue no. 879, 2 Kislev, 5760, p. 82.

21 Rabbi Sholom Ber Levin, *Toldot Chabad BePolin, Lita, VeLatvia (History of Chabad in Poland, Lithuania, and Latvia)* (Brooklyn, NY: Kehot Publication Society, 2011), 138; *Reshimat HaYoman,* 445.

22 Cheshvan 5692 (November 3, 1931).

23 It is difficult to determine the exact date that the yeshivah opened in Riga, but by the summer of 1932 it was fully operational. In a letter dated 22 Av, 5692 (August

24, 1932), Feigin tells Jacobson that the Chabad community "was moved to establish a yeshivah. Students who are from chasidic backgrounds are coming from the Lithuanian yeshivas. It is thought that if it's successful, it might prompt the Rebbe to remain in Riga." But the effort was short lived. On November 9, 1932 (10 Marcheshvan, 5693) the Riga Yiddish paper *Evening Post* reported, "The yeshivah of the Lubavitcher Rebbe is closed." Feigin wrote to Yechezkel Zuber in December 1932, "We have given up on the yeshivah and the Rebbe is considering relocating. Many of the students were unable to receive a deferment from military service." See *Sefer HaSichos*, 5692–95 (Brooklyn, NY: Kehot Publication Society), 3.

24 *Igrot Kodesh*, vol. 15, letter to the Rebbe's daughter Chaya Mushka dated 26 Sivan, 5693 (June 20, 1933). The Rebbe left Riga, spent some of the summer at the resort in Marienbad, then went to Otwock for the holidays, and finally, moved to Warsaw after the holidays.

25 For a detailed overview of the Rebbe's visits, see Levin, *Toldot Chabad BePolin, Lita, VeLatvia*, chap. 9.

26 During the visit, Ida Haberman, then ten years old, was brought to the Rebbe at the train station by her father. Ida's eyesight was fading, and he worried she was going blind. Though he was not a Chasid, he asked the Rebbe to bless her that she would regain her sight, and amazingly, she did. During the Holocaust, Ida was hidden by non-Jews; after the war, she immigrated to the US. Her daughter is a member of my community in Orange County, California. At the weddings of two of Ida's grandchildren, I retold the story of the Rebbe's remarkable miracle in her presence and noted the divine providence that a follower of the Rebbe was conducting the weddings of her grandchildren that she was able to witness decades after receiving the Rebbe's blessing in the train station of Glubok.

27 The conflict over the appointment of a community rabbi divided the local Chasidim and Zionists. See Glenn Dynner, *The Light of Learning: Hasidism in Poland on the Eve of the Holocaust* (Oxford University Press, 2023), chap. 4.

28 *Igrot Kodesh*, vol. 15, letter dated 26 Sivan, 5693 (June 20, 1933).

29 It is intriguing that this was written in the first weeks of the Rebbe's visit to the US, where he had been welcomed with much hoopla. Writing in his diary on the same day, he expresses a disdain for all the fanfare: "I am weary of a life of emptiness." Personal diary, entry dated 6 Tishrei, 5690 (October 10, 1929).

30 Simcha Elberg, *Varsha Shel Maalah* (Bnei Brak: 1969).

31 Dynner, *The Light of Learning*, chap. 4.

32 Interview with JEM, Oral History Project.

33 Rabbi Nachum Greenwald, *Shaar HaAmerot* (Machon HaRav, 5775), 2015.

34 Yisrael Gutman, ed., et al., *The Jews of Poland Between Two World Wars* (University Press of New England, 1989), 20–35.

35 Mizrachi, the religious Zionist organization, was founded in 1902 in Vilnius at a world conference of religious Zionists called by Rabbi Yitzchak Yaakov Reines. Bnei Akiva, which was founded in 1929, is the youth movement associated with Mizrachi.

36 For an overview of Jewish life in the interwar years, see Celia Heller, *On the Edge of Destruction* (Columbia University Press, 1977).

37 The chasidic courts of Belz and Bobov did not join Agudath Israel.

38 In Riga, Chabad Chasid Mordechai Dubin was the head of Agudath Israel as a leader of the local Jewish community. The Rebbe himself never formally joined Agudath Israel in Latvia.

39 David Biale, et al., *Hasidism: A New History* (Princeton University Press, 2018), chap. 23.

40 Dynner, *The Light of Learning*, chap. 2.

41 Yosef's dreams caused his brothers to become jealous (Gen. 37:11). The seventh Rebbe explains that the Rebbe had three periods of leadership: The first was under the adversity of the Communist regime, the second was during his time in Riga and Poland, and the third was during the last decade of his life, in the United States. *Likkutei Sichot* 18:304 (Brooklyn, NY: Kehot Publication Society).

42 Ibid. This statement of the seventh Rebbe was quite unusual, as he would rarely speak disparagingly about others. One can speculate regarding what he means by saying that the Rebbe acted with self-sacrifice in Poland. He might be referring to the effort the Rebbe had to exert to bring the teachings and culture of Chabad to an environment that was not always welcoming.

43 For a detailed list of students, including names, hometowns, and backgrounds, see Levin, *Toldot Chabad BePolin, Lita, VeLatvia*, 126.

44 Otwock had the largest number at 450, with the remaining students distributed amongst the ten other branches of the yeshivah in Poland and Lithuania, including 250 in Warsaw and 150 in Lodz. The census was originally printed in *HaPardes* 5702 (1942), 3rd edition, 10. Reprinted in Levin, *Toldot Chabad BePolin, Lita, VeLatvia*, 205. See chap. 17–52 of *Toldot Chabad BePolin, Lita, VeLatvia* for a detailed history of the yeshivah and its branches in Poland and Lithuania from 1920–39. The relocation of the yeshivah caused by the war led to new branches in Japan, China, and other European cities. For more on the yeshivah during the war years, including its reconstitution in the US and Canada, see chap. 9–10.

45 David E. Fishman, "The Musar Movement in Interwar Poland," in Yisrael Gutman, Ezra Mendelsohn, Yehuda Reinharz, and Chone Shmeruk, eds., *The Jews of Poland Between Two World Wars* (Hanover and London: University Press of New England, 1989), 247–71.

46 *Igrot Kodesh*, vol., Letter 15 Sivan, 5793, June 9, 1933.

47 *Igrot Kodesh*, vol. 2, letter to Yehuda Leib Nemutim dated 14 Kislev, 5691 (December 4, 1930).

48 Rabbi Yisrael Salanter (1786–1883) was a student of Rabbis Chaim Volozhin and Akiva Eiger. He instituted the study of classics such as *Mesilas Yesharim*.

49 Dovid Zaklikowski, *The People's Rabbi: The Life and Legacy of Rabbi Leib Kramer* (Brooklyn, NY: 2021).

50 Yitzchak Hendel (1916–2007) was born in Komarov, the son of Yisrael Yosef Hendel, a Chasid of the Husiatyn Rebbe. Hendel studied in Tomchei Temimim in Warsaw, Otwock, and Vilnius. He escaped Europe to Japan and Shanghai. Before the attack on Pearl Harbor in 1941, he traveled to Montreal as one of the nine students who established Chabad there. He was appointed the rabbi of the Chabad community in Montreal after his marriage in 1944, and went on to serve on Montreal's rabbinical court.

51 Recorded recollections of Rabbi Kramer.

52 Levin, *Toldot Chabad BePolin, Lita, VeLatvia*, 102.

53 Interview with Rabbi Chaim Meir Bukiet and students of the yeshivah of Shanghai by Rabbi Avraham Holzberg, Tishrei 5758 (September 1998).

54 *Kfar Chabad*, issue no. 328, p. 71.

55 Interview with Rabbi Avraham Yitzchak Garfinkel, JEM Oral History Project.

56 Letter to Rabbi Yisrael Jacobson dated 26 Tishrei, 5694 (October 16, 1933).

57 Letter from Feigin dated 9 Iyar, 5694 (April 24, 1934).

58 Memoirs of Avraham Garfinkel, quoted in Levin, *Toldot Chabad BePolin, Lita, VeLatvia*, 143.

59 *The Lives and Legacy of Zaidy and Bubby Tenenbaum* (Brooklyn, NY: 2018).

60 Rabbi Yitzchak Hendel, family video, Los Angeles, 2006.

61 Garfinkel notes that at that time, "when the Rebbe talked, we understood everything." In later years, after he suffered a stroke, the Rebbe's speech was difficult to understand.

62 Hendel, family video, 2006.

63 Dovid Zaklikowski, *Kosher Investigator* (Brooklyn, NY: Hasidic Archives, 2017), "American in Poland."

64 The Rebbe took a great personal interest in the Americans. When the administration reported to the Rebbe that Berel Levy had a library of secular English books, the Rebbe called him in for a meeting. Levy told the Rebbe, "I read them because I don't want to forget my mother tongue, which I expect to resume speaking naturally when I return home after my studies in Otwock." The Rebbe responded, "If they are scholarly books, it is a *shad der moach* (a waste of mental efforts). If they are novels, then it's a *shad de hertz* (a waste of emotional efforts)." The Rebbe then suggested that Berel's mother send him the "News in Brief" from *The New*

York Times so that he could "read the news reports in English from there." Ibid Zaklikowski.

65 Interview with Yankel Goldstein, son of Yosef. Yosef Goldstein (1906–87) was sent to a concentration camp; his first wife and the rest of his family were killed by the Nazis. After the war, he remarried and immigrated to the US with the help of Rabbi Eliezer Silver in 1947. He became a *shochet.*

66 See Levin, *Toldot Chabad BePolin, Lita, VeLatvia,* chap. 32, for a detailed history of the yeshivah in Chmielnik.

67 Goldstein was fortunate to have a group of local community leaders who underwrote most of the budget. The yeshivah continued to flourish until 1939, when the Nazis invaded and killed most of the Jews of Chmielnik.

68 Interview for the Shoah Foundation conducted by Stella Eliezrie with Rabbi Chaim Meir Bukiet, available at: https://www.youtube.com/watch?v=eawO9ECN8jo&list=PLmtfqxE37fAB3f4cxA__idUecsPoir-fG.

69 When the war broke out, Chaim Meir Bukiet escaped to Vilna and was a student in the yeshivah in Shanghai, immigrating to the US after the war. See "Our Heroes: Rabbi Chaim Meir Bukiet (1919–1998)," available at: https://crownheights.info/blogs/370015/our-heroes-rabbo-chaim-meir-bukiet-1919-1998/.

70 *Igrot Kodesh* 11:148.

71 *BeKhol Batei Ne'eman* (Kfar Chabad, Israel: Machon Razag), chap. 3.

72 The Novardok yeshivas were originally started in Russia in 1896 by Rabbi Yosef Yozel Horwitz, known as the Alter (literally, "elder" rabbi). With the Russian revolution, they transferred to Poland and expanded into a network across the country. The Novardok yeshivas followed the tradition of Rabbi Yisrael Salanter, stressing the study of *musar,* ethics.

73 Levin, *Toldot Chabad BePolin, Lita, VeLatvia,* chap. 45.

74 Interview with Garfinkel, JEM Oral History Project.

75 Dovid Zaklikowski, *The Atvotzkers,* available at: https://files.anash.org/uploads/2021/01/The-Atvotzkers.pdf.

76 Ibid.

77 *Igrot Kodesh,* vol. 11, letter dated April 29, 1930 (1 Iyar, 5690). The letter was written during the Rebbe's visit to Detroit and refers to a meeting that took place when the Rebbe was in New York earlier that year.

78 Peter Wiernik (1865–1936) was born in Vilna and immigrated to the US in 1885. He settled in Chicago, where he wrote for the Yiddish *Chicago Daily Courier.* From 1901 to 1936, he was the editor of New York's important Yiddish-language daily, *The Jewish Morning Journal,* a Modern Orthodox, pro-Zionist newspaper. Wiernik is the author of *The History of the Jews in America* (1931, reprinted in 1972 by Herman Press).

79 *Igrot Kodesh,* vol. 1, letter dated 15 Tamuz, 5664 (June 28, 1904).

80 Rabbi Dovber (1773–1827) was the second Chabad-Lubavitch Rebbe, succeeding his father Rabbi Schneur Zalman in 1812. He is called the Mitteler Rebbe ("the Middle Rebbe") as the Rebbe in between the Chabad founder and Rabbi Menachem Mendel, the third Rebbe. He was the first Rebbe to live in the town of Lubavitch. Chabad Chasidim who immigrated to *Eretz Yisrael* began moving to Hebron as early as 1816 upon the encouragement of the Mitteler Rebbe. He raised funds in Russia to purchase a synagogue in Hebron. The Mitteler Rebbe's daughter, Menucha Rochel, moved to Hebron with her family in 1845.

81 *Igrot Kodesh*, vol. 1, letter dated 10 Kislev, 5665 (November 18, 1904).

82 "In 1921, the Department of State Libraries under the auspices of the People's Committee of Education issued a resolution approving the return of the books to me." Letter in Russian from the Rebbe to the director of the Rumyantsev Museum, November 22, 1922, Archives of Chabad of California.

83 The library reneged on the agreement due to the intervention of Shmuel Eizenstat, a librarian in the Moscow library who objected to the Rebbe's views on Zionism. See *Igrot Kodesh* 11:82, where the Rebbe writes, "It was an act of personal retribution because the historic stand of the Lubavitcher Rebbes on Zionism was known." *Sifriyat Lubavitch*, Rabbi Berel Levin (Brooklyn, NY: Kehot Publication), 84–85.

84 *Igrot Kodesh* 16:98, letter to the Russian Ambassador to Latvia (translated into Hebrew), dated October 27, 1927.

85 In the same letter, the Rebbe mentions that "due to communal concerns, I held back from pressing the issue," alluding to the priority he gave to lobbying Western governments to alleviate the suffering of Russian Jews after he exited Russia. However, in this letter written in early 1932, he writes, "Now I have resolved to make a major effort on this." *Igrot Kodesh*, vol. 15, letter to the Ramash dated 11 Shevat, 5693 (January 19, 1932).

86 As the Soviet Union weakened in 1988, the seventh Rebbe sent his secretary Dr. Nissan Mindel and the library's director Rabbi Berel Levin to Russia to search for the historic collection. With time, he appointed a committee comprised of Levin and three distinguished *shluchim*, Rabbis Shlomo Cunin of California, Yitzchak Kogan of Moscow, and Yosef Aronoff of Israel, to redeem the library on behalf of its legal owner, Agudas Chassidei Chabad, based in New York. To quell the controversy, the Russian National Library opened an official branch in the Jewish Museum of Moscow, where it placed a selection of the books. This was unacceptable to Agudas Chassidei Chabad, and it demanded the library be returned to its rightful owners, the historic Chabad library, located in Brooklyn. As Russia became more recalcitrant, the issue moved into federal court, where sanctions were imposed on Russia. For a detailed overview of the efforts to free the library, see *Sifriyat Lubavitch*, chap. 12; Graham Bowley, "Russia Fined $44 Million for Refusing to Hand Over

Jewish Books," available at: https://www.nytimes.com/2015/09/12/books/russia-fined-44-million-for-refusing-to-hand-over-jewish-books.html.

87 The Rebbe purchased this collection from Shmuel Weiner, who had a large personal collection and was librarian of the Asiatic Museum of the Imperial Academy of Sciences. He wanted to emigrate from Russia, and the Communist government refused to grant him permission to take his collection with him. Having no choice, he parted with his valuable collection for just five thousand dollars. In this way, the Rebbe acquired a very valuable collection at low cost; he made payments over time.

88 Testimony, Chaim Lieberman, book trial transcript, p. 1,262.

89 The government sent an investigator who understood the value of Jewish books and historical manuscripts. He urged the government to block the export of the library. Mordechai Dubin was able to arrange a second investigator who lacked knowledge of Jewish books and authorized the license for export. *Likkutei Dibburim* 6:237.

90 Testimony, Lieberman, p. 1,262.

91 *Igrot Kodesh*, vol. 2, letter to Dovid Frankel dated 17 Iyar, 5688 (May 7, 1928).

92 The library even included publications from the Yevesektzia that were very antireligious. Librarian Berel Levin explains that this was done "so people would know how to respond" to these types of allegations. The Rebbe also asked one of his followers in *Eretz Yisrael* to gather calendars and other materials published by institutions in the country. *Igrot Kodesh*, vol. 2, letter to Chanoch Hendel Havlin dated 16 Iyar, 5688 (May 16, 1928).

93 *Igrot Kodesh*, vol. 2, letter to Dovid Frankel dated 17 Iyar, 5688 (May 7, 1928).

94 Letter from Feigin to Simpson dated 21 Av, 5696 (August 9, 1936). See Ibid Levin, *Sifriyas*, 107.

95 *Igrot Kodesh*, vol. 3, letter to Rabbi Eliyahu Simpson dated 11 Av, 5696 (July 30, 1936).

96 Letter from Feigin to Ashkenazi dated 28 Nisan, 5693 (April 24, 1933). Rabbi Meir Ashkenazi (1891–1954) was a student of the yeshivah in Lubavitch. He was a prominent scholar, first serving as a rabbi in Vladivostok before becoming chief rabbi of Shanghai, with the Rebbe's encouragement. During the war, he saved many refugees. Afterward, he immigrated to the US.

97 *HaOlam*, 22 Elul, 5688/September 7, 1928.

98 *Igrot Kodesh* 16:143.

99 Microfilm copies of the Polish Library collection were discovered in Canada in 1983. This led to a investigation that revealed their whereabouts. Two years later, a Canadian student visiting the library in Warsaw was given an actual manuscript of the Rebbe's; it eventually reached the hands of Chabad rabbis in Toronto. This sparked an initiative to repatriate the library. After a major diplomatic effort, the

collection was returned to Chabad in 1988. See "Rescue of the Library," available at: https://derher.org/wp-content/uploads/17-adar-2-5774-04.pdf.

100 Rabbi Shalom Dovber Levine, "The Library Exhibitions: The 15 Exhibitions Held at the Library's Exhibition Hall, 1994–2025," available at: http://s3.wasabisys.com/chabadlibrary/pdf/EXHIBITIONS-E.pdf.

101 In 2020, Kehot Publication Society published *Treasures from the Chabad Library*, a 564-page book on the special collections of the library, authored by Rabbi Shalom Dovber Levine. See Menachem Posner, "11 Treasures of the Chabad Library and the Stories They Tell," available at: chabad.org/4601125.

102 Available at: https://www.chabadlibrary.org/.

103 Nora Levin, *The Jews in the Soviet Union Since 1917*, vol. 1 (New York University Press, 1987), chap. 10.

104 David Fishman, "The Fate of Religious Education," in Yaacov Ro'i, ed., *Jews and Jewish Life in the Russia and the Soviet Union* (Ilford England: Frank Cass & Co.).

105 Some of Rabbi Lazaroff's children survived, and today many of his descendants are Chabad *shluchim*. His grandson and namesake is the head of Chabad in Texas.

106 Irina Osipova, *Hasidim – Saving Thy People: The Resistance of Hasidic Jews to Soviet Oppression During the Stalin Era*, trans. Malcolm Gilbert, chap. 3. There were numerous other arrests throughout Russia during this period. Osipova describes them in detail using information gleaned from files of the KGB that have come to light in the post-Soviet era.

107 Due to the secrecy involved, there are sparse details on how the Rebbe communicated with and transferred funds to Rabbi Morozov and other activists in Russia.

108 Osipova, ibid.

109 Richard Pipes, *Russia Under the Bolshevik Regime* (Vintage Books, 1995). For details on the Yevesektzia's closure, see Zvi Gitelman, *Jewish Nationality and Soviet Politics*, 472–81. The Soviets had also supported the creation of an alternative leadership for the Russian Orthodox church that was loyal to Communism. Once the church was weakened, the pro-Communist church group was dismantled.

110 See chap. 3.

111 Throughout the 1920s, there had been ambiguity and at times tension between government policies and the zealousness of the Yevesektzia. The Rebbe had exploited this in many cities, prompting government officials to intervene to restrain the activists of the Yevesektzia. With the closure of the Yevesektzia, government restraint ended. As Fishman writes, "In 1930, it became painfully evident that the anti-religious persecution emanated from the state and not renegade Jewish Communists." Jack Wertheimer, ed. *The Uses of Tradition* (New York: Jewish Theological Seminary, 1992), 116.

112 In addition to working as editors of the Yevesektzia newspaper *Der Emes*, Litvakov and Frumkin together translated Lenin's works into an eight-volume Yiddish publication.

113 Letter to Jacobson dated 24 Tevet, 5693 (January 24, 1933).

114 Fishman argues in Wertheimer, ed. *The Uses of Tradition,* that after 1930, "the struggle to preserve tradition in the USSR ultimately failed." But the fact that one thousand Chasidim exited Russia twenty-six years later in the Great Escape disproves this assertion, as it shows that secret yeshivas and synagogues continued to operate until the fall of the Soviet Union, then emerging to spark a renaissance of Judaism.

115 For a detailed overview on the yeshivas in the 1930s, see Levin, *Toldot Chabad BeRusia HaSovietit,* chap. 72.

116 *Igrot Kodesh,* vol. 11, letter to Peter Wiernik dated 29 Tevet, 5691 (January 18, 1931).

117 *Harif,* letter dated 20 Sivan, 5691 (June 5, 1931), 148.

118 Shmuel Menachem Mendel Butman, *The Rebbe in Paris* (Chazak Publishing, 2024), chap. 1; *Igrot Kodesh* 11:378, letter to chief rabbi of Paris; *Igrot Kodesh* 11:380, letter to Menachem Rothstein. These letters do not have exact dates, but they seem to have been written while the Rebbe was in Paris in 1933–34.

119 The JDC did subsidize some of the shipments. *Igrot Kodesh* 17:80, letter to Aharon Teitelbaum dated late winter 5693 (1933–34).

120 It is not known who was behind the arrest – the Latvians themselves, concerned with the suspicious activity, or the Russian government, which had perhaps gotten wind of the project.

121 At the time, the Rashag was in *Eretz Yisrael.* With the help of Agudath Israel and Israel's Chief Rabbi Avraham Yitzchak Kook, immigration certificates were issued, and the four Chasidim left Latvia with their families.

122 Dovber Chaskind and the two Gurary brothers were joined by their brother-in-law Eliezer Karasik. They advertised in newspapers in *Eretz Yisrael* that they could arrange shipments of food to Russia. Chaskind eventually immigrated to the US, where he set up a similar operation, sending packages from New York.

123 Levin, *Toldot Chabad BeRusia HaSovietit,* chap. 42.

124 Maxim Litvinov (1876–1951) joined the Russian Social Democratic Labor Party in 1898. He fled Russia in 1906 when the Russian government began arresting Bolsheviks, spending time overseas as an arms dealer for the revolution. In 1917, Lenin appointed him the Soviet representative to London, and in 1930, Stalin appointed Litvinov as People's Commissar for Foreign Affairs. He negotiated US recognition with the new Roosevelt government in 1933. During World War II, he served as Soviet ambassador to the US. See "Maxim M. Litvinov, Russian Commissar of Foreign Affairs arrives in United States," video clip available at: https://www.youtube.com/watch?v=DVUEKDXOWXO.

125 The Rebbe drafted a letter with seven demands: not to close religious schools, to permit Hebrew instruction, to allow immigration for rabbis, to allow ration cards for rabbis and teachers, not to close synagogues and study halls, not to prohibit kosher slaughter, and not to ban ritual circumcision. *Igrot Kodesh* 3:62, footnote.

126 Some of the others included were Yaakov Rosenheim and Y. M. Levin of Agudath Israel, Rabbi Alter from Agudas Harabonim, and Professor Shur on behalf of Liberal Jewish leaders.

127 *Igrot Kodesh,* vol. 3, letter to Menachem Mendel Lokshin dated 5 Cheshvan, 5694 (October 24, 1933). The Rebbe writes there that he is enclosing letters to be forwarded to leading American rabbis, including Rabbi Eliezer Silver. "I am asking you to act expeditiously and push the Agudas Harabonim to the task, to prepare for when the Soviet representatives are coming to Washington." See also *Igrot Kodesh* 11:205.

128 *Igrot Kodesh,* vol. 3, letter to Rabbi Chaim Ozer dated 4 Tevet, 5694 (December 22, 1933). He writes, "I am enclosing copies of the letters for Senators Borah and King, Congressman Dickstein, and Professor Cyrus Adler."

129 *Igrot Kodesh* 11:405, letter to Agudas Harabonim, Rabbis Teitelbaum, Silver, Rosenberg, Lokshin, Kramer, Telushkin, dated 5 Cheshvan, 5644 (October 24, 1933). The Rebbe wrote that there were unusual circumstances when public protest could help, referring to an incident in 1929 when he wrote: "For instance, when the Rabbis were imprisoned in Minsk and protests overseas brought about their release."

130 In general, the policy of the Rebbe and his successor the seventh Rebbe was one of quiet diplomacy with regard to the Soviet Union. This policy of secrecy that they practiced makes it difficult for us to learn about many of the initiatives to help Russian Jews throughout the decades. The seventh Rebbe would discuss ideas for operations in the Soviet Union only in face-to-face private meetings with the principals involved. His own secretaries were not aware of much of the activity he orchestrated behind the Iron Curtain.

131 *HaOlam,* London, January 18, 1934.

132 "Recognition of the Soviet Union, 1933," Office of the Historian, available at: https://history.state.gov/milestones/1921-1936/USSR.

133 Levin, *Toldot Chabad BeRusia HaSovietit,* chap. 113.

134 It can be argued that the Rebbe took different strategies in regard to the issues of returning his library and religious freedom for Russian Jews, using different channels for each one. When it came to the question of religious freedom in Russia, he urged major Jewish organizations and prominent international Jewish leaders to intervene with the US government to get the issue onto the agenda in the Russian negotiations for US diplomatic recognition. The issue even received some press attention. In the case of the library, the Rebbe operated more discretely, asking Rabbi Axelrod, a Chabad follower in Baltimore, to approach the State Department personally. Perhaps the Rebbe feared that if the matter of the library would have

been presented along with the question of religious freedom, the US government would advocate for the library's return instead of giving attention to the issue of religious freedom.

135 Levin, *Sifriyas Lubavitch*, letter dated December 19, 1933, p. 87.

136 *Igrot Kodesh*, vol. 11, letter dated 7 Cheshvan 5699 (November 1, 1938).

137 Rabbi Yisrael Zuber (1896–1953) studied in Lubavitch. He was a rabbi in Stockholm and immigrated to the US after the war, where he was appointed as a rabbi in Boston. Tragically, he was killed in December 1953. Rabbi Zuber assisted the Rebbe with the immigration of Chasidim from Russia and many other projects. See Gefen Yisrael, *Bnei Brak: The Life and Legacy of Rabbi Yisrael Zuber*; Chana (Zuber) Sharfstein, "The Life and Legacy of Rabbi Yakov Yisroel Zuber," available at: https://www.youtube.com/watch?v=7460C6XRylg.

138 *Igrot Kodesh*, vol. 3, letter dated 7 Teves 5695 (December 13, 1934).

139 *Igrot Kodesh*, vol. 3, letter to Moshe Sterlin dated 29 Adar Alef 5695 (April 23, 1935).

140 Moshe Zalman Feiglin (1875–1957) came from a Chabad family. He left Palestine to escape the Turkish draft at the onset of World War I, moving to Australia. Despite geographic separation, he was an ardent Chasid of the Rebbe and the seventh Rebbe. He established a successful business and helped bring Chasidim to Australia after World War II. Feiglin was instrumental in establishing Chabad in Australia and has been called "the Avraham Avinu of Australia." See "Moshe Zalman Feiglin and Chabad Australia," available at: https://www.youtube.com/watch?v=fyKNy-Rijco.

141 *Igrot Kodesh*, vol. 3, letter dated 21 Cheshvan, 5696 (November 17, 1935).

142 Rabbi Azriel Zelig Slonim (1897–1972) was born in Hebron, a great-grandson of Rebbetzin Menucha Rochel, a granddaughter of the Alter Rebbe who moved to Hebron in 1845. As a student in Yeshivas Tomchei Temimim who was a relative of the Rebbe Rashab, Rabbi Slonim enjoyed the special privilege of being invited to the Rebbe's home for holiday and Shabbat meals. He studied in Russia for seven years, first in Lubavitch and then in other cities as the yeshivah moved due to the disruptions of the war and revolution. He returned to *Eretz Yisrael*, married, and began to travel on behalf of the Rebbe Rayatz. In 1948, the Rebbe appointed him director of Colel Chabad, the historic charitable fund based in Jerusalem. He took a lead in Chabad in Israel and in Jerusalem in particular. In 1957, he was visiting the US when the seventh Rebbe instructed him to join other Chabad rabbis at a meeting in the White House concerning Israel's security. The Rebbe instructed the group to introduce Rabbi Slonim to President Eisenhower "as a Jew born in the historic city of Hebron." Throughout his life, Rabbi Slonim had a close relationship with three Chabad Rebbes, beginning in his youth with his connection to the Rashab, then traveling globally for the Rayatz, and later heading Chabad institutions in Israel on behalf of the seventh Rebbe.

143 In 1924, Slonim traveled to the US for two years. This was not a personal mission from the Rebbe; it seems to have been a fundraising trip for Colel Chabad, the charity based in Jerusalem. While the Rebbe encouraged Rabbi Slonim to go and urged him to strengthen the fledgling Chabad community in the US, it was primarily a trip to raise funds.

144 Rabbi Shalom Ber Wolpa, *Eved HaMelech* (5765), chap. 12.

145 Anna Diamond, "The 1924 Law That Slammed the Door on Immigrants and the Politicians Who Pushed it Back Open," available at: https://www.smithsonianmag.com/history/1924-law-slammed-door-immigrants-and-politicians-who-pushed-it-back-open-180974910/.

146 Rabbi Mordechai Gutnick (1896–1931) studied in Lubavitch and was sent by the Rebbe Rashab to Soviet Georgia. He was appointed rabbi in London with the help of Rabbi Zelig Slonim in 1926 and passed away at the age of 35. Two of his sons were refugees in Australia and became leading rabbis there. See *Igrot Kodesh*, vol. 1, letter to Slonim dated 26 Adar, 5686 (March 12, 1926).

147 Wolpa, *Eved HaMelech*, chap. 13.

148 *Sydney Jewish News*, June 23, 1939. The paper noted that Slonim was "a scholar from a distinguished scholar" and that he had the endorsements of the Sephardic chief rabbi of Palestine and the chief rabbis of the UK and South Africa.

149 Some of the rabbis in these countries were outstanding; others were not top caliber. Slonim himself was very careful in following the dictates of Jewish law. While in Australia, he could only find a *shochet* who did not have a beard, a serious breach of religious standards in the chasidic community. Even though the *shochet* was proficient in the laws of slaughter, Slonim wondered whether he should eat his meat and only did so after receiving instructions from the Rebbe.

150 *Igrot Kodesh*, vol. 4, letter dated 18 Tamuz, 5768 (July 17, 1938). In a long, self-reflective letter, the Rebbe confides in Rabbi Dovid Rabinowitz of Boston about his medical history and the challenges he was facing in Poland at the time. See also *Igrot Kodesh* 2:272, where the Rebbe discusses his visit to Marienbad on the way back to Riga.

151 Located in northern Czechoslovakia, Marienbad was a spa town with kosher hotels and restaurants that attracted many chasidic Rebbes and prominent rabbis. Located between Eastern and Western Europe, it became a venue for prominent Jewish conferences, including the third Knessiah Gedolah of Agudath Israel in 1937. For a history and memoir, see Dovid Leitner, *Marienbad & Beyond* (2020).

152 In a November 5, 1930 newspaper report cited in the introduction to *Igrot Kodesh*, vol. 2, the headline reads, "Belzer Rebbe Visits Lubavitcher Rebbe." The story goes on to say that the Rebbe also met with the Aleksander and Gerrer Rebbes. Because Marienbad was so popular amongst prominent rabbis, it became a venue

for leaders from different countries and different segments of the Jewish community to meet.

153 Letter to Jacobson dated 25 Cheshvan, 5693 (November 24, 1932).

154 Zusha Wolf, *Admorei Chabad VeYahudut Germania* (Jerusalem: Hekhal Menachem, 2006), 86–87.

155 *Igrot Kodesh,* vol. 4, letter to Rabbi Dovid Rabinowitz.

156 Jews from around the world wrote to the Rebbe asking for advice and blessings, often sharing their greatest problems with the hope that the Rebbe could provide advice and spiritual blessing. The Rebbe himself acknowledged that the letters were withheld because the doctors feared they would cause stress at a time when he needed to conserve his energy. See *Igrot Kodesh,* vol. 4.

157 Wolf, *Admorei Chabad VeYahudut Germania,* letters from Rabbi Yechezkel Feigin, 86–87.

158 *Igrot Kodesh* 11:209.

159 *Igrot Kodesh,* vol. 4, letter to Rabinowitz.

160 Ibid.

161 Deposition of Chaya Moussia Schneerson, book trial, November 12, 1985, p. 21.

162 Chaim Miller, *Turning Judaism Outward* (Brooklyn, NY: Kol Menachem).

163 See appendix 2 for a timeline of the Rebbe's travels in the 1930s.

164 Letter from Feigin to Simchovitch dated 13 Tamuz, 5696 (July 3, 1936), cited in Rabbi Mordechai Ashkenazi, *HaRav Ashkenazi* [Hebrew], vol. 2, chap. 8.

165 *Igrot Kodesh,* vol. 3, letter to "My dear and beloved daughter" dated 16 Shevat, 5695 (January 15, 1935). Known as "*Der Longa Brief*" (The Long Letter), it outlined the historical background of the genesis of the chasidic movement. It was written during the time that the Rebbe was in the sanatorium in Purkersdorf.

166 See "Translator's Introduction," available at: https://www.sie.org/templates/sie/article_cdo/aid/2420993/jewish/Translators-Introduction.htm.

167 Levin, *Toldot Chabad BePolin, Lita, VeLatvia,* 205. Also see a detailed description of the branches, chap. 39–53.

168 Author's interview with Moshe Binyamin Kaplan's son, Rabbi Nochum Kaplan. This unpublished letter from the Rebbe is in the family's possession.

CHAPTER NINE

1 The audience with the Rebbe was on Saturday evening, August 26, 1939 (11 Elul, 5799) in Otwock. The war broke out the following Friday morning, September 1, 1939. "Journey to America," *Di Yiddishe Heim,* issue no. 33, Autumn 5726 (1966).

2 Dovid Zaklikowski, *Kosher Investigator: How Rabbi Berel Levy Built the OK and Transformed the World of Kosher Supervision* (Brooklyn, NY: Hasidic Archives, 2017), 28.

3 *Kfar Chabad*, issue no. 1,362, p. 30. It seems the Rebbe was apprehensive about the Jewish future in Poland even earlier. When Simcha Yitzchak Zajac asked the Rebbe about moving to Brazil in 1934 to be a *shochet*, the Rebbe told him, "Poland is not a place for Jews anymore. You should go to Brazil and improve kosher slaughter." Interview with Mordechai Zajac, JEM Oral History Project.

4 *Di Yiddishe Heim*, issue no. 64, Summer 1975; *Zikhron Livnei Yisrael – Memoirs of Rabbi Yisrael Jacobson: 1907–1939* [Hebrew] (Brooklyn, NY: Kehot Publication Society, 1996), 226.

5 Recalled by Rabbi Jacobson to Rabbi Shalom Ber Levitan, author's interview with Levitan.

6 August 31, 1939 (16 Elul, 5799).

7 Interview with Avraham Garfinkel, JEM Oral History Project.

8 Rabbi Avraham B. Hecht, *My Spiritual Journey* (Brooklyn, NY: 2006), 65.

9 Rabbi Pinchas Hirschsprung (1912–98), born in Poland, was a brilliant student at Yeshivas Chachmei Lublin. He became a renowned scholar and the chief rabbi of Montreal. His memoir, *The Vale of Tears*, was originally published in Yiddish in 1944. It is unique in Holocaust literature since it was published during the war, while the memories were still fresh.

10 Hecht, *My Spiritual Journey*, 47–48.

11 Jacobson personally escorted six students from the US to Poland to attend the yeshivah. They departed the US on August 9, 1939 (24 Av, 5699).

12 Author's interview with Avraham Hecht.

13 Ibid.

14 That Shabbat was Chai (18) Elul on the Jewish calendar. It marks the birthday of the founder of the chasidic movement, Rabbi Yisrael Baal Shem Tov in 1698, and Chabad's founder Rabbi Schneur Zalman of Liadi in 1745.

15 At the hotel, the students had a heated discussion about whether they should transgress Shabbat by signing the forms. Meir Greenberg and Mottel Altein walked to the home of Warsaw's leading rabbi, Menachem Ziemba, to ask him what to do. Rabbi Ziemba insisted that they should first make *Kiddush*, and he ruled that past 11:00 p.m. it was dangerous to go outside, saying that at that point they should sign in a manner that would entail breaking the rules of Shabbat based on a rabbinic decree, not an actual biblical prohibition.

16 The students repaid him when they got to America.

17 *Der Morgen Journal*, March 27, 1940, March 29, 1940, and April 5, 1940, reprinted in Rachel Altein and Rabbi Eliezer Y. Zaklikovsky, *Out of the Inferno* (Brooklyn, NY: Kehot Publication Society, 2002), appendix 4.

18 *Der Morgen Journal*, reprinted in Altein and Zaklikovsky, *Out of the Inferno*.

19 "Rabbi Barry Gourary's Life and History | Full Testimony | USC Shoah Foundation," September 10, 1997, video available at: https://www.youtube.com/watch?v=CFnvFTTyTok.

20 Rabbi Yosef Wineberg (1918–2012) was a student of the yeshivah in Otwock. From Poland he escaped to Lithuania and then to Shanghai. Later, he was one of the nine students who established the yeshivah in Montreal. He served as the vice chairman of the United Lubavitcher Yeshivah and traveled the world on behalf of the Rebbe. Diary of Rabbi Yosef Wineberg, "With the Lubavitcher Rebbe in Warsaw, under the hail of German bombs," original Hebrew version published in Refael Nachman Kahan, *Shemuot VeSippurim* (Brooklyn, NY: 1977), 3:118–20. English translation published in *Out of the Inferno*, appendix 3.

21 Judaism teaches that we can ask the deceased to intercede on high for the welfare of those in this world. See Taanit 16a; *Shulchan Arukh, Orach Chaim* 579:3, *Mishnah Berurah* (14) ad loc: "We go to graves so the deceased will invoke mercy on us." For a broader discussion, see Tzvi Freeman, "Is It OK to Ask a Deceased Tzaddik to Pray for Me?" available at: chabad.org/562222.

22 Altein and Zaklikovsky, *Out of the Inferno*, appendix 4.

23 Shmotkin was one of the Rebbe's Chasidim in Poland. The house was located at 32 Muranowska Street. Two apartments were emptied to provide space for the Rebbe and his extended family.

24 For a description of the German siege of Warsaw, see: https://www.youtube.com/watch?v=hohsP-hK1sQ.

25 September 13, 1939 (29 Elul, 5699).

26 Altein and Zaklikovsky, *Out of the Inferno*.

27 Rabbi Feigin and the Shmotkin brothers worried that the Rebbe's eighty-year-old mother would be unable to flee on foot if the area was bombed. They moved her on a stretcher to an area where there was no bombing.

28 Shoah Foundation interview, September 10, 1997.

29 September 21, 1939 (8 Tishrei, 5700).

30 September 27, 1939 (14 Tishrei, 5700).

31 Shoah Foundation interview, September 10, 1997.

32 https://vimeo.com/528071660.

33 Rabbi Pinchas Hirschsprung, *The Vale of Tears*.

34 Interview with Moshe Feder, JEM Oral History Project.

35 Dovid Zaklikowski, *The People's Rabbi: The Life and Legacy of Rabbi Leib Kramer* (Brooklyn, NY: Hasidic Archives, 2021), part 3.

36 Levin, *Toldot Chabad BePolin, Lita, VeLatvia*, chap. 54.

37 *The Mashpia: The Life and Teachings of Reb Volf Greenglass* (Montreal, Canada: Ezras Achim Organization, 2023), chap. 3.

38 Kramer was a prominent attorney who, while not chasidic in his outward appearance, had a strong family loyalty to Chabad. He was an observant Jew, active in a variety of Jewish causes. He organized annual fundraisers for Chabad at his synagogue, the prominent New York Jewish Center located on Manhattan's Upper West Side. See Dovid Margolin, "Milton Kramer, 99, a Third-Generation Pillar of Chabad in America," available at: chabad.org/4124407.

39 Letter from Robert Wagner to Secretary of State Cordel Hull dated September 22, 1939, in Altein and Zaklikovsky, *Out of the Inferno*, 31.

40 Sol Bloom (1870–1949) was a prominent Jewish congressman from New York. As chair of the House Foreign Affairs Committee, he had an influence on US policy. He supported Roosevelt's policy toward European Jews, which was against open immigration, putting him at odds with Jewish activists who lobbied for more strident US action.

41 *Di Yiddishe Heim*, issue no. 64, Summer 1975.

42 Growing up, Cohen "attended services from time to time" and had a "smattering of Hebrew and a passing acquaintance with Jewish holidays." William Lasser, *Benjamin V. Cohen: Architect of the New Deal* (The Century Foundation, 2002), chap. 2.

43 Cover available at: https://content.time.com/time/magazine/0,9263,7601380912,00.html.

44 Author's interview with William Lasser.

45 Cable Sept. 26, 1939. He also shared Shmotkin's address, 32 Muranowksa, where the Rebbe found refuge during the first days of the bombings. By now, it had been destroyed, and the Rebbe had relocated to a nearby building, but that information had not made its way from Poland to Latvia and then on the US.

46 Recollection by Yisrael Gordon to his great-granddaughter Rivkah Levitan. Due to the doubt that a government official was calling, Rabbi Jacobson felt it was a lesser transgression for a minor to break Shabbat. Once it was clear that it was a government official on the phone, and that it was an issue of life and death, Jewish law is clear that Shabbat must be transgressed. It seems fair to assume that if young Gordon were not present, Rabbi Jacobson would have answered the call despite not being sure that it was connected to saving the Rebbe. Jewish law dictates that a Jew must transgress Shabbat even in a case when it is doubtful if a life can be saved.

47 Psalm 34, recited at the beginning of the service on Erev Rosh HaShanah. Rabbi Mordechai Ashkenazi, *HaRav Ashkenazi* [Hebrew], vol. 2, chap. 1.

48 *Haaretz*, November 12, 1939.

49 *Haaretz*, November 14, 1939. Two days later, on November 16, *Haaretz* reported that the Chabad Chasidim in Tel Aviv had received a telegram from Rabbi Chaim Ozer Grodzinski in Vilnius reporting that the Rebbe was alive in Warsaw.

50 Russia had seized Latvia in 1710, only withdrawing in 1920. There was great fear that they would retake Latvia. Those fears were realized when Russia invaded on June 17, 1940, a few months after the Rebbe departed to the US. Latvia regained its independence in 1991 after the fall of the Soviet Union.

51 Max Rhoade (1898–1964) was a graduate of George Washington Law School. An active Zionist, he was one of the founders of Avukah at Harvard in 1924, which developed into a national student Zionist organization. He was national president for four years, later becoming honorary president. See "Avukah, Zionist Student Federation, Concludes Convention in Buffalo," JTA, July 7, 1926, available at: https://www.jta.org/archive/avukah-zionist-student-federation-concludes-convention-in-buffalo.

52 Rafael Medoff, *Jewish Americans and Political Participation: A Reference Handbook* (ABC-CLIO, September 1, 2002), 117.

53 Jonathan D. Sarna and Zev Eleff, "The Immigration Clause that Transformed Orthodox Judaism in the United States," in *American Jewish History*, vol. 101, no. 3 (July 2017), 357–76.

54 Breckinridge Long (1881–1958) was born to an affluent family in St. Louis and was a lawyer by training. After losing two bids for the Senate, he was appointed Under Secretary of State by his friend FDR. Long attempted to block immigration by Jews fleeing the Holocaust.

55 A copy of the infamous memo and background information on Long are available at: https://exhibitions.ushmm.org/americans-and-the-holocaust/personal-story/breckinridge-long.

56 Shalom Ber Levin, *Toldot Chabad BeArtzot HaBrit* (Brooklyn, NY: Kehot Publication Society, 1988), chap. 4.

57 Jacobson would struggle to find the funds to pay Rhoades's legal fees.

58 Dept. of State, Memorandum of conversation, October 3, 1939, Subject: Rabbi Schneersohn, Participants: Mr. Benjamin V. Cohen, Mr. Robert T. Pell, European division. Published in Altein and Zaklikovsky, *Out of the Inferno*, 48.

59 The conference was held in Evian, France, in July 1938. Delegates of thirty-two countries assembled to discuss saving Jewish refugees from Nazi persecution. The Evian Conference resulted in almost no change in the immigration policies of most of the attending nations. The major powers – the United States, Great Britain, and France – opposed unrestricted immigration, making it clear that they intended to take no official action to alleviate the German-Jewish refugee problem.

60 Raymond Herman Geist (1885–1955) was the first secretary and consul in the US Berlin mission. In that capacity, he was instrumental in helping Jews leave the country. He joined the US consular service in 1919 while he was teaching at Harvard. During his long tenure in Berlin, he cultivated important relationships with German government officials and provided the US administration with an insightful analysis of internal German politics. Geist was well connected in German government circles,

even negotiating with Heinrich Himmler, Reinhard Heydrich, and Hermann Goering. In 1938, in the aftermath of Kristallnacht, he warned US government officials that German Jews "were condemned to death." For more on Geist, see Richard Breitman, *The Berlin Mission: The American Who Resisted Nazi Germany from Within* (PublicAffairs, 2019). Strangely, the author omits Geist's important role in saving the Rebbe.

61 Telegram, Pell to Geist, October 2, 1939, Washington National Records Center.

62 In the telegram, Pell noted that the Rebbe was a Latvian citizen. "While the government does not wish to intervene in the case of a citizen of a foreign country, you might in the course of conversation with Wohlthat...." Pell emphasized that this issue needed to be handled with diplomatic sensitivity.

63 Joachim von Ribbentrop (1893–1946) was the foreign minister of Germany from 1938 to 1945. He played a key role in negotiating the German-Soviet nonaggression pact that made possible the German invasion of Poland in September 1939. He also directed diplomatic efforts to persuade Germany's Axis partners to deport their Jews to German concentration camps.

64 Film, "The Chabad Rebbe and the German Officer," Larry Price, director (Israel: Price Communications Inc., 2011), 56 minutes.

65 Yisrael Jacobson wrote in 1968 that Hermann Goering gave his approval to the plan to save the Rebbe; see *Di Yiddishe Heim*, issue no. 34, Winter 5728 (1968). Others have argued that Wohlthat did not dare approach Goering, since that could have put the whole mission at risk, even causing the expulsion of US Consul Geist. See Ralf Vogel, *Journey to America* (Germany: 1977). An excerpt titled "A Part of Ourselves: German Jews in the German Army" is translated in Altein and Zaklikovsky, *Out of the Inferno*, 160.

66 Richard Bassett, *Hitler's Spy Chief* (New York: Pegasus Books, 2012).

67 Michael Bar-Zohar, *Hitler's Jewish Spy* (London: Sidgwick & Jackson, 1985), 92.

68 "The Brutal Execution of Wilhelm Canaris – Hitler's Spymaster," available at: https://www.youtube.com/watch?v=QVVO7qH-t-s.

69 Cornelia Shockweiler in "The Chabad Rebbe and the German Officer."

70 These included a ban on citizenship, outlawing non-Jewish employees in a Jewish home, and a ban on marriage between Jews and non-Jews. These laws began the cascade of anti-Semitic laws and policies that degraded Jews in Germany and eventually led to the policy of annihilation.

71 There were soldiers of Jewish background who served in the German army. Some only had Jewish fathers; others were very assimilated, their ancestry hidden. Canaris kept some of those with Jewish background on his staff.

72 November 11, 1939.

73 Altein and Zaklikovsky, *Out of the Inferno*, 109.

74 Lieberman wrote in mid-November, before the Rebbe was found. Altein and Zaklikovsky, *Out of the Inferno*, appendix 2.

75 Cable from Lieberman in Riga to Jacobson in New York, November 17, 1939, in Altein and Zaklikovsky, *Out of the Inferno*, 101.

76 Kahan, *Shemuot VeSippurim* 3:134, reprinted in Levin, *Toldot Chabad BePolin, Lita, VeLatvia.*

77 Interview with Barry (Berke) Gurary, Amud Aish Memorial Museum archives.

78 Letter from Max Rhoade to Sam Kramer, November 27, 1939, following up on a phone conversation earlier that day. Richard Pell had received a cable from the US Embassy in Berlin with the news the Rebbe was safe: "He has been ill and is recovering." It noted that a German officer "has been assigned to look after him" and said he should be able to travel. Altein and Zaklikovsky, *Out of the Inferno*, 113.

79 Ibid.

80 These were the most prominent Chabad rabbis in the US, including Rabbis Jacobson, Levitan, Kazanofsky, and Rivkin. See "Memo of Conference, Thursday, November 23, 1939," in Altein and Zaklikovsky, *Out of the Inferno*, 110.

81 Letter from Rabbi Chaim Lieberman, published in Rabbi Shalom Ber Levin, *Toldot Chabad BePolin, Lita, VeLatvia* (Brooklyn, NY: Kehot Publications, 2011), 343.

82 While Lieberman was aware of Bloch's Jewish background, it seems he did not know that only his father was Jewish. Its seems that Bloch must have shared some information about his family history with the Rebbe or with others in his entourage. This would have calmed those who feared being escorted by a German soldier.

83 The Rashag told the story at the *farbrengen* in honor of 18 Elul, 5706 (September 1946). Unpublished manuscript, *Nitzutzei Ohr*, the diaries of Rabbi Avraham Weingarten.

84 *Igrot Kodesh* 15:361, letter from the Rebbe to the Ramash and his daughter describing the trip, dated 9 Tevet, 5700 (December 20, 1939).

85 *Dos Vort* was a Labor Zionist Yiddish newspaper published in Kaunas. The article was headlined, "With the Lubavitcher Rebbe on the Train," December 20, 1939.

86 Bloch returned to the Abwehr, where he was promoted to the rank of colonel. In 1943, he was appointed as a battalion commander in Russia. In February of 1945, the SS prompted his dismissal from the army, due to his Jewish background. When the Russian army reached the edge of Berlin in April 1945, Bloch returned to the front and lost his life just a few days before the end of the war.

87 Sunday, 5 Tevet, 5700 (December 17, 1939).

88 *Di Yiddishe Heim*, issue no. 6.

89 Letter to Rabbi Sholom Posner dated 10 Tevet, 5700 (December 22, 1939).

90 Letter to Rabbi Moshe Sheyivich of Chicago dated 19 Tevet, 5700 (December 31, 1939).

91 Letter from Rhoade to Cohen, November 4, 1939, in Altein and Zaklikovsky, *Out of the Inferno*.

92 Cable from Jacobson to Cheifetz and Lieberman, December 21, 1939, in Altein and Zaklikovsky, *Out of the Inferno*, 170.

93 Letter from Rhoade to Pell, December 21, 1939, in Altein and Zaklikovsky, *Out of the Inferno*, 173.

94 Letter from Rhoade to Cohen, December 29, 1939, in Altein and Zaklikovsky, *Out of the Inferno*, 192. The letter was marked "very urgent."

95 These fears were not unfounded. The Soviets invaded Latvia on June 16, 1940.

96 The meeting took place on January 10, 1940. See Memorandum of Investigation of Agudas Chassidei Chabad, in Altein and Zaklikovsky, *Out of the Inferno*, appendix 6.

97 "I am happy to advise you a cable has been received from Rabbi Schneersohn to the effect all immigration visas to the United States have been granted to all the rabbis in Riga." Letter from Samuel Kramer to Henry Butler, February 13, 1940, in Altein and Zaklikovsky, *Out of the Inferno*, 262.

98 *Igrot Kodesh*, vol. 5, letter "To our friends, *anash* across the world" dated 5 Tevet, 5700 (December 17, 1939).

99 *Igrot Kodesh*, vol. 5, letter "To our Jewish brethren" dated 5 Tevet, 5700 (December 17, 1939).

100 Letters to Morris C. Troper, Chairman European Executive Council, American Jewish Joint Distribution Committee, Paris, dated January 10, 1940 and January 13, 1940. Mindel Archives.

101 The JDC representative, Dr. Schwartz, explained "the United States immigration regulations which prohibit any organization or corporation from furnishing funds for assisting immigration to this country." Nor was the JDC willing to cover the costs incurred by relocating the yeshivah to Vilnius. It did agree to provide a grant to the Rebbe to use at his discretion, "in view of Rabbi Schneersohn's leadership and his contribution to Polish Jewry." In addition, "in view of the imminent approach of the Passover holidays, it was urged that a prompt decision be made with respect to a sum required for matzos for Russian rabbis." JDC memorandum, meeting with representatives of Agudas Chassidei Chabad and JDC, February 27, 1940. JDC Archives.

102 *Igrot Kodesh*, vol. 5, letters to Jacobson, the Kramer family, and Dr. Jung dated 14 Tevet, 5700 (December 26, 1939).

103 Letter to Rabbi Yisrael Jacobson dated 21 Tevet, 5700 (January 2, 1940).

104 During the Holocaust, there were other heroic efforts to preserve great Jewish libraries and artifacts, most notably the collection of the YIVO Institute in Vilnius. Its staff and others, known as "The Paper Brigade," risked their lives during the war to hide the collection. After the war, it was discovered and transferred to the YIVO Institute in New York. See "The Paper Brigade: Smuggling Rare Books and Documents in Nazi-Occupied Vilna," available at: https://www.yivo.org/The-Paper-Brigade.

A similar case was the Aleppo Codex, a tenth-century handwritten copy of the Torah used by Maimonides and brought to Syria by his son. Through the centuries it was held in trust by the Aleppo Jewish community. The community was endangered in 1948 after riots broke out in Syria to protest the establishment of the State of Israel. The Israeli government made major efforts to save the Codex, but some of it was lost. Today it is in the National Library of Israel. See Matti Friedman, *The Aleppo Codex: A True Story of Obsession, Faith, and the Pursuit of an Ancient Bible* (Algonquin Books, 2012).

105 *A Chassidisher Derher*, issue no. 17, available at: https://derher.org/wp-content/uploads/2016/03/adar25774.pdf.

106 Friday, 6 Shevat, 5700 (January 26, 1940).

107 *Igrot Kodesh*, vol. 15, letter dated 25 Adar Alef, 5700 (March 5, 1940).

108 Interview with Yehoshua Wolosow's grandson, Rabbi Mordechai Einbinder. Wolosow arrived in New York before the Rebbe.

109 Leibel Zisman, *I Believe: The Story of One Jewish Life* (Brooklyn, NY: GJCF, 2012), 56.

110 Ibid Zikoron Bes Yisrael.

111 Uri Kaploun, trans., *Sefer HaSichos*, 5705 (Brooklyn, NY: Kehot Publication Society, 2014), 134.

112 In May 1924, due to threats from the Yevesektzia, the Rebbe was forced to leave Riga for St. Petersburg. In October 1927, he was forced out of Russia due to the threat to his life. In August 1933, he relocated to Warsaw to be near the yeshivah and strengthen chasidic life in Poland. Due to health concerns, he relocated to Otwock in 1934.

113 Uri Kaploun, trans., *Sefer HaSichos*, 5696–5700, p. 408.

114 Levin, *Toldot Chabad BePolin, Lita, VeLatvia*, 345.

115 Zisman, *I Believe*, 56.

116 *Igrot Kodesh* 5:34, letter to "My dear friends, *anash* in the Holy Land and Europe" dated 24 Adar Alef, 5700 (March 4, 1940). In the letter, the Rebbe showers them with blessings and encourages them to continue their commitment to Torah study and Jewish observance. It is important to note that at this time, in early 1940, no one imagined the nefarious intent of the Nazis to annihilate the Jewish people. Many thought that Jews under their regime would face difficulties, but the notion that millions would be killed was beyond comprehension.

117 The eleven were the Rebbe, his wife, his mother, the Rashag, the Rashag's wife, and the Rashag's son Berel, joined by Rabbi Hodakov and his wife, the Rebbe's secretaries, Rabbis Nissan Mindel and Chaim Lieberman, and the Rebbe's nurse Manya.

118 "Historic Treasures Rabbi S.B. Schapiro," #146, video available at: https://www.youtube.com/watch?v=MfGfuUCNpvw&t=17s.

119 Interview with Barry (Berke) Gurary, Amud Aish Memorial Museum archives.

120 "America Is No Different: A Selection of Vintage Film Clips of Rabbi Yosef Yitzchak of Lubavitch in the United States," JEM, chap. 4; *Sefer HaSichos*, 5700 (Brooklyn, NY: Kehot, 2015), appendix A: "The Voyage to America."

CHAPTER TEN

1 The voyage from Gothenburg, Sweden, to New York Harbor took twelve days, arriving on Monday, March 18 at 4:00 p.m. Port regulations required the ship to wait overnight until it docked. The Rebbe departed the next day, Tuesday, March 19 (9 Adar II) at Pier 97 on West 57th Street in Manhattan. "America Is No Different: A Selection of Vintage Film Clips of Rabbi Yosef Yitzchak of Lubavitch in the United States," JEM (Brooklyn, NY: 1999); Video of the Rebbe's arrival, "The Previous Rebbe's Arrival to America," available at: chabad.org/363468; for a personal account of one of the travelers, see Introduction, *Sefer HaMaamarim*, 5700.

2 Talk by Rabbi Groner, Sydney, Australia, Rosh Chodesh Kislev, 5747, tapes of Rabbi Groner.

3 Author's interview with Risya Kazarnovsky.

4 Author's interview with Aaron Rakeffet. Shoen recalled the details of the day to his niece and her husband, Rabbi Aaron and Malka Rakeffet.

5 *The Wonder Rabbi*, a biographical sketch of the Rayatz with handwritten annotations of the seventh Rebbe. There is no author's name on this work, but by comparing it to other documents in the Mindel Archives it is clear that the author is Gershon Kranzler.

6 Both became pioneering emissaries of the Rebbe. Groner was sent by the Rebbe to Australia in 1947 for six months, and in 1958 the seventh Rebbe sent him there permanently. He led Chabad in Australia until he passed away in 2008. See Dovid Zaklikowski, "Rabbi Yitzchok Dovid Groner (1925–2008)," available at: chabad.org/698882. Risya Kazarnovsky married Rabbi Zalman Posner. They were the first Chabad *shluchim* in Nashville, Tennessee, arriving in 1949. Risya passed away in 2007. See Sue Fishkoff, "Pioneering Chabad Emissary, Mother, and Grandmother Passes Away in Nashville," available at: chabad.org/585088.

7 Agudas Harabonim, the Union of Orthodox Rabbis, was a prominent rabbinical association in the US. Mizrachi also sent a large delegation to greet the Rebbe. *Der Tog*, March 20, 1940.

8 Interview with Edith Block, JEM Oral History Project.

9 *Der Tog*, March 20, 1940.

10 Uri Kaploun, trans., *Sefer HaSichos*, 5700 (Brooklyn, NY: 2015), chap. 6.

11 Kaploun, trans., *Sefer HaSichos*, 5700, chap. 7.

12 For the full statement, see Kaploun, trans., *Sefer HaSichos*, appendix B, "A Call to American Jewry."

13 *Brooklyn Eagle*. The assertion that Hodakov would be in the US for just six months indicates that the fear for the welfare of Jews in Poland did not extend to all of Europe. Apparently, Hodakov was still planning to return to Latvia.

14 *Di Yiddishe Heim*, issue no. 33, Autumn 5728 (1968).

15 Kaploun, trans., *Sefer HaSichos*, 5700, chap. 24.

16 Rabbi Dr. Aaron Rakeffet, "Post-1939 – The Change in American Torah Judaism," audio lecture available at: https://www.yutorah.org/sidebar/lecturedata/968804/Post-1939The-Change-in-American-Torah-Judaism.

17 *Farbrengen, Motza'ei Shabbat*, 10 Shevat, 5734 (February 2, 1974).

18 Uri Kaploun, trans., *Likkutei Dibburim*, vol. 3 (Brooklyn, NY: Kehot Publication Society, 2012), chap. 24a.

19 *The Wonder Rabbi*.

20 Author's interview with Rabbi Avraham Hecht.

21 Professor Jonathan Sarna, *American Judaism* (Yale University, 2004), 227.

22 In 1913, there were just twenty-two synagogues that were members of the Conservative association United Synagogue. In 1929, that number had grown tenfold to 229. In the postwar era, the Conservative movement grew even more, fueled by the move of many Jews from the urban core to the suburbs. Sarna, *American Judaism*, 238.

23 Marshall Sklare, *Conservative Judaism: An American Religious Movement*.

24 Considered by many the "mother yeshivah of American Jewry," it was founded in 1918 in the Williamsburg section of Brooklyn.

25 Rabbi Shraga Feivel Mendlowitz (1886–1948) immigrated to the US in 1913, first to Philadelphia and then to Scranton, where he headed the Talmud Torah. In 1921, he became principal of Torah Vodaath. It was a small school at that time, but under his leadership it expanded to include a high school and college-level yeshivah program. By 1936, it had 751 students and "spawned several imitators and competitors," Professor Jonathan Sarna writes. Rabbi Mendlowitz was instrumental in establishing Torah Umesorah in 1944 and supported other Torah institutions as well. See Sarna, *American Judaism*, 228. For a full biography, see Yonoson Rosenblum, *Reb Shraga Feivel: The Life and Times of Rabbi Shraga Feivel Mendlowitz, the Architect of Torah in America* (Brooklyn, NY: Mesorah Publications, 2001).

26 Jeffrey Gurock, *Orthodox Jews in America* (Indiana University Press, 2009), chap. 6.

27 Sarna, *American Judaism*, 232.

28 For an overview of the growth of traditional Judaism, see Menachem Keren-Katz, "The Haredization of American Orthodoxy in the Early Twentieth Century" in *Tradition*, Winter 2022.

29 Agudas Harabonim, the Union of Orthodox Rabbis, was founded in 1902 by European rabbinic scholars.

30 The Rabbinical Council of America (RCA) was founded in 1923 to unify American Orthodox rabbis, primarily graduates of Yeshiva University. It has close ties with the Orthodox Union.

31 US immigration law had a special clause permitting the entry of clergy, which facilitated the immigration of these scholars. See Jonathan Sarna and Zev Eleff, "The Immigration Clause that Transformed Orthodox Judaism in the United States," in *American Jewish History*, vol. 101, available at: https://www.brandeis.edu/hornstein/sarna/immigration/Sarna,%20Eleff%20IMMIGRATION%20CLAUSE%20THAT%20TRANSFORMED%20ORTHODOX%20JUDAISM.pdf.

32 Rabbi Feinstein was *rosh yeshivah* of Mesivta Tifereth Jerusalem, Rabbi Soloveitchik was *rosh yeshivah* of Yeshiva University, and Rabbi Kamenetsky was *rosh yeshivah* of Torah Vodaath. Rabbi Breuer became the leader of the German Jewish community in Washington Heights, Manhattan.

33 Other prominent scholars arrived in the US after the Rebbe, including Rabbi Aharon Kotler, who founded Beth Medrash Govoha in Lakewood, and Rabbi Moshe Shatzkes (the Lomzer Rav) and Rabbi Dovid Lifshitz, who both joined Yeshiva University as *roshei yeshivah*.

34 Rabbi Moshe Soloveichik (1879–1941) was the son of the legendary Rabbi Chaim Soloveitchik and *rosh yeshivah* of Yeshiva University. Speech cited in *HaPardes*, May 1940. *HaPardes* was a monthly rabbinic magazine that started publishing in the 1920s in Chicago and later moved to New York.

35 Author's interview with Herschel Fogelman.

36 *Ad Bli Dai* [Hebrew] (Jerusalem: Maggid, 2021).

37 Rabbi Adin Even-Yisrael Steinsaltz, *My Rebbe* (Jerusalem: Maggid, 2014), chap. 5.

38 Rabbi Abraham Hecht, *My Spiritual Journey* (Brooklyn, NY: 2006).

39 Students from New York yeshivas, in particular Torah Vodaath, had been studying chasidic philosophy with Rabbi Jacobson and became attached to Chabad. Some joined the new yeshivah right away, and others transferred in the coming years. Rabbi Shalom Ber Levin, *Toldot Chabad BeArtzot HaBrit* (Brooklyn, NY: Kehot Publication Society, 1988), chap. 29.

40 The Rebbe took an active interest in the students' progress. The administration sent him regular reports and he met regularly with the yeshivah staff.

41 Kaploun, trans., *Sefer HaSichos*, 5700, chap. 9.

42 Steinsaltz, *My Rebbe*, chap. 5; *Farbrengens* with Rabbi Steinsaltz.

43 A committee was formed by Agudas Chassidei Chabad. It included Chaim Kramer, Avraham Dovber Kramer, Dovber Chaskind, and Rabbis Shlomo Aharon

Kazanofsky, Shmuel Levitin, Moshe Dovber Rivkin, Eli Simpson, Yisrael Jacobson, and Menachem Mendel Cunin.

44 A local doctor commissioned renowned architect Edwin Kline to create a home and clinic for him. It was completed in 1936, but the doctor was indicted and the bank seized the property. For more on the property's history, see Andrew Silverstein, "How 770 Eastern Parkway Became the World's Most Recognizable Jewish Building," available at: https://forward.com/culture/474642/how-770-eastern-parkway-chabad-lubavitch-rebbe-schneerson-history-jewish/#:~:text=Around%20the%20world%2C%20construction%20is,on%20every%20continent%20except%20Antarctica.

45 The house had an elevator, an important feature for the Rebbe, since his mobility was limited.

46 Letter to the Chabad community in the United States dated 12 Av, 5700 (August 16, 1940), the day of the purchase. Levin, *Toldot Chabad BeArtzot HaBrit*, 174.

47 Replicas have been built in over thirty locations around the world, including Australia, Israel, California, and Texas. The profile of 770 is also used in the creation of Judaica. See Barbara Eldredge, "This Crown Heights Building Has Doppelgängers All Over the Globe," available at: https://www.brownstoner.com/architecture/770-eastern-parkway-brooklyn-chabad-lubavitch-building-crown-heights/.

48 The three families were Chaskind, Popak, and Gordon. Charles Roth.

49 Ibid.

50 The purchase was completed by Agudas Chassidei Chabad on August 16, 1940 (12 Av, 5700).

51 Letter from Avraham Pariz, reprinted in Levin, *Toldot Chabad BeArtzot HaBrit*, chap. 35.

52 Hecht, *My Spiritual Journey*.

53 Kaploun, trans., *Sefer HaSichos*, 5702 (Brooklyn, NY: 2017), chap. 13.

54 *Igrot Kodesh*, vol. 5, Introduction.

55 For a detailed overview of the yeshivah during the war years, see Rabbi Shalom Ber Levin, *Toldot Chabad BePolin, Lita, VeLatvia* (Brooklyn, NY: Kehot Publication Society, 2001), chap. 54–62.

56 *Igrot Kodesh*, vol. 5, letter dated 14 Tevet, 5700 (December 26, 1939). The letter from Riga was following up on a telegram the Rebbe had sent to Jacobson.

57 *Igrot Kodesh*, vol. 5, letter dated Nisan 5700 (April 1940). The appeal was addressed "To my beloved brothers and sisters, the Jews of United States." The Rebbe listed *Eretz Yisrael* and America as appropriate locations to resettle the students.

58 Rabbi Meir Ashkenazi (1892–1954) served as chief rabbi of Shanghai from 1926 to 1949. He studied in Yeshivas Tomchei Temimim in Lubavitch; later he was a rabbi in Harbin and then moved to Shanghai. After the war, he relocated to Brooklyn, where he passed away. See *Igrot Kodesh*, vol. 5, letter to Rabbi Meir Ashkenazi

dated 26 Sivan, 5700 (June 4, 1940). In the same letter, the Rebbe lauds Ashkenazi for establishing a Talmud Torah with Jewish education programs for refugees who arrived in Shanghai. "You should make every effort to organize programs for the youth, designed for the needs of each group," he wrote, possibly referring to the fact that refugees were arriving from different countries, speaking different languages and with varied levels of Jewish knowledge. For more on Rabbi Ashkenazi's life, see Yehuda Geberer, "Shliach to Shanghai: The Life & Heroics of Rabbi Meir Ashkenazi," podcast available at: https://jsoundbites.podbean.com/e/the-shliach-to-shanghai-the-life-heroics-of-rabbi-meir-ashkenazi/.

59 Two students with Dutch backgrounds, Nathan Gutwirth and Leo Sternheim, came up with the plan to escape Europe via Japan. Interview with Rabbi Yisroel Chanovitz by Rabbi Avrohom Holzberg of *Kfar Chabad* magazine in which Holzberg spoke with students of the yeshivah in Shanghai. See also Steven Lapidus, "Memoirs of a Refugee: The Travels and Travails of Rabbi Pinchas Hirschsprung," available at: file:///C:/Users/rabbi/Downloads/editorcjs,+Vol+27,+8,+Lapidus.pdf.

60 Russia's policy of hostility toward religious observance caused prominent rabbis, including Rabbis Chaim Ozer Grodzinski and Aharon Kotler, to advise against traveling via Russia. See Marc Shapiro, "The Mir Yeshivah's Incredible Escape to Shanghai," audio lectures available at: https://torahinmotion.org/programs/e-tim-the-mir-yeshivas-incredible-escape-to-shanghai.

61 While in Riga after leaving Warsaw, the Rebbe sent Rabbi Yehoshua Bick to serve as the *mashpia* (spiritual mentor) of the yeshivah in Vilnius. He instructed him to seek counsel with the Amshinover Rebbe if needed. Interview with Michoel Seligson by Rabbi Avrohom Holzberg of *Kfar Chabad* magazine; Seligson's father was one of the students in Shanghai.

62 Interview with Rabbi Chaim Meir Bukiet by Rabbi Avrohom Holzberg of *Kfar Chabad* magazine.

63 Interview with Rabbi Herschel Fuchs by Rabbi Avrohom Holzberg of *Kfar Chabad* magazine. Fuchs was a student in the yeshivah in Poland and Shanghai. After the war he was a teacher in the Lubavitcher yeshivah in Brooklyn.

64 *Igrot Kodesh*, vol. 5, letter dated 3 Tamuz, 5700 (July 9, 1940).

65 In addition to the funds remitted to the Russian government, there were other expenses, bringing the total to around five hundred dollars each.

66 Gore was a Russian Jew who succeeded in the oil business in Wichita. *Igrot Kodesh*, vol. 5, letter dated January 6, 1941 (7 Tevet, 5701).

67 *Igrot Kodesh*, vol. 5, letter dated 15 Tevet, 5701 (January 14, 1941). It seems the number of visas fluctuated as the US changed its policy.

68 *Igrot Kodesh*, vol. 5, letter to Yaakov Schector of Pittsburgh dated 14 Tevet, 5700 (January 13, 1941). In the letter, the Rebbe also thanks Schector for helping to establish a Ladies Auxiliary in Pittsburgh and for supporting the Chabad yeshivas.

69 *Igrot Kodesh* 5:243, letter to Binyamin Disin dated 20 Tevet, 5701 (January 19, 1941).

70 Levin, *Toldot Chabad BePolin, Lita, VeLatvia*, chap. 56.

71 During the stop in Moscow, the students visited the Choral Synagogue, the main congregation in Moscow. Avraham Garfinkel recalls that local Jews could not believe that a Jew could depart from Russia and feared conversing with the students. They made contact there with some Chabad Chasidim "who we secretly gave *siddurim* and chasidic publications."

72 Tamar Engel, "The Jews of Kobe," available at: https://xenon.stanford.edu/~tamar/Kobe/Kobe.html. Today Jewish life continues in Kobe; see: https://jewishkobe-osaka.com/.

73 Rabbi S.D. Raichik, "The Lubavitcher Yeshivah in Kobe, Japan 1," available at: chabadofla.com/1409449.

74 For an overview of the history of the Mir Yeshivah in Shanghai, see Marc Shapiro, "The Mir Yeshivah's Incredible Escape to Shanghai," audio lectures available at: https://torahinmotion.org/programs/e-tim-the-mir-yeshivas-incredible-escape-to-shanghai.

75 For more, see Rabbi S.D. Raichik, "The Lubavitcher Yeshivah in Shanghai," available at: chabadofla.com/1409453

76 It was constructed by Silas Hardoon (1851–1931), an affluent assimilated Jew, in memory of his father Aharon. The facility sat unused until the arrival of the yeshivah students.

77 The Chabad yeshivas integrated the study of Talmud and chasidic philosophy. The Mir Yeshivah followed the classic Lithuanian mode of study that focused almost entirely on Talmud, accentuated by *musar* (ethics).

78 There was very occasional, limited communication via Stockholm in neutral Sweden between the students in Shanghai and the Rebbe in New York. After the attack on Pearl Harbor, communication became almost impossible. Rabbi Yisrael Zuber, a Chabad Chasid who served as the rabbi in Stockholm, facilitated the connection. Students would refer to the Rebbe as "Davidson" (son of Sholom Dovber). See interview by *Mishpacha* magazine, November 2010. For more on the Stockholm connection, see *Igrot Kodesh* 5:41.

79 Interview by *Mishpacha* magazine, November 2010.

80 The ghetto was administered by Japanese official Sgt. Kano Ghoya. He called himself the "king of the Jews" and treated the refugees brutally. See Henny Bauer's video testimony, available at: https://sfi.usc.edu/video/chhenny-bauergen.

81 Established in 1939 to assist yeshivah students and rabbis in war-torn Europe, it was originally named "Emergency Committee for War-Torn Yeshivas." When the route via Japan opened, the Vaad Hatzalah raised money to transport students of the Mir

Yeshivah and support them in Japan and Shanghai. Later in the war, as the scope of the Holocaust became known, it expanded its work to save Jews in Hungary and other countries. In the postwar era, it took a leading role in helping refugees. It was led by Rabbis Eliezer Silver, Avraham Kalmanovich, and Aharon Kotler. See "An Inventory to the Vaad Hatzala Collection, 1940–1963," available at: https://archives.yu.edu/xtf/view?docId=ead/vaad/vaad.xml;query=;brand=default; Alex Grobman, *Battling for Souls: The Vaad Hatzala Rescue Committee in Post-War Europe* (Jersey City, NJ: Ktav); Efraim Zuroff, "Rabbis' Relief and Rescue: A Case Study of the Activities of the Vaad ha-Hatzala (Rescue Committee) of the American Orthodox Rabbis, 1942–1943," available at: https://www.museumoftolerance.com/education/archives-and-reference-library/online-resources/simon-wiesenthal-center-annual-volume-3/annual-3-chapter-5.html.

82 *Igrot Kodesh*, vol. 8, letter to Shlomo Palmar dated 11 Adar, 5704 (March 6, 1944). Palmar was a Chabad supporter in Chicago.

83 Interview with Rabbi Chaim Meir Bukiet by Rabbi Avrohom Holzberg of *Kfar Chabad* magazine.

84 In the same letter, the Rebbe states that he is under tremendous financial strain and has debts totaling more than $20,000 (over $350,000 today).

85 *Igrot Kodesh*, vol. 8, letter to Shlomo Palmar dated 11 Adar, 5704 (March 6, 1944).

86 Unlike Vaad Hatzalah, other US Jewish organizations such as the JDC were unwilling to transfer funds to Jewish refugees in Shanghai. This contravened US law banning the transfer of funds to areas under enemy control. In the eyes of Vaad Hatzalah, this was a matter of life and death, and Jewish law dictates *pikuach nefesh docheh et hakol* –to save a life, all is permitted (other than taking other lives). In this case, the Vaad Hatzalah believed that this Jewish principle trumped US law, a concept that was foreign to the more secular Jewish groups.

87 Other methods were also used. Local Jews provided funds for the yeshivah, and Vaad Hatzalah would reimburse their friends or relatives in other countries. Communications between Rabbi Shmuelevitz and Vaad Hatzalah was done in code. For a detailed of view of these efforts, see Efraim Zuroff, "Rabbis' Relief and Rescue: A Case Study of the Activities of the Vaad ha-Hatzala (Rescue Committee) of the American Orthodox Rabbis, 1942–1943," available at: https://www.museumoftolerance.com/education/archives-and-reference-library/online-resources/simon-wiesenthal-center-annual-volume-3/annual-3-chapter-5.html.

88 Rabbi Avraham Kalmanowitz, one of the leaders of Vaad Hatzalah, convinced Morgenthau to make this exception. David Kranzler, *Thy Brother's Blood* (Brooklyn, NY: Mesorah Publications, 1987), chap. 4.

89 Letter from the yeshivah students in Shanghai to the Rashag dated 26 Tishrei, 5706 (October 3, 1945). The first part of the letter provides a general review of the yeshivah and its academic achievements, noting that it continued the same mode of study as

when the yeshivah was in Poland. The second part outlines the polices of the Vaad Hatzalah and states that not only did it discriminate against Chabad students, but also against the Amshinover Rebbe. "They did not provide the Amshinover Rebbe with funds, claiming he was not a yeshivah student, while providing funding to the Litvish [Lithuanians] who are far from that [yeshivah students]. Only after harsh protest did it change." This letter revealed the full details of the Vaad Hatzalah's scandalous policy to Chabad leaders in New York. This prompted the New York rabbis to write to Chabad leaders in Israel asking them to meet with leading scholars of the Lithuanian yeshivah community in Israel to share their distress about what had occurred in Shanghai. They asked them to rein in some of the antagonistic activities of the leaders of Vaad Hatzalah toward Chabad. See Rabbi Chaim Dalfin, *Lakewood and Lubavitch* (Brooklyn, NY: Jewish Enrichment Press, 2018), 19.

90 Rabbi Shimon Goldman, *From Shedlitz to Safety: A Young Jew's Story of Survival* (Brooklyn, NY: 2004).

91 After the war, when the Rebbe became aware of Aryeh Leib Brailovsky's generosity, he sent a letter to Rabbi Ashkenazi asking him to express the Rebbe's appreciation for his kindness to the students. See *Igrot Kodesh*, vol. 9, letter dated 12 Adar Bet, 5706.

92 Rabbi Ashkenazi relocated to New York in 1948. There, members of the Vaad Hatzalah initiated a *din Torah*, a case in rabbinical court, against Rabbi Ashkenazi. They accused him of improperly diverting some of the funds sent during the war to Shanghai for the Mir Yeshivah, so that they went to the Chabad yeshivah students instead. Since Ashkenazi was a foreigner, he was able to pick up the funds at a neutral embassy in Shanghai and bring the money to the Mir Yeshivah. He argued that if the Japanese had discovered that the funds came from the US, which was at war with Japan at the time, he could have been killed. Because of the risk, he claimed that it was permitted to take a percentage, which he gave to the Chabad students. When Ashkenazi went to the embassy to collect the funds, he would wear *takhrikhim* (burial shrouds) under his clothes, fearing that if the Japanese arrested him, he would never have a proper Jewish burial. The rabbinical court ruled in Ashkenazi's favor. See Rabbi Yosef Ashkenazi, *HaRav Ashkenazi* (Israel: Chazak Publishing, 2017), 193–94.

93 Members of the Vaad Hatzalah attempted to justify their actions by claiming that the Rebbe had his own fund for *pidyon shvuyim*. That fund's purpose was to support Jews suffering under Communism in Soviet Russia, and it operated clandestinely. The Rebbe's involvement with Soviet Jewry was a long-standing fact, well known to those who stood at the helm of Vaad Hatzalah. Shimon Goldman, one of the students in Shanghai, wrote in his memoir, "Some postulated that members of Vaad Hatzalah were irate over a second fund established by the Rebbe Rayatz. Called Pidyon Shvuyim, the Rebbe raised money to support Jews suffering from

Nazi Germany and Communist Russia. Needless to say, the legalities of such a fund were not straightforward and this prevented the Rebbe from revealing the true nature of the fund. Neither could the Rebbe show other *gedolim* (prominent rabbis) an accounting of the funds that he distributed to German and Russian Jewry. Apparently, certain *gedolim* resented this secrecy and retaliated by excluding suffering Chabad students from the Vaad Hatzalah fund." The Rebbe's financial support of Russian Jews was done with the utmost secrecy, as the discovery of the transfer of funds to support religious life in Russia would have prompted the arrest of the recipients.

94 Rabbi Eliyahu of Vilna, known as the Vilna Gaon, was the leading rabbinic scholar in Lithuania and the head of the *mitnagdim* (opponents) of Chasidism. In 1777 and again in 1781, he issued a *cherem* (ban of excommunication) against Chasidim. In the nineteenth century, cooperation between Chasidim and *mitnagdim* lowered those tensions; still, they existed with less intensity. Fuchs, one of the Shanghai students, says the unwillingness to provide funds to the Chabad yeshivas "was connected to a degree of the hostility of *mitnagdim* to Chasidim." See interview with Rabbi Herschel Fuchs by Rabbi Avrohom Holzberg of *Kfar Chabad* magazine.

95 Author's interview with Rabbi Chaim Gutnick. Gutnick was a student of the Telz Yeshivah in Lithuania who found refuge in Australia during the war, eventually becoming one of the country's leading rabbis. He was visiting the Rebbe from Australia at the time of their conversation. See "Rabbi Chaim Gutnick talks about his youth in the Telzer Yeshivah," video available at: https://www.youtube.com/watch?v=m2VHcb1Jzgk&t=2701s.

96 There is a dramatic contrast between the Rebbe and his successor, the seventh Rebbe. The Rebbe was deeply expressive, many times sharing his most intimate thoughts and feelings with others. The seventh Rebbe was much more reserved, rarely speaking of himself, making personal observations, or expressing criticism of others. Rabbi Yoel Kahn noted that the seventh Rebbe was by nature an introvert and had to transform himself to assume the position of leadership. Author's interview with Kahn.

97 Steven Lapidus, "Memoirs of a Refugee: The Travels and Travails of Rabbi Pinchas Hirschsprung," available at: file:///C:/Users/rabbi/Downloads/editorcjs,+Vol+27,+8,+Lapidus.pdf.

98 The Rebbe reached out to the Polish ambassador in Tokyo, writing, "I respectfully appeal to you to kindly provide Canadian visas for the thirty-eight students of Tomchei Temimim." The Rebbe also cabled Jewish leaders such as Rabbi Abramsky in the UK, who had apparently been involved in lobbying Canada to issue the visas, to include the Chabad students. See *Igrot Kodesh* 5:456.

99 Dovid Zaklikowski, *The People's Rabbi: The Life and Legacy of Rabbi Leib Kramer* (New York: 2001), part IV.

100 The ship's route would have taken them across the date line on Yom Kippur, creating a halakhic dilemma regarding whether to fast one or two days. After the ship departed Shanghai, the issue became moot when it was diverted to Hong Kong, causing it to cross the date line after Yom Kippur.

101 Other prominent scholars who came on that ship included Rabbi Pinchas Hirschsprung, who was appointed Montreal's chief rabbi in 1969.

102 Some of the students of the Mir Yeshivah waited and took the next ship. Sadly, the war broke out while they were traveling, and they were interned in the Philippines, where they suffered greatly. Memoir of Rabbi Yitzchak Hendel.

103 Zaklikowski, *The People's Rabbi.*

104 Memoir of Rabbi Yitzchak Hendel.

105 There had been a community meeting upon the arrival of the students to discuss the issue, and there was a concern that supporting two institutions would be challenging. There was also a degree of opposition to the traditional religious education offered by the yeshivah. With time, the community saw its value. In 1942, S. Greenfeld, president of the Federation of Polish Jews of Canada, who had strongly opposed having two yeshivas, publicly stated that Rabbi Jacobson had been correct. See Zaklikowski, *The People's Rabbi*, part IV.

106 By 1954, Mercaz HaTorah had 140 students. In the mid-1980s, Mercaz HaTorah merged with the newly established Yeshivah Gedolah and today is a major center of Jewish scholarship in Montreal. The Chabad yeshivah became the foundation for Chabad's growth in the city. Today Montreal boasts a large network of Chabad institutions, including schools, synagogues, and community and campus centers. The yeshivah continues to be a center of learning till today. See Steven Lapidus, "Memoirs of a Refugee: The Travels and Travails of Rabbi Pinchas Hirschsprung," available at: file:///C:/Users/rabbi/Downloads/editorcjs,+Vol+27,+8,+Lapidus.pdf.

107 Memoir of Rabbi Yitzchak Hendel.

108 Goldie Morgentaler, "The Jewish People's School of Montreal," available at: https://www.tabletmag.com/sections/arts-letters/articles/jewish-peoples-school-montreal.

109 Just 1.9 percent of Canadian Jewish children were attending a Jewish day school in 1940. For an overview of Canadian Jewish life at the time that the Shanghai students arrived in Montreal, see the comprehensive survey: Louis Rosenberg, *Canada's Jews: A Social and Economic Study of Jews in Canada in the 1930s*" (Montreal: McGill-Queens University Press, 1941). For more on the Yiddish schools in Montreal, see "Dr. David Fraser speaks about the history of the Jewish school question in Montreal," available at: https://www.youtube.com/watch?v=sxQDAPN4wRw.

110 In Quebec, religious groups operated public schools. At the time there was no Jewish school system, and many Jewish parents opted for the Protestant schools. With

time, Jewish schools received government support. See Dorothy Zalcman Howard, "Jewish School Question," available at: https://www.thecanadianencyclopedia.ca/en/article/jewish-school-question#:~:text=In%201923%2C%2012%2C000%20Jewish%20children,to%20serve%20as%20school%20commissioners.

111 This includes children enrolled in once-a-week Sunday schools or afternoon schools. Rosenberg, *Canada's Jews*, chap. 23, section 4.

112 *Igrot Kodesh* 6:198, letter dated 28 Shevat, 5702 (February 15, 1942).

113 Zaklikowski, *The People's Rabbi*, part IV.

114 The yeshivah in New York had opened eighteen months earlier in March 1940 with only a small number of students. The influx of nine senior students, alumni of the yeshivah in Poland, would have enhanced it considerably.

115 Dovid Zaklikowski, *Advorkers*.

116 *Igrot Kodesh*, vol. 7, letter to Bronfman dated 23 Adar Bet, 5703 (March 30, 1943).

117 Zaklikowski, *The People's Rabbi*.

118 Interview with Shmuel Rodal, JEM Oral History Project.

119 Rodal was born in 1918 and was twenty-eight at the time that he married. He had been a senior student in the yeshivah in Otwock. His father passed away before the war. One brother survived, and his mother and remaining nine siblings lost their lives in the Holocaust.

120 Letter to Rabbi Hendel dated 13 Tishrei, 5704 (February 12, 1943), Hendel family archive.

121 For a detailed account of the effort to save the Rebbe's family, see Levin, *Toldot Chabad BePolin, Lita, VeLatvia*, chap. 64.

122 The couple adopted their nephew, Yaakov Yosef Lis. See the *teshurah* (wedding memento) of Eliyahu and Chaya Mushka Shivacha, chap. 7.

123 After the war, the Ramash conducted an inquiry into the fate of Mendel and Sheina Horenstein. In August 1949 he received confirmation of the date of their passing from Mordechai Unrad, who had been in the same barracks as Mendel in Treblinka. He wrote that Sheina was killed on the second day of Rosh HaShanah 1942 and her husband Mendel was killed seven weeks later, on 25 Cheshvan. Due to the fear over the grief the news would cause the Rebbe, who was in ill health, the Ramash withheld this information. Only two years later, in 1951, did the seventh Rebbe reveal the dates of their passing. Annually he recited *Kaddish* on the second day of Rosh HaShanah in memory of his sister-in-law, Sheina. For copies of the correspondence, see "Amazing Discovery: The Rebbe's Attempts to Find Out About Rebbetzin Sheina," available at: https://collive.com/amazing-discovery-the-rebbes-attempts-to-find-out-about-rebbetzin-sheina/.

124 Undated letter from Feigin to Jacobson. It seems that it was written in February or March 1940 while the Rebbe was en route to the United States. Feigin writes that the Ramash is "strong in his own opinions" and that if he comes to the US, "much

good could come from this." He requests that Jacobson write to him to encourage his relocation. *Kfar Chabad* magazine, issue no. 671.

125 Shmuel Menachem Mendel Butman, *The Rebbe in Paris* (Chazak Publishing, 2024), section 2.

126 *Farbrengen* of Rabbi Yitzchok Groner at Oholei Torah, Sydney, Australia, tapes of Rabbi Groner.

127 "*Gaon*" is an honorific title reserved for great Torah scholars. The Rebbe referred to the Ramash the same way in his personal diary. In private notations to himself in sections of the diary from 1946 and 1948 that have been published, every time he mentions the Ramash, he uses title "*HaRav HaGaon* – The Rabbi and Great Scholar" before his name. See Rabbi Shalom Dovber Levine, *Treasures of the Chabad Library* (Brooklyn, NY: Kehot Publication Society, 2009).

128 Memo about the Machne Israel program, visit to Jewish farmers, Mindel Archives.

129 By 1944, the annual budget of Merkos L'Inyonei Chinuch had reached $39,991 (more than $700,000 today). Financial statement, Merkos L'Inyonei Chinuch, June 1943–44, Mindel Archives.

130 Yoel 2:13.

131 Midrash Esther Rabbah, cited in "Who Should Teach the Children?" available at: chabad.org/1130179/.

132 Berakhot 5a.

133 In the Temple in Jerusalem, trumpets – and according to some, a shofar – were sounded. See Maimonides, *Hilkhot Taanit* (Laws of Fasting) 1:1. Four of the five chapters of *Hilkhot Taanit* outline the spiritual response that Jewish tradition dictates in times of crisis.

134 The monthly magazine was published from October 1940 to September 1945.

135 Publication stopped the month that the war ended. One could argue that the object of the magazine was to provide a spiritual response to the war, and now that issue was moot.

136 In 1967, on the eve of the Six-Day War, the seventh Rebbe inaugurated a tefillin campaign as a spiritual response to the threats to Israel's survival.

137 Author's interview with Rabbi Groner. This practice of not eating chocolate during the war years became so ingrained that he did not indulge in chocolate throughout the rest of his life.

138 The one-time success of saving the Rebbe did not translate into long-term political access. The key government figure who advocated behind the scenes of the US government intervention to the save the Rebbe was White House official Benjamin Cohen. There is no record of meetings between Cohen and Chabad leaders once the Rebbe arrived in the US. According to Rabbi Dovid Edelman of Springfield, Justice

Brandeis enlisted Cohen, whom he knew well, after the Rabinowitz brothers asked for his help to save the Rebbe. Though Cohen was not religious, he cared about the Jewish people, at times working quietly to advance Jewish interests. In 1938, Cohen met with British officials in London about the plight of Jewish refugees and afterward with Ben-Gurion in Paris. In 1948, when US officials were debating whether to recognize the State of Israel, Cohen worked behind the scenes to prod the White House to support the new state. Still, he believed that the United States should focus on winning the war, and he did not make special efforts to rescue European Jews. In a postwar interview, he stated, "To imagine Roosevelt could come up with a magic wand to solve the Jewish problem might be expecting too much. When you are in a dirty war some will suffer more than others." William Lasser, *Benjamin V. Cohen: Architect of the New Deal* (The Century Foundation, 2002), chap. 11, 14–15.

139 Many see Chabad today as a global Jewish powerhouse and have difficulty understanding the small scope and limited resources of Chabad in the early 1940s. The Rebbe's yeshivas in Poland had been devastated, from 1,500 students before the war to fewer than fifty who found refuge first in Lithuania and later in Shanghai. The majority of his students and Chasidim in Poland were suffering under Nazi tyranny, and ultimately, many would be victims of the Holocaust. The largest concentration of Chasidim remained in Soviet Russia, unable to practice their religion freely. In the United States, the actual number of Chasidim probably did not exceed one hundred families. In the war years, the Rebbe had just four small college-level yeshivas with a few hundred students between the United States, *Eretz Yisrael*, Canada, and Shanghai. Unlike his father the Rashab, who had a network of affluent supporters in czarist Russia, the Rebbe did not have many supporters in the US. With limited financial resources, a paucity of political connections, government policy blocking immigration, and opposition by the American Jewish establishment, the Rebbe's ability to orchestrate rescue was severely restricted.

140 Rabbi Feigelstock (1922–2020) came from a non-chasidic religious family in Vienna; he met the Rebbe when he was there for medical treatment in 1933. The Feigelstock family fled Austria with the onset of the war, and Herschel and his brother made their way to England. Arrested as a foreign national, he was interned in Canada, and upon his release he joined the yeshivah. He later became the principal of the Chabad yeshivah in Montreal. See interview with Rabbi Herschel Feigelstock, JEM Oral History Project; Menachem Posner, "Rabbi Herschel Feigelstock, 98, Devoted Montreal Educator For 75 Years," available at: chabad.org/4953637.

141 Professor Jonathan Sarna, *American Judaism* (Yale University, 2004), chap. 5.

142 In 1938, Rabbi Meir Bar Ilan, leader of Mizrachi, the religious Zionists, visited the US and opened a Mizrachi Washington office. This raised the ire of Rabbi Stephen Wise, who orchestrated a condemnation by the Emergency Committee for Zionist

Affairs and forced its closure. Medoff, *Jewish Americans and Political Participation*, chap. 4.

Today, the three major Orthodox groups, Agudath Israel, the Orthodox Union, and Chabad, all have a presence in Washington. Agudah and the OU are active on the political front, advocating for important issues. Chabad retains its policy of nonpartisanship and focuses on educational programs.

143 Stephen Wise (1874–1949) was born in Hungary to an Orthodox family. He immigrated to the US as a child and became a Reform rabbi. A close confidant of FDR, he was the most influential figure in US Jewry in the 1930s and 1940s. The Rebbe had met Wise during his 1929 visit, when Wise visited him on Simchat Torah. The Rebbe refers to him in his correspondence during the 1929–30 US visit a number of times. There are no historical records indicating that Wise assisted with saving the Rebbe from the Nazis, nor any indication that he helped the Rebbe with his efforts to save European Jewry. It seems his door was closed to the Rebbe and to other Orthodox leaders, which forced the Rebbe to find other avenues such as the Quakers to gain access to decision makers in Washington.

144 Peter Bergson (1915–2001) was originally known by the name Hillel Kook. A nephew of Chief Rabbi Avraham Yitzchak Kook, Bergson was a Zionist activist who came to the US in 1940 to organize American Jews to defend Palestine. As the fate of European Jewry became known, he organized protests and stood up to the complacency of liberal Jewish leaders such as Weiss. See Stephanie Flanders, "Peter Bergson, Who Helped European Jews, Dies at 86," available at: https://www.nytimes.com/2001/08/20/us/peter-bergson-who-helped-european-jews-dies-at-86.html.

145 Medoff, *Jewish Americans and Political Participation*, 187.

146 The American Friends Service Committee based in Philadelphia was a pacifist group founded by the Quaker community. While it is unclear how the connection to them was established, it may have been arranged by Rabbi Ephraim Yolles, a prominent Philadelphia rabbi who was close to the Rebbe, or by the Kramer brothers, Chaim Zalman and Avraham Dov.

147 Clarence E. Pickett, head of the AFSC, appealed directly to Mrs. Roosevelt after meeting with "three distinguished Orthodox rabbis of the bearded sort" (apparently referring to the Rashag, Yolles, and another rabbi) on March 4, 1941. Letter from Pickett to Roosevelt dated March 5, 1941.

148 Memorandum #2 for the First Lady Eleanor Roosevelt, March 18, 1941. The document details the request to facilitate the immigration of Chasidim under threat in Soviet-controlled areas, including Latvia and Lithuania. One of those Chasidim, Sholom Levitan, forged many documents for the yeshivah students who escaped via Japan, and he was being held in a Soviet jail in Vilnius. He was later killed by the Nazis.

149 Medoff, *Jewish Americans and Political Participation*, chap. 8.

150 "The United States and the Holocaust: Why Auschwitz Was Not Bombed," available at: https://encyclopedia.ushmm.org/content/en/article/the-united-states-and-the-holocaust-why-auschwitz-was-not-bombed.

151 In response to Klatzkin's call for public demonstrations, the Rebbe writes, "I don't know from demonstrations, and for whom and why," reflecting his view that quiet diplomacy was usually the most effective means of advancing an agenda with government authorities. He lamented the silence and apathy of the media, government, and others. The Rebbe reflects on the Jewish leadership that has lost its way, calling them "false prophets." He also mentions the fate of "children of Tehran" and the group of religious children that the Jewish Agency forced into secular schools in Palestine. Klazkin had influence in Zionist circles; perhaps the Rebbe hoped he would speak up on the issue.

152 Dr. Jacob Klatzkin (1882–1948) came from a rabbinic family. In his youth, he attended yeshivah; later he became a university-educated Jewish scholar, writing extensively on Spinoza. He was a Zionist activist but rejected the concept that the Jewish people were chosen for a special mission. Despite clear theological differences, the Rebbe wrote respectfully of him, referring to him as "a serious person… who has not been infected [with the idea] that in America all is permitted…. [He] searches for truth." *Igrot Kodesh*, vol. 7, letter dated 24 Adar Bet, 5703 (March 31, 1943).

153 The Rebbe quotes from Klatzkin's original letter in his response.

154 Ashley Rindsberg, *The Gray Lady Winked: How The New York Times's Misreporting, Distortions and Fabrications Radically Alter History* (Midnight Oil Publishers, 2021).

155 The Rebbe was not well and was relegated to a wheelchair.

156 The Rebbe was provided with a list of potential delegates for the march and selected the four he wished to attend. The full list of suggested participants is available in the Mindel Archives. See also Partial List of Rabbis in Pilgrimage to Washington, Jabotinsky Archives, Tel Aviv; this list includes the names Gurary, Levitin, Mindel, and Quint.

157 Levitin accompanied the Rebbe on the voyage from Europe. He was a personal assistant to the Rebbe from 1940 to 1946.

158 Dr. Nissan Mindel retained notes with impressions of the day; see the Mindel Archives. See also "When 500 Rabbis Marched in Washington, DC," video available at: https://collive.com/when-500-rabbis-marched-in-washington-dc/.

159 Medoff, *Jewish Americans and Political Participation*, chap. 5.

160 *Sefer HaSichos*, 5702 (Brooklyn, NY: Kehot Publication Society), chap. 12.

161 "Historic Treasures by Rabbi Sholom Ber Schapiro," video available at: https://www.youtube.com/watch?v=Q28r77rwxq8.

162 In February 1943, Wallace met with prominent Zionist leader Rabbi Meir Berlin and refused to acknowledge that European Jews were threatened with extinction; he also failed to recognize Zionism. See Medoff, *Jewish Americans and Political Participation*, 162.

163 *Time*, October 18, 1943.

164 Jewish leaders attempted to deter this effort. New York Jewish Congressman Sol Bloom (who helped save the Rebbe) tried to block the hearings. Wise testified in favor of the War Refugee Board, adding conditions for immigration to Palestine that he knew would torpedo the plan. Privately, he told associates that he was against it and fumed that Bergson had been able to orchestrate these hearings. See Medoff, *Jewish Americans and Political Participation*, chap. 5.

165 At the time of the Rabbis' March, there was a growing awareness in the US of the plight of European Jews. The march and the increasing publicity about the fate of the Jews helped Bergson lobby Congress to call for official US government intervention. This prompted a series of public hearings about creating the War Refugee Board. Secretary of State Breckinridge Long opposed the board. Secretary of the Treasury Henry Morgenthau ultimately convinced the president to authorize it.

166 The Vaad Hatzalah was also involved in rescue efforts. Until this point, its focus had primarily been supporting yeshivah students in war-torn Europe and Japan. Following the march, the focus shifted to efforts to save Jews in Europe.

167 Rabbi Lipa Steimetz had been living in Paris adjacent to the Ramash, who advised Steimetz to seek refuge in the Dominican Republic in 1939. A prominent scholar and *mohel*, he built up Jewish life on the island, reaching out to the Rebbe in 1940. The Rebbe responded with a series of ten questions about the state of Jewish affairs on the island and pledged his assistance; he remained in contact with the community.

168 The Kindertransport brought children from Nazi-controlled Europe to Britian; some of the children were later transferred to Canada. See "Kindertransport, 1938–40," available at: https://encyclopedia.ushmm.org/content/en/article/kindertransport-1938-40.

169 *Igrot Kodesh*, vol. 6, letter to Rabbi Shumel Levitin dated 26 Cheshvan, 5702 (November 16, 1941).

170 One thousand Jewish refugees, many of them concentration camp survivors, were admitted to the US and placed in the camp in Oswego. The refugees arrived on August 5, 1944, and eleven days later, on August 16, the Rebbe's delegation visited the camp to meet with them. The camp was established by the War Relocation Authority, which had operated camps for Japanese refugees during the war; this was the only camp for Europeans. The refugees were not given US immigration status. When the camp was closed in 1946, some refugees remained in the US, some reunited with their families in Europe, and some immigrated to Israel. See *Token*

Shipment: The Story of America's War Refugee Shelter, United States Department of Interior, *kovetz* Lubavitch 4, cited in Levin, *Toldot Chabad BeArtzot HaBrit,* 385. See also "The Secret History of America's Only WWII Refugee Camp," available at: https://www.nytimes.com/2020/09/11/nyregion/oswego-jewish-refugees-world-war-two.html.

171 *Igrot Kodesh,* vol. 5, letter dated 15 Kislev, 5701 (January 14, 1941). In 1940, the British shipped a large group of Jewish German refugees to Australia, where they were interned. See "Refugee Internment," available at: https://ergo.slv.vic.gov.au/explore-history/australia-wwii/home-wii/refugee-internment.

172 The seventh Rebbe took the lead in assisting the Rebbe during his many medical treatments in Europe. In the same talk, he states that a certain medical consultation took place "eighteen years before his passing." It seems he is referring to the period that the Rebbe was receiving medical care in Berlin. Transcript, *farbrengen,* 13 Tishrei, 5738.

173 In Riga, despite reservations, the Rebbe supported the local Orthodox schools that integrated secular and religious subjects. He still greatly favored the classic *cheder* system of exclusive religious education, but in the US he chose a strategy of building schools that offered both religious and secular studies.

174 The Jewish school system was an official part of the educational programs in Latvia. Hodakov was a government employee and responsible for overseeing all Jewish schools in the country.

175 As retold by Rabbi Yehuda Krinsky. "I worked side by side with Rabbi Hodakov for many years," Krinsky said. "Once he recalled to me about the time he was on the ship with the Rebbe." *Umaleh Haaretz Farbrengens* (Brooklyn, NY: Office of the Kinus Hashluchim, 2022), 235.

176 Hodakov was supposed to come to the United States for a short while. "I had not taken vacation for three years, so I had accumulated vacation time," he recalled. The Rebbe urged him to use that time now. He did, leaving behind his wedding gifts and other possessions. The trip "turned out to be my salvation." Shortly after his arrival in the US, Latvia was invaded by Russia and then Germany. See family Chanukah recording of Rabbi Hodakov.

177 *Sefer HaSichos,* 5702, address to male and female teachers, Chicago.

178 For a history of the initiatives to improve Hebrew schools in the non-Orthodox community, see Jonathan Krasner, *The Benderly Boys and American Jewish Education* (Brandeis University Press, 2011).

179 Kaploun, trans., *Sefer HaSichos,* 5702, chap. 13.

180 Hecht, *My Spiritual Journey.*

181 Kaploun, trans., *Sefer HaSichos,* 5702, chap. 13.

182 *The Wonder Rabbi.*

183 *Igrot Kodesh* 8:221, letter to "my dear students" dated 12 Adar, 5704 (March 7, 1944). The Rebbe writes that those who want to be "*mekusharim* (bound to him as Chasidim) must make an effort to assist in one of the institutions I have established… to make their environment filled with the light of Torah and *yiras Shamayim* (G-d-fearing spirit)."

184 Each of these ideologies had its own solution. Many Jews were drawn away from observance and stood at the leadership of these causes. See David Biale, et al., *Hasidism: A New History* (Princeton University Press, 2018).

185 *Igrot Kodesh*, vol. 6, letter to Yosef Flier dated 24 Tevet, 5703 (January 1, 1943).

186 The seventh Rebbe would also face internal resistance in the early years of his leadership. Some Chabad parents were not enthusiastic about his plan to send their children to communities across the globe. While the sixth Rebbe tasked students with specific missions, such as opening a school or becoming the rabbi of an existing synagogue, the seventh Rebbe broadened this by instructing the couples he began dispatching in the late 1950s to transform their new communities with whatever was needed. That could mean revitalizing existing institutions or building new ones from the ground up. He charged them with the responsibility for the welfare of every Jew. As Rabbi Hodakov famously told a young rabbi heading out to a new community, "If there are a hundred Jews there and you have reached ninety-nine, you have not completed your mission." Both the sixth and seventh Rebbes created a new paradigm in Jewish leadership, sending young couples rooted in the teachings of Torah to be Jewish leaders. Permanent emissaries were always couples.

The women, too, were entrusted with equal responsibility in these missions, propelling women to a larger Jewish leadership role that shattered historical stereotypes.

187 Author's interview with Avraham Hecht.

188 Author's interview with Elye Gross's son Noochie.

189 There was a debate between the Rebbe and other prominent rabbinic scholars. The Rebbe's priority was to abate assimilation in the US. Once his students had developed broad Jewish knowledge, he wanted them to take responsibility for the Jewish destiny. Other rabbinic scholars argued that the most important goal was to establish in the US great centers of learning; they felt it was important for students to remain in yeshivah for a longer period of time. This led to the development of kollels, centers of learning where married yeshivah students spent many years. This debate reflected historical differences reaching back centuries: On one side were the teachings of Rabbi Yisrael Baal Shem Tov, who stressed the spiritual potential of every Jew. On the other side was the belief of classic Lithuanian yeshivas that the pursuit of scholarship by an elite would ensure the Jewish future. Author's interview with Hecht.

190 Yaakov Ort, "Rabbi Mordechai Altein, 100, a Leading Chabad Rabbi in North America," available at chabad.org/4567611.
191 Author's interview with Altein.
192 The nineteenth of Kislev is a chasidic holiday marking the release of Chabad's founder from czarist prison.
193 *Igrot Kodesh*, vol. 6, letter to Schiff dated third night of Chanukah 5702 (December 16, 1941).
194 *Igrot Kodesh*, vol. 6, letter to Altein dated third night of Chanukah 5702 (December 16, 1941).
195 *Igrot Kodesh* 6:180–81, letters to Altein and the community dated 3 Shevat, 5702 (January 21, 1942). From the letters it seems the Rebbe sent Rabbi Jacobson to Pittsburgh to restructure the Chabad organization and prepare the way for Altein to begin a variety of programs.
196 Rabbi Sholom Posner was born in 1895 and died in 1994.
197 Leibel Estrin, "Righteous Lives," available at: https://www.academia.edu/40639749/RIGHTEOUS_LIVES_THE_STORY_OF_RABBI_SHOLOM_AND_REBBETZIN_CHAYA_POSNER_AND_THE_YESHIVA_SCHOOLS.
198 Interviews with Rabbi Sholom and Chaya Posner conducted by the National Council of Jewish Women in 1974. Audio recording available at: https://historicpittsburgh.org/islandora/object/pitt:ais196440.353.
199 Miriam Rosenblum recalls that Chaya Posner told this story at a convention of Chabad women in Pittsburgh. Interview with JEM, Oral History Project.
200 Today the yeshivah has more than four hundred students on two campuses in Pittsburgh.
201 Shlomo Zalman, Moshe Yitzchak, Avraham, and Yankel (J.J.) all became rabbis. Shalom opened a Judaica bookstore, and Peretz was a businessman.
202 Rivkah Hecht nee Krinsky was born in 1919 and died in 2010. For more information, see "Senior Chabad Representative, Mrs. Rivkah Hecht, 91," available at: https://www.lubavitch.com/senior-chabad-representative-mrs-rivkah-hecht-91/.
203 Author's interview with Rivkah Hecht.
204 This was a major innovation. In Europe, Chabad did not operate schools for girls. Perhaps the Rebbe felt it was not needed in Poland due to other schools that had been opened along the lines of the one established by Sarah Schenirer.
205 Author's interview with Rivkah Hecht.
206 Released Time began in Indiana in 1914. By 1922, the program was in twenty-three states. In New York the statute approving Released Time was signed into law on April 9, 1940 by Governor Lehman. In November that year, the Board of Education of the City of New York published regulations for program. See *Shiurei Limud HaDas* (Brooklyn, NY: Kehot Publication Society, 2006), appendix.
207 *Shiurei Limud HaDas*, chap. 2.

208 Ibid., letter dated 19 Shevat, 5703 (February 14, 1943).

209 Saul Adelson, "How Can Jewish Children Be Given a Jewish Education?" in *Jewish Life*, February 1946.

210 "Central Conference of American Rabbis Opposed 'Released Time' in Public Schools," JTA, June 27, 1947, available at: https://www.jta.org/archive/central-conference-of-american-rabbis-opposes-released-time-in-public-schools.

211 "Opposition to Released Time Religious Teaching Voiced at Jewish Congress Parley," JTA, January 20, 1949, available at: https://www.jta.org/archive/opposition-to-released-time-religious-teaching-voiced-at-jewish-congress-parley.

212 "Jewish Organizations File Brief in N.Y. Court Against Release Time Program in Schools," JTA, June 1, 1951, available at: https://www.jta.org/archive/jewish-organizations-file-brief-in-n-y-court-against-release-time-program-in-schools.

213 In 1952, the Supreme Court ruled in Zorach v. Clauson with Justice William Douglas writing for the majority, "The Released Time program involves neither religious instruction in public school classrooms nor the expenditure of public funds." Justice Felix Frankfurter, who was Jewish, was in the minority that did not support Released Time in public schools. See Zorach v. Clauson, https://www.oyez.org/cases/1940-1955/343us306. To read the court's decision, see *Shiurei Limud HaDas*, appendix.

214 *Igrot Kodesh* 9:205, letter dated Tu BeShevat 5707 (February 5, 1947).

215 Interview with Rabbi Yitzchok Groner, JEM Oral History Project.

216 The first Lag BaOmer parade was held in 1953 on Eastern Parkway. See Phreddy Nosanwisch, "Recalling Lag BaOmer 1953, Montreal Rabbi Marches On," available at: chabad.org/3672868.

217 E.L. Tenenbaum, *Rabbi J.J. Hecht* (Mosaica Press, 2022), 37.

218 Even then, the strategy was profoundly different from that of Chabad, which sends young couples to communities devoid of religious structure with a mandate to build from the bottom up. The approach of the Lithuanian yeshivah community to outreach is to establish kollels, centers of learning, with a group of young couples. These centers are usually only in areas with an existing Orthodox community. In essence, it is an extension of their worldview of "fortress Judaism," much like the idea of the US cavalry creating forts on the prairie during the Indian wars. Chabad rabbis and rebbetzins create new communities in the areas they move to and become an integral part of those communities. In more recent years, the yeshivah community has set up outreach programs at universities. Here their strategy is dramatically different than Chabad. They attempt to enroll as many students as possible in study programs in Israel and other locations. Chabad campus centers, on the other hand, are an essential part of Jewish life on campus, creating many gateways for Jewish identity by designing programs that reflect the needs of the students while encouraging a stronger bond with tradition. While Chabad also

promotes Jewish study programs in yeshivas, it connects all Jewish students with their heritage. Other outreach programs, such as the flagship teen network NCSY, created by the Orthodox Union, would not be established until the 1950s. As a rule, NCSY is based in existing Orthodox synagogues. It does outstanding work bolstering Jewish identity among teens, including public school students.

219 Author's interview with Rivkah Hecht.

220 The remarkable success of Jewish learning is reflected in the vast numbers studying Torah today in such yeshivas as Lakewood, proving that the insular approach has great merit. At the same time, these institutions have a marginal influence on Jewish life beyond their communities.

221 Sarna, *American Judaism* (New Haven, CT: Yale University Press, 2004), chap. 5.

222 Many of those schools established by the Rebbe, such as in Pittsburgh, Worcester, and Boston, continue till today. Others closed after a time. Merkos L'Inyonei Chinuch established a network of girls' schools in tandem with the yeshivas. For a detailed overview of the system the Rebbe founded, see Levin, *Toldot Chabad BeArtzot HaBrit,* chap. 41–58.

223 Jung was one of the leading Orthodox rabbis of the first half of the twentieth century, eventually serving as rabbi of the Jewish Center in New York. He was active in the construction of aesthetically pleasing *mikvehs*. See Dovi Safier, "Man of Action: The Life & Times of Rabbi Leo Jung," available at: https://mishpacha.com/man-of-action/.

224 *Igrot Kodesh* 5:41, letter dated Purim 5700 (March 25, 1940). The Rebbe had written to Jung on other occasions. While he was in Riga, he sent him a letter thanking him for his efforts to help him escape from Warsaw. Lookstein was a prominent modern Orthodox New York rabbi. Neither was part of the chasidic community. The Rebbe's involvement reflects an interest in advancing traditional Judaism in a variety of ways. It's difficult to ascertain why the Rebbe felt he should prod Jung in particular to help with the project. Perhaps the Rebbe's personal interest would inspire him to assist with a project that it seems he had been hesitant to support.

225 While Rabbi Shraga Feivel Mendlowitz came from a chasidic background and for years gave a class in *Tanya,* he was not a Chabad follower. He had great respect for the Rebbe but differed with him on many issues. He made a donation to the opening of Tomchei Temimim in the US. According to Avraham Hecht, when some Torah Vodaath students transferred to the newly opened Chabad yeshivah, he was dismayed. To a degree, Torah Vodaath was in competition with the newly opened US Chabad yeshivah, but the Rebbe saw the greater value of Torah and recognized the unique role of Torah Vodaath as a vital center of Jewish learning. See Jacobson, *Zikhron Livnei Yisrael*; Dalfin, *Lakewood and Lubavitch.*

226 The exact date of the crisis remains unclear. It seems to have occurred in the early 1940s; Rabbi Shmuel Knopfler says it was 1941. Interview with Knopfler, JEM Oral History Project.

227 Rabbi Shmuel Kuselewitz was the author of *Netivot Shmuel* and ordained the rabbis at Yeshivah Torah Vodaath. The yeshivah conducted an annual memorial program on the yahrzeit of Rabbi Shlomo Hyman (1893–1944), who became *rosh yeshivah* of Torah Vodaath in 1936. At the 1958 memorial, Kuselewitz recalled that the Rebbe had lauded Rabbi Hyman as a true scholar. He then shared the story of how the Rebbe intervened to save the yeshivah. Kuselewitz had an affinity for Chabad and made a bequest to Chabad yeshivas in his will. See Dalfin, *Lakewood and Lubavitch,* chap. 4.

228 Mayer Plotkin, a student of Torah Vodaath at that time, was present at the speech. He says he and his fellow students were surprised to hear the story. Interview with Plotkin, JEM Oral History Project.

229 Rabbi Shmuel Knopfler verified the story of the Rebbe's role in saving the yeshivah with Rabbi Yosef Wilner, who served as principal of Torah Vodaath when Knopfler's son attended school there in 2002. Interview with JEM Oral History Project.

230 Shortly before he passed away on September 7, 1948 (3 Elul), Mendlowitz told the story to a group of close friends who had gathered at his bedside. He said he did not want to take the secret to his grave. See Rabbi Shmuel Knopfler, "Lubavitcher Rebbe Saved Yeshivah Torah Vodaas from Foreclosure," available at: https://dusiznies.blogspot.com/2016/06/lubavitcher-rebbe-saved-yeshiva-torah.html. For additional details, see Dalfin, *Lakewood and Lubavitch,* chap. 1; JEM Oral History Project interview with Knopfler.

231 "About Our History," available at: https://www.ariecrown.org/apps/pages/index.jsp?uREC_ID=274544&type=d&pREC_ID=547914.

232 *Igrot Kodesh,* vol. 12, letter to Nachum Dovber Reisch dated 2 Elul, 5700 (September 5, 1940). This volume includes extensive correspondence to Jewish leaders in Chicago about the school.

233 The exceptionally long letter – ten pages – is replete with encouragement to strengthen Judaism in Chicago. *Igrot Kodesh* 8:31, letter dated 12 Marcheshvan, 5704 (November 10, 1943).

234 JEM Oral History Project interview with Ephraim Fishel Katz, nephew of Yaakov Katz.

235 Rabbi Yosef Dov Soloveitchik (1903–83) was born in Russia to a distinguished rabbinic family. His grandfather was Rabbi Chaim Brisker and his great-grandfather was the Netziv, Rabbi Naftali Tzvi Yehudah Berlin. Rabbi Yosef Dov studied in Berlin under Rabbi Chaim Heller and received a doctorate in 1932. That year he immigrated to the US, settling in Boston. As *rosh yeshivah* of Yeshiva University, Rabbi Soloveitchik would emerge as one of the leading rabbinic figures in postwar

Jewry, ordaining over two thousand rabbis. See Rabbi Aaron Rakeffet, *The Rav: The World of Rabbi Joseph B. Soloveitchik* (Ktav Publishing).

236 The Rebbe's intervention to secure the appointment of Rabbi Soloveitchik is more interesting because there is no question that the Rebbe's views on Torah study were different than those advocated by Yeshiva University. In college-age Chabad yeshivas, there is no secular education; it's a classic approach to Jewish learning with an exclusive focus on Torah study. Yeshiva University departed from that model by integrating college-level academics with Torah study. Many leading rabbis were highly critical of this innovation. Still, the Rebbe, while not endorsing the educational philosophy of Yeshiva University, took a different view. It seems he wanted to ensure that YU would be the best institution possible and that it would be led by an outstanding scholar like Rabbi Soloveitchik. The Rebbe visited YU during his 1929 trip to the US, according to Rabbi Zevulun Charlop, former dean of YU. He says that his father "brought the Frierdiker Rebbe to Yeshivas Rabbeinu Yitzchak Elchonon (YU)." The Rebbe had been invited by Dr. Revel, and he gave "a very good *shiur*." Interview with Rabbi Zevulun Charlop, JEM Oral History Project.

237 Rabbi Soloveitchik shared with Rabbi Chaim Cement, a Chabad rabbi in Boston, a humorous anecdote from the time he spent with the Ramash in Berlin. One Purim, the Rebbe was celebrating until late into the night, and he went out to speak publicly in the street. This caused a disruption, and he was arrested; his friend Soloveitchik was contacted to bail him out. When the Ramash was freed, Rabbi Soloveitchik remarked to him that his great-grandfather Rabbi Menachem Mendel, the third Rebbe, had been in prison, and other Chabad rabbis had also been in prison. Now that he had been in prison too, one day he could become a Rebbe! (The first three Rebbes of Chabad were imprisoned in czarist Russia, and the sixth Rebbe was imprisoned by the czarist regime and the Communists.) See "Purim in Berlin," video available at: chabad.org/640817.

238 Rabbi Sholem Kowalsky, a student of Rabbi Soloveitchik, assisted him with many of his personal affairs. He writes, "The Rav told me that he was a great admirer of the Rebbe. He said that their relationship began when they met in Berlin where they were both studying at the University of Berlin. During that period, they would often meet at the home of the Torah scholar Rabbi Chaim Heller. It was in the course of these meetings that a strong friendship developed between the two men, both of whom were destined to become outstanding spiritual leaders of the century." See Sholem Kowalsky, "The Rebbe and the Rav," available at: chabad.org/529444. See also David Holzer, *The Rav: Thinking Aloud* (Holzer Seforim, 2009).

239 Rabbi Dr. Aaron Rakeffet, one of the leading students of the Rav, documents his conversations with the Rav about both the sixth and seventh Rebbes. See Rakeffet, "The Rebbe and the Rav," available at: https://jewishaction.com/jewish-world/people/rebbe-rav/.

240 Rakeffet, *The Rav.*

241 Yeshiva University Archives.

242 By using the term "*gaon*" the Rebbe was endorsing Rabbi Soloveitchik as a world-class scholar.

243 Dalfin, *Lakewood and Lubavitch,* chap. 7.

244 In that letter, the Rebbe recalled his father sharing a *maamar* with Soloveitchik's grandfather, Reb Chaim Brisker, whom the Rebbe held in great esteem. Chasidic historian Chaim Dalfin opines that "the Rebbe wanted to impress on him that the number one thing he should be concerned about as a newly appointed *rosh yeshivah* was to instill in his students a G-d-fearing spirit." See Dalfin, *Lakewood and Lubavitch,* chap. 7; *Igrot Kodesh* 5:345.

245 *Igrot Kodesh* 6:253, letter to Irving Bunim dated 29 Adar, 5702 (March 18, 1942).

246 This remarkable letter begins with recollecting the visit of the Rebbe Rashab in Paris, where Herzog's father (a distinguished rabbi) and mother acted with kindness – "your mother baking challah" for the Rebbe Rashab. He recalls that the Rebbe Rashab had told him that he was impressed when he met the "young Rabbi Herzog in Paris. He is a clear-thinking Torah scholar who not only has vast Torah knowledge but also languages and wisdom [i.e. secular education]." The Rebbe had the letter hand-delivered by one of his prominent Chasidim "who has no knowledge of its contents" and told Herzog that once he read the letter, he should seal it and return it. *Igrot Kodesh,* vol. 5, letter dated 25 Adar, 5701 (March 24, 1941).

247 A telegram from the Rebbe to Rabbi David De Sola Pool of the Jewish Welfare Board (JWB) dated March 9, 1943 expresses concern about a Purim celebration being held in Camp Grant at which milk and meat were to be served together. This communication prompted a series of letters and telegrams between the Rebbe and the JWB that caused the event to be modified according to Jewish tradition. The JWB also clarified that the event was not actually sponsored by the JWB, but rather by the local B'nai Brith chapter and the United Service Organizations (USO). Subsequently, the Rebbe wrote a long letter to the JWB about the need to provide proper religious services, qualified chaplains, and prayer books to Jewish serviceman. Letter dated April 4, 1943 (28 Adar Bet, 5703), author's archive.

248 On February 18, 1943, a total of 1,228 refugee children arrived in Palestine. Russia permitted the transit of these children as a result of the Stalin-Sikorski agreement between Poland and Russia.

249 Zvi Zameret, *The Melting Pot in Israel: The Commission of Inquiry Concerning the Education of Immigrant Children During the Early Years of the State* (State University of New York Press, 2002).

250 Zameret, *The Melting Pot,* chap. 1.

251 Rabbi Avraham Mordechai Alter (1865–1948), also known as the Imrei Emes.

252 Letter to Agudas Chassidei Chabad, also sent to Orthodox leaders, dated 24 Adar Bet, 5703 (March 31, 1943).

253 *Igrot Kodesh*, vol. 6, public letter dated 20 Adar Bet, 5703 (April 5, 1943).

254 "Rabbis Protest the Settling of Refugee Children in Non-religious Colony," JTA, March 7, 1943, available at: https://www.jta.org/archive/rabbis-protest-the-settling-of-refugee-children-in-non-religious-colony.

255 Cable to Agudas Harabonim, April 7, 1943 (2 Nisan, 5703).

256 *Igrot Kodesh*, vol. 6, letter to Rabbi Herzog, including a list of the rabbis, dated 23 Iyar, 5703 (May 28, 1943). See also "Lubavitcher Rebbe Wants Jewish Refugee Children Placed in Religious Institutions," JTA, May 4, 1943, available at: https://www.jta.org/archive/lubavitcher-rebbe-wants-jewish-refugee-children-placed-in-religious-institutions.

257 Letter with a series of proposals "To the Committee of Rabbis" dated 25 Av, 1943 (August 26, 1943). The actual meeting of Jewish leaders was held at the Rebbe's office on September 6, 1943 (6 Elul, 5703). The follow-up letter, dated 19 Elul, 5703 (September 19, 1943) includes minutes of the meeting.

258 "Rabbis Protest the Settling of Refugee Children in Non-Religious Colony," JTA, March 7, 1943, available at: https://www.jta.org/archive/chief-rabbi-of-england-supports-palestine-rabbis-in-conflict-with-jewish-agency.

259 The public controversy prompted the Jewish Agency to create a Commission of Inquiry in 1943. It was heavily criticized for a lack of objectivity. In 1950, due to the insistence of the religious community, the government set up a second investigation called the Frumkin Commission. It was chaired by Gad Frumkin, whose father was a Chabad Chasid who had welcomed the Rebbe during his 1929 Palestine visit. Frumkin was a judge on the Supreme Court under the British Mandate. The commission reviewed the actions of the Jewish Agency in regard to the children of Tehran, as well as immigrant children from Yemen and other countries. Among its conclusions was that "it was a fatal error" to have secular teachers. It also found that accusations such as the forcible removal of *peyos* and interference with religious studies were true. It noted that the policies toward the children were driven by "a desire to prepare the immigrants and the youth for membership in the Histadrut (the Labor Zionist Workers organization) and not to strengthen the religious parties." See Zameret, *The Melting Pot*, book 2 for the full report.

260 In 1942, the JDC allocated for $334,000 for Polish refugees, primarily in Russia and Persia (many Polish Jews made their way overland to Persia). However, they did not fund projects for Russian Jews, claiming in their annual report "that J.D.C per se was unable to conduct any program on behalf of Russian Jews. Its officers, directors, and contributors have, in their individual and private capacities, supported the work of the Russian War Relief Society, which has appealed to all Americans." Report Aiding Jews Overseas, 1942. JDC Archives, folder 158, Administrative Reports.

261 *Igrot Kodesh* 6:215, letter to the JDC headquarters in New York, dated 12 Adar, 5702 (March 1, 1942). During this period, the Rebbe had extensive correspondence (see *Igrot Kodesh*, vol. 6) with many Jewish groups to pressure the JDC to change its policy. This included Young Israel, Agudath Israel, the Zionist Federation, and notable public figures such as Chief Rabbi Isaac Herzog. At the time, the United States and Russia were allies, and the Rebbe believed that with the proper approach, they would permit direct aid to Russian Jews from the JDC, as it was nonpartisan and already active in Russia in helping Polish Jews.

262 The Rebbe argued that the JDC should galvanize American Jewish groups. See letter to the JDC (New York) dated 15 Adar, 5702 (March 4, 1942); *Igrot Kodesh* 6:230–32, letter to Rabbi Ephraim Yolles dated 16 Adar, 5702 (March 5, 1942).

263 Letter to Ephraim Yolles dated 24 Adar 5702 (March 13, 1942). The Rebbe wrote that the JDC should have begun efforts to assist Russian Jews months earlier. "We will sit and eat at our tables in peace and our brothers and sisters will sit crying without a piece of matzah."

264 JDC press release dated September 24, 1947, "JDC Sends 27 Rabbis to Dublin." Interview with Rabbi Benjamin Gorodetsky, "The JDC sends Lubowitscher *shochtim* to prepare kosher meat for the survivors." JDC Archives.

265 Levine, *Treasures of the Chabad Library*, chap. 19.

266 Rabbi Yaakov Yisrael Twerski was a chasidic Rebbe in Milwaukee from Hornistopoli in Russia. *Igrot Kodesh*, vol. 13, letter dated Cheshvan 5705 (October 1944).

267 *Igrot Kodesh* 8:238, letter dated 21 Cheshvan, 5705 (November 10, 1944).

268 The heart attack took place on 26 Cheshvan, 5705 (November 12, 1944). See Levine, *Treasures of the Chabad Library*.

269 At the beginning of the summer of 1945, Rabbi Shlomo Aharon Kazarnofsky visited Montreal to raise funds to install air conditioning in the Rebbe's apartment during the humid summer, a very costly undertaking at the time. The doctors felt it would be a great help to the Rebbe's health, which was still precarious. During the Montreal visit, Kazarnofsky told Rabbi Yitzchak Hendel about the letter that had precipitated the Rebbe's heart attack. Memoir of Rabbi Yitzchak Hendel.

270 Riga's Choral Synagogue was burned on July 4, 1941, with many Jews locked inside. A government memorial with senior government officials is held annually on the site of the ruined synagogue. It is unclear if the initial report the Rebbe received stating that the Chasidim were killed in the synagogue was correct, or if they were murdered in a nearby concentration camp.

271 *Igrot Kodesh*, vol. 8, letter addressed to "My dear friends *anash* and the lovers of disseminating Torah, G-d-fearing spirit, and strengthening Judaism," dated 24 Kislev, 5705 (November 10, 1944).

272 Levine, *Treasures of the Chabad Library*, diary entry dated 7 Tevet, 5705 (December 23, 1944).

273 Ibid., diary entry dated 18 Cheshvan, 5705 (November 4, 1944); *Sefer HaMaamarim*, 5705.

274 *Igrot Kodesh*, vol. 8, letter dated 15 Tevet, 5705 (December 31, 1944); Kaploun, trans., *Sefer HaSichos*, 5705, appendix A.

275 Harold Berman, *Toronto Hebrew Journal*, June 10, 1945.

CHAPTER ELEVEN

1 Rabbi Moshe Chaim Yehoshua Schneersohn-Twerski (1867–1957) was a descendant of the second Rebbe, Rabbi Dovber. He immigrated to the United States in 1924 and lived on Eastern Parkway near the Rebbe's shul.

2 *Igrot Kodesh*, vol. 9, letter to "My dear beloved students from Poland," sent upon their arrival in the US from Shanghai, dated 15 Av, 5706 (August 12, 1946).

3 *Igrot Kodesh*, vol. 10, letter dated 7 Shevat, 5700 (January 25, 1950).

4 Telz was one of the outstanding centers of Jewish scholarship in Poland. For a history of the yeshivah, see Shmuel Natanowitz, "The Telshe Yeshivah – Its Rabbis and Its Institutions," available at: https://www.jewishgen.org/yizkor/Telsiai/tel057.html.

5 Rabbi Chaim Gutnick (1921–2003) was born in Ukraine and raised in London, where his father was the rabbi of the Chabad synagogue. Gutnick would emerge as one of the most influential rabbis in Australia. He founded the Rabbinical Council of Australia and Elwood Talmud Torah Hebrew Congregation. His children and grandchildren have continued his legacy and are leading rabbis in the country. For more on the Gutnick family, see "Memento from the Wedding of Yaakov and Chaya Basya Gurkov," available at: https://collive.com/wp-content/uploads/2019/08/Master-GUTNIK-26-Av-5779-ENGLISH.pdf.

6 The students had received visas from the Japanese consul in Kovno, Chiune Sugihara. They were led by Rabbi Chaim Stein, who settled in Cleveland. See Hana Levi Julian, "Telshe Y. Rabbi Chaim Stein, 98," available at: https://www.israelnationalnews.com/news/145319.

7 Rabbis Mordechai Katz and Eliyahu Meir Bloch, *roshei yeshivah* of Telz, traveled to the US in 1940 to explore options for relocating the yeshivah. They chose Cleveland and reopened Telz there in October 1941. The group of ten students who came via Australia were the nucleus for the rebirth of Telz on American soil.

8 His father, Rabbi Schneur Gutnick, passed away in London in 1931 when he was just eleven. Rabbi Yechezkel Abramsky took an interest in the orphan and encouraged his attendance at Telz. He joined after his mother received a blessing from the Rebbe for him to join the yeshivah.

9 Author's interview with Chaim Gutnick.

10 Ibid. For an amazing story about Rabbi Gutnick and the seventh Rebbe, see "Video of Rabbi Chaim Gutnick Z"L in 2000," available at: https://elirab.me/video-of-rabbi-chaim-gutnick-zl-in-2000/.

11 After the war, the students of Mir were instrumental in the rebirth of the yeshivah, both in New York and Israel. The influence of the Mirrer students was felt in many parts of the American Orthodox community. Rabbi Dr. Aaron Rakeffet recalls that the Shanghai students of the Mir Yeshivah had a powerful impact on him as a young student at Yeshiva University. He recalls, "We had never seen real European yeshivah students in America, and they became role models" for his generation at YU. Aaron Rakeffet, *From Washington Avenue to Washington Street* (Gefen Publishing, 2011).

12 Author's interview with Azriel Chaikin.

13 *Igrot Kodesh*, vol. 9, letter to Rabbi Shmuel Levitin dated 8 Tevet, 1946 (December 12, 1945). For a facsimile of the letter, see Rabbi Binyamin Gorodetsky, *Light in the Darkness* (New York: Sheingold Publishers, 1986), 91.

14 Rabbi Shalom Friedland, *Pe'ilut Chotzei Gevulot* (Kfar Chabad, Israel: Kehot Publication Society), chap. 3.

15 Gorodetsky, *Light in the Darkness*, chap. 11.

16 Gorodetsky, *Light in the Darkness*, chap. 12.

17 Permission was needed from Ovir, the division of the Ministry of Internal Affairs that issued exit visas.

18 Brichah, Hebrew for "fleeing," was an organized effort by Holocaust survivors in Europe and Zionist activists from Palestine. Their heroic activities saved many lives. Rebbetzin Chaya Mushka Schneerson called them "*tzaddikim* that did not put on tefillin." Zvi Nesher describes the interaction of Brichah with Chabad: "The Bricha men were amazed by their ingenious escape from Russia and very impressed by the discipline, the sense of solidarity, and the reverence for their Rebbe in New York." Ephraim Dekel, *Briha: Flight to the Homeland* (New York: Herzl Press), chap. 6.

19 Such a large convocation was unprecedented. Usually, rabbinical courts consist of three judges; at times, of five. The gravity of the situation and the risk of death demanded a serious deliberation based on Jewish law.

20 For lists of those who succeeded in leaving Russia, see Friedland, *Pe'ilut Chotzei Gevulot*.

21 The gathering took place on May 18, 1947.

22 *Yemei Melekh*, vol. 3, chap. 5; Friedland, *Pe'ilut Chotzei Gevulot*. The story was also recounted by Efraim Zalman Sudakevitch, who was at the *farbrengen* in Paris. Numerous other attendees of the *farbrengen* have retold this story as well.

23 *Igrot Kodesh*, vol. 9, letter "To *anash* and the students of Tomchei Temimim" dated 15 Kislev, 5707 (December 8, 1946).

24 *Igrot Kodesh*, vol. 9, letter "To my dear student Rabbi Binyamin" dated 15 Kislev, 5707 (December 8, 1946).

25 The office became known in the Chabad community as "the *lishkah*" (the bureau) and continues to operate today. See https://www.loubavitchfrance.fr/.

26 *Igrot Kodesh* 14:393–94; Rabbi Eliyahu Matosov, *HaYetziah MiRusia* (Israel, 2019), 202–3.

27 January 28, 1947.

28 Mendel Futerfus (1907–95) was a legendary figure in the Chabad community. He played a leading role in the secret Jewish underground in Russia. After his arrest, he was sentenced to nine years in prison. On May 7, 1947 (17 Iyar, 5707). Futerfas was brought into interrogation. Years later, he told his grandson Yosef Yitzchak Liberov that at that moment of crisis he envisioned himself writing a letter to the Rebbe asking for a blessing, conjuring up the image of the last time he saw the Rebbe on Simchat Torah in Leningrad in 1927, the day before the Rebbe departed from Russia. Shortly afterward, Futerfas's wife, who had escaped Russia, received a letter addressed to Reb Mendel, dated 17 Iyar, 5707, beginning with the words "Your telegram has been received." Confused, she thought that perhaps her husband had escaped Russia and been able to send a telegram to New York. In the fall of 1963, the Soviet Union allowed Reb Mendel to reunite with his wife and children, who lived in England. When his wife showed him the letter that had always perplexed her, Reb Mendel recounted how during the interrogation, he had conjured up the image of the Rebbe and imagined himself sending a letter to the Rebbe. On that same day, the Rebbe responded to Reb Mendel, as if an actual telegram had been sent from prison. Interview with Yosef Yitzchak Liberov, JEM Oral History Project.

29 Sara Katzenelenbogen (1880–1952) was a primary organizer of the Great Escape. After the Russians assassinated her husband Michoel in 1937, she took a lead in financing the clandestine Chabad educational network in Russia. Russian authorities put her on the most wanted list; she was eventually captured in Uzbekistan. She died in prison of a heart attack.

30 Dovid Margolin, "Memo to Secret Police Chief Reveals Hunt for Chabad's Soviet Underground," available at: chabad.org/5619816.

31 Letter to Rabbi Shalom Mendel Kalmenson dated 8 Iyar, 5707 (April 28, 1947). The letter appears in Shalom Ber Levin, *Toldot Chabad BeRusia HaSovietit* (Brooklyn, NY: Kehot Publication Society, 1989), chap. 117.

32 *Avnei Chein: History of the Chein Family Dynasty* (Kehot Publication Society, 2020), chap. 22.

33 For the full details of the remarkable clandestine effort to free the three prisoners from jail in Russia, see the letter to Kalmenson in Levin, *Toldot Chabad BeRusia HaSovietit*.

34 Author's interview with Yehudis Groner.

35 Shula Kazen (1922–2019) was brought up in Russia. Her father was arrested in 1937 and never seen again. Her mother-in-law was the legendary Sara Katzenelenbogen. In 1952, the Kazen family received US visas and wanted to settle in Brooklyn's chasidic enclave in Crown Heights. Instead, the seventh Rebbe insisted they live in Cleveland, where they pioneered the Chabad community. See Rebbetzin Shula Kazen with Henya Laine, *The Queen of Cleveland: A Life of Self-Sacrifice and Courage* (Brooklyn, NY: Hasidic Archives, 2022), part 3.

36 The Rebbe sent a series of letters to Jewish leaders and the Chabad community in England asking them to assist Dr. Mindel in his mission. *Igrot Kodesh*, vol. 9, letters dated 14 Elul, 5705 (August 23, 1945) and 15 Elul, 5705 (August 25, 1945).

37 For Jacobson's report on his mission, see Levin, *Toldot Chabad BeRusia HaSovietit*, chap. 117.

38 It was up to the individual Chasid to ask the Rebbe for advice on where to settle. There was no coercion from the Rebbe or the community.

39 Shemtov was sent in October 1947.

40 When Jacobson came to Rostov in 1919, he was on the way to a training program in Italy. The Rashab advised him to stay in the yeshivah in Rostov, telling him, "You will eventually get to Italy." Indeed, he later visited Italy as part of his mission on behalf of the Rebbe, according to his grandson Rabbi Simon Jacobson.

41 In 1949, the Rebbe met with two students of his yeshivah, Shlomo Carlebach and Zalman Schachter, and asked them to go to Brandeis University to reach out to the students. This was the first formal foray of Chabad into college campuses. The seventh Rebbe would greatly expand Chabad's outreach to college students, evolving into a global network of Chabad Houses, starting with UCLA in 1969. Carlebach and Schachter each broke away from the Chabad community in different ways. Carlebach remained observant and developed a new style of Jewish music. Schachter departed from tradition and created the Jewish Renewal movement. Both pushed the boundaries of halakha, creating controversy and setting themselves apart from Chabad. Interview with Schachter about Chabad, available at: https://www.youtube.com/watch?v=E9iJFoeXzD4.

42 Uri Kaploun, *Avraham Avinu of Australia: The Life of Reb Moshe Feiglin* (AAA Publications, 2002).

43 Letter dated 23 Iyar, 5709 (May 22, 1949). In this letter sent to Gurewicz before he departed from Europe for Australia, the Rebbe wished mazel tov to Gurewicz on his son's bar mitzvah, which would be celebrated on board the ship as it was docked in Port Said, Egypt. See Ian Grinblat, *Nachum Zalman Gurewicz: A Life* (Caulfield South, Australia: Makor Jewish Community Library, 2003).

44 Letter dated 17 Elul, 5709 (September 11, 1949). The letter appears in Grinblat, *Nachum Zalman Gurewicz.*

45 *Igrot Kodesh*, vol. 10, letter dated 26 Iyar, 5709 (May 25, 1949).
46 *Igrot Kodesh*, vol. 10, letter dated 7 Marcheshvan, 5709 (November 9, 1948).
47 Letter dated 19 Kislev, 5709 (December 21, 1948). The Rebbe praised Gurewicz after learning about the educational programs he created in Cuba. A few months later, the Rebbe remarked to Rodshtein, "It's time to tell Tzemach to come." He did not arrive in New York until June of 1950, after the Rebbe's passing. Also see "Service & Discretion: The Life and Times of the Legendary Mazkir, Reb Moshe Leib Rodshtein," available at: https://derher.org/wp-content/uploads/105-iyar-5781-9.pdf.
48 *Igrot Kodesh*, vol. 10, letter dated 13 Tamuz, 5709 (July 10, 1949).
49 Interview with Winnie Gourarie, JEM Oral History Project, N'shei Chabad Journal, Nisan 2018. Also see audio recording of Rabbi Aloy speaking at a *farbrengen* (South Africa, 1962) celebrating 12 Tamuz, the anniversary of the Rebbe's release from Russian prison, available at: https://www.youtube.com/watch?v=kd04_J4bLuo&t=1282s.
50 Letter to Rabbi Shalom Mendel Kalmenson dated 8 Iyar, 5707 (April 28, 1947).
51 *Igrot Kodesh*, vol. 9, letter to the Chasidim and students in Paris, 28 Iyar, 5709 (June 3, 1948).
52 Kohen's brother-in-law was the father of yeshivah student Herschel Feigelstock. JEM Oral History Project interview.
53 In that meeting, the Rebbe also told him, "Eventually you will move to *Eretz Yisrael*." Later in life, he relocated there, as the Rebbe had predicted.
54 Grinblat, *Nachum Zalman Gurewicz*.
55 After Gurewicz's passing, Smorgon dedicated a building at the Yeshivah Center in Melbourne in his memory. See Grinblat, *Nachum Zalman Gurewicz*.
56 "Israel's Oldest Charity," available at: chabad.org/2098354.
57 Zalman Shazar (1889–1974) was born Schneur Zalman Rubashov to a Chabad family in Mir, near Minsk in Belorussia. As a young man he became involved in Poalei Tzion, a Zionist group. He immigrated to Palestine in 1924, taking a leadership role in Zionist activities. He was a member of the Zionist Council, the Jewish National Fund, and the Histadrut. In his later years he returned to his chasidic roots, visiting the seventh Rebbe on a variety of occasions, even during his tenure as president, which caused some public controversy. Israeli Diplomat Yehuda Avner accompanied Shazar on one of those visits. He recalled a conversation he had in the limousine with Shazar on the way to Brooklyn. "Golda [referring to Prime Minister Golda Meir] called me today and said, 'The Rebbe should come to the president, not the president to the Rebbe.'" Shazar exclaimed, "But what does Golda understand about a Rebbe!" (Meir came from a secular background). Author's interview with Yehuda Avner.

58 According to Rabbi Shmuel Chefer, a Chabad leader in Israel and a close confidant of Shazar, there were multiple meetings between Shazar and the Rebbe. Interview with Shalom Magidman for *Kfar Chabad* magazine.

59 Shazar documented his early years growing up in the warmth of chasidic life in his memoir, *Morning Stars* (Jewish Publication Society, 1967; originally published in Hebrew as *Kokhvei Boker*, Am Oved Publishers, 1950). For more on Shazar, see: https://youtu.be/VNDHtG-jN1Y.

60 The British had assumed control over Palestine in 1917 during the First World War. Exasperated by the conflict between the Jews and Arabs, the UK turned to the United Nations to find a solution. The UN committee recommended a partition of Palestine into Jewish and Arab states. The UN proposal needed a two-thirds majority for approval.

61 Shazar recounted the events numerous times. This account is from a chasidic *farbrengen* in Paris marking the tenth yahrzeit of the Rebbe, on January 19, 1960 (10 Shevat, 5720). Shazar, then Israel's minister of education, was visiting Paris at the time, and Rabbi Binyamin Gorodetsky invited him to the *farbrengen*. It was held at the Modern Hotel, which served as a base for Chabad activities in Paris. One of the participants at the *farbrengen*, Rabbi Shalom Mendel Kalmenson, wrote a brief account of the evening to the seventh Rebbe in New York, after which the Rebbe requested a more detailed description. A copy of the second (longer) letter is printed in Friedland, *Pe'ilut Chotzei Gevulot*, vol. 2, chap. 24. Excerpts are reprinted in *Kfar Chabad* magazine, issue no. 1,693.

62 Shazar says he understood the idea of a Rebbe, a person with a deeper spiritual insight. Etched in his memory was his grandfather's regular pilgrimages to Lubavitch to see the Rebbe. Shazar remembered his grandfather jokingly saying to him, "I'd like to bring you in my suitcase."

63 On November 29, 1947, the UN General Assembly adopted the partition plan, thirty-three votes to thirteen with ten abstentions. See "November 29, 1947: The Story of a Vote," available at: https://www.youtube.com/watch?v=QrIjzUKOFKg&t=128s.

64 Interview with Shalom Magidman for *Kfar Chabad* magazine.

65 Rabbi Menachem Greenglass recalls a poignant moment in the *farbrengen* when the Rebbe quoted the Talmud's statement that an indentured servant can perform acts of indiscretion with no legal ramifications (*"Avda behekeira niecha lei,"* Gittin 13a). Greenglass says, "Shazar banged on the table and exclaimed, 'Rebbe! It is true the slave is behaving in an anarchic manner, but he's not enjoying it.'" Perhaps he was reflecting on an internal conflict over drifting from religious observance. This interaction is not recorded in *Sefer HaSichos*, but it was reported by Greenglass, who was present.

66 Yud Tet Kislev (19 Kislev) marks the release of Rabbi Schneur Zalman from czarist prison in 1798. Accusations against him had been orchestrated by the *mitnagdim*,

those opposed to the growing chasidic movement. One of the allegations was his fundraising for Jews living in *Eretz Yisrael*, then part of the Ottoman Empire, an enemy of czarist Russia. The prison release was a vindication of his teachings and is celebrated as the Rosh HaShanah of Chasidism. See Eli Rubin, "The Historic Significance of Yud Tes Kislev," video available at: chabad.org/3884665.

67 *Sefer HaSichos*, 5706–10 (Brooklyn, NY: Kehot Publication Society, 2001), 19 Kislev, 5708.

68 It seems there was an earlier interaction between the Rebbe and Shazar regarding the idea of an agricultural settlement for Chabad Chasidim. Three weeks before the UN vote, the Rebbe wrote to Shazar about other issues, noting at the end of the letter: "As was discussed, if he could inform me a few days in advance of his visit where we will be able to discuss the suggestion of some *anash*, including the refugees in *Eretz HaKodesh*, working the land." *Igrot Kodesh*, vol. 13, letter to Schneur Zalman Rubashov (Shazar) dated 27 Cheshvan, 5708 (November 10, 1947).

69 *Zalman Shazar* [Hebrew], ed. Hagai Tzoref, available at: https://kotar.cet.ac.il/KotarApp/Viewer.aspx?nBookID=95155801#5.1166.6.default.

70 "The Rebbe's Capital City: The Founding of Kfar Chabad," available at: https://derher.org/wp-content/uploads/73-Tishrei-5779-05.pdf.

71 Fifty families founded the community. Today there are more than seven thousand residents. The town serves as the headquarters of Chabad in Israel and boasts a large array of educational institutions.

72 *The Jewish Observer and Middle East Review*, July 3, 1959.

73 *Igrot Kodesh*, vol. 18, letter dated 21 Iyar, 5709 (May 20, 1949).

74 *Igrot Kodesh*, vol. 10, letter dated 11 Marcheshvan, 5710 (November 3, 1949).

75 In 1882, BILU was established in the wake of pogroms in Russia to organize immigration to Palestine and to establish agricultural communities. The first group of BILU immigrants arrived on the port of Jaffa in 1882; this is referred to as the beginning of the First Aliyah. See "Zionism: BILU," Jewish Virtual Library, available at: https://www.jewishvirtuallibrary.org/bilu.

76 Isaiah 2:5 is part of Isaiah's prophecy about messianic times.

77 Uri Kaploun, trans., *Sefer HaSichos*, 5705 (Brooklyn, NY: 2014), chap. 13.

78 Writings of Nachman Syrkin (Berlin: Hashar, 1903).

79 Bialik's remarks at a writers' conference in 1927, available in Hebrew at: https://benyehuda.org/read/191.

80 At the *farbrengen* in Paris, Shazar recalled that in one of his conversations with the Rebbe, "I spoke with enthusiasm about the early pioneers and disparaged some of the chasidic Rebbes who had opposed the Zionist efforts. The Rebbe interrupted me, saying, "Your passion is pleasing to me, but don't think they were not correct."

81 In the same talk, the seventh Rebbe emphasized that there is a role for Jews in both the Diaspora and *Eretz Yisrael,* clearly not supporting *aliyah* for all Jews. He also noted that everything must be done in Israel to uplift the spiritual state of the county and that farming should be conducted according to Jewish law. *Farbrengen,* 11 Shevat, 5728 (February 10, 1968).

82 Israeli society at the time was very different from what it is today. The Mapai Party (Labor), rooted in socialist ideology, was in full command of the country. It dominated the government, the Histadrut (national labor union, which held great sway over the county's economy), academia, the legal system, and much of the media. If you did not follow the party line, it could be difficult to find employment. That only began to change with the election of Menachem Begin in 1977. He was a traditional Jew, and his election represented a shift in focus in modern Israel toward classic Jewish values, as well as the shift toward a free market economy. Today, one-third of Israelis are Shabbat observant, one-third traditional, and the balance secular.

83 This is a foundational idea in Jewish belief, as articulated in Maimonides's *Principles of Faith*: "I believe with complete faith in the coming of *Mashiach,* and although he may tarry, nevertheless, I wait every day for him to come." See Nissan Dovid Dubov, "What Is the Jewish Belief About Moshiach (Messiah)?" available at: chabad.org/108400.

84 On a few occasions, the Rebbe expressed praise for those protecting Jews in *Eretz Yisrael*: "Those who are sacrificing their lives for Jews are doing great work. Hashem should strengthen their hands with success"; "We need benevolence for all the Jews in the world. We are not talking only about those Jews who are complete in their observance of Torah and mitzvot, but all Jews in the world. They are fulfilling the divine intent, even though they may have areas that need improvement (Rosh HaShanah 5708/September 17, 1947).

85 A fourth (smaller) school of thought, supported by the Satmar Chasidim in New York and some Chareidim in Israel, boycotted any involvement with the state. They believed that Zionism was intrinsically hostile toward traditional Jewish observance and refused to vote in elections or accept money from government institutions.

86 For more on Mizrachi and the Chareidi response, see Rabbi Chaim Navon, "The Morning After Ideologies," available at: https://iyun.org.il/en/article/toward-a-haredi-middle-class/the-morning-after-ideologies/.

87 For an overview of the ideals of Mizrachi, see Rabbi Doron Perez, *The Jewish State: From Opposition to Opportunity* (Jerusalem: Gefen/Mizrachi Press, 2023).

88 Students attend the Hesder program for five years, splitting their time between Torah study and army service. The first Hesder yeshivah, Kerem B'Yavneh, was established in 1953. Today there are sixty-eight Hesder yeshivas in Israel with more than eight thousand students between them.

89 Ben-Gurion came from a religious family in Poland. Golda Meir had little sympathy for tradition, despite the fact that her grandparents were observant. Levi Eshkol attended a traditional *cheder* as a child. Shimon Peres was not observant, but felt warmly toward tradition. Yitzchak Rabin came from a secular family. See David Hartman, "Israel & Judaism's Future: Secular Zionism in Revolt," available at: https://www.hartman.org.il/israel-and-judaisms-future-part-1-secular-zionism-in-revolt-2/.

90 In 1952, Israeli Prime Minister David Ben-Gurion met with Rabbi Avraham Yeshaya Karelitz, known as the Chazon Ish, the most prominent Chareidi leader in Israel, at his home in Bnei Brak. The meeting was precipitated by the government's plan to draft young women, an action that was universally opposed by the Chareidi community. The meeting represented the clash of two worldviews. Despite their differences, it was conducted with great respect, and Ben-Gurion was impressed by the modesty of the rabbi's home. The Chazon Ish demanded that the modern state defer to the Chareidi way of life. Ben-Gurion asked him about the broader responsibilities of the state, such as defense and absorption of immigrants, and the Chazon Ish argued that they benefited spiritually from the Torah study of their fellow Jews. After the meeting, Ben-Gurion decided to offer deferments for yeshivah students, who at the time numbered just a few hundred. The Chazon Ish and others in the Lithuanian yeshivah community advocated that men should spend their lives in Torah study. In the decades that followed, the number of those receiving military exemptions and studying Torah full-time has grown to tens of thousands. Ben-Gurion also decided to exempt religious women from military service due to the adamant opposition by many religious Jews. Many young women of the religious Zionist community choose to serve in Sheirut Leumi, national civil service, in place of joining the military. See Chen Malul, "When David Ben-Gurion Met the Chazon Ish," available at: https://blog.nli.org.il/en/hoi_bg_chazon/.

91 The segment of Chareidim called *mitnagdim*, from the Lithuanian yeshivah background, advocate lifelong learning. Chasidic groups such as Ger, Belz, and others encourage their members to seek employment. The majority of Chareidim do not serve in the military. In the early decades of the state, the army was viewed as a tool to instill secular values in youth; that fear still lingers. The IDF has instituted some programs that are respectful of religious observance, but much more needs to be done. In recent years, the number of Chareidim joining the army has been slowly increasing, but there still remains a strong opposition to joining the army.

92 "The Lubavitcher Rebbe's View on Zionism," available at: chabad.org/498520/; Menachem Shlomo, "Walking a tightrope: Chabad's complicated relationship with Zionism," available at: https://www.jpost.com/israel-news/walking-a-tightrope-chabads-complicated-relationship-with-zionism-589020.

93 *Igrot Kodesh*, vol. 9, letters dated 14 Adar Alef, 5708 (February 24, 1948) and 19 Adar Alef, 5708 (February 29, 1948). Today Chabad in Israel has an agreement with the

army permitting yeshivah students to pursue their studies, including a year of study in Brooklyn, and later serve in the IDF. The Knesset passed a special provision allowing a small number of Chabad students to perform alternative national service by helping in Jewish communities in remote countries. Chabad, along with many other parts of the religious community in Israel, supported the exemption of women from the military and did not endorse Sheirut Leumi (national civil service) as an alternative. See "In Landmark Deal, Chabad Men to Enlist in IDF," available at: https://crownheights.info/chabad-news/36580/in-landmark-deal-chabad-men-to-enlist-in-idf/.

94 *Igrot Kodesh*, vol. 10, letter dated 5 Kislev, 5709 (December 7, 1948).

95 The lack of formal representation in the Knesset remains a major handicap for Chabad, as political parties hold sway over funding. State funding is a major component of budgets for educational and social services and religious activities. Without a party to represent its interests, and no seat at the table, Chabad struggles to be treated equitably.

96 The Chabad *bet din* (rabbinical court), whose members are distinguished rabbinic scholars, is responsible for overseeing Chabad activities and setting policy for the movement in Israel. It does not endorse any party in Israeli elections. Chabad policy worldwide is the same, never issuing statements on political issues or endorsing candidates or political parties.

97 Chabad did support parties in two elections due to unusual circumstances. The first time was in 1988, when the seventh Rebbe made a one-time intervention endorsing Agudath Israel because of internal conflicts in the Orthodox community. The second case, in 1996, was due to a dangerous security situation. For details, see David Eliezrie, *The Secret of Chabad*, chap. 11.

98 According to a study by the Jewish People Planning Institute, three percent of Israelis, over 200,000 people, formally identify as Chabad Chasidim. Close to one million Jews in Israel, while not fully chasidic or observant, are active in the network of one thousand Chabad synagogues and educational, social service, and community institutions. If Chabad chose to create a party – something the Rebbe and the seventh Rebbe were against – it would easily earn a few seats in the Knesset. That would ensure a far larger amount of funding to Chabad institutions than they presently receive. See Shmuel Rosner and Camil Fuchs, *Israeli Judaism: Portrait of a Cultural Revolution* (Jerusalem: JPPI, 2019).

99 When Shas, the Sephardic party, was founded in 1984, it created its own system, Bnei Yosef.

100 Prime Ministers Moshe Sharett, Menachem Begin, Yitzchak Rabin, Shimon Peres, Ariel Sharon, and Binyamin Netanyahu met with the Rebbe, all on multiple occasions, except for Sharett and Peres. The Rebbe also met with six of Israel's presidents: Zalman Shazar, Chaim Herzog, Moshe Katzav, Shimon Peres, Reuven Rivlin, and Isaac Herzog. For more, see "The Rebbe & Israel," available at: chabad.org/628305.

101 For the Chabad directory in Israel, see: https://www.chabad.org/jewish-centers/search?query=israel.

102 Letter to Rabbi Lipa Steinmetz dated 1 Iyar, 5700 (May 9, 1940), Steinmetz family wedding memento.

103 *Igrot Kodesh*, vol. 10, letter dated 18 Shevat, 5709 (February 17, 1949).

104 *Igrot Kodesh*, vol. 10, letter dated 7 Marcheshvan, 5709 (November 9, 1948).

105 *Igrot Kodesh*, vol. 10, letter dated 1 Adar, 5709 (March 2, 1949).

106 *Igrot Kodesh*, vol. 10, letter dated 4 Shevat, 5700 (January 22, 1950).

107 *Igrot Kodesh*, vol. 9, letter to Rabbi Eliezer Silver dated 3 Nisan, 5706 (April 7, 1946) and letter to Rabbi Binyamin Gorodetsky dated 5 Nisan, 5707 (March 26, 1947).

108 In the letter to Silver dated 3 Nisan, 5706 (April 7, 1946), the Rebbe mentions telegrams sent to the United Nations Relief Agency and President Truman.

109 Rabbi Yitzchok Zev Soloveitchik (1886–1959) was the son of Rabbi Chaim Soloveitchik and a prominent Chareidi leader in Israel. He opposed Zionism, advocating a complete withdrawal from participation with the newly established Israeli government. He believed that the secular ideals and values of the new state were antithetical to the principles of Judaism. This worldview was at odds with the Rebbe's perspective. While he didn't endorse secular nationalism, the Rebbe believed that one should engage in modern Israeli society, and he encouraged his Chasidim to serve in the army and vote in elections.

110 Porush recalls that the Rebbe was surprised to receive the request from Rabbi Soloveitchik. See excerpt from JEM's interview with Porush, video available at: https://www.youtube.com/watch?v=chzsPZzi7Qs. In 1962, Porush recalled this story in Yiddish at a chasidic gathering in Johannesburg in honor of 12 Tamuz, the anniversary of the Rebbe's release from Russian prison. Audio recording available at: https://www.youtube.com/watch?v=kdo4_J4bLuo&t=1282s.

111 Zalman Shazar, "My Last Shabbat with Grandfather," available at: chabad.org/710368.

112 Interview with Rabbi Yitzchok Groner, JEM Oral History Project.

113 Remarks by Rabbi J.J. Hecht on the ninetieth anniversary of Yeshivas Tomchei Temimim, video available at: https://www.youtube.com/watch?v=P-461HY1wdQ.

114 For an overview of chasidic life in the pre-war era, see Ira Robinson, *Translating a Tradition: Studies in American Jewish History* (Boston: Academic Studies Press, 2010), section 2. Robinson claims that the rabbis who came in the pre-war era were not of high caliber: "Most of the Chasidic spiritual leaders who settled in North America in this period tended to be more of the second ranks, unable to establish themselves satisfactorily in Europe." There were notable exceptions to this, but these Rebbes tended to have a local community following and were not involved in world Jewry.

115 After the war, other prominent chasidic Rebbes relocated to the US. The most well-known of these were the Satmar Rebbe and the Bobover Rebbe. Both established

large communities in Brooklyn, Satmar in Williamsburg and Bobov in Crown Heights and then Borough Park.

116 Jerome Mintz, *Legends of Hasidim: An Introduction to Hasidic Culture and Oral Tradition in the New World* (Chicago University Press, 1968), 37.

117 In the early 1940s, the Rebbe would say *maamarim* on Tuesdays to allow people to come from different places. He spoke on the first floor of 770 in the room that eventually became the office of the seventh Rebbe.

118 The Rebbe did venture out a few times. On Passover 1940, he went to Lakewood, New Jersey, and during the summer months of 1943, he spent some time in Morristown, New Jersey.

119 When the Rebbe spoke on weekdays, Chasidim gathered on the ground floor synagogue to listen through a speaker system. On a few occasions, he spoke to larger crowds in special venues, but his health made those events rare.

120 Moshe Lazar, who was a young child at the time, recalls that children would play ball in the courtyard and the Rebbe would observe them from his second-story balcony. In December of 1942, the yeshivah administration banned ball playing because they thought it was disruptive. This upset the students, and the Rebbe became aware of it. A few days later, upon the Rebbe's instruction, Rebbetzin Nechama Dina and her two daughters stood on the balcony and tossed over thirty red balls to the children below. To the joy of the children, the decree of the yeshivah administration was nullified. JEM Oral History Project interview.

121 In 1945, the Rebbe suffered a heart attack and fell behind in his responses to letters. He noted this in his diary. See Rabbi Shalom Dovber Levine, *Treasures of the Chabad Library* (Brooklyn, NY: Kehot Publication Society, 2009).

122 *Igrot Kodesh*, vol. 7, letter dated 9 Cheshvan, 5703 (October 20, 1942). For a copy of the letter in English and background on Sara Feigelstock, see E.L. Tenenbaum, "Sara Esther Feigelstock: The Woman Who Ran Away at 12, Became a Judaic Scholar and Raised 10 Kids," available at: chabad.org/4529915.

123 JEM Oral History Iinterview with Sara Esther Feigelstock (1932–2016), Oral History Project. Also see Menachem Posner, "Sara Esther Feigelstock, 85, Pioneer of Jewish Education in North America," available at: chabad.org/3474082.

124 Interview with Rabbi Herschel Feigelstock, JEM Oral History Project. In the Chabad community, there are no arranged marriages. Friends, family members, and at times, *shadkhanim* (matchmakers) suggest ideas for marriage. The young couple decides who they want to meet and date, and it's clear to both parties that the purpose of dating is matrimony. As the Rebbe wrote to Sara, each person makes their own decision to marry. Once the couples resolved to marry, they requested a blessing from the Rebbe prior to becoming formally engaged.

125 Schneur Zalman Berger, *Chasid Ne'eman: The Story of Rabbi Eliyahu Simpson* (Brooklyn, NY: 2008), chap. 13.

126 The Rebbe called Simpson a *baal sod*, keeper of secrets. Despite overhearing people's most intimate problems as they shared them with the Rebbe, he never revealed anything to others.

127 Rare audio recording of the Rebbe, available at: https://collive.com/audio-recording-of-frierdiker-rebbe-transcribed-in-english/.

128 Video tour of the Rebbe's study narrated by Rabbi Berel Levin, available at: https://www.youtube.com/watch?v=RXPpeA4ZczU&t=33s.

129 Interview with Rabbi Azriel Chaiken, JEM Oral History Project.

130 Interview with Rabbi Chaim Baruch Halberstam, JEM Oral History Project. The rebbetzin outlived the Rebbe by twenty-one years, and Halberstam assisted her in her later years. He says she rarely confided in him about the Rebbe; it was quite unusual for her to speak about such personal matters.

131 *The Wonder Rabbi.*

132 Interview with Chaya (Rosenfeld) Hecht, JEM Oral History Project.

133 Interview with Tzivia Lipsker, JEM Oral History Project.

134 Interviews with Zalman and Leibel Posner, JEM Oral History Project.

135 Rabbi Mordechai Mentlik (1912–87) studied in Otwock. In 1945, he was appointed *rosh yeshivah* of 770 by the Rebbe Rayatz. He recounted this story to Herschel Chitrik in an interview for the JEM Oral History Project.

136 Chana was from Fürth, Germany, and was one of the children on the Kindertransport to England. After the war, she came to New York and married Dovid Tennenhaus in February 1949. The couple lived in New Brunswick and then Montreal. They had four children. After Dovid Tennenhaus's passing in 1993, Chana told this story to her son Rabbi Rafael Tennenhaus, a Chabad *shliach* in Florida. Interview, JEM Oral History Project.

137 "The Previous Rebbe's Plea to Our Rebbe," video available at: https://www.youtube.com/watch?v=NnxrjFTBr8o.

138 Leibel Zisman, *I Believe: The Story of One Jewish Life* (Brooklyn, NY: GJCF, 2012), chap. 5.

139 *Yechidut* was considered confidential. There are some brief notations the Rebbe made about some of his meetings and references in letters that he sent following up on these meetings. See Levine, *Treasures from the Chabad Library.*

140 Rabbi Yekusiel Yehudah Halberstam (1905–94) was known as the Klausenberger Rebbe. *Igrot Kodesh*, vol. 10, letter dated 5 Iyar, 5709 (June 14, 1949).

141 The Rebbe was impressed with the potential of Young Israel to influence young people, and he wrote about Young Israel in letters to his wife during his visit in 1929. Irving Bunim was a noted Jewish activist. He met the Rebbe on numerous occasions and maintained an active correspondence with him. *Igrot Kodesh,* vol. 10, letter dated 27 Sivan, 5709 (June 24, 1949).

142 Interview with Rabbi Yehuda Krinsky, JEM Oral History Project.

143 Interview with Mordechai Zajac, JEM Oral History Project. Zajac's father immigrated to Brazil in 1934. He sent his sons, including teenage Mordechai, to study in 770 in 1947.

144 Kislev 5710 (December 1950).

145 In the early 1940s, the Rebbe said *maamarim*, but as his physical condition became more challenging, he wrote them down instead, and they were published in honor of Jewish and chasidic holidays. The six published volumes of *maamarim* encompass the years 1940 to 1950.

146 At each *farbrengen* there was a *chozer*, a person who memorized and later documented the Rebbe's talks. These talks were originally published in Yiddish and more recently translated into English.

147 *Sefer HaSichos*, 5700–05, Foreword.

148 *Sefer HaSichos*, 5702, Introduction.

149 *Sefer HaSichos*, 5705, vol. 5, Introduction.

150 Adar 5709 (March 17, 1949).

151 Levine, *Treasures from the Chabad Library*.

152 The meeting was held on 4 Cheshvan, 5710 (October 27, 1949). Diary entry recorded in *Yemei Bereishit* (Kehot Publication Society, 1993).

153 The Jewish population was sizable at the time. According to the American Jewish Yearbook survey of world Jewry of 1950, the number of Jews in North Africa totaled 280,000 in Morocco; 130,000 in Algeria; 90,000 in Tunisia; 75,000 in Egypt; and 25,000 in Libya. With the establishment of the State of Israel in 1948, Jews from North African counties began immigrating to Israel as well as other countries. See American Jewish Yearbook, vol. 51 (American Jewish Committee and Jewish Publication Society, 1950), world Jewish population.

154 This was the first correspondence of his after the passing of the Rebbe. For a copy of the letter, see *Yemei Bereishit*.

155 Some schools had already been established by the Alliance Israelite Universelle, an agency of French Jewry that created educational programs in Sephardic countries, opening its first school in Morocco in 1862. The focus of the schools was secular; the Jewish educational component was limited. Part of the philosophy of secular French Jews was to assimilate into the broader society. This put them in conflict with many of the rabbis in Morocco, who wanted a more classic education with a greater focus on Torah study. These rabbis, starting with Rabbi Baruch Toledano of Meknes, welcomed Chabad efforts in Morocco. See Eliezrie, *The Secret of Chabad*, chap. 3.

156 *Igrot Kodesh*, vol. 17, letter dated 7 Shevat, 5700 (January 25, 1950).

157 *Igrot Kodesh*, vol. 10, letter dated 7 Shevat, 5700 (January 25, 1950).

158 *Yemei Bereishit*.

159 It would take some years for the blessings to be realized. At one point, the seventh Rebbe told Rhoda, "If my father-in-law said you will have children, you will have

children." When doctors recommended surgeries that would have left Rhoda unable to have children, the seventh Rebbe advised her not to accept their advice and instead seek other medical opinions.

160 When Rhoda finally gave birth to a son, the first of their three children, Rabbi Hecht was indeed the *sandek* (the person honored with holding a child at his circumcision). To hear Rhoda's story in her own words, see the video available at: https://www.youtube.com/watch?v=mMZPWpB52Cg.

161 While in Riga in 1928, the Rebbe sent Dubov to Manchester. He was hesitant to go and lamented to the Rebbe, "When will I see the Rebbe?" The Rebbe responded, "We will see each other again." When he entered the Rebbe's room that night, the Rebbe said, "I told you we would see each other again." Interview with Sholom Weiss, JEM Oral History Project.

162 Due to the tragic passing of the Rebbe, Avraham Weingarten asked chasidic elder Rabbi Shmuel Levitin whether the engagement should still be celebrated. He referred him to the Ramash, who told him not to cancel the engagement, but to make it a very small affair (on that Saturday night, as scheduled). Interview with Shimshon Stock, JEM Oral History Project.

163 As per custom, the Rebbe would meet with brides and grooms and their families before the engagement and often on the day of the wedding to offer his blessings.

164 The next day, Friday, Rabbi Naftali Dolinski was leaving on a ship set for Israel and met with the Rebbe before his departure. He was the last person to have a formal *yechidut* with the Rebbe. See *Yemei Bereishit.*

165 Author's interview.

166 See "Rabbi Groner On What Happened After Yud Shvat 5710," Yiddish video available at: https://collive.com/rabbi-groner-on-what-happened-after-yud-shvat-5710/.

167 Interview with Moshe Lazar, JEM Oral History Project.

168 The Ramash instructed the Chasidim to use the wood from the Rebbe's *shtender* (prayer podium) for the casket and to place his black silk Shabbat *kapota* on top of the casket.

169 Interview with Aaron Lichtenstein, JEM Oral History Project.

170 Gershon Kranzler, *The Lubavitcher,* Mindel Archives.

171 Jewish law dictates that when a great Jewish leader passes away, it is a collective loss and every Jew should sit *shivah* for a brief time, usually an hour. After the funeral, the Chasidim returned from the cemetery and, along with Jews around the world, paused, tore their clothes, sat in mourning, and reflected on the tremendous loss.

172 Author's interview with Uri Kaploun.

173 Interview with Yehudis Groner nee Gurewicz.

174 *Igrot Kodesh*, vol. 1, Introduction.

175 Seventeen volumes of the Rebbe's letters were published between 1982 and 2011. The vast majority were written after he became Rebbe in 1920; few letters written

prior to that time have survived. Before 1920, the Rayatz was deeply involved in community affairs on behalf of his father, the Rashab. Levin writes that when the Rayatz traveled, "he would write his father daily." During his visit to the US in 1929–30, the Rebbe also wrote to his wife almost daily. The letters to his wife were seized by the Russian army after the invasion of Latvia in 1941 and are presently in the hands of the Russian National Library.

176 Until the Rebbe's arrival in the US, there was no national system of Jewish day school education. Others, such as Torah Umesorah, which was established in 1944, followed in the path the Rebbe pioneered. The Rebbe created a broad base of innovations, arguing for upgrading Hebrew schools, ensuring that the teachers were role models of observance, creating programs such as Released Time, producing curriculum guides, and publishing educational material, including magazines for children.

177 David Eliezrie, "US Jewry is shifting profoundly and Chabad is on rise – Pew research," available at: https://www.jpost.com/opinion/pew-us-jewry-is-shifting-profoundly-chabad-is-on-rise-669549.

178 Today, Chabad has centers in over fifty US states and 110 countries. No other Jewish organization has such a vast international presence. For a list of centers, see: chabad.org/centers.

179 See "The Yud Shvat Story (5766)," audio recording available at: https://insidechassidus.org/the-yud-shvat-story-5766/.

180 Here the Rebbe used the term "*kotz shel yod.*" This is a classic Hebrew expression referring to the line on the smallest letter in the Hebrew alphabet, *yod,* meaning that not even something as small as that line should be modified. See *Sefer HaSichos,* 8 Tevet, 5710 (January 11, 1949).

AFTERWORD

1 Author's interview with Rabbi Yoel Kahn.

2 *Yemei Bereishit.*

3 Greenglass, "The 22nd of Shevat"

4 "The Rebbe's First *Maamar,*" available at: chabad.org/2333961.

5 In the years that followed, on 10 Shevat, his father-in-law's yahrzeit, the seventh Rebbe would teach a *maamar* built on a concept from the Rayatz's last *maamar.*

6 *Yemei Bereishit.*

7 The seventh Rebbe passed away in Brooklyn on 3 Tamuz, 5754 (June 3, 1994) at ninety-two years old. His teachings and ideas continue to inspire the movement. Both Rebbes are interred in Montefiore Cemetery in New York. Close to one million people, Jews and non-Jews alike, have visited the Ohel (the resting place of the Rebbes) to offer prayers. See ohel.com and therebbe.org.

Index

770 Eastern Parkway, 133, 170, 281, 349, 353, 356, 361, 365, 366, 519n117, 520n135, 521n143

Achot Hatemimim (The Sisterhood of the Temimim), 153–154
in Riga, 154
of Greater New York, 436n14
Adler, Cyrus, 187, 188, 190, 193, 201, 431n66, 453n84, 453n87, 457n135
Agro-Joint, 189, 191, 456n117, 456n121
Agudas Chassidei Chabad, 230, 249, 252, 272, 278, 423n90, 437n121, 443n64, 444n1, 451n73, 466n86, 485n50
Agudas Chassidei Chabad (a Union of the Chabad Chasidim) in Poland, Lithuania, and Latvia, 146, 200, 201, 206, 484n29, 484n43
Agudas Harabonim (Union of Orthodox Rabbis), 192, 286, 298, 307, 430n60, 470n127, 470n129, 482n7
Agudath Israel, 82, 148, 160, 213, 278, 345, 346, 405n72, 426n10, 426n11, 432n82, 433n87, 439n22, 447n28, 463n37, 463n38, 469n121, 470n126, 472n151, 495n142, 507n261, 517n97
ahavas Yisrael, concept of, 12
aid packages, 128
Aizik, Rabbi Yekusiel, 12
akedah, 23
Albert, Judah, 288
Alexander II (Czar), 44, 418n29
Alexander III (Czar), 24
Alexandria, Egypt, 177–178, 183–184, 469n66
Alliance Israélite Universelle, 143
Aloy, Rabbi Yirmiyahu, 338–339
Alter Rebbe. *See* Schneur Zalman
Altein, Mordechai, 242, 306–307, 350,
Altein, Mottel, 474n15, 500n195
Althaus, Pinchas, 251

Althaus, Rabbi Eliyahu Chaim, 83, 97, 98, 101–103, 106, 107, 110, 115, 119, 121, 122, 124, 154, 158, 161–162, 163, 167, 250–251, 427n97, 411n134, 412n135, 512n136, 412n137, 414n1, 417n19, 440n32
American Friends Service Committee, 296, 495n146
American Jewish Committee, 193, 295, 298, 311, 457n131
American Jewish Congress, 193, 295, 311, 457n130, 457n131,
American Jewish Yearbook, 521n153191,
American Yeshivas Tomchei Temimim, 279
Amin al-Husseini, Mohammed, 182, 450n57
Amskislav, 93
anash (the Chabad community), 56, 58, 63, 64, 65, 124, 136, 152, 206, 217, 231, 232, 281, 305, 339, 359, 422n83, 445n6, 460n4, 480n98, 507n271, 481n116, 509n23, 524n68
Anti-Defamation League, 295
anti-Semitism, 32, 46, 54, 69, 79–80, 141, 190, 213, 247, 295, 296, 324, 362, 330, 416n10
Arie Crown Hebrew Day School (Chicago), 317
aron Kodesh, 22–23
Asherov, Rabbi Avraham Eliyahu, 154
Ashkenazi, Rabbi Meir, 223, 231, 283, 287, 288, 467n96, 485n58, 489n91, 489n92
assimilation, 44, 45, 48, 137, 268, 308, 312, 323, 340, 343, 362, 444n73, 499
Auschwitz, 250, 266, 296
avodah (service of G-d), 11, 20, 21, 30, 66, 151, 176, 211,
Axelrod, Rabbi Avraham, 230, 470n134

Baal Shem Tov, Yisrael (the Maggid), 12, 78, 152, 186, 242, 281, 392n50, 406n78, 422n79, 435n104, 452n82, 474n14
gravesite, 390n27
Baeck, Dr. Leo, 117, 144, 418n40
Baku, 79
Bar, Rabbi Nachman, 199–200, 459n156, 494n142
Barnetsky, Avraham, 219
Bashkov, Aryeh Shlomo, 92
Bashkov, Mark Semyonovitch, 91–93
Baskov, Shimon, 92
Bauer, Zvi, 189, 191
Beilis affair, 52–53
Beilis, Mendel, 52–53, 396n106, 397n124
Beis Rivkah schools, 154
beit din (rabbinical court), 64, 399n5
Beit HaMikdash, 15, 179
Beit HaRav, 56, 398n131
Beit Romano (large property in Hebron), 42, 448n41
Beizer, Michael, 83, 189, 289, 411n133
Ben Hillel, Mordechai, 48
Benjamin of Tudela, 181
Ber, Rabbi Dov, 16, 178, 186, 386n72
Ber, Rabbi Joseph, 77,
Berenbaum, Michael, 125
Bergelson, David, 133
Beria, Lavrentiy, 88
Berlin, Rabbi Meir, 497n162

Berlin, Rabbi Naftali Tzvi Yehudah, 29, 503n235
Berlin, Yeshaya, 19, 36, 38, 47, 391n44, 427n24
Berman, Harold, 323
Bertoldi, (Zeev) Latski, 133
Biale, David, 213
Bialik, Chaim Nachman, 31, 343, 5124n79
Bibliothek Lybubawithc, 223
BILU, 45, 343, 524n75
bimah (podium on which the Torah is read), 36, 37, 87
Birobidzhan, 80, 192, 408n85, 456n123
Bliner, Shimon
Bloch, Ernst, 254–255
blood libel, 52, 53, 397n124
Bloom, Sol, 249, 476n40, 497n164
Bnei Brak, 183, 398n134, 516n90
Bobruysk (Belarus), 66, 383n28, 383n29, 400n17, 408n92, 413n144
Bolivke (resort town), 21, 22, 24, 28, 41, 388n4
Bolshevik Party, 416n6
Bolshevik Revolution (1917), 5, 54, 79, 229,
Bolshoi Moskovsky Hotel, 91
Borah, William (US Senator from Idaho), 117, 229, 470n128
Boxer, Lewis, 197, 198, 199, 458n153
Brailovsky, Aryeh Leib, 287, 489n91
Brandeis University, 337
Brandeis, Justice Louis, 117–118, 180, 184, 192–193, 249, 250, 251, 252, 256, 419n49, 457n130, 457n132, 459n163, 494n138, 511n41
Brawer, Naftali, 32, 34
Bressler, David, 193
Breuer, Rabbi Joseph, 278, 484n32
British Mandate Palestine, 176, 180, 229, 324
Bronfman, Menachem, 150–151
Bronfman, Samuel, 289, 290
Bronstein, Zalman, 125, 423n92
Brooklyn Eagle, 273, 274
Brooklyn Jewish Center, 184
Brownsville, 184, 185, 261, 281
Bryski, Rabbi Mottel, 219
Bukjet, Chaim Meir, 216, 219, 248, 283, 286–287, 465n69
Bundism, 39
Bunim, Irving (Simcha), 318, 355, 520n141

Cairo, Egypt, 451n65, 451n66
Canadian Jewish Congress, 288
Chabad Chasidism, 6, 53, 135, 150, 275–276, 402n39
Chabad Rabbinical Court in Israel, 94
Chachmei Lublin, 162, 474n9
chadarim (traditional Jewish school), 76, 147, 214, 225, 236, 301, 421n63, 432n84
Chaikin, Azriel, 329
Chaikin, Rabbi Meir, 338
Chaim Berlin, 277
Chaim, Rabbi Shmuel, 322
chasidic courts:
Belz, 134, 236, 444n33, 463n37, 516n9
 Ger, 213, 236, 436n119, 441n33, 516n91
 Novominsk, 134
 Radomsk, 134

chasidic historiography, 149, 150–151, 363
chasidic teachings, broadening the dissemination beyond the chasidic community, 151–152
Chasidut, 18, 20, 32, 59, 60, 95, 120, 153, 167, 215, 390n27
chasidut (chasidic discourses), 5, 17, 19, 59, 83, 366
Chaskind, Rabbi Dovber, 469n122, 484n43
chatzer (courtyard of the Rebbes' synagogue), 6, 7, 10
cheder (elementary school), 2, 12, 75, 121, 147, 405n69, 432n84, 516n89498n173,
Cheifer, Rabbi Shmuel, 341–342
Cheifetz, Mordechai, 153, 154, 208, 242, 267, 321
Chein, Berke, 334
Chein, Rabbi Dovid, 126, 384, 423
Chein, Rabbi Meir Simcha, 126
Chein, Yehuda, 126
Cheka (secret police), 74, 404n61, 417n15
Chelyabinsk, 91, 92
Chernihiv, 226
Chernov, Vasily, 52
Chernow, Ron, 188
Chevrah Mefitzei Haskalah (Chamah, Society to Promote the Enlightenment), 48
Chevronim (special fund to help Jews in Hebron), 42
Chicago Courier, 195
Children of Tehran, 319, 445, 96n151, 506n259
Chimka (Soviet official), 112–113
Chitrik, Herschel, 354, 520n135
Chitrik, Rabbi Yehudah, 70, 122, 161, 401n37
Choral Synagogue (Moscow), 127
chozrim (oral scribes), 33, 217, 423n98
chuppah, 28, 132, 162, 164, 389n9
Churchill, Winston, 57
Cohen, Benjamin V., 249–250, 252–253, 256, 260–261, 262, 476n42,
493–494n138
Cohen, Rabbi She'ar Yashuv, 159, 438n17
Cohn, Dr. Oscar, 117, 124
Colel Chabad, 178, 180, 181, 341, 393n64, 446n21, 448n38, 448n39, 448n40, 471n142, 472n143
Committee for the Protection and Care (of Russian Jewry), 139
Committee of Rabbis, 81, 98, 225,
Communism, 4, 39, 45, 68, 72, 76, 77, 78, 79, 156, 189, 225, 275, 305, 328, 362, 407n81, 416n10, 427n25, 444n73, 468n109, 489n93,
Communist Party, 69
  Jewish section, 71, 380n8
Communist Revolution, 160
Congregation Adas B'nei Israel, 200
Congregation Oneg Shabbat, 274, 280
Conservative movement, 307, 459n159, 483n22
Crimea, 141, 142, 393n70
Crown Heights, 184–185, 279, 281, 311, 511n35, 519n115

crown rabbis, 50–51

Dalfen, Arnold, 290
Davzik, Berel, 39, 40
Depression, 187, 205
Der Emes (Yevesektzia newspaper), 123, 226, 403n53, 410n113, 469n112
Der Moment (Yiddish daily published in Warsaw), 164, 442n43
Der Morgen Journal (New York Yiddish newspaper), 202, 362
Der Tag (New York Yiddish daily), 178, 179, 447n28
Derech Eretz School, 134, 147, 148
Detroit Jewish Chronicle, 134, 139
Dimenstein, Semyon, 72, 73, 141, 403n49, 403n50, 403n55, 403n56
Dnipropetrovsk, 166
Dos Vort (Yiddish paper), 479n85
Druya, northern Belorussia, 85
Dubin, Rabbi Mordechai, 124, 125, 127, 133, 134, 144, 147–148, 184, 242, 243, 250, 300, 422n80, 422n86, 422n87, 422n88, 451n69, 463n38, 467n89
Dubrashvili, Yaakov, 165
Dubrovno, 49
Duchman, Rabbi Zalman, 17, 102, 103, 108, 120, 126
Dvinsk, 145, 163, 428n39
Dvorkin, Rabbi Michoel, 118, 119, 121, 250–251, 420n57
Dynner, Glen, 211–212

Edelman, Rabbi Dovid, 419n48, 419n49, 420n50, 443n70, 493–494n138
Edelstein, Yuli, 128–129
Eidah HaChareidit, 177
Eisenstadt, Moshe, 227
Elberg, Rabbi Simcha, 211
Eliazrov, Rabbi Shlomo Leib, 181, 448n41
Elituv, Rabbi Shimon, 184, 451n66
Emanual Synagogue (Detroit, Michigan), 194–195
emergency campaign, 143–144
England, 87, 92, 106, 115, 125, 140, 231, 232, 335, 360, 366, 416n7, 430n63, 494n140, 510n28, 511n36, 520n136
Enlightenment (Haskalah), 30, 39, 41, 44, 45, 47–48, 50, 51, 53, 96, 116, 381n14, 134, 390n21, 395n87, 406n80, 411n133
secular, 134, 381n14, 411n122
epidemic: typhus, 67, 70, 71, 157
ethical will, 14
Etkin, Rabbi Chanoch Henoch, 159,
Evian Conference 1938, 253
exit visas, 125, 257. *See also* visas

Fallaci, Oriana (Italian reporter), 128, 424n101
famine of 1921–1922, 71, 72, 76, 143, 157, 190
Farley, James, 252
Fasman, Rabbi Oscar, 288
Fast of Esther, 70
Feigelstock, Rabbi Herschel, 294, 351, 494n140, 512n52, 519n123
Feinstein, Rabbi Moshe, 77, 278, 404–405n69, 484n32
Finkel, Rabbi Nosson Tzvi, 29, 390n20
Fisher, Mordechai, 241, 279

Fishman, David, 68, 81, 224, 406n80, 468n111, 469n114
Fogelman, Herschel, 170, 279, 309, 443n71
Fogelman, Rabbi Chaim, 200
Frankenheim, Paul, 254
Frankfurter, Felix, 250, 501n213
Franz Ferdinand of Austria, 54
Freud, Sigmund, 252
Frimorgen (left-wing newspaper), 133, 149, 163, 414n1
Frumkin, Esther, 226
Frumkin, Gad, 180, 183, 450n61, 469n112, 506n259
fundraising campaign, 35, 39, 144, 193, 196, 227, 234, 235, 286, 310, 312, 427n22, 431n67, 456n118, 472n143, 514n66
Futerfas, Rabbi Mendel, 334, 424n105, 510n28

Garfinkel, Avraham, 211, 216–217, 218, 241, 285, 464n61, 487n71
Geberer, Yehuda, 137
Geist, Raymond Herman, 253, 256, 477–478n60, 478n65
General Zionists, 213
Gerlitzky, Avraham, 290
Gerlitzky, Moshe, 210, 220–221, 461n18
Gerrer Rebbe, 51, 220–221, 234, 319, 396n103, 450n51, 472n152
Gershoni, Avraham, 79, 407n81
Gerson, Charlotte, 235
Gerson, Dr. Max, 235, 375
Gitelman, Zvi, 73, 189
Glitzenstein, Rabbi Shimon, 183
Glubok, 146, 212, 374
Gluboker Lebn (Yiddish paper), 211
Gluckowsky, Rabbi, Mendel, 94
Goldin, Avraham, 166
Goldin, Reb Yitzchak, 40, 69–70, 334, 401n29, 402n38, 402n44, 442n53
Goldman, Shimon, 287, 489n93
Goldshmidt, Shalom Ber, 182
Goldstein, Rabbi Yosef, 219, 228, 248, 465n65, 465n67, 489n93
Gordon, Shalom Ber, 209
Gordon, Yisrael, 250
Gordon, Rabbi Yochanan, 164, 209, 250, 436n114, 461n12, 476n46
Gorky, Maxim, 418
Gorodetsky, Rabbi Binyamin, 94, 98, 329, 330, 333, 359, 413n144, 420n57, 513n61
Gorodetsky, Simcha, 411n114
GPU (secret police), 91, 105, 106, 107–108, 111, 115, 118–119, 120, 121, 122, 190, 415n1, 417n25
Great Escape (1946), 237, 333, 469n114
Great Purge, 71
Greenberg, Meir, 242–243, 474n15
Greenberg, Meyer, 306
Greenberg, Yehoshua, 185, 243
Greenwald, Rabbi Nachum, 212
Greystone Hotel, 274, 276, 280, 348, 349
Grodzinski, Rabbi Chaim Ozer, 51, 72, 134, 139, 143, 146, 158, 175, 211, 229, 396n101, 426n16, 438n18, 444n2, 470n128, 476n49,
Gronem, Rabbi Shmuel, 34, 391n32

Groner, Yitzchok, 272, 273, 292, 309, 311, 348, 423n94
Gross, Tzipora, 306
Grossman, Rabbi Asher, 19, 27, 35
Gruzenberg, Oscar, 52–53, 397n111
Gunzburg, Baron David, 45, 394n73, 396n105
Gunzburg, Baron Horace (Naftali Hertz), 48, 395n84, 395n87
Gurary, Berke, 243,
Gurary, Herschel, 247
Gurary, Judah, 261
Gurary, Rabbi Moshe, 228
Gurary, Rabbi Shmaryahu (Rashag), 75, 76, 121, 144, 157, 365, 428n41
Gurary, Rabbi Shmuel, 69, 69, 70, 71, 401n27, 427n24,
Gurary, Rabbi Zalman, 157, 163, 220, 258, 294, 298, 437n5
Gurewicz , Rabbi Nachum Zalman, 340
Gurewicz, Berel, 333, 334
Gurewicz, Lev, 96, 409n98, 411n133
Gurewicz, Rabbi Itche "der masmid," 70, 201, 207, 208, 228, 235, 321, 325
Gurewicz, Tzemach, 331, 338
Gurock, Jeffry, 277
Gutnick, Chaim, 287, 327, 508n5, 509n10
Gutnick, Rabbi Mordechai, 232, 472n 146
Gutnick, Rabbi Schneur, 508n8

Habima, 73, 403n55, 403n56, 404n57
Hadoar (US Hebrew-language newspaper), 142, 430n55,
Haffkine, Waldemar, 140, 438n43, 428n44, 429n45
HaGomel (blessing), 124, 421n73
Hakafot, 36, 149, 167, 392n46
HaKriah VeHaKedushah (magazine), 294
Halberstam, Benzion, 296, 520n130
Hanukkah, 72, 243, 258, 307, 321, 364, 461n12, 498n176,
HaOlam (London Newspaper), 223
Harris, Nathan, 172
Haskalah (Enlightenment). *See* Enlightenment
Hatomim (magazine), 168, 434n91
Havlin, Rabbi Zalman, 42–43, 56, 59–60, 61–62, 64–65, 393n67
Hebrew Parochial School (Chicago), 317
Hebrew Theological College, 199, 459n158
Hecht, J. J., 359–360
Hecht, Rabbi Avraham, 208, 241, 242, 273, 276, 280, 281, 301, 302, 304, 305–306, 308, 312, 502n225, 522n160
Hecht, Rivkah, 309, 313
Hecht, Yankel, 310, 312, 349
Hecht, Shlomo Zalman, 219, 242, 350
Heint (Yiddish daily published in Warsaw), 164
Hellenist Jews, 94
Hemshekhim (a series of *maamarim* following a common theme), 33
Hendel, Reb Tzvi Chanoch, 15
Hendel, Rabbi Yitzchak, 216, 217, 218, 288, 290, 291, 464n50, 507n269, 15
Henkin, Rabbi Eliyahu, 278

Herald Tribune, 273
Hertz, Rabbi Dr. Yosef, 140, 428n42
Herzog, Rabbi Isaac, 236, 283, 318–319, 319–320, 505n246, 507n261, 517n100
High Holidays, 6, 34, 100, 124, 146, 152, 167, 203, 205, 207, 208, 217, 298, 321, 332, 358, 387n80, 413n154, 448n33
Hildesheimer, Rabbi Dr. Meir, 117, 139, 144, 418n40, 430n63
Hillel, Rabbi Yosef, 322
Hirschsprung, Rabbi Pinchas, 241, 247, 474n9,
Hirshorn, Yehoshua, 291
Hodakov, Rabbi Chaim Mordechai Aizek, 148, 156, 173, 275, 300, 301, 311, 406n80, 436n120, 444n73, 481n117, 483n13, 498n174, 498n175, 498n176, 499n186
Holocaust, 6, 220, 247, 266, 323, 326, 328, 337, 338, 339, 344, 355, 359, 391n36, 399n6, 416n11, 428n40, 431n76, 450n57, 462n26, 474n9, 477n54, 480n104, 488n81, 492n119, 494n139, 509n18
Hoover, Herbert, 184, 200, 249, 420n50
Horenstein, Moshe, 162, 164, 184,
Horenstein, Rabbi Mendel, 158, 263, 268, 291
Horowitz, Reb Aharon, 427n23
Horowitz, Rabbi Yehuda Leib, 227
Horowitz, Rabbi Yitzchak, 207, 228, 235, 325
Horowitz, Yaakov, 47
Horowitz, Yisroel, 352
Hotel Britannia, 242
Hull, Cordell, 249, 253, 261
Hyman, Joseph, 187–188, 190, 191, 192, 431n66, 452n84, 454n89, 455n108, 457n135
Hyman, Rabbi Shlomo, 503n227

Igrot Kodesh, 23, 379
Iron Curtain, 205, 324, 364, 424n104, 470n130, 48

Jacobson, Rabbi Simon, 95, 336, 409n103, 511n40
Jacobson, Rabbi Yisrael, 48, 76, 89, 101, 117, 127, 136, 149, 160–161, 169, 176, 185, 193, 201, 207, 208, 210, 219, 239–241, 248–250, 251, 252, 254, 256, 260, 261, 262, 264, 266, 275, 279–280, 282, 288, 289, 292, 336–337, 419n46, 422n80, 427n23, 436n114, 445n3, 458n146, 462n13, 474n11, 476n46, 477n57, 478n65, 479n80, 484n39, 484–485n43, 491n105, 492–493n124, 500n195, 511n40
Jacobson, Rabbi Yosef Yitzchak, 87, 89
Jacobson, Sholom, 95
Jewish Agency, 229, 319–320, 341, 359, 496n151, 506n259
Jewish Colonial Association (JCA), 48
Jewish Communist youth club, 149
Jewish Community Center (Berlin), 259
Jewish Quarter, Old City, 179, 447n26
Jewish Telegraphic Agency (JTA), 189, 415n4, 433n87

Jewish Welfare Board (JWB), 319, 505n247
Joint Distribution Committee (JDC), 81, 140

Kabbalah, 8, 56, 74, 293, 384n37, 449n44
Kagan, Rabbi Yisrael Meir (Chafetz Chaim), 77, 134, 139, 143, 405n72
Kahn, Bernard, 142, 187
Kahn, Rabbi Yoel, 162, 365, 441n34, 452n84, 490n96
Kahn, Rabbi Rafael, 417n19
Kaiser Wilhelm, 54
Kalinin, Mikhail, 116
Kalish, Rabbi Shimon, 283
Kamenetsky, Rabbi Yaakov, 278, 484n32
Kantaroff, Shmuel, 273
Kaplan, Moshe Binyamin, 237,
Kaplan, Rabbi Aryeh Leib, 79, 186, 407n83, 408n84
Kaplan, Rabbi Shmuel, 200
Kaploun, Uri, 150, 357, 414n1
Karlisker, Rabbi Avraham, 178
Katz, Rabbi Binyomin, 406n80
Katz, Rabbi Mordechai, 508n7
Katz, Rabbi Yosef, 181, 199–200
Katz, Yankel, 317
Katzenelenbogen, Rabbi David Tevel, 83, 409n99
Katzenelenbogen, Sara, 334, 510n29
Katzenelson, Judah Leib, 50
Katzman, Shmuel, 40
Kazarnovsky, Moshe, 311
Kazarnovsky, Rabbi Shlomo Aharon, 272, 300
Kazarnovsky, Risya, 272, 273, 482n6
Kazarnovsky, Yisrael, 436n114
Kazen, Shula, 335, 511n35
Kehillah (community), 71, 133, 144, 213
Kehot Publication Society, 169, 293
Keller, Yossi, 18
Kfar Chabad, 341, 342, 343–344, 345, 346, 444n73
Kharkiv, 13, 54, 76, 86, 87, 122, 161, 226, 403n53
King David, 19, 181, 229, 402n37, 449n48
King Herod, 181
King Shlomo, 19
King, William, 229
Kipnis, Rabbi Zev, 99, 100
kiruv penimi (Rashab), 21
Kislovodsk (town), 158–159
kivrei tzaddikim, 176
Klatzkin, Jacob, 297, 298, 299, 496n151, 496n152
Klatzkin, Rabbi Moshe, 40
Klonski, Rabbi Shlomo Zalman, 182
Kohen, Herman, 339, 512n52
kollels, 42, 390n20, 499n189, 501n218
Kolyma (remote region of Siberia), 106
Konikov, Dvorah, 126
Konikov, Rabbi Chaim Tzvi, 310
Kook, Rabbi Avraham Yitzchak, 177
Kopust, 7, 39, 180, 382n25, 383n28, 393n64, 400n17, 408n92, 426n18, 428n39
Korosten, Ukraine, 86, 99

kosher slaughter, 87, 95, 321, 470n125, 474n3
Kostroma, 119–120, 121, 122, 416n12, 416n14, 420n58,
Kotkin, Stephen, 106
Kotlarsky, Tzvi Hirsch, 216, 284, 288, 405n76
Kotler, Rabbi Aharon, 77, 106, 484n33, 486n60, 488n81
Kovno, 45, 259, 265, 283, 355, 430n63, 508n6
Kramer, Aryeh Leib, 210
Kramer, Hyman S., 172
Kramer, Leibel, 216, 291, 358,
Kramer, Max, 418n43
Kramer, Milton, 476n38
Kramer, Rabbi Moshe, 200
Kramer, Samuel, 249, 250, 251, 252
Kramer, Yosef, 248
Kramer, Sam, 117, 256, 257, 418n43
Kramers, Chaim Zalman and Avraham Dov, 127, 484n43, 495n146
Kranzler, Gershon, 24, 49, 272, 273, 276, 303, 352, 361
Kremenchuk, Ukraine, 69, 228, 383n31
Krinsky, Rivkah, 208, 500n202
Krinsky, Shmaya, 208
Krinsky, Yehuda, 356, 498n175
kritat brit, 84
Krivoy Rog (town), 142
Krotov, 92–93
ktav hitkashrut, 65
Kugel, Yerachmiel, 121
Kuselewitz, Rabbi Shmuel, 315, 316, 503n227
Kutaisi (town), 87, 139, 226, 409n103, 428n34

Labor Zionist Jewish People's School, 289
Lag BaOmer, 13, 311, 332, 501n216
Lakewood, New Jersey, 280, 405n76, 484n33, 502n220, 519n118, 60
Landau, Yaakov, 398n134, 437n4
Landwarow, Poland, 133, 158, 193–194
Lasser, William, 249, 250
Latvian Chasidim, 132
Lazaroff, Rabbi Shimon, 225, 468n105
Leibowitz, Rabbi Baruch Ber, 79, 390n20, 437n6
Lenin, Vladimir, 57, 72, 73, 106, 118, 119, 120, 397n126n 420n53, 422n79, 469n112
Leningrad (now St. Petersburg), 83, 86, 90, 91, 93, 96, 97, 98, 99, 100, 115, 118, 122, 124, 125, 131, 139, 143, 159, 225, 226, 409n97, 413n141, 413n152, 415n1, 415n4, 416n13, 417n15, 422n79, 423n92, 423n93, 428n34, 438n13, 438n15, 469n124, 510n28
Leningrad, Jewish Conference, 412n134, 415n4
Leningrad Jewish Religious Community (LERO), 409n998
Leningrad University, 106
Levertov, Rabbi Berel, 95
Levertov, Rabbi DovBer, 95
Levertov, Rabbi Moishe, 95, 424n105
Levik, Avraham [Slavin], 139, 158
Levin, Nora, 71, 140, 190, 192, 224, 397n125, 401n24, 406n80

Levin, Rabbi Hillel, 122
Levin, Rabbi Shalom Ber, 138, 209, 237, 282, 400n23, 407n80
Levitin, Rabbi Shmuel, 86, 78, 201, 208–209, 239, 281, 289, 291, 298, 325, 329, 330, 356, 360, 410n110, 460n167, 460n167, 484–485n43, 496n156, 496n257, 522n162
Levy, Berel, 219, 464n64
Levy, Yitzchak, 358
Liadi (town), 7, 39, 136, 379n5, 380n14, 381n26, 383n3, 393n64, 422n79, 426n18, 474n14
Lieberman, Rabbi Chaim, 107, 108, 110, 222, 223, 256–257, 258, 351, 401n37, 417n15, 478n74, 479n82
Lieblis, Zalman, 14
Likkutei Dibburim (published talks and Chasidic lore), 150, 230, 414n1,
Lilienthal, Max, 47, 134, 394n83, 426n13
Lipshitz, Rabbi Mottel, 129
Lipskar, Rabbi Shalom Ber, 417n23
Lipsker, Michoel, 329, 359
Lipsker, Tzvia, 353
Litvakov, Moshe, 88, 226, 410n113
Litvinov, Maxim, 229, 230, 320, 469n124
loan fund, 1, 2, 4
Loewenthal, Naftali, 153–155, 436n119
Lokshin, Yehuda, 175, 444n1, 470n129
Long, Breckinridge, 251–252, 296–297, 477n54, 497n165
Lookstein, Rabbi Joseph, 315, 502n224
Lowenthal, Gabriel, 199
Lubavitch World headquarters, 224
Ludmir, Poland, 146, 211
Lulov, Grigory, 106, 107, 110, 115 116, 119, 166, 116n12, 417n15, 442n53
Lulov, Noach, 166
Lunacharsky, Anatoly, 138
Luria, Ilia, 29, 31, 38, 39, 41, 48, 394n73, 395n86, 407n80
Lyuban, Belorussia, 77

Maccabees, 94
Machne Israel (Chabad's social service agency), 169, 293,
Machon Levi Yitzchak (an organization dedicated to publishing the talks of the seventh Rebbe in Hebrew), 86
Mack, Julian, 250
Maimonides, 181, 293, 404n60, 418n39, 451n66, 481n104, 493n133, 515n83
Malakhovka (small town outside Moscow), 124
Manischewitz company, 431n72
Margolin, Dovid, 125, 133, 407n80, 422n84, 423n87, 423n88, 430n58, 431n72, 476n38,
Marienbad spa, 177, 203, 472n151
Marina Rosche Chabad Synagogue, 76–77
Mark, Mendel, 148, 400n15
Marshall, Hyman, 453n84
Marshall, Louis, 430n54, 453n84
mashpia (spiritual mentor), 33, 34, 154, 388n93, 486n61
maskil (maskilim) (secularists, a proponent of the Enlightenment), 31, 39, 115–116

May Laws, 44, 393n69, 394n79
Mazeh, Chief Rabbi Jacob, 53
Mazer, Abraham, 318
Me'arat Hamakhpelah (Tomb of the Patriarchs), 176, 181, 182, 183, 389n6
Medoff, Rafael, 296
Meir, Golda, 127, 512n57, 516n89
Meir, Rabbi Yaakov, 179
Meisel, Rabbi Mendel, 120
Meisel, Rabbi Yisrael, 431n67, 431n68
melamed (teacher), 13, 147
Melamed, Roza, 121, 122
Meltzer, Rabbi Isser Zalman, 77
Menachem Mendel of Vitebsk, 178, 181, 322
Menachem Mendel, the Tzemach Tzedek, 5, 16, 18, 23
Mendlowitz, Rabbi Shraga Feivel, 277–278, 313, 315–316, 483n25, 502n225, 503n230
Mentlik, Rabbi Mordechai, 280, 353, 354, 355, 520n135
Menzhinsky, Vyacheslav, 116, 120
Mercaz HaTorah, 289, 491n107
Merkos L'Inyonei Chinuch (Central Organization for Jewish Education), 169, 293, 305, 310, 405n77, 437n121, 493n129, 502n222
Mesibot Shabbat clubs, 303, 307, 350
mesirat nefesh (self-sacrifice), 23, 58, 84, 103, 129, 275, 322
Mesivta Tiferes Yerushalayim, 277
Messing, Stanislav (Jewish Communist), 122, 421n69
Metzger, Alter B., 115
Mezeritch, 16, 386n72, 390n27, 422n79
mikveh, 17, 18, 22, 56, 81, 84, 86, 88, 121, 196, 233, 315, 316, 335, 429n50, 445n5, 458n149, 458n150, 502n223
Miller, Rabbi Chaim, 235
Mindel, Nissan, 156, 173, 257, 298, 299, 300, 335, 436–437n121, 441n36, 466n86, 481n117, 511n36,
Minkowitz, Yitzchak, 120, 421n62
Minsk, 139, 189, 408n92, 455n105, 470n129, 512n57
Mir (town), 29, 512
Mir yeshiva, 199, 285, 286, 287, 288, 358, 408n92, 440n24, 487n77, 487–488n81, 489n92, 491n102, 509n11
misnagdishe shtick, 28
mitboded, 20
Mizrachi, 213, 278, 344, 345, 346, 426n10, 463n35, 482n7, 494n142, 515n86, 515n87
Mogilev-Podolski, 178
Montifiore, Judith, 52
Montefiore, Simon, 57,
Montfiore, Moses, 181, 447n26, 454n99
Mordechai, Reb Meir, 15
Mordechai, Yosef, 11
Morgenthau, Henry, 181, 286, 488n88, 497n165, 221
Morning Journal (Chicago), 195
Morning Journal (New York), 221
Morozov, Rabbi Elchonon Dov, 76, 82, 85, 89–91, 102, 225, 401n24, 402n39, 414n157, 468n107
Mossad, 128, 156, 437n122
multiple sclerosis, 235

musar, 30, 214, 215, 390n20, 390n21, 412n136, 436n120, 487n77

Nablus, 181, 448n43
Nachmanson, Mikhail, 106, 107–109, 110–111, 113, 115, 118, 416n12, 416n13, 416n14
National Committee for the Furtherance of Jewish Education (NCFJE), 310
nationalism:
  Jewish, 302
  Russian, 52
  secular, 45, 176, 343, 392n56, 5128n109
Neubort, Shimon, 236
New Deal, 250
New York Times, The, 138, 297,
Nicholas I (czar), 44, 46, 57, 92, 106, 411n122, 454n99
Nicholas II (czar), 394n76, 397n124
Nikolayev (town), 97
Nizhyn (town), 7, 383n28, 402n38
Noach, Rabbi Yisrael, 7, 383n28
Novardok (yeshiva), 405n75, 465n72
Novgorod, 106, 416n13, 416n14
Nusach Ari (Chabad) synagogue (London), 232
Nusach Ari Congregation (Pittsburgh), 306

Ohel, 14, 22, 28, 70, 397n119
Ohel David, 223
Old Montefiore Cemetery, 362, 523n7
Oneg Shabbat Synagogue, 274, 280
Orsha (city in Belorussia), 92, 383n28
Orthodox Union (OU), 178
Ovruch, Ukraine, 4, 380n12, 383n28

Pale of Settlement, 44, 55, 79, 393n70, 416n10
Palmer, Chaim, 355
Palmer, Shlomo, 342
Paltiel, Rabbi Yossi, 9, 20, 23, 25, 354, 362, 364
Pasternak, Boris, 224
Pell, Robert T., 252–253, 255, 256, 257, 260–261, 262, 477n58, 278n62, 479n78
Perchtoldsdorf, 167
Peretz, 117, 149, 221, 249
Peshkova, Madam Yekaterina, 118–119, 120, 122, 124, 420n53
Pesner, Berke (false name for Morozov), 90
Petach Tikvah, 183, 229
Pevsner, Rabbi, 190
Philadelphia, Pennsylvania, 184, 187, 192, 194, 197, 198, 309, 458n153, 458n154, 483n25, 495n146
Phillips, William, 230
Potsdam, 57
Poalei Tzion, 39–40, 41, 380n8, 392n57, 512n57
Pobedonostsev, Konstantine, 47, 394n78, 394n79
Pogroms, 44, 46, 49, 68, 185, 397n114, 416n10, 457n137, 514n75
Polish Jewry, 213–214, 263, 274, 480n101
Polish National Library, 224
Polonsky, Antony, 50

Poltava, 76, 404n66
Polyakov, Samuel, 7, 49, 382n26, 382n27
Porush, Menachem, 348, 518n110
Posner, Rabbi Sholom, 307
Pri Etz Chaim, 56
Purim, 56, 58, 64, 70, 102, 105, 146, 315, 319, 348, 349, 356, 357, 398n128, 398n132, 502n224, 504n237, 505n247

Quint, Rabbi Eliyahu, 298

Rabbi Akiva, 101, 181, 414n156
Rabbi Shimshon the *melamed*, 13
Rabbi Yochanan ben Zakkai, 48
Rabbinical College of Greater Miami, 94
Rabbinical Committee, 81–82, 83, 160
Rabbinical Council of America, 278, 484n30
Rabbinical Council of Australia, 508n5
Rabbinical Council of Russia, 408n92
Rabbinical Seminary of Berlin, 160
Rabinowitz, Asher, 172, 200, 249, 256
Rabinowitz, Peretz, 419n50
Rabinowitz, Rabbi Dovid, 117, 187, 192, 209, 249, 284, 419n47, 456n127, 457n130, 459n163, 472n150,
Rabinowitz, Shimon, 1
Rabinowitz, Rabbi Shmuel, 81
Rachmistrivka, 77
Ragolin, Menachem Shmuel, 92
Raichik, Rabbi Shmuel Dovid, 337
Rakeffet, Rabbi Aaron, 156, 157, 275, 318, 437n122, 504n239, 509n11
Rapoport, Ada, 150, 151, 153
rav mitaam, 50
Reb Dovid, 2, 3
Reb Hertzl der Schreiber, 16
Reb Itche der Masmid, 70, 207, 230, 321, 325
Reb Nissan, 2, 16, 17, 19, 386n74,
Reb Saadia, 2
Rechovot, 183, 450n61
Red Square (Moscow), 364
Reese, Avraham, 317
Released Time (a weekly after school program), 303, 310–311, 359, 500n206, 501n213, 523n176
Revel, Rabbi Dov, 278
Rhoade, Max, 251, 252, 256, 257, 258, 260, 261, 262, 477n51, 479n78
Rivkin, Rabbi Moshe Dovber (Berel), 58, 61, 63, 64, 67–68, 398n131, 398n132
Rivkin, Shalom Dovber, 161
Rivlin, Rabbi Eliyahu Yosef, 179
Rochel, Rebbetzin Menucha, 41, 178, 385n59, 405n69, 448n41, 450n55, 466n80, 471n142
Rodal, Yosef, 248, 291
Rodshtein, Rabbi Moshe Leib, 338, 512n47
Rokiškis, Lithuania, 146, 153, 432n84
Romanov, 40
Roosevelt, Eleanor, 296, 495n147, 495n148
Roosevelt, Franklin Delano, 57, 229, 249, 251, 254, 260, 294, 296, 299, 300, 456n119, 469n124, 476n40, 494n138
Roseman, Samuel, 298, 299

Rosen, Dr. Joseph, 82, 91, 139, 145, 187, 191, 192, 250, 25, 429n50, 429n54, 438n15, 452n84, 455n108
Rosen, Rabbi Yosef, 428n39
Rosenberg, Samuel, 298, 299
Rosenblum, Rabbi Moshe, 29, 31, 36, 37, 38, 389n16
Rosenblum, Yosef, 228
Rosenson, Zelig Alekseyevich, 121
Rosh HaShanah, 7, 17, 20, 28, 35, 45, 68, 87, 101, 127, 185, 187, 206, 216, 240, 244, 245, 247, 250, 389n6, 391n46, 410n112, 424n101, 435n104, 437n7, 492n123, 514n66,
"royal wedding," 157–170
Rubin, Rabbi Eli, 52, 65, 385n47
Rudnya, 7
Rupo, Nissan, 57
Russian National Library, 221, 385n47, 397n117, 446n13, 466n86, 523n175
Russian Orthodox Church, 46, 57, 72, 394n79
Russian Revolution, 52
Rykov, Alexei, 116, 120

Salanter, Rabbi Yisrael, 30, 215, 412n136, 464n48, 465n72
Sapochinksy, Chaim, 285
Sarna, Jonathan, 141, 277, 278, 295
Sassonkin, Shmaryahu, 7
Sassoon, Rabbi David Solomon, 223
Schapiro, Rabbi Yehuda Leib, 94
Schiff, Yaakov, 307
Schneersohn, Rabbi Avraham, 27, 383n28
Schneersohn , Chaya Mushka (Chaya Moussia), 107, 133, 203, 158, 177, 203, 236, 263, 292, 356, 417n19, 492n122
Schneersohn, Feivel, 52
Schneersohn, Joseph Isaac, 249
Schneersohn, Nechama Dina, 27–28, 115, 173, 352, 383n28, 388n2, 519n120
Schneersohn, Rabbi Shmaryahu Noach, 66, 383n29, 408n92
Schneersohn, Shterna Sara, 4, 5, 19, 22, 28, 70, 94, 109, 265, 380n12, 380n13
Schneersohn, Zalman Aharon, 3, 8, 9, 12
Schneersohnovschina, 138, 428n31
Schneersohn-Twerski, Rabbi Moshe Chaim Yehoshua, 508n1,
Schneerson, Rabbi Levi Yitzchak, 158, 161, 399n3, 407n83, 419n49, 440n29
Schneur Zalman, the Alter Rebbe, 5, 12, 16, 18, 24, 61, 92, 152, 355
Schwartz, Yardena, 182, 480n101
Schwei, Rabbi Mordechai, 165
Second Temple, 181
"secret covenant," 84, 95
Sfas Emes, 221
Shaare Tzedek Synagogue, 196
shadkhan (matchmaker), 158
Shainberg, David, 181
Shamir, Yitzhak, 128
Shapiro, Rabbi Meir, 134, 162, 441n35, 441n36
Sharfstein, Mussi, 95, 437n6
Shazar, Zalman, 341–342
Sheftel, Shmuel Betzalel (Rashbatz), 20, 387n93

Shehechiyanu (blessing), 273, 367
Shemtov, Rabbi Bentzion, 84–87, 89, 99, 100, 336, 409n101, 409n106, 409n107, 413n150, 511n39
shluchim, 128, 169, 220, 231, 233, 341, 405n76, 443n64
Shmotkin, Zalman, 244–245
Shmuelevitz, Rabbi Chaim, 285, 287
shochet (kosher slaughterer), 87, 99, 121, 129, 465n65, 472n149
Shpalerka Prison, 4, 110, 111, 112
Shteif, Yonason, 339
Shuss, Mendel, 247
Shusterman, Tzvi, 309
Siberia, 80, 85, 86–87, 89, 100, 106, 124, 142, 285, 328, 456n123
Silver, Rabbi Eliezer, 229, 278, 299, 347, 465n65, 470n127, 488n81
Simchovich, Alter, 235
Simmon bar Yochai, 181
Simpson, Rabbi Eliyahu, 223, 351, 355–356, 422n80, 423n98, 427n22, 520n126
Six-Day War, 128, 345, 424n103, 434n88, 447n26, 493n136
Sklare, Marshal, 277
Slonim, Azriel Zelig, 471n142, 472n143
Slonim, Eliezer Don, 182
Slonim, Rabbi Yaakov Yosef, 221
Slonim, Schneur Zalman, 12, 385n59, 392n53
Slonim, Rabbi Zelig, 231–233, 384n35, 472n 146, 472n148, 472n149
Smorgon, Victor, 340, 512n55
Sofer, Rabbi Moshe, 277
Sokolow, Nahum, 229
Soloveichik, Rabbi Moshe, 278, 317, 484n34
Soloveitchik, Rabbi Chaim (the Brisker Rav), 29, 51, 99, 318, 396n103, 396n105, 484n34, 503n235, 504n236, 504n237
Soloveitchik, Haym, 318
Soloveitchik, Rabbi Joseph (Yosef Dov), 278, 317–318, 440n27
Soloveitchik, Rabbi Yitzchok Zev, 348, 518n109
Sonnenfeld, Rabbi Yosef Chaim, 143, 177, 179, 431n69
Sonnenfeld, Yosef Chaim, 445n9
Sovetish Heymland, 192
Soviet Council of Chelyabinsk, 91
Soviet gulag, 89
Spanish and Portuguese Synagogue (Montreal), 289
SS *Drottningholm*, 267, 271
Stalin, Joseph, 57, 71, 80, 88, 95, 106, 118, 143, 190, 191, 205, 226, 316, 335, 340, 362, 398n126, 398n128, 398n129, 403n49, 410n1123, 411n 124, 415n6, 416n7, 416n13, 455n105, 455n106, 455n115, 456n117, 469n124, 505n248
Starkenstein, Moshe, 284
Starr, Isadore, 196–197
Steinsaltz, Rabbi Adin Even-Israel, 279
Stolypin, Pyotr, 46, 51, 394n76, 394n78
Sudakevitch, Efraim, 333
Sugihara, Chiune, 283

Tablung, David, 217
Talks and Tales (monthly children's magazine), 303
Tanya, 23, 210
Tbilisi, Soviet Georgia, 88, 165,
tefillin, 74, 109, 111, 113–115, 116, 128, 148, 170, 198, 231, 434n88, 493n136, 509n18
Teitelbaum, Rabbi Aron, 142, 430n60,
Telushkin, Rabbi Nissan, 195
Telz Yeshivah (Cleveland, Ohio), 327
Temple Emanuel, 191
Temple Mount, 179, 181
The Canadian Eagle (Yiddish newspaper), 289
The Jewish Record, 194
The Lubavitcher Rebbe's Memoirs, 16
"The New Book of Lamentations," 142
The Society of the Sisters of the Temimim, 154
Tikkun Chatzot, 15
Tomarkin, Rabbi Aharon, 123
Tomb of the Patriarchs, 176, 181, 418n28
Torah im derekh eretz, 147
Torah Umesorah, 313
Torah Vodaath, 185, 208, 243, 272, 277, 279, 315, 398n131, 451n71, 483n25, 484n32, 484n39, 502n225, 503n227, 503n229
Toras Emes, 42, 43, 398n131, 448n41
Toronto Hebrew Journal, 323
Tractate Gehinnom (purgatory), 111
Treblinka, 158, 263, 292, 437n7, 492n123
Troper, Morris, 263,
Trotsky, Leon, 57, 398n126
Truman, Harry S, 57, 347, 518n108
tuberculosis, 9
Twerski, Rabbi Yaakov Yisrael, 321
typhoid, 60
typhus, 67, 70, 157
tzaddikim, 5, 15, 150, 196, 211, 242, 384n38, 509n18
Tze'irei Agudath Israel, 147

Ukraine, 4, 69, 76, 77, 86, 99, 122, 141, 161, 165, 178, 188, 212, 224, 393n70, 398n131, 408n90, 415n6, 422n79, 429n54, 438n8, 459n166, 508n5
Ulmanis, Kārlis, 148
underground network, 78, 80, 136, 201, 237, 404

Vaad Magen UMekhaseh, 139
Vad, Eliyahu, 259
Vilensky, Rabbi Getche, 129
Vilna, 45, 50, 51, 72, 134, 178, 251, 387n93, 390n20, 465n69, 465n78
Vilna Gaon, 287, 334, 446n22, 490n94
Vilnius, 143, 146, 158, 163, 210, 211, 216, 247, 248, 259, 264, 265, 284, 290, 334, 396n101, 426n16, 437n4, 463n35, 464n50, 476n49, 480n101, 486n61, 495n148
Vitebsk, 9, 35, 40, 41, 75, 178, 181, 392n57
Volhynia, 86, 220
volost (local police station), 3
Volozhin (town), 29, 31, 428n40, 446n10

Voskhod (secular paper), 50, 392n55
Voykov, Pyotr, 106, 415n6

Wagner, Robert, 249
Wall Street crash, 192, 197
Wallace, Henry, 299, 497n162
Wallach, Dr. Moshe, 184, 452n68
War Refugee Board, 300, 497n164, 497n165
Warburg, Felix, 187–189, 191, 193, 201, 429–430n54, 453n86, 454n94, 455n112, 455n113 455n108
Weinberg, Rabbi Yechiel Yaakov, 160, 439n23, 440n24, 440n25
Weinstein, Gedalia, 39, 392n55
Westend Sanatorium (Purkersdorf), 167, 235
Western liberal society, 137
Western Wall, 176, 179, 182, 447n31
White Russia, Ukraine, 1, 7, 88, 212, 221, 227
White Sea, 119
Wiernik, Peter (Peretz), 221, 227, 465n78,
Wilshanski, Reb Betzalel, 338
Wineberg, Rabbi Yosef, 244–245, 246, 255, 327, 359, 475n20
Wise, Rabbi Stephen S., 186, 193, 251, 295–296, 298–299, 457n132, 494–495n142, 495n143, 497n164
Wohlthat, Helmuth, 253–254, 256, 478n62, 478n65
Wolofsky, Hirsch, 289
Wolosow, Yehoshua, 265
women, empowering in the realm of Jewish study, 152–155
Women's organizations, establishment of, 153–155
Workers' Party, 72, 227
World Agudath Israel, 426n11
World War I, 5, 42, 68, 185, 213, 247, 253, 254–255, 405n72, 419n49, 422n79, 440n24, 445n7, 448n41, 471n140
World War II, 6, 44, 57, 76, 133, 167, 237, 278, 436n121, 442n58, 450n57, 451n66, 469n124, 471n140

Yakovshvili, Simon, 85, 87–89
Yalta, 12, 13, 57, 385n57, 386n66
Yanivskiek (village), 86
yechidut (private audience), 8, 9, 20, 56, 94, 146, 210, 217, 219, 265, 292, 349, 351–352, 355–356, 359, 520n139, 522n164
Yehuda Leib, Rabbi (Maharil), 7
Yekaterinoslav (today known as Dinipo), 92, 158, 159
yeshivah ketanah (high school), 147, 307
Yeshivah Torah Vodaath (Williamsburg), 185, 398n131, 451n71
Yeshiva University, 278, 371, 372, 451n71, 484n30, 484n32, 484n33, 484n34, 503n235, 504n236
Yeshivas Rabbeinu Yitzhak Elchonon (Washington Heights), 185, 439n18, 452n71, 504n237
Yiddish movement, 45, 148, 289, 433n84, 433n86, 433n87
Yiddish Peretz School, 289, 443n86
Yiddishes Tageblatt (New York), 65
Yiddishists, 148

Yitzchaki, Rabbi Zalman Moshe, 118, 420n52
yoshvim ("those who sit and study"), 29, 34
Young Israel, 278, 318, 355, 507n261, 520n141
Young Israel Viewpoint, 275
Yushchinksy, Andrei, 52

Zajac, Avraham, 120
Zajak, Mordechai, 521n143
Zajac, Motel, 356
Zajac, Simcha Yitzchak, 474n3, 521n143
Zaklikowski, Dovid, 220
Zaklikowski, Eliezer, 299
Zaks, Rabbi Mendel, 216
zal (large study hall), 28, 38, 40, 389n10
Zalman, Chaim Schneur, 7, 383n28
Zalman, Reb Nachman, 322
Zalmanov, Rabbi Shmuel, 440n32, 441n36
Zalmanov, Rabbi Shraga, 431n75
Zeffren, Faye, 196, 458n149
Ziemba, Rabbi Menachem, 134, 474n15
Zembin, 34, 38, 385n41, 391n36
Zemel, Rabbi Mordechai, 216
Zevin, Rabbi Shlomo Yosef, 408n92
Zevin, Rabbi Yosef, 99, 160, 359, 412n139, 438n15
Zhytomyr, 50
Zigelbaum, Menachem, 132
Zionism, 31, 39, 45, 72, 80, 213, 289, 302, 305, 343, 343, 392n56, 392n57, 403n52, 406n80, 419n49, 426n11, 433n86, 450n57, 457n131, 466n83, 497n162, 515n85, 518n109
secular, 90
Zionists, 39, 133, 177, 213, 346, 426n10, 462n27, 463n35, 494n142
Marxist, 41
Zisman, Berel, 355
Zisman, Leibel, 267
Zisman, Shraga Feivel, 265, 267
Zuber, Rabbi Yisrael, 231, 267
Zvogin, Anshel, 135
Zwartendyk, Jan, 283

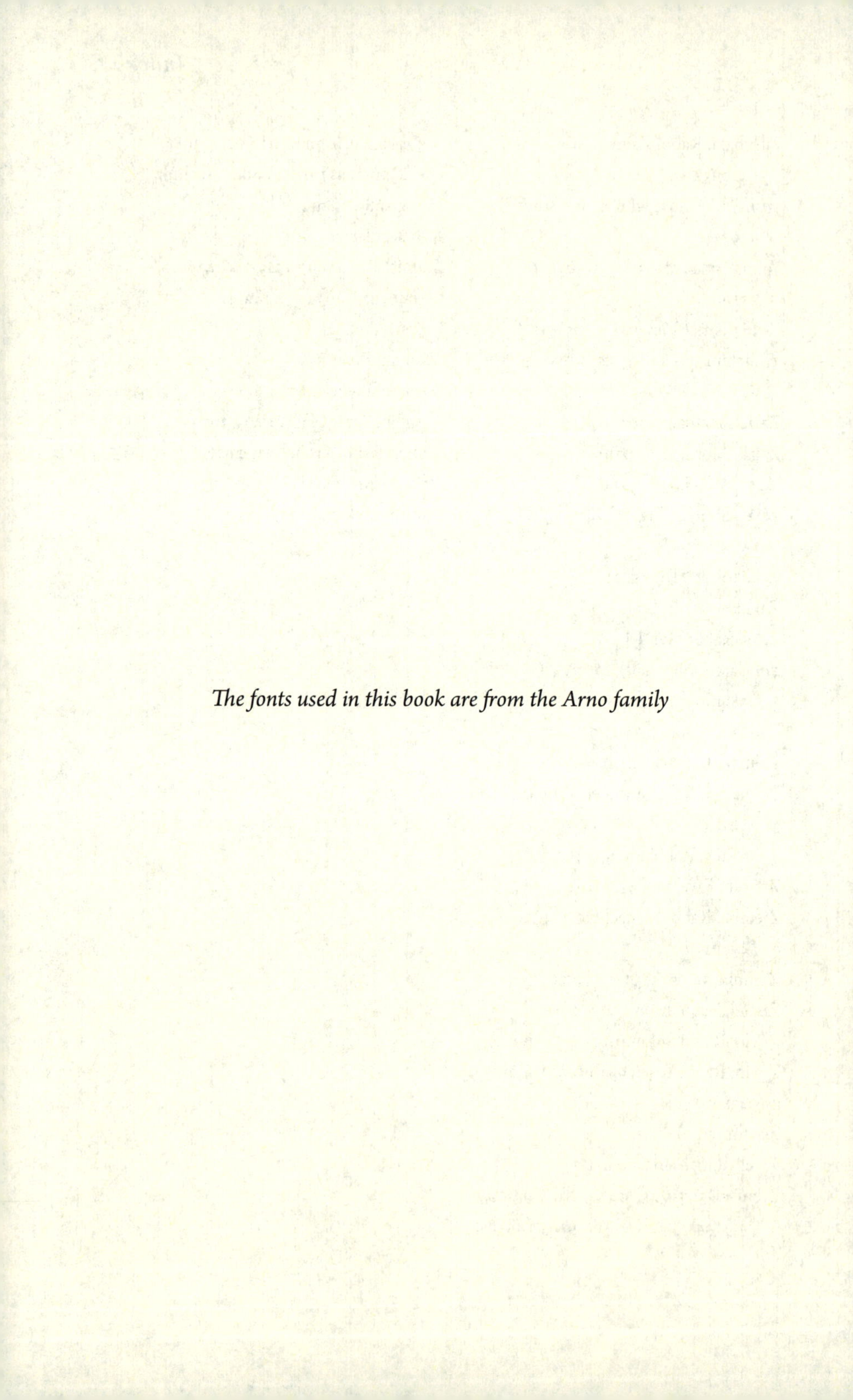

The fonts used in this book are from the Arno family